THE OXFORD HANDBOOK OF

# AMERICAN PUBLIC OPINION AND THE MEDIA

# THE
# OXFORD
# HANDBOOKS
# OF
# AMERICAN
# POLITICS

### GENERAL EDITOR: GEORGE C. EDWARDS III

*The Oxford Handbooks of American Politics* is a set of reference books offering authoritative and engaging critical overviews of the state of scholarship on American politics.

Each volume focuses on a particular aspect of the field. The project is under the General Editorship of George C. Edwards III, and distinguished specialists in their respective fields edit each volume. The *Handbooks* aim not just to report on the discipline, but also to shape it as scholars critically assess the current state of scholarship on a topic and propose directions in which it needs to move. The series is an indispensable reference for anyone working in American politics.

# THE OXFORD HANDBOOK OF

# AMERICAN PUBLIC OPINION AND THE MEDIA

*Edited by*

ROBERT Y. SHAPIRO

*and*

LAWRENCE R. JACOBS

OXFORD
UNIVERSITY PRESS

*This book has been printed digitally and produced in a standard specification*
*in order to ensure its continuing availability*

# OXFORD
UNIVERSITY PRESS

Great Clarendon Street, Oxford OX2 6DP
United Kingdom

Oxford University Press is a department of the University of Oxford.
It furthers the University's objective of excellence in research, scholarship,
and education by publishing worldwide.
Oxford is a registered trade mark of Oxford University Press in the UK
and in certain other countries

British Library Cataloguing in Publication Data
Data available

Library of Congress Cataloging in Publication Data
Data available

ISBN 978-0-19-954563-6

# PREFACE

................................................

PUBLIC opinion and the media form the foundation of representative democracy in the United States. They are the subject of enormous scrutiny by scholars, pundits, and ordinary citizens. This volume takes on the "big questions" about public opinion and the media in popular debates and in social scientific research. The volume brings together the thinking of leading academic experts, delivering fresh assessments of what we know about public opinion, the media, and their interconnections. This volume is particularly attentive to the changes in the mass media and communications technology and the sharp expansion in the number of cable television channels, websites and blogs, and the new social media, which are changing how news about political life is collected and conveyed. The changing dynamics of the media and public opinion have created a process that we call *informational interdependence*. These extensive interconnections exert a wide range of influences on public opinion as the processes by which information reaches the public have been transformed.

In addition to encompassing critical developments in public opinion and the media, this volume brings together a remarkable diversity of research from psychology, genetics, political science, sociology, and the study of gender, race, and ethnicity. Many of the chapters integrate analyses of broader developments in public opinion and political behavior with attention to critical variations based on economic status, education and sophistication, religion, and generational change, drawing on research that uses survey data and experimental designs. Moreover, the book covers the variations in public opinion and media coverage across domestic and foreign policy issues.

As academics well know—and as we tell our students—every project takes longer than you think. This book was no exception. We thank Dominic Byatt, Jennifer Lunsford, Sarah Parker, and Elizabeth Suffling at Oxford University Press, and copyeditor Laurien Berkeley, for their patience and superb assistance in moving this volume to publication. We are especially grateful to our good colleague George Edwards for proposing to Oxford that we undertake this volume. We share credit for what we have put together with him, but take full responsibility for any shortcomings. Stephen Thompson and Michael Scott provided able assistance as we scrambled to finish the volume, as did the proofreader, Debbie Sutcliffe, and indexer, Michael Tombs.

We thank most of all the outstanding scholars who agreed readily and with good cheer to write chapters for us. We stole their valuable time so that we and this volume's readers would benefit from their highly engaged research and collective expertise.

Columbia University's Department of Political Science, its Institute for Social and Economic Research and Policy, and the University of Minnesota's Humphrey Institute of Public Affairs and Center for the Study of Politics and Governance have provided us with strong academic homes and support. We began work on this volume while Shapiro was finishing the 2006/7 year as a Visiting Scholar at the Russell Sage Foundation, which supported work that is reflected in this volume's final chapter regarding political leadership, "pathologies," and partisan conflict.

And as always, each of us is indebted to our soul mates, Nancy Rubenstein and Julie Schumacher, who were patient as we worked on this volume—and let us know that.

R.Y.S.
L.R.J.

*New York and St Paul*
*August 2010*

# Contents

## PART I INTRODUCTION: THE NEW INTERDEPENDENCE OF PUBLIC OPINION, THE MEDIA, AND POLITICS

## PART II THE MEDIA

# PART III PUBLIC OPINION

## PART IV  ISSUES AND POLITICS

# PART V  DEMOCRACY UNDER STRESS

# Lists of Figures and Tables

## Figures

## Tables

# About the Contributors

**Jason Barabas**, Associate Professor of Political Science in the Department of Political Science, Florida State University.

**Aimee Barbeau**, Ph.D. candidate in the Department of Government, Georgetown University.

**Jackie Bass**, Ph.D. candidate in political science at the University of California, Berkeley.

**Matthew A. Baum**, Marvin Kalb Professor of Global Communications and Professor of Public Policy and Government in the John F. Kennedy School of Government, Harvard University.

**W. Lance Bennett**, Professor of Political Science and Ruddick C. Lawrence Professor of Communication at the University of Washington, Seattle, where he also directs the Center for Communication and Civic Engagement.

**Adam J. Berinsky**, Associate Professor of Political Science at the Massachusetts Institute of Technology.

**Bruce Bimber**, Professor of Political Science at the University of California, Santa Barbara.

**Bradford H. Bishop**, graduate student in political science at Duke University.

**George Franklin Bishop**, Professor of Political Science and Director of the Graduate Certificate Program in Public Opinion and Survey Research at the University of Cincinnati.

**Yaeli Bloch-Elkon**, Lecturer/Assistant Professor of Political Science and Communications at Bar Ilan University, and an Associate Research Scholar at the university's Begin-Sadat Center for Strategic Studies and at the Institute for Social and Economic Research and Policy, Columbia University.

**Ted Brader**, Associate Professor of Political Science at the University of Michigan and Research Associate Professor in the Center for Political Studies, Institute for Social Research.

**Katherine Ann Brown**, Ph.D. candidate in communications at Columbia University.

**Erin Cassese**, Assistant Professor of Political Science at West Virginia University.

**Dennis Chong**, John D. and Catherine T. MacArthur Professor of Political Science at Northwestern University.

**Rodolfo O. de la Garza**, Eaton Professor of Administrative Law and Municipal Science in the Department of Political Science and the School of International and Public Affairs, Columbia University.

**Michael X. Delli Carpini**, Dean of the Annenberg School for Communication at the University of Pennsylvania.

**James N. Druckman**, Payson S. Wild Professor of Political Science and a Faculty Fellow at the Institute for Policy Research, Northwestern University.

**Patrick J. Egan**, Assistant Professor of Politics and Public Policy at New York University.

**Douglas C. Foyle**, Douglas J. and Midge Bowen Bennet Associate Professor of Government at Wesleyan University, Middletown, Connecticut.

**Carolyn L. Funk**, Associate Professor in the L. Douglas Wilder School of Government and Public Affairs, Virginia Commonwealth University.

**Brian J. Gaines**, Associate Professor at the University of Illinois, with appointments in the Department of Political Science and the Institute of Government and Public Affairs.

**Todd Gitlin**, Professor of Journalism and Sociology, and Director of the Ph.D. program in communications, at Columbia University.

**Doris A. Graber**, Professor of Political Science and Communication at the University of Illinois at Chicago, and founding editor of *Political Communication*.

**John G. Gunnell**, Distinguished Professor Emeritus at the State University of New York at Albany and currently a Research Associate at the University of California, Davis.

**Kathleen Hall Jamieson**, Professor at the Annenberg School for Communication at the University of Pennsylvania and Director of its Annenberg Public Policy Center.

**Bruce W. Hardy**, Senior Research Analyst at the Annenberg Public Policy Center, University of Pennsylvania.

**Fredrick C. Harris**, Professor of Political Science and Director of the Center on African-American Politics and Society, Columbia University.

**Susan Herbst**, President of the University of Connecticut and Professor of Political Science.

**D. Sunshine Hillygus**, Associate Professor of Political Science at Duke University and Director of the Duke Initiative on Survey Methodology.

**Matthew Hindman**, Assistant Professor in the School of Media and Public Affairs, George Washington University.

**Gregory G. Holyk**, Visiting Professor of Politics in the Williams School of Commerce, Economics, and Politics at Washington and Lee University, and survey consultant for the Chicago Council on Global Affairs.

**Leonie Huddy**, Professor of Political Science and Director of the Center for Survey Research, Stony Brook University.

**Muzammil M. Hussain**, doctoral student in the Department of Communication, University of Washington.

**Vincent Hutchings**, Professor of Political Science at the University of Michigan and Research Professor at the Institute for Social Research.

**Shanto Iyengar**, Professor of Communication and Political Science at Stanford University.

**Lawrence R. Jacobs**, Walter F. and Joan Mondale Chair for Political Studies in the Hubert H. Humphrey Institute and the Department of Political Science, University of Minnesota.

**William G. Jacoby**, Professor in the Department of Political Science at Michigan State University and Research Scientist at the University of Michigan, where he is Director of the Inter-University Consortium for Political and Social Research Summer Program in Quantitative Methods of Social Research.

**Angela Jamison**, visiting scholar in the Department of Sociology, University of Michigan.

**Seung-Jin Jang**, Assistant Professor, Department of Political Science and International Relations, Kookmin University, Seoul, Korea.

**Jennifer Jerit**, Associate Professor in the Department of Political Science, Florida State University.

**Jane Junn**, Professor of Political Science at the University of Southern California.

**Marion R. Just**, William R. Kenan, Jr., Professor in the Department of Political Science, Wellesley College, and an Associate of the Joan Shorenstein Center at the John F. Kennedy School of Government, Harvard University.

**James H. Kuklinski**, Matthew T. McClure Professor of Political Science at the University of Illinois at Urbana-Champaign.

**Taeku Lee**, Professor and Chair in the Department of Political Science and Professor in the School of Law, University of California, Berkeley.

**Leslie McCall**, Associate Professor of Sociology and Faculty Fellow of the Institute for Policy Research, Northwestern University.

**Rose McDermott**, Professor of Political Science at Brown University.

**Jeff Manza**, Professor and Department Chair of Sociology at New York University.

**George E. Marcus**, Professor of Political Science at Williams College.

**Kristyn L. Miller**, Ph.D. candidate in the Department of Political Science, University of Michigan.

**Patricia Moy**, Christy Cressey Professor of Communication and Adjunct Professor of Political Science at the University of Washington.

**John Mueller**, Woody Hayes Chair of National Security Studies, Mershon Center, and Professor of Political Science at Ohio State University.

**Brigitte L. Nacos**, journalist and Adjunct Professor of Political Science at Columbia University.

**Thomas E. Nelson**, Associate Professor of Political Science at Ohio State University.

**W. Russell Neuman**, John Derby Evans Professor of Media Technology in Communication Studies and Research Professor at the Institute for Social Research, University of Michigan.

**Costas Panagopoulos**, Assistant Professor of Political Science and Director of the Center for Electoral Politics and Democracy, Fordham University.

**Spencer Piston**, Ph.D. student in the Department of Political Science, University of Michigan.

**S. Karthick Ramakrishnan**, Associate Professor of Political Science at the University of California, Riverside.

**Carin Robinson**, Assistant Professor of Political Science at Hood College.

**Michael Schudson**, Professor of Communication at the Columbia Journalism School, Columbia University.

**Robert Y. Shapiro**, Professor of Political Science at Columbia University and a Faculty Fellow at its Institute for Social and Economic Research and Policy.

**Laura Stoker**, Associate Professor of Political Science at the University of California, Berkeley.

**Charles S. Taber**, Professor of Political Science and Director of the Laboratory for Experimental Research in Political Behavior, Stony Brook University.

**Michael Traugott**, Professor of Communication Studies and Research Professor in the Center for Political Studies at the Institute for Social Research, University of Michigan.

**Lynn Vavreck**, Associate Professor of Political Science at the University of California, Los Angeles. She is Director of the UCLA Center for the Study of Campaigns and Co-Principal Investigator of the Cooperative Campaign Analysis Project.

**Clyde Wilcox**, Professor of Government at Georgetown University.

**Nicole Willcoxon**, Ph.D. candidate and Chancellor's Diversity Fellow in the Department of Political Science at the University of California, Berkeley.

**Janelle Wong**, Associate Professor of Political Science and American Studies and Ethnicity at the University of Southern California.

# PART I

## INTRODUCTION

### THE NEW INTERDEPENDENCE OF PUBLIC OPINION, THE MEDIA, AND POLITICS

..........................................................................................

# CHAPTER 1

# INFORMATIONAL INTERDEPENDENCE

*Public Opinion and the Media in the New Communications Era*

..........................................................................................

LAWRENCE R. JACOBS
ROBERT Y. SHAPIRO

WE have grown accustomed to the steady parade of new devices for communications and novel uses of them. In the historic span of human communications, this transition has been extraordinary in its impact and speed. The Internet expanded and took off in its use just fifteen years ago, sparking a renaissance of new communication software and machines that extended beyond computers to highly mobile PDAs—personal digital assistants—that connect millions to the Internet in their everyday activity. Google's search engine transformed access to information on the Internet, starting a mere dozen years ago and subsequently becoming a dominant corporate presence. Facebook and Twitter stitched together millions of people but were only created in 2004 and 2006, respectively. Slate and the Drudge Report helped launch the deluge of online news sites just over a decade ago, during the late 1990s; the Huffington Post and other hard-edged partisan news and news-aggregating websites have proliferated in the early years of the twenty-first century.

Most of the traditional media froze with uncertainty as communication and infor-mation-sharing technologies took off, and they struggled to understand and anticipate the consequences for their industry. An ongoing period of transition enveloped the traditional media as they labored to adapt to a chaotic swirl of change: audience and readership declined, as did advertising revenue, which coincided with successive economic downturns in the first decade of the twenty-first century that forced cost cutting; and a legal battle broke out over the free use of the mainstream press's content

vibrant bodies of research on the media and public opinion. Rarely has one volume provided such a broad-ranging compendium; more than forty chapters review the latest research in the study of public opinion and the media and offer accessible introductions to those new to these fields as well as insightful essays for more seasoned readers. Second, this volume develops a unique and critical synthesis of the transformations in today's media world as creating systems of informational interdependence. The social relations of public opinion and mass media are a common theme in many of the chapters, as is the heterogeneity of media messages. Third, this volume raises profound questions about the normative consequences of the new information environment: to what extent have the proliferation of news and information sources, their co-production, and other new developments provided a boon for democracy and genuine public deliberation; or intensified existing threats to democratic processes—or created new ones?

The sections that follow go into greater depth in outlining the new model of information interdependence that emerges from this volume's chapters. We also discuss the distinctive features of public opinion and the media that, according to the latest research, define the conditions under which the two interact. The last section considers some of the broader implications of the new information interdependence for democracy and public deliberation.

## INFORMATIONAL INTERDEPENDENCE

This new interdependence of the media and public opinion is based on three mutually beneficial relationships: ecological symbiosis, the co-production of political news, and the new social relations of political news.

## Ecological Symbiosis

First, the information environment feeds off the symbiosis of government elites, media, and mass public. Chapter 3, by Brian J. Gaines and James H. Kuklinski, approaches the "informational environment holistically," focusing on the "strategic interactions between politicians and members of the media" and, one might add, ordinary individuals. "Politicians . . . need the media to convey particular messages to the public," they reason, and "the media need access to politicians to generate news . . . [and] to make money, which requires that they report stories of interest to ordinary citizens." These symbiotic relationships "[shape] what is and what is not included in the news . . . and how ordinary citizens react." Chapter 2, by W. Russell Neuman, Bruce Bimber, and Matthew Hindman, stresses a similar dynamic of interconnection created by new information technology and its use—"the interoperability, interactivity, intelligence, portability, and increased information bandwidth of these networked devices."

Younger generations are often most engaged in the new information and technology, creating the potential (as Laura Stoker and Jackie Bass describe in Chapter 28) to "positively influence the civic and political engagement of young people."

The chapters in this volume specify the processes and mechanisms that co-join the media, politics, and public opinion. Thomas E. Nelson (Chapter 12) examines the double action of framing: framing organizes government decisions and news reports on them into "compact, easily digested summaries" and responds to the demands of consumers for certain types and forms of information. It both serves the information needs of the public and provides the media with a way of describing complex news or information.

The mutual interests of the press and government are well known, although their interactions with public opinion are subject to increasingly sophisticated analysis. Douglas C. Foyle's chapter on foreign policy (Chapter 40) traces the interplay of Washington elites, who often monopolize information about national security, with the media that depend on government elites as sources. Although the press follows the broad contours of the Washington policy debates and attitudes, "political actors (e.g., the president, Congress, foreign policy experts) and the media interact to shape and control how an issue, problem, or situation is understood." Framing, priming, and agenda-setting are the mechanisms that shape the content of policy-relevant information and how it is consumed by individuals, often serving as "powerful tools in strengthening or weakening public support for foreign policies." Foyle explains why, even as Washington elites control critical information, both public opinion and the media can react independently of leaders in response to foreign policy.

Matthew A. Baum and Angela Jamison (Chapter 8) trace the interdependence of elites, media, and public opinion in the production and consumption of "soft news"—namely, human interest, dramatic, or entertaining press reports of politics that appeal to those less attentive to public affairs, as distinct from "hard news" coverage of leaders in government and business, major national and international issues, or disasters or developments that can alter daily life. Rejecting claims that soft news deprives citizens of the information they need to make informed choices among candidates or policies, Baum and Jamison describe the impact of soft news on individual attentiveness, knowledge, attitudes, and behavior. Not only does soft news affect individuals, it can also loop into the decisions of the media and politicians. Searching to expand their audiences, the organizations producing soft news "cater not only to those with little interest in or attentiveness to politics but also to more politically attentive, ideological, and active citizens." Politicians seeking votes are acutely aware of the opportunity, as is evident by their appearance on daytime and late-night talk shows like *The View* and *Late Night with David Letterman*, as well as John Stewart's news satire the *Daily Show*. Baum and Jamison conclude that informational interdependence is defined, in part, by the "interaction of the supply and demand sides of soft news—that is, on the ways that politicians understand and then take advantage of soft news, and in turn the ways that audiences seek or respond to the resulting content."

The interactions of elites, media, and public opinion have been exploited by international terrorists. Brigitte L. Nacos and Yaeli Bloch-Elkon (Chapter 42) dissect and explain the strategies of terrorists to accomplish what they seek (massive publicity) by exploiting the needs of media for must-see coverage and by grabbing the public's undivided attention. In this way, "terrorists and media organizations feed off each other." The spread of global television networks and Internet news coverage has accelerated the symbiotic relationship among terrorists, media, and public opinion.

## The Co-Production of Political News

The second aspect of today's informational interdependence is that political news is increasingly being co-produced—often in uncoordinated and unplanned ways—by news organizations, ordinary citizens, and government officials. Individuals (including high-level White House and congressional officials) and a variety of novel organizations and collaborations have generated a new supply of political news through online sites (from Politico to Slate and the Drudge Report), blogs, YouTube videos, and themed aggregators (such as liberal or conservative compilations of like-minded news stories), as well as online feedback to the stories filed by traditional reporters. One of the most important features of the Internet is its social networking through Facebook, Twitter, and others new capabilities. Where news media used to be a static bulletin board, they have become sites of dynamic exchanges with some posts going "viral" as it is linked to, forwarded, and commented on by hundreds of thousands or more (such as a YouTube video of a Virginia senator using racially derogatory language or Iranian police shooting a young, innocent bystander at a protest).

Reflecting on these changes in the supply of political news, Marion R. Just (Chapter 7) reports that "the audience has invaded the newsroom and is shaping the definition of news," not only by "contributing news content and comments," but also by "taking on the roles of distribution and editorial signaling via social network computing." As the new era arrives in which political news "will necessarily be collaborations between the professionals and the audience," control over news content has slipped from the grasp of traditional news organizations and their editors and journalists as untrained individuals and new organizations and collaborations emerge and evolve.

Michael Schudson (Chapter 4) approaches the changing nature of news production from the perspectives of normative political theory and the history of news reporting, but in the end also concludes that it is "increasingly originated by citizens, rank amateurs." He points to the shift away from "a largely 'vertical' mass medium—from the journalists to the readers and viewers—... [toward a relationship that is] increasingly 'horizontal.'" Schudson suggests that the co-production of news in the era of the Internet ushered in several significant changes—the velocity and speed of new production and the number of people participating on a global level have grown substantially. In the process, traditional news organizations have had to evolve; the "horizontal circulation of news acts back quickly on the consciousness of the journalists and helps to shape what they choose to cover." As the distinction between news producers and audience breaks down, the earlier tendency toward treating individuals as passive receivers of news is also giving way to research on individuals as co-producers.

## The New Social Relations of Political News

The third component of informational interdependence is its radically social and relational dynamics. In the previous era of traditional media, the audience was often conceptualized as disconnected individuals. In the new era, the production and consumption of political news occurs within webs of social relations.

Patricia Moy and Muzammil M. Hussain (Chapter 14) stress the social implications of news organizations adopting technology that facilitates interactivity and the "blurring of mass and interpersonal communication." The audience now produces news content and comments on stories filed by traditional media; journalists both receive online feedback and track audience interest. The result appears to intensify the social interactions and political discussions in which citizens engage and to facilitate "talking about politics alongside consuming political news from the media."

## New Research Approaches to Study New Forms of Political Communications

The distinctive motivations and resources of the media, political actors, and everyday citizens generate patterns of news production, consumption, and political behavior. Studying today's information environment in isolation misses significant interactive relationships that account for both political communications and the activities of each actor.

The emergence of informational interdependence requires, according to a number of chapters, a new research methodology. Gaines and Kuklinski recommend analysis of the entire context within which citizens learn about and respond to politics. Moy and Hussain call for new research that focuses on the "interpersonal discussion" in "non-face-to-face settings" and on "what actually transpires within these discussions." Kathleen Hall Jamieson and Bruce W. Hardy (Chapter 15) also recommend that research adjust to "citizens now build[ing] their own media experiences" and to the increasing social production and distribution of news by tracking "who sent what information to whom in what form through what channel."

In addition, analysis is shifting from static models of one-way causation in which the media influence the public's agenda, to research on the simultaneity of news production and consumption (Bennett and Iyengar 2008, 2010). Moreover, the earlier tendency to examine print as opposed to broadcast media or the distinctive features of individual organizations is shifting toward the diffuse and widening array of old and new media formats. Furthermore, research using a range of methodologies will be necessary to track the new political communications systems. Lynn Vavreck and Shanto Iyengar (Chapter 10) suggest that the diffusion of the Internet and rapid evolution of new media has "chang[ed] the real world of political communication" and reshaped how researchers use experimental and survey methodologies in political communication research. They project that "as technology diffuses still further, the generalizability gap between experimental and survey methods will continue to close." Other authors in this volume also emphasize the increasing importance of experimental designs (often in conjunction with other research approaches) to study public opinion, political behavior, and the media.

In short, an era of informational interdependence requires new approaches to research that reconsider causality and connectedness between media and public opinion.

## THE MEDIA AND PUBLIC OPINION

Understanding today's informational interdependence requires moving beyond broad generalizations to specifying the nature and conditions of the interactions between the media and public opinion. The specific characteristics of each affect the terms on which they interact and to what end. This volume's contributors elaborate on the interdependence of the media and public opinion and also identify the distinctive traits of each and the mechanisms that link them. A new generation of research makes clear that the media do not dictate public opinion but rather engage in more subtle processes in which they respond to how individuals acquire and process information and trigger cognitive and affective reactions by the public. Research has moved beyond the homogeneous categorizations of "the media" and "public opinion" to distinguish disparate news sources and platforms and different subgroups of the public.

### The Public and Information Processing

Decades of research demonstrate that public opinion is not an epiphenomenon of the media or elite discourse. Individuals and the aggregate public have durable attitudes and capacities to interpret information on politics and policy. Illustrating a particularly dramatic case, John Mueller (Chapter 41) stresses how media coverage of war can have limited impact on public opinion: "In general, the media do not seem to have much independent impact on public attitudes toward war"; the public is "substantially set [ting] its own agenda" and being "quite selective." Delving deeper into the psychological processes by which individuals form opinions, Dennis Chong and James N. Druckman (Chapter 11) argue that the impact on individuals of communications and crafted messages from political elites are mediated by prior attitudes and their degree of availability, accessibility, and applicability. "A consideration highlighted by a communication frame cannot impinge on an attitude," they reason, "unless it is available in memory." Elite strategies of communication will have more impact on more knowledgeable individuals, though strong prior attitudes will mitigate the impact. This more nuanced approach to opinion change is reinforced by Neuman, Bimber, and Hindman (Chapter 2), who suggest that the effects of the information revolution on mass public opinion vary (depending in part on interactions with preexisting political attitudes and policy preferences) and may not be as extensive as assumed: "The dramatic changes in technology have not led to similarly dramatic changes in the political psychology of the average citizen."

A building block, then, for research on informational interdependence is that the content of public attitudes and mechanisms of opinion formation matter and that analyzing the heterogeneity of individuals is critical. Whether, how, and to what extent individuals use, produce, and are influenced by political information is not uniform but rather varies. Four broad features of public opinion and dimensions of individuals' variability are identified by the contributors to this volume.

## Four Features of Public Opinion

First, individuals are not blank slates when they are exposed to political information. Rather, they harbor beliefs, affiliations, and interests that have profound effects on how they perceive the world, what information they accept as credible, and how they interpret it. William G. Jacoby (Chapter 27) reviews the large body of research on individual attitude structures and belief systems and, in particular, ideology and partisanship, which form the "organizational foundations for many individuals' political beliefs and attitudes" and an "integral element of public opinion." Jason Barabas (Chapter 36) emphasizes that political attitudes and affiliations with political parties "shape how people look at the world" and their "perceptions of reality," even if they contradict the objective facts. This kind of partisan cuing may affect perceptions of the economy as well as policy debates. For example, when President George W. Bush pushed for expanding Medicare to cover prescription medications, a number of self-identified Republicans reversed their earlier opposition while some Democratic partisans flipped in their support for the expansion even though they had long favored this change. During the presidency of Barack Obama, Democrats and Republicans have reversed their assessment of the economy and this has affected their quite divergent evaluations of his job performance. Shifts in public attitudes and evaluations based on partisanship and which party is in power occurred in the past (see Page and Shapiro 1992) but may have intensified more recently owing to the dynamics of informational interdependence—a topic that we return to in the volume's final chapter (Chapter 43).

Second, individuals differ across several critical dimensions, which open up significant disparities in how information is processed and what impact it delivers. Vincent Hutchings and Spencer Piston (Chapter 35) report that levels of knowledge and sophistication among Americans are lower than those found in other Western countries, and, as Leslie McCall and Jeff Manza (Chapter 34) note especially, information and knowledge are unequally distributed across classes owing to "differences in education and family background." McCall and Manza connect these disparities to the acquisition and processing of information by associating "socioeconomic differences . . . in the formation of public opinion" with "class biases in political participation and media framing."

In addition to differences across individuals in knowledge, sophistication, and socioeconomic background and class, there are distinctive attitudinal patterns and beliefs across racial and ethnic groups in America that are replacing the black–white divide with a more wide-ranging multiracial politics. Rodolfo O. de la Garza and Seung-Jin Jang (Chapter 31) trace the mix of generally liberal views of Latinos toward government and self-identification as moderate and conservative. Jane Junn, Taeku Lee, S. Karthick Ramakrishnan, and Janelle Wong (Chapter 32) find variations among Asians based on whether they immigrated or were born in the US and their nation of origin. While noting that Asian Americans tend to identify with the Democratic Party (especially Asian Indians, Japanese, and Koreans), they observe that "partisanship . . . is clearly a social identity up for grabs among Asian Americans . . . [because] a large proportion of this newest group of Americans says that they do not think in partisan terms." Although there are distinctive racial and ethnic attitudes and beliefs, these intersect with individual differences in knowledge and sophistication as well as in class and socioeconomic status.

African Americans, as Fredrick C. Harris explains (Chapter 30), are loyal supporters of Democratic Party candidates and at the same time harbor diverse policy attitudes: compared to whites, they are more liberal on government social policies but more conservative on social issues such as gay marriage, prayer in schools, and abortion rights. The history of African Americans has contributed to group solidarity, support for independence from whites, and a consistent belief in the "linked fate" of blacks— namely, the sense of individual blacks that they share a common experience with other blacks and are jointly impacted as a group by politics and government policies. Linked fate has been a persistent influence on policy preferences and political attitudes, helping to account for the similarity of African-Americans' perceptions, attitudes, and opinions regardless of levels of education and income. Harris suggests that the election of Barack Obama both reflected changing attitudes about identity and will "shape black public opinion for years to come."

Gender also conditions attitudes toward policy issues, support for candidates, and political participation. Leonie Huddy and Erin Cassese (Chapter 29) report that women have been less supportive than men of government use of force and more supportive of social welfare spending and the Democratic Party (reflected in a roughly 8 to 10 percentage point "gender gap" in voting). Although women have turned out at higher rates than men for elections, they participate at lower rates in other political activities and express less interest in and knowledge about campaigns. Gender has also influenced the broad perceptions of male and female candidates: voters have associated political leadership by presidents and legislators more with stereotypes of men (strength, determination, and confidence) than with feminine personality traits of warmth and compassion.

Religion affects political attitudes and behavior and broader contours of American politics. There are differences in the political attitudes and behaviors of Protestant and

Catholic voters (with important subgroup differences relating to the greater religiousness of women). As Aimee E. Barbeau, Carin Robinson, and Clyde Wilcox (Chapter 33) explain, white evangelicals now play an influential role in Republican Party politics and are critical to understanding conservative beliefs and political attitudes. They stress that "the relationship between religion and politics is reciprocal: religion influences political attitudes, but political debates influence religion as well."

New generations and changes in socialization are generating significant changes in public opinion that, in general, point to a trend of greater egalitarianism and social liberalism. Barbeau, Robinson, and Wilcox note that "Americans of all religious traditions hold more egalitarian attitudes toward women and toward gays and lesbians in 2010 than they did in 1980, and they are also somewhat less pro-choice on abortion" (Patrick J. Egan, in Chapter 38, also discusses these issues). Stoker and Bass report that, compared with older generations, "Generations X and (especially) Y . . . hold more liberal attitudes on . . . gender roles, homosexuality, and gay rights, and . . . are stronger advocates of civil liberties and hold more egalitarian or progressive attitudes on . . . immigration and racial equality. Environmental conservation and clean energy are [also] a higher priority."

In the newest wave of research, genetics is a third dimension of public attitudes and opinion formation. Acknowledging that research in this area "is still in its infancy," Carolyn L. Funk (Chapter 26) reports that genetics may help to explain the durability of political attitudes and beliefs and the variations in their heritability. For instance, she reports that genetics exerts a strong and consistent impact on ideological orientations, perhaps more so than on party affiliation. Stoker and Bass agree with Funk that research on the effects of genetics is an important and growing area of research regarding political behavior and public opinion and, specifically, political socialization.

A fourth important aspect of public opinion involves differences among issue or policy areas. Chapters on economic issues and well-being (Barabas, Chapter 36), race relations (Taeku Lee and Nicole Willcoxon, Chapter 37), social issues more broadly (Egan, Chapter 38), "big government" (Costas Panagopolous and Robert Y. Shapiro, Chapter 39), foreign policy (Foyle, Chapter 40), and war making (Mueller, Chapter 41) identify attitudinal patterns that vary by policy domain and by time period. For many of these issues, though, recent public opinion has been increasingly shaped by partisan and ideological conflict in the United States.

## The Susceptibility of Public Opinion

These four features of public attitudes and opinion formation define the terms on which individuals process and co-produce information and are influenced by it. The durability of public attitudes and beliefs make them difficult to change rapidly, which presents a barrier to short-term manipulation of public opinion. But extensive research identifies and measures the susceptibility of the public's evaluations of policies and politicians to six forms of influence: priming and framing; online information processing; perceptions of risk; the effects of emotions; the impact of elite mobilization efforts; and inadvertent media effects.

*Priming and framing.*    The processes of priming and, especially, framing are widely discussed by authors in this volume as a subtle but potent influence on opinion formation and the processing of new information (see especially the chapters by Chong and Druckman, Nelson, and Foyle; Chapters 11, 12, and 40, respectively). Priming occurs when new information accesses existing attitudes in memory to trigger individuals to use particular standards of evaluation: President Richard Nixon developed a strategy for improving his approval rating by frequently referencing in his speeches his popular foreign policy breakthroughs such as his opening up to China (Druckman and Jacobs 2006). Framing involves the organization of information into simplifying story lines.

*Online information processing.*    Our understanding of priming and framing grows out of political psychology and research on how individuals process information. Charles S. Taber (Chapter 23) explains that even busy, distracted individuals whose cognitive capacities are impaired routinely use heuristic cues (such as political parties and interest groups) and "online" processing (such as a real-time running tally of political parties based on economic and foreign policy circumstances). Taber suggests that these processes enable everyday individuals to simplify cognitively taxing demands and to respond quickly to new information. He warns, though, of "considerable uncertainty . . . about whether such shortcuts allow them to behave competently" and the "strong likelihood of bias and susceptibility to manipulation." He concludes, in particular, that studies of "motivated reasoning" have found "that citizens are unable to treat new information evenhandedly; rather, they find agreeable information more convincing and actively counter-argue what they disagree with. . . . " Moreover, motivated reasoning occurs especially among the better educated and those most engaged in politics; the result can be misperceptions and mistakes about facts—tendencies that have long been assumed to be least likely among these groups. We consider the implications of motivated reasoning for American democracy in the final chapter (Chapter 43) as well.

*Perceptions of risk.*    Rose McDermott (Chapter 25) reviews research on "Prospect Theory," which suggests that individuals are more attentive to the risk of loss than the potential for gain. For instance, in the debate over President Barack Obama's health reform or President George Bush's push to partially privatize Social Security, opponents had the advantage in the battle for public opinion because the threat of loss matters more to individuals than the potential for gain. Beyond this broad generalization, McDermott catalogues the variations in how individuals differentially assess and respond to the allocation of risk and the perception of threat. One of the implications is that threat is, in part, a social construction based both in hard facts (such as the genuine threat of terrorist attacks) and in perception (terrorist attacks are imminent and require immediate decisions to curtail certain civil freedoms).

*The effects of emotions.*    Generations of political thought and research on the process of opinion formation and political choice have focused on cognition and neglected the role of emotion, which was often considered a pernicious component of politics that had to be controlled and avoided in order to protect political stability, tolerance, and justice (as, for instance, the Framers of the US Constitution argued). Ted Brader, George E. Marcus, and Kristyn L. Miller (Chapter 24) set aside the view of cognition as insulated from emotion; instead, they point to the interaction and two-way causal relationships between affective and cognitive processes. Emotion and its intertwined connections to cognition may create opportunities for the new media (in conjunction with the efforts of political elites) to affect the mass public.

*The impact of elite mobilization efforts.*    Elected officials, including presidents, party leaders, interest groups, and other political elites, deliberately capitalize on priming, framing, online processing, and risk perceptions to mobilize support for or against policies or politicians—though of course they rarely use these terms. Bradford H. Bishop and D. Sunshine Hillygus (Chapter 13) explain that campaigns often accept existing beliefs, affiliations, and interests and instead focus on adding new information, heightening the attention or weight attached to certain preexisting considerations, and drawing on established views to mobilize voters who irregularly turn out to cast a ballot. In identifying a variety of campaign effects, they note that the candidate and their strategists devise messages and advertisements that prompt voters to "sort through and prioritize complex and often competing predispositions, shaping how those predispositions are brought to bear in selecting a preferred candidate."

Jacoby (Chapter 27) stresses that durable attitude structures and belief systems are influenced by their "ongoing interplay" with political leadership not only during campaigns, as Bishop and Hillygus explain, but also in policy debates during the governing phase. In particular, he suggests that highly prominent political divisions (namely, today's sharp partisan polarization among elites in Washington) have prompted the "public's reactions to a broad array of issues . . . [to become] organized in ways that are consistent with individual attachments to the respective parties—self-identified Democrats are taking consistently liberal stands on issues, while Republican identifiers adhere to conservative policy positions." He suggests that "the increasing polarization in public opinion appears to be almost entirely due to the enhanced clarity in the parties' respective policy positions, rather than to increases in sophistication or ideological awareness among individual citizens" (see also Chapter 43).

McDermott also points to the ability of politicians and interest groups to "skew the debate toward preferred solutions through the strategic or incidental manipulation of how risks are presented." Calculated efforts to heighten the perceptions of risk and threat associated with Obama's health care reform and Bush's Social Security privatization illustrate the capacity of political elites to affect public evalutions. Liberals and conservatives rely on a similar strategy of invoking risk to defeat policy proposals they oppose; the overall result is that Americans receive a steady stream of efforts to "communicate frightening risks," which in turn "exacerbate[s] the difficulty of establishing trust between individuals and the government charged with protecting them."

*Inadretant media effects.*   Although research does not find consistent evidence that the media deliberately set out to indoctrinate Americans, they do influence the public by inadvertently triggering many of the processes that political elites target. Barabas (Chapter 36) reports the disproportionate press coverage of negative as opposed to positive economic developments, which primes Americans "by over-weighting bad economic information" in the news. Moy and Hussain (Chapter 14) find that media framing are "extremely effective in shaping ... political trust and political engagement." They stress the media's impact in "shaping what citizens know and how they feel about the world around them" through how they report neighborhood crime and a range of state and national news and political debates.

## Challenges for Future Research

The revolution in communications and growing interconnections of everyday Americans and the political media both reinforces the need to address enduring challenges in research and raises new ones.

There have been perennial methodological issues in accurately measuring public opinion. Michael Traugott (Chapter 20) reviews the ongoing efforts to improve the accuracy of polls measuring candidate choice before Election Day. Although preelection polls have consistently been accurate and increasingly so, there have been a few embarrassing episodes (such as the failure of most polls to estimate Hillary Clinton's lead over Barack Obama in the New Hampshire primary), which precipitated investigations and revisions to improve accuracy. Adam J. Berinsky (Chapter 21) examines "non-response bias"—errors in measurement related to systematic biases in who responds to surveys. Non-response bias reflects social economic status; individuals with higher levels of education and income answer surveys at a higher rate, which undermines the broad representativeness of survey results. George Franklin Bishop (Chapter 22) describes the distorting effects of question wordings and formats, and also the context effects related to the order of survey questions. Traugott, Berinsky, and Bishop all emphasize the relentless efforts of survey researchers, especially through the use of survey experiments, to identify the sources of error, and to correct them in order (as Bishop concludes) "to arrive at reasonably valid conclusions about aggregate-level trends in public opinion."

Michael X. Delli Carpini (Chapter 18) reviews the evolution of survey research and the impact of new computer technology on sampling, database management, survey design, and the analysis of the data. One of the most recent innovations is the Internet survey, which makes it possible to develop more complicated question formats (such as tradeoffs among competing budget choices) and to substantially reduce costs. Among the challenges to this innovation is that the use of recruited, self-selected Internet "samples" raises questions about the representativeness of survey findings.

John G. Gunnell (Chapter 17) steps back from questions about how to measure public opinion and its interactions with the new information environment to examine how it is conceptualized. He explains that the now widely accepted conception of public opinion as "an aggregation of individual and group preferences" is, in fact, a relatively recent invention of the twentieth century. He suggests that this understanding is narrower than the earlier conception of public opinion as a "collective entity" and departs from the notion of an "organic people" as the foundation of popular sovereignty, which was embraced by leaders of the American Revolution and the Framers of the US Constitution.

## Media Organization and News Reporting

Political reporting is a function of how the media is organized and for what purpose. Doris A. Graber and Gregory G. Holyk (Chapter 6) review the enduring organizational forces and norms that have long influenced what is defined as "newsworthy" and how it is reported. The chapters in this volume go a step further to identify important new developments as the media undergoes a rapid and transformative evolution.

A number of chapters review the reinvention of the media through the Internet. Susan Herbst (Chapter 19), Moy and Hussain (Chapter 14), Jamieson and Hardy (Chapter 15), and other contributors trace the spawning of new formats for generating information about politics and policy. Jennifer Jerit and Jason Barabas (Chapter 9) discuss the "continually evolving media environment—in particular, the increased availability of news sources as well as the ease with which people can select their information source. . . ." The traditional definition of the mass media with television networks and cable and with family newspapers has been radically redefined by new forms of media that are produced and distributed online.

Media organization has also evolved to reflect demographic changes in American society. As the country has become more multiethnic and multiracial, media tailored for distinct populations has emerged. Chapter 32, by Junn, Lee, Ramakrishnan, and Wong, points to Asian-language media, while de la Garza and Jang (Chapter 31) note the Spanish press.

A persistent theme is the consequence of changes in old and new media for expanding the diversity of information available to citizens and their opportunities for fruitful deliberation. Schudson (Chapter 4) suggests that the astonishing changes in the media offer "many more reasons for hope than for despair." Vavreck and Iyengar (Chapter 10) point to our new era of "people interact[ing] with political 'media' and information in many new ways" and believe that it "opens doors for real political communication." Herbst (Chapter 19) observes that the "Web enables more rhetorical activity than any communication technology has ever allowed, in the history of human expression," which equips citizens to "connect with others, spread ideas, and get a sense of public opinion on any issue." She is hopeful that it facilitates and enriches the opportunities for citizens to make "public argument with those who oppose us, and [organize] with those who think like us. . . ."

The optimistic view of the greater openness, access, and diversity of news is, however, challenged in this volume. Graber and Holyk (Chapter 6) express great concern about the rise of "opinionated reporting and the shift toward soft interpretive news away from harder factual formats" that are "essential for citizens' political deliberations." The decline of in-depth and investigative reporting, they report, "widen[s] gaps in knowledge . . . [and] erode[s] our common information bases and the ability to communicate and understand one another." Jamieson and Hardy expand on concerns that the new media landscape has created "the potential to reside in a self-protective enclave of reinforcing information" as Americans "customize their news repertoire" and as media organizations "[shift] away from wide-ranging broadcast messages to focus in on niche markets." They share the worry of others about the damage to our democracy when "deliberation over a policy issue between groups may become more difficult as those coming to the table will have incompatible information repertoires." Moy and Hussain (Chapter 14) worry that the new social media may "[improve] access to political information and institutions" when in fact they are "promoting 'thin citizenship,'" in which "Citizens may feel more engaged and efficacious, but [do] not actually participate effectively."

Although information interdependence has broken the monopoly of the mainstream press and opened up opportunities for individuals to generate political information for potentially wide distribution, it may also foster—as W. Lance Bennett (Chapter 16) suggests—negative "feedback between publics and politicians." Bennett's particular concern is how polls have been used by the news media to construct a misleading and "symbolic public" that marginalizes opposition, prompts dissidents to "tune out social deliberations because they perceive that they are in a minority," and induce "news organizations [to] avoid critical examination of ever more dominant news frames. . . ." The result, Bennett warns, is "managerial democracy," in which messages are framed by communication professionals and passively accepted by journalists.

Some chapters reach more ambivalent conclusions. The chapters by Schudson (Chapter 4) and by Katherine Ann Brown and Todd Gitlin (Chapter 5) recalibrate the dire warnings about the threat of the new media by emphasizing the limitations of the older, traditional media. Brown and Gitlin warn against "oversimplify[ing] and romanticiz[ing] the actual news media and their part in everyday life [in the course of American history]" given its record of "frequently fail[ing] to challenge abuses of power" and its mixed record on "encourag[ing] meaningful civic engagement." Noting the demise of the 1970s "fierce truth-bound independence" and the media's current "symbiotic relations with the powerful," they close by warning that the "current weaknesses of journalism cannot, on balance, be good news for democratic prospects."

## Challenges for Future Research

The transformation of the media requires innovations in research on it. Jerit and Barabas (Chapter 9) call for "new and better ways of identifying the causal impact of the mass media on public opinion" in an era when there are disparate sources of political information. Several authors also insist that research adapt to increasingly heterogeneous media. The proliferation of traditional media offerings and new media models has produced a plethora of information sources and highly selective patterns of consumption that require new methodologies for measuring and detecting media effects (Bennett and Iyengar 2008, 2010). As Gaines and Kuklinski (Chapter 3) explain,

The number of media sources began to expand at an unprecedented rate, which not only gave citizens more news options from which to choose, but also increased the overall activity in the environment. Together, these two consequences of media expansion translated into more factors to be taken into account, thus increasing the difficulty of properly specifying regression and other statistical models.

The heterogeneity of information and how it is consumed by individuals may well require new disciplinary approaches and methodologies that combine the specialization of today's research with a return to earlier participant observation and more integrating frameworks to "holistically" analyze the strategic interactions of politicians, the full universe of information sources, and public opinion.

# THE BATTLE FOR AMERICAN DEMOCRACY: FROM GRAND THEORY TO ENGAGED THEORY

The beginning of the twenty-first century witnessed extraordinary breakthroughs in mass communications and precipitated vibrant debate about whether the proliferation of information sources, their co-production, and informational interdependence created a boon for democracy and genuine public deliberation or intensified existing threats or created new ones.

The storming of the Bastille sparked the French Revolution; the acceleration of the online information revolution has broken the stranglehold that the traditional media and its government sources once held on what information was produced and disseminated, fundamentally affecting what citizens know. Today, the audience not only has far more choices of information but also can participate in its production and distribution. (Think of the profound impacts of such disparate self-directed newsmaking as the online leaking of top-secret US–Afghan memorandums and the spontaneous videoing of Iranian protesters attacked by their government's forces.) These trends in production and consumption have introduced a degree of emancipation and equality in information production and dissemination that is unprecedented and opens the door to a resurgence of popular sovereignty in both publicly scrutinizing government and rallying pressure on it.

The opening of information flow may directly foster collective deliberation (Page 1996) through social media communications and reactions and counterreactions. News articles or online posts now regularly generate "threads" of comments from hundreds and even thousands of readers who largely interact free of policing. The information revolution may also fuel what appears to be vigorous public deliberation within many communities. The first comprehensive empirical study of reason-based public talk about matters of community concern finds that deliberation, as a form of public activity, is as prevalent as more widely discussed and studied forms of political expression such as voting (Jacobs, Cook, and Delli Carpini 2009). The wide-ranging and highly accessible revolution in online information production and distribution appears to support and encourage decentralized and uncoordinated public deliberation including organized meetings that rely on facilitators to include diverse voices and guide discussion toward reason-based claims.

Although styles of argumentation and scholarly reputations are enhanced by the drawing of sharp polarities, conclusions about the emancipatory potential of information interdependence are too sweeping and, indeed, are contradicted by notable barriers to public deliberation and democratic oversight. The co-production of Internet-based information has opened up mass communication, but it has also scattered the shared public square of debate into innumerable and cloistered silos and has put informed and knowledgeable news producers (such as skilled journalists) on the same footing as individuals with limited competency and understanding of public issues. While vibrant online exchanges might well chase out the ignorant or extreme partisans, the process of self-correction is more difficult in the new fragmented information environment. In addition, economic, cultural, and technical capacities to follow online debates and to engage in them vary across racial, ethnic, and socio-economic groups, which adds yet another level of inequality of voice and influence in politics. The better-established groups are more engaged in the world of information interdependence. Moreover, affluent organizations and political actors have seized on the Internet as a new strategic tool to distort debate, distract attention, and selectively rally supporters. The crafted talk of twentieth-century political operatives has now become a more potent weapon to orchestrate public deliberation and influence government.

As claims about the emancipatory power of the new media are too sweeping, so are conclusions about the complete "corruption" of public life and American democracy. New information capacities both open up opportunities for citizen engagement and trigger countervailing effects that minimize some of these new possibilities for influence. The disaggregating of news sources, the selectivity of individuals about which sources they use, the embedded attitudes and preference of ordinary citizens, and the countervailing effects of news sources and strategic maneuvering by media organizations and political actors may be bastions against the most significant threats to democracy and deliberation—and they may well, going forward, create promising opportunities for strengthening both.

Nonetheless, overly optimistic championing of the new information revolution is not justified. The final chapter outlines the confluence of a series of pathological developments that limit and threaten authentic public deliberation and vigorous democracy. Even mixed effects of the new media on citizens and on political elites deserve careful attention, especially as they may (individually or in combination) weaken democratic governance.

# REFERENCES

*American Journalism Review.* 2009. AJR's 2009 Count of Statehouse Reporters. *American Journalism Review*, Apr.–May.

ANSOLABEHERE, S., BEHR, R., and IYENGAR, S. 1992. *The Media Game: American Politics in the Television Age.* New York: Longman.

BENNETT, W. L., and IYENGAR, S. 2008. A New Era of Minimal Effects? The Changing Foundations of Political Communication. *Journal of Communication*, 58: 707–31.

————— 2010. The Shifting Foundations of Political Communication: Responding to a Defense of the Media Effects Paradigm. *Journal of Communication*, 60: 35–9.

DRUCKMAN, J. N., and JACOBS, L. R. 2006. Lumpers and Splitters: The Public Opinion Information that Politicians Collect and Use. *Public Opinion Quarterly*, 70 (Dec.), 453–76.

FIORINA, M., with ABRAMS, S., and POPE, J. 2005. *The Culture War? The Myth of a Polarized America.* New York: Pearson Longman.

GAMSON, W. 1992. *Talking Politics.* Cambridge: Cambridge University Press.

JACOBS, L. R., COOK, F. L., and DELLI CARPINI, M. X. 2009. *Talking Together: Public Deliberation in America and the Search for Community.* Chicago: University of Chicago Press.

NEUMAN, W. R., JUST, M. K., and CRIGLER, A. N. 1992. *Common Knowledge: News and the Construction of Political Meaning.* Chicago: University of Chicago Press.

PAGE, B. I. 1996. *Who Deliberates? Mass Media in Modern Democracy.* Chicago: University of Chicago Press.

—— and JACOBS, L. R. 2009. *Class War? What Americans Really Think about Economic Inequality.* Chicago: University of Chicago Press.

—— and SHAPIRO, R. Y. 1992. *The Rational Public: Fifty Years of Trends in Americans' Policy Preferences.* Chicago: University of Chicago Press.

PRIOR, M. 2007. *Post-Broadcast Democracy: How Media Choice Increases Inequality in Political Involvement and Polarize Elections.* New York: Cambridge University Press.

Technology executives, government regulators, and even key innovators themselves did not realize until quite late the implications of these technological shifts. When physicist Tim Berners-Lee developed technical refinements in the early 1990s in order to share academic information over the Internet, he hardly expected to lay the foundation of a new mass medium (Berners-Lee 1999). He wasn't alone. As late as 1995, Bill Gates's vision of "the road ahead" hardly mentioned the Internet. The monumental 1996 US Telecommunications Act, which set the regulatory ground rules for competitive telephony and digital television, famously ignored the Internet (Neuman, McKnight, and Solomon 1998).

The Internet, of course, now constitutes a large and still growing portion of the American media diet. As of 2009, over 80 percent of US households had home Internet access (Pew Internet & American Life Project 2009). About 63 percent of households had broadband, about 85 percent of all Americans had cellphones, and about a third had used the Internet from a smartphone or other portable device (Horrigan 2009a, 2009b). In 2006, for the first time, the number of Americans reporting that they went online for news at least three times per week exceeded the number regularly watching nightly network news, and by 2008 exceeded the number reading the newspaper on a daily basis (Pew Research Center for the People & the Press 2008).

The Internet is also entangled in the economic travails of the newspaper and magazine industries. Though rates of newspaper readership have been slowly declining since the 1980s, revenue had been largely stable until the recent and precipitous declines. Between 2006 and 2008 the newspaper industry saw a 23 percent decline in advertising revenue, and by the end of 2008, massive layoffs placed newsroom staffing levels 20 percent below the level of 2001 (Pew Project for Excellence in Journalism 2009). Readers shifting news consumption from print to the Internet explains some of the fall: Web editions now account for half of all newspaper readership, but provide only 10 percent of revenues. Even bigger culprits are sites like Craigslist and eBay, which have gutted newspaper classified advertising, the largest profit center for many small- and mid-sized papers. A wave of highly leveraged mergers has made matters worse by saddling many newspapers with steep debts, turning a long-term problem into an immediate crisis.

# THREE CAUTIONARY PRINCIPLES

The dynamics of how media shape citizenship are clearly in flux. In considering the implications of these technologies and their accompanying economic shifts for citizenship, it is worth reviewing three analytic principles from the study of technological evolution and media effects that have helped illuminate previous technological changes. The first is the *diffusion principle*. Everett Rogers engaged in a lifetime study of communication and the diffusion of innovation (1986, 2003). He developed and popularized the notion that early adopters of new technologies are systematically different from mainstream adopters and laggards. Accordingly, for studies conducted in the United States in the 1990s and early 2000s, one needs to take great care in parsing the impact of the technologies themselves from the characteristics of the atypical citizens who are early adopters. Strikingly few of the publications we have reviewed address this issue seriously. Furthermore, new technical architectures sometimes take decades to change behaviors, expectations, and institutions. The Model T as a mass-produced and accessibly priced automobile was introduced in 1908, but it was not until after the Second World War that the full impact of the automobile was realized (Kline and Pinch 1996). Observations that the Internet has not, for example, challenged the dominance of broadcast-television-based spot advertising in electoral politics need to be seen in historical perspective.

The second, related cautionary principle is the existence of *differential effects*. Often when a new technical resource becomes available the most active and best-resourced members of society are quick to take advantage while marginal members are unable or uninterested in doing so. Under these circumstances, inequality can be magnified. This widely acknowledged dynamic is sometimes identified as positive feedback, accumulated advantage, or "the Matthew Effect" (Merton 1968). Unlike the diffusion principle, this theme is frequently addressed in the literature on Internet effects (Norris 2000, 2001; Bimber and Davis 2003; Hindman 2009; and others). As we will see below, the answers to basic questions about the Internet and political participation or knowledge require accounting for differential effects. This principle is particularly important in assessing hypotheses about the Internet as leveler and mobilizer of previously marginal strata of the citizenry.

The third principle is the prospect of *conditional effects*. The literature in general is quite careful to avoid simplistic technological determinism and uses phrases like "the facilitation by" and "the affordances of" new technologies. Accordingly, under some social and cultural conditions and for some especially motivated strata of society, the Internet's capacities for interactivity, diversity, and information abundance may be transformative. The Internet certainly makes an impressively broad array of political information and misinformation available, and it dramatically changes who can communicate with whom. For those citizens with the motivation and interest to seek political information or to engage in communication about public affairs, the Internet is likely to have much different effects than for those who are relatively disinterested in politics or unmotivated about public life. Indeed, a key emphasis in recent work on the Internet and citizenship is accounting for conditional effects and interactions.

# CITIZEN DELIBERATION AND THE PUBLIC SPHERE

The cautionary principles above are a start—but only a start—in addressing perhaps the most basic and difficult-to-answer question about the Internet: what does it mean for the fate of the public sphere in the twenty-first century? Few scholars of political communication have been more influential than Jürgen Habermas. His concepts of the public sphere and the ideal speech situation have been a popular lens through which to evaluate the Internet's impact on public life. Habermas, of course, argues that the participatory bourgeois public sphere of nineteenth-century salon culture was subverted by the rise of commercialized mass media (1989). Might not the Internet, which grants any citizen the technical means to communicate their views directly to other citizens, move us closer to Habermas's "ideal speech situation" (1981)?

At first glance, one might posit that the Internet is optimally designed to provide a structural *re*transformation of the public sphere along the lines Habermas idealizes. The key elements Habermas sets out concern the capacity of citizens to express their attitudes, desires, and needs, and their ability to challenge the assertions of others without fear of retribution (1990a). The hope is that, as with the widely used metaphor of a marketplace of ideas, the better argument will win out (Napoli 2001). Interestingly, Habermas himself has addressed the question of the Internet and the public sphere several times, and acknowledged that the ideal of a face-to-face collective of mutually consenting members may be also made possible by new technical means (Habermas 1990b; Peters 1993). But Habermas remains highly skeptical. He acknowledges in a recent footnote that "The Internet has certainly reactivated the grassroots of an egalitarian public of writers and readers" but notes that "the rise of millions of fragmented chat rooms across the world tend[s] instead to lead to the fragmentation of large but politically focused mass audiences into a huge number of isolated issue publics" (Habermas 2006, 423). Bruns in a challenging review presses further:

So what is it with Habermas and the Net? A similarly critical (and similarly questionable) negative stance towards the Net can be found in his (German-language) speech on the occasion of the Bruno Kreisky Award in March 2005: here, he suggests that while the Net "has led to an unforeseen extension of the media public and to an unprecedented thickening of communications networks," this "welcome increase in egalitarianism . . . is being paid for by the decentralization of access to unedited contributions. In this medium the contributions of intellectuals lose the power to create a focus." Overall, therefore, "use of the Internet has both extended and fragmented communication connections."    (Bruns 2007)

Habermas's assessment appears to be that the Internet's fundamental openness, and its lack of knowledgeable moderators to structure debate, precludes the sort of deliberation he hopes for. This view arises in large part from his position that every "competent speaker" should participate, rather than every possible speaker. The question of which citizens might qualify as competent remains troublingly unanswered.

In addition to Habermas himself, a small army of scholars has been attracted to the question of whether online deliberation does, or can, approach a Habermasian ideal (among them: Bimber 2003; Brants 2005; Bruns 2007; Castells 2009; Coleman and Blumler 2009; Dahlberg 2004; Davis 2009; Hauser 1999; Hindman 2009; Papacharissi 2004; Poster 1997; Price 2009; Sey and Castells 2004; Thornton 2002; Wilhelm 2000; and Wright and Street 2007). Two elements are common to nearly all of these essays. First, the scholars expand upon or add some conditions to Habermas's original list of prerequisites for ideal speech. Second, they conclude that they too are skeptical that the Internet could produce such an idealized vision of democratic practice.

Our reading of this body of scholarship suggests that, with variations in terminology, Habermas's original criteria for an ideal speech situation have been expanded into six with respect to online communication. But it is worth emphasizing from the start that the online public sphere is not just a function of the technical facilities of the Internet and related technologies—even when (as rarely happens) these are assessed completely and correctly. Conclusions about the public sphere, as Habermas's own work makes clear, require us to examine the actual practices of debate.

His original criteria for the celebrated ideal speech situation are frequently summarized as: (1) every subject with the competence to speak and act is allowed to take part in a discourse; (2) everyone is allowed to express their attitudes, desires, and needs and to introduce or question any assertion whatever; and (3) no speaker may be prevented, by internal or external coercion, from exercising the rights as laid down in (1) and (2) above (see Habermas 1990a). In some ways, this list underspecifies speech situations in real contexts of all kinds, whether they involve the Internet or not. In the literature on the public sphere and the Internet, these have been elaborated to address in more detail issues of inclusiveness, equality, rationality, agendas, power, and the absence of distraction from substantive discourse. This work can be summarized as follows.

The first criterion for a successful online public sphere is *the inclusion of a broad array of citizens in rational deliberation*. Habermas famously concludes that the one-way commercial media dulled the capacity of the bourgeoisie to engage in critical discussion in public forums such as coffee houses and salons. One problem with the Internet and especially the blogosphere, according to this follow-on literature, is a continuing digital divide. Despite the great extent of Internet diffusion cited above, economically and culturally marginalized citizens represent a big portion of those who do not use the Internet (Bonfadelli 2002; Norris 2001; Servon and Pinkett 2004). And among those already online, large differences in skill levels may represent a second-level digital divide affecting both the elderly and a surprising number of younger citizens (Hargittai 2002, 2007).

But if the hope is to include a broad array of citizens in discussion, overcoming divides in access and skills is only a start. One place discussion takes place is on blogs. It is estimated that there are approximately 900,000 new blog posts every day (Technorati 2010) but most of them are about celebrity and culture. Only one blog in ten discusses politics on a regular basis (Lenhart, Purcell, Smith, and Zickuhr 2010). And only a few hundred bloggers can count on readership levels measured in the thousands of visitors per day. This small set of A-list bloggers is hardly a broad cross-section of the public, and this elite group remains overwhelmingly white, disproportionately male, and replete with the alumni of Ivy-League-caliber institutions (Hindman 2009). Bloggers who attract a significant audience certainly have the smarts and schooling necessary to serve as Habermasian moderators; whether they have the necessary temperament is more debatable.

key advantage and the gap between them persists. The most compelling possibilities are not in such settings, but within formal organizations themselves as these adapt to new possibilities and expectations from citizens, and also in new kinds of groups that bring new issues to the political agenda and that engage in politics outside highly institutio-nalized contexts.

This pattern is confirmed in numerous studies, including Phil Howard's detailed ethnography of political mobilization and campaign organizations in the early 2000s:

A decade ago, only the wealthier lobbyists and presidential campaigns could afford the services of Databank.com [a pseudonymous political strategy and data analysis firm], but now the firm also sells detailed relational databases to the country's nascent grassroots movements and individuals eager to start a small campaign of their own. Political data became a marketable product, something that could be sold to grassroots movements, elite campaigns or corporate lobbyists. (Howard 2006, 29)

Political scientists have been especially curious about the impact of the new media on the structure and prominence of the dominant political parties. Nelson Polsby and others have characterized the last five decades as the mass media age of party politics (Polsby 1984). Polsby noted that structural reforms after the 1968 election reduced the power of the party insiders in the iconic "smoke-filled rooms" and made winning the party nomination the product of a media-saturated primary process. So we ask, will new technology weaken the mass media, reenergize party organizations, or even freshly empower third party efforts? Several scholars have argued that, while the Internet may lessen dependence on big media and facilitate cheaper and more narrowly targeted political communication, it will neither reenergize the major parties nor hasten their decline (Norris 2000).

So, for the most part, the Internet does not look likely to alter the distribution of power among major players much, particularly for political contests taking place in traditional institutionalized forums. A different question is: what happens when political organizing happens outside traditional venues and organizations, in cam-paigns other than for national office, or where organizing takes alternative forms such as protest or political consumerism? Though these sorts of cases have received less study, the Internet has played an essential role in many recent and varied instances of political activism, from the 2006 student immigration walkout in Los Angeles high schools to the demonstrations at the 2010 Copenhagen climate change conference. The Internet increases the speed of mobilization and the ability of organizers to shift scale from the local to the global and back (Bennett, Breunig, and Givens 2008). It permits activists to mobilize people who become interested in one issue, even if temporarily, and who do not necessarily "belong" to anything but their own personal social net-works. Structurally, this is a substantial change in how mobilization can work. The Internet also affects the structure of organizers themselves, permitting organizational hybridity (Chadwick 2007) and contributing to a profusion of new organizational forms that are less dependent for their existence upon traditional resources and infra-structure, or on traditional practices of "membership" (Bimber, Stohl, and Flanagin

2009). All this means that the menu of participatory opportunities for interested citizens is expanding, and to a large degree it is doing so on citizens' own terms. What to participate in, when, and even how, are decisions increasingly in the hands of citizens themselves, rather than the formal leadership hierarchy of interest groups or political campaigns. These developments suggest that significant changes may be coming in the structure of collective action broadly, even if highly institutionalized election campaigns for high office remain dominated by elites and campaign professionals. How citizens choose among options for engagement and political expression in this changing, expanding, and less well-bounded environment remains to be seen.

## THE CHANGING CONTEXT FOR CITIZENSHIP

In the study of media and politics, the media have often played the role of convenient whipping boy. When US survey data began showing declines in political trust and efficacy during the 1960s and 1970s, television was seen as the obvious culprit (Robinson 1976). There is a long tradition of attributing negative dimensions of the human condition to the mass media, most notably violence and irresponsible sexual behavior. But in the case of the Internet and politics the dominant theme has been surprisingly positive. Scholars have been inclined to believe that the expanded media environment will be able to engage, inform, and enrich the political consciousness of the otherwise easily distracted citizenry.

One of the earliest book-length studies reviewing these issues was published in 2000 and concluded that the null hypothesis had won out: the Internet environment represented nothing more than "politics as usual" (Margolis and Resnick 2000). Perhaps they spoke too soon. Online and mobile media are becoming intimately integrated into the daily flow of political information and occasional waves of citizen mobilization. The dramatic changes in technology have not led to similarly dramatic changes in the political psychology of the average citizen. But Internet-facilitated changes in citizenship are numerous, subtle, conditional, and still evolving.

We have been using the term "Internet" to try to capture the diverse elements of interoperability, interactivity, intelligence, portability, and communicative capacity commonly associated with the digital revolution. When many of the studies in the extant literature were being conducted, the term "Internet" conjured up a desktop computer with a bulky monitor tethered to a wall. Now laptops outsell desktops, and to many people the Internet means Facebook and Twitter on a smartphone. It will likely mean something else in another decade. Those analyzing the Internet are attempting to assess a moving target as new stages of Internet diffusion arrive.

In this chapter we have reviewed four dimensions of citizenship of particular salience in these literatures. In each of the four dimensions we have documented a changing information environment and subtle but important responses by the public. The most consistent finding across all four domains is that the Internet has not changed the US

GARRETT, R. K. 2009. Politically Motivated Reinforcement Seeking: Reframing the Selective Exposure Debate. *Journal of Communication*, 594: 676–99.

GATES, B. 1995. *The Road Ahead*. New York: Viking Press.

HABERMAS, J. 1981. *The Theory of Communicative Action*, i and ii. Boston: Beacon Press.

—— 1989. *The Structural Transformation of the Public Sphere*. Cambridge, MA: MIT Press. First published 1962.

—— 1990a. *Moral Consciousness and Communicative Action*. Cambridge, MA: MIT Press.

—— 1990b. Vorwort zur Neuauflage 1990. In *Strukturwandel der Offentlichkeit*. Frankfurt: Suhrkamp.

—— 2006. Political Communication in Media Society: Does Democracy Still Enjoy an Epistemic Dimension? The Impact of Normative Theory on Empirical Research. *Communication Theory*, 16: 411–26.

HARGITTAI, E. 2002. Second Level Digital Divide: Differences in People's Online Skills. *First Monday*, 7/4 (Apr. 1). At <http://firstmonday.org/htbin/cgiwrap/bin/ojs/index.php/fm/article/view/942/864>. Accessed Oct. 2010.

—— 2007. The Social, Political, Economic, and Cultural Dimensions of Search Engines. *Journal of Computer Mediated Communication*, 12/3. At <jcmc.indiana.edu/vol12/issue3/hargittai.html>. Accessed Oct. 2010.

HAUSER, G. A. 1999. *Vernacular Voices: The Rhetoric of Publics and Public Spheres*. Columbia: University of South Carolina Press.

HEWITT, H. 2006. *Blog: Understanding the Information Reformation that's Changing your World*. Nashville: Thomas Nelson.

HIGHTON, B. 2009. Revisiting the Relationship between Educational Attainment and Political Sophistication. *Journal of Politics*, 71: 1564–76.

HINDMAN, M. S. 2009. *The Myth of Digital Democracy*. Princeton: Princeton University Press.

HORRIGAN, J. 2009a. Home Broadband Adoption 2009. Pew Internet & American Life Project. At <http://www.pewinternet.org>. Accessed Oct. 2010.

—— 2009b. Wireless Internet Use. Pew Internet & American Life Project. At <http://www.pewinternet.org>. Accessed Oct. 2010.

HOWARD, P. N. 2006. *New Media Campaigns and the Managed Citizen*. New York: Cambridge University Press.

IYENGAR, S., and HAHN, K. S. 2009. Red Media, Blue Media: Evidence of Ideological Selectivity in Media Use. *Journal of Communication*, 57: 19–39.

JENNINGS, M. K., and ZEITNER, V. 2003. Internet Use and Civic Engagement. *Public Opinion Quarterly*, 673: 311–34.

JONES, D. A. 2002. The Polarizing Effect of New Media Messages. *International Journal of Public Opinion Research*, 14: 158–74.

KENSKI, K., and STROUD, N. J. 2006. Connections between Internet Use and Political Efficacy, Knowledge, and Participation. *Journal of Broadcasting & Electronic Media*, 502: 173–93.

KERBEL, M. 2009. *Netroots: Online Progressives and the Transformation of American Politics*. Boulder, CO: Paradigm.

KIPPEN, G., and JENKINS, G. 2004. The Challenge of E-Democracy for Political Parties. In *Democracy Online: The Prospects for Political Renewal through the Internet*, ed. P. M. Shane. New York: Routledge.

KLINE, R., and PINCH, T. 1996. Users as Agents of Technological Change: The Social Construction of the Automobile in the Rural United States. *Technology and Culture*, 374: 763–95.

KROSNICK, J. A. 1990. Government Policy and Citizen Passion: A Study of Issue Publics in Contemporary America. *Political Behavior*, 12: 59–92.

—— and TELHAMI, S. 1995. Public Attitudes toward Israel: A Study of the Attentive and Issue Publics. *International Studies Quarterly*, 39: 535–54.

LENHART, A., PURCELL, K., SMITH, A., and ZICKUHR, K. 2010. *Social Media and Young Adults.* Washington, DC: Pew Internet & American Life Project.

LESKOVEC, J., BACKSTROM, L., and KLEINBERG, J. 2009. Meme Tracking and the Dynamics of the News Cycle. *Proceedings of the 15th ACM SIGKDD International Conference on Knowledge Discovery and Data Mining.* Association for Computing Machinery 978-1-60558-495-9/09/06. At <www.cs.cornell.edu/home/kleinber/kdd09-quotes.pdf>. Accessed Oct. 2010.

McCHESNEY, R. W. (ed.) 2007. *Communication Revolution: Critical Junctures and the Future of Media.* New York: New Press.

MANSBRIDGE, J. 1983. *Beyond Adversary Democracy.* Chicago: University of Chicago Press.

MARGOLIS, M., and RESNICK, D. 2000. *Politics as Usual: The Cyberspace Revolution.* Thousand Oaks, CA: Sage.

MERTON, R. K. 1968. *Social Theory and Social Structure.* New York: Free Press.

MOSSBERGER, K., TOLBERT, C. J., and MCNEAL, R. S. 2008. *Digital Citizenship: The Internet, Society, and Participation.* Cambridge, MA: MIT Press.

NAPOLI, P. M. 2001. *Foundations of Communications Policy: Principles and Process in the Regulation of Electronic Media.* Cresskill, NJ: Hampton Press.

NEUMAN, W. R., McKNIGHT, L., and SOLOMON, R. J. 1998. *The Gordian Knot: Political Gridlock on the Information Highway.* Cambridge, MA: MIT Press.

NORRIS, P. 2000. *A Virtuous Circle: Political Communications in Post-Industrial Societies.* New York: Cambridge University Press.

—— 2001. *Digital Divide: Civic Engagement, Information Poverty, and the Internet Worldwide.* New York: Cambridge University Press.

PAPACHARISSI, Z. 2004. Democracy Online: Civility, Politeness, and the Democratic Potential of Online Political Discussion Groups. *New Media and Society*, 62: 259–83.

PETERS, J. D. 1993. Distrust of Representation: Habermas on the Public Sphere. *Media, Culture and Society*, 15: 541–71.

Pew Internet & American Life Project 2009. March 2009 Poll. At <http://www.pewinternet. org>. Accessed Oct. 2010.

Pew Project for Excellence in Journalism. 2009. The State of the News Media: An Annual Report on American Journalism. At <http://www.stateofthemedia.org/2009/index.htm>. Accessed Oct. 2010.

Pew Research Center for the People & the Press. 2006. Online News. At <http://people-press. org/reports/pdf/282.pdf>. Accessed Oct. 2010.

—— 2008. Key News Audiences Now Blend Online and Traditional Sources. At <http:// people-press.org/report/444/news-media>. Accessed Oct. 2010.

POLSBY, N. W. 1984. *Political Innovation in America: The Politics of Policy Initiation.* New Haven: Yale University Press.

POSTER, M. 1997. Cyberdemocracy: The Internet and the Public Sphere. In *Virtual Politics: Identity and Community in Cyberspace*, ed. D. Holmes. Thousand Oaks, CA: Sage.

PRICE, V. 2009. Citizens Deliberating Online: Theory and Some Evidence. In *Online Deliberation: Design, Research, and Practice*, ed. T. Davies and S. P. Gangadharan. Chicago: University of Chicago Press for the Center for the Study of Language and Information.

—— NIR, L., and CAPPELLA, J. N. 2002. Does Disagreement Contribute to More Deliberative Opinion? *Political Communication*, 19: 95–112.

PRICE, V., NIR, L., and CAPPELLA, J. N. 2006. Normative and Informational Influences in Online Political Discussions. *Communication Theory*, 16: 47–74.

PRIOR, M. 2007. *Post-Broadcast Democracy: How Media Choice Increases Inequality in Political Involvement and Polarizes Elections*. New York: Cambridge University Press.

PUTNAM, R. D. 2000. *Bowling Alone: The Collapse and Revival of American Community*. New York: Simon & Schuster.

REYNOLDS, G. 2006. *An Army of Davids: How Markets and Technology Empower Ordinary People to Beat Big Media, Big Government, and Other Goliaths*. Nashville: Thomas Nelson.

ROBINSON, M. J. 1976. Public Affairs Television and the Growth of Political Malaise: The Case of "the Selling of the Pentagon." *American Political Science Review*, 70: 409–32.

ROGERS, E. M. 1986. *Communication Technology: The New Media in Society*. New York: Free Press.

—— 2003. *Diffusion of Innovations*, 5th edn. New York: Free Press.

SERVON, L. J., and PINKETT, R. D. 2004. Narrowing the Digital Divide: The Potential and Limits of the US Community Technology Movement. In *The Network Society*, ed. M. Castells. Northampton, MA: Edward Elgar.

SEY, A., and CASTELLS, M. 2004. From Media Politics to Networked Politics: The Internet and the Political Process. In *The Network Society*, ed. M. Castells. Northampton, MA: Edward Elgar.

SHAH, D. V., KWAK, N., and HOLBERT, R. L. 2001. "Connecting" and "Disconnecting" with Civic Life: Patterns of Internet Use and the Production of Social Capital. *Political Communication*, 18: 141–62.

SIGELMAN, L., and KUGLER, M. 2003. Why Is Research on the Effects of Negative Campaigning So Inconclusive? Understanding Citizens' Perceptions of Negativity. *Journal of Politics*, 6501: 142–60.

STARR, P. 2004. *The Creation of the Media*. New York: Basic Books.

SUNSTEIN, C. 2001. *Republic.com*. Princeton: Princeton University Press.

Technorati. 2010. Technorati's State of the Blogosphere. At <http://technorati.com/state-of-the-blogosphere>. Accessed Oct. 2010.

THORNTON, A. 2002. Does Internet Create Democracy? Sydney: University of Technology. At <http://www.zipworld.com.au/~athornto>. Accessed Oct. 2010.

TREMAYNE, M., ZHENG, N., LEE, J. K., and JEONG, J. 2006. Issue Publics on the Web: Applying Network Theory to the War Blogosphere. *Journal of Computer-Mediated Communication*, 121: 15.

VAN DE DONK, W. B. H. J., LOADER, B. D., NIXON, P. G., and RUCHT, D. (eds.) 2004. *Cyberprotest: New Media, Citizens, and Social Movements*. New York: Routledge.

WILHELM, A. 2000. *Democracy in the Digital Age: Challenges to Political Life in Cyberspace*. New York: Routledge.

WOJCIESZAK, M. E., and MUTZ, D. 2009. Online Groups and Political Discourse: Do Online Discussion Spaces Facilitate Exposure to Political Disagreement? *Journal of Communication*, 59: 40–56.

WRIGHT, S., and STREET, J. 2007. Democracy, Deliberation and Design: The Case of Online Discussion Forums. *New Media Society*, 95: 849–69.

XENOS, M., and MOY, P. 2007. Direct and Differential Effects of the Internet on Political and Civic Engagement. *Journal of Communication*, 57: 704–18.

ZITTRAIN, J. 2008. *The Future of the Internet and How to Stop It*. New Haven: Yale University Press.

·············································································

# CHAPTER 3

# A POSSIBLE NEXT FRONTIER IN POLITICAL COMMUNICATION RESEARCH

*Merging the Old with the New*

·············································································

BRIAN J. GAINES
JAMES H. KUKLINSKI*

THE study of political communication has reached new and once inconceivable heights in the past twenty years. The field can claim its own American Political Science Association section and its own journal, both of which have flourished. Scholars ask more penetrating questions than ever before, and apply increasingly sophisticated methods to answer them. Scholars' detailed understandings of the relationships between media, politicians, and information, on the one hand, and citizens' beliefs and opinions, on the other, have increased as a result. In 1948 Harold Lasswell, one of the founders of the political communication field, and a master of aphorisms, proposed a working definition of communication—"who says what to whom (in what channel) with what effect" (1948, 37)—that has shaped more than sixty years of research. Today's embarrassment of riches stands in contrast to the state of affairs that existed when Lasswell wrote, as the chapters in this volume convincingly testify.

"More" does not automatically translate into progress, and in the first part of this chapter we assess where the study of political communication has improved with the passage of time and where it has not. To order the discussion, we loosely distinguish

* We thank the editors of this volume for their patience and helpful comments on earlier versions of this chapter.

three generations of research.[1] These generations reflect and are products of three broad changes that have occurred throughout the past ninety years, and mostly in the past fifty years: increasing methodological rigor in the social sciences; increasing specialization in the social sciences; and a changing environment that went from simple and homogeneous to multifaceted and heterogeneous. All three factors have shaped the study of political communication, and thus all three must be taken into account when trying to assess that progress, or the lack thereof. After describing a conundrum that afflicts political communication research, we offer three recommendations to advance the enterprise. All three entail a return to earlier approaches to research, without relinquishing the accumulated methodological gains of the past fifty years. None of them serves as a magical wand to overcome the conundrum.

First, we recommend that students of political communication gain substantial training in both institutions and behavior. The organization of this volume underlines the specialization that characterizes the current study of political communication. Institutionally oriented scholars tend to be lumped together in some subsections, behaviorally oriented scholars in others. We would expect to find few common references. At least on the behavioral side, if the study of political communication is to be more than the study of public opinion with a different name, a marked change in training must occur.

Second, we urge more in-the-field observation of politicians and members of the media as they interact to shape the news. Only by directly observing the selection processes that determine what does and does not become news can researchers begin to decompose the proximate and ultimate sources of citizens' beliefs and opinions. No matter how sophisticated they might be, methodological tools alone cannot substitute for a keen understanding of how news comes about.

Finally, if the goal is to understand real-world political communication, researchers need to begin to characterize the environment holistically, even when they purport to be interested in only select aspects of it. Most contemporary political communication scholars, like social scientists generally, adopt a reductionist approach to their research, i.e., they segment the whole into smaller parts and analyze the parts individually. Unfortunately, while this approach increases tractability, it comes at a cost of distortion. Citizens normally see and hear "it all," clearly or unclearly, not just a part that interests the researcher. Experimentalists, especially, can increase the complexity of their designs without undermining the leverage that random assignment into control and treatment groups affords.

## THREE GENERATIONS OF RESEARCH

The study of political communication underwent a remarkable transformation during the approximately ninety years included in our analysis. As we noted above, increasing

---

[1] Because of space limitations, we refrain from citing all of the research that merits mention, hopeful that other chapters will give this work the attention it deserves.

methodological sophistication and substantive specialization within the social sciences, along with an increasingly complex environment, combined to effect this transformation. These three contextual changes undergird our categorization scheme, which should be construed as no more than an arbitrary organizational structure by which to facilitate the following discussion. In reality, distinct and non-overlapping generations of research do not exist. If they did, trying to place this review under a single umbrella would make little sense. Of course, others might propose different and equally valid (or equally invalid) categorization schemes.

## The First Generation (Early 1900s to Mid-1940s)

Two world wars and an undeniable growth in mass-mediated information after the turn of the century catapulted the term "propaganda" to the fore in all the social sciences, with Walter Lippmann and Harold Lasswell serving as the intellectual leaders in political science. In *Public Opinion*, Lippmann distinguished, in his now famous words, between "the world outside and the pictures in our heads" (1922, ch. 1). Emphasizing that people do not observe most events directly, he set the stage for the capacity of the media and politicians to influence, by means of propaganda, what people think about and how they think about it.

Five years later, Harold Lasswell published *Propaganda Technique in the World War* (1927), ensuring that the words "Lasswell" and "propaganda" would be forever linked. Lasswell borrowed heavily from psychology, and construed propaganda as one actor's conscious manipulation of symbols for purposes of evoking a particular response from another actor. This manipulation can take the form of associating the object of the manipulation (the enemy) with a value (safety), or of attributing the object (a president's decision to order invasion of country X) as the cause of something favorable (removing any chance of it attacking the United States) or unfavorable (reducing domestic supplies of metal). Although Lasswell acknowledged the use of propaganda as conscious manipulation, he did not view it as inherently negative. To the contrary, he viewed it as consistent with democracy, as long as all sides of a public debate had an equal opportunity to propagate their particular views. Indeed, Lasswell's conception of propaganda seems to be little more than the media-filtered and -reported rhetoric that elected officials and others currently employ to win policy debates.

Scholars writing on propaganda and its persuasive effects on public opinion during these early years shared an important and unqualified conclusion: the effects were large. Rarely did they offer systematic evidence in support of this conclusion, since rigorous social scientific methodologies began to emerge only near the end of this first generation. Arguably, such methodologies were not necessary for academic observers to reach their conclusions; the effects were usually self-evident, in good part due to the nature of the environment. For one thing, nearly everyone listened to the same (radio) news reports, so that the implication of different people listening to different sources was largely hypothetical. For another, during each of the two wars, the focus was singularly, or nearly so, on the war itself, including its threats to freedom. Finally, politicians generally spoke as a single supportive voice during this time, so observers did not face the task of separating the effects of contradictory elite messages. During the First World War, in fact, President Wilson established the Committee on Public Information for the sole purpose of ensuring that the government spoke in a single voice that demonized the enemy and evoked the "right" emotions. Of course, focusing narrowly on activities during a major world war helped researchers to delimit their research scope, albeit it at the cost of raising questions about the relevance of their conclusions beyond a war setting.

Lippmann, Lasswell, and others working during this first period were as interested in the media's internal dynamics, and public officials' use of the media, as they were in how the media shaped public opinion. More to the point, these scholars assumed that one could not understand the media's effect on public opinion without knowing how the media actually worked. They were simultaneously students of the mass media and students of public opinion, or, more simply, students of political communication. To be sure, they were not methodologically well-trained, but they could nonetheless legitimately lay claim to the title "social scientist."

## The Second Generation (Mid-1940s to Early 1980s)

Research conducted during the second generation reported a seemingly wide range of conclusions about how much "the media" shaped public opinion, from not at all to a little to a lot. One might conclude, as some have, that this wide range of conclusions underlines the lack of research progress and, at an extreme, the futility of studying political communication. We agree with Neuman and Guggenheim (2009), however, that such a determination would be premature.

Consider, for example, the widely cited works of two research teams that seemingly reached conflicting conclusions. First are Paul Lazarsfeld and colleagues' contextually rich studies of single communities (Berelson, Lazarsfeld, and McPhee 1954; Lazarsfeld, Berelson, and Gaudet 1944), with which scholars associate the verdict that what people see and hear via formal communication channels shapes their beliefs, perceptions, and attitudes only minimally, if at all. Conducting their survey-based panel studies during actual presidential campaigns, the Columbia University scholars focused heavily on people's votes, and found that interpersonal communication more strongly influenced them than did anything emanating from the mass media. Their explanation anticipated Zaller's later and more developed theory (1992): while the better-educated and more strongly partisan closely attend to mass media reporting of presidential campaigns, they also use the reported information to justify their existing choices; the less educated and weakly partisan, who presumably would be susceptible to mediated reports, pay scant attention to campaign coverage.

Second is the 1972 McCombs and Shaw study of 100 voters in Chapel Hill, North Carolina, during the 1968 presidential campaign. It would become a classic, perhaps because it produced a conclusion that seemingly differed from those of Lazarsfeld et al. Media-disseminated information, McCombs and Shaw argued, strongly influences what aspects of politics come to people's minds. In reaching this conclusion, the authors studied initially undecided voters only, and examined agenda-setting effects rather than changes in vote preference. In other words, they asked whether media coverage of certain issues caused undecided voters to emphasize those issues in their own minds. To show the agenda-setting effects, they asked their undecided voters to express what they believed to be the key issues and then determined whether those responses reflected prior media content.

Does the McCombs and Shaw study contradict the Columbia studies? Not necessarily. For one thing, people's presidential preferences and the issues on which they focus are not one and the same. That the two sets of authors use different dependent variables makes comparison difficult if not impossible. For another, associating people's reported beliefs about the key issues with prior media content does not preclude the possibility that this association arose because of interpersonal communication. McCombs and Shaw do not directly consider this mechanism. Moreover, in limiting their study to undecided voters only, McCombs and Shaw increased the likelihood of uncovering statistically significant results.

Different questions, different variables, different measures of them, and different types of analysis; these are the methodological obstacles that make it difficult if not impossible to compare across any two studies, or collections of studies, undertaken during this period. Ironically, perhaps, the very exponential increase in available methodological tools that afforded individual scholars and research teams a new-found opportunity to display their creative prowess also made it more difficult, if not impossible, to characterize the collective enterprise. This problem, we will see, continues to plague the study of political communication, with no remedy in sight.

Much of this generation's research reflects the rise of statistical methods in the social sciences. During the 1960s and 1970s, the statistical analysis of observational data increasingly became the method of choice. In the minds of most scholars conducting research back then, correlations and regression coefficients came close to revealing true cause and effect, despite the oft-repeated words "correlation does not equal causation." The recognition and serious discussion of problems arising from misspecification, selection processes, the lack of unit homogeneity, the effects of unobserved variables, and possible mutual causation between independent and dependent variables would come later. Moreover, the lack of across-time data led researchers to rely heavily on cross-sectional data, whose limitations are now widely recognized.

Increasing disciplinary specialization also characterized the second generation of research. Students of political communication began to split into those who studied the media from a purely institutional perspective and those who studied how "the media" shape public opinion. Fewer and fewer scholars could claim the comprehensive understanding of both arenas that Lippmann and Lasswell could claim at the time they wrote. As in political science generally, "institutions or behavior" had begun to replace "institutions and behavior." At least among those trained in the behavior tradition, two unintended consequences followed: a lack of attention to the strategic maneuvers of the media and public officials and, relatedly, a lack of interest in observing actual interactions between the two sets of actors as they try to shape news reporting.

Significant changes also occurred outside academia. The environment became increasingly complex and heterogeneous. The number of media sources began to expand at an unprecedented rate, which not only gave citizens more news options from which to choose, but also increased the overall activity in the environment. Together, these two consequences of media expansion translated into more factors to be taken into account, thus increasing the difficulty of properly specifying regression and other statistical models. Perhaps researchers included all of the right variables in their models and excluded the wrong ones, perhaps they did not. A betting person would assume the latter. A provocative question is whether the rapidly increasing heterogeneity of the environment, and the research challenges associated with it, outdistanced disciplinary methodological advances, resulting in a "net loss."

## The Third Generation (Mid-1980s–Present)

The statistical analysis of survey data that dominated the second generation arguably reached its apex during the late 1980s and early 1990s. Some of the most idea- and theory-rich observational studies, including Mutz (1998), Page and Shapiro (1992), Popkin (1994), Sniderman, Brody, and Tetlock (1993), and Zaller (1992), were published within six years of each other. Meanwhile, a group of young scholars, many with formal training in psychology, began to employ experiments to study the effects of various aspects of communication on people's beliefs and attitudes. The emergence of new, general, and influential theories that were based on and tested primarily with observational data and the rapid proliferation of survey and laboratory experiments together characterize the third generation and distinguish it from the second.

The theoretical studies cited immediately above share two assumptions. First, all the authors adopted a top-down perspective, with information moving from the environment to citizens. Second, all assumed that people heuristically use what the environment provides them. For Mutz, Popkin, and Sniderman, looking to relevant others serves as a means for people to compensate for, albeit it not to overcome, informational deficiencies. Zaller emphasized elites, broadly defined, and his theory distinguished between messages on which elites agree from those on which two groups of elites disagree. Page and Shapiro, too, emphasized political elites, in particular, how elites interpret major events. Significantly, none of these influential works, Zaller partially excepted, undertook a thorough and careful analysis of the actual environment. When people take cues from interest groups, members of Congress, and the like, for example, just how clear and plentiful are the cues? Are there times when cues do not exist at all? Do people sometimes receive conflicting cues from trusted sources?

On the experimental front, Iyengar and Kinder (1987) conducted the pioneering and still unrivaled study, pioneering because it weakened political scientists' resistance to experimental research and unrivaled because, unlike most researchers who followed them, Iyengar and Kinder used actual (archived) network television evening newscasts into which they inserted manipulations that allowed them to test for priming and framing effects. The authors reported compelling evidence of both types of effect in *News That Matters*, which in turn brought discussions of minimal media effects to a halt. Since the publication of this landmark study, political scientists have used experiments to study a variety of specific topics falling under the general rubric of political communication. Chong and Druckman's recent across-time study of framing effects (2008) epitomizes the progress that the experimental study of political communication has made.

One might ask whether an experimental approach to the study of political communication represents an advance over an approach based on observational data, especially since social scientists have begun to specialize in one or the other. In some respects, the answer is yes. In others, it is not clear.

Those working in the observational tradition try to capture some of the complexity of the environment by employing complicated models that include many control variables. Those working in the experimental tradition eliminate the complexity via random assignment. They focus on a single explanatory factor and then try to determine its effects. As Holland (1986) famously put it, the statistical analysis of observational data typically estimates the causes of an effect whereas experiments estimate the effects of a cause.

At first glance, one might be tempted to conclude that experimental studies represent a considerable advance over observational studies. Users of observational data always face the likelihood of improperly specified statistical models, and thus biased estimates. Because random assignment in principle eliminates all potentially confounding factors, experimenters can be more confident that they have discovered true cause and effect, at least within the experimental context. On the other hand, one of the very strengths of experiments—simplification—also increases the likelihood that researchers will overestimate the real-world effect of the single explanatory variable they choose. In an environment characterized by multiple and simultaneously occurring stimuli, the signal of any single stimulus might be more faint than it is in an experimental context. Notable exceptions are highly visible events, which, Page and Shapiro (1992) show in their analysis of aggregated survey data, move ordinary citizens in expected directions.

Gone unnoticed, users of observational and experimental data are often answering different questions, even though they proceed as though they are not. When researchers analyze observational data to study political communication, they implicitly assume that not everyone will receive the media stimulus of interest. In other words, they answer the question "what are the effects of a stimulus given that not everyone chooses to receive it?" When researchers conduct experiments, they implicitly answer a different question: "what are the effects given that everyone receives the relevant stimulus?"[2] The two types of study address the same question only when either of two conditions is met in the real

---

[2] In fairness, Iyengar and Kinder (1987) make every effort to simulate television watching as it exists in people's living rooms.

world that researchers are seeking to understand: no one in the real world selects out of receiving the stimulus or, while some select out, they would have, overall, reacted to it just as those who received the stimulus reacted.

In this regard, consider Zaller's highly influential study of media influence on public opinion (1992). First formulating a theory of opinion change and then testing it using a combination of survey data and issue counts from the *New York Times*, Zaller demonstrates convincingly the restricted impact of information on attitude change. Because some people lack media exposure, the information does not (directly) change their beliefs and attitudes.[3] On the other end are those who pay much attention to media reporting of politics; because these individuals are also politically sophisticated and strongly partisan, they screen information that is incompatible with their existing beliefs and attitudes. Only those who receive some media exposure and who also lack the skills to counter information that conflicts with their existing beliefs, then, respond to mediated information. The average treatment effect generated by a typical random assignment experiment would not reveal this crucially important pattern. Of course, neither would observational data had Zaller not first formulated a theory axiomatically.

While users of observational data have often been limited to coarse measures of media behavior and activity—the number of times various issues are mentioned during a specified time period, for example—experimenters usually create their own measures of media behavior and activity. In the study of framing effects, for example, researchers choose the frames to use. When this research began, scholars chose the frames seemingly with little reference to the frames actually reported by the media. This practice has begun to change (Chong and Druckman 2007), although politicians' strategic use of, and the media's strategic reporting of, frames have not yet fully entered experimental research. Experimenters, like users of observational data, continue to ignore the strategic behavior of politicians and members of the media. Ironically, perhaps, while the growing use of experiments has led students of political communication to focus more than ever before on a single causal variable, the real-world information environment has continued to grow, such that it is more complex and more heterogeneous than it was even a decade ago.

# A Conundrum in the Study
## of Political Communication

Reading across the chapters in this volume, one would conclude that students of political communication view information, media, and statements from politicians as

---

[3] Zaller uses the term "information" (1992), which we use here. See the following section for an elaboration of the distinctions among information, media, and politicians' statements.

distinct factors that independently shape citizens' beliefs and attitudes.[4] This thinking has intuitive appeal. The three factors are, in both reality and the abstract, separate entities. Yet, a simple mental exercise reveals the difficulty, if not impossibility, of separating their effects, a fundamental and unstated conundrum in the study of political communication.

Imagine a hypothetical experimenter who controls the world completely and sets in motion a bare-bones "politics" consisting only of legislative roll-call votes. "Information" means objective, verifiable fact, in this case, the member's roll-call vote itself. It does not include any explanations of why a member's vote was cast or predictions about the consequences of a bill passing or failing. "Media" includes all news accounts and commentaries, including not only those purporting to be strictly objective and descriptive but also those explicitly offering opinions and editorials. It encompasses traditional news sources and modern alternatives, such as blogs, twittering, and the like. Finally, the researcher construes political rhetoric to include only those statements coming directly from the politicians themselves.

This researcher then creates three dichotomous, real-world treatments: information is available (roll-call votes are recorded), or not; media report on the votes, or not; and, politicians issue statements, or not. It is not hard to imagine, given this hypothetical $2 \times 2 \times 2$ experiment, the eight possible combinations. In one cell of the experimental world, official documents record all roll-call votes, for anyone interested in consulting the public record, but there are no media reports of any kind on the votes, and politicians offer no statements or discussion of their actions. In another, politicians wax eloquent about their behavior, there is media coverage of the votes, but the actual votes are not officially recorded or in any way verifiable. And so on.

Then, for a set of interesting dependent variables describing public opinion, the researcher could obtain multiple observations from each environment, as from surveys administered to simple random samples of the local populations. He or she would then proceed to isolate direct and interactive effects for each factor by appropriate analysis of the data. Even as a thought experiment, there are at least two more caveats. First, all of this analysis would be conditional on the environment, that is, the ongoing political activities being chronicled (or not), described and analyzed by media (or not), and defended (or not) by politicians. So another researcher with equally awesome control over environments in a different polity, with different roll-call votes, might reach different conclusions. Second, time is absent from the description above. These researchers might be in the role of gods, creating worlds *de novo*, or they might be intervening in a modern democracy, suspending some (or all) of these three factors selectively. Either of those versions of the thought experiment suffices for our present purposes, because the point is, the research design is purely imaginary.

---

[4] Even when "media" and "politicians" are understood very broadly, this three-way scheme omits an important category of sources of influence on opinion, subjective statements from friends, relatives, neighbors, and coworkers. Mondak's study of Pittsburgh and Cleveland (1995) illustrates convincingly that media use and informal discussion interact in complicated ways.

Returning to the real world, all of the data scholars analyze are generated from one cell, where information, media reporting, and statements from politicians simultaneously exist. On rare occasions, a researcher can use a creative design to overcome the problem, as, for example, Mondak did in his study exploiting a newspaper strike in Pittsburgh (1995). Even then, Mondak's good fortune was a glimpse of one extra cell (media, in a far, far narrower sense than above, temporarily suspended), not the whole set of combinations that would allow fine discrimination of all possible effects.

In a typical experiment, then, whatever manipulation is undertaken, the subjects are drawn from a world where all three sources are on, not off. By exposing a random subset of subjects to a stimulus or treatment (an editorial or TV ad, say), and contrasting them in some manner with a random subset not exposed, one can attempt to identify causal effects for the treatment. But all conclusions will be conditional on the subjects existing in a real world, distinct from the experimental simulation thereof, in which whatever phenomenon is under study does exist. In other words, the "control" group will have seen newscasts or read editorials or heard politicians speak in their real lives before they were ever recruited into the experimental study. Even with carefully designed and/or highly stylized scenarios, it is difficult, if not impossible, to avoid real-life pre-treatment. In turn, experimental results will normally not reveal the effects of some factor (seeing an advertisement, hearing a speech) so much as the marginal effects of one extra instance of the factor.

Currently, neither the generation of experimental data nor the statistical analysis of observational data can fully overcome these problems; they inhere in the environment that the researcher seeks to understand. It is not surprising, therefore, that individual researchers have tended to be less than fully explicit about distinguishing the effects of information, media, and politicians. In his deservedly influential study, for example, Zaller uses count data collected from the *New York Times* to show the effects of one-sided and two-sided information flows. Although he explicitly uses the term "information" flows, all of this "information" is mediated by the *New York Times*, and, moreover, much of the "information" consists of statements from Democrat and Republican members of Congress. In essence, Zaller uses data from one cell: information on, media on, and politicians on. He does so because this is the only cell for which the real world generated data.[5]

We cited Zaller not to criticize his work, but to show that the nature of the environment creates challenges for even the best of scholars. Some of these challenges look nearly insurmountable, even from the perspective of our current methodological arsenal. These challenges should not, and surely will not, deter researchers from moving forward, which, we propose, should entail merging some of the old with the new.

---

[5] As we noted above, Zaller (1992) also shows that, for many people, the effects of prior beliefs and opinions dominate all other effects (also see Gaines et al. 2007), which, as an empirical matter, reduces the sting of our observations.

# ADDING THE OLD TO THE NEW IN THE STUDY OF POLITICAL COMMUNICATION

The study of political communication today barely resembles the study of political communication as it existed when Lippmann and Lasswell conducted their research. To most contemporary scholars, the early work surely looks simplistic and lacking in rigor. To reject it out of hand, however, would be a costly mistake. In our view, students of political communication can benefit from revisiting Lippmann, Lasswell, and other writers of the period, and identifying and adopting those things they did well, most of which have been forgotten, unnecessarily, in the forward march called "progress." This they can do without losing the rigor that characterizes contemporary research. Such a merger will not cure all that ails the study of political communication, but it can begin to plug a few holes in current research.

## Less Disciplinary Specialization

Disciplinary specialization is inevitable, and, for the most part, it is also beneficial. It affords a depth of understanding that would otherwise not be possible. A cursory glance at the list of chapters included in this volume underlines the extent to which specialization has shaped the contemporary study of political communication. In particular, the first half dozen or so chapters focus heavily on institutional workings while most of the following chapters fall easily under the "political behavior" label. We doubt that the authors of the early chapters could have written the behaviorally oriented chapters, and vice versa. Such is the cost of specialized training.

But perhaps a handbook such as this one represents the best possible solution; the benefits of specialization are fully realized within any particular chapter, and a reading of all the chapters provides a comprehensive view of political communication. To put it another way, a reader of this volume gains all of the insights of a Lippmann or Lasswell, but with the added sophistication that comes with specialization.

The problem with this logic is that political communication entails strategic inter-actions between politicians and members of the media. Politicians, especially party leaders, need the media to convey particular messages to the public; the media need access to politicians to generate news; the media need to make money, which requires that they report stories of interest to ordinary citizens. Each one of these requirements shapes what is and what is not included in the news, and thus to what, and how, ordinary citizens react.

Take, specifically, the matter of issue framing. It is one thing for a behaviorally oriented scholar to select two or three frames and then use them as manipulations in experiments to determine whether people in fact react to the frames. It is quite another for that same scholar to begin with a game-theoretic model that derives predictions about when competing party leaders will continue to use a frame and when they will abandon it, then tests the model's predictions experimentally, and, finally, determines which types of frames, broadly speaking, persist, and with what effects. The first approach does not require an understanding of institutions and institutional behavior; the second, which has greater value for understanding politics, does.

Early scholars like Lippmann and Lasswell were not trained in game theory; but they did understand how the media went about their business, including how media members strategically interacted with politicians. Their analyses of how the media and politicians shaped public opinion began with this understanding. Most contemporary students of political communication trained in the behavioral tradition take the media and politicians as given, an assumption that takes the politics out of the study of political communication. Increased training in institutions and game theory would help to put it back in.

## Increased Field Observation

We noted, above, that neither observational nor even experimental studies can deliver on the promise fully to separate the effects of information, media, and politicians. What, then, is a researcher to do? A crucial step, in our view, consists of grappling with the unobserved selection processes that control how objective information and various sources of subjective information mix in normal life.

Consider the BP Gulf oil spill, which was big news during the final writing of this chapter. The various opinions about this series of events (e.g., who is to blame? How well has President Obama handled the crisis?, etc.) form in diverse and complicated ways. A number of people had opinions about offshore oil drilling before the accidents; others did not. A very small number, by virtue of professional background, possessed relevant specialized knowledge (e.g., petroleum engineers, environmental activists); most did not. As people encountered news reports, discussed the events with friends, sought out news and information from BP and/or various governmental actors, sorted through online debates, and so on, "media," "information," and "political rhetoric" were constantly intertwined. In any given newscast, producers chose content and framing. No one individual had first-hand experience with all objective facts, and the meaning of the facts was subject to much interpretation. Even a narrowly framed question like "how much damage will be done to the shrimp stock in the Gulf?" probably cannot be answered in a strictly objective manner, in so far as there is necessarily a predictive element to the response.

We recite the obvious to draw an also obvious yet rarely stated implication for students of political communication. The information that ordinary citizens obtain when they watch television, listen to the radio, talk to friends, read a blog, magazine, or newspaper, and so on, has already been shaped by interactions between media and politicians. Politicians convey some messages directly, as when they speak to a small crowd. But most of their communication will take place through the media. Thus, to identify "media effects" and the "effects of politicians" requires knowledge of multiple selection processes that cannot generally be observed directly. Even more daunting, the two tasks require, in principle, a specification of all the news that might have been reported. Moreover, the effects of prior information—as a source distinct from the flow of communication from political actors and the media—will vary greatly across the population.

We see two ways to proceed, neither of which will provide the leverage of our earlier hypothetical experiment. First, when faced with seemingly intractable empirical tasks, scholars routinely call for better theory. It is much easier, of course, to urge theory than to do it; and formal models are not cure-alls. Nevertheless, greater use of game-theoretic or agent-based models would help researchers to derive useful equilibrium implications, as Bovitz, Druckman, and Lupia (2002; also see Chong and Druckman 2007) show in their exemplary study.

Second, Lippmann, Lasswell, and others of their generation showed the value of direct observation. Many of the founders of political communication held, at one time or another, positions in government, which gave them a vantage point from which to see how politicians and the media interacted. They represented government in meetings with members of the media, and thus personally saw how the media identified all possible topics to include in their news presentations, how the media then selected some topics and not others, and how events and other factors constrained their choices.

Contemporary social scientific research places considerably less value on direct observation, and with good reason. Direct observation opens the door to subjectivity, arbitrary interpretation, and a host of vulnerabilities that can reduce the validity of the collected evidence. Complete isolation from the object of research, on the other hand, reduces insight and opens the door to assumptions that have no basis in reality. We do not recommend a return to the "good old days" and the lack of rigor that characterized them. We do recommend, however, that today's well-trained social scientists also find a way to use their eyes and ears, in relevant settings, to supplement their research.

## Holistic View of the Information Environment

Throughout this chapter, we have emphasized the changing nature of the information environment, especially its increasing complexity and heterogeneity. The amount of news available at any moment far exceeds anything that Lippmann, Lasswell, and their contemporaries experienced, or could have envisioned. Prior (2007) has documented these changes in detail, and, as he notes, people today can pick and choose as they wish. What they seemingly cannot easily do is ignore everything; information overload is no longer just a sexy term, it is a reality.

An irony, we suggested earlier, is that students of political communication are increasingly adopting random-assignment experimental designs, which entail isolating a single explanatory factor and determining its effects on the selected dependent variable. Such designs generate "clean" estimates of the treatment effect. But, given the nature of today's information environments, those clean estimates come at a price; the environmental simulation in the experiment barely resembles the true, far more complex and heterogeneous environment.

The remedy, we propose, entails bringing a more holistic measure of the information environment into the experiment itself. This requires, first, that the researcher carefully characterize the true environment. Returning to the case of the Gulf oil spill, not every single news story focused on it. Bad economic news continued throughout the time period. After having regained some of its earlier losses, the stock market plummeted, largely in response to widely disseminated information, accompanied by declarations from politicians that Greece, Spain, and Portugal were approaching financial insolvency. Although political leaders from around the world, led by United States officials, tried to put the best possible spin on the economic struggles of these and other countries, their reassurances seemed to fall on deaf ears. In the United States, unemployment continued to hover around 10 percent, with more and more commentators suggesting that, for many across the globe, the unemployment would be permanent. There were also ongoing reports of the Obama administration offering lucrative federal jobs to two US Senate candidates in exchange for their willingness to drop out of primaries. Few suggested that such offers were illegal or unprecedented, but many politicians and members of the media suggested that they raised doubts about Obama's ethics. Around the same time, reports that the United States was paying Afghan warlords and militia leaders $2.1 billion to protect its convoys raised eyebrows, given that the warlord's primary target was the very central government that US troops were supposedly protecting.

Suppose, now, that a team of researchers undertakes a typical experiment to determine the extent to which news about the oil spill affected people's evaluations of President Obama. They randomly assign some of their subjects to the treatment group, and ask them to read two or three stories about the spill that appeared in, say, the *New York Times*. Those assigned to the control group read the same number of stories, but none refers to the oil spill.

Given the purpose of the experiment, to estimate how much news stories about the Gulf oil spill influenced evaluations of the President, this manipulation will not suffice. A proper manipulation should include, in both the treatment and the control condition, all of the other stories covered in the news, from the economic news to news about unethical job offers and payments to Afghan warlords. Since these are constant across the two conditions, they should not affect the estimate of the treatment, except to the extent that they interact with news about the oil spill. But allowing for these interactions is precisely what is needed for the experimental simulation to approximate the state of the actual information environment.

Early researchers viewed the information environment holistically, but lacked the kinds of analytical tools currently available to researchers. Today's scholars have the tools, but thus far have failed to adopt holistic conceptions of the information environment. They can easily take the latter step, thus merging the best of the past and future.

# FINAL COMMENT

The study of political communication has a seemingly limitless scope of inquiry. Geographically, it includes the whole world, and beyond, as evidenced by coverage of various nations' space shuttles in outer space. Substantively, nearly every conceivable topic, from local zoning problems to international drug and human trafficking to multi-country conflicts, falls under its umbrella. Academically, many of the individual scholars who contributed to this volume study highly specialized topics, such as, for example, memory, affect and emotions, information processing, and elite framing of issues. Across all contributors, areas of study vary markedly, from the preceding to the history of the media in society.

A revealing exercise would be to ask each contributor whether he or she considers him- or herself first and foremost a student of political communication. We would expect some unhesitatingly to say yes, others to say no. Many, we predict, would respond more slowly, ultimately offering answers such as "maybe," "I guess so," "I doubt it," and so on. If we are right about this latter group, then section status in the American Political Science Association and the existence of the journal *Political Communication* say less about the emergence and maturity of an intellectual endeavor than they say about the emergence of a loose federation of scholars, all of whom are chipping away at small and different pieces of a phenomenon that is real and crucially important, and whose name rings a bell of familiarity, yet that must fringe on the incomprehensible from the standpoint of any randomly chosen member of that scholarly federation intending to conduct a study of it.

## REFERENCES

BERELSON, B. R., LAZARSFELD, P. F., and MCPHEE, W. N. 1954. *Voting: A Study of Opinion Formation in a Presidential Campaign.* Chicago: University of Chicago Press.

BOVITZ, G. L., DRUCKMAN, J. N., and LUPIA, A. 2002. When Can a News Organization Lead Public Opinion? Ideology versus Market Forces in Decisions to Make News. *Public Choice*, 113/1–2: 127–55.

CHONG, D., and DRUCKMAN, J. N. 2007. Framing Public Opinion in Competitive Democracies. *American Political Science Review*, 101/4: 637–55.

—— —— 2008. Framing Effects over Time. Paper presented at the Annual Meeting of the International Society of Political Psychology, Paris.

GAINES, B. J., KUKLINSKI, J. H., QUIRK, P. J., PEYTON, B., and VERKUILEN, J. 2007. Same Facts, Different Interpretations: Partisan Motivation and Opinion on Iraq. *Journal of Politics*, 69/4: 957–74.

HOLLAND, P. W. 1986. Statistics and Causal Inference. *Journal of the American Statistical Association*, 81/396: 945–60.

IYENGAR, S., and KINDER, D. 1987. *News that Matters: Television and American Opinion.* Chicago: University of Chicago Press.

LASSWELL, H. 1927. *Propaganda Technique in the World War.* New York: Knopf.

—— 1948. The Structure and Function of Communication in Society. In *The Communication of Ideas*, ed. L. Bryson. New York: Institute for Religious and Social Studies.

LAZARSFELD, P. F., BERELSON, B., and GAUDET, H. 1944. *The People's Choice: How the Voter Makes Up his Mind in a Presidential Campaign.* New York: Columbia University Press.

LIPPMANN, W. 1922. *Public Opinion.* New York: Macmillan.

McCOMBS, M. E., and SHAW, D. L. 1972. The Agenda-Setting Function of Mass Media. *Public Opinion Quarterly*, 36/2: 176–87.

MONDAK, J. J. 1995. *Nothing to Read: Newspapers and Elections in a Social Experiment.* Ann Arbor: University of Michigan Press.

MUTZ, D. 1998. *Impersonal Influence: How Perceptions of Mass Collectives Affect Political Attitudes.* New York: Cambridge University Press.

NEUMAN, R., and GUGGENHEIM, L. 2009. The Evolution of Media Effects Theory: Fifty Years of Cumulative Research. Paper presented at the Annual Meeting of the International Communication Association, Chicago.

PAGE, B. I., and SHAPIRO, R. Y. 1992. *The Rational Public: Fifty Years of Trends in Americans' Policy Preferences.* Chicago: University of Chicago Press.

POPKIN, S. L. 1994. *The Reasoning Voter: Communication and Persuasion in Presidential Campaigns*, 2nd edn. Chicago: University of Chicago Press.

PRIOR, M. 2007. *Post-Broadcast Democracy: How Media Choice Increases Inequality in Political Involvement and Polarizes Elections.* New York: Cambridge University Press.

SNIDERMAN, P. M., BRODY, R. A., and TETLOCK, P. E. 1991. *Reasoning and Choice: Explorations in Political Psychology.* Cambridge: Cambridge University Press.

ZALLER, J. R. 1992. *The Nature and Origins of Mass Opinion.* Cambridge: Cambridge University Press.

# PART II

# THE MEDIA

# SECTION ONE:
# FOUNDATIONS

......................................................................

# CHAPTER 4

# TOCQUEVILLE'S
# INTERESTING ERROR

## *On Journalism and Democracy*

......................................................................

MICHAEL SCHUDSON

ALEXIS DE TOCQUEVILLE is widely quoted for any number of brilliant observations about American society. No more perceptive work has ever been written about the United States than his *Democracy in America*. But Tocqueville could be wrong as well as right about what he saw when he visited America in 1831–2, and he was wrong, I will suggest, about the role of newspapers in democratic life.

Journalism in our day is regularly honored for its importance to democracy. The greatest heroes of journalism in the field's own image of itself and in favorable portraits of it in the general culture ferret out information difficult or dangerous or even life-threatening; they move into places where angels fear to tread. They do so for various reasons (adventure, ego, the pleasures of travel or of writing, curiosity about people, wanting to make a difference in the world), but among this long list, one of the most important is the journalists' commitment to the belief that there is a public value to providing citizens with reliable information necessary to making democracy work.

Does journalism help make democracy work? In particular, does it help make democracy work by fearless investigations and reliable reporting that inform citizens about what their elected officials are doing and how their political institutions are working? This is a fundamental assumption today and it is on this point that Tocqueville's frequently cited writings about the newspapers in America are misleading. I want to show where Tocqueville's view of the press went astray and to suggest that news organizations, as monitors of government, can only be understood as part of a multi-institutional complex of monitorial institutions and activities that hold government accountable. Particularly in light of the shifting character of accountability practices in recent years, this recognition is the necessary first step in rethinking journalism's democratic force.

Like other visitors to young America, Tocqueville was impressed by the sheer quantity of American papers. It was phenomenal. Estimates vary but they are all in the same direction: the United States at the time of Tocqueville's visit supported five times as many dailies as Britain, three and a half times as many newspapers altogether (dailies, weeklies, and others), and a total circulation two to three times that of the mother country. A later nineteenth-century estimate for newspaper circulation in 1840, while it cannot be confirmed, could well be about right—that the United States, population 17 million, had a greater weekly newspaper circulation than the whole of Europe with its 233 million (Starr 2004, 86–7).

How to understand this? Here is where Tocqueville made his mistake. He found the broad prevalence of newspapers to be explained by the large number of governmental units in America. If citizens elected only state or national representatives, he wrote, there would be no need for so many newspapers. In that case, there would be few occasions when people acted together politically. But the many governmental units responsible for local administration means that "the lawmaker has thus compelled every American to join forces daily with a few of his fellow citizens on community projects and each of them needs a newspaper to inform him of what the others are doing" (Tocqueville 2003, 603).

Tocqueville assumed that people turned to the news for guidance about local affairs, but that is not what Americans did with newspapers in 1832. It was the rare newspaper of Tocqueville's day that told citizens very much at all about what their neighbors were doing or what their local government was considering. Tocqueville recognized a striking correlation: many local governments, many local newspapers. He then imagined a causal connection—that the presence of local governments in a democracy that called on the citizens to participate provoked a need for local political information. As a result, newspapers thrived.

This was a reasonable surmise, but it turns out to have been wrong. There simply was very little local political news in the local newspapers that most people read in this overwhelmingly agricultural, minimally urbanized society. The *Macon Telegraph* in Georgia in 1831 provided "virtually no news about Macon" (Baldasty 1992, 179). In Virginia, even congressional elections received only sporadic coverage in the state's newspapers in the first decades of the century (Jordan 1983, 149). Local items in the papers of a thriving provincial city, Cincinnati, made up less than a fifth of all news items (Nerone 1989, 57). In fact, many "country" newspapers did not feel compelled to print local news at all until improved mail service in the 1820s brought city papers more expeditiously to the towns; only then did the provincial press scramble to find something—local news—the city papers could not do better (Kielbowicz 1989, 57). In the village of Kingston, New York, the local press did not so much as mention local elections in the early 1800s and did not report on the operation of village government at all until 1845. Were there issues? Were there campaigns? There is no way to know from Kingston's newspapers (Blumin 1976, 126–49).

If Tocqueville's surmise is wrong, what accounts for the flourishing of American newspapers at the time of his visit?

Tocqueville presumed a demand-driven model where reader interest gave rise to a market response. In fact, it appears, there were several supply-side reasons the United States gave birth to so many newspapers. First, there was a generous supply of newspaper proprietors. There were motives for merchants and others to start newspapers to advertise their towns to a wider world, to advertise their printing business to people who might pay for job printing services, and to generally promote the fortunes of their communities to stimulate economic growth. Small towns boasted of newspapers, grand hotels, and even colleges all as part of a "shoeshine and a smile" salesmanship—not responding to demand but trying to manufacture demand (Boorstin 1965, 141). The founders of the town of Emporia, Kansas, in 1857, anti-slavery activists, started a newspaper in the first few months and mailed nearly all of the first copies back to the east to attract new residents. Setting up a newspaper was a form of real estate development (Griffith 1989, 14). The first two newspapers in Milwaukee were established in 1836 and 1837 by leading landowners on either bank of the Milwaukee River, each singing of the advantages of his own side of the river (Watrous 1909, 431–2).

Second, there was a connection between the many governmental units and the many newspapers, but the mediating element was not citizen demand for local knowledge but the supply of government advertising. Governments placed legislatively required legal advertising in newspapers, especially in newspapers that had proved faithful to the party then in power. Legal advertising was a substantial and reliable source of newspaper income.

Third, a general ideological underwriting of the importance of popular information to representative government helped the growth of newspapers in early America. The ideological orientation of the Founding Fathers helped secure newspapers' economic success. The Postal Act of 1792 provided federal funds to establish post offices, to support the building of roads to connect them, and singled out newspapers for a special subsidy, providing them with very low rates for use of the mails and providing mailing privileges free when one newspaper sent copies to another newspaper (John 1995). This free newspaper exchange provided a crucial source of news for a provincial press that had scarcely any news-gathering resources of its own.

Tocqueville's error has been compounded in the way his remarks on newspapers have been read: we assume that the newspapers he praised took their function to be the reporting of news. This is so only in the wildest stretch of what one might mean by "reporting news." In 1832 few American newspapers employed anyone to "report." Most of the papers were very small operations whose proprietors were rightly known as "printers." They set type and operated the printing press. They gathered national and foreign news by taking (free through the post) the major metropolitan daily papers and reprinting from them what they found of interest (or simply what would fill space). What local news they printed was incidental. "Covering" local government was not a routine activity. "Investigating" a local issue was essentially unheard of. Local newspapers simply did not have "a significant relationship to the communities where they were printed," as historian David Paul Russo put it, until a generation after Tocqueville (Russo 1980, 2). Even then, the local press tended to avoid politicizing local news. Local items were typically "user-generated content," with newspaper readers themselves providing news of who was ill or who had harvested their crops. Narrating the local in these papers meant avoiding mention of political conflict, preserving the apolitical image of country life, and implying (rather than reporting) great local economic opportunity.

All of this is to say that newspapers have not always been about, nor are they necessarily today about, providing the information to make democracy work in the communities they most directly serve. Newspapers have not arisen in response to the demands of citizens for local political information. Nor have they regularly provided or even sought to provide local political information on which citizens might be expected to act. In fact, as sociologist Herbert J. Gans has written, "If the truth be told, America's journalists have done less in behalf of the country's democracy than they believe. However, they operate with a theory of democracy and a conception of their own responsibility which only require them to present as much political and when relevant, economic and other news as is commercially feasible" (Gans 2009, 95).

An exception must be noted for the "associational press" of the nineteenth century, newspapers and magazines that in Tocqueville's day spoke for and to a geographically dispersed body of readers united by allegiance to a cause (like abolitionism or temperance) or to a religion (Nord 2001). The associational papers were an important part of nineteenth-century journalism and they were indeed a mechanism for bringing people together for collective political action. They were essential to creating a "virtual" community of people joined not by their cohabiting in a common place within a common political unit but by their connecting people spread across a large country who shared a common ideological, religious, or political orientation.

The relationship of news or journalism to democracy, then, is more complicated and far more attenuated in practice than in normative theory. Even in theory, it is journalism theory and not political theory that attributes great weight to journalism, and the self-love of journalists in this celebration is obvious.

Tocqueville's error deserves reconsideration today when the entire shape of journalism is dramatically changing. The primary employers of journalism professionals from Tocqueville's day to our own have been newspapers. The business model that enabled them to become both large, prosperous enterprises closely identified with their communities and also symbolic mascots for those communities emerged with the urban penny papers. The first of these, the *New York Sun*, appeared in 1833, just after Tocqueville returned to France; others quickly followed in the largest cities of the eastern seaboard: Boston, Philadelphia, Baltimore, and New York. The new model, coming to maturity in the late nineteenth century, made papers cheaply available for single purchase or by subscription to attract a large readership to win advertisers willing to pay good money to the paper for having assembled a large audience. Advertising would in time provide two-thirds or three-quarters or more of the newspaper's income.

This model is now in jeopardy. Online advertising sites for jobs, for cars, for household items and household services, and for real estate, have stripped newspapers of the classified ads that contributed 20 to 40 percent of their income. On the heels of this loss, the sharp economic decline of 2007–9 and further loss of advertising revenue forced some newspapers to go out of business, others to reduce the number of days of the week they print and deliver papers, and led nearly every ambitious metropolitan daily newspaper to cut back on expenses by closing bureaus and laying off reporters, editors, and photographers.[1]

These developments are alarming since newspapers have come to serve democracy in important ways and while the hundreds of small weeklies at the time of Tocqueville's visit did little to report on local government, the profitable metropolitan and regional dailies that have been the mainstay of the American system of journalism for more than a century have covered the basics of local politics—sometimes (but by no means regularly) aggressively. But can this continue? Will it continue? Many observers in and out of journalism have serious doubts as newspapers with rapidly declining advertising revenue and gradually shrinking paid readership struggle to cut costs.

It is not satisfactory to reply that the press has never stood alone as a way to keep tabs on power. If the democratic job of the press in the United States has come to be holding government accountable (although it is much more than this—a point I will return to) we should ask what other ways there are to keep government accountable. Political scientists studying Latin American governments have developed a simple and useful typology of forms of accountability. The typology—which I want to use but also to complicate—is as follows.

The most basic form of accountability in democratic politics is vertical accountability—that elected government officials and by extension those who serve under them are held accountable to the citizenry through elections. Electoral systems differ from one democracy to another; sometimes it is the individual officeholder who is directly responsible to the electorate and sometimes it is the party he or she is a member of. Sometimes this accountability operates frequently with regular elections repeated at short intervals and sometimes elections are infrequent. But in any event the elected officials by this mechanism become accountable to the people they serve and in an extremely powerful way: if they don't please the voters as much as a challenger does, they lose the election and they have to pack up their personal effects and walk out the door and find another job.

The second familiar form of accountability is horizontal accountability; that is, one branch of government is accountable to another branch of government. Guillermo O'Donnell writes that horizontal accountability refers to "the existence of state agencies that are legally enabled and powered, and factually willing and able, to take actions that span from routine oversight to criminal sanctions or impeachment in relation to actions or omissions by other agents or agencies of the state that may be qualified as unlawful" (2003, 34). It is horizontal accountability that the Senate exercised when it investigated Watergate, the legislature keeping a watchful eye on the executive.

---

[1] The literature on the current economic crisis of the news media is burgeoning and I make no attempt to summarize it here. But summaries are available in Breaux Symposium (2008), Downie and Schudson (2009), Jones (2009), McChesney and Nichols (2010), Pickard, Stearns, and Aaron (2009), and Pew Project for Excellence in Journalism (2009).

Horizontal accountability comprises a set of mechanisms for one branch of government to effectively monitor and partially control another branch.

The third form of accountability is social accountability. A variety of institutions of civil society have come to play a role in keeping governments accountable. Although this form of accountability does not have legal standing, it still has real power, as Smulovitz and Peruzzotti emphasize, for two reasons:

First, because the disclosure of illegal or corrupt practices can destroy a fundamental resource of electoral politics: the symbolic capital or reputation of a politician or institution. Second, because very often these symbolic sanctions are needed for the activation of the mechanisms that have "teeth." That is, societal strategies are able to activate horizontal mechanisms because they can threaten public officials with the imposition of reputational or electoral consequences.   (2003, 311)

In the US, social accountability operates through various mechanisms, among them, litigation. The civil rights movement involved the work of a national voluntary association, the National Association for the Advancement of Colored People (NAACP), which had the money and the legal power to initiate lawsuits against bus companies that operated across state lines and against municipalities that operated segregated school systems in what the NAACP claimed—ultimately successfully—was a violation of the Fourteenth Amendment. Voluntary associations have also brought their authority to bear in holding the government accountable through the force of public opinion. For instance, organized groups of spouses of those who died in the 9/11 attacks forced a reluctant Bush administration to a more public accounting of its own failures and pressured Secretary of State Condoleezza Rice to testify to the 9/11 Commission, something she initially refused to do. The spouses had privileged access to Capitol Hill lawmakers and used that access to push Rice to the witness stand. In this case, social accountability operated to make horizontal accountability more effective.

Social accountability has existed from the beginning of the American republic—any organized or ad hoc protest or voluntary group participation in politics is a form of social accountability. The political party is the most important institution of social accountability—a voluntary association oriented to politics that seeks to hold government actors accountable, even though it is equally an organization that seeks to acquire the reins of governmental authority. Labor unions, chambers of commerce, professional and trade associations, and other standing organizations that seek to influence government as well as social movements, policy think tanks, and advocacy groups also participate in social accountability. The number, expertise, and sophistication of these groups in sharing information, applying pressure, gathering data, and managing publicity has grown greatly, especially since the 1960s.

The news media can be subsumed under the rubric of social accountability, but media accountability might be set aside as a fourth category of accountability. While journalism is often a medium through which other instruments of accountability work, it also operates on its own terms. The media sometimes initiate inquiries unprompted by elections, by conflicts between various branches of government, or by the efforts of advocacy groups.

Media accountability, like other sorts of accountability, is far from a perfect mechanism. The weight of research in sociology and political science makes it clear that much media coverage of government does little more than provide publicity for what political incumbents want the public to know. When government officials are relatively unified in their views on public issues, the media typically do not probe far. It is primarily when government elites are divided that the general commercial media offer a variety of sharply differentiated opinions and analyses of policy options. This, for instance, is what Daniel Hallin (1986) found in his classic study of US news media coverage of the Vietnam War; the media took up critical voices slowly and largely after, not before, there was significant opposition to the Vietnam War in the US Congress itself. W. Lance Bennett's work (1991) has likewise shown that the range of opinion in the mainstream media is "indexed" to the range and diversity of opinion among political elites. The media rarely serve as what sociologists call "moral entrepreneurs," advancing a new ethic or new set of values or new way of seeing the world unprompted by other social forces.

The position that the media generally reflect the range of views in the political elite must be qualified. Some research indicates that the ethics and customs of independent journalism modify this picture of a relatively slavish regurgitation of official views (or official conflicts). A study of New York Times coverage of the US–Libya crisis of 1985–6 finds that news did not mirror official government opinion but, in fact, gave more weight to critics of the administration than can be accounted for by the degree of prominence of the critics in Congress. Moreover, the newspaper cited many foreign sources, many of them critical of the US position. The researchers concluded that in a "decentered, destabilized international political system" this is a trend likely to endure (Althaus, Edy, Entman, and Phalen 1996, 418). Furthermore, journalists' attraction to "event-centered" rather than "institution-centered" occasions for news also weakens the hold of government on the media. And, as Regina Lawrence has written in her study of media coverage of police brutality, "Event-driven discourse about public issues is often more variable and dynamic than institutionally driven news, ranging beyond established news beats and drawing on a wider variety of voices and perspectives" (Lawrence 2000, 9).

When journalists cover spontaneous events, rather than predictable or staged occasions, they may have a real effect on the agenda of public policy. Media coverage of sexual or financial scandal in which standard conventions of behavior are violated can command broad attention and can lead to public embarrassment, resignations from office, and legal prosecutions of alleged criminal behavior. These are typically status quo police actions—important but not socially transformative. Transformative activity—not revealing a crime, say, but identifying that what was once regarded as normal and acceptable is now deserving of criminal sanction (say, sexual harassment in the workplace)—is the sort of thing that happens when activist organizations or social movements successfully champion new social values. The media follow up with news coverage.

The news media may also follow up accidents and scandals in ways that turn apparently unique or eccentric events into signs of something larger. The media are first responders, in a sense, at a moment of emergency, accident, or scandal. For instance, within a few weeks of Hurricane Katrina and the public revelation that the Bush administration's chief of the Federal Emergency Management Agency, Mike Brown, had no relevant experience for the responsible job he was appointed to, *Time* Magazine ran an article headlined "How Many More Mike Browns Are Out There?" which profiled several other prominent Bush administration officials whose advancement came exclusively from their political allegiances and personal connections (Tumulty, Thompson, and Allen 2005). A single incompetent official became the media emblem of an administration that seemed unusually contemptuous of ordinary requirements of relevant experience for responsible government positions.

A fifth type of accountability is something I will call executive self-surveillance or executive self-accountability. This may sound ridiculous on its face and certainly it would not seem to be good institutional design to delegate guarding the henhouse to the foxes. But executive self-accountability is worth taking seriously, all the more so because so much of it has arisen only in the period since the 1960s as the product of reform legislation. It is not more important than the other types of accountability, but it is for the most part newer, less visible, less studied, and a vital resource for media and civil society efforts to monitor government.

By executive self-surveillance, I mean simply that the executive branch of government has mechanisms for keeping account of itself in a public way. Reform legislation of the 1970s and 1980s provided large new capacities for monitoring government through federal agencies themselves. Think of the importance of environmental impact statements and the public airing of them required by law—a law (the National Environmental Policy Act) that went into effect in 1970. Think of the public disclosure of campaign finance contributions and expenditures through laws passed in 1971 and 1974. Think of the important reports of the federal inspectors general (IGs) critical of the actions of agencies from the FBI to the Corporation for Public Broadcasting, from the Interior Department to the CIA. These reports are normally public and readily available to journalists, advocacy organizations, and any citizens interested enough to download them from government websites. None of them were available before the Inspector General Act of 1978.

The 1978 legislation and its extensions today authorize more than sixty statutory IGs with 12,000 staff members whose job is to investigate the agencies to which they are assigned and report to both the agency head and Congress on their findings, with recommendations for change, recommendations for prosecution, and a report on money recovered. Usually the IGs are looking for waste and fraud and other financial mismanagement, but sometimes their efforts are far more extensive. While the name "inspector general" suggests an individual, IGs at the larger departments oversee very large offices; the IG at the Department of Justice manages a staff of some 400 criminal investigators, auditors, and lawyers.

All Cabinet-level agencies and most other major government agencies have an IG who is responsible for submitting semi-annual reports to Congress that cannot be altered by the agencies. In fiscal year 2006, the IGs collectively made recommendations that would account for $9.9 billion in savings for the government. They recovered directly $8.6 billion in monies owed to the government by contractors, employees, or others. Their reports led to 6,500 criminal indictments, 950 successful civil suits, and, 300 suspensions or disbarments—and untold numbers of news stories.

To get a sense of how the work of the inspectors general reaches the news media and thus the general public, consider the following examples.

In September 2008 the Justice Department IG issued "a blistering critique" of the political motives in the firing of US attorneys but "stopped short" of urging criminal indictments of former Attorney General Alberto Gonzales or his aides (Lichtblau and Otterman 2008).

Also in September 2008 the IG at Health and Human Services reported that more than 90 percent of nursing homes had been cited for violation of federal health and safety standards in 2007 and 17 percent of them had deficiencies that caused "actual harm or immediate jeopardy." The problems were greater in for-profit homes than in non-profits (Pear 2008).

In December 2008 the special IG for the Reconstruction of Iraq, a Bush appointee, made available a 513-page history of the reconstruction that the *New York Times* held, in its lead story, "depicts an effort crippled before the invasion by Pentagon planners who were hostile to the idea of rebuilding a foreign country, and then molded into a $100 billion failure by bureaucratic turf wars, spiraling violence and ignorance of the basic elements of Iraqi society and infrastructure" (Glanz and Miller 2008).

The IG is doing self-surveillance; he or she works within the executive branch of government and reports on the executive branch—to both the executive and Congress. It is possible to pervert the job, but not as easily as it may seem. The most vital protection of the integrity of the IG function is that the IG must report not only to the agency but to Congress. In other words, self-surveillance as constituted by the 1978 law provides an automatic trigger to Congress to keep its eyes trained on executive accountability, too. The IG reports become public and thereby invite media attention and the attention of various non-profit, advocacy, and political groups.

All of these types of accountability matter. All help make democracy work. All work better when each is working well. None is sufficient by itself.

What follows from placing the news media in this broader context, as one of a set of vital forms of holding government accountable? We end up with a better understanding of the impact of the news on our politics. We know that sometimes news makes a big difference. From Watergate on, there are streams of examples that demonstrate that publicity in the news media or investigation by the news media has forced a politician to resign or stopped some legislation or executive initiative in its tracks. We know from a US study that the presence of news organizations in local areas providing more coverage of representatives to Congress makes representatives more sensitive to and more accountable to the desires and preferences of local constituents and more responsive to their interests (Snyder and Stromberg 2008). Cases from around the world show that press coverage of corporate malfeasance has powerful effects on corporate behavior (Fisse and Braithwaite 1983). News matters. But how much does it matter? And how much does its influence depend on the health of the four other types of accountability systems discussed above? And what do we know, if anything, about the relative effectiveness of different kinds of news: regular informational reporting of government proceedings? Advocacy journalism that champions the policies of one party or another? Muckraking investigations? Social empathy reporting that evokes sentiments on behalf of one or another outcast, downtrodden, or neglected group in society?

At this moment, there is much more interest in the future of news than in its past. The past—meaning the world or worlds we knew or thought we knew from the middle of the nineteenth century when commercial newspapers began to be independent of political parties in the United States to 2003 or 2004 or 2005 or certainly 2007–8—seems to have vanished. There is still news. There are still newspapers; some of them are even making money. The vast majority of others, although bloodied, are still kicking. But the old economic premises of news are out the window.

News that came from a largely "vertical" mass medium—from the journalists to the readers and viewers—has turned increasingly "horizontal." People always passed along news and often passed along newspapers themselves, but in the online world the "pass along" factor operates so swiftly and with so many people involved that it changes the game. And since news organizations archive and attend to what is passed along ("most emailed story,") this horizontal circulation of news acts back quickly on the consciousness of the journalists and helps to shape what they choose to cover.

News is increasingly global. News is increasingly originated by citizens, rank amateurs, even though, increasingly, professional news organizations are sponsoring or soliciting the amateurs to participate in their own activities in a variety of experiments that have been labeled "pro-am" journalism (Downie and Schudson 2009). Journalists at mainstream news organizations (that are increasingly referred to as "legacy" media) read analysis and even reporting from bloggers whose primary investment is their time and who make their reputations not from the prestige of institutions they work for (they work for themselves and usually without pay) but from the cogency of their work alone. Journalists at commercial news organizations were never alone in keeping government accountable but now they are reduced in number, reduced in future prospects, and competing with (or sometimes cooperating with) and dependent on a growing variety of other journalists and other institutions in the accountability business.

In the end, does Tocqueville's error matter? Should we care that the prevalence of newspapers in the United States had little to do with what enlightened public opinion demanded and more to do with the convictions of elites that public information should circulate as widely as possible, the inclinations of political parties in power to reward their friends by advertising in their newspapers and providing government jobs for them and their families, and the desire of entrepreneurs to make money in the news business whether they published much political news or not?

There is something to be said for correcting the historical record for its own sake, but in this case, more is at stake: revising Tocqueville helps us understand the complex—and impure—tradition from which the contemporary media descend. We will be better able to contemplate what are and are not the best directions for the media if we have a more sensible appreciation of where the media have stood in the past, and how and why they have mattered. They have mattered as one—of five—significant mechanisms for holding government accountable. They have mattered in other ways, too. They do this not only by providing information but by providing analysis and perspective. They have also been a forum for public expressions of opinion—from letters to the editor to "op ed" contributions to tips and leaks that citizens provide journalists, to the many forms of public expression the Internet now makes possible and makes convenient. They have mattered, too, in giving public recognition to various groups in society; as philosopher Joseph Raz has put it, the media contribute to a pluralistic democracy when they portray and thereby legitimize various styles of life in society, giving them a "stamp of public acceptability" (Raz 1994, 140). There is much that the news media do, or sometimes do, for a democratic society beyond the specific, delimited service of providing information to hold government to account (Schudson 2008, 11–26).

Journalism is one necessary contributing factor to an effective democracy, but it has a set of partners in keeping government accountable. If one is interested in the survival of journalism for the accountability function it serves, one should also be interested in the integrity of the electoral process; the security of checks and balances within the government; the viability of civil society organizations that monitor the government— from political parties to think tanks, partisan or non-partisan, to various non-profit organizations that advocate government transparency or that keep the Freedom of Information Act a living institution by using it to get government documents publicly released; and the effective exercise of executive self-surveillance through the IGs and the processes that preserve the IGs' willingness to critically examine the operation of the departments to which they are assigned. It is in the interests of journalism, and of democracy, that journalists inform, educate, and remind the public about all of these matters—not only about the role of journalism.

As we move into a world of astonishing change for the news media, there are many more reasons for hope than for despair—but the losses at the moment are real and the possibilities for a reconstruction that could leave us better off than we were before are easier to see after shedding a few illusions about the quality and character of American journalism of the past, some of which misled even so subtle an observer as Alexis de Tocqueville.

## References

ALTHAUS, S., EDY, J., ENTMAN, R., and PHALEN, P. 1996. Revising the Indexing Hypothesis: Officials, Media, and the Libya Crisis. *Political Communication*, 13: 407–21.

BALDASTY, G. 1992. *The Commercialization of News in the Nineteenth Century*. Madison: University of Wisconsin Press.

BENNETT, W. L. 1991. Toward a Theory of Press–State Relations. *Journal of Communication*, 40: 103–25.

BLUMIN, S. 1976. *Urban Threshold: Growth and Change in a 19th-Century American Community*. Chicago: University of Chicago Press.

BOORSTIN, D. 1965. *The Americans: The National Experience*. New York: Random House.

*Breaux Symposium*. 2008. *New Models for News*. Baton Rouge: Manship School of Mass Communication, Louisiana State University.

DOWNIE, L., JR., and SCHUDSON, M. 2009. The Reconstruction of American Journalism. *Columbia Journalism Review* (Nov.–Dec.), 28–51. At <http://www.columbiajournalismreport.org>. Accessed Oct. 2010.

FISSE, B., and BRAITHWAITE, J. 1983. *The Impact of Publicity on Corporate Offenders*. Albany: State University of New York Press.

GANS, H. J. 2009. News and Democracy in the United States: Some Observations on Current Problems and Future Possibilities. In *Routledge Companion to News and Journalism Studies*, ed. S. Allan. New York: Routledge.

GLANZ, J., and MILLER, T. C. 2008. Official History Spotlights Iraq Rebuilding Blunders. *New York Times*, Dec. 13, A1.

GRIFFITH, S. F. 1989. *Home Town News: William Allen White and the Emporia Gazette*. New York: Oxford University Press.

HALLIN, D. 1986. *The "Uncensored War": The Media and Vietnam*. New York: Oxford University Press.

—— 1994. *We Keep America on Top of the World*. New York: Routledge.

JOHN, R. 1995. *Spreading the News*. Cambridge, MA: Harvard University Press.

JONES, A. 2009. *Losing the News*. New York: Oxford University Press.

JORDAN, D. P. 1983. *Political Leadership in Jefferson's Virginia*. Charlottesville: University Press of Virginia.

KIELBOWICZ, R. 1989. *News in the Mail*. Westport, CT: Greenwood, 1989.

LAWRENCE, R. 2000. *The Politics of Force: Media and the Construction of Police Brutality*. Berkeley: University of California Press.

LICHTBLAU, E., and OTTERMAN, S. 2008. Special Prosecutor Named in Attorney Firing Case. *New York Times*, Sept. 29, A12.

MCCHESNEY, R. W., and NICHOLS, J. 2010. *The Death and Life of American Journalism*. New York: Nation Books.

NERONE, J. 1989. *The Culture of the Press in the Early Republic: Cincinnati, 1793–1848*. New York: Garland.

NORD, D. P. 2001. *Communities of Journalism*. Urbana: University of Illinois Press.

O'DONNELL, G. 2003. Horizontal Accountability: The Legal Institutionalization of Mistrust. In *Democratic Accountability in Latin America*, ed. S. Mainwaring and C. Welna. New York: Oxford University Press.

PEAR, R. 2008. Violations Reported at 94% of U.S. Nursing Homes. *New York Times*, Sept. 30, A20.

Pew Project for Excellence in Journalism. 2009. State of the News Media 2009. At <http://www.journalism.org>. Accessed Oct. 2010.

PICKARD, V., STEARNS, J., and AARON, C. 2009. Saving the News: Toward a National Journalism Strategy. At <http://www.freepress.net/files/saving_the_news.pdf>. Accessed Oct. 2010.

RAZ, J. 1994. *Ethics in the Public Domain*. Oxford: Clarendon Press.

RUSSO, D. P. 1980. *The Origins of Local News in the U.S. Country Press, 1840s–1870s*. Journalism Monographs, 65 (Feb.). Minneapolis, MN: University of Minnesota.

SCHUDSON, M. 1978. *Discovering the News: A Social History of American Newspapers*. New York: Basic Books.

—— 2008. *Why Democracies Need an Unlovable Press*. Cambridge: Polity Press.

SMULOVITZ, C., and PERUZZOTTI, E. 2003. Societal and Horizontal Controls: Two Cases of a Fruitful Relationship. In *Democratic Accountability in Latin America*, ed. S. Mainwaring and C. Welna. New York: Oxford University Press.

SNYDER, J. M., JR., and STROMBERG, D. 2008. *Press Coverage and Political Accountability*. National Bureau of Economic Research Working Paper 13878. Cambridge, MA.

STARR, P. 2004. *The Creation of the Media*. New York: Basic Books.

TOCQUEVILLE, A. de. 2003. *Democracy in America*. London: Penguin.

TUMULTY, K., THOMPSON, M., and ALLEN, M. 2005. How Many More Mike Browns Are Out There? *Time* (Oct. 3), 49–54.

WATROUS, J. (ed.) 1909. *Memoirs of Milwaukee County*, i. Madison: Western Historical Association.

CHAPTER 5

........................................................................................

# PARTISANS, WATCHDOGS, AND ENTERTAINERS

## The Press for Democracy and its Limits

........................................................................................

KATHERINE ANN BROWN
TODD GITLIN

EVEN as the financial health of the American press can no longer be taken for granted, it is commonly said that the press—or the media—is the lifeblood of democracy. Toward this end, Thomas Jefferson's 1787 remark is widely quoted (especially in newspapers): "If it were left to me to decide whether we should have a government without newspapers or newspapers without a government, I should not hesitate for a moment to prefer the latter" (Jefferson 1903–4). Is it not self-evident that an open press conveys information, that information produces public knowledge, and that knowledge is power?

But the press's cheerful self-congratulation is a rampant simplification, and so is the notion that the press protected by the First Amendment was a mannerly, balanced, objective press. The press whose freedom was guaranteed against infringement was an unbridled affair, much of it opinionated, scurrilous, vicious, and flagrantly partisan. In 1807 President Jefferson, with much more experience under his belt, wrote: "The man who never looks into a newspaper is better informed than he who reads them, inasmuch as he who knows nothing is nearer to truth than he whose mind is filled with falsehoods and errors" (Jefferson 1903–4).

The standard progress narrative of journalism connects a reliable press directly with good government. The argument runs as follows. As the press evolved from partisanship to objectivity, its ability to serve as a watchdog improved. As it came to elevate rationality and reliable information over unbridled opinion, it became more useful as a curb on abuses of power, encouraging the people to take part in politics and to influence powerful institutions in the direction of sensible policy.

This chapter, examining the evolution of the American media from their colonial origins to today, argues that the standard tribute to the democratic uses of journalism oversimplifies and romanticizes the actual news media and their part in everyday life. We begin with the newspaper's changing form in the eighteenth and nineteenth centuries—from partisan rags crafted for political elites to popular publications that democratized information—and the role newspaper partisanship and sensationalism played in America's social and political development. Turning to the twentieth century, we examine media independence and its watchdog role, reflected most acutely in the muckraking magazines of the 1900s and 1910s and the newspapers and broadcast outlets of the 1960s and 1970s, when rigorous investigative reporting successfully challenged government malfeasance. Today, however, partisanship, often thought to belong strictly to the early days of the republic, is becoming more pronounced, while popular faith in the objectivity of the news media is embattled. Moreover, the news media frequently fail to challenge abuses of power, and it is by no means clear that they encourage meaningful civic engagement. Partisan journalism, sensational journalism, deferential journalism, and watchdog journalism all coexist in proportions that can be expected to fluctuate over time.

## Boisterous Beginnings

During colonial times, the writing, printing, and distribution of newspapers was a one-man operation, limited in scope and deeply opinionated. Foreign news outweighed local news, which often was reprinted without verification (Downie and Schudson 2009, 4). Whatever the rebellious reputation of such publishers as John Peter Zenger, who in 1735 was successfully defended against a charge of seditious libel brought by the governor of New York, the Founding Fathers did not expect newspapers to play a central role in the republic (Leonard 1986, 5, 7).

In post-revolutionary America, the press enjoyed more freedom than anywhere else in the world (Mott 1941, 143). Debate was freewheeling over the adoption of the Constitution, over taxes and state debts, over the peace treaty with Britain. Political leaders found the press useful for amplifying their platforms. Beginning in the 1790s, "no politician dreamed of mounting a campaign, launching a new movement, or winning over a new geographic region without a newspaper" (Pasley 2001, 9). Printing was subsidized by political candidates, factions, and—in the form of post office subsidy—the government. The Postal Act of 1792 ensured that newspapers could be mailed at much lower rates than letters, and that printers could mail their papers to all other papers free of charge (John 1995, 36–42).

Between 1783 and 1801, 450 newspapers were started—some dying quickly, others surviving (Mott 1941, 113). They were, in the main, personal and acrimonious. During this period, one historian summarized, "the character of no man was safe from the assaults of anonymous scribblers, who as easily changed their allegiance as their coat, and who gained a precarious living from personalities, half-truths and untruths, expressed in the most outrageous terms" (Ford 1905, 81). Partisanship was intense and reckless. The *Federalist Papers* accused Jefferson's allies of being "filthy Jacobins" and "monsters of sedition," only to be accused, in turn, of being "Tory monarchists" and "British-loving aristocrats." John Adams was called "a mock Monarch" who was "blind, bald, toothless, querulous" and "a ruffian deserving of the curses of mankind"; Adams, in return, charged that he had suffered "the most envious malignity, the most base, vulgar, sordid, fish-woman scurrility, and the most palpable lies" to which any official had ever been subjected (Wood 2009, 256). In 1798 President Adams signed into law the Sedition Act, which made it a crime to publish "false, scandalous, and malicious writing" against the government or its officials (*United States Statutes*).

Fact was frequently held hostage to opinion. When, in 1800, Hamiltonians and Jeffersonians created the Federalist and Republican (later Democratic) parties, respectively, both founded newspapers to reach their sympathizers, advocate their opinions, and mobilize voters (Cook 1998, 26). During the 1800 campaign, "The Federalist newspapers printed any anti-Jefferson smear they could find" (Lerche 1948, 471). Many Americans saw this press as "corroding the basis for rational public discussion and fraying the bonds of civility that held the nation together" (Daniel 2009, 284–5). But partisanship was congruent with diversion, a prime purpose of the press. In 1816 an erudite Massachusetts clergyman named William Bentley, who wrote biweekly newspaper columns to help "all classes of readers" grasp "the causes which produce interesting events," concluded that news about fires, accidents, and like ephemera was crowding out judicious analysis, driving the public mind "into a sea of mediocrity" (Wood 2009, 732).

More than three times as many newspapers were mailed in 1820 as in 1800. Wood summarizes the growth of America's papers:

In 1790 the country contained only 92 newspapers, only eight of them dailies. By 1800 this number had more than doubled, to 235, twenty-four of which were dailies. By 1810 Americans were buying over twenty-two million copies of 376 newspapers annually— even though half the population was under the age of sixteen and one-fifth was enslaved and generally prevented from reading. This was the largest aggregate circulation of newspapers of any country in the world.   (2009, 479)

As in the eighteenth century, however, the literature that dominated mass circulation was religious, not political. Well into the nineteenth century, religious publishers outproduced the emerging commercial press. By the 1830s, the American Tract Society alone "had presses that produced five pages of religious information each year for every adult and child in America" (Leonard 1986, 58). Simultaneously, profound changes in nineteenth-century political culture and institutions strengthened the partisan press and allowed it to follow the religious press's lead in mass publication.

As party politics became increasingly contentious during the opening decades of the nineteenth century, Americans became increasingly hungry for political news. Political parties and voluntary organizations contributed to robust public debates (Leonard

1986, 58; Keyssar 2000, 40). The party press, spurred by a new enthusiasm for politics, increased its output, which was more opinionated than reportorial. Sometimes news was fabricated. During the presidential campaign of 1828, newspapers supporting Andrew Jackson went so far as to circulate an invented smear to the effect that his chief opponent, John Quincy Adams, while serving as minister to Russia, had pimped for the Tsar (Cole 2009, 28, 150). Some editors used newspapers to promote themselves as political candidates; if successful, they kept their editorships while holding government office (Cook 1998, 26). Journalists' talents were judged not by their fidelity to fact, but "by the subjective values of wit, eloquence, ability to attract readers, and talent in stirring popular agitation" (Sheppard 2008, 196).

## THE DEMOCRATIZING OF INFORMATION

As political interest and democratic spirit grew, information mattered to growing numbers of Americans, yet neither the party nor commercial papers satisfied them. It was common knowledge that political parties, factions, and candidates financed newspapers and dictated their editorials (Schudson 1981, 15; Andrews 1970, 24). The party press was intended for, and read by, political elites—and their content, correspondingly, was confined to information on politics (Schudson 1981, 15)—while the commercial papers were intended for the mercantile class. The reach of the press was decidedly limited. Both party and commercial papers were expensive: they cost 6 cents per issue when the average daily wage for non-farm labor was less than 85 cents. Newspapers were often sold only by annual subscription, costing $8 to $10. In 1833 the combined circulation of all of New York City's eleven dailies was 26,500, for an urban population of approximately 200,000 people (Schudson 1981, 18).

Enter the penny press, a newly egalitarian approach to news delivery that fed the growing public curiosity about leaders and fellow citizens, broke from the partisan approach to news, and contributed to the proliferation of both newspapers and readers. On September 3, 1833, the first penny paper, the *New York Sun*, was published; soon, the *Evening Transcript* and the *New York Herald* followed. The media historian Michael Schudson claims that the middle class penny press provided the foundation for the press, as we know it today (Schudson 1995, 38; for a dissenting view, see Nerone 1987). Costing a single cent, such papers aimed to attract a broad readership with a wide array of political, social, and economic news, and without much partisanship (Schudson 1981, 60). James Gordon Bennett, the publisher of the *Herald*, understood deeply that "partisanship of any sort, whether political, economic, or social, whether acknowledged or underground, was simply too limiting for a businessman who wanted to sell to all comers" (Tucher 1994, 17). Within two years, the three penny papers' combined circulation alone was 44,000 (Schudson 1981, 18).

As citizens in the early to mid-nineteenth century "understood their own ordinary lives to be of value and of possible interest to others," Schudson writes, "they both sought strangers as audiences or publics and avoided them to protect a private space for the self" (Schudson 1981, 60). Newspapers brought news of strangers, enlarging the popular sense of the scope of the world at large—even if they tended to reduce the world to stereotypes. In particular, readers relished windows into the world of crime, sin, and the unexpected. The penny press provided a broad array of news while simultaneously allowing urban newsreaders to glimpse the spectacle of the world. The growing public demand for news was also manifested in multiple editions (Lee 1937, 277), or what later became known as "extras." The first multiple-edition paper came out in April 1836, during the murder investigation of the prostitute Ellen Jewett in New York City. By 1840 the *Herald* "frequently 'made over' its news content as many as three times" per morning (Lee 1937, 277).

The act of reading news was becoming habitual; keeping up with the news was a sort of everyday piety. By 1840 the number of penny press dailies had grown from eleven to 138 (Schudson 1981, 14); by 1850 total daily newspaper circulation in the United States exceeded 750,000. Daily newspapers reached one fifth of all American households (McCombs, Einsiedel, and Weaver 1991, 54).

During the antebellum decades, a contentious press accompanied increasingly contentious politics. Electoral politics became public theater; election days became "climaxes of public excitement" (Leonard 1986, 7). The consolidation of polarized parties and the growth of the press furthered political mobilization. Voter turnout more than doubled, from 27 percent in 1824 to 57.6 percent in 1828, and then, with the democratization of the Jacksonian period, rose to 80.2 percent in 1840 (Leonard 1986, 7; Keyssar 2000, 40). Readers were voters; voters were readers. At the same time, observers were struck by the papers' ability to serve as public watchdogs. Ralph Waldo Emerson celebrated "the power of the newspaper" for its "relentless inquisition.... turn[ing] the glare of this solar microscope on every malfeasance... forewarn[ing]... the whole people" (Emerson 1856).

The Civil War catalyzed an increase in the demand for news in both the North and the South. Both populations felt a stake in military developments and craved up-to-the-minute reports (Andrews 1970, 506). The telegraph permitted news to be transmitted via wire, helping to standardize its form (Dicken-Garcia 1989, 53). With the end of the war, the federal government stopped providing presses with printing contracts for stationery and congressional records, a form of subsidy that had begun in the eighteenth century (Baldasty 1992, 20). Publishers adapted by reducing costs with high-speed printing, cheaper newsprint, railroad shipping, and advertising, all permitting increased circulation and growing profits (McGerr 1986, 109).

In the late 1860s and early 1870s, urban newspapers grew prosperous. Increased demand, lower prices per copy, and more enticing content allowed them to free themselves from party ties (Briggs and Burke 2005, 155). Although some papers remained staunchly partisan, others proclaimed political independence and affirmed a responsibility to society as a whole (Dicken-Garcia 1989, 62). Editors and publishers of the *New York Tribune*, the *New York Evening Post*, the *Springfield Republican*, the

*Chicago Tribune*, and the *Cincinnati Commercial* declared themselves above party loyalty and "devoted to the impartial reporting of news" (McGerr 1986, 114). These reformers wanted good government and promoted educational campaigns, asking voters to make informed rather than emotional decisions at the ballot box (Schudson and Tifft 2005, 23). Newspapermen aimed to present voters with empirical knowledge and factual information; subjective responses to news, they deemed, should be sequestered on the editorial page (McGerr 1986, 118). An elite press took root, claiming superior knowledge and a privileged vantage point.

In 1810 independent papers had numbered 5 percent of the total. In 1850 they made up 9 percent. But by the mid-1870s, a full 25 percent of newspapers could be considered independent, rising to 28 percent in 1880 and 36 percent in 1892 (Sheppard 2008, 198). While still not outnumbering the partisan press, they "had broken the partisan monopoly on public discourse" (McGerr 1986, 120). This was not to say that the independent press was free of partisan tendencies. In 1872 independent editors from the *Cincinnati Commercial*, *Springfield Republican*, and *Louisville Courier-Journal*, aiming to defeat President Ulysses S. Grant in his reelection bid, joined together to find another presidential candidate at the short-lived Liberal Republican Party's convention (McGerr 1986, 116; Summers 1994, 255).

Independence went only so far. Writes Michael McGerr: "the crusading independent papers were quite willing to choose stories to serve their political goals." They "deplored the notion of political neutrality" (McGerr 1986, 115–19). Still, the independent press was a significant departure from the party press. Disguised partisanship was the tribute that partisanship paid to objectivity. Professing fairness and fact-based impartiality, they "reach[ed] the common denominator of an increasingly large readership" (Muhlmann 2004, 6, 10).

By the mid-1880s, sensational journalism challenged both the partisan and the independent press for readership (Schudson and Tifft 2005, 23). Foreshadowed in the early penny press, sensationalist newspapers (called the "yellow press" after their comic strips) focused on "human interest"—political gossip, celebrity scandals, murders, believe-it-or-not stories, and the like, all descended from traditional folklore (Hughes 1940). Dramatic narratives attracted the attention of those who wished to be informed and entertained at the same time. The essentially a- or anti-political journalism of Joseph Pulitzer and William Randolph Hearst, designed for working class men and women (especially immigrants unfamiliar with English), made ample use of illustrations, cartoons, comic strips, cooking and etiquette tips, and punchy, stripped-down prose (McGerr 1986, 107, 125, 126; Campbell 2001, 52–3). Such features, along with scandal reports and investigative exposés, built circulation. By 1892 Pulitzer's *World* was an extraordinary success, contributing to the depoliticization of the working classes yet simultaneously making politics more accessible to them by sparking interest in political affairs through human interest stories (McGerr 1986, 127). With his *Journal*, Hearst, too, aimed to reach less educated readers put off by the "dry intellectualism" of the independent press (McGerr 1986, 127).

# MUCKRAKING AND POLITICAL LIFE

At the same time, there developed a black (or "Negro") press enlarging upon the antebellum abolitionist papers. Frederick Douglass had established the *North Star* in 1847; it both campaigned against slavery and embraced the emancipation of women. (Its motto: "Right is of no Sex—Truth is of no Color—God is the Father of us all, and we are all brethren.") After the Civil War, the journalist Ida B. Wells went from editing a Memphis newspaper called *Free Speech* in 1889 to writing investigative reports about lynching during the 1890s, acquiring a national readership and an international reputation. These papers, however, were weeklies; they could not compete with white-owned dailies on the general run of news (Detweiler 1922, 5).

The independent, sensationalist, and partisan papers, and to a lesser degree the black press, in various permutations and combinations, shaped the American news land-scape into the Progressive era. The independent press took the moralistic high ground, focusing on facts of the public world; the sensationalist press depicted the world as a strange and wondrous spectacle; the party-funded partisan press, and the black press, combined sensational and fact-based elements (McGerr 1986, 130). Around the turn of the century, these forms were joined by exposé journalism—long-form investigations prefigured by Ida B. Wells, chiefly published in monthly magazines. It was an adver-sary, not an advocate, who dubbed this work "muckraking": President Theodore Roosevelt in 1906, deeming investigative reporting dangerous to a fragile democracy (Feldstein 2006, 106; Steffens 1931, 357).

Muckrakers dug for facts and embedded them in extended narratives to challenge authority, expose government corruption and corporate abuse, and ignite public outrage against injustice (Feldstein 2006, 105). While investigative reporting was not new, nineteenth century muckraking had been largely partisan, exposing malfeasance on the part of the opposition rather than letting chips fall where they may (Feldstein 2006, 108–9). By contrast, the muckrakers of the early twentieth century disdained party loyalty. Between 1903 and 1912, they produced over 2,000 investigative articles in American magazines read mainly by the middle classes (Aucoin 2005, 33). Writing for commercial organs supported by circulation, not political party subsidies, they were free to choose their targets as they liked (Leonard 1986, 223; Schudson and Tifft 2005, 23–4; Tichi 2004, 63). The antagonists in muckrakers' narratives on corruption and greed were municipal leaders—Lincoln Steffens's 1904 exposé of the mayor of Min-neapolis was typical—and corporate giants, as in Ida Tarbell's 1904 investigation of John D. Rockefeller's business practices (Tichi 2004, 84–5, 97).

The muckrakers stirred reformist sentiment and spurred politicians to pass laws like the Pure Food and Drug Act of 1906 (Bennett and Serrin 2005, 176). But much of the time, the attitude of most of their readers seems to have been spectatorial. They were interested in what they read, but not necessarily moved to take remedial action. Arguably, in fact, the muckraking exposés had the unintended consequence of discrediting the democratic process and producing disenchantment with the prospects of reform politics. As the historian Thomas Leonard has argued, the muckrakers' work delivered something that was, at once, "both shocking (as the authors intended) and (as they did not wish) a message to pull back from political life" (Leonard 1986, 197). This is, of course, an interpretation. All that can be said firmly is that there is no evidence that muckraking, by itself, brought citizens into active political life. In any event, by 1917, when the United States entered the First World War, the muckrakers' heyday was over.

The Progressive era, the historian Richard Hofstadter maintained (1955, 186), was fueled by journalism. Muckrakers were feared, and sometimes repressed, by powerful enemies. The black press was especially targeted. In 1919 a black-edited newspaper wrote of a town outside Memphis:

White people of this city have issued an order that no "colored newspapers" must be circulated in this town, but that every "darkey," the petition reads, must read the *Falcon*, a local white paper edited by a Confederate veteran. The whites stated this step was being done in order to keep the "nigger from getting besides himself, and to keep him in his place." (Detweiler 1922, 1)

But the limits of muckraking also deserve attention. It was during Progressivism's upsurge, in the first two decades of the twentieth century, that a paradox emerged. During this period, newspapers grew dramatically. The average circulation of daily newspapers "climbed from 2,200 a day in 1840 to 8,007 in 1904" (McGerr 1986, 108). But as circulation increased, so did political apathy. Popular participation in politics waned, for the most part, after 1900. Voter turnout in presidential elections, which had averaged 78 percent of eligible voters in the 1880s and 1890s, fell to 73.2 percent in 1900 (the last time it exceeded 70 percent), to 65.2 percent in 1904, then to 58.8 percent in 1912. In 1920, with women newly eligible to vote and the pool of potential voters thus enlarged by a factor of two, voter turnout fell to 49.2 percent. Yet, in that same year, more than 2,000 daily newspapers were published. An estimated 27 million Americans read them daily, and 1.34 copies of a daily newspaper were sold for every household in the United States (Drowne and Huber 2004, 139; McCombs, Einsiedel, and Weaver 1991, 54). Plainly there was no direct correlation between newspaper circulation and political participation. Voter turnout did not exceed 50 percent again until 1928.

During the first two decades of the twentieth century, in other words, voter turnout sank back to those of a century earlier, before the ascent of the penny press, back to the level that prevailed at a time of flagrant partisanship and reckless scandalmongering. It seems a strong working hypothesis that increased exposure to news, whether in the daily press, muckraking magazines, or the radio broadcasts that began in the 1920s, did not translate into political activity. If it strengthened democracy, it did so by influencing elites, not arousing public participation. Increasingly, Americans were reading or hearing about the larger world, but reading about it was not necessarily a prologue—or even an accompaniment—to political engagement. News empowered political elites, unearthing useful material for congressional investigations, regulatory agencies, and law enforcement. But for most of the public, news was a spectator sport, not necessarily an effective tool for improving public involvement in political life. Down to the present, it is difficult to disagree with the conclusion of Herbert J. Gans: "Much of the audience is interested in keeping up with the news rather than being politically involved citizens" (2003, 21).

# THE AGE OF THE WATCHDOG

The Second World War was good for newspapers and for broadcast reporting. Between 1940 and 1946, total daily newspaper circulation rose by 24 percent, and total Sunday circulation by 35 percent. Beginning in 1938, Edward R. Murrow's team of CBS foreign correspondents provided original reportage on events in Europe for American listeners, adapting a literary style to news for radio (Cloud and Olson 1998, 3). Total daily newspaper circulation continued to rise non-stop from 1946 to 1984. During this time, of course, television also became integral to both government and opposition.

Defenders of the excellence and efficacy of the press point to waves of watchdog journalism during this period, exemplified in Edward R. Murrow's anti-McCarthy broadcasts, the rise of the dissenting underground press in the 1960s, and the "journalism review" movement among disgruntled reporters (Peck 1985). According to journalists' own balance sheets, the coverage of 1954–74—from the televised army–McCarthy hearings through Watergate—helped spur a virtual revolution in civil rights and shattered the grip of two presidents. Of course, the news media's treatment of dramatic conflicts is easier to discern than their lapses. (In other words, journalism is judged by the same standard that journalists use for newsworthiness.)

The press's claim to a significant role in America's democratic life during the years following the Second World War rests heavily on its record in covering the civil rights movement; the Vietnam War; and Watergate and the Nixon administration's abuses of power.

## Civil Rights

Mainstream journalism's achievement is best appreciated against the background of the not so benign neglect that newspapers practiced for decades in the face of the wretched conditions of blacks, north and south. In 1938, according to the journalist–historians Gene Roberts and Hank Klibanoff:

No major publication had a news bureau in the South. Even so thorough a paper as *The New York Times* wrote about antisegregationist leaders and organizations almost entirely on the inside pages, when it reported on them at all. Only once between 1935 and 1940 . . . did the *Times* run a front-page story mentioning the name of any of the country's leading Negro racial reformists.    (2006, 10)

Not until 1947 was the first major national bureau established in the South—a *New York Times* bureau in Chattanooga (Roberts and Klibanoff 2006, 34). But even with a bureau, *Times* coverage of white supremacy was spotty (Roberts and Klibanoff 2006, 106). The paper emphasized stories of progress. The "race story" in the South was left to a handful of black-owned newspapers and magazines, along with left-wing weeklies from the North, notably pouring into Mississippi to cover the 1955 murder of Emmett Till and the subsequent trial, while local white-owned papers obscured racist violence (Roberts and Klibanoff 2006, 76, 89–105, 80–1). When the Montgomery bus boycott began in December 1955, mainstream papers were slow to appreciate the extent and depth of what was taking place (Roberts and Klibanoff 2006, 111–12). The national press's conception of objectivity downplayed the steadfast non-violence of the demonstrators. "The wire services . . . became fixated on declaring whether or not incidents provoked violence but studiously avoided suggesting whether whites or Negroes were responsible" (Roberts and Klibanoff 2006, 225).

Still, mounting coverage of civil rights actions by the *Times* and other outlets was enough to incur the wrath of segregationists. In March 1960, after the *Times*'s Harrison Salisbury filed a front-page story that ran under the headline "Fear and Hatred Grip Birmingham," the *Birmingham News* reprinted it under a different headline: "*New York Times* Slanders Our City" (Roberts and Klibanoff 2006, 232–3). City officials filed criminal libel charges against Salisbury. Fearing more of the same, the paper withdrew its reporters from Alabama for two and a half years (Roberts and Klibanoff 2006, 234–5). Reporters were often the targets of violent racists; in Oxford, Mississippi, in 1962, a French reporter was assassinated, shot in the back, during a riot against a black man's attempt to be admitted to the university (Roberts and Klibanoff 2006, 294).

During the early 1960s, civil rights coverage improved in both quantity and quality. Northern newspapers played up the brutality of white supremacists. News photos dramatically reinforced print reports. Television coverage of confrontations—vicious attacks on the integrated buses of Freedom Riders (1961), marching children met with fire hoses and snarling dogs in Birmingham (1963), assaults on peaceful demonstrators in Selma, Alabama (1965)—cast the movement against riotous racists and barbarian police in a national melodrama. Civil rights organizers orchestrated projects to heighten this imagery. The Mississippi Summer Project of 1964, which flooded the state with mainly white civil rights workers, attracted reporters to cover a state where racist terror was normal and normally invisible to the rest of the country. *Newsweek* reported at the beginning of the summer that eighty "race reporters" were at work "among the magnolias and cattle prods" (Roberts and Klibanoff 2006, 365).

The coverage galvanized the movement, spreading its iconography and its appeal to potential supporters, intensifying the public impression of a polarization between good and evil (Gitlin 1980, 243). Once amplified, white supremacists' violence isolated them, serving the cause of reform. The immediacy of the pictures electrified a critical mass of viewers. Members of Congress reacted viscerally to televised pictures of brutality in Selma, Alabama, as did many of their constituents (Garrow 1978, 178).

Congressman John Lewis, once a leading civil rights worker in the South, summarized the results this way: "If it hadn't been for the media—the print media and television—the civil rights movement would have been like a bird without wings, a choir without a song" (Roberts and Klibanoff 2006, 407).

## Vietnam

Journalism's achievement with respect to Vietnam also needs to be juxtaposed to its defaults and deficits. During the early years of the American military intervention, reporters tended to defer to the official government position. But their view on the ground collided with the official line. From 1962 on, as the political scientist Daniel C. Hallin writes, *New York Times* reports from South Vietnam "reflected very closely the views of Americans in the field. . . . for the most part, the *Times* reporters of this period focused on the views of field-level officers. Their reporting was 'pessimistic' where these officers were pessimistic, and enthusiastic where they were enthusiastic." Altogether, "there was simply very little coverage of the character of the Diem regime or the opposition to it until these became the focus of a major debate among American officials" (Hallin 1986, 39–40, 45).

At the decisive moment of escalation, with the so-called Gulf of Tonkin incident of August 1964, Lyndon Johnson and other top officials lied and stretched the truth (Alterman 2004, 184–212). Almost all of the press was credulous (Hallin 1986, 15–21, 70–5), even if, by January 1965, most of the major papers opposed further escalation (Alterman 2004, 171; Hallin 1986, 93). As news coverage mounted, the impression grew that the war was a difficult slog and that victory was indefinitely postponed. Television news, which expanded to thirty minutes nightly on CBS and NBC in 1963 (ABC didn't follow until 1967), adopted the frame that the war was legitimate, but routine coverage was punctuated by muckraking episodes, most famously Morley Safer's CBS report in 1965 of Marines setting fire to the thatched roofs of a village (Hallin 1986, 132). Also exceptionally, the *Times*'s Harrison Salisbury traveled to North Vietnam in December 1966 and reported the widespread damage done by American bombing. But for the most part, the enemy was faceless (Hallin 1986, 147). Regular readers and viewers of the news probably formed the overall impression that the war was justified in principle, at least at first, but was nevertheless brutal and, at any rate, unsuccessful. This sense that the war was an unjustifiable grind grew with the Tet Offensive of 1968 (Hallin 1986, 161), which startled both journalists and the government. Revelations of war crimes, starting with Seymour Hersh's 1969 reportage on the My Lai massacre, in which hundreds of civilians were slaughtered by American troops, poured into the mainstream press. But President Nixon's unacknowledged bombing of Cambodia and Laos did not feature on television, and barely in newspapers. "For the most part," Hallin concludes, "television was a follower [of public opinion and political debate] rather than a leader" (1986, 163).

By the time the leaked Pentagon Papers were published by the *New York Times, Washington Post, Boston Globe*, and *St. Louis Post-Dispatch*, in 1971, public opinion had long since turned against the war. Coverage, especially on television, focused on the judicial showdown between the government and the press, not the content of the leaked documents themselves, which ratified the oppositional view that what the government had told the people diverged markedly from what it told itself; that the Kennedy and Johnson administrations had systematically lied about the war.

## Watergate

The *Washington Post*'s intensive investigation of the Watergate crimes—supplemented at times by other newspapers and occasionally well summarized on television news—is probably the most successful muckraking episode ever. It is certainly the most celebrated—and for good reason, for it exemplifies journalism stepping up to compensate for the political system's inability to cope with the executive's abuse of power. Most of the revelations originated with government leaks and the investigations by Judge John Sirica, among others highly placed in the criminal justice system. But it remains the case that Bob Woodward and Carl Bernstein's bold, dogged, and protracted pursuit of the crimes into the heights of the administration exposed Nixon's criminality and badgered Congress into revivifying its watchdog function. Unsurprisingly, it was not an inside-dopester political reporter but a crime reporter (Woodward) and a general assignment reporter (Bernstein) who partnered to dog the criminals' trails. Nixon's resignation in 1974 confirmed the view of 1960s rebels that journalists and their employers had a high calling even—or especially—when their publishers tried to dampen the zeal of their employees. For a time, journalists were lionized, encouraged to aerate governmental transgressions.

During the age of the watchdog, the courage of reporters and their employers was unmistakable. Addressing civil rights and the Vietnam War, they took legal and physical risks. Reporting the Pentagon Papers and Watergate, the publishers of the *New York Times* and *Washington Post* withstood formidable government pressures. Their reportage exerted significant pressure on government, framed issues, moved public opinion, and helped set agendas. They improved the quality of public discussion, helped produce reforms, and inspired generations of young journalists.

## Entertainment, Deference, Investigation, and Partisan Scurrility

And yet, the fierce truth-bound independence of the mainstream press in the 1970s failed to hold. Under pressure to compensate for the ample weaknesses of the American political system, journalism fell short. Highly paid celebrity journalists formed symbiotic relations with the powerful. The tabloid spirit flourished in mainstream journalism, as with the arrest, investigation, and trial of O. J. Simpson (1994–5). The critical spirit tended to focus on what the historian Sean Wilentz has called "pseudoscandals" (Wilentz 2002), which were helped along by the Internet's Drudge Report (Halperin and Harris 2006, 52–64) and similar right-wing enterprises. The profusion of delivery systems for information—from talk radio to cable television to the Internet—left mainstream news at times accommodating the tabloid spirit and at times defending a high moral ground, an embattled ideal of objectivity, as growing percentages of Americans gravitated toward either entertainment or ideological confirmation (primarily on the right). The partisanship of the nineteenth century was resurrected by Rupert Murdoch, Matt Drudge, Rush Limbaugh, Bill O'Reilly, Sean Hannity, Glenn Beck, and Fox News overall, with occasional and irregular counterbalance on the left from MSNBC and Air America (launched in 2004, bankrupted in 2010). Most journalistic skepticism collapsed into deference when the administration of George W. Bush set out to take the United States to war in Iraq in 2002–3 (Massing 2004). Business journalism tended to cheerlead as financial bubbles jeopardized the world economy (Starkman 2009).

The financial troubles of journalism have further weakened the watchdog function. Television news investigations have shriveled. The growth of online access undermined a business model already damaged by corporate consolidation. While journalism's current plights—in financing, organization, competition, and philosophy—deserve separate treatment (for recent surveys, see Gitlin 2009 and Downie and Schudson 2009), some online efforts in recent years have been serious. Whether they compensate for general decline or suggest a new start for journalism is far from evident. But it cannot be good for the health of the republic that the capacity of powerful institutions to endanger the public good routinely outruns journalism's ability to expose them. It cannot improve the quality of public debate when the press surrenders to the formula of he-said-she-said "balance," in an effort to insulate itself from the charge of partisanship, while an outright partisan press observes no such scruples.

The news today mixes partisanship, sensationalism, and deference, along with the watchdog role enshrined in conventional definitions of the First Amendment. New delivery systems make partisanship profitable. Zealous, informed, comprehensive journalism is not the salvation of popular self-government all by itself, but the current weaknesses of journalism cannot, on balance, be good news for democratic prospects. Manifestly, scholars owe American journalism continuing scrutiny.

## References

ALTERMAN, E. 2004. *When Presidents Lie: A History of Official Deception and its Consequences.* New York: Viking Press.

ANDREWS, J. C. 1970. *The South Reports the Civil War.* Princeton: Princeton University Press.

AUCOIN, J. L. 2005. *The Evolution of Investigative Journalism.* Columbia, MO: University of Missouri Press.

BALDASTY, G. J. 1992. *The Commercialization of News in the Nineteenth Century.* Madison: University of Wisconsin Press.

BENNETT, W. L., and SERRIN, W. 2005. The Watchdog Role. In *The Press*, ed. K. H. Jamieson and G. Overholser. New York: Oxford University Press.

BRIGGS, A., and BURKE, P. 2005. *A Social History of the Media*. Malden, MA: Polity Press.

CAMPBELL, W. J. 2001. *Yellow Journalism: Puncturing the Myths, Defining the Legacies*. London: Praeger.

CLOUD, S., and OLSON, L. 1998. The Murrow Boys—Broadcasting for the Mind's Eye. In *Defining Moments in Journalism*, ed. N. J. Woodhull and R. W. Snyder. London: Transaction.

COLE, D. B. 2009. *Vindicating Andrew Jackson: The 1828 Election and the Rise of the Two-Party System*. Lawrence: University Press of Kansas.

COOK, T. 1998. *Governing with the News: The News Media as a Political Institution*. Chicago: University of Chicago Press.

DANIEL, M. 2009. *Scandal and Civility: Journalism and the Birth of American Democracy*. Oxford: Oxford University Press.

DETWEILER, F. G. 1922. *The Negro Press in the United States*. Chicago: University of Chicago Press.

DICKEN-GARCIA, H. 1989. *Journalistic Standards in Nineteenth-Century America*. Madison: University of Wisconsin Press.

DOWNIE, L., and SCHUDSON, M. 2009. The Reconstruction of American Journalism. *Columbia University School of Journalism*. At <http://www.journalism.columbia.edu/cs/ContentServer?pagename=JRN/Render/DocURL&binaryid=1212611716626>. Accessed Nov. 24, 2009.

DROWNE, K. M., and HUBER, P., *The 1920s*. Westport, CT: Greenwood Press.

EMERSON, R. W. 1856. English Traits. In *Essays and English Traits: The Harvard Classics*, v. Cambridge, MA: Harvard University Press.

FELDSTEIN, M. 2006. A Muckraking Model: Investigative Reporting Cycles in American History. *Harvard International Journal of Press/Politics*, 11: 105–20.

FORD, W. C. 1905. Jefferson and the Newspaper. *Records of the Columbia Historical Society, Washington, D.C.*, 8: 78–111.

GANS, H. J. 2003. *Democracy and the News*. New York: Oxford University Press.

GARROW, D. J. 1978. *Protest at Selma: Martin Luther King, Jr., and the Voting Rights Act of 1965*. New Haven: Yale University Press.

GITLIN, T. 1980. *The Whole World Is Watching: Mass Media in the Making and Unmaking of the New Left*. Berkeley: University of California Press.

—— 2009. Journalism's Many Crises. openDemocracy. At <http://www.opendemocracy.net/article/a-surfeit-of-crises-circulation-revenue-attention-authority-and-deference>. Accessed Nov. 21, 2009.

HALLIN, D. C. 1986. *The "Uncensored War": The Media and Vietnam*. New York: Oxford University Press.

HALPERIN, M., and HARRIS, J. F. 2006. *The Way to Win: Taking the White House in 2008*. New York: Random House.

HOFSTADTER, R. 1955. *The Age of Reform: From Bryan to FDR*. New York: Vintage.

HUGHES, H. M. 1940. *News and the Human Interest Story*. Chicago: University of Chicago Press.

JEFFERSON, T. 1903–4. *The Writings of Thomas Jefferson*, Memorial Edition, xx, ed. A. A. Lipscomb and A. E. Bergh. Washington, DC: Thomas Jefferson Memorial Association of the United States.

JOHN, R. R. 1995. Spreading the News: The American Postal System from Franklin to Morse. Cambridge, MA: Harvard University Press.

KEYSSAR, A. 2000. *The Right to Vote: The Contested History of Democracy in the United States.* New York: Basic Books.

LEE, A. M. 1937. *The Daily Newspaper in America.* New York: Macmillan.

LEONARD, T. C. 1986. *The Power of the Press: The Birth of American Political Reporting.* New York: Oxford University Press.

LERCHE, C. O., JR., 1948. Jefferson and the Election of 1800: A Case Study in the Political Smear. *William and Mary Quarterly,* 5: 467–91.

MCCOMBS, M. E., EINSIEDEL, E. F., and WEAVER, D. H. 1991. *Contemporary Public Opinion: Issues and the News.* Hillsdale, NJ: Lawrence Erlbaum.

MCGERR, M. E. 1986. *The Decline of Popular Politics: The American North, 1865–1928.* New York: Oxford University Press.

MASSING, M. 2004. *Now They Tell Us: The American Press and Iraq.* New York: New York Review of Books.

MOTT, F. L. 1941. *American Journalism: 1690–1940.* London: Routledge, Thoemmes.

MUHLMANN, G. 2004. *A Political History of Journalism.* Malden, MA: Polity Press.

NASAW, D. 2000. *The Chief: The Life of William Randolph Hearst.* Boston: Houghton Mifflin.

NERONE, J. C. 1987. The Mythology of the Penny Press. *Critical Studies in Mass Communication,* 4: 376–404.

PASLEY, J. L. 2001. *The Tyranny of Printers: Newspaper Politics in the Early American Republic.* Charlottesville: University Press of Virginia.

PECK, A. 1985. *Uncovering the Sixties: The Life and Times of the Underground Press.* New York: Pantheon.

ROBERTS, G., and KLIBANOFF, H. 2006. *The Race Beat: The Press, the Civil Rights Struggle, and the Awakening of a Nation.* New York: Knopf.

SCHUDSON, M. 1981. *Discovering the News.* New York: Basic Books.

—— 1995. *The Power of News.* Cambridge, MA: Harvard University Press.

—— and TIFFT, S. E. 2005. American Journalism in Historical Perspective. In *The Press,* ed. K. H. Jamieson and G. Overholser. New York: Oxford University Press.

SHEPPARD, S. 2008. *The Partisan Press: A History of Media Bias in the United States.* London: McFarland.

STARKMAN, D. 2009. Power Problem. *Columbia Journalism Review.* At <http://www.cjr.org/cover_story/power_problem.php>. Accessed Jan. 3, 2010.

STEFFENS, L. 1931. *The Autobiography of Lincoln Steffens.* New York: Harcourt Brace Jovanovich.

SUMMERS, M. W. 1994. *The Press Gang: Newspapers and Politics: 1865–1878.* Chapel Hill: University of North Carolina Press.

TICHI, C. 2004. *Exposés and Excess: Muckraking in America, 1900/2000.* Philadelphia: University of Pennsylvania Press.

TUCHER, A. 1994. *Froth & Scum: Truth, Beauty, Goodness, and the Ax Murder in America's First Mass Medium.* Chapel Hill: University of North Carolina Press.

*United States Statutes.* Act for the Punishment of Certain Crimes against the United States [Sedition Act]. *United States Statutes at Large,* vol. i, sects. 1–4.

WILENTZ, S. 2002. Will Pseudo-Scandals Decide the Election? American Prospect. <http://www.prospect.org/cs/articles?article=will_pseudoscandals_decide_the_election>. Accessed Jan. 3, 2010.

WOOD, G. S. 2009. *Empire of Liberty: A History of the Early Republic, 1789–1815.* New York: Oxford University Press.

# CHAPTER 6

........................................................................

# THE NEWS INDUSTRY

........................................................................

DORIS A. GRABER
GREGORY G. HOLYK*

NEWS industries are vital parts of democracies, which, by definition, need politically informed citizens. News industries selectively gather information about the political world, frame it into news stories, and distribute it through print and broadcast media. News reports then permit people to learn about events and facts near and far, as seen through the lenses of their chosen media. Enormous changes are currently reshaping US news industries' operations, with substantial consequences for American democracy.

This chapter begins by outlining the structure and main political functions performed by news industries, including the role played by the Federal Communications Commission, which regulates some aspects of news dissemination. The second section covers adaptations and challenges for the news industry in the twenty-first century. It addresses the consequences for the industry and for American politics. The third section highlights significant changes in the news industry climate such as the explosive growth of opinionated reporting and the shift toward soft interpretive news away from harder factual formats. In the last section, we speculate about future challenges for the news industry including assessing the viability of traditional business models and the Internet's changing impact.

## FUNCTIONS

........................................................................

The mass media's vital political functions in the United States include: (1) providing information for citizens, (2) serving as political tools for public and private elites, and

* The authors wish to thank the PEW Project for Excellence in Journalism for the treasure trove of data about the news industry that the Project provides to social scientists. This chapter has relied heavily on the 2009 Project.

(3) alerting citizens when government malfunctions or misbehaves (Overholser and Jamieson 2005). Because these functions are so essential for governing democratically, press freedom is crucial. Hence the First Amendment to the Constitution provides that "Congress shall make no law . . . abridging the freedom of speech, or of the press." Although that provision does not preclude all types of government regulation of news media, it has sharply limited governments' ability to meddle with news content.

## Informing Citizens

Most people agree that the news media's primary function is presenting citizens with a broad array of information. This means taking millions of Americans from all walks of life, to the world's main political and military arenas. Through spoken and printed words, sounds, and pictures, news stories allow citizens to observe unfolding election contests from afar and scrutinize them from varied perspectives. Media offer glimpses of congressional investigations and show the consequences of environmental disasters. They focus on freshly breaking events or provide retrospective judgments about past happenings. The stream of news topics is endless, with reporters and editors acting as gatekeepers who decide what events constitute "news." Their choices differ. Just as no single person can pay attention to everything, so too media organizations must ignore many important events and messages or omit salient details and contextual information. Consequently, media stories often create skewed impressions.

Media not only survey political events. They also frame events for citizens, interpreting meanings and speculating about consequences. Since most events lend themselves to a variety of often discordant interpretations, the specific interpretation that is chosen may determine the political consequences of media reports. As part of contextualizing the news, reporters often suggest which views and behaviors are compatible with mainstream thinking, which issues different groups deem important or unimportant, and how events are related to each other. Portions of the audience are likely to be persuaded by the arguments offered in news media stories because media attention bestows gravitas on people and issues. The ability to influence the political views of large audiences of ordinary people, as well as influential political elites, is a major ingredient in the power of the mass media and makes them extraordinarily important for the individuals and groups whose stories and causes receive publicity or are denied attention.

The media also play a crucial role in political socialization. Young people lack established attitudes and behaviors. Apart from their families and immediate experiences, most information that they acquire about their political world comes directly or indirectly from the mass media. It becomes one of the bases for developing their opinions. Likewise, most of the new opinions that adults form during their lifetime are constructed from information drawn from the mass media. That makes the mass media major contributors to adult political socialization.

# Supporting Political Actors

Political actors succeed in their missions if they can present persuasive stories to their target audiences and if the political environment that news stories depict lends relevance to their pleas. This is why political actors devote a goodly portion of their resources to gaining favorable attention from reporters. Major tactics include framing press releases tailored to media needs and conducting news briefings. If these tactics are well executed, the news media are likely to create a political reality that favors political actors. For example, racial segregation in the American South persisted for many decades, with most people in other parts of the country unaware of its ugly manifestations. The situation changed when the civil rights movement finally managed to attract nationwide media attention.

The news industry and political actors are Siamese twins whose fates are linked because political actors generate much of the information that news media need to report about important political developments, while political actors are dependent on the media to reach mass audiences. Public officials are deemed the most legitimate sources of information about political events. At the same time, the news media and public officials are traditional enemies. In the United States, political reporters are expected to serve the public as watchdogs on the lookout for government misbehavior. That role requires them to avoid entangling personal relations with government officials.

Media dependence on information known to government officials and other elites leaves reporters open to manipulation. Political actors are well aware of the power that they hold as the most legitimate sources for news reports. Officials also know that reporters must produce stories quickly because of the journalistic norm that news must be as recent as possible. Reporters must therefore meet deadlines, especially for stories that will also be covered by their competitors. The need for rapid publication makes it likely that reporters will transmit the carefully prepared messages of government officials very much in their original formats.

# Monitoring Governments

Acting as a watchdog on government and the powerful in general is considered a major professional obligation by journalists and the public. Media in the United States are quite free to oppose incumbent government officials, weaken them, and occasionally even drive them from office. This power is protected by the First Amendment to the Constitution because unfettered criticism is essential in fighting government corruption and misbehavior. When *Washington Post* journalists Bob Woodward and Carl Bernstein uncovered and reported the Watergate political corruption scandal that led to the downfall of the Nixon administration in 1974, their work became the stuff of legend. However, toppling a president is an extreme example. The extent to which journalists have acted as watchdogs has varied over time, but there is generally strong support for this role, which has become a journalistic norm in the United States.

## Regulating the News Industry

The First Amendment was inspired by fear that government would use the press to suppress opposition and maintain itself in power. The founders of the country believed that the news industry could not perform its democratic duties properly unless it was free from government control over news content. However, because of the critical importance of news media as information providers, and because of the limited broadcast space that was initially available for broadcast news, some regulation of the news industry became unavoidable.

In the United States, the Federal Communications Commission (FCC) regulates radio and television broadcasting. The Commission is structured as an independent regulatory body that is insulated from government influence. In reality, this is only partly the case. The president and Senate control the appointment of Commission members. Congress controls the Commission's budget, and the Commission is subject to a great deal of pressure from the substantial cadre of strong lobby groups.

The FCC consists of five members: three are allotted to the party that controls the White House and two represent the opposing party. The Commission's vague mandate is to "serve the public interest, convenience, and necessity." What exactly is implied by this mandate has been open to a wide latitude of interpretations. What, for instance, constitutes "the public interest" that must be served? What is meant by "convenience?" What is truly a "necessity?" Past and present members of the FCC and government officials have interpreted the mandate in quite different ways that entail greater or lesser government regulation of the media industry. Democrats tend to favor more control, while Republicans opt for less. The FCC's performance over the years in protecting the "public interest" and acting as a watchdog leaves much to be desired, partly because of the vagueness of the mandate and partly because the Commission deals with very controversial issues that mobilize strong lobbies who seek to control communications policies.

Lobbies like the National Association of Broadcasters and the American Newspaper Publishers' Association have had tremendous influence on FCC policies. Regulation tends to be light because news industries want it that way and because Congress caters to them, hoping for their support. Politicians cannot afford to alienate an industry that controls the political messages that reach the public. For example, a career lobbyist in Washington had this to say about the Communications Act of 1996: "In all my years of walking the halls of Congress, I have never seen anything like the Telecommunications Bill . . . the silence of public debate is deafening. A bill with astonishing impact on all of us is not even being discussed" (quoted in McChesney 1996: 3).

In addition to substantial business lobbying, many "public" interest groups influence media policy. These include groups such as Fairness & Accuracy in Reporting, Citizens for the American Way, and the Parents' Television Council, among others. These groups generally seek influence over content, including the accuracy of news stories. Their efforts have led to retractions of incorrect information, guidelines for "offensive" content on television, and laws that protect the interests of children.

The chances for adopting strong regulations are further weakened because of disagreements about the merits of particular rules. Federal laws must be balanced with strict state and local requirements for cable television. Disagreements between the policy goals of Republicans and Democrats have already been mentioned. In addition, strong action is discouraged by the knowledge that FCC rulings can be appealed to the courts, which have overturned them frequently.

The extent of regulations varies by industry depending on the modality of message transmission. The print news industry is least regulated but must comply with antimonopoly laws. Broadcast media are regulated to a greater degree, largely because access to scarce broadcasting channels requires licenses. FCC regulations for broadcasting fall into four categories: (1) limitations on the number of stations controlled by a single organization, (2) periodic scrutiny of the goals and performance of stations, (3) requirements to offer public service and local interest programming, and (4) rules to ensure that the media will air a variety of viewpoints about controversial issues. No rules prescribe specific content because that would violate press freedom.

To assure news diversity, the FCC limits the number of radio and television stations that a media enterprise can control and the size of the audience that it may reach within a single news market. However, a news supplier may operate in multiple markets. Markets are geographic areas in which a medium attracts a substantial audience. They vary in population size.

The FCC is very superficial in its scrutiny of station performance, including checks that stations are meeting their public service and local programming requirements. The main reason is fear of being accused of undue meddling with message content. Even if the FCC wanted to be more rigorous, its small size would limit its activities. The Commission has been quite zealous in enforcing the rules that guarantee access to the media to proponents of differing views, including candidates during an election campaign and supporters of clashing policies. Nonetheless, space and time constraints inevitably bar many viewpoints.

The fact that the FCC is explicitly barred from regulating news media content invests the news industry with huge influence over the nation's supply of political information. In fact, it has often been called the 'Fourth Branch' of government because, like the president, Congress, and the courts, its messages powerfully influence the thrust of politics. But, unlike the other branches, it is not subject to formal checks and balances, and it does not undergo periodic review through the electoral process. Truth-in-advertising laws protect citizens from false advertising of consumer goods but not from false political claims or improper news selection or reporters' biases. Courts are likely to uphold the news media's power to freely choose and frame news on constitutional grounds. The responsibility of serving the public's interests well therefore rests squarely on the shoulders of the news industry.

## Structure

The news industry's structure is quite varied. Some news organizations perform all news functions, from gathering information, to writing stories, to editing and producing them and transmitting them to audiences. Other news enterprises may concentrate on a single function, or they may use various combinations. For example, the Associated Press and United Press International function as collectives who gather news for their members. News organizations may operate independently or they may combine with like organizations in networks or chains. They may also undertake joint ventures. The possibilities for creating various structures are limited by anti-monopoly rules designed to keep specific business enterprises from dominating their slice of media industry. Cross-ownership constraints ensure that no business enterprise controls all types of news channels in a particular market. Historical precedents also limit choices. For example, it would be difficult to overcome the traditional preference for private rather than public ownership of news industries, or to make government subsidies the media's chief revenue source.

## Ownership Patterns

In the United States, news media intended for the general public have largely been in private hands. The government has exercised little direct control over the activities of these private entrepreneurs, especially when it comes to news content and news production methods. The hands-off policy reflects the belief that diverse owners will produce a broad array of views, sustaining a sound democracy (Baker 2007). In the past, individually owned private media companies predominated in the industry. That pattern has given way to much larger organizations and conglomerates; some, like CNN, have an international reach. In many of the huge corporate entities, like the General Electric Company, news media holdings are only a small part of a large array of diverse enterprises that are unrelated to political communication.

Newspapers are free to operate in an unlimited number of media markets; most belong to large regional newspaper chains. Television and radio ownership is more restricted because demand for channels exceeds supply despite tremendous expansion. Broadcasters are assigned to specific frequencies. The 'big three'—NBC, CBS, and ABC—and their affiliates have traditionally dominated the television market. However, their control over news broadcasting is shrinking because of cable television competition. CNN, Fox News, and MSNBC are attracting large audiences and advertising revenues with their popular 24/7 commentary-centered formats. The greater partisanship of cable channels allows consumers to choose information that conforms to their identities and established beliefs. In turn, the channels' slant of the news shapes the audience's beliefs in a complex interactive relationship (Zaller 1992). Media content choices and framing thus shape public perceptions of societal problems (Iyengar and Kinder 1989). Overall, the Internet is the strongest rival for audience attention because it provides a wealth of news and entertainment. It remains an open, uncontrolled forum where no single news provider holds sway over a huge slice of the audience. Still, sites linked to traditional mainstream media enjoy the greatest popularity.

Does private ownership of news media actually accomplish the goal of providing an information-rich open marketplace for discussing public issues? The answer is moot. In the United States, for example, most private owners are business entrepreneurs who are motivated by economic goals rather than public service aims. According to Hamilton (2004), profit-making is the main determinant of content chosen to attract the audiences that advertisers prefer. Advertising rates rise or fall based on audience size and demographic composition. To attract the largest audiences, and thereby earn the largest advertising fees, programming is structured to suit audience preferences. The societal importance of news is secondary, as is the need to keep the public well informed enough to perform citizenship functions effectively. Since light entertainment programming has the broadest audience appeal, news enterprises feature it. Even serious news is framed in 'infotainment', human interest formats.

To compensate for major shortcomings of privately controlled broadcast enterprises, the government has reserved small parts of the radio and television spectra for public broadcasting. The Public Broadcasting Act of 1967 established a public broadcasting system that focuses on unprofitable programming that private broadcasters neglect. Educational broadcasts, ethnic entertainment, and classical music are examples of the kinds of offerings that public broadcasting features. The main organizational structures are the Public Broadcasting System for television and National Public Radio for radio. Overall, public broadcasting in the United States remains a very small player on the broadcasting scene.

## Modalities

The news media are segmented into multiple modalities—newspapers, magazines, radio, television, and a mixture of offerings on the Internet. Within each of these categories, there are subcategories. For example, one can distinguish between over-the-air, cable, or satellite televisions; one can categorize media by their contents as either mainstream or tabloid or partisan or neutral. One can look at the frequency of publication and talk about hourly or daily or monthly or intermittent publication cycles within each medium. All of these different modalities compete for audiences and financing.

Media establishments face different problems depending on the type and format of their publications. Their political impact varies as well. Print media, including media featuring printed text on the Internet, generally supply the largest amounts of factual political information. Their readers must have advanced reading skills to fully grasp story details. News presented by broadcast media, especially television, has a broader appeal. Many Americans have limited reading skills and find it far easier to capture meanings from visuals and spoken language than from printed texts. Audiovisual broadcasts excel in presenting non-verbal images, including people's body language and facial expressions. They also provide a greater sense of reality and are more likely to arouse attention and emotions.

Structural constraints in news production result in a more constricted marketplace of information than one might expect in the face of public policies designed to keep news offerings diverse. Because news gathering is expensive, only a few media companies actually do it. Most news providers rely on wire services for non-local stories or follow the lead of prestigious news organizations. The inability to finance independent news gathering, coupled with "follow-the-leader" journalism, sharply narrows the spectrum of news and opinions readily available to mass publics. That explains why, despite mushrooming of broadcast enterprises, the news diet of most Americans has remained surprisingly uniform in the Internet age.

# THE IMPACT OF TECHNOLOGY CHANGES
# AND NEW MEDIA FORMATS

Thanks to advancing technologies, the news industry has become much more diversified. Many of the new media allow substantial public participation in creating news content. The key question is whether the traditional news media will be able to adapt and survive in this new environment. In this section, we highlight some of the most pressing and interesting developments in the news media industries.

## Technology Changes

The meteoric rise of Internet usage in general, and specifically for news consumption, represents by far the greatest challenge. It threatens the survival of legacy news companies—long-standing, respected, traditional format news institutions such as the *New York Times* and NBC's *Nightly News*—and their modes of operation. News consumers, who have grown up with the Internet as an integral part of their lives, have been turning away from traditional news suppliers in favor of newer formats (Bennett 2008). Search engines permit them to look for information on a specific topic of interest, choose trusted sources, and access single news articles or videos without having to scan through a whole newspaper or watch a whole broadcast. Blogs, microblogs, email, and social networking websites allow average citizens to send and receive personalized information, rather than accepting standardized offerings. These new news consumers' preferences will determine the fate and thrust of news industries in the years to come.

In the short term, television news remains the preferred news format, although legacy broadcast audiences have diminished steadily. Twenty-four-hour cable news networks and video available on the Internet have been the beneficiaries. Platform choices are growing and they offer broader content and ideological orientations than in the past. News consumers can choose between national or local network news, cable news channels, as well as video clips on the Internet, in addition to massive amounts of worldwide cable, satellite, and Internet news options.

Technological change has increased public participation in news production, creating online "digital citizenship" (Mossberger, Tolbert, and McNeal 2008). Members of the public and individual journalists can frame their own information and opinions and broadcast them inexpensively through blogs. Amateur news providers can enter the field without any professional preparation. Their forte is commentary and distribution, rather than news gathering, which has largely been left to legacy news outlets with the financial and organizational resources to gather news. But their financial strength is ebbing. They are losing audience to venues that use their information without any compensation for the substantial costs of news gathering. Obviously, a new system of news-gathering cost distribution will have to be developed, based on substantial changes in the news industry. For example, if news gatherers charged bloggers for news, the costs would thin the ranks of bloggers, decimating the variety of opinions circulating on the Internet.

Social networking websites such as Facebook, MySpace, and Twitter, and video posting sites such as YouTube, have become very important for Generation Y and beyond, for sharing news with friends or the general public. The news offerings of social websites—which are for-profit, advertiser-dependent organizations—have become serious competitors for legacy media. At times, they even pressure legacy media to devote time to topics that dominate the social networks' agenda.

Social website publicity can cause a story to go "viral," spreading very quickly to thousands or perhaps millions of recipients, just like a computer virus. Social websites do not necessarily broaden viewers' perspectives because users tend to interact with like-minded users. However, the networks do facilitate social activism.

Video posting sites such as YouTube allow users to place and view video content free of charge. Some of the content consists of news and other political topics. Miniblog sites such as Twitter and social networking sites such as Facebook and MySpace also provide links to political news and information, along with brief opinions and political statements. Even legacy media now use Twitter or their own blogs to transmit breaking news and to advertise their offerings.

New technologies have liberated news disseminators and consumers from many of the constraints of time and space. News can be broadcast and received around the clock so that audiences can access it whenever they want with stationary or portable instruments. Cable news channels, for example, offer a constant news flow twenty-four hours a day, seven days a week, covering important events as they happen from around the world. The consequences of this revolution in news delivery remain to be assessed. Greater availability may translate into more extensive coverage, larger audiences, and, possibly, a speed-up in politicians' responses.

Search engines like Google and Yahoo, bookmarks, email news updates, and personalized home pages enable individual news consumers to check for customized news online multiple times throughout the day. Personalized home pages on Yahoo or Google allow users to automatically control the kind of content brought to their attention. People can now take their cellphones, computers, and other wireless devices to virtually any location. Many phones are equipped with Internet access, allowing users to obtain news and information from online news sources anywhere and any time.

## Democratizing Effects

Messianic proclamations about transformative effects often surface in the wake of new technological developments. The claims tend to be exaggerated (Cranor and Greenstein 2002). Average citizens' empowerment to compete with other news providers is strong in theory, but almost negligible in practice. Most personal websites and blogs have tiny audiences. Teens are the most prolific bloggers. Most aggregator news sites, such as Yahoo and Google, link predominantly to legacy media sites. Legacy media retain control over most news gathering and their familiar and trusted brand names retain a credibility advantage over most amateur-based news sources. The web versions of legacy media have become exceptionally attractive because blogs vary widely in reliability and quality.

By contrast to private citizens' blogs, interest groups have been empowered by the availability of websites and blogging. That is particularly true for interest groups that lack the financial resources to conduct traditional lobby operations and public relations campaigns. For example, college students can now afford to establish their own websites and blogs to mobilize students around the country, or even around the world, for specific political purposes. Causes may range from personal interests to narrow or broad social interests. College students have, for example, protested a mass murderer's forthcoming execution, or urged governments to ban the use of land mines worldwide. Most interest groups continue to work through legacy media, legacy websites, and major non-legacy websites. Each of these platforms has its own distinct advantages along with drawbacks.

# THE NEW MEDIA CLIMATE

## Partisan Punditry

US news media continue to take pride in providing "objective" coverage, presenting opposing versions of stories and avoiding personal interpretations and opinions. Nonetheless, neutrality and objectivity are declining. Much of today's partisan news verges on "propaganda" masquerading as objective facts and analysis (Pavlik 2008). One important reason for the explosive growth of commentary is the twenty-four-hour cable news cycle. It is difficult and expensive to fill twenty-four hours with well-researched news that features multiple perspectives. It is also difficult to attract audiences to updates of previously covered events. The solution to these challenges is spicy commentary about the evolving political scene.

While cable broadcasts are thriving, news-gathering operations have been sharply curtailed at the legacy media and elsewhere, with the most expensive operations suffering the sharpest cuts. Foreign news gathering is the primary casualty. The major news organizations have closed most of their foreign bureaus or completely reorganized them so that they operate with only one or two individuals. Overall, there are now far fewer professional reporters, production personnel, and editors producing the news. All news enterprises, including legacy media, have increased interpretive stories delivered by "pundits" who often are exceptionally outspoken, partisan, provocative, and sometimes even outrageous. Audiences do not seem to mind the increased partisanship. News channels that are confrontational and partisan are psychologically attractive, lure larger audiences, and hold their attention for longer spans of time. But the quality of democracy suffers. Democratic governance benefits from civil discourse in the public sphere based on news that is accurate, fair, and free from deliberate distortion. The overall consequence is an increasingly confrontational political climate, less willingness to compromise, and greater disrespect for opposition views.

## Soft News Growth

Along with the increase in punditry and partisanship, "soft news" is overwhelming "hard news" (Baum 2003). The dividing line between soft news and its hard news counterpart is fuzzy. Soft news deals with human interest stories that focus on episodes in the lives of particular individuals or groups. Stories are framed so that the audience can identify with some of the people in the story and empathize with their problems. Hard news deals with societal problems in a more thematic, less personalized way. It reports happenings in a matter-of-fact style that encourages dispassionate analysis and general conclusions about the issues involved in the case. Soft news, with its emphasis on specific episodes in identified individuals' lives, encourages people to think in terms of individual cases, whereas thematic framing encourages them to take a broad view of social issues and look for society-wide resolutions.

To compete successfully in the fight for audiences' attention, news industries must couch political fare in appealing entertainment formats. For example, local news, which ranks highly in popularity, spends very little time reporting hard news topics. Instead, the focus is on weather, sports, entertainment, crime, disasters, and human interest stories.

The blurring of lines between entertainment and news is well illustrated by the merger between politics and low-cost comedy offerings. Comedy shows like the *Daily Show* have large audiences that relish the satirical accounts of current political events (Baym 2010). Entertainment programming has also become a routine part of election campaigning (Panagopoulos 2009). Candidates regularly appear on late night talk shows and comedy shows like *Saturday Night Live*. That would have been completely politically taboo in the past.

Research on the impact of entertainment programming on citizens' political views confirms that they learn political information from popular nighttime dramas which base their stories on current problems and ways to cope with them. Crime shows and hospital shows are examples. Juries commonly refer to crime show happenings as rationales for their decisions, and traffic escalates sharply on AIDS health advice sites when hospital shows recommend such consultations.

## QUESTIONS IN SEARCH OF ANSWERS

We now turn to the arguably most pressing issues facing news industries in the twenty-first century. We believe that these issues warrant attention from media researchers and practitioners alike.

### Coping with Shrinking Budgets

Legacy news industries are in deep financial trouble. They have become unable to adequately finance their operations through advertising. The traditional advertising revenue model has been a failure thus far, even online. According to the 2009 Pew Report *The State of the News Media*, "the problem facing American journalism is not fundamentally an audience problem or a credibility problem. It is a revenue problem—the decoupling . . . of advertising from news." These financial troubles are occurring in tandem with sharpening competition between a growing number of news outlets, declining advertising revenues, and news audience empowerment to control content (Pavlik 2008). More and more people rely on the Internet as a news source each year.

News budgets continue to wither. Newspapers, local and national broadcast television, and radio are investing less in news gathering, infrastructure, and staff. Until the legacy news organizations figure out how to make money from news distributed via the Internet, they will remain financially strapped (Alexander et al. 2003). Many will not survive. Shrinking revenues mean smaller profit margins, and small profit margins will drive investors away. The value of news industries has plummeted when owners try to sell them and there are few buyers. Obviously, inventing a new business model has become a survival issue for news industries in the United States.

To cope with problems created by insufficient revenues, news organizations have started to partner in ways that would have been unthinkable in the past. They are sharing news gathering and story production to cut the costs of producing news stories. They cover the same news beats with fewer people. They gather news more cheaply through satellite technology, which allows foreign reporters to transmit messages with fewer staff and production costs. Some television stations have even consolidated reporting teams so that a single individual functions as reporter, camera person, editor, and producer.

All of the changes designed to reduce costs raise questions about the overall quality of the news that is produced in this downsized environment. Will news industries be able to supply a broad spectrum of viewpoints that is essential for a vigorous democracy or will the news consist largely of polarized left- and right-wing diatribes? If news organizations are sharing news gathering and production, will the number of available perspectives contract sharply? Will the surviving news providers offer high-quality, palatable news for the masses? When television reporters are doing unaccustomed jobs, will story quality deteriorate? When amateurs become broadcasters on their own or on invitation from professionals, will the range of topics and the thoroughness of coverage change for better or for worse? What will be the consequences of sparse coverage of foreign affairs? The end result of cost-cutting maneuvers, coupled with greater input by non-professional news providers, may be a news environment that few news veterans would recognize or appreciate.

## New News and Democracy

The changes in the news industry that are popular and are taking hold raise serious issues about the quality of news for the general public. Hard news, which is essential for citizens' political deliberations, is declining and infotainment is gaining popularity. How well will the news media perform their watchdog function when they dwell on soft news and dedicate fewer resources to gathering serious news? How will these changes affect the quality of democracy in the United States? Can we really expect private, for-profit news industries to spend time on unprofitable public education in a period of economic contraction? Would non-profit private organizations or publicly financed, possibly publicly operated, news organizations do any better? These are questions that require answers.

Individual citizens' power to broadcast their own information on the Internet is a positive step that strengthens each citizen's right to be heard and to hear what others have to say. However, it does not mean that equality will truly be achieved. Most people will not seize the opportunity to become information providers. Even if they did, there is little to no audience for a cacophony of voices. Nearly all will be drowned out by the vast number of competing messages.

Likewise, the increased diversity of the news supply that cable television provides is a positive change that may be a mixed blessing. The traditional news media stressed the nation's common political culture. Cable news, operating in a super-competitive environment, is more partisan, more opinionated, more conflict-provoking in efforts to maximize the size of its audiences. What will be the impact on the shared political socialization that made it possible in the past to reach agreements acceptable to majorities and minorities alike? Will the fragmented nature of cable news create a new political and cultural environment that encourages societal division and destroys common bases of understanding? Preliminary evidence suggests that new media technologies widen gaps in knowledge, splinter news audiences along partisan lines, and erode our common information bases and the ability to communicate and understand one another (Prior 2007).

## Controlling Internet Excesses

The openness of the Internet as an interactive mass communication medium has encouraged a wide array of positive developments, but it also comes with some difficult realities (Pavlik 2008). Short of rigid censorship, it is nearly impossible to control socially damaging content on the Internet. Hate messages, exploitation of children and adults, deliberate misinformation, unverified anonymous information, and criminal activities are downsides of the openness of the medium. Internet messages are largely free of any regulation by internal norms or government rules so that anyone can post anything they like, useful or harmful. There are no procedures to ensure the quality of the information that is presented. There are no guarantees that Internet postings meet any professional standards of research, veracity, or objectivity. Consumers face a vast wilderness of information with no guide about its merits. Are new sets of norms needed to maintain reasonable standards of quality of content and format? Or are most people satisfied with an Internet where hate messages abound, unverified allegations flourish, and where the number of pornographic tales far exceed stories in other categories of news?

The traditional news media developed norms and procedures for gathering high-quality news and presenting it appropriately because they valued their credibility and good reputations. Norms relate to matters such as using multiple sources and identifying them, fact checking, and a commitment to reporting conflicting viewpoints objectively and fairly. They also include avoiding libel, privacy invasion, and impairment of the fairness of judicial proceedings. The shortcoming of the legacy media, compared to non-professional journalism on the Internet, was and is that legacy media are elite organizations controlled by a small cadre of private owners, editors, and journalists with no direct input by average citizens whose interests they claim to represent.

Not only is the quality of the information that is flooding the Internet suspect, there actually may be too much information. Information is only useful to the extent that it is easily identifiable and accessible. Too much information can be very difficult to navigate. It becomes almost impossible to know where to start and when to stop. Search engines such as Google and Yahoo help to narrow down the unmanageable mass of information, but the criteria these search engines use to filter information lack transparency. Furthermore, many people are not adept at Internet searching.

## Digital Divide Hurdles

Who will be the dominant actors in news production in the years to come? Will news collection, production, and dissemination remain profitable enough to attract private investors? Will for-profit enterprises be replaced by non-profit ventures? Will the elites who dominated political discourse in the past by controlling news industries seize control of the Internet marketplace? Clearly, the Internet has enormous capability to democratize control over the political information supply (Dahlgren 2009). However, the persistence of the "digital divide"—the gap in access to the Internet and in Internet literacy and skills—suggests that members of the "attentive public" will continue to run the show, as in the past (Hindman 2009). Most members of the attentive public are well-educated, economically secure individuals who care deeply about politics for a multiplicity of reasons, including economic gain. Thanks to the Internet, they will be better informed than ever before. The inattentive public, with important excep- tions, is likely to remain less informed and interested, except during political crises (Ferdinand 2000).

The Internet, open to all, has the potential to become the news and information medium that levels the playing field between the socially and economically privileged sectors of the public and those who lack these resources. At this point in time, that goal remains unfulfilled, and there are serious doubts whether the goal is reachable so that citizens from all walks of life will fully enjoy the benefits of the Internet information feast.


## An Uncertain Media Future

To sum up, the media environment has undergone tremendous changes recently, mostly due to changes in technology. Six features of the new technologies have the potential for generating major political changes. They are: (1) the advent of non- professional journalism that competes with traditional journalism; (2) the Web 2.0 interactivity tools that have created a new global public sphere; (3) the leveling of barriers to communication created by time, space, and political constraints; (4) the multiplication of communication channels that have created a hyper-competitive media world; (5) the modernization of legacy journalism; and (6) the emergence of new approaches for financing the creation and distribution of news.

Although legacy news media have been unable to adapt the traditional advertising business model to the Internet, they are unlikely to disappear in the near future. Most of the new media still rely upon legacy media for a steady stream of quality content that enjoys credibility and legitimacy. At the societal level, the US public must determine who benefits and who is hurt by the changing technologies and how damages can be mitigated. There are no easy solutions for Internet age problems. They demand a great deal of research and experimentation with continual adjustments to cope with an unstable environment. The nature of changes in the news industries will hinge on general economic and social challenges. Larger societal problems will have to be addressed in order to tackle political communication issues, like true equality of access to the Internet. The extent to which American elites and the public are willing to address these larger societal issues remains uncertain.

## REFERENCES

ALEXANDER, A., OWERS, J., CARVETH, R., HOLLIFIELD, C. A., and GRECO, A. N. (eds.) 2003. *Media Economics: Theory and Practice*, 3rd edn. Mahwah, NJ: Lawrence Erlbaum.

BAKER, C. E. 2007. *Media Concentration and Democracy: Why Ownership Matters*. New York: Cambridge University Press.

BAUM, M. A. 2003. *Soft News Goes to War: Public Opinion and American Foreign Policy in the New Media Age*. Princeton: Princeton University Press.

BAYM, G. 2010. *From Cronkite to Colbert: The Evolution of Broadcast News*. Boulder, CO: Paradigm.

BENNETT, W. L. (ed.) 2008. *Civic Life Online: Learning How Digital Media Can Engage Youth*. Cambridge, MA: MIT Press.

CRANOR, L. F., and GREENSTEIN, S. (eds.) 2002. *Communications Policy and Information Technology: Promises, Problems, Prospects*. Cambridge, MA: MIT Press.

DAHLGREN, P. 2009. *Media and Political Engagement: Citizens, Communication, and Democracy*. New York: Cambridge University Press.

FERDINAND, P. (ed.) 2000. *The Internet, Democracy and Democratization*. Portland, OR: Frank Cass.

HAMILTON, J. T. 2004. *All the News that's Fit to Sell: How the Market Transforms Information into News*. Princeton: Princeton University Press.

HINDMAN, M. S. 2009. *The Myth of Digital Democracy*. Princeton: Princeton University Press.

IYENGAR, S., and KINDER, D. R. 1989. *News that Matters: Television and American Opinion*. Chicago: University of Chicago Press.

McCHESNEY, R. W. 1999. *Rich Media, Poor Democracy: Communication Politics in Dubious Times*. Urbana: University of Illinois Press.

MOSSBERGER, K., TOLBERT, C. J., and MCNEAL, R. S. 2008. *Digital Citizenship: The Internet, Society, and Participation*. Cambridge, MA: MIT Press.

OVERHOLSER, G., and JAMIESON, K. H. (eds.) 2005. *The Press*. New York: Oxford University Press.

PANAGOPOULOS, C. (ed.) 2009. *Politicking Online: The Transformation of Election Campaign Communications*. New Brunswick, NJ: Rutgers University Press.

PAVLIK, J. V. 2008. *Media in the Digital Age*. New York: Columbia University Press.

Pew Project for Excellence in Journalism. 2009. *The State of the News Media: An Annual Report on American Journalism*. At <http://www.stateofthemedia.org/2009/index.htm>. Accessed Mar. 19, 2009.

PRIOR, M. 2007. *Post-Broadcast Democracy: How Media Choice Increases Inequality in Political Involvement and Polarizes Elections*. New York: Cambridge University Press.

ZALLER, J. 1992. *The Nature and Origins of Mass Opinion*. New York: Cambridge University Press.

CHAPTER 7

........................................................................

# WHAT'S NEWS

## A View from the Twenty-First Century

........................................................................

MARION R. JUST

## NEWS AND CIVIC COMPETENCE
........................................................................

DEMOCRATIC citizens depend on the press to be their witness in the corridors of power. News—about government achievements or failures, honesty or corruption—gives citizens the information they need to hold the government to account. At a minimum, citizens are responsible for hiring or firing public officials. The chief function of a democratic press is to give citizens the means to make electoral decisions and to participate in politics.

In its democratic role, the press is responsible for the continuing education of citizens. The news reinforces what people learned in school and continually updates them. At its best, the news can be a great educator, but its success depends on people's willingness to pay attention and the journalists' ability to engage them. When the public is uninformed or confused about crucial political issues, such as the reasons for the invasion of Iraq, the media are often blamed—and not without cause. The press shares responsibility for the public's level of knowledge or misinformation. For example, when surveys showed that a substantial number of Americans believed that invading forces actually found weapons of mass destruction (WMDs) in Iraq, researchers looked back at the coverage. Content analysis revealed that Fox News commentators were the most likely to predict that WMDs would be found and downplayed or ignored the fact that the U.S. failed to find WMD's in Iraq (see for example, Rampton and Stauber 2006). A PIPA/Knowledge Networks poll found that people who watched networks with the least coverage of dissenting opinions about the war, such as Fox News, were the most likely to be mistaken about the WMDs (2003). In this case, watching Fox News was associated with a mistaken view about a central fact of the war.

As new media emerge and the process of news gathering changes, observers are concerned about the quality of information available to citizens. Until the turn of the twenty-first century news production was a one-way street. Power lay in the hands of the reporters and editors who decided "what's news" (Gans 1980). With the rise of the Internet and attendant technologies, power over the news agenda is passing from the control of professional journalists and media organizations to amateurs and volunteers. In the twenty-first century the audience has invaded the newsroom and is shaping the very definition of news.

Cellphone cameras allow members of the audience to produce news, or at least the raw materials of news, in real time. In some war-torn or inaccessible places, audience-produced content is the only source of news. Up to now, established media institutions have reluctantly collaborated with the audience with suspicion and resignation, but technology has forced their hands. Not only are citizens contributing news content and comments, but the audience is also taking on the roles of distribution and editorial signaling via social network computing. What impact will these changes have on the democratic function of news? Will citizens become more or less informed with the proliferation of news formats? Will citizens be more or less able to participate mean-ingfully in the democratic process? To answer these questions, this chapter traces the evolution of news values over time and explores the impact of new media on the democratic function of the press.

## EVOLVING NEWS VALUES

Since news content is potentially infinite and print and television news outlets are limited, reporters and editors must be selective. The ability to pick out the news from the tumult of daily life is a skill generally taught on the job (Neal 1942, 57). Good reporters have a "nose for news," i.e., the ability to find good stories and choose the newsworthy aspects of events or speeches. By choosing what to include, journalists are in effect the gatekeepers of public discourse (Alger 1996, 148).

Most observers agree that the news should report information that is new to the audience and of consequence to them in negotiating their personal and political lives. Without the element of newness, surprise, or novelty, the information is not news. Colloquially, "man bites dog" is news, but "dog bites man" is not. In addition to novelty, specific news selection criteria include overall importance or impact on the audience, timeliness, involvement of important people, relevance to the audience, as well as an element of drama or inherent interest (Alger 1996, 150; Graber 1980, 63–5; McManus 1994, 19–20; Mencher 1977, 54). The news value of conflict, as opposed to consequence, disturbs some news observers. The overall impression that the new is "bad" turns off a significant portion of the audience (Patterson 2000, 9).

Doris Graber reports a survey with editors and television producers that identified conflict, timeliness, and proximity as the three of news values most highly rated by practitioners (1980, 63–5). Relevance to the audience is a requisite of all news, but particularly of local news in any form—print, broadcast, or online. By this measure, news about happenings in one's local town or city is most proximate, followed by news from the state and nation. News about what is happening in the wider world is distant, but news about culturally related nations is more relevant than news about culturally different places. So, for example, news about the United Kingdom or western Europe is more likely to be carried in the US than news about South America, Africa, or Asia. In fact, Johan Galtung and Marie Ruge claimed that there was a mathematical relationship between distance and number of deaths that would be required for an international disaster to be reported in the news. The further away the disaster, the higher the death threshold for making the news (1965). The journalist's ability to show the relevance of a distant story is, therefore, a critical professional skill.

## Consequence and Impact

It is more difficult for journalists to convey the relevance of news about distant countries or technical policy debates than about the local community or everyday problems. Journalists recognize, however, that to equip the audience with consequential information they have to cover some less proximate events and difficult topics. Herbert Gans suggests that what makes a story consequential derives from the relative importance of the actor(s) in the story, its effect on the whole country or on large numbers of people, or the expected impact (2004, 147–52; Alger 1996, 150). As a local television news director put it: "There are some stories you do because you educate people . . . They're not done always to be what people choose to want to watch, because you're doing an important job" (Rosenstiel et al. 2007, 20).

## Event-Centered News

News stories are commonly—perhaps too commonly—defined as events. A news event may be the government's release of information or just published academic research, "planned" events, even "non-events," as well as circumstances or significant trends that have just now come to light. In the words of Walter Lippmann: "The news does not tell you how the seed is germinating in the ground, but it may tell you when the first sprout breaks through the surface" (1957, 216). Some critics worry that by promoting events as news, the resulting product is "episodic" and disconnected, making it difficult for the audience to put a unique event into any knowable context (Gilliam and Iyengar 2000).

## Timeliness

Professional gatekeepers select news that is about very recent "'hard events'—developments that have taken a clear and definable shape *within the past twenty- four hours*" (Patterson 1998, 57; my emphasis). The prominence given to news "just in," i.e., information most recently acquired, is a characteristic of news from the town crier to the Daily Kos. If the story is about an event that has just occurred or, even better, is ongoing, it meets the definition of news. The first media outlet to report a story is credited with the "scoop." Beating the opposition, however, carries the danger of reporting inaccurate or misleading information.

The classic misadventure in the race to report the news was the 2000 presidential election night decision by CBS and CNN, followed by other networks, to declare George W. Bush the winner in Florida. News reports of the Bush victory, even though they were later retracted, fed the Bush narrative that he had won the election and that Gore was just delaying the inevitable (Jamieson and Waldman 2003, 97–129). The 2000 debacle reflects the dangers of striving to be "first" with the news (Mason, Frankovic, and Jamieson 2001).

The emergence of cable television put even more pressure on journalists. Cable news can report breaking news at any hour of the day, seven days a week. In order to put their own stamp on the news, other media outlets have to "advance the story." In the Internet age, timing is now measured not in days, or hours, but minutes. The *New York Times* home page, for example, lists the exact time that breaking news stories are put up on the website. Other stories are tagged with the relative time they were put up that day, e.g., "28 minutes ago" or "5 minutes ago" (*New York Times*, August 14, 2009). Note that stories do not have to be late-breaking to merit the time stamp on the Web. The purpose of the stamp is to show that the user is getting the very latest news.

## Variation in News Values by Medium

While general news values, such as timeliness, have remained constant, what makes a news story publishable or prominent on a given day depends on the medium's news cycle. A story that is new in that particular twenty-four-hour period may come too late in the afternoon to make it onto the evening TV news or too late in the evening to make it into the morning newspaper. Stories that break late on a Friday afternoon may be reported on Saturday, when the fewest people follow the news in newspapers or on television. A Friday afternoon story will likely be gone by Sunday and is almost certain to be regarded as "old news" by Monday. Even big stories rarely get top billing for more than three days because of the competition with fresher news (Graber 1980 63).

The selection of what to air, print, or post on a particular day also depends on the medium. Gate keeping is most stringent on television, where the evening "news hole" is about twenty-two minutes, or the same number of words as on the front page of the *New York Times*. Whether a story gets more than headline space on television depends largely on the availability of video (Alger 1996, 149). As Lynn Sherr explained, TV reporters want visual "wall-paper" to make their stories interesting to the viewer (Moyers 1994). Stories with good video are more likely to make air than stories of similar consequence but only a talking head. Television stories with exciting visuals are also much longer than other stories with similar content (Rosenstiel et al. 2007, ch. 3).

Print news does not require great pictures, so newspapers carry a wider selection of news than television. Newspaper editors assume that consumers will not read all of the stories. By turning the page, the newspaper reader edits the news for personal consumption, while the TV viewer is expected to passively accept the news package selected to interest the widest possible audience. National Public Radio's two-hour news programs offer a news hole more like print than television.

In spite of format differences, the persistence and consensus about news values means that the news is remarkably similar across platforms and outlets (Mencher 1977, 57). In one study of the 1992 presidential campaign, the relative amount of news about the candidates—their chances, campaign strategies, organizations, and positions on issues—was the same across three national networks, newspapers, and local television broadcasts in four different-size media markets (Just et al. 1996, ch. 5). Local news, which one might expect to differ markedly from one city to another, not only has similar content (predominantly crime, accidents, and disasters) but a similar look and feel (Rosenstiel et al. 2007, 35).

## Soft News versus Hard News

While sameness characterizes news selection at any given time, the types of stories have changed. In the past twenty years, both practitioners and news critics have deplored the decline of "hard news" and the rise of "soft news." "Hard news" generally refers to important political and economic news, while soft news amounts to "everything else." Most news about government, policy issues, and foreign affairs falls under the rubric of hard news. Soft news is more practical ("news you can use") or entertaining, including human interest stories or features.

The vaunted appeal of human interest stories does not mean that hard news cannot be entertaining as well. Stories about political scandals or widespread disasters are both consequential and dramatic. But the details of public policy proposals, no matter how important the outcome, may not automatically appeal to the audience. A study by the Pew Research Center showed that there is a mismatch between the stories heavily covered in the press and the stories most followed by the news audience. For example, only between 2 and 14 percent of the public claimed to have "followed closely" the most heavily covered stories of 2007, such as a report on the situation in the Iraq War or the verdict in the Scooter Libby trial. Conversely, the stories that the public followed most closely, such as gas prices (51 percent) or Chinese toy recalls (33 percent), did not make it into the top twenty most covered stories in 2007 (Pew Research Center for the People & the Press 2007a). All of the heavily covered stories were "hard news," while many of the "most closely followed" stories were soft news.

Exacerbating the growth in soft news is an overall decline in the news audience. Newscasts have suffered from the competition of entertainment programming. News audiences were greatest when newscasts blocked the early evening 7 p.m. time slot. In the past twenty years most stations moved national news to 6.30 p.m. in order to increase local advertising revenue. The time change, coupled with longer audience commutes and two working parents, means that families are not watching television when national news airs. The emergence first of UHF stations and then of cable programming during the common news slot wreaked havoc on the "inadvertent," blocked news audience. The multitude of entertainment choices available today means that only a minority of the TV audience tunes in to the evening news.

News gatekeepers, under pressure to maintain audience and improve the bottom line, have increasingly relied on sensational and soft news to attract the audience (Alger 1996, 148; Miel and Faris 2008, 12; Patterson 2000, 4; McManus 1994). An analysis by Thomas Patterson shows that in the period 1980–2000 non-policy news increased from about a third of news stories to almost half. Specific categories of soft news, such as sensational, human interest, crime and disaster, and lifestyle news have all increased linearly and across all news platforms (Patterson 2000, 5). Local TV news has been particularly vulnerable to the depredations of the soft news formula. A five-year study carried out by the Project for Excellence in Journalism (PEJ) found that "crime, accidents and disasters lead the newscast and 'soft news' concludes the program . . . Only after the sixth story in an average local news broadcast does civic news (politics/government, social issues, science/technology, etc.) . . . appear" (Rosenstiel et al. 2007, 35).

It is ironic that most media cut hard news coverage when the audience declined. A study by Thomas Patterson found that people who mostly choose soft news will pay attention to hard news, but hard news consumers don't want to watch soft news. Patterson argues that the news media should reverse course and cater to hard news consumers, because they represent the most "reliable" part of the news audience (2000, 7).

Research based on TV ratings rather than self-reports supports Patterson's view. PEJ researchers found that local hard news stories about political figures were more likely to draw and maintain audience than stories about celebrities. In election news, stories about candidate policy proposals got more audience attention than campaign strategy stories. The PEJ study showed that hard news stories, such as politics, education, and health, can draw viewers' attention when the stories include good sources, a balance of opinions, and interviews with key players (Rosenstiel et al. 2007, chs. 5 and 6). In spite of these research findings, however, hard news continues to get short shrift in local programming.

## Infotainment and "Faux News"

Soft news has a home not only on newscasts; programs devoted to soft news are popular around the clock. Morning television news programs have a mix of public affairs and features, but soft news predominates in the second hour. Morning and afternoon talk shows, such as *Oprah*, are mostly concerned with soft news topics, but have some public affairs content, as do news magazine shows. Matthew Baum showed that the public affairs programming on soft news shows actually helps to inform viewers about foreign affairs (2005). Baum argues that infotainment programs draw in members of the audience who would otherwise have no exposure to public affairs news at all. (See Chapter 8 in this volume for a discussion of soft news programs.) Markus Prior counters, however, that the audience for soft news programs used to watch hard news, so that the total impact of soft news programs is to decrease hard news consumption in a high-choice media environment (2007, 281).

A new kind of infotainment program, comedy news, draws an enthusiastic audience. For more than three decades *Saturday Night Live* included some public affairs satire. More recent programs such as the *Daily Show* with Jon Stewart and the *Colbert Report* focus entirely on public affairs and media criticism. Political comedy shows attract public figures, who converse with the anchors about policy issues (Baym 2005, 260). An analysis by PEJ found that comedy shows do not cover the breadth of topics that traditional news programs do, but they do include substantial public affairs content (Project for Excellence in Journalism 2008c). Surveys show that as many as 20 percent of young people get their news primarily from comedy and late night programs (Gans 1980, xii; Baym 2005, 260).

# New Media: The Internet
## as a Game Changer

Young people generally have less overall interest in news than older age cohorts. Comedy news and online news figures prominently in the news consumption of younger people. According to a Pew Research Center survey, 59 percent of young people rely on Internet news; but older cohorts are catching up. During the 2008 presidential election, the proportion of people relying on the Internet for campaign news actually surpassed the percentage using newspapers (2008). The Internet has changed the delivery of news.

The Internet has penetrated the great majority of households, and even broadband connections are widely accessible throughout the US and in many countries in the world. The Internet includes a huge, if not overwhelming, number of news sites. News can be tailored to the consumer's specific interests, such as politics in Arizona or technology in India. It is not surprising that the Internet has contributed to the increasing fragmentation of the news audience, worrying some observers that the result will be the "Daily Me" and diminished concern for the community and nation (Sunstein 2009).

An Internet news site can contain an unconstrained number of stories. The gatekeeping role of reporters and editors fades if every story appears somewhere on the website. Editorial signaling is not a meaningful task if the package has no boundaries. Aggregating sites, such as Yahoo and Google, present hyperlinked snippets of news from sources around the globe. These news aggregator sites are the most popular political sites on the Internet (Hindman 2008, 64).

Because the Internet makes almost all content available free, it has had a devastating effect on the primary engine for public affairs information: newspapers and television news. In the early days of the Internet, major newspapers decided that the Internet culture required free distribution of content. Only the *Wall Street Journal* charged for online subscriptions. Since access to the *Journal* is usually a business expense, the subscription model worked for it. Other newspapers are now struggling to find a way to support their news-gathering operations, while continuing to provide content online. There are hints that the free lunch may be coming to an end, but in the meantime, Internet news is eating into the audience for print news.

## Interactive News

In the early days of Internet news, traditional media simply uploaded stories that were already in digital format onto their webpages. Items that did not make the cut for the print or on-air edition of the news still could be included on the website to give the Internet version added value. But this approach did not take advantage of the built-in interactive capability of the Web. The appearance of Internet bloggers in the mid-1990s challenged the passive audience model of the legacy media. By 2009 online news sites, such as the *New York Times*, were chockablock with interactive features, searchable archives, commentary, Internet-only content, and blogs.

### Blogging

Blogs, like newspaper columns, are personal versions of the news. A blog entry consists of a brief and sometimes edited selection from a news story—often a quote and hyperlink—accompanied by uniquely voiced commentary. A key ingredient is the invitation to readers to post comments. In 1999 simple free programs appeared on the Internet to make it easy for amateurs to set up blogs.

Interactive blogging takes up where letters to the editor and call-in talk shows leave off. Letters to the editor normally take up no more than a few inches of print space a day (or a few minutes a week on *All Things Considered*). The content of interactive blogs, however, is overwhelmingly originated by the readers. Another difference between blog posts and letters is that the voice of the audience is unmediated. By way of contrast, the *New York Times* often selects letters from elite contributors, such as officers of relevant organizations. On talk radio programs a "delay" protects hosts from cranks, while producers pre-screen calls to fit the host's topic and, usually, point of view. A few opposition calls are permitted after giving ample time to the host to prepare a catchy comeback.

The blog world has more of a Wild West culture compared to letters to the editor or call-in radio. Some of the posted comments consist of four-letter words, while still others insult the blogger's intelligence or heredity. Blogging is not for the squeamish. The saving grace is that most blogs are invisible and remain monologues rather than conversations. Starkey describe blogging as "onanistic" (2007, 47). Generally the pressure to provide up-to-date content is so great that most bloggers abandon their posts within days or weeks (Caslon Analytics 2009).

Some bloggers, however, have established a continuing presence on the Web and draw large daily audiences. Many political bloggers have sought legitimacy as news professionals and in recent years they have succeeded. Bloggers were credentialed at the

2004 presidential conventions, and in 2009 President Obama called on a blogger at a White House press conference. Traditional journalists are wary of these new entrants into the field. Many reporters worry that without an institutional reputation at stake, bloggers are careless and prone to make false accusations or disseminate false information. Some bloggers have admitted changing their blog archives to make their previous incorrect predictions appear true (Rainey 2009). While professional journalists have deplored bloggers' casual attitude to truth and accuracy, bloggers point out that they are under constant scrutiny from their readers and the blogosphere.

Bloggers further counter that professional journalists have their own biases in news selection. An example of bloggers challenging the traditional news agenda occurred in reporting Strom Thurmond's hundredth birthday party. In this public event, with many reporters present, Senate Majority Leader Trent Lott praised Thurmond's Dixie-crat platform of 1948. Lott implied that continuing segregation might have been better for the country than racial integration. The birthday celebration was aired on C-SPAN, meaning that a large audience of non-professionals, including bloggers, also had front-row seats and a record of the proceedings. Traditional news about the birthday party characterized it as a tribute to a very elderly member of the Senate, but the blogosphere put the focus on Lott. The left-leaning bloggers were outraged by Lott's apparent endorsement of segregation, while the right-leaning bloggers saw this as an opportunity to get rid of Lott altogether (Scott 2004, 24). One traditional news outlet, ABC News, covered Lott's remarks on an early morning news program and also on *The Note*, ABC's web chronicle of the day's political events cum blog. Eventually the commotion in the blogosphere reached traditional media and Lott was forced to resign. The birthday party story demonstrates the potential of blogs as a resource for and pressure on traditional journalists, while also showing that the greatest impact of blogs comes when their content is embraced by traditional media. The birthday story also featured a new kind of crossover blog, *The Note*, which is sponsored by legacy media and written by professional journalists.

## Audience Participation In the News

By 2008 virtually all newspapers had at least one professional blog (Miel and Faris 2008, 15). The Internet began to permeate other aspects of legacy media online. Each week on the NewYorkTimes.com one of the editors takes audience questions. Reporters list their email addresses at the bottom of stories so that readers can send them comments directly. This new openness to the audience marks a major shift for editors and reporters and the beginning of journalism's two-way street. In the past, reporters were protected from audience reaction, in part because of the effort required to contact the news outlet or to find a particular reporter or editor. Journalists used to regard citizen oversight as an infringement of freedom of the press. The interactivity inherent in the Internet, however, changed all that. The opening of traditional media to two-way communication has proved popular with the audience. Most online news outlets provide opportunities for the audience to contribute ideas for stories, news tips, comments, and even home videos. In the face of severe budget cuts, some news outlets are hoping that audience volunteers will take up the slack in news gathering.

A study by the Harvard University's Berkman Center for Internet & Society finds, however, that "digital media's low barriers to entry have led to an explosion of content on topics broadly defined as 'soft' news" (Miel and Faris 2008, 12). Most of the blogs and niche communities on the Internet are not concerned with public affairs. Audience attention to online news reflects a preference for soft news or information about personal interests, such as technology, health, or cooking. A glance at the "most emailed" or "most accessed stories" of the day (computer-generated features) indicates that the appetite for political news is sporadic at best. On August 18, 2009, for example, three of the *New York Times*'s ten "most emailed" stories were public affairs commentary, four were health news or commentary, and only one was a regular hard news story, "Mental Stress Training Is Planned for U.S. Soldiers" (*New York Times* 2009), albeit with a health theme.

# AUDIENCE-GENERATED NEWS

Not only can the Internet news audience cater to their particular interests, they can follow what other people find interesting. Digg.com and similar sites report which news items are currently most popular. These sites in effect construct an audience-edited news product. Audience-generated news, however, leans heavily to soft news and funny pictures. A week-long study by the Project for Excellence in Journalism found that the news agenda on Digg, Reddit, and Delicious covered a wider range of topics and more soft news than professionally edited news, but had less hard news and almost no international stories (Project for Excellence in Journalism 2007).

This is not to say that the audience cannot play a role in gathering public affairs news. While miniaturization of video cameras and small satellite hookups made it possible for TV journalists to report from the front lines, the same technology is available to consumers. Perhaps the most ubiquitous and often overlooked technological development is the versatile cellphone with built-in camera and video capability. Not only can bystanders record images, but they can distribute video instantly. The possibility that every person you meet is a potential reporter has significant consequences for society. For example, when a fellow partygoer took a picture of Olympic champion Michael Phelps smoking pot, dissemination on YouTube created an international incident.

## YouTube and Video-Sharing

YouTube, which was founded in 2005, has become one of the top five or six websites in most industrialized countries. YouTube was intended to be a site where users could easily upload and almost instantly share their personal videos and v-logs. In a few short years it has become a major information resource. Users can find demonstrations about how to do almost anything from driving a stick shift to cooking salmon. Even academic experiences, such as Leo Strauss's 1966 lecture on Plato's *Meno*, are available. In the political arena, YouTube puts candidate speeches, advertisements, and debates at the fingertips of any interested citizen. In the 2008 presidential election all of the major party candidates posted their ads on YouTube as well as on their websites. Candidate speeches were available along with parodies and critiques. One of the most widely viewed videos in the 2008 campaign was "Yes We Can," a version of a speech by Barack Obama set to music. Perhaps the most notable innovation of the 2008 election was the CNN–YouTube presidential debate, where members of the virtual audience asked the candidates questions via YouTube.

In 2008 YouTube received a Peabody award in electronic journalism for providing a public commons. Indeed YouTube represents the Internet's great potential for many-to-many communication. YouTube videos may be viewed not only on a computer, but via cellphones and even on television screens. YouTube videos can be embedded on social networking sites, such as Facebook, or shared via email. Forwarding from "friend" to "friend" allows YouTube videos to spread virally across the Internet. YouTube is a powerful tool for user-generated news. Because of YouTube's ease of dissemination, police brutality or other forms of oppression or violation of human rights have been revealed to the world outside.

*Chi-Town Daily News*, a non-profit online newspaper in Chicago, encourages amateur "grassroots" reporters to be its eyes and ears around the city. *Chi-Town* offers training to its citizen journalists, recruiting them from another Internet phenomenon, Craigslist. *Chi-Town* covers news at the neighborhood level and has documented examples of police misconduct (Hempel 2008). International advocacy organizations, such as Human Rights Watch and Amnesty International, have trained local volunteers to use video cameras to publish eyewitness accounts of political oppression abroad (Miel and Faris 2008, 18).

### Twitter: 140-Character News

While one of YouTube's virtues is easy accessibility, it has been challenged by an even newer, more instantaneous form of social networking. Twitter, founded in 2006, has become the thirteenth most popular site in the US and is growing exponentially. Twitter messages are limited to 140 characters and can be viewed within a circle of friends or open to the public. One of the contributions of Twitter is to crowd-source news. When numerous users "tweet" about an earthquake, the news is in real time. Twitter is an international service and has proved valuable in organizing protests on the fly—as in the 2009 Moldova demonstrations (Barry 2009). In Iran, post-election protesters used several Internet reporting platforms (cellphones, Facebook, and Twitter) to help organize banned demonstrations and to report on the regime's response (Cohen 2009). The Iranian government shut down Facebook, but it could not keep up with the short tweets from multiple platforms on Twitter. The US government took the unusual step of asking Twitter to defer maintenance on its site to permit continuous use of the service by Iranian protesters (Kafka 2009; Stone and Cohen 2009; Landler and Stelter 2009). Real-time blogs, Twitter feeds, and cellphone images reenergized the protesters. The riveting video of a young woman shot to death by the Iranian police was posted on YouTube and drew support for the protests from around the world (Worth and Fathi 2009).

At first, some traditional news outlets were reluctant to air the video, blogs, and tweets coming from Iran. The slow response of the 24/7 cable news networks led to a massive number of cyber complaints, causing CNN to publicly defend its decision to hold the video. The Iranian protests crystallize the vast change in defining, reporting, gate keeping, distributing, and critiquing news that has resulted from recent technological changes. Bystanders decided what was important, recorded the events, and distributed the news around the world. When traditional media fretted about the sourcing and reliability of the Iranian content, the online community effectively made the case against editors. One could argue that the cable news channels were applying the typical professional standards. No cellphone video comes with a date stamp to verify when the recorded events took place. Who were these unknown reporters whose accounts of events were coinciding on the Internet? Were they real or fabricated? The enormous demand for news about the Iranian protests, however, caused traditional journalists to retreat from their routine gate-keeping and editorial judgments—and paid homage to the user revolution in news.

Journalists have been learning to accommodate the loss of control over the news process. In the past, the audience was able to filter the news—by turning the page in the newspaper or changing the channel. But selecting from professionally produced stories is a far cry from actually generating news. The audience has welcomed its role in news production and it is unlikely that this trend will be reversed.

## Collaborative News

The two-way street between the audience and the professionals means that not only are the professionals allowing the audience to contribute to the news; journalists are also consulting the audience for editorial signaling. Journalists check Twitter, Facebook, and even Google Trends to see what people are talking about and what concerns them (personal communication with ABC producer, August 19, 2009). When editors and reporters see increased interest in a topic, they feel encouraged to pursue those stories. Journalists monitor audience reports from around the world, especially in places where they do not have staff. A Project for Excellence in Journalism survey shows that editors today think that "print and website versions of today's daily newspapers can be complementary and mutually strengthening" (2008b). The *New York Times* describes a two-track process in which their blogs carry the raw information from Twitter and YouTube while traditional reporters try to authenticate the sources or triangulate versions from several sources. Once the story is verified, the *Times* publishes the reports as news (Stelter 2009).

Journalists are still needed to cover the hard news—the public affairs topics—that does not grab the audience's interest. Sadly the sharp decline of newspapers throughout the country means that a great deal of city hall and state house reporting is already dying, gutting the watchdog function of the press (Dorroh 2009). There were half or fewer state house beat reporters in 2008 than the year before. In the state of Nevada the number is down to one. It is not clear how the gap in reporting public affairs will be met, although the Associated Press maintains a presence in most states. One concern is that if the sentinel effect of state house reporters is gone, political corruption will follow (Schudson 2008, 14; Dorroh 2009).

At the national level, major television networks and national newspapers such as the *New York Times* have the resources and audience attention to continue to report news—although the format may shift to the Web—but staffs have been slashed everywhere. The result is an overall decline in foreign news (Gans 2004, p. xiv; Project for Excellence in Journalism 2008b). In the future, Americans may have to rely on international sources for foreign news. One experiment to fill the lacuna in international affairs is GlobalPost, a for-profit online international news service employing freelance journalists. It is too early to tell whether this model will succeed in becoming profitable. Another potential resource for foreign news is Current TV, which sends a crew of semi-professional reporters to places difficult to access. Some of them run foul of local governments. According to the Committee to Protect Journalists, in 2008 "at least 56 of the 125 jailed journalists worked for online outlets and . . . 45 of the total were freelancers." Without media institutions and resources to back them up, the fate of some of these semi-professional journalists is precarious. The gaps left by declining traditional media may be difficult to fill by amateur, accidental, or freelance journalists.

## INTO THE TWENTY-FIRST CENTURY

The democratic function of continuous oversight at home and abroad seem to require professional journalists, but the news products of the twenty-first century will necessarily be collaborations between the professionals and the audience. Future research in media and public opinion should pair what we know about changes in content with studies about the impact of decreased professionalization on citizens' knowledge and the democratic process.

One pressing need for future research concerns news credibility. As the lines between professionals and amateurs blur, which versions of news will people believe? While the audience for online news in increasing, the audience trusts the Internet less than other media. As we go forward, a lot will depend on how well new media perform as civic educators and watchdogs. Will amateur reporters fill in the gaps left by smaller professional staff? Can bloggers provide the kind of oversight that will keep government corruption at bay? The answers to these questions are crucial for democratic accountability in the twenty-first century.

# References

ALGER, D. 1996. *Media and Politics*. Belmont, CA: Wadsworth.

BARRY, E. 2009. Protests in Moldova Explode, with Help of Twitter. *New York Times*, Apr. 7.

BAUM, M. 2005. *Soft News Goes to War: Public Opinion and American Foreign Policy in the New Media Age*. Princeton: Princeton University Press.

BAYM, G. 2005. *The Daily Show*: Discursive Integration and the Reinvention of Political Journalism. *Political Communication*, 22: 259–76.

Caslon Analytics. 2009. Blogging: Ephemerality, Feb. At <http://www.caslon.com.au/weblog-profile1.htm#ephemerality>. Accessed Oct. 29, 2010.

COHEN, N. 2009. Twitter on the Barricades. *New York Times, Week in Review*, June 20. At <http://www.nytimes.com/2009/06/21/weekinreview/21cohenweb.html>. Accessed Oct. 29, 2010.

DORROH, J. 2009. Statehouse Exodus. *American Journalism Review*, Apr.–May.

GALTUNG, J., and RUGE, M. H. 1965. The Structure of Foreign News. *Journal of Peace Research*, 2/1: 64–91.

GANS, H. J. 1980. *Deciding What's News: A Study of CBS Evening News, NBC Nightly News, Newsweek, and Time*. Evanston, IL: Northwestern University Press.

GILLIAM, F. D., JR., and IYENGAR, S. 2000. Prime Suspects: The Influence of Local Television News on the Viewing Public. *American Journal of Political Science*, 44/3 (July), 560–73.

GRABER, D. A. 1980. *Mass Media and American Politics*. Washington, DC: CQ.

——1988. *Processing the News: How People Tame the Information Tide*. Chicago: University of Chicago Press.

HEMPEL, M. *The Chi-Town Daily News: Creating a New Supply of Local News*. Media Re: Public: Case Studies 2008. Cambridge, MA: Berkman Center for Internet & Society at Harvard University.

HINDMAN, M. 2008. *The Myth of Digital Democracy*. Princeton: Princeton University Press.

HUGHES, H. M. 1939. *News and the Human Interest Story*. Chicago: University of Chicago Press.

JAMIESON, K. H., and WALDMAN, P. 2003. *The Press Effect*. New York: Oxford University Press.

JUST, M. R., CRIGLER, A. N., ALGER, D., COOK, T., KERN, M., and WEST, D. 1996. *Citizens, Candidates and the Media in a Presidential Campaign*. Chicago: University of Chicago Press.

KAKFA, P. 2009. Why Twitter Did Not Go Down: The State Department Told It Stay Up (But Not Forever!). All Things Digital. Media Memo. *Wall Street Journal*, June 16. <http://mediamemo.allthingsd.com/20090616/why-twitter-didnt-go-down-the-state-department-told-it-stay-up/?mod=ATD_search>. Accessed Oct. 30, 2010.

LANDLER, M., and STELTER, B. 2009. Washington Taps into a Potent New Force in Diplomacy. *New York Times*, June 16. At <http://www.nytimes.com/2009/06/17/world/middleeast/17media.html>. Accessed Oct. 30, 2010.

LIPPMANN, W. 1957. *Public Opinion.* New York: Macmillan.

McMANUS, J. H. 1994. *Market Driven Journalism: Let the Citizen Beware?* Thousand Oaks, CA: Sage.

MASON, L., FRANKOVIC, K., and JAMIESON, K. H. 2001. CBS News Coverage of Election Night 2000: Investigation, Analysis, Recommendations. *CBS News,* Jan.

MENCHER, M. 1977. *News Reporting and Writing,* 5th edn. New York: W. C. Brown.

MIEL, P., and FARIS, R. 2008. *News and Information as Digital Media Come of Age.* Cambridge, MA: Berkman Center for Internet & Society at Harvard University.

MOYERS, B. 1994. *The Public Mind with Bill Moyers: The Truth about Lies.* VHS. Clayton, DE: Prestwick House.

NEAL, R. M. 1942. *News Gathering and News Writing.* New York: Prentice-Hall.

*New York Times* 2009. Mental Stress Training Is Planned for U.S. Soldiers. At <http://www.nytimes.com/2009/08/18/health/18psych.html?scp=1&sq=mental+stress+training+for+soldiers&st=nyt>. Accessed Oct. 30, 2010.

PATTERSON, T. E. 1998. Time and News: The Media's Limitations as an Instrument of Democracy. *International Political Science Review,* 19/1: 55–67.

—— 2000. *Doing Well and Doing Good: How Soft News and Critical Journalism Are Shrinking the News Audience and Weakening Democracy.* Joan Shorenstein Center. Cambridge, MA: Harvard Kennedy School.

Pew Research Center for the People & the Press. 2007a. *Gas Prices, Disasters Top Public's News Interests in 2007,* Dec. 19. At <http://people-press.org/report/380/gas-prices-disasters-top-publics-news-interests-in-2007>. Accessed Oct. 29, 2010.

—— 2007b. *Biggest Stories of 2008: Economy Tops Campaign; Internet Overtakes Newspapers as News Outlet,* Dec. 23. At <http://people-press.org/reports/pdf/479.pdf>. Accessed Oct. 29, 2010.

—— 2008. *Key News Audiences Now Blend Online and Traditional Sources,* Aug. 17. At <http://people-press.org/report/?pageid=1358>. Accessed Oct. 30, 2010.

PIPA/Knowledge Networks. 2003. *Misperceptions, the Media, and the Iraq War,* Oct. 2. At <http://www.pipa.org/OnlineReports/Iraq/IraqMedia_Oct03/IraqMedia_Oct03_rpt.pdf>. Accessed Oct. 29, 2010.

PRIOR, M. 2007. *Post-Broadcast Democracy.* Cambridge: Cambridge University Press.

Project for Excellence in Journalism. 2007. *The Latest News Headlines—Your Vote Counts,* Sept. 12. At <http://www.journalism.org/node/7493>. Accessed Oct. 29, 2010.

—— 2008a. *The Changing Newsroom: The Influence of the Web,* July 21. At <http://www.journalism.org/node/11966>. Accessed Oct. 30, 2010.

—— 2008b. *The Changing Newsroom: Changing Content,* July 21. <http://www.journalism.org/node/11963>. Accessed Oct. 30, 2010.

—— 2008c. *Journalism, Satire or Just Laughs: The Daily Show with Jon Stewart Examined,* May 8. At <http://www.journalism.org/node/10954>. Accessed Oct. 30, 2010.

RAINEY, J. 2009. On the Media: Being Relentless and Harsh Pays Off for Deadline Hollywood Daily's Nikki Finke. *Los Angeles Times,* July 15.

RAMPTON, S., and STAUBER, J. 2006. *The Best War Ever: Lies, Damned Lies, and the Mess in Iraq.* New York: Tarcher/Penguin.

ROSENSTIEL, T., JUST, M., BELT, T., PERTILLA, A., DEAN, W., and CHINNI, D. 2007. *We Interrupt this Newscast: How to Improve Local News and Win Ratings, Too.* New York: Cambridge University Press.

SCHUDSON, M. 2008. *Why Democracies Need an Unlovable Press.* Cambridge: Polity Press.

Scott, E. 2004. *"Big Media" Meets the Bloggers: Coverage of Trent Lott's Remarks at Strom Thurmond's Birthday Party.* Kennedy School of Government Case Program. Reference C14-04-1731.0. At <http://www.hks.harvard.edu/presspol/publications/case_studies/1731_0_scott.pdf>. Accessed Oct. 2010.

Starkey, G. 2007. *Balance and Bias in Journalism.* New York: Palgrave Macmillan.

Stelter, B. 2009. Journalism Rules Are Bent in News Coverage from Iran. *New York Times,* June 28. At <http://www.nytimes.com/2009/06/29/business/media/29coverage.html>. Accessed Oct. 30, 2010.

Stone, B., and Cohen, N. 2009. Social Networks Spread Defiance Online. *New York Times,* June 15. At <http://www.nytimes.com/2009/06/16/world/middleeast/16media.html?scp=1&sq=social%20networks%20spread%20defiance%20on%20line&st=cse>. Accessed Aug. 19, 2009.

Sunstein, C. 2009. *Republic.com 2.0.* Princeton: Princeton University Press.

Worth, R. F., and Fathi, N. 2009. Iranians Gather in Grief, then Face Police. *New York Times,* July 30. At <http://www.nytimes.com/2009/07/31/world/asia/31iran.html?scp=1&sq=iranians%20gather%20in%20grief&st=cse>. Accessed Aug. 19, 2009.

## CHAPTER 8

## SOFT NEWS AND THE FOUR OPRAH EFFECTS

MATTHEW A. BAUM
ANGELA JAMISON

## INTRODUCTION

ON September 21, 2009, President Barack Obama took to the stage of the *Late Show with David Letterman*, only the second time a sitting US president had appeared on a network late-night comedy show.[1] This appearance—Obama's sixth on *Letterman*—capped an intensive media push by the President to promote health care reform, including interviews on five Sunday news shows the previous day. The interview addressed a variety of topics, ranging from the state of the economy to the war in Afghanistan, as well as how the President's children were adjusting to life in the White House.

Why would a sitting president add a late-night comedy-oriented talk show to his already crowded weekend itinerary of five appearances on traditional news and interview shows? One obvious answer concerns the audience magnitude: nearly 7.2 million Americans watched the President on *Letterman*. Only 3.1 million watched Obama's interview the day before on ABC's *This Week with George Stephanopoulos*.

A second, less obvious answer concerns the *nature* of Letterman's audience. Compared to the typical audience for traditional news and interview programs, Letterman's audience is less politically engaged, ideologically extreme, or partisan (Baum 2003a, 2005; Baum and Jamison 2006). Consequently, Letterman's viewers are more likely to

---

[1] Obama also made the *first* such appearance, on the *Tonight Show with Jay Leno*, six months earlier, on March 18, 2009.

be persuaded by a presidential appeal than the relatively more partisan and ideological audiences of typical traditional news outlets (Zaller 1992).

Finally, such interviews present candidates in a more favorable light than traditional political interview shows. For example, commenting on another 2008 presidential candidate's talk show appearances, Gold (2007) observes, "John and Elizabeth Edwards got substantially gentler treatment from Leno on 'The Tonight Show' than they did from Katie Couric on '60 Minutes.'" In short, late-night entertainment talk shows or other soft news programs afford politicians one of their best opportunities to reach a large group of potentially persuadable voters in a relatively sympathetic venue.

If the combination of audience size, demographics, and anticipated interview content accounts for Obama's interest in appearing six times on Letterman, as well as on other decidedly non-political programs, such as the *Tonight Show with Jay Leno*, the *Oprah Winfrey Show*, *The View*, and the *Tyra Banks Show*, it does not tell us what viewers take away from these appearances. The increasing frequency of presidential candidate appearances on daytime and late-night talk shows (Baum 2003a, 2005; Gold 2007) strongly suggests they believe such appearances are politically beneficial. Are they correct? What do viewers learn, and with what effects? These are the primary topics of the present chapter.

Numerous scholars (for example, Patterson 1994, 2000; Bennett 2003) and journalists (for example, Jones 2009) have decried what they consider the increasingly bleak state of political news, and its implications for the capacity of voters to fulfill their basic responsibilities as democratic citizens. Proponents of this perspective—termed *participatory democratic theory* by Clawson and Oxley (2008)—frequently cite the proliferation of soft news as evidence of the news media's failure to equip citizens with proper or sufficient information. Patterson (2000), for instance, implicitly argues that hard news—defined as coverage of breaking events involving top leaders, major issues, or significant disruptions in the routines of daily life—is of higher quality than soft news, which lacks a public policy component, featuring instead human interest themes and dramatic subject matter. As Zaller (2003: 129) states, "soft news is information that is either personally useful or merely entertaining." In short, a prevalent scholarly critique is that the contemporary news media offer too little hard news and too much soft news, thereby making it difficult for citizens to obtain sufficient information to make informed vote choices.[2]

But could soft news shows help citizens better perform their democratic responsibilities? Stated differently: is there an *Oprah Effect* and if so, what is it? Or is there, perhaps, more than one such effect? In fact, scholars investigating this question have identified and begun to grapple with at least four distinct categories of potential soft news effects on consumers. These include effects on *attention* to and *knowledge* about politics, as well as political *attitudes*, and *behavior*. Numerous studies find what might be termed Oprah Effects that fit into more than one of these categories, and they are by no means absolute. Nonetheless, we employ this schema to enhance analytic clarity and to provide a framework for integrating the growing literature on the political

---

[2] The distinction between hard and soft news in the academic literature appears to date back to Tuchman's (1973) sociological investigation of newsroom values.

implications of soft news. Viewing the large quantity of literature through this schema also reveals that as the size and complexity of the soft news market increase, a second effective distinction is emerging—between more traditional soft news talk programs such as *The View* or the *Late Show with David Letterman*, and explicitly satirical comedy productions hosted by dramatic characters, particularly Jon Stewart and Stephen Colbert.

The remainder of this chapter reviews the literature in each of these four categories, drawing linkages between several of them, as well as assessing their implications for the behavior of and policies provided by politicians. We conclude by suggesting directions for future research.

# FOUR OPRAH EFFECTS

Baum and Jamison (2006) define the Oprah Effect as the influence of consuming soft news political content on vote choice. Yet it is possible to conceptualize the Oprah Effect from the perspective of either the suppliers or the consumers of political information. As the introduction makes clear, the two are intimately related. Without citizen interest (the demand side), it is unclear why politicians would bother tailoring their appeals to soft news formats. It is also possible to conceptualize the Oprah Effect in terms of influence on public policy outcomes. After all, changes in the tenor of political discourse could lead to consequential changes in the substance, rather than merely the style, of politics (Popkin 2006; Baum 2007). Consequently, in the final substantive section we assess research into the supply side. However, in order to anticipate likely supply-side effects, it is first necessary to explicate the demand side. In other words, to assess how politicians may adapt their behavior or policy agendas as a consequence of soft news coverage of politics, one must first determine how consuming political information via soft news affects citizens. Therefore, we now discuss each of the four potential demand-side political effects of soft news.

## Attention

Basic attentiveness to political information is arguably the lowest threshold of learning of the four Oprah Effects. Baum (2002, 2003a) characterizes attentiveness as a precursor to knowledge or understanding, making attention an important element of political learning. He reports evidence from a variety of public opinion surveys suggesting that politically unengaged individuals who consume soft news are more attentive to major political events than their counterparts who do not consume soft news. Conversely, consuming soft news does not influence highly politically engaged individuals. Baum explicates an *Incidental By-product* model, which holds that soft news makes political information accessible (that is, interesting and entertaining) for politically inattentive individuals, thereby increasing the likelihood that they will attend to it if exposed. In essence, soft news "piggybacks" substantive political news to information consumed for purposes of entertainment.

Additional research supports this contention. For instance, Van Zoonen et al. (2007) find that "infotainment"—operationalized as appearances by presidential candidates George W. Bush and John Kerry on the *Dr. Phil Show*—does enhance viewers' overall attention to politics. Yet, based on a qualitative analysis, they report that viewers of these candidate interviews were even *more* attentive to non-political subjects like seating arrangements, body language, and candidates' physical appearance. This suggests that the political-attentiveness-enhancing effects of watching political candidates on entertainment-oriented talk shows may be somewhat limited.

Moy, Xenos, and Hess (2005) find, consistent with Baum, that exposure to political humor on late-night comedy shows enhances political engagement. However, contrary to Baum's findings, they argue that such effects are limited to viewers with sufficient political sophistication to "get the joke."

This is an area in the literature where potentially important differences between soft news programs are increasingly apparent. This seeming discrepancy stems from differences in content across soft-news-oriented outlets, a distinction Moy, Xenos, and Hess (2005) emphasize. Some outlets, like the *Daily Show with Jon Stewart* (henceforth the *Daily Show*) or the *Colbert Report*, offer relatively sophisticated satire clearly aimed at politically attentive consumers, while others, including most daytime talk shows (e.g., *The View*) and some late-night talk shows (e.g., the *Tonight Show*) and entertainment news magazine shows (e.g., *Entertainment Tonight*), target less politically sophisticated audiences. It thus seems reasonable to presume, and is largely consistent with the findings of both Baum and Moy, Xenos, and Hess, that beneficial attentiveness or engagement effects among politically unsophisticated audiences would be strongest for venues that do not assume high levels of political knowledge.

The previous discussion illustrates the importance of drawing clear distinctions between different types of media outlets and content aimed at distinct audiences. Most research into the effects of soft news on public opinion finds any such effects to be contingent on media venue, topic, and audience characteristics. Such venues vary in the sophistication of their content and hence the likely learning effects among different types of viewers, while some issues are more easily framed in accessible terms than others. Moreover, different types of viewers differ in their propensity to learn about politics via such outlets. Scholars have only partially disentangled these distinctions. Much of the research in this area thus suffers from imprecise definitions of the independent (soft news exposure) and/or dependent (public opinion) variables.

## Knowledge

Communication scholars (Blumler and McQuail 1969; Wamsley and Pride 1972; Fitzsimmons and Osburn 1968; Robinson 1974) have shown that television allows individuals to learn passively, even if they are neither interested in a topic nor motivated to learn about it. This is possible because individuals are more likely to accept information presented in a non-conflictual manner that does not arouse excitement (Krugman and Hartley 1970). Television arguably represents the ideal instrument of passive learning. Individuals learn passively by first choosing to expose themselves to some type of information, such as network television news, and then surrendering control of the specific information to which they are exposed (Zukin and Snyder 1984). TV watchers can thereby gain knowledge via consuming television, without necessarily intending to do so.

More recently, Popkin (1993) extended the conceptualization of passive learning to explicate a by-product theory of political knowledge. He argues that individuals learn about politics through everyday experiences having little direct connection with politics. Passive learning incidental to seeking entertainment via soft news could allow consumers to gain political knowledge, even without their intending to do so (Baum 2003a).

Political communication scholars have sought to determine more precisely *what* political knowledge consumers glean from soft news and *who* is most likely to gain it. This has produced a schism between those arguing that consuming soft news produces relatively limited political knowledge gain, primarily among individuals who might not otherwise gain such information, and others arguing that soft news has little political informational value. In the former camp, some argue that soft news can facilitate political learning either directly, via exposure to substantive information in soft news venues (Baum 2003a, 2003b; Brewer and Cao 2006), or indirectly, through a gateway effect, whereby exposure to small amounts of information on soft news outlets motivates viewers to consume additional related information via traditional news venues (Baum 2003a; Young and Tisinger 2006). In both cases, political learning effects appear strongest among individuals who are relatively uninterested in, and hence unmotivated to learn about, politics.

In the latter camp, some scholars, notably Markus Prior (2003, 2005, 2007), have argued that consuming soft news does not contribute to consequential gains in political knowledge. Prior does not dispute that soft news programs cover political issues. Instead, he challenges Baum's (2002, 2003a) contention that consequential numbers of consumers learn about politics from such shows. He argues (2005) that extreme media fragmentation in recent years has reduced incidental exposure to politics among entertainment-seeking viewers. The reason is that viewers who prefer entertainment to news are increasingly able to avoid the latter. As evidence, Prior conducted a series of survey experiments in which he found that individuals who claim to prefer soft news to political news programs typically gain at most sporadic factual knowledge about a variety of political topics from consuming soft news.

Baum (2003b), though not disputing Prior's finding of limited factual knowledge gains in his experiments, countered—drawing on the online model of information processing (McGraw and Lodge 1995; Lodge, Steenberger, and Brau 1995)—that factual knowledge is an insufficient measure of political learning. According to this perspective, typical individuals rapidly discard factual details regarding the objects to which they devote their attention. But they maintain an online summary evaluation of how they feel about them. Each new piece of information about a given object is tagged with a positive or negative emotional "charge." The individual then discards the information and retains the emotional tag, which is added to his or her running tally. If a majority of the emotional tags in the running tally are positive, the individual will have a net positive summary evaluation of the object, and vice versa. Through this process, individuals can remember what they support or oppose, or like or dislike, without necessarily remembering *why*. This suggests that soft news exposure *could* lead to political learning without necessarily enhancing an individual's capacity to recall political facts.

Parkin (2010) presented information about 2004 presidential candidate John Kerry's position on Iraq to different groups of participants in the context of either a late-night entertainment talk show (*Letterman*) or a traditional political interview show (*Face the Nation*). He finds that young, politically disinterested viewers who read the Letterman version of the transcript—that is, a transcript embedded in a webpage designed to appear like the show's website—reported increased political engagement and demonstrated increased knowledge about Kerry's policy positions. However, the *exact same* information presented in a traditional news context had virtually no effect on younger viewers. Parkin concludes that by making political information entertaining, soft news can at minimum supplement the political learning engendered by consuming traditional news, both directly and via the gateway effect. In a complementary study, Pfau, Houston, and Semmler (2006) also find that watching late-night comedy during a political campaign increases a person's general political "expertise" during that campaign.

In his aforementioned study, Parkin (2010) combines experimental research on exposure to *Letterman* with content analysis of particularly engaging features of the program. He demonstrates that relatively disengaged viewers not only learn and process new political information through consuming soft news, but are more able to recall this information later because of the manner in which they were exposed to it. Finally, Young (2004) notes that, *ceteris paribus*, regular viewers of the *Daily Show* are more politically knowledgeable than non-viewers.

These studies find a fairly clear link between consuming soft news and gaining political knowledge. However, other studies have found more limited and contingent effects. For instance, Brewer and Cao (2006) find that viewing late-night comedy shows is associated with greater knowledge of political candidates' biographies, but not of their policy positions. Hollander (2005), in turn, reports evidence from public opinion surveys suggesting that viewers—particularly *younger* viewers—who watch late-night talk and comedy shows are more likely to recognize campaign issues if subsequently encountered, but are *not* more likely to recall political events. In other words, soft news enhances *recognition* but not *recall* of political issues.

Taken together, these findings suggest that at least *some* consumers do learn about politics via soft news, but that *what* they are learning, *how much*, and *how long lasting* remain subject to debate. Also unresolved is whether such learning influences consumers' attitudes or behavior. It is to these questions that we now turn, beginning with the possibility of attitudinal effects.

## Attitudes

For soft news to affect politics, it must first influence the attitudes of voters. After all, if any information voters glean from soft news does not influence their attitudes, then it would make little sense for politicians to court them via soft news outlets. Nor would it seem likely that such exposure would alter the substance of public policy. Some democratic theorists might applaud any increases in political knowledge and attention resulting from soft news consumption. Yet, even if consumers do increase their political attention and knowledge via soft news, such increases only matter for the state of democracy or democratic citizenship if they influence citizens' attitudes in *some* meaningful way.

In fact, some research suggests that exposure to soft news does influence the attitudes of consumers. Some of this literature focuses on the complexity and critical thinking elements of soft news—particularly its more coarse, comedic elements. For instance, Brewer and Marquardt (2007), in a detailed content analysis of 222 episodes of the *Daily Show*, find a profusion of educational content. They argue that such material increases viewers' attention to world affairs and encourages critical thinking, rather than engendering a knee-jerk cynical attitude toward political figures and institutions. Baym's (2005) analysis of the same program reaches a similar conclusion. Envisioning this form of soft news as an experiment in journalism, the author argues for its potential as a forum for deliberative democracy.

Other studies probe more deeply the causal mechanisms by which such content could actually shape the attitudes of citizens—particularly the typical soft news consumer who may not be seeking novel political information. For instance, Baum (2005) investigates survey data from the 2000 presidential election and finds that politically inattentive individuals who frequently watched daytime talk shows during the campaign were likely to find the candidates that appeared on those shows more likeable than their non-viewing counterparts. Baum and Jamison (2006) find, based on an analysis of the same election, that politically inattentive daytime talk show viewers did better than inattentive non-viewers at figuring out which candidate best represented their own interests and preferences. In both cases, the authors posit that soft news consumers arrived at their political viewpoints not by deliberation or concerted critical thinking, but incidentally, as a by-product of pursuing entertainment.

While this last finding appears somewhat hopeful from the perspective of democratic theory—as it suggests soft news can at least partially level the political information playing field—some research on political attitudes casts a darker shadow on the possible effects of soft news consumption. The findings of these studies, taken together, suggest that there may be a stark difference between the effects of watching daytime soft news such as the *Oprah Winfrey Show* and those associated with watching the late-night in-character comedy shows, particularly the *Daily Show with Jon Stewart*.

For instance, Baum (2004) reports evidence from the 2000 American National Election Study that among less politically informed individuals, but not their better-informed counterparts, consuming daytime talk shows is associated with enhanced isolationism and reduced support for then-President Bill Clinton's (avowedly multilateralist) management of foreign policy. In a possibly related phenomenon, Elenbaas and De Vreese (2008) report, based on an experiment demonstrating significant possibilities for cross-cultural comparison of soft news effects, that increased exposure to soft news enhances political cynicism. Similarly, Baumgartner and Morris (2006) find that experiment-based exposure to *Daily Show* jokes about the 2000 presidential candidates led viewers to rank *both* candidates more negatively. They also found, contrary to the assertions of Brewer and Marquardt (2007), that watching this program increased subjects' cynicism about the electoral system as well as the news media.

Pease and Brewer (2008) also report experimental findings suggesting that soft news exposure enhances political cynicism. They find that while celebrity endorsements (such as Oprah Winfrey's endorsement of Barack Obama) increase participants' perceptions of candidate viability, they do not increase perceptions of likeability. In other words, celebrity endorsements were largely unpersuasive to their student participants, only causing them to expect that the endorsed candidate was more likely to win.

Overall, there is little evidence that soft news causes viewers to swing to a different side of the political spectrum or to support particular policies. Yet, a main tension in the literature on the attitudinal Oprah Effect concerns how soft news shapes perceptions of the legitimacy of political institutions. While some scholars report evidence that at least some soft news should bolster a sense of enfranchisement in and an enhanced perception of overall importance of the political system, other experimental research suggests the contrary. These studies suggest that soft news may increase cynicism toward both political leaders and institutions.

# Behavior

Finding that soft news influences political attention, knowledge, and even attitudes only takes us part of the way to linking soft news consumption to political outcomes. An additional intermediate step concerns mass political behavior—the fourth Oprah Effect. On this score, evidence is emerging that soft news may influence the political behavior of at least some citizens.

The most basic act of democratic citizenship is voting. It is here that scholars interested in locating soft news behavioral effects have concentrated the bulk of their investigations. Such research can be usefully divided into two questions. First, are soft news consumers likely to vote differently than comparable non-consumers? Second, are they likely to vote differently, contingent on showing up at the polling station?

Beginning with the former question, Baumgartner and Morris (2006) argue that exposure to soft news alienates viewers from the political process and thus depresses political participation. Prior (2007) also argues that soft news may depress voting, though he proposes a different causal mechanism. Rather than attributing reduced participation to disaffection, he points to an indirect media selection process. Prior argues that media fragmentation and the resulting proliferation of choices allows politically uninterested consumers to avoid political information altogether, in favor of pure entertainment. Consequently, he argues, these individuals have become less likely to vote over time. Conversely, people interested in politics are now better able to inform themselves than ever before. These individuals, he argues, are thus increasingly likely to vote. Because they are also more partisan and ideological, this alters the mix of voters who show up at the polls, leading to more polarized political outcomes. Though not a story directly *about* soft news, the inescapable implication is that greater access to entertainment media—presumably including soft news—depresses the political partic-ipation of otherwise inattentive individuals.

Other research has more directly measured the effects of soft news consumption on voting behavior, though it has not added to our knowledge on turnout. Cao and Brewer (2008) find that the one in four citizens who report learning about a campaign from political comedy shows were also more likely to attend a campaign event and to join a campaign-related organization. Similarly, in an experiment, Xenos and Becker (2009) find that exposure to political comedy shows on television is associated with various additional information-seeking behaviors, albeit only among highly politically engaged subjects.

Baum (2005), in turn, reports that not only do politically inattentive individuals who watch presidential candidates on daytime talk shows come away liking those candi-dates better, they also become more likely than their non-talk-show-consuming coun-terparts to cross party lines and vote for the opposition party candidate. This is because likeability can trump party loyalty among these relatively less partisan voters. As Bill Geddie, executive producer of *The View* (a daytime talk show that in 2008 featured presidential aspirants Hillary Clinton, Barack Obama, and John McCain) commented, "There have been a hundred debates, and who's seen them? Voters operate on two fronts: 'Do I like this person?' and 'Do I agree with this person?' A talk show is the first step toward helping them decide if they like a person" (quoted in Gold 2007).

Baum and Jamison (2006) extend Lau and Redlawsk's (1997) "correct voting" model and find that the same politically inattentive talk show consumers that Baum (2005) investigated are also more likely to vote for the candidate who best matches their own self-described preferences on public policy and values issues. This suggests that the likeability heuristic (Sniderman, Brody, and Tetlock 1991) can help relatively unin-formed voters figure out which candidate is likely to best represent their interests. It also suggests that the party switching identified by Baum (2005) may represent rational responses to newly gained information.

In one sense, Prior's findings seem somewhat inconsistent with those of Baum and Baum and Jamison. Unfortunately, because Prior addresses turnout while the latter studies address vote choice *contingent on turning out*, it is difficult to compare the two directly. Notwithstanding the aforementioned debate concerning soft news effects on attention and knowledge, it is possible that the proliferation of soft news might cause fewer politically inattentive individuals to vote, while still improving the reasoning process and accuracy of the vote choice among those who, despite their increased capacity to ignore politics, nonetheless continue to turn out.

# POLITICIANS' RESPONSES TO THE
# FOUR OPRAH EFFECTS

Arguably, the most crucial step for research into soft news effects on politics is determining whether and to what extent soft news—via its various effects on public opinion—ultimately influences politics and public policy. One can draw inferences from effects on attention, knowledge, attitudes, and behavior, on the one hand, to outcomes, on the other. Indeed, if a previously inattentive individual becomes attentive, gains new knowledge, and thus changes her opinions and subsequently her vote choice due to soft news consumption, then, if enough such individuals follow suit, candidate strategies, and perhaps electoral outcomes, might change too.

While research in this area is preliminary, suggestive evidence has emerged concerning soft news effects on the behavior of candidates, electoral outcomes, and even public policy initiatives. For instance, Popkin (2006) argues that the mix of policy issues salient to the public has changed since the advent of soft news, with the topics most often covered in soft news outlets—such as foreign crises, crime, scandal, and morality—growing increasingly salient among citizens and hence more prominent in the public policy agenda. Baum (2003, 2007), in turn, presents evidence that these salience effects are most pronounced among soft news consumers.

Popkin (2006) further characterizes democratic politicians as "crowd-seeking missiles" who are responsive to such changes in public priorities. He provides historical examples of politicians responding to changes in public priorities, which he argues are traceable to changes in communication technology that enhanced the political knowledge of previously marginalized citizens. Baum (2007) offers several contemporary examples in this regard. For instance, when Bush administration Secretary of State Condoleezza Rice traveled abroad, she often arranged airport photo opportunities with local celebrities. In Tokyo she posed for photographs with a popular Japanese American sumo wrestling champion; in Romania she met with Olympic legend Nadia Comaneci. These "photo ops" were intended to attract the local media, so that they would pay more attention to the Secretary's visit and, in so doing, transmit her messages to segments of the local population that might otherwise ignore her visit. One official predicted that Romanians would "go crazy" over the Secretary's meeting with Comaneci (Brinkley 2005).

A second example concerns presidential communication. In the current era of fragmented media and polarized politics, presidents can no longer rely on nationally televised prime time speeches or Sunday morning talk show appearances to communicate with the public. Instead, they must increasingly tailor their messages to the sensibilities of soft news audiences, who constitute a large pool of relatively persuadable potential voters (Baum 2005; Baum and Jamison 2006).

It is therefore unsurprising that politicians court the soft news media. For instance, in a series of pre-9/11 episodes, the *Oprah Winfrey Show* covered the plight of women in autocratic countries. Following the US invasion of Afghanistan in November 2001, President Bush—presumably with an eye toward appealing to her vast, mostly female, audience—asked Oprah Winfrey to be the US special envoy to Afghanistan for women's issues, an honor she declined.

In the run-up to the March 2003 US invasion of Iraq, in turn, the Pentagon granted coveted reporting slots "embedded" within US combat units to entertainment-oriented media outlets like MTV, *Rolling Stone*, and *People* magazine. Bryan G. Whitman, Deputy Assistant Secretary of Defense for Media Operations, explained the Pentagon's rationale: "It is a recognition that not everyone gets their news from *The Washington Post* and *The Wall Street Journal*. . . . We consciously looked at those news organizations that have reach and impact and provided them with the greatest possible opportunities. . . . Each of them [embedded reporters] reach a different audience. Our goal was to dominate the information market" (quoted in Carr 2003).

During the 2000, 2004, and 2008 primary and general presidential election campaigns, virtually all candidates appeared on daytime and late-night entertainment-oriented talk shows. Consequently, many Americans who might otherwise have largely ignored the presidential campaign encountered at least *some* information about the candidates. Perhaps presaging President Obama's September 2009 *Letterman* appearance, then-President George W. Bush and Vice-President Dick Cheney appeared on the celebrity entertainment news magazine *The Insider*. This suggests even sitting presidents are now enlisting the soft news media in their efforts to persuade Americans to support their policies.

Baum (2007) offers an anecdote from the 2005 State of the Union Address that appears to substantiate Popkin's (2006) assertion that soft news can alter the public policy agenda. In the run-up to the address, President Bush presented a major speech outlining an ambitious agenda for space exploration. The issue, however, failed to capture the public's interest. In contrast, a second pre-address "trial balloon" focusing on steroid abuse *did* capture the public's imagination. Consequently, at the last moment, the President substantially altered his address to drop any mention of space exploration in favor of condemning steroid abuse among professional athletes.

The President's focus on steroid abuse paid political dividends. The nation's sports media covered the story extensively. Taking up the President's call to arms, Congress quickly arranged a series of high-profile hearings on the subject. These hearings, involving some of the nation's most celebrated athletes, generated a feeding frenzy of media coverage. By focusing on steroids, the President reached a vast audience of sports enthusiasts who might otherwise never have heard about his address. He also generated considerable post-address attention by continuing to promote the issue, even as his allies in Congress arranged public hearings on the subject. Those hearings attracted a large nationwide audience thanks to predictable media fascination with the lifestyles (and foibles) of celebrities, including star athletes.

Some scholars interpret the aforementioned patterns as suggesting a darker side to the effects of soft news on political outcomes. For instance, there is evidence of a trend in the United States toward politicians growing increasingly responsive to wealthier, more politically sophisticated citizens, at the expense of relatively less advantaged citizens (APSA 2004; Jacobs and Skocpol 2005). Since less politically engaged citizens tend to be most attentive to soft news, this implies some limitation on politicians' responsiveness to the policy preferences of soft news consumers. In the US context, this could reflect a shift either in *responsiveness to* or in the *preferences of* typical voters. Prior (2007) favors the latter explanation, arguing that the current high media choice environment brought about by cable and the Internet has effectively shifted the preferences of the median voter toward those of more politically sophisticated citizens.

Of course, citizens' political priorities are not necessarily always driven by policy preferences. Exposure to politics via soft news might also cause consumers to focus relatively more on image- or personality-centric dimensions of candidate evaluation (Baum 2003, 2005; Druckman, Jacobs, and Ostermeier 2004). This could also help account for the aforementioned shift in representation without assuming a change in overall responsiveness by politicians.

Direct evidence of soft news influencing electoral outcomes in the United States remains elusive. However, suggestive evidence has emerged in other nations. For instance, Salmond (2007) reports that parliamentary question times with rules allowing more unstructured debate tend to attract larger and less politically sophisticated audiences than those with more highly structured rules. This is because freewheeling debates are more entertaining. By changing the audience mix, in turn, question time rules also influence who turns out on Election Day. This alters electoral outcomes. Politically inattentive voters are more likely to be working class and ideologically left-of-center. Consequently, permissive question time rules lead to increased support for labor governments.

Additional research (Taniguchi 2007; *Japan Today* 2004) suggests that soft news has influenced the political fortunes of individual candidates in Japan. For instance, former Japanese Minister of Foreign Affairs Makiko Tanaka—daughter of former Prime Minister Kakuei Tanaka—built her political constituency in significant measure through repeated appearances on soft news shows. In particular, Tanaka benefited from public exposure via Japan's so-called *Wide Shows*—Japan's analog to daytime talk shows in the United States. Taniguchi finds that *Wide Show* viewers consistently rated Tanaka more positively than viewers of traditional TV news shows or newspapers.

Taniguchi argues that the types of politicians who court soft news outlets, like former Prime Minister Junichiro Koizumi, tend to be more reform-minded. He also presents evidence that appearing on soft news increases legislators' chances of reelection.

Perhaps most importantly, Taniguchi argues that soft news changes the policy process and political outcomes in Japan. In the former case, he cites Koizumi's success in overriding strong legislative opposition to a postal reform program by reaching out to the Japanese public via appearances on *Wide Shows* and other entertainment-oriented TV programs. He argues that Japan's dominant political party, the LDP, is undergoing substantial organizational change due to the proliferation of politics into the soft news media. He further credits intensive *Wide Show* coverage of foreign policy crises—such as a diplomatic row between Japan and North Korea—with pressuring Japanese leaders to take a harder line than they would otherwise prefer.

Shirk (2007) reports evidence that similar developments are under way in China. She notes that commercialization of the media has led to more audience-appealing stories about Japan, Taiwan, and the United States. This tends to stoke popular nationalism in China, thereby complicating the government's efforts at diplomacy with those nations.

Finally, Baum (2007) notes that in Saudi Arabia the *Oprah Winfrey Show* is the nation's highest-rated English-language TV program. The show is particularly popular among young Saudi women. According to Hana Balaa, director of the TNS Female Research Center in Saudi Arabia, the popularity of *Oprah* is part of a growing trend in the region. Largely due to the availability of satellite TV, Bala notes that "Women are increasingly seeking ways to express themselves and their individuality... They're expressing their opinions more" (quoted in El-Rashidi 2005).

## Conclusion

The literature on soft news has begun to address two types of new complexity in the production and consumption of such content. First, as the market for soft news grows, the genre is becoming more diverse. In particular, the audience for late-night political comedy programs like the *Daily Show* tripled from 2001 to 2005 (Xenos and Becker 2009). A subsequent surge in content analyses and experimental studies on the potential effects of such programming suggests it may differ in key respects from other soft news programming. Holbert (2005), for instance, identifies two main contrasts between satirical political comedy and more traditional soft news. That is, political satire is *primarily* political in content, rather than incidentally so, and contains few explicit statements of political fact. In contrast, when other soft news genres report on politics they do introduce new factual information.

Since the 2008 presidential election, the satirical comedy subgenre of soft news, and the scholarly attention to it, have continued to grow. It is thus possible to lose sight of the fact that this is only one of several varieties of soft news, one with a relatively ideological and sophisticated audience and so perhaps limited possibilities for shaping the behavior of politicians. Meanwhile, the more traditional soft news outlets—lighter on political content and heavier on human interest, and aiming to entertain not by satire but by providing unchallenging fare—have continued apace, catering to consumers with relatively limited interest in politics.

What has been their effect on the political attention, knowledge, attitudes, and behavior of citizens? It seems possible that these two genres might have quite distinct effects on quite different groups of consumers, as well as on politicians' strategic behavior. For instance, traditional soft news may be of most value to politically inattentive audiences and politicians seeking to persuade them, while satiric late-night comedy shows may facilitate greater political learning and engagement among relatively sophisticated segments of the public.

In any case, as the soft news landscape grows larger and begins to cater not only to those with little interest in or attentiveness to politics but also to more politically attentive, ideological, and active citizens, it is important that scholars recognize the changing and potentially increasing power of soft news on the larger political landscape. It may ultimately become difficult to explain politicians' actions without an intimate knowledge of soft news content and the ways that consumers use it.

This highlights the *second* emerging complexity identified by the literature on soft news: the fragmentation of news audiences into ever smaller self-selected niches of news consumption. Not only is the content of soft news growing more varied, but so too are the ways that consumers get their news. Due to technological innovations and shifts in audience behavior, the organization of news consumption is increasingly personalized and subject to consumer preferences regarding what, when, and where they entertain themselves or expose themselves to politically themed news.

Some scholars (Xenos and Becker 2009) have speculated that these changes—particularly web-based delivery of news and filtering technologies consumers can use to set their own daily news menus—will preempt inattentive citizens' incidental political learning. Gone are the days of passive learning and incidental by-products, or so the logic goes. But so far the evidence for such a trend is limited at best. While changes in consumer technologies and habits may be dramatic, thus far scholars know relatively little about the effects of this fragmentation on consumers' political attentiveness, knowledge, attitudes, and behavior. Given the enormity and speed of the changes in this marketplace, as well as the potential consequences for democratic participation and the strategic landscape for politicians, this is a key area for future research.

New research on the interaction of the supply and demand sides of soft news—that is, on the ways that politicians understand and then take advantage of soft news, and in turn the ways that audiences seek or respond to the resulting content—demonstrates that soft news has become a critical arena for the playing out of the democratic process. This is taking place not only in the United States, but worldwide.

For instance, soft news may facilitate leaders' efforts to emphasize politically advantageous personal images, rather than policies (Druckman, Jacobs, and Ostermeier 2004). This may increase the extent to which, at least in some institutional contexts, politicians contest politics more along *personalistic* than *policy* dimensions (Downs 1957). Indeed, increased comparative research would lend much to the scholarly understanding of the root mechanisms at play, that is, the effects on *both* the consumers *and* the producers of soft news—politicians and media actors alike. Politicians and potential voters have limited time and energy, and although delivered with guffaws or by sleight of hand, or packaged as inconsequential entertainment, soft news can be a serious channel of communication in the fast-moving, complex, political landscapes of the present day.

# REFERENCES

APSA (AMERICAN POLITICAL SCIENCE ASSOCIATION). 2004. *America in an Age of Rising Inequality: Task Force on Inequality and American Democracy.* Washington, DC: American Political Science Association.

BAUM, M. A. 2002. Sex, Lies and War: How Soft News Brings Foreign Policy to the Inattentive Public. *American Political Science Review*, 96 (Mar.), 91–109.

——2003a. *Soft News Goes to War: Public Opinion and American Foreign Policy in the New Media Age.* Princeton: Princeton University Press.

——2003b. Soft News and Political Knowledge: Evidence of Absence or Absence of Evidence? *Political Communication*, 20 (Apr.), 173–90.

——2004. Circling the Wagons: Soft News and Isolationism in American Public Opinion. *International Studies Quarterly*, 48 (June), 313–38.

——2005. Talking the Vote: Why Presidential Candidates Hit the Talk Show Circuit. *American Journal of Political Science*, 44 (Apr.), 213–34.

——2007. Soft News and Foreign Policy: How Expanding the Audience Changes the Policies. *Japanese Journal of Political Science*, 8/1: 109–38.

——and JAMISON, A. 2006. The Oprah Effect: How Soft News Helps Inattentive Citizens Vote Consistently. *Journal of Politics*, 68: 946–59.

BAUMGARTNER, J., and MORRIS, J. 2006. The Daily Show Effect: Candidate Evaluations, Efficacy and American Youth. *American Politics Research*, 34 (May), 341–67.

BAYM, G. 2005. The *Daily Show*: Discursive Integration and the Reinvention of Political Journalism. *Political Communication*, 22 (July–Sept.), 259–76.

BENNETT, W. L. 2003. The Burglar Alarm that Just Keeps Ringing: A Response to Zaller. *Political Communication*, 20 (Apr.–June), 131–8.

BLUMLER, J. G., and McQUAIL, D. 1969. *Television in Politics.* Chicago: University of Chicago Press.

BREWER, P., and CAO, X. 2006. Candidate Appearances on Soft News Shows and Public Knowledge about Primary Campaigns. *Journal of Broadcasting & Electronic Media*, 50 (Mar.), 18–35.

——and MARQUARDT, E. 2007. Mock News and Democracy: Analyzing the *Daily Show*. *Atlantic Journal of Communication*, 15 (Nov.), 249–67.

BRINKLEY, J. 2005. The Man behind the Secretary of State's Rock Star Image. *New York Times*, Dec. 5, A3.

CAO, X., and BREWER, P. 2008. Political Comedy Shows and Public Participation in Politics. *International Journal of Public Opinion Research*, 20 (Spring), 90–9.

CARR, D. 2003. War News from MTV and *People* Magazine. *New York Times*, 27 Mar., B14.

CLAWSON, R. A., and OXLEY, Z. M. 2008. *Public Opinion: Democratic Ideals, Democratic Practice*. Washington, DC: CQ Press.

DOWNS, A. 1957. *An Economic Theory of Democracy*. New York: Harper & Row.

DRUCKMAN, J. N., JACOBS, L. R., and OSTERMEIER, E. 2004. Candidate Strategies to Prime Issues and Image. *Journal of Politics*, 66: 1205–27.

ELENBAAS, M., and DE VREESE, C. 2008. The Effects of Strategic News on Political Cynicism and Vote Choice among Young Voters. *Journal of Communication*, 58: 550–67.

EL-RASHIDI, Y. 2005. "Oprah" Is Attracting Young, Female Viewers to TV in Saudi Arabia, Dec. 1. *Wall Street Journal*, online edn. At <http://online.wsj.com/public/article/SB113339300437910675-YTXuo84JPhOwH2DogtmFGhityiM_20061130.html?mod=blogs>. Accessed Oct. 19, 2010.

FITZSIMMONS, S. J., and OSBURN, H. G. 1968. The Impact of Social Issues and Public Affairs Television Documentaries. *Public Opinion Quarterly*, 32 (Autumn), 379–97.

GOLD, M. 2007. Candidates Embrace the Chat: Daytime Gabfests and Latenight Comedy TV Become Essential Stops on the Presidential Trail to Reach "Regular Folks." *New York Times*, Sept. 29.

HOLBERT, R. L. 2005. A Typology for the Study of Entertainment Television and Politics. *American Behavioral Scientist*, 49 (Nov.), 436–53.

HOLLANDER, B. 2005. Late-Night Learning: Do Entertainment Programs Increase Political Campaign Knowledge for Young Viewers? *Journal of Broadcasting & Electronic Media*, 49 (Dec.), 402–15.

JACOBS, L. R., and SKOCPOL, T. (eds.) 2005. *Inequality and American Democracy: What We Know and What We Need to Learn*. New York: Russell Sage Foundation Press.

*Japan Today*. 2004. Tanaka and the Dumbing Down of Japanese Politics. *Japan Today*, online edn., May 29. At <http://japantoday.com/e/?content=kuchikomi&id=174>. Accessed Apr. 14, 2005; no longer available.

JONES, A. 2009. *Losing the News*. Oxford: Oxford University Press.

KRUGMAN, H. E., and HARTLEY, E. L. 1970. Passive Learning from Television. *Public Opinion Quarterly*, 34 (Summer), 184–90.

LAU, R., and REDLAWSK, D. 1997. Voting Correctly. *American Political Science Review*, 91 (Sept.), 585–98.

LODGE, M., STEENBERGEN, M., and BRAU, S. 1995. The Responsive Voter: Campaign Information and the Dynamics of Candidate Evaluation. *American Political Science Review*, 89 (June), 309–26.

MCGRAW, K. M., and LODGE, M. 1995. Information Processing Approaches to the Study of Political Judgment. In *Political Judgment: Structure and Process*, ed. M. Lodge and K. M. McGraw. Ann Arbor: University of Michigan Press.

MOY, P., XENOS, M. A., and HESS, V. K. 2005. Communication and Citizenship: Mapping the Political Effects of Infotainment. *Mass Communication and Society*, 8 (May), 111–31.

PARKIN, M. 2010. Taking Late Night Comedy Seriously: How Candidate Appearances on Late Night Television Can Engage Viewers. *Political Research Quarterly*, 63/1: 3–15.

PATTERSON, T. 1994. *Out of Order*. New York: Vintage.

——2000. *Doing Well and Doing Good*. Research Report. Cambridge, MA: Joan Shorenstein Center on the Press, Politics and Public Policy, Harvard University.

PEASE, A., and BREWER, P. 2008. The Oprah Factor: The Effects of a Celebrity Endorsement in a Presidential Primary Campaign. *International Journal of Press/Politics*, 13 (Oct.), 386–400.

PFAU, M. J., HOUSTON, B., and SEMMLER, S. M. 2006. *Mediating the Vote: The Changing Media Landscape in U.S. Presidential Elections*. Boulder, CO: Rowman & Littlefield.

POPKIN, S. 1993. *The Reasoning Voter*. Chicago: University of Chicago Press.

——2006. Changing Media, Changing Politics. *Perspectives on Politics*, 4: 327–41.

PRIOR, M. 2003. Any Good News in Soft News? The Impact of Soft News Preference on Political Knowledge. *Political Communication*, 20 (Apr.–June), 149–71.

——2005. News vs. Entertainment: How Increasing Media Choice Widens Gaps in Political Knowledge and Turnout. *American Journal of Political Science*, 49 (May), 577–92.

——2007. *Post-Broadcast Democracy: How Media Choice Increases Inequality in Political Involvement and Polarizes Elections*. Cambridge: Cambridge University Press.

ROBINSON, M. 1974. The Impact of the Televised Watergate Hearings. *Journal of Communication*, 24: 17–30.

SALMOND, R. 2007. Parliamentary Question Times: How Legislative Accountability Mechanisms Affect Citizens and Politics. Dissertation, Department of Political Science, University of California, Los Angeles.

SHIRK, S. 2007. Changing Media, Changing Foreign Policy in China. *Japanese Journal of Political Science*, 8 (Apr.), 43–70.

SNIDERMAN, P. M., BRODY, R. A., and TETLOCK, P. E. 1991. *Reasoning and Choice: Explorations in Political Psychology*. New York: Cambridge University Press.

TANIGUCHI, M. 2007. Changing Media, Changing Politics in Japan. *Japanese Journal of Political Science*, 8 (Apr.), 147–66.

TUCHMAN, G. 1973. Making News by Doing Work: Routinizing the Unexpected. *American Journal of Sociology*, 79: 110–31.

VAN ZOONEN, L., MULLER, F., ALINEJAD, D., DEKKER, M., DUITS, L., VAN ROMONDT, P., and WITTENBERG, W. 2007. Dr. Phil Meets the Candidates: How Family Life and Personal Experience Produce Political Discussions. *Critical Studies in Mass Communication*, 24 (Oct.), 322–38.

WAMSLEY, G. L., and PRIDE, R. A. 1972. Television Network News: Re-Thinking the Iceberg Problem. *Western Political Quarterly*, 25 (Sept.), 434–50.

XENOS, M., and BECKER, A. 2009. Moments of Zen: Effects of the *Daily Show* on Information Seeking. *Political Communication*, 26 (July), 317–32.

YOUNG, D. G. 2004. *Daily Show Viewers Knowledgeable about Presidential Campaign, National Annenberg Election Survey Shows*. Issue paper. Philadelphia: Annenberg Public Policy Center.

——and TISINGER, R. M. 2006. Dispelling Late-Night Myths: News Consumption among Late-Night Comedy Viewers and the Predictors of Exposure to Various Late-Night Shows. *Harvard International Journal of Press/Politics*, 11 (Summer), 113–34.

ZALLER, J. 1992. *The Nature and Origins of Mass Opinion*. New York: Cambridge University Press.

——2003. A New Standard of News Quality: Burglar Alarms for the Monitorial Citizen. *Political Communication*, 20 (Apr.–June), 109–30.

ZUKIN, C., and SNYDER, R. 1984. Passive Learning: When the Media Environment Is the Message. *Public Opinion Quarterly*, 48 (Autumn), 629–38.

# SECTION TWO: MEASUREMENT AND METHOD

# CHAPTER 9

EXPOSURE MEASURES AND
CONTENT ANALYSIS IN
MEDIA EFFECTS STUDIES

JENNIFER JERIT
JASON BARABAS

SCHOLARS typically study media effects in one of two ways. First, there is the individual-level approach, in which the researcher relies on media "exposure" or "usage" measures in public opinion surveys. Second, there is the environmental-level approach, which involves measuring media content and possibly even includes media data as a predictor in empirical models. Because the first method is more common, many studies purporting to study media effects do not actually include explicit measures of the media. While this state of affairs may seem unusual, analyzing media content is not straightforward, especially when it comes to integrating media messages and public opinion survey data. In this chapter we consider how media exposure has been studied, focusing on criticisms of media use measures and the main alternative to this approach: incorporating media content in the empirical analyses of public opinion data. We conclude with a discussion of some of the practical considerations regarding content analysis as well as the analytical challenges associated with estimating the causal effects of media messages on public opinion.

## MEDIA EXPOSURE MEASURES

Researchers employ media exposure variables to capture the extent to which individuals encounter or are influenced by messages appearing in outlets such as television, newspapers, radio, and the Internet. While the evidence for direct persuasion effects may be hard to find (Berelson, Lazarsfeld, and McPhee 1954; Katz and Lazarsfeld 1955), information carried in the mass media can have a powerful effect on opinions by influencing the ideas that are foremost in a person's mind as they make political judgments (for example, Iyengar and Kinder 1987; Krosnick and Kinder 1990; Zaller 1992). Likewise, features of media coverage such as the amount, breadth, and prominence of news stories are related to levels of political knowledge (for example, Barabas and Jerit 2009).

One of the most common ways to document the effect of the mass media is with a "media use" question, which asks respondents to categorize their news acquisition behavior. For example, the 2008 American National Election Study (ANES) asked respondents, "During a typical week, how many days do you watch news on TV, not including sports?" There were eight answer choices, from zero to seven days. The same question was asked about newspapers, radio, and the Internet. In the 2008 ANES, on average, respondents report watching television news 4.89 days per week. Other activities, such as reading a newspaper, listening to the radio, or obtaining news from the Internet, are more infrequent, taking place about two and a half days a week.[1] Despite the explosive growth of the Internet, television remains the most common form of media exposure, a pattern that has been reported in many commercial polls (for example, Pew Research Center for the People & the Press News Savvy Poll, February 2007).

## Critiques of the Exposure Measure

Given the challenge of identifying media effects (Bartels 1993; Zaller 1996), the intellectual community has subjected media use questions to extensive examination over the past several decades. One of the first such attempts occurred in the late 1990s when Vincent Price and John Zaller explored the ANES media use measures (Price and Zaller 1990, 1993). More recently, Althaus and Tewksbury (2007) examined a variety of different media exposure measures and summarized their findings in a detailed report to the ANES Board of Overseers.

Based on an extensive series of analyses, Althaus and Tewksbury urged the ANES Board of Overseers to (1) continue the use of self-reported media exposure questions along with questions that measure political knowledge since each has unique effects; (2) employ media exposure items pertaining to newspapers, television, radio, and news sources on the Internet; (3) standardize the measures of exposure to each of the four news media as days in a typical week; and (4) include a measure of political discussion formatted to match the days per week scale. In addition, Althaus and Tewksbury advocate adding a new media exposure question that asks respondents to identify

---

[1] We calculated survey averages using the sampling weights provided by the ANES. For details on the administration of the ANES, see <http://www.electionstudies.org>.

where they have been getting most of their information about the presidential campaign.

After the publication of the Althaus and Tewksbury report, other scholars were invited to comment on their recommendations. While most of the commentators support the continued use of the media exposure measures, they raised a number of important substantive and methodological issues. For example, some scholars question whether the traditional ANES exposure measures will hold up across generations, especially as media content is delivered via cellphones, portable electronic devices, or even smart automobiles that may escape standard categorizations (Shapiro 2008). Others believe that it is essential to combine media use questions with measures of media attention in order to get at the differential effects of motivation and opportunity (Eveland, Hively, and Shen 2008).[2] Even within a single medium such as television there are numerous programs that provide political information, each varying by content and audience (Fowler, Goldstein, and Shah 2008). Accordingly, adapting the traditional media use questions to allow for some differentiation of television programs might be necessary. Lumping together viewership across programs without distinguishing who watches what and how often may introduce measurement error into studies that seek to determine the effects of television viewing (Fowler, Goldstein, Hale, and Kaplan 2007).[3]

Finally, Barabas (2008) identified several challenges with using individual-level measures of media exposure. He highlighted the following issues:

*Social desirability.* When answering media use questions, respondents may overreport their media usage, thinking that this is the socially desirable answer. Americans overreport other behaviors, such as voting (Burden 2000; Karp and Brockington 2005) and church attendance (Hadaway, Marler, and Chaves 1998; Presser and Stinson 1998). Although Althaus and Tewksbury find no evidence of social desirability bias in the ANES exposure measures (2007, 16), other studies conclude that overreporting takes place. For example, Prior (2009a) compared survey estimates of evening network news usage to Nielsen estimates, which are based on automated recordings of usage, and found evidence of considerable overreporting (also see Bechtel, Achepohl, and Akers 1972; Prior 2009b; Robinson 1985).

*Selection bias.* Self-reported media exposure in cross-sectional surveys like the ANES is not randomly assigned. Thus, patterns attributed to media exposure could instead be due to underlying differences between those who opt to use one medium versus another. Although analysts often include demographic variables to control for some of these differences, it is difficult to eliminate selection threats. As a result,

---

[2] This might entail asking people how much attention they pay to particular types of news (e.g., "How much attention do you pay to news on national news shows about the campaign for president—a great deal, quite a bit, some, very little, or none?").

[3] Here, scholars have had some success with an alternative format that asks respondents to state which particular source they use to get information about politics (Barabas and Jerit 2010; also see Freedman, Franz, and Goldstein 2004 for an innovative approach to measuring exposure).

associations between media exposure and other outcome measures may be due to differences in sample composition or omitted factors that predict both exposure and the dependent variable.

*Reverse causality.* Employing a media usage term as a predictor in a regression equation does not necessarily mean that it is a causal variable. Knowledge, or whatever outcome one is trying to explain, could be influencing media usage. In fact, two-way, or reciprocal, causation is even a possibility (Eveland, Shah, and Kwak 2003). While recent studies have reported evidence of a unidirectional relationship between media use and political knowledge (Eveland, Hayes, Shah, and Kwak 2005), endogeneity is a long-standing concern in media studies (for example, Mondak 1995). In general, it can be challenging to estimate the causal effects of media coverage in cross-sectional studies (but see Barabas and Jerit 2009 for one approach).

The preceding issues represent inferential threats, particularly from the standpoints of construct validity and internal validity (Shadish, Cook, and Campbell 2002). Media exposure items in cross-sectional surveys also may face problems related to statistical conclusion validity. That is, studies that seek to document media effects (via the typical media use measures) may suffer from low statistical power. Simulations with known media effects have revealed that power often is too low to recover statistically significant effects with typical sample sizes (e.g., $n = 1,000$ to 1,500; see Zaller 2002). Thus, documenting meaningful media effects—even when they really exist—can be difficult in the public opinion polls that researchers often employ.

## Exposure Alternatives

In light of these potential problems, some scholars resort to experiments in which media content is delivered randomly to treatment and control groups. There is a long tradition of studying media effects via randomized experiments and we do not intend to survey that literature here (for exemplars, see Iyengar and Kinder 1987; Iyengar 1991; Neuman, Just, and Crigler 1992). Compared with scholars who rely on the media use measure, experimenters are on firmer ground when it comes to asserting the causal effect of a media treatment. However, critics often question the external validity of experiments. Such critiques focus on the convenience samples that are used in many experiments (for example, Sears 1986) or on the possibility that the experimental setting might exaggerate the impact of the stimulus (for example, Kinder 2007). The second point is particularly relevant to researchers interested in media effects, as the complex nature of the information environment can be difficult to capture in a randomized experiment (see Barabas and Jerit 2010 for discussion).

As another alternative to self-reported media exposure, many scholars use political awareness, which is measured by asking people factual questions about politics (Price and Zaller 1993; Zaller 1992). Typically, such questions ask about civic facts (e.g., the percentage required to overturn a veto), the assumption being that "[people] who are knowledgeable about politics in general are habitually attentive to communications on most particular issues as well" (Zaller 1992, 43). Across a number of different analyses, Zaller (1992) demonstrates that individuals with high levels of political awareness internalize more information from the mass media (e.g., in the form of considerations) than people with low levels of awareness. In a related, and widely cited, study Price and Zaller (1993) show that when it comes to explaining news recall, political awareness outperforms self-reported media exposure and other measures (e.g., education).[4]

# INCLUDING THE MEDIA IN STUDIES
# OF MEDIA EFFECTS

The fundamental limitation of the individual-level approach to studying media effects is that it says little about the precise elements of media coverage that affect public opinion. Even if we could "correct" some of the problems identified earlier, such as measurement error (Bartels 1993), we still would not know what it is about media coverage that affects the mass public. In many cases simply knowing that someone used a particular style of media such as print or television is not enough; the researcher's theory necessitates knowing something about media content (e.g., what kind of information was provided?)

Typically, scholars have taken one of two approaches when it comes to using media data in studies of media effects. With the first approach, data from a media content analysis complements, but does not directly factor into, the analysis of public opinion. For example, in studies of political knowledge, information from media content analyses may be used to inform the researcher's expectations regarding learning patterns (for example, Druckman 2005; Graber 1988; Patterson and McClure 1976). Other researchers have adopted this same basic approach in studies of attitudes and candidate evaluations (for example, Althaus 2003; Druckman and Parkin 2005; Gilens 1999).

The other method of studying media effects is to incorporate media data *directly* in the analysis as a variable. This approach involves merging media content with public opinion data and treating the media variables as predictors. Oftentimes, this is done in analyses of aggregate opinion (for example, Althaus and Kim 2006; Barabas and Jerit 2009; Duch, Palmer, and Anderson 2000; Holbrook and Garand 1996; Jerit 2008; Simon and Jerit 2007). It also is possible to include media variables in individual-level studies of public opinion (for example, Barabas and Jerit 2009; Dalton, Beck, and Huckfeldt 1998; Jerit and Barabas 2006; Jerit, Barabas, and Bolsen 2006; Kahn and Kenny 2002; Price and Czilli 1996). There are important analytical issues to consider when media

---

[4] As a proxy for political awareness, some analysts employ interviewer ratings of the respondent's level of political knowledge (but see Martin and Johnson forthcoming for a critique of this practice).

variables appear alongside of individual-level predictors. We discuss these issues in greater detail later.

The key point is that in both situations, the central concept of interest—information from the mass media—is incorporated in the empirical analysis either directly or indirectly. There is much to recommend with either of these approaches and both offer advantages over media use variables. In the rest of this chapter, we address some of the practical considerations that come into play when a researcher seeks to incorporate media data into studies of media effects.

# Online Media Databases

Assuming investigators want to include media content in a media effects study, a natural question becomes what source to use. To date, most scholars rely on online archives to identify and collect the texts they will later analyze.[5] For researchers interested in documenting media effects, the two most popular archives are LexisNexis Academic Universe and the Vanderbilt Television News Archive, though many other sources have become available in recent years (e.g., NewsBank, ProQuest). As discussed below, a number of important issues arise with the use of online archives, all potentially affecting the quality of one's data.[6]

## *Choosing a Source*

The first and perhaps most obvious consideration when using an archive that contains hundreds of sources is choosing a source(s) to content-analyze. There is some evidence that different newspapers cover the same topic differently (Woolley 2000), but there has been little sustained empirical analysis of the matter. Consequently, the common practice is to use a single source such as the *New York Times* or the Associated Press on the grounds that it leads the coverage in other outlets and/or provides the raw material for stories and broadcasts appearing around the country (for example, Jerit 2008; Simon and Jerit 2007).

Like many of the issues that will be raised in this section, the choice of source depends on the goals of a study. If the purpose is to capture general trends in news coverage, relying on a news "leader" might make sense. For example, in a study that examines media coverage of recent political developments, Barabas and Jerit (2009) report similar results regardless of whether they operationalized media coverage with story counts from the Associated Press or from specific broadcast and print sources

---

[5] Some have voiced concern that online databases differ from the published record (for example, Snider and Janda 1998; Woolley 2000). Nevertheless, most scholars continue using electronic news archives rather than coding the actual stories (but see Page 1996, who employs both methods).

[6] Our discussion assumes that researchers intend to analyze the full text versions of a story rather than relying on indices or other proxy measures (see Althaus, Edy, and Phalen 2001 for a treatment of that topic).

(*CBS Evening News, USA Today*). In contrast, in an earlier study, Jerit, Barabas, and Bolsen (2006) hypothesized that the type of outlet mattered for the phenomenon they were studying (the "knowledge gap" between individuals with low and high levels of socioeconomic status). Consistent with their expectations, they found that higher levels of newspaper coverage exacerbated the knowledge gap between low and high socio-economic groups. Increases in the amount of television coverage had no effect on the knowledge gap.

Depending on one's research question, then, it may be appropriate to use a small number of sources (or even a single source) as an indicator of the larger information environment. Even in this situation, however, it is useful to demonstrate that the results hold when other sources are interchanged for the proxy measure (for example, Simon and Jerit 2007).

## Identifying Stories

Once a researcher has settled upon a source or sources, he or she has to come up with a method for identifying news stories on their topic. Typically, this is done through a keyword search, but that simple description belies the challenge of identifying appro-priate keywords. On the one hand, if keywords are too general, the search may turn up thousands of "hits," many of which are only tangentially related to the topic at hand. On the other hand, keywords that are overly specific may generate too few hits, causing the researcher to miss wide swaths of media coverage. Even after one settles upon an appropriate level of generality, slight changes in the choice of keywords can result in dramatically different search results. In light of these challenges, an iterative approach to keyword selection often works best. The procedures described by Chong and Druckman (2010) should serve as a model for other researchers. For each of the issues in their study, they settled upon an optimal set of keywords by "experimenting with alternative word combinations and locations (e.g., in the headline or lead paragraph of the article) and reading a sample of articles generated by each combination to ensure that all major articles were captured" (Chong and Druckman 2010, 18; also see Jacobs and Shapiro 2000, app. 3).

## What are You Counting and Over What Period of Time?

Decisions regarding the unit of analysis and the time period for a content analysis are important matters that must be guided by theory. Whether one is coding entire stories, individual paragraphs, or some smaller unit, like a sentence, is a decision that must flow from one's research question and theoretical argument. For example, in her analysis of the 1993–4 health care reform debate, Jerit (2008) used weekly measures of rhetoric based on a content analysis of the Associated Press. The weekly unit of analysis allowed her to examine the give and take between opposing political elites, which was essential for evaluating the hypotheses of her study. In other cases, the researcher may be interested in looking at trends in media coverage over a longer period of time, in which case monthly or even yearly data may make more sense (for example, Jacobs and Shapiro 2000).[7]

In addition to the unit of analysis, researchers also must specify a time period for their content analysis. For example, Jerit, Barabas, and Bolsen (2006) examine media coverage over the six-week period preceding a public opinion survey. This particular time frame was chosen to correspond with the wording of the knowledge questions they were examining. These items asked people about recent political developments (e.g., events that had occurred in the "past month" or "past month or so"). At a more general level, choices about the time period of a content analysis entail assumptions about information processing and, in particular, human memory.

As the preceding discussion suggests, the ease and availability of online archives belie the complexity of issues that surrounds their use. There also are limits to the kind of information one can obtain from online archives. As we will discuss in more detail below, information about images is absent from the transcripts of most electronic archives. Additionally, other important details (e.g., did an article appear "above the fold"?) are not apparent from the transcripts in LexisNexis and similar online archives. As a result, stories obtained from these sources are an imperfect representation of the information to which people are exposed. Given that the rationale for combining media content analysis with survey data often has to do with analyzing realistic media treatments, it is important that scholars keep this potential limitation in mind.

## Human versus Computer-Based Coding

After identifying a body of text to be coded, the researcher must decide whether he or she will do manual or machine-based coding. The manual approach involves trained human coders analyzing the textual elements of a news story. Although this has been the most common way of conducting content analysis (Graber 2004), the explosion in content analysis software programs has encouraged an increasing number of scholars to try computer-based coding (for examples, see Fan 1988; Nadeau, Niemi, Fan, and Amato 1999; or Shah, Watts, Domke, and Fan 2002). Today, it is possible to automate many of the tasks previously assigned to human coders, including simple story counts as well as comparisons of entire texts to identify their similarities and differences. Many programs can even detect textual themes as well as specific words and strings of words (Graber 2004, 53).

In order for scholars to take advantage of computer-based coding, however, the text must be in computer-readable format. Now that many news stories, speeches, and other political texts are archived electronically, this requirement is not as onerous as it once was. But machine-based coding still involves some work on the part of the analyst.

---

[7] Regardless of what the researcher is counting, intercoder reliability checks should be done at the unit of analysis. Intercoder reliability analysis is a topic that could easily fill an entire chapter on its own; we refer interested readers to Neuendorf (2001) and Krippendorf (2003).

To the extent that one is interested in something beyond a simple count of stories, it is necessary to specify what the software program is looking for, whether that be a word, phrase, or frame.

For example, Kellstedt (2000, 2003) tracks the use of two media frames—individualism and egalitarianism—in the mass media. In order to do that, he created a dictionary of words and phrases that indicated the presence of each of these broad, thematic frames. Next, a content analysis software program examined the presence of these words and phrases in thousands of *Newsweek* and *New York Times* articles over a forty-year period (see Shah, Watts, Domke, and Fan 2002 for another example). As the previous example makes clear, dictionary-based coding makes it possible to analyze large amounts of political text. But as scholars have observed, computerized coding does not dispense with the need for human input, given the start-up costs involved in developing and testing a coding dictionary. Thus, dictionary-based computerized coding is to some extent theory-driven, based on a priori expectations of what concepts are relevant and how they fit together. Increasingly, researchers are developing ways to let the text speak for itself (Laver, Benoit, and Garry 2003; Quinn et al. 2010; Simon and Xenos 2004).

In many instances, the research question demands that the researcher make a qualitative judgment about a news story or political text, such as the extent to which it emphasizes political strategy over substance (for example, Jacobs and Shapiro 2000; Lawrence 2000), or whether facts are accompanied by contextual information (Jerit 2009; Neuman, Just, and Crigler 1992). In this situation, human coding often is preferred because the coding task involves some sort of *interpretive* judgment about a political text.

Consider a recent study by Chong and Druckman (2010) that examines how various political issues were framed in the mass media over differing time periods. Chong and Druckman used human coders to identify the presence or absence of a frame, as well as the frame's position (pro or con) relative to the issue, the incidence of a refuting argument or frame in the same article, the reference to statistical or numerical data, and episodic evidence pertaining to individual cases or experiences. It is hard to envision how one would direct a computer or piece of software to make such fine-grained judgments. Thus, the primary advantages of manual coding, and the reason why many researchers continue to use this approach, are its greater flexibility and the rich data that human coding generates. To the extent that a researcher is interested in how some feature of news reporting affects audiences (say, the tone of a story or the effect of a facial display), there may be few alternatives to human coding.

Having said that, manual coding comes with some disadvantages. The most obvious is the tremendous cost in terms of time (and ultimately money) that it takes to train human coders. Regardless of how well trained or experienced a coder may be, it is essential to demonstrate the reliability of one's data, which will necessarily involve some redundancies in coding (and further increases in the time-cost of the coding effort). All of this means that researchers who choose the manual approach probably cannot undertake coding projects of the same magnitude as those relying on computer-based programs.

## Going beyond Volume

Many content analyses use counts, such as the number of stories over a particular time period. Aside from the topics raised in the previous section, there are some concerns specific to frequency-based content analyses. For example, Woolley (2000) describes the necessity of "deflating" counts when one uses an index such as *The Readers' Guide to Periodical Literature* over long periods of time because counts in one era may not mean the same thing in another. More generally, researchers should place information about story counts in context, either by noting the presence of other important events (for example, Barabas and Jerit 2010; Jerit and Barabas 2006) or by examining the volume of coverage relative to some other benchmark, such as the top story of the year (Woolley 2000).

As the title of this subsection suggests, there is a growing appreciation that public opinion scholars need to look beyond the frequency of a message and to consider other aspects of news coverage. For example, Althaus and Kim (2006) show that the content and tone of news stories moderate priming effects. Work by Chong and Druckman (2007) indicates that the strength of a frame may be just as important as its prevalence in real-world political debate. More generally, the recognition that people face complex information environments (for example, Althaus and Kim 2006; Chong and Druckman 2007; Sniderman and Theriault 2004) means that scholars will continue to conduct fine-grained analyses of media coverage. This in turn ensures that human coding will persist even as automated coding programs become more widespread.

## New Frontiers of Content Analysis

Given the rate at which computer-based content analysis software programs and online archives are proliferating, the field of content analysis is likely to change rapidly over the coming years. Here we highlight two issues that will be important for the next wave of researchers seeking to do content analysis: the necessity of incorporating audiovisual information in media content analyses, and methods for content-analyzing "new" or hard-to-obtain sources such as webpages, blogs, and radio programs.

### Audiovisual Content

The analysis of audiovisual content has not kept pace with the importance of visual information in televised and print news stories (but see Graber 2001 or Grabe and Bucy 2009 for exceptions). Television is a case in point. Despite the importance of TV as a source of political information, scholars have analyzed this medium mainly in terms of its *verbal* content—that is, through analysis of the spoken word (but see Sulkin and

Swigger 2008 for an analysis of campaign ad visuals). The same charge can be leveled against the analysis of print sources (e.g., newspapers, news magazines), though the visual component of a print source is by definition a more minor element of the story. Even though an increasing amount of information is conveyed through visuals, content analysis of images and audiovisuals is seldom undertaken.

This bias in research practices is troubling. Scholars have shown that the visuals that accompany news stories may reinforce or contradict the text (Messaris and Abraham 2001). Thus, when researchers ignore the visual component of the news, they may mischaracterize the message that people take away from the information environment. Consequently, much of what we "know" about public opinion may be subject to change once we take into account the role of visual information (Grabe and Bucy 2009). This point relates to the second topic we wish to highlight: how to find information about new media or hard-to-find sources.

### New and Hard-to-Find Sources

It can be challenging to content-analyze particular sources such as Internet webpages, blogs, and many radio shows because the coverage of these sources in online archives is not as extensive as it is for print and broadcast outlets. Moreover, in the case of the Internet, the appearance of websites changes throughout the day, making it difficult to characterize the content on these pages even with Internet-capturing technology such as the Wayback Machine.[8]

This situation poses a significant challenge to anyone seeking to content-analyze such sources (though see Hopkins and King's (2010) mixed hand-computer approach to coding blogs). We suspect it will only be a matter of time before there is an equivalent to LexisNexis for the Internet. Until then, however, researchers are at the mercy of news websites, some of which have extensive archiving systems and others that do not. This state of affairs makes it difficult to follow an earlier recommendation about using detailed media use questions; e.g., asking people about the particular source they use.[9] In our experience, respondents sometimes name Internet sites or radio stations that are difficult to find.

## Analytical Challenges

When researchers combine media content with individual-level public opinion data, they usually treat the media data as a proxy for the larger information environment that respondents were exposed to in the weeks (or months) before they entered an opinion poll. But this can present difficulties for assessing the causal impact of media coverage on public opinion. First, by including media data (e.g., story counts) as variables in one's analyses of individual-level data, the researcher is effectively

---

[8] <http://www.archive.org/web/web.php>. Accessed Feb. 8, 2010.
[9] See n. 3.

assuming that survey respondents were exposed to that information. Naturally, what-ever media effects exist should be strongest among the subset of the sample that was exposed to such information. Here, any of the previously mentioned indicators of media exposure (self-reported media use, political awareness, and education) may be useful in helping researchers to identify media effects (for example, Barabas and Jerit 2010).

The second complication that arises from combining media data with opinion polls is the resulting "clustering" that occurs in one's data (with individuals from the same survey "nested" in whatever information environment preceded the survey). In this situation the researcher effectively has data at two levels. The first is the level of the individual survey respondent; the second corresponds to the information environment preceding the survey. Because individuals in any given survey confront similar infor-mation environments, there are statistical dependencies in the resulting data set. This is a problem in so far as most statistical models assume that one observation is unrelated to another (Steenbergen and Jones 2002). In these situations "multilevel" or "hierarchical" models may be necessary (Raudenbush and Bryk 2002).

Finally, no discussion of analytical challenges would be complete without mention-ing statistical power. When researchers combine media content and public opinion surveys, there may be thousands of survey respondents in the resulting data set, but the effective $n$ is actually much lower (it is equivalent to the number of "media environ-ments"; see Stoker and Bowers 2002). Complicating the issue further, researchers often are interested in how particular subgroups respond to media messages. But answering this question necessitates statistical interaction terms (Kam and Franzese 2007) and thus splits the individual-level data into increasingly smaller groups—both of which reduce statistical power (Zaller 2002).

# Conclusion

Researchers tend to study media effects in one of two ways: using an individual-level measure of media exposure or linking media content with public opinion data. Each approach helps one understand the effect of the mass media. Like any method, however, each comes with distinctive strengths and weaknesses. We have tried to highlight some of the key issues that scholars might consider in this regard. Yet the continually evolving media environment—in particular, the increased availability of news sources as well as the ease with which people can select their information source—presents challenges for anyone seeking to understand the nature of media effects (Bennett and Iyengar 2008). We can only hope that these changes in the media landscape will inspire researchers to find new and better ways of identifying the causal impact of the mass media on public opinion.

# References

ALTHAUS, S. L. 2003. *Collective Preferences in Democratic Politics: Opinion Surveys and the Will of the People*. Cambridge: Cambridge University Press.

—— and KIM, Y. M. 2006. Priming Effects in Complex Information Environments: Reassessing the Impact of News Discourse on Presidential Approval. *Journal of Politics*, 68: 960–76.

—— and TEWKSBURY, D. H. 2007. Toward a New Generation of Media Use Measures for the ANES. American National Election Studies Pilot Study Report, No. neso11903. Unpublished.

—— EDY, J. A., and PHELAN, P. F. 2001. Using Substitutes for Full-Text News Stories in Content Analysis: Which Text Is Best? *American Journal of Political Science*, 45 (July), 707–24.

BARABAS, J. 2008. Measuring Media Exposure in the 2006 ANES Pilot Study and Beyond. In *Commentary on Media Measures for the ANES Sponsored by the Political Communications Sections of the International Communication Association and the American Political Science Association*. Political Communication Report 18/1. At <http://www.jour.unr.edu/pcr/1801_2008_winter/roundtable_barabas.html>. Accessed Oct. 16, 2010.

—— and JERIT, J. 2009. Estimating the Causal Effect of Media Coverage on Policy-Specific Knowledge. *American Journal of Political Science*, 53 (Jan.), 73–89.

—— —— 2010. Are Survey Experiments Externally Valid? *American Political Science Review*, 104 (May), 226–42.

BARTELS, L. M. 1993. Messages Received: The Political Impact of Media Exposure. *American Political Science Review*, 87 (June), 267–85.

BECHTEL, R., ACHEPOHL, C., and AKERS, R. 1972. Correlates between Observed Behavior and Questionnaire Responses in Television Viewing. In *Television and Social Behavior*, iv: *Television in Day-to-Day Life*, ed. E. A. Rubinstein, G. A. Comstock, and J. P. Murray. Washington, DC: US Government Printing Office.

BENNETT, W. L., and IYENGAR, S. 2008. A New Era of Minimal Effects? The Changing Foundations of Political Communication. *Journal of Communication*, 58: 707–31.

BERELSON, B. R., LAZARSFELD, P. F., and McPHEE, W. N. 1954. *Voting: A Study of Opinion Formation in a Presidential Campaign*. Chicago: University of Chicago Press.

BURDEN, B. 2000. Voter Turnout and the National Election Studies. *Political Analysis*, 8 (Autumn), 389–98.

CHONG, D., and DRUCKMAN, J. N. 2007. Framing Public Opinion in Competitive Democracies. *American Political Science Review*, 101 (Nov.), 637–56.

—— —— 2010. Identifying Frames in Political News. In *Sourcebook for Political Communication Research: Methods, Measures, and Analytical Techniques*, ed. E. P. Bucy and R. L. Holbert. Florence, KY: Routledge.

DALTON, R. J., BECK, P. A., and HUCKFELDT, R. 1998. Partisan Cues and the Media: Information Flows in the 1992 Presidential Election. *American Political Science Review*, 92 (Mar.), 111–26.

DRUCKMAN, J. N. 2005. Media Matter: How Newspapers and Television News Cover Campaigns and Influence. *Political Communication*, 22: 463–81.

—— and PARKIN, M. 2005. The Impact of Media Bias: How Editorial Slant Affects Voters. *Journal of Politics*, 67: 1030–49.

DUCH, R. M., PALMER, H. D., and ANDERSON, C. J. 2000. Heterogeneity in Perceptions of National Economic Conditions. *American Journal of Political Science*, 44 (Oct.), 635–52.

EVELAND, W. P., JR., HAYES, A. F., SHAH, D. V., and KWAK, N. 2005. Understanding the Relationship between Communication and Political Knowledge: A Model Comparison Approach Using Panel Data. *Political Communication*, 22: 423–46.

——HIVELY, M. H., and SHEN, F. 2008. Extending Validation Efforts to the Concept of Media Use. In *Commentary on Media Measures for the ANES Sponsored by the Political Communications Sections of the International Communication Association and the American Political Science Association*. Political Communication Report 18/1. At <http://www.jour.unr.edu/pcr/1801_2008_winter/roundtable_eveland.html>. Accessed Oct. 16, 2010.

——SHAH, D. V., and KWAK, N. 2003. Assessing Causality in the Cognitive Mediation Model: A Panel Study of Motivations, Information Processing, and Learning during Campaign 2000. *Communication Research*, 30 (Aug.), 359–86.

FAN, D. P. 1988. *Predictions of Public Opinion from the Mass Media: Computer Content Analysis and Mathematical Modeling*. New York: Greenwood.

FOWLER, E. F., GOLDSTEIN, K. M., HALE, M., and KAPLAN, M. 2007. Does Local News Measure Up? *Stanford Law and Policy Review*, 18/2: 410–31.

————and SHAH, D. 2008. The Challenge of Measuring News Consumption. In *Commentary on Media Measures for the ANES Sponsored by the Political Communications Sections of the International Communication Association and the American Political Science Association*. Political Communication Report 18/1. At <http://www.jour.unr.edu/pcr/1801_2008_winter/roundtable_fowler.html>. Accessed Oct. 16, 2010.

FREEDMAN, P., FRANZ, M., and GOLDSTEIN, K. 2004. Campaign Advertising and Democratic Citizenship Author. *American Journal of Political Science*, 48 (Oct.), 723–41.

GILENS, M. 1999. *Why Americans Hate Welfare: Race, Media, and the Politics of Anti-Poverty Policy*. Chicago: University of Chicago Press.

GRABE, M. E., and BUCY, E. P. 2009. *Image Bite Politics: News and the Visual Framing of Elections*. New York: Oxford University Press.

GRABER, D. 1988. *Processing the News: How People Tame the Information Tide*, 2nd edn. New York: Longman.

——2001. *Processing Politics: Learning from Television in the Internet Age*. Chicago: University of Chicago Press.

——2004. Methodological Developments in Political Communication Research. In *Handbook of Political Communications Research*, ed. L. L. Kaid. Mahwah, NJ: Lawrence Erlbaum.

HADAWAY, C. K., MARLER, P. L., and CHAVES, M. 1998. Overreporting Church Attendance in America: Evidence that Demands the Same Verdict. *American Sociological Review*, 63: 122–30.

HOLBROOK, T., and GARAND, J. C. 1996. Homo Economus? Economic Information and Economic Voting. *Political Research Quarterly*, 49: 351–75.

HOPKINS, D. J., and KING, G. 2010. A Method of Automated Nonparametric Content Analysis for Social Science. *American Journal of Political Science*, 54 (Jan.), 229–47.

IYENGAR, S. 1991. *Is Anyone Responsible?* Chicago: University of Chicago Press.

——and KINDER, D. 1987. *News that Matters: Television and American Opinion*. Chicago: University of Chicago Press.

JACOBS, L. R., and SHAPIRO, R. Y. 2000. *Politicians Don't Pander: Political Manipulation and the Loss of Democratic Responsiveness*. Chicago: University of Chicago Press.

JERIT, J. 2008. Issue Framing and Engagement: Rhetorical Strategy in Public Policy Debates. *Political Behavior*, 1: 1–24.

——2009. Understanding the Knowledge Gap: The Role of Experts and Journalists. *Journal of Politics*, 71: 442–56.

—— and BARABAS, J. 2006. Bankrupt Rhetoric: How Misleading Information Affects Knowledge about Social Security. *Public Opinion Quarterly*, 70 (Fall), 278–303.

—— —— and BOLSEN, T. 2006. Citizens, Knowledge, and the Information Environment. *American Journal of Political Science*, 50 (Apr.), 266–82.

KAHN, K. F., and KENNEY, P. J. 2002. The Slant of the News: How Editorial Endorsements Influence Campaign Coverage and Citizens' Views of Candidates. *American Political Science Review*, 96/2: 381–94.

KAM, C. D., and FRANZESE, R. J., JR. 2007. *Modeling and Interpreting Interaction Hypotheses in Regression Analysis*. Ann Arbor: University of Michigan Press.

KARP, J. A., and BROCKINGTON, D. 2005. Social Desirability and Response Validity: A Comparative Analysis of Overreporting Turnout in Five Countries. *Journal of Politics*, 67: 825–70.

KATZ, E., and LAZARSFELD, P. F. 1955. *Personal Influence: The Part Played by People in the Flow of Mass Communications*. Glencoe, IL: Free Press.

KELLSTEDT, P. 2000. Media Framing and the Dynamics of Racial Policy Preferences. *American Journal of Political Science*, 44 (Apr.), 245–60.

—— 2003. *The Mass Media and the Dynamics of American Racial Attitudes*. New York: Cambridge University Press.

KINDER, D. 2007. Curmudgeonly Advice. *Journal of Communication*, 57: 155–62.

KRIPPENDORF, K. H. 2003. *Content Analysis: An Introduction to its Methodology*. Beverly Hills, CA: Sage.

KROSNICK, J. A., and KINDER, D. R. 1990. Altering the Foundations of Support for the President through Priming. *American Political Science Review*, 84: 497–512.

LAVER, M., BENOIT, K., and GARRY, J. 2003. Extracting Policy Positions from Political Texts Using Words as Data. *American Political Science Review*, 97 (May), 311–31.

LAWRENCE, R. G. 2000. Game-Framing the Issues: Tracking the Strategy Frame in Public Policy News. *Political Communication*, 17: 93–114.

MARTIN, B., and JOHNSON, M. Forthcoming. Civic Norms and Surveys: Are Interviewer Evaluations Affected by Respondent Voting Behavior? *Public Opinion Quarterly*.

MESSARIS, P., and ABRAHAM, L. A. 2001. The Role of Images in Framing News Stories. In S. D. Reese, O. H. Gandy, Jr., and A. E. Grant (eds.), *Framing Public Life: Perspectives on Media and Our Understanding of the Social World*. Mahwah, NJ: Lawrence Erlbaum.

MONDAK, J. J. 1995. Newspapers and Political Awareness. *American Journal of Political Science*, 39 (May), 513–27.

NADEAU, R., and LEWIS-BECK, M. S. 2001. National Economic Voting in U.S. Presidential Elections. *Journal of Politics*, 63: 159–81.

—— NIEMI, R. G., FAN, D. P., and AMATO, T. 1999. Elite Economic Forecasts, Economic News, Mass Economic Judgments, and Presidential Approval. *Journal of Politics*, 61: 109–35.

NEUENDORF, K. A. 2001. *The Content Analysis Guidebook*. Thousand Oaks, CA: Sage.

NEUMAN, W. R., JUST, M. R., and CRIGLER, A. N. 1992. *Common Knowledge: News and the Construction of Political Meaning*. Chicago: University of Chicago Press.

PAGE, B. I. 1996. *Who Deliberates? Mass Media in Modern Democracy*. Chicago: University of Chicago Press.

PATTERSON, T. E., and McCLURE, R. D. 1976. *The Unseeing Eye: The Myth of Television Power in National Politics*. New York: Putnam.

PRESSER, S., and STINSON, L. 1998. Data Collection Mode and Social Desirability Bias in Self-Reported Religious Attendance. *American Sociological Review*, 63: 137–45.

PRICE, V., and CZILLI, E. J. 1996. Modeling Patterns of News Recognition and Recall. *Journal of Communication*, 46: 55–78.

—— and ZALLER, J. 1990. Evaluation of Media Exposure Items in the 1989 NES Pilot Study. American National Election Studies Pilot Study Report, No. nes002283. Unpublished.

—— —— 1993. Who Gets the News? Alternative Measures of News Reception and their Implications for Research. *Public Opinion Quarterly*, 57(Summer), 133–64.

PRIOR, M. 2009a. The Immensely Inflated News Audience: Assessing Bias in Self-Reported News Exposure. *Public Opinion Quarterly*, 73 (Spring), 130–43.

—— 2009b. Improving Media Effects Research through Better Measurement of News Exposure. *American Journal of Political Science*, 71 (July), 893–908.

QUINN, K. M., MONROE, B. L., COLARESI, M., CRESPIN, M. H., and RADEV, D. R. 2010. How to Analyze Political Attention with Minimal Assumptions and Costs. *American Journal of Political Science*, 54 (Jan.), 209–28.

RAUDENBUSH, S. W., and BRYK, A. 2002. *Hierarchical Linear Models*. Thousand Oaks, CA: Sage.

ROBINSON, J. P. 1985. The Validity and Reliability of Diaries versus Alternative Time Use Measures. In *Time, Goods, and Well-Being*, ed. F. T. Juster and F. P. Stafford. Ann Arbor: University of Michigan Survey Research Center, Institute for Social Research.

SEARS, D. O. 1986. College Sophomores in the Laboratory: Influences of a Narrow Data Base on Social Psychology's View of Human Nature. *Journal of Personality and Social Psychology*, 51: 515–30.

SHADISH, W. R., COOK, T. D., and CAMPBELL, D. T. 2002. *Experimental and Quasi-Experimental Designs for Generalized Causal Inference*. Boston: Houghton Mifflin.

SHAH, D. V., WATTS, M. D., DOMKE, D., and FAN, D. P. 2002. News Framing and Cueing of Issue Regimes: Explaining Clinton's Public Approval in Spite of Scandal. *Public Opinion Quarterly*, 66 (Autumn), 339–70.

SHAPIRO, R. Y. 2008. Comment: Media Use Measures for New Generations. In *Commentary on Media Measures for the ANES Sponsored by the Political Communications Sections of the International Communication Association and the American Political Science Association*. Political Communication Report 18/1. At <http://www.jour.unr.edu/pcr/1801_2008_winter/roundtable_shapiro.html>. Accessed Oct. 16, 2010.

SIMON, A., and JERIT, J. 2007. Toward a Theory Relating Political Discourse, Media, and Public Opinion. *Journal of Communication*, 57: 254–71.

—— and XENOS, M. 2004. Dimensional Reduction of Word-Frequency Data as a Substitute for Intersubjective Content Analysis. *Political Analysis*, 12: 63–75.

SNIDER, J. H., and JANDA, K. 1998. Newspapers and Bytes and Bits: Limitations of Electronic Databases for Content Analysis. Paper presented at the Annual Meeting of the American Political Science Association, Boston.

SNIDERMAN, P. M., and THERIAULT, S. M. 2004. The Structure of Political Argument and the Logic of Issue Framing. In *Studies in Public Opinion: Attitudes, Nonattitudes, Measurement Error, and Change*, ed. W. E. Saris and P. M. Sniderman. Princeton: Princeton University Press.

STEENBERGEN, M. R., and JONES, B. S. 2002. Modeling Multilevel Data Structures. *American Journal of Political Science*, 46 (Jan.), 218–37.

STOKER, L., and BOWERS, J. 2002. Designing Multi-Level Studies: Sampling Voters and Electoral Contexts. *Electoral Studies*, 21: 235–67.

SULKIN, T., and SWIGGER, N. 2008. Is There Truth in Advertising? Campaign Ad Images as Signals about Legislative Behavior. *Journal of Politics*, 1: 232–44.

WOOLLEY, J. T. 2000. Using Media-Based Data in Studies of Politics. *American Journal of Political Science*, 44 (Jan.), 156–73.

ZALLER, J. R. 1992. *The Nature and Origins of Mass Opinion*. New York: Cambridge University Press.

—— 1996. The Myth of Massive Media Impact Revived: New Support for a Discredited Idea. In *Political Persuasion and Attitude Change*, ed. D. Mutz, P. Sniderman, and R. Brody. Ann Arbor: University of Michigan Press.

—— 2002. The Statistical Power of Election Studies to Detect Media Exposure Effects in Political Campaigns. *Electoral Studies*, 21: 297–329.

..................................................................................................

# CHAPTER 10

# THE FUTURE OF POLITICAL COMMUNICATION RESEARCH

## Online Panels and Experimentation

..................................................................................................

LYNN VAVRECK

SHANTO IYENGAR*

A CENTRAL aim of political communication research is to assess the effects of different forms of media on public attitudes and behaviors. In the 1970s and 1980s, "media effects" researchers concentrated on television because that was where most Americans got information (see Patterson and McClure 1976; Iyengar and Kinder 1987). As new forms of media and alternative types of news programming gained audience share, researchers expanded the focus. We are now concerned with cable news programming, infotainment shows, blogs, chat rooms, and websites. Today, people interact with political "media" and information in many new ways and it only makes sense that the way we examine the effects of political communication should also change.

Luckily, these technology-driven changes in actual political communication make it possible to extend our research agenda in productive ways. The Internet not only opens doors for real political communication, it provides a platform that improves our ability to measure a key concept of interest: exposure to information. It also increases external validity and mundane realism, while sharpening our conclusions about causation through the increased power that comes from experimenting on thousands of represen-

* We thank the editors for the invitation to participate in the *Handbook* and for their helpful comments. Vavreck has worked as a consultant for the online survey research firm YouGov/Polimetrix, Inc., Palo Alto, California. Both Iyengar and Vavreck have been clients of YouGov/Polimetrix and Knowledge Networks.

tative cases. The Internet is not only changing the real world of political communication, it is changing research about political communication as well—and for the better.

Scholars have already begun to recognize the opportunities that online randomized experimentation provides (on this topic, see Mutz forthcoming). Geer and Brooks (2007) use the Internet to expose respondents to randomly selected advertisements with varying levels of incivility in the content. Similarly, Gottfried, Ben-Porath, Gibson, and Jamieson (2010) and Gottfried (2009a, 2009b) investigate the effects of advertisements in judicial races. Hill, Lo, Vavreck, and Zaller (2010) demonstrate the rapid decay in the effectiveness of advertisements during a mid-term election; and Baum and Gussin (2008) investigate the specific effect of images in media. The effects of news content are also in focus as Baum and Groeling (2009a, 2009b) demonstrate the effects of the news organization (as represented by the network bug at the bottom of the screen) and other signals on opinions about war; and Baum, Groeling, and Haselton (2006) bravely head into the territory of tabloid news effects. But it is Prior (2007) who foreshadows the effects of this new media age in his aptly titled *Post-Broadcast Democracy*, which contains online experiments conducted through the Time Sharing Experiments in the Social Sciences (TESS) project—a National Science Foundation sponsored project. His argument illustrates one of our concerns very well: with so many media choices available to news consumers, people can select in to exposure to "news" that fits with their preexisting proclivities—in other words, concerns over endogeneity have never been more relevant.

Other scholars are exploiting the Internet's capabilities and paying attention to direct kinds of political communication, like terrorist threats (Merolla and Zechmeister 2009), candidate position-taking (Tomz and Van Houweling 2008a, 2008b), presidential rhetoric (Tomz 2007, 2009; Trager and Vavreck 2010), or the desire to meet with and deliberate with your elected representatives (Neblo et al. 2010). Finally, some scholars are investigating the information contained in cues about race and ethnicity (Berinsky and Mendelberg 2005; Hutchings, Walton, and Benjamin forthcoming; Tesler and Sears 2010).

All of these investigations, whether about the audience costs a president suffers when he backs down from an international declaration to use force or the effects of attack advertising in congressional campaigns, have one thing in common: they all use randomized online experiments to support part of the argument. Despite the apparent recent popularity of this method for investigating the effects of political communications, questions remain about the quality of samples generated from opt-in Internet panels, even those originally built through probabilistic sampling methods. In this chapter, we discuss the benefits of experimentation, highlight previous experimental work and creative manipulations that have been carried out using online panels, and then investigate two 2008 online election studies to demonstrate the attractive properties of the samples and data. We demonstrate that Internet technology is redefining the methodology of political communication research with major improvements to some of the fundamental weaknesses of previous methods.

# WHY EXPERIMENTS? MEASUREMENT
# AND ENDOGENEITY

The most basic challenge for political communication researchers is obtaining accurate and precise measures of exposure to media messages. Self-reports on media exposure— long the preferred measure—are likely to yield highly exaggerated and hence inaccurate estimates of media effects (Vavreck 2007). In addition, researchers must deal with the thorny issue of endogeneity (or two-way causation) between exposure to media programming and political predispositions, which makes it difficult to disentangle the causal effects of messages on the opinions and actions of the audience and vice versa.

Problems of imprecise measurement and weak causal inference have proven intractable in observational research such as surveys. Political communication researchers have increasingly turned to experimental methods that substitute actual exposure to media messages for self-reported exposure, and which neutralize the issue of endogeneity by assigning individuals to particular audiences on a random basis. The combination of manipulation control and random assignment yields unequivocal causal evidence. The rise of Internet panels has helped researchers make advances in both areas by providing low-cost options that increase power and external validity. Moreover, the gains come with an increased range of possible manipulations delivered on a platform that people now routinely use to consume political information.

Online experiments make it very easy to abandon self-reports of exposure. How biased are self-reported measures of media exposure? Unfortunately, there is considerable evidence that the bias is profound, exaggerating the impact by as much as 600 percent (Vavreck 2007; Ansolabehere and Iyengar 1994; Price and Zaller 1993). In 2002 Vavreck randomly assigned half of her Knowledge Networks sample to receive advertising treatments, including a non-partisan get-out-the-vote ad. Each respondent's registration and turnout record was located after the 2002 election from official statewide databases. The true effect of the ad (the effect of actual exposure on actual turnout) was to increase turnout by less than 1 point. But, when self-reports of ad recall were used, the impact on reported turnout went up by a factor of 8.

In "The Exaggerated Effects of Advertising on Turnout: The Dangers of Self-Reports," Vavreck (2007) shows that it is not forgetfulness among people who were assigned to treatment that makes this difference.[1] In fact, false recall among people in the control group contributes more to the inflation of the treatment effect. Prior (2009) presents similar findings. Both Vavreck and Prior conclude that observational data can

---

[1] In the Ansolabehere and Iyengar experiments on campaign advertising (which spanned the 1990, 1992, and 1994 election cycles), over 50 percent of the participants who were exposed to a political advertisement were unable, *some thirty minutes later*, to recall having seen the advertisement (Ansolabehere and Iyengar 1994).

be salvaged with careful attention to survey design and modeling, but in their own future work on political communication, both go on to use experimental methods, suggesting a preference they do not *explicitly* articulate in their pieces on observational methods. In order to understand how exposure to political communication affects people, we need to know who is exposed without relying on self-reports.

This experimental control not only cleans up the measure of exposure, but it helps researchers isolate specific causal mechanisms and exploit individual-level heterogeneity in the effects—it helps us get a handle on the endogeneity or recursive effects between exposure to certain news sources and political attitudes. The principal advantage of the experiment over the survey is the researcher's ability to isolate the effects of specific components of political messages. At the aggregate level, campaigns, for example, encompass a concatenation of messages, channels, and sources, all of which may influence the audience, often in inconsistent directions. The researcher's task is to identify specific causal factors and delineate the range of their attributes. Even at the narrow level of campaign advertisements, for instance, there are an infinite number of potential causal factors, including images, audio, written text, music, and the interaction of all these things. To isolate the effects of one of these things, control over manipulations is needed. Some researchers have been very creative in the way they have manipulated causal factors. The Internet provides new opportunities to deliver creative treatments that were previously impossible to administer to large numbers of nationally representative samples.

More validity and realism, more power, less measurement error, and improved confidence in our inferences—these are the most obvious benefits of online survey experimentation. But online surveys also make randomization easier and more accurate—and this is of great benefit to researchers. Respondents can be randomized into conditions at the time they accept the survey invitation, which is an improvement over methods that assign subjects to conditions before they agree to participate in the project. Randomizing at the start of the survey ensures that there will be no bias due to unequal response rates across the treatment and control groups. Furthermore, online vendors can link specific treatments to specific respondents because firms generally know basic information about the respondents before invitations are accepted (or sent). For example, if a researcher wants a treatment to contain a map of the respondent's city block or the name of their member of Congress, these things can be pre-programmed and delivered to respondents as they accept survey invitations in real time. This capability opens up a new set of possible treatments to scholars, embedding the heterogeneity of the population in the treatment in order to standardize the treatment.

As an example of a treatment that uses information about the respondent at the point of randomization, we turn to a project that leverages the "look" of a respondent's face by incorporating an image of the respondent into the treatment. In this experiment, Bailenson, Iyengar, Yee, and Collins (2009) want to know whether voters are attracted to candidates who look like them. We know that voters prefer candidates who resemble them on questions of ideology, policy, or partisanship, but what about physical resemblance? Several lines of research suggest that physical similarity in general, and facial similarity in particular, is relevant for political choice. In particular, evolutionary psychologists argue that physical similarity is a kinship cue and humans are motivated to treat their kin preferentially (see, for instance, Burnstein, Crandall, and Kitayama 1994).

In order to isolate the effects of facial similarity on voting preferences, researchers obtained digital photographs of 172 registered voters selected at random from a national Internet panel (for details on the methodology, see Bailenson, Iyengar, Yee, and Collins 2009). Participants were asked to provide their photographs approximately three weeks in advance of the 2004 presidential election. One week before the election, these same participants were asked to participate in an online survey of political attitudes that included a variety of questions about the presidential candidates (President George W. Bush and Senator John Kerry). The computer screens on which these candidate questions appeared also included photographs of the two candidates displayed side by side. Within this split-panel presentation, participants had their own face either morphed with Bush or Kerry at a ratio of 60 percent of the candidate and 40 percent of the participant.[2]

The results of the face-morphing study revealed a significant interaction between facial similarity and strength of the participant's party affiliation. Among strong partisans, the similarity manipulation had no effect; these voters were already convinced of their vote choice. But weak partisans and independents whose voting preferences were not as entrenched moved in the direction of the more similarly morphed candidate (see Bailenson, Iyengar, Yee, and Collins 2009). Thus, the evidence suggests that non-verbal cues can influence voting, even in the most visible and contested of political campaigns.[3]

The ability to launch experiments online has further strengthened the ability of political communication researchers to draw causal inferences by providing more precisely calibrated indicators of audience reactions to media messages. Online experiments permit observation of information-seeking behavior as well as user reactions to visual, verbal, and audiovisual stimuli such as the material encountered in campaign advertisements.

Researchers have long assumed that people possess an innate preference for attitude-consistent messages or sources of information. According to this "selective exposure" hypothesis, voters seek to avoid information that clashes with their preexisting beliefs (for example, Festinger 1957) and instead put themselves in the path of information they expect to agree with. In the words of Lazarsfeld, Berelson, and Gaudet:

---

[2] They settled on the 60:40 ratio after a pre-test study indicated that this level of blending was insufficient for participants to detect traces of themselves in the morph, but sufficient to move evaluations of the target candidate.

[3] Facial similarity is necessarily confounded with familiarity—people are familiar with their own faces. There is considerable evidence (see Zajonc 2001) that people prefer familiar to unfamiliar stimuli. An alternative interpretation of these results, accordingly, is that participants were more inclined to support the more familiar-looking candidate.

In recent years there has been a good deal of talk by men of good will about the desirability and necessity of guaranteeing the free exchange of ideas in the market place of public opinion. Such talk has centered upon the problem of keeping free the channels of expression and communication. Now we find that the consumers of ideas, if they have made a decision on the issue, themselves erect high tariff walls against alien notions.    (1948, 89)

Given the practical difficulties of delivering large quantities of information, the typical study on selective exposure provides participants with only a limited range of choice. Indeed, Cotton (1985) observed that the selective exposure literature had failed to address "how people actively seek and avoid information on their own" (1985, 29) in naturalistic settings. However, digital technology now makes it possible to deliver voluminous quantities of information in a compact and easy-to-navigate format.

In a study of selective exposure during the 2000 presidential campaign, researchers provided a representative sample of registered voters with a multimedia CD containing extensive information about candidates Bush and Gore—including text of all of their stump speeches delivered between July 1 and October 7, a full set of televised ads, and the texts of the Democratic and Republican party platforms. The CD also included the soundtrack and transcripts of the candidates' nomination acceptance speeches as well as the first televised debate. All told, the information amounted to over 600 pages of text and two hours of multimedia (see Iyengar, Hahn, Krosnick, and Walker 2008).

The campaign CD was delivered to a representative sample of American adult Internet users two weeks before Election Day. Participants were informed in advance that their use of the CD would be examined by the researchers (and they were asked not to share the CD with members of their family or friends). As the user navigated through the CD offerings, a built-in tracking feature recorded every visited page (in the order of visit), the number of total times the CD was accessed, and the length of each browsing session in a log file on the user's hard drive. Upon completing a post-election questionnaire, participants were given instructions for finding and uploading their log files (600 people were invited to participate in the study; of these, 226 actually used the CD for a response rate of 38 percent). From these files, they were able to monitor the degree to which CD users gravitated to information provided by the candidate they preferred. The findings revealed only partial evidence of selective exposure based on partisanship; Republicans (and conservatives) showed a preference for information concerning Bush, but Democrats (and liberals) proved more even-handed in their information-seeking behavior.

The tendency for partisans on the right to show greater avoidance of attitude-discrepant information may be attributable to both dispositional and contextual factors. In comparison with liberals, conservatives may have a more intense sense of group identity, thus heightening their need to avoid dissonance. On the other hand, the greater selectivity among Republicans may reflect habituation over time. Since the launch of the Fox News network in 1986, Republicans have enjoyed easy access to television news with a pro-Republican tilt. The tendency to avoid attitude-discrepant information encouraged by Fox News may have promoted similar information-seeking behaviors in a non-news context.

Moving from presidential elections to more local levels, campaign advertising is the major source of information for voters in non-presidential elections. Understanding voters' reactions to ads is thus fundamental to understanding the effectiveness of campaigns. Most researchers who investigate the effectiveness of ad campaigns typically rely on verbal measures to gage the influence of ads. Viewers might be asked if they agreed or disagreed with the ad in question, or if the ad elicited positive or negative feelings concerning the sponsoring candidate. These measures ask respondents to provide a post hoc summary or "averaged" assessment of their reaction to the content and imagery of ads.

With the diffusion of online technology, it is possible to monitor viewer response to advertising on a continuous basis, over the entire playing of the ad (see Iyengar, Jackman, and Hahn 2007). Rather than asking for a summary assessment *after* viewers have watched the ad, researchers can use an online "dial" (or sliding scale) procedure that synchronizes viewers' self-reported feelings concerning the soundtrack and visual imagery they encounter at any given moment *during* the playing of the ad.

Ad dial methodology was implemented online in a study of the 2006 US Senate elections in six battleground states. A sample of approximately 1,900 registered voters with Internet access was selected at random from a nationwide online panel. Participants were instructed (and given a practice task) on how to move a slider located immediately below the video in accordance with their feelings about the content of the ad. The specific instruction was: "If what you see or hear makes you feel good, or you agree with the speaker, indicate this by moving the slider towards the green end. If, however, your reaction is negative, and you dislike what you see or hear, then move the slider to the red zone." Special software recorded the position of the slider once a second by evenly dividing the range of dial positions into 100 intervals, with zero indicating the left or negative end of the dial, and 100 the right or positive end. Thus, as the ad played, we could monitor voters' reactions in real time from beginning to end. At the start of each ad, the slider was positioned at the neutral, or "50," position, and this was the first dial value recorded for each respondent.

The results from this study indicated that most ads polarize partisan viewers; over the course of the ad, Democrats and Republicans inevitably move in opposite directions. This pattern is consistent with prior research showing that exposure to campaign ads strengthens viewers' partisan predispositions (Ansolabehere and Iyengar 1994). While partisans responded rapidly to the content of advertising, independents were typically unmoved, remaining lukewarm over the entire playing of the ad.

A further finding from this study was that the rate of polarization proved variable across the partisanship of the sponsoring candidate. Democrats consistently converged (arrived at their stable end point) faster in response to Democratic ads than did Republicans in response to Republican ads. In effect, Democratic ads resonated more powerfully with Democrats than Republican ads did with Republicans. Perhaps this effect was due to the partisan appeal of the ads' messages. Democratic ads, which tended to highlight the state of the war in Iraq and the fallout from the Abramoff ethics scandal linking the Republican candidate with President Bush mobilized the

Democratic base more effectively than generic Republican appeals on national security, immigration, and taxes. These manipulations illustrate some of the more creative manipulations researchers have delivered to date using online experimentation.

## THE FUTURE OF EXPERIMENTATION

Because of the need for tight control over exposure to the stimulus, the laboratory setting in which an experiment used to occur was often quite dissimilar from the setting in which subjects ordinarily experience the "target" phenomenon. The inherently artificial properties of lab experiments led researchers to turn to designs in which the procedures and settings more closely reflected ordinary life. In the lab experiments of the 1990s (Ansolabehere and Iyengar 1996), care was even taken to decorate the room as if it were a living room, leaving a remote control on the coffee table, and allowing subjects to bring friends or family with them.

The days of such heroic efforts toward mundane realism are over. Put simply, since campaigns now use the Internet to send political information to people, and people use the Internet to get political information, researchers can use the Internet to test the effects of political information with fewer challenges to realism or validity. When respondents in an online survey click on a link to play a randomly selected advertisement, they may be doing something that they routinely do on a daily basis: clicking on a link to get more information about something.

While online surveys help with external validity and realism, there is still substantial concern over the subject pools. This is not unlike the common refrain made about lab experiments (Sears 1986). Typically, laboratory experiments are administered upon "captive" populations—college students who must serve as guinea pigs in order to gain course credit. College sophomores may be a convenient subject population for academic researchers, but they are hardly comparable to "real people."

Fortunately, technology has both enlarged the pool of potential participants and reduced the per capita cost of administering an experimental study. With the significantly lowered per respondent cost, online panels of respondents and the firms that build them make it possible to track opinion over long periods of time for a set of impaneled people, or track people every day for a few weeks at a time. The technology helps with the measurement issues; and the substantial increase in sample size that one gets from the Internet and the ability to track the same survey respondents over prolonged periods of time help observational researchers gain traction on the endogeneity and power problems.

The benefits from moving online to study political communication are many, but some still question whether the value is as real as it seems. Critics of online survey research argue that because most of the online panels are not recruited through probability sampling methodologies, the resulting data sets are of no use to scholars interested in making inferences about a target population. But it is precisely because the large pools of potential respondents do not have to be recruited through expensive and low-yielding probability methods that online survey research is so affordable. The question is whether these opt-in recruiting methods produce a pool of people from which representative samples can be assembled. We believe the answer is yes. In our research we have mainly used Knowledge Networks (KN) and YouGov/Polimetrix (YGP) and consequently we will focus on those two firms as we compare the sample attributes of these online panels to other probabilistic non-Internet surveys (the American National Election Study and the Census).

Most people understand probability-based sampling methodologies. Made familiar to scholars through decades of use by telephone polling firms, methods like random digit dialing (RDD), list-based sampling, and the post-stratification weighting procedures that come along with these sampling methods now seem routine and acceptable to most users of survey data. We are less familiar with the methods used by online survey vendors largely because there are a variety of methods in use and few of them are as straightforward as RDD or random selection off a list. KN, one of the oldest online survey vendors in the academic business, uses a traditional RDD sampling method to invite household residents to join their "Knowledge Panel" and provides Internet access to selected respondents who do not currently have it. This seems straightforward enough. The sampling frame includes households without Internet access, and selection is based on a probabilistic method. This method, however, will also boast the weaknesses of any RDD method: low response rates and relatively high cost. The low response rate combined with panel attrition over time means that even after the probabilistic exercise, users of the data generated for any *specific* project must still weight the data to account for selection biases. Even when online vendors use probabilistic recruitment methods to build special samples for specific projects, the resulting pool of respondents is not demographically representative.

In contrast to the low-yield probabilistic recruitment methods, other online survey research firms have abandoned the random recruitment of panelists into their panels and allowed people to "opt in" to the panel at will. Some firms buy ads on popular webpages inviting people to join their panels, others send email invitations to lists of people who indicate they are interested in online offers, still others buy ads in online editions of newspapers. Some firms use combinations of these methods, others may use a completely different set of tools.

YGP mainly uses online advertising about topics of interest to recruit panelists (see Vavreck and Rivers 2008 for a complete description of recruiting methods). To construct a specific sample from the pool of over 1 million panelists, YGP uses a sample matching methodology. To begin, YGP constructs a synthetic sampling frame from the American Community Study (ACS), a high-quality probability-based survey conducted by the US Census. For the Cooperative Campaign Analysis Project (CCAP), a 2008 presidential election study run by Simon Jackman and Lynn Vavreck (Jackman and Vavreck 2009a), YGP used the 2005–7 ACS. Variables from the Current Population Study (CPS) Registration and Voter Supplement (for 2004 and 2008), the Pew Study of Religious Life, and state voter lists are matched to the ACS using nearest-neighbor matching. The key to a matched sample is having very many people in nearly any category determined by the cross-classification of the frame variables. YGP has 1.4 million people in its PollingPoint panel; this means that they can populate every cell of the cross-classification generated by the frame variables. The size of the pool is critical to the quality of the final matched sample (see Rivers and Bailey 2009 for details).

Rivers and Bailey (2009) use the 2008 CPS November Voting Registration Supplement as a baseline to compare data sets produced by KN (for the American National Election Study) and YGP (for CCAP) during the 2008 election to the ANES face-to-face survey. Overall, the online samples come close to the population estimates in the CPS, and in some cases (gender and less than high school education), the online samples are closer than the face-to-face data. The CCAP matched sample does well across the race categories providing the closest match in all categories to the CPS. Similarly, the CCAP sample most closely estimates gender and marital status. The matched sample has bigger misses on education, slightly overrepresenting the lower levels of education and underrepresenting the higher levels.

Still, some skeptics may wonder whether these people are representative of voters in the population in terms of their political attitudes and behaviors, not just their demographics. In other words, are the less educated women in online panels "the same" as similarly educated women in the population or are they different, specifically on the characteristics we care about (interest in politics, political attitudes, etc. . . . )? Rivers and Bailey (2009) show the percentage of each sample reporting a vote for Obama in the 2008 presidential election for the three categories of race and compare it to National Exit Poll data. This helps us learn whether the Latinos in the online panels behave the same way in the voting booth (something we care about) as the Latinos in the population. Once again, the matched sample of CCAP does very well, especially among Hispanic and black voters. For white voters, the KN sample does slightly better, but CCAP does just as well as the face-to-face method. A similar trend can be seen across categories of income. Others have demonstrated this same level of similarity across the data sets for things like the effect of racial attitudes on vote choice (Tesler and Sears 2010; Jackman and Vavreck 2010) and for the effects of political information on the level of attitude constraint (Hill, Lo, Vavreck, and Zaller 2006; Jackman and Vavreck 2009b).

Our purpose here is not to demonstrate the representativeness of matched samples for the sake of survey research generally, but to show that affordable Internet surveys can provide high-quality data, at least in terms of demographics and dependent variables in which we are interested. We have a single purpose in doing so: to argue that these platforms are a natural way forward for research on political communication as they provide realistic settings in which to conduct experimentation. Internet survey experiments provide large doses of mundane reality and external validity because respondents experience political communications this way in the modern campaign age—and because the experiments can be conducted on large samples that are representative of target populations. This is a significant improvement from the days of gathering thirty-five people in a small room and having them huddle around a television set. We can now show thousands of people different pieces of media on a platform on which they view political media regularly. And the results of our controlled tests are generalizable to the population.

# CONCLUSION

The standard comparison of experiments and surveys favors the former on the grounds of precise causal inference and the latter on the grounds of greater generalizability. As we have suggested, however, traditional experimental methods can now be effectively and rigorously replicated using online strategies which have the advantage of reaching a participant pool that is more far-flung and diverse than the pool relied on by conventional experimentalists. The development of online research panels makes it possible to administer experiments on broad cross-sections of the American population. As technology diffuses still further, the generalizability gap between experimental and survey methods will continue to close.

## REFERENCES

ANSOLABEHERE, S. D., and IYENGAR, S. 1994. Messages Forgotten: Mis-reporting in Surveys and the Bias toward Minimal Effects. Unpublished paper. Department of Political Science, University of California, Los Angeles.

——1996. *Going Negative*. New York: Free Press.

BAILENSON, J. N., IYENGAR, S., YEE, N., and COLLINS, N. A. 2009. Facial Similarity between Candidates and Voters Causes Influence. *Public Opinion Quarterly*, 72: 935–61.

BAUM, M., and GROELING, T. 2009a. Shot by the Messenger: The Effects of Party Cues on Public Opinion regarding National Security and War. *Political Behavior*, 31: 157–86.

——2009b. *War Stories: The Causes and Consequences of Citizen Views of War*. Princeton: Princeton University Press.

——and GUSSIN, P. 2008. In the Eye of the Beholder: How Information Shortcuts Shape Individual Perceptions of Bias in the Media. *Quarterly Journal of Political Science*, 3/1: 1–31.

——GROELING, T., and HASELTON, M. 2006. Political Scandal, Gender, and Tabloid News: An Experimental Examination of News Preferences for Scandalous News. Unpublished working paper. University of California, Los Angeles.

BERINSKY, A., and MENDELBERG, T. 2005. The Indirect Effects of Discredited Stereotypes in Judgments of Jewish Leaders. *American Journal of Political Science*, 49/4: 845–64.

BURNSTEIN, E., CRANDALL, C., and KITAYAMA, S. 1994. Some Neo-Darwinian Decision Rules for Altruism: Weighing Cues for Inclusive Fitness as a Function of the Biological Importance of the Decision. *Journal of Personality and Social Psychology*, 67: 773–89.

COTTON, J. L. 1985. Cognitive Dissonance in Selective Exposure. In *Selective Exposure to Communication*, ed. D. Zillman and J. Bryant. Hillsdale, NJ: Lawrence Erlbaum.

FESTINGER, L. 1957. *A Theory of Cognitive Dissonance*. Evanston, IL: Row, Peterson.

GEER, J. G., and BROOKS, D. 2007. Beyond Negativity: The Effects of Incivility on the Electorate. *American Journal of Political Science*, 51/1: 1–16.

GOTTFRIED, J. A. 2009a. Judicial Campaign Advertising and Partisan Cueing: An Experimental Study of the 2007 Pennsylvania Supreme Court Election. Paper presented at the 2009 Annual Meeting of the International Communication Association, May 20–5, Chicago.

——2009b. "Pigs in Robes": An Experimental Study of the Influence of Negative Judicial Campaign Messages. Paper presented at the 2009 Annual Meeting of the American Political Science Association, Sept. 3–6, Toronto.

——BEN-PORATH, E. N., GIBSON, J. L., and JAMIESON, K. H. 2010. How Judicial Advertising Can Mobilize Voters: An Experimental Study of the 2007 Pennsylvania Judicial Election. Unpublished working paper. University of Pennsylvania.

HILL, S. J., LO, J., VAVRECK, L., and ZALLER, J. R. 2010. How Quickly We Forget. Unpublished working paper. University of California, Los Angeles.

HUTCHINGS, V. L., WALTON, H., JR., and BENJAMIN, A. Forthcoming. The Impact of Explicit Racial Cues on Gender Differences in Support for Confederate Symbols and Partisanship. *Journal of Politics*.

IYENGAR, S., and KINDER, D. 1987. *News that Matters: Television and American Opinion*. Chicago: University of Chicago Press.

——HAHN, K., KROSNICK, J. A., and WALKER, J. 2008. Selective Exposure to Campaign Communication: The Role of Anticipated Agreement and Issue Public Membership. *Journal of Politics*, 70: 186–200.

——JACKMAN, S., and HAHN, K. 2007. Polarization in Less than 30 Seconds: Continuous Monitoring of Voter Response to Campaign Advertising. Paper presented at the Annual Meeting of the American Political Science Association, Chicago.

JACKMAN, S., and VAVRECK, L. 2009a. The Cooperative Campaign Analysis Project 2007–8. Release 2.0. Palo Alto, CA: YouGov/Polimetrix.

————2009b. How Does Obama "Match-up"? Attitudes about Race, the Economy, and Cross-partisan Appeal in the 2008 Election. Unpublished working paper. University of California, Los Angeles.

————2010. Primary Politics: The Role of Gender, Age, and Race in the 2008 Democratic Primary. *Journal of Elections, Public Opinion, and Parties*, 20/2: 153–86.

LAZARSFELD, P., BERELSON, B., and GAUDET, H. 1948. *The People's Choice: How the Voter Makes up his Mind in a Presidential Campaign*, 2nd edn. New York: Columbia University Press.

MEROLLA, J. L., and ZECHMEISTER, E. J. 2009. *Democracy at Risk: How Terrorist Threats Affect the Public*. Chicago: University of Chicago Press.

MUTZ, D. C. Forthcoming. *Population-Based Experimentation for the Social Sciences*. Princeton: Princeton University Press.

NEBLO, M. A., ESTERLING, K. M., KENNEDY, R., LAZER, D. M. J., and SOKHEY, A. 2010. Who Wants to Deliberate, and Why? Unpublished working paper. University of California, Riverside.

PATTERSON, T. E., and McCLURE, R. D. 1976. *The Unseeing Eye: The Myth of Television Power in National Politics*. New York: Putnam.

PRICE, V., and ZALLER, J. R. 1993. Who Gets the News? Alternative Measures of News Reception and their Implications for Research. *Public Opinion Quarterly*, 57: 133–64.

PRIOR, M. 2007. *Post-Broadcast Democracy: How Media Choice Increases Inequality in Political Involvement and Polarizes Elections*. New York: Cambridge University Press.

PRIOR, M. 2009. Improving Media Effects Research through Better Measurement of News Exposure. *Journal of Politics*, 71/3: 893–908.

RIVERS, D., and BAILEY, D. 2009. Inferences from Matched-Samples in the 2008 U.S. National Elections. Paper presented at the Joint Statistical Meetings, Chicago.

SEARS, D. O. 1986. College Sophomores in the Laboratory: Influences of a Narrow Data Base on the Social Psychology View of Human Nature. *Journal of Personality and Social Psychology*, 51: 515–30.

TESLER, M., and SEARS, D. O. 2010. *Obama's Race: Pathway to a Post-Racial America?* Chicago: University of Chicago Press.

TOMZ, M. 2007. Domestic Audience Costs in International Relations: An Experimental Approach. *International Organization*, 61/4: 821–40.

——2009. The Foundations of Domestic Audience Costs: Attitudes, Expectations, and Institutions. In *Expectations, Institutions, and Global Society/Kitai, Seido, Gurobaru-shakai*, ed. M. Kohno and A. Tanaka. Tokyo: Keiso-Shobo.

——and VAN HOUWELING, R. P. 2008a. The Electoral Implications of Candidate Ambiguity. *American Political Science Review*, 103/1: 83–98.

————2008b. Candidate Positioning and Voter Choice. *American Political Science Review*, 102/3: 303–18.

TRAGER, R. F., and VAVRECK, L. Forthcoming. Presidential Approval during International Crises: The Role of Rhetoric, Party, and Opposition Support. *American Journal of Political Science*.

VAVRECK, L. 2007. The Exaggerated Effects of Advertising on Turnout: The Dangers of Self-Reports. *Quarterly Journal of Political Science*, 2: 325–43.

——and RIVERS, D. 2008. The 2006 Cooperative Congressional Election Study. *Journal of Elections, Public Opinion, and Parties*, 18: 355–66.

ZAJONC, R. B. 2001. Mere Exposure: A Gateway to the Subliminal. *Current Directions in Psychological Science*, 10: 224–8.

# SECTION THREE: EFFECTS

CHAPTER 11

.................................................................................................

# PUBLIC–ELITE
# INTERACTIONS[*]

*Puzzles in Search of Researchers*

.................................................................................................

DENNIS CHONG
JAMES N. DRUCKMAN

THE dynamics of public–elite interactions has been the focus of one of the most progressive research agendas in political science over the past twenty years. Under this rubric, scholars have studied how elites influence public opinion, elaborated on the conditions promoting or constraining elite influence, identified strategies motivating elite behavior, and explored the impact of mass media on the relationship between elites and the public. Considering the advances made on these topics, we feel Bartels's (1993, 267) indictment, made over fifteen years ago, that research in this area is "one of the most notable embarrassments of modern social science" no longer applies.

Nonetheless, important questions remain to be addressed. In this chapter, we identify the most pressing puzzles in research on the effect of elite rhetoric on public opinion. In particular, we discuss theoretical and empirical issues in four realms: (1) the conceptualization of communication effects, (2) elite strategies of communications, (3) conditions that moderate elite influence, and (4) the implications of political communications research on democratic theory. For each topic, we offer our perspective, frequently citing examples from our own work, and then present what we view as key questions deserving further exploration. We acknowledge that, like most others, we give disproportionate attention to how elites shape public preferences compared to how the public's opinions affect elite

* Parts of this chapter come from Chong and Druckman (2007a, 2007c, 2010) and Druckman (2010). We adopted our subtitle from D. Druckman's (2003) paper. We thank Thomas Leeper for research assistance.

behavior (which is a topic treated by a somewhat distinct literature on responsiveness). We will discuss the implications of this asymmetry, especially for normative theory.

## Defining Communication Effects

Our interest ultimately lies in understanding how public opinion is affected by elite communications. A useful basis for comparing types of communication effects is the expectancy value model of an attitude (for example, Ajzen and Fishbein 1980; Nelson, Oxley, and Clawson 1997). In this model, an attitude toward an object equals the weighted sum of a set of evaluative beliefs about that object. Specifically, $Attitude = \sum v_i^* w_i$, where $v_i$ is the evaluation of the object on attribute $i$ and $w_i$ is the salience weight ($\sum w_i = 1$) associated with that attribute. For example, suppose one's overall attitude, $A$, toward a new housing development consists of a mix of negative and positive evaluations, $v_i$, of the project on different dimensions $i$. An individual may believe that the project will *favor* economic growth by creating jobs ($i = 1$) but *harm* the environment by impinging on existing green spaces ($i = 2$). Assuming this individual places a positive value on both the economy and the environment, then $v_1$ is positive and $v_2$ is negative, and his attitude toward the project will depend on the relative magnitudes of $v_1$ and $v_2$ discounted by the relative weights ($w_1$ and $w_2$) assigned respectively to each attribute (Nelson and Oxley 1999).

The following examples illustrate how this conceptualization of an attitude applies to any object of evaluation: (1) a voter's preference between two candidates may vary according to whether the voter evaluates them on economic or foreign policy issues (see Enelow and Hinich 1984). In the 2008 US presidential election, a voter might have preferred John McCain to Barack Obama when evaluating them on their foreign policy positions, but preferred Obama to McCain when comparing their economic platforms. (2) An individual's attitude toward welfare recipients may depend on the extent she believes their plight is explained by their personal failures or by social and economic disadvantages (see Iyengar 1991). (3) One's tolerance for allowing a hate group rally may hinge on the value one places on defending free speech versus maintaining public safety. Ultimately, the attitude or preference in each of these situations depends on the valences and weights given to the competing considerations.

Individuals typically base their evaluations on a subset of dimensions, rather than on the universe of possible considerations. In the simplest case, they focus on a single dimension ($w_i = 1$) such as foreign policy or economic affairs in evaluating a candidate, free speech or public safety when considering a hate group rally request, or lives saved or lives lost in assessing medical programs. Even when they incorporate more than one dimension, cognitive limitations and economies of thought may cause most individuals to rely on no more than a few considerations (for example, Simon 1955). The dimensions underlying one's attitude are *available* (i.e., an individual comprehends the meaning and significance of the dimension), *accessible* (i.e., the consideration *unconsciously* enters the individual's working memory), and *applicable* or appropriate (i.e., the individual *consciously* views the dimension as a relevant or important basis of opinion) (see Althaus and Kim 2006; Chong 2000; Chong and Druckman 2007a; Price and Tewksbury 1997; Winter 2008).

Two points are particularly noteworthy. First, accessibility increases with chronic use of a consideration over time *or* from temporary contextual cues—including repeated exposure to communications. Second, individuals assess the applicability of a dimension only when motivated by incentives (e.g., a desire to make the correct decision) or by contextual factors such as the presence of directly conflicting or competing information.

## Conceptual Clarification

This model of attitude formation can be used to compare alternative conceptions of communication effects. We refer to the dimension or dimensions, $i$, that affect an individual's evaluation as an individual's *frame in thought*. For example, an individual who believes economic considerations trump all other concerns in making decisions about the proposed housing development has an "economic" frame in thought on that issue. Or, if free speech dominates all other considerations in deciding a hate group's right to rally, the individual's frame would be free speech. Individuals may also constitue issues using more complex frames in thought that combine multiple considerations, such as concern for free speech, public safety, and the community's image in contemplating whether a hate group should be allowed to hold a rally.[1]

The frames on which an individual bases his or her attitude have their origin in past experiences, ongoing world events, interpersonal discussions, and so on. Of particular relevance, given our focus, is the impact of communications from politicians and the media—whom we label "elites" (see Zaller 1992, 6). The importance of elite communications to citizens' opinions is clear, and perhaps most powerfully demonstrated by Vavreck's (2009) recent book that shows that even the impact of the economy on vote choice—a dimension of evaluation that may seem to require no external prompting to be employed—depends on exposure to campaign messages.

As we will discuss, elites employ a variety of approaches to purposefully influence the public's opinions. The most obvious strategy they employ is using rhetoric to affect how citizens construe political issues and candidates. A speaker emphasizes one interpretation of an issue to encourage the public to evaluate the issue on the same terms; for example, a news outlet states that a hate group's planned rally is "a free speech issue," or a politician describes welfare in terms of its humanitarian effects rather than its impact on taxes. When such *frames in communication* influence an individual's frame in thought, it is called a *framing effect*.

---

[1] We focus exclusively on what scholars call "emphasis" frames, "issue" frames, or "value" frames, and not equivalency or valence frames (for discussion, see Druckman 2004, forthcoming).

Political communication scholars often distinguish framing effects from "priming," "agenda setting," and "persuasion" (for example, Scheufele 2000; McCombs 2004). The term "priming" entered the field of communication, from related psychological work, when Iyengar and Kinder (1987, 63) defined it as follows: "By calling attention to some matters while ignoring others, television news influences the standards by which governments, presidents, policies, and candidates for public office are judged. Priming refers to changes in the standards that people use to make political evaluations." For example, individuals exposed to news stories about defense policy tend to base their approval of the president on their assessment of the president's performance on defense. If, in contrast, these individuals watch stories about energy policy, their overall evaluations of the president's performance will tend to be based on his handling of energy policy. Clearly, political elites will have strategic incentives to prime the public to think in terms that are most favorable to themselves.

The expectancy value model presented above can be generalized to priming by assuming each consideration constitutes a separate issue dimension or image (J. N. Druckman and Holmes 2004) used to evaluate candidates. When a mass communication places attention on an issue, that issue will receive greater weight through increased accessibility and, possibly, applicability. If this is correct, then framing effects and what communication scholars have called "priming effects" share common processes and the two terms can be used interchangeably.

A similar argument applies to agenda-setting, which occurs when a speaker's (e.g., a news outlet or politician) emphasis on an issue or problem leads the audience to give higher priority to the issue (for example, McCombs 2004). For example, when a news outlet's campaign coverage focuses on the economy, viewers come to believe the economy is the most important campaign issue. Agenda-setting therefore refers to the change in weights ($w_i$) given to different issues. We thus view framing, priming (as used by communication scholars), and agenda-setting as equivalent processes, which we prefer to uniformly call "framing."[2] Much of the remainder of this chapter focuses on framing, with the understanding that we view it as enveloping these other processes.

A final conceptual distinction concerns framing and persuasion. Nelson and Oxley (1999) differentiate framing from persuasion by referring to the former as a change in the weight component, $w_i$, of an attitude in response to a communication, and the latter as a change in the evaluation component, $v_i$ (W. Wood 2000). For example, in assessing a candidate, framing takes place if a communication causes voters to give more attention to the candidate's economic positions than to her foreign policy platform. Persuasion occurs if the communication alters one's evaluation of the candidate on one of those dimensions. In practice, framing and persuasion strategies often go hand in

---

[2] We prefer the overarching term "framing effects," in part because priming refers to a related but distinct procedure in psychology (used strictly to increase accessibility; see J. N. Druckman, Kuklinski, and Sigelman 2009), and agenda-setting is widely used in political science to refer to institutional agendas (e.g., in elections or in Congress; see Cox and McCubbins 2005).

hand, as campaign communications simultaneously steer voters to focus on certain issues in the campaign while also trying to persuade them to believe the candidate has a strong (or weak) record on those issues.

## Puzzles

The political science and communication literature on framing, priming, agenda-setting, or persuasion is immense. A search of thirteen prominent disciplinary journals, from 1994 through August 2009, reveals 308 articles that mention one or more of the concepts in the title and/or abstract.[3] Yet, a number of basic issues remain unresolved. First, our argument about the equivalency of these concepts contrasts with common portrayals (for example, McCombs 2004; Scheufele 1999). More research is needed, particularly to *determine whether the concepts involve distinct mediators and moderators* (evidence to date suggests they do not; see Miller and Krosnick 2000; Nelson, Clawson, and Oxley 1997). Along similar lines, the extent to which persuasion and framing differ remains unclear; the current distinction stems in part from a focus in most persuasion research on the evaluation component of an attitude. Do the processes (i.e., mediators and moderators) underlying changes in the weight and evaluative components of an attitude differ?

Second, more work is needed to document the psychological processes of the expectancy value model. Two important recent contributions accentuate the need for and difficulty of such research. Bullock and Ha (forthcoming) show that the conventional (Baron–Kenny) approach to documenting psychological mediation generates statistical bias, leading to misestimates. They emphasize the need to manipulate potential mediators as part of the experiment protocol—a task which they admit is not straightforward. Third, Lenz (2009) shows that the bulk of observational evidence for priming effects (e.g., increases in the weight attached to a dimension) is not priming at all, but rather reflects individuals changing the evaluation component of their attitude (for example, people change their own preference or their perception of the object's position) (also see Slothuus 2008).

Not only would resolving these puzzles signify a considerable advance, but it would have practical implications. First, if the concepts are the same, research should be merged and redundancy avoided. Second, identification of precise psychological processes facilitates the specification of conditions under which effects take place, an empirical question with significant normative implications.

---

[3] The journals include: *Public Opinion Quarterly, American Journal of Political Science, American Political Science Review, Journal of Politics, Political Behavior, Political Psychology, Journal of Communication, Communication Research, Political Communication, Journalism and Mass Communication Quarterly, Mass Communication and Society, Media Psychology,* and *Science Communication.*

# DETERMINING WHAT ELITES SAY

Scholars and pundits have long recognized the role of frames in shaping public opinion (Riker 1996; Schattschneider 1960, 70). The power of framing is also not lost on politicians, who spend considerable time determining the frames most advantageous to them (Bai 2005; Lakoff 2004).

The process by which speakers determine which frames to employ is often called "frame building" or "agenda building" (for example, Scheufele 1999). Here we provide three examples of how political elites choose frames (i.e., dimensions of emphasis). Our point is to highlight the driving role of strategic incentives. We then briefly discuss media framing and what we see as the key puzzles when it comes to work on determining elite rhetoric.

Our first example comes from Druckman and Holmes's (2004) study of President Bush's first post-2001 State of the Union Address (delivered on January 29, 2002). According to the January 2002 Gallup poll, 35 percent of respondents named terrorism or related problems as the most important problem facing the nation compared to 33 percent who named some sort of economic problem (followed by education at 6 percent). Prior to Bush's address, analysts predicted that he would focus equally on terrorism/homeland security and the economy. For example, CNN predicted that Bush would "focus on war, economy," while MSNBC described Bush as preparing for a "balancing act . . . [dealing] with terrorism, recession" (Druckman and Holmes 2004: 760).

These predictions seemed to ignore that Bush's issue-specific approval on security (roughly 86 percent) was substantially higher than on the slumping economy (roughly 31 percent) (Druckman and Holmes 2004). There was much greater incentive therefore for Bush to emphasize an issue that he was perceived to be managing well. Contrary to pre-debate expectations, but consistent with his strategic incentives, Bush framed the bulk of his policy discussion (49 percent based on content analysis of policy statements) in terms of terrorism/homeland security. In contrast, he devoted only 10 percent apiece to the economy and to the war in Afghanistan. The *New York Times* headline the day after the address reinforced the President's theme: "Bush, Focusing on Terrorism, Says Secure U.S. Is Top Priority."

Additional evidence suggests that Bush's behavior reflects a general pattern. Druckman, Jacobs, and Ostermeier (2004) examined Nixon's rhetorical choices during his first term in office (1969–72). The authors coded a large sample of Nixon's public statements and counted the amount of space devoted to distinct issues (e.g., welfare, crime, civil rights). Linking the rhetorical data with polling results from Nixon's private archives, they find that, on domestic issues, Nixon chose to accentuate issue positions that attracted public support. For example, if public support for Nixon's position on a particular domestic issue (e.g., Nixon's tax plans, which a large percentage of the public supported) increased by 10 percent over the total average, then, holding other variables at their means, Nixon increased attention to that domestic issue by an average of 58 percent (Druckman, Jacobs, and Ostermeier 2004, 1217–18). Nixon was not, however, responsive to changes in the public's issue priorities, choosing instead to prime those issues that worked in his favor (for example, he would promote his tax policy even if most of the public did not see taxes as an important problem). As Nixon's chief of staff, H. R. Haldeman, explained, using frames that highlight "issues where the President is favorably received" would make "Americans realize that the President is with them on these issues" (Druckman, Jacobs, and Ostermeier 2004, 1218).

Congressional candidates also follow predictable rules in framing their election campaigns. Because incumbents enjoy up to a 10 percentage point advantage (Jacobson 2004), they have a strategic incentive to highlight their experience, ties to the district, and benefits they have brought to constituents. In contrast, challengers will frame their campaigns around alternative considerations that tend to matter in congressional elections, including their issue positions, partisanship, endorsements, and viability.

Druckman, Kifer, and Parkin (2009) tested these predictions by content-analyzing candidate websites from a representative sample of US House and Senate campaigns from 2002, 2004, and 2006. They find clear evidence of strategic framing: incumbents play their strong suit by emphasizing their experience in office, familiarity to constituents, and district ties, while challengers frame the campaign in alternative terms. The normative implications are intriguing, since campaign frames that often establish subsequent policy agendas (for example, Jamieson 2000, 17) are driven, in no small way, by strategic considerations that may bear little relationship with pressing governmental issues.

All three examples focus on the framing tactics of a single elite actor without taking account of strategic interactions among competing elites or between elites and the media. Following Bush's 2002 State of the Union Address, Democrats predictably emphasized the troubled economy in their public statements, just as they tried, during Nixon's presidency, to turn public attention to issues that reflected poorly on Nixon. While congressional incumbents champion their experience, congressional challengers will attempt to exploit any perceived weakness in the voting records or personal reputations of the incumbents they are trying to unseat. To measure the extent to which competing frames are represented in news coverage of political issues, Chong and Druckman (forthcoming a) content-analyzed major newspaper coverage of fourteen distinct issues over time, counting the number of frames put forth on each issue (as well as other features of the frames).[4] While the data do not provide insight into strategic incentives, the findings reveal a complex mix of frames for each issue.

---

[4] Issues included the Patriot Act (*New York Times*, Sept. 12, 2001–Dec. 31, 2005); global warming (*New York Times*, Jan. 2, 2000–Dec. 31, 2004); intelligent design (*New York Times*, Nov. 1, 2004–Dec. 31, 2005); same-sex marriage in the US (*New York Times*, Aug. 1, 2003–Dec. 31, 2005) and in Canada (*Globe and Mail*, Aug. 1, 2003–Dec. 31, 2005); Social Security at two points in time (*New York Times*, June 1, 1997–June 31, 2000); the *Bush* v. *Gore* Supreme Court case (*New York Times*, Nov. 9–Dec. 13, 2000); the Abu Ghraib controversy (*New York Times*, Mar. 20–Sept. 30, 2004); an immigration initiative (*San Francisco Chronicle*, Nov. 1, 1993–Dec. 31, 1998); a Nazi rally (*Chicago Tribune*, Jan. 1–Dec. 31, 1978); two Ku Klux Klan rallies (*Lancaster New Era*, Aug. 1–Sept. 31, 2001; *Commercial Appeal*, Jan. 1–Feb. 28, 1998); and a proposal for a state-sponsored casino (*Chicago Tribune*, Aug. 24–Nov. 7, 2006). Rationale for these specific sources and dates are explained in Chong and Druckman (forthcoming a).

Chong and Druckman computed a score to capture the weighted number of frames used on a given issue (for example, frames employed more often receive greater weight). Across the fourteen issues, the average number of weighted frames is 5.09 (standard deviation = 1.19). The issue for which the fewest weighted frames were employed was coverage of a 1998 Ku Klux Klan rally in Tennessee (with 3.03 weighted frames including free speech, public safety, and opposing racism). The issue with the most frames was coverage of the 2004 Abu Ghraib controversy concerning prisoner abuse by members of the United States Armed Forces (with 6.9 weighted frames, several of which centered on different attributions of responsibility).

On each issue, there were competing frames that implied or explicitly recommended positions on the issue. For example, framing the Abu Ghraib incidents in terms of either renegade individual actions or the policies promulgated by the administration or military may contribute to widely varying public perceptions of responsibility. How individuals process these mixes of frames is a topic we address below.

Although competition proliferates alternative approaches to framing issues, it does not appear that issue frames change significantly over time. Baumgartner and his colleagues (2009) explored the rate at which ninety-eight issues on which lobbyists were active (for a full list, see Baumgartner et al. 2009, 17) were reframed (i.e., understood using a wholly or partially new frame) by interest groups, media, and other elite sources during a two-year period. They report that, "The results are surprising. Of the 98 issues that fell into our sample, we judged just 4 issues to have undergone some degree of re-framing over the period studied" (2009, 176). They point to several challenges of reframing elite understandings including limitations in resources, political constraints (e.g., political alignments), and failed lobbyist strategies. The lack of change also is consistent with macro-level studies that show that "system-wide definitions of most issues remain relatively constant through time" (B. D. Wood and Vedlitz 2007, 553). A question to explore further on this subject is: what proportion of issues would benefit from reframing from the perspective of competing parties? This requires examining the subset of issues for which there were elite incentives to engage in reframing. Of this smaller subset of cases, how frequently did elites have the necessary resources to attempt to reframe the issue? And when elites possess both incentives and resources, are they able to accomplish their objective? Answers to these questions would suggest whether limitations on reframing of issues can be explained by the absence of elite incentives, shortages of resources to carry out the task, or entrenched public opinion on the issues.

## Puzzles

The evidence thus shows that political elites strategically choose their frames and that the media offers competing frames on most issues. Beyond these intuitive findings, a number of issues remain unclear. First, *in addition to anticipating the public's response, how do elites incorporate expectations about other relevant actors, such as opponents, interest groups, and news outlets?* Campaigns for candidates or policies typically prepare for elite debate by using polling to test opposing messages in order to gage how the public will respond to competing frames. If support does not waver substantially following exposure to the strongest arguments of the opposition, this is taken as evidence that the campaign message can withstand the pressure of competition (Stonecash 2003).

While there is work on communication strategies (e.g., the media bias literature, the media indexing literature, ethnographic studies), there is scant theory of how political actors interact with the media to ensure that their chosen frame receives coverage (see Entman 2004). For example, the evidence about Nixon shows he was responsive to the public, but did he also consider likely media coverage? One promising area worth pursuing is explicit integration with the somewhat distinct literature on interest group framing (see Polletta and Ho 2006).

Second, *how does new media proliferation (and more direct communication opportunities) affect strategy?* This is an interesting dynamic insofar as cable television initially stripped prominent politicians of predictable access (Baum and Kernell 1999), but now the Web and other direct communication technologies may restore opportunities to address limited publics. This may, in turn, increase precise targeting when frames are chosen.

Third, the bulk of work on elite influence takes a unidirectional approach: elites take actions that influence public opinion. Even if they anticipate that response, the elites are influencing the public. A separate literature explores whether elite actions, such as policy or roll-call votes, reflect public opinion (for example, J. N. Druckman and Jacobs 2009; Erikson, Mackuen, and Stimson 2002), which is treated as an exogenous influence on elites' choices. There is undoubtedly a reciprocal process in which elites influence opinion, opinions influence policy choices, policy choices influence opinion and rhetoric, and so on. We are certainly not the first to recognize this dynamic (for example, Page and Shapiro 1992), but we continue to have a limited understanding of it (although see Soroka and Wlezien 2009). For example, *when does an elected official treat opinions as given and respond to them as opposed to trying to change opinions?* Or do politicians "respond" to the public simply by framing their policies to make them consistent with the public's values (Jacobs and Shapiro 2000)? Elites are likely to employ mixed communication strategies geared toward different audiences depending on their susceptibility to persuasion and framing. It is also worth exploring how framing and persuasion strategies differ across issues of varying salience. More generally, work on elite influence could benefit from considering the conditions that tend to affect responsiveness (for example, see J. N. Druckman and Jacobs 2006).

## DETERMINING INFLUENCE

The history of research on elite influence on the public's opinions has followed a well-known evolution, from maximal effects to minimal effects to "strong" effects, and a possible return to minimal effects (see Bennett and Iyengar 2008). Understanding the conditions under which elite rhetoric shapes opinions depends, to a large extent, on the psychological processes at work and the context of the communication. The psychological model we posited above—based on availability, accessibility, and applicability—leads straightforwardly to predictions about when influence occurs.

As explained, a consideration highlighted by a communication frame cannot impinge on an attitude unless it is available in memory (i.e., it can be comprehended). By definition, this requires knowledge, and thus, all else constant, framing will have a *greater effect on more knowledgeable individuals* (for evidence, see J. N. Druckman and Nelson 2003; Nelson, Oxley, and Clawson 1997; Slothuus 2008; although see Togeby 2007). The proviso that everything else be held constant is critical to this prediction because knowledgeable individuals are more likely to hold strong prior opinions that resist the influence of framing (for example, Brewer 2001; Iyengar 1991). Therefore, it is necessary to control for the strength of prior opinions when examining the influence of knowledge on framing.

In addition to individual factors that qualify elite influence, the nature of the message matters. All else constant, *increased repetition will enhance a frame's effect*, because repetition can facilitate learning and increase the accessibility of a consideration (for example, Bless, Fiedler, and Strack 2004, 61). The impact of repetition, however, is reduced when individuals evaluate the applicability of frames. As mentioned, this occurs either when an individual is motivated or when competition between contrasting messages stimulates more deliberate processing of information. Therefore, in competitive political environments, *a frame's impact tends to increase with an individual's perception of the frames' applicability or strength* (for evidence, see Chong and Druckman 2007b; J. N. Druckman 2010; also see J. N. Druckman 2004; Sniderman and Theriault 2004). The effect of competition highlights the importance, when studying elite communications, of looking beyond individual psychology to take account of the context of elite–public interactions (Schattschneider 1960). That individuals tend to resolve competing frames in favor of the stronger frame also reiterates the importance of a frame's strength in determining its effect.

## Puzzles

There are many unresolved puzzles concerning the conditions of elite influence. First is the obvious question of what factors make a frame strong. Chong and Druckman (2007a) explain that strong frames emphasize available considerations; a frame focused on unavailable considerations cannot have an effect (i.e., it is inherently weak). The other factor is the judged persuasiveness or effectiveness of the frame. This is commonly assessed, in both political science (for example, Chong and Druckman 2007b) and psychology (for example, Petty and Cacioppo 1986) by asking respondents who do not participate in the main part of the study to rate the effectiveness of different frames or arguments, with more effective frames being treated as stronger. But, why are some frames perceived as strong and others weak? Even the large persuasion literature provides limited insight: "Unhappily, this research evidence is not as illuminating as one might suppose ... It is not yet known what it is about the 'strong arguments' ... that makes them persuasive" (O'Keefe 2002, 147, 156). A parallel question applies to priming and agenda setting as it cannot be assumed that elites can elevate with equal ease the priority given to any issue. At any given time, some issues are undoubtedly easier to prime or place on the agenda and in this sense are "stronger" than other issues.

The slight evidence to date on the underpinnings of strength is not encouraging as it appears individuals often ignore criteria seen as normatively desirable (e.g., logic, facts) while focusing on factors that are more difficult to justify. For example, Arceneaux (2009, 1) finds that "individuals are more likely to be persuaded by political arguments that evoke cognitive biases." Specifically, he reports that frames that highlight averting losses or out-group threats resonate to a greater extent than do other, ostensibly analogous arguments. J. N. Druckman and Bolsen (2009) report that adding references to scientific studies to frames does nothing to enhance their effectiveness in influencing opinions. Other work suggests frame strength increases with activation of specific emotions (Aarøe 2008; Petersen forthcoming), use of multiple repetitive arguments (Baumgartner et al. 2008), attribution to a credible source (Chong and Druckman 2007b), and familiarity (Edy 2006). The initial studies on frame strength make clear that one should not confuse "strength" with superiority on rational or normative grounds.

A second puzzle of elite effects concerns the role of time. Political campaigns and debates over issues occur over extended periods in which citizens receive continual messages. Research, however, has concentrated overwhelmingly on the immediate impact of communications and paid little attention to the dynamics of public opinion formation over time. Most studies that have monitored respondents over time find rapid decay of communication effects (for example, De Vreese 2004; J. N. Druckman and Nelson 2003; Mutz and Reeves 2005, 12); however, these studies have largely ignored individual variation and not examined how attitudes respond to the pressure of competing messages received over the course of a campaign. A likely source of heterogeneity is how individuals process information (Chong and Druckman forthcoming b; Druckman, Hennessy, St Charles, and Weber 2010; Matthes 2008). Those who engage in online formation of opinions update their opinions when they receive a new communication (e.g., a frame) and are able to retrieve the summary evaluation subsequently. These individuals are more likely to express stable attitudes because past learning extends into the future and each additional piece of information has a smaller marginal effect. In contrast, the effects of past communications tend to fade rapidly among memory-based processors who draw disproportionately on immediately accessible considerations. A related process that affects attitude stability is motivated reasoning: simply put, the stronger one's opinions, the more one is motivated to dismiss communications that contradict those opinions. Therefore, online processors will have more stable opinions not only because their attitudes reflect cumulative exposure to information, but also because they increasingly resist new information that might change those attitudes (see Lodge and Taber 2000).

A third area that would benefit from further research is the analysis of other relevant political factors (for example, Togeby 2007). A paradigmatic example of this type of work comes from Slothuus's (2009) study of party frames. He notes that framing research has not adequately investigated how party sources qualify the impact of frames. In an ingenious study that exploits a shift in frames among parties in Denmark on the issue of early retirement benefits, he finds that while people are more influenced by frames sponsored by their preferred party, they do not automatically adopt their party's frame. Rather, the frames must also be consistent with their more general beliefs (also see Lecheler, De Vreese, and Slothuus 2009). Other relevant dynamics that are in need of further study include competition with distinct types of communication such as direct endorsements (J. N. Druckman, Hennessy, St Charles, and Weber 2010) and interpersonal discussion (for example, J. N. Druckman and Nelson 2003). Also important is the need to devise research strategies that account for ongoing technological and social transformations. Bennett and Iyengar (2008) state: "it is clear we are entering another important turning point not just in communication technologies [e.g., increased media choice, outlets] but in social structure and identity formation [e.g., decline of group memberships and the rise of multiple identities] that affect the behaviors of audiences" (2008, 716). The authors then provide a blueprint on how researchers can begin to address these new political realities.

Finally, more research is needed on how self-selection of information affects the impact of communications. Most communication studies take exposure as given (for example, in an experiment, participants are captive audiences who view the stimuli), whereas in reality people can and do ignore information. Arceneaux and Johnson (2008) show that when participants in communication experiments can choose whether to receive a communication (i.e., the captive audience constraint is removed), communication effects are diminished (also see Barabas and Jerit forthcoming).

# NORMATIVE PUZZLES

We raise two normative puzzles that follow from the work on elite influence we have reviewed: (1) what are the normative implications of elite influence over public opinion? and (2) what do the results imply for normative theory itself?

## Normative Implications

Early research on elite influence, particularly on framing, suggested that political elites can manipulate popular preferences to serve their own interests. It is this perspective, with all the negative connotations it entails for democratic processes, that led researchers to search for mechanisms that condition effects (e.g., source credibility, deliberation, competition) and make individuals less vulnerable to framing (Sniderman and

Levendusky 2007). More recently, researchers have come to recognize that framing and related communication effects are intrinsic to the formation of attitudes. Indeed, public opinion formation involves the selective acceptance and rejection of competing frames that contain information about candidates and issues. Discussion and debate over the appropriate frames for conceptualizing an issue ultimately lead to common perceptions and judgments about the consequences of a policy (Chong 2000).

Framing effects, however, undermine the validity of public preferences if individuals never acquire a basis for discriminating among frames and remain constantly vulnerable to changing representations of issues. Alternatively, individuals who are impervious to framing because they refuse to consider alternative perspectives suffer from closed-mindedness, or "motivated reasoning," which might be as problematic as unstable preferences (for example, J. N. Druckman and Bolsen 2009; Lodge and Taber 2000). In short, at one extreme are citizens without sufficiently strong attitudes and cognitive defenses to resist elite manipulation, while at the other extreme are citizens whose attitudes are held so rigidly that they seek only to reinforce their existing views. The ideal public is surely somewhere in between, capable of differentiating between relevant information and misleading arguments.

No consensus, however, exists about the standards that should be applied to evaluating the quality of public opinion. Features of superior or more sophisticated opinions that have been suggested include choices that are ideologically coherent, based upon deliberation, consistent with individual interests, or consistent with values (see J. N. Druckman 2001 for discussion). The most noted standard against which public opinion is compared is a decision that takes account of full, unbiased, or the best available information (for example, Lau and Redlawsk 2006; Page and Shapiro 1992, 356; Zaller 1992, 313). In the absence of clear standards, discussions about ways to improve the quality of public opinion can produce conflicting conclusions. For example, according to some researchers, voters who use cues or cognitive shortcuts make better decisions than those who are uninformed (Popkin 1994), but others have argued that relying on cues produces poor decisions by most normative standards (for example, Kinder 1998; for extended discussion, see J. N. Druckman, Kuklinski, and Sigelman 2009). Likewise, when Iyengar and Kinder (1987) introduced priming to the discipline in experimental studies, it was construed as a form of manipulation that undermined the public's role in keeping elected representatives in check; more recently, however, Lenz (2009) laments the limited evidence for priming effects in actual political campaigns on the grounds that priming can lead people to base their opinions on issues rather than on less substantive criteria (e.g., images and symbols).

These reflections on framing and priming lead us to conclude that normative assessments of communication effects must evaluate details of individuals' psychological processing and the substantive basis of their decisions. In terms of process, it is important to be realistic in one's normative standards for the public (see, for example, Schattschneider 1960, 134). Citizens will use a mix of shortcuts and substantive information depending on individual and contextual circumstances, but generally fall well short of possessing full information (however we define this ideal). In addition to studying what information people process, scholars also need to assess how people evaluate information. It is again not straightforward what standards should apply in judging whether people's preferences are the product of good procedures; for example, although motivated reasoning is problematic because it can negate the influence of relevant information, a realistic theory of reasoning must recognize that the beliefs underlying people's preferences will usually reflect some degree of motivated reasoning, especially in polarized political settings (for example, Lodge and Taber 2000). Identifying the substantive basis on which citizens *should* form their preferences is challenging, lest theorists end up making unrealistic, ill-defined, and elitist demands on citizens. As Lupia explains, "those who write about voter competence might recognize the differences between their interests and the interest of the people whom they study" (2006, 219).

Our perspective leads us to focus on the nature of the frames on which individuals base their opinions. We introduced the distinction between strong and weak frames, with the exclusive focus being on the citizens' perceptions of strength. One could apply an analogous distinction between normatively desirable and undesirable frames. Desirable frames presumably have some logical basis and are correlated with an objective reality—for instance, to return to the example of the proposed housing development we began with, those who frame their support in terms of future economic benefits should be willing to alter their judgments if no valid studies can support claims that the project will have an impact on local employment.

## Implications for Normative Theory

Identifying clear guidelines to assess frame quality requires engagement with normative theory. This, in turn, may require a reorientation of dominant normative approaches. Canonical theory treats citizens' preferences as exogenous to the political process and focuses on whether elites respond to these preferences, whereas the entire corpus of framing research shows that public preferences are highly contingent on how alternatives are represented to citizens and, as such, are far removed from the consistent individual preferences assumed in economic theory (Bartels 2003).

A democratic theory based on exogenous public preferences ignores the issue of where citizens are supposed to obtain information on which to form preferences. It is perhaps implicit that they are supposed to rely on some objective experiences, but in an age of mass communication the theory seems dated. In other words, we posit that normative theory move beyond what Disch describes as "the 'bedrock' norm of representative democracy: the commonsense notion that political representation is democracy only to the extent that it takes citizens' preferences as the 'bedrock for social choice'" (2009, 2). A democratic theory needs to recognize the reality of endogenous preferences that depend on the actions and rhetoric of politicians even if, as Bartels notes, a "successful normative resolution may require a style of theorizing unfamiliar to political philosophers and political scientists alike" (2003, 74).

We are not the first to recognize this normative–empirical disjuncture and the concomitant challenges (for example, Disch 2009). The issues we encourage others to consider are neatly captured in Schattschneider's lament:

It is an outrage to attribute the failures of American democracy to the ignorance and stupidity of the masses. The most disastrous shortcomings of the system have been those of the intellectuals whose concepts of democracy have been amazingly rigid and uninventive . . . Unless the intellectuals can produce a better theory of politics than they have, it is possible that we shall abolish democracy before we have found out what it is! The intellectuals have done very little to get us out of the theoretical trap created by the disparity between the demands made on the public by the common definition of democracy and the capacity of the public to meet these demands. The embarrassment results from the reluctance of intellectuals to develop a definition that describes what really happens in a democracy.   (1960, 132–3)

# CONCLUSION

As technological and societal changes continue, mass communication researchers face a host of challenges. Addressing how these transformations affect elite–public interactions will be imperative (Bennett and Iyengar 2008). However, it also is important that researchers consider various other longer-standing challenges that have yet to be resolved. We identified many of these, including puzzles revolving around basic conceptual questions and mediational processes, elite strategy, political context, and the normative implications of proven communications effects. In pursuing some of these research questions, scholars should recognize that some of the technological transformations that may interest them from a substantive perspective can facilitate methodological applications as well. For example, the profusion of new media offers researchers novel opportunities to measure elites' and citizens' behaviors (for example, J. N. Druckman, Kifer, and Parkin 2009). We have little doubt that progress will continue and hopefully it will do so at a rate approaching that of the last fifteen years.

## REFERENCES

AARØE, L. 2008. Investigating Frame Strength. Unpublished paper. Aarhus University.
AJZEN, I., and FISHBEIN, M. 1980. *Understanding Attitudes and Predicting Social Behavior.* Englewood Cliffs, NJ: Prentice-Hall.
ALTHAUS, S. L., and KIM, Y. M. 2006. Priming Effects in Complex Environments. *Journal of Politics*, 68: 960–76.
ARCENEAUX, K. 2009. Cognitive Biases and the Strength of Political Arguments. Unpublished paper. Temple University.

—— and JOHNSON, M. 2008. Choice, Attention, and Reception in Political Communication Research. Paper presented at the Annual Meeting of the International Society for Political Psychology, Paris, July 9–12.

BAI, M. 2005. The Framing Wars. *New York Times Magazine*, July 17.

BARABAS, J., and JERIT, J. Forthcoming. The External Validity of Treatments. *American Political Science Review*.

BARTELS, L. M. 1993. Messages Received. *American Political Science Review*, 87/2: 267–85.

—— 2003. Democracy with Attitudes. In *Electoral Democracy*, ed. M. B. MacKuen and G. Rabinowitz. Ann Arbor: University of Michigan Press.

BAUM, M. A., and KERNELL, S. 1999. Has Cable Ended the Golden Age of Presidential Television? *American Political Science Review*, 93/1: 99–114.

BAUMGARTNER, F. R., BERRY, J. M., HOJNAACKI, M., KIMBALL, D. C., and LEECH, B. L. 2009. *Lobbying and Policy Change.* Chicago: University of Chicago Press.

—— DE BOEF, S. L., and BOYDSTUN, A. E. 2008. *The Decline of the Death Penalty and the Discovery of Innocence.* New York: Cambridge University Press.

BENNETT, W. L., and IYENGAR, S. 2008. A New Era of Minimal Effects? *Journal of Communication*, 58: 707–31.

BLESS, H., FIEDLER, K., and STRACK, F. 2004. *Social Cognition.* New York: Psychology Press.

BREWER, P. R. 2001. Value Words and Lizard Brains. *Political Psychology*, 22: 45–64.

BULLOCK, J., and HA, S. Forthcoming. Mediation Analysis Is Harder than it Looks. In *Cambridge Handbook of Experimental Political Science*, ed. J. N. Druckman, D. P. Green, J. H. Kuklinski, and A. Lupia. New York: Cambridge University Press.

CHONG, D. 2000. *Rational Lives.* Chicago: University of Chicago Press.

—— and DRUCKMAN, J. N. 2007a. A Theory of Framing and Opinion Formation in Competitive Elite Environments. *Journal of Communication*, 57: 99–118.

—— —— 2007b. Framing Public Opinion in Competitive Democracies. *American Political Science Review*, 101/4: 637–55.

—— —— 2007c. Framing Theory. *Annual Review of Political Science*, 10/1: 103–26.

—— —— 2010. Dynamics in Mass Communication Effects Research. In *The Sage Handbook of Political Communication*, ed. H. Semetko and M. Scammell. Thousand Oaks, CA: Sage.

—— —— Forthcoming a. Identifying Frames in Political News. In *Sourcebook for Political Communication Research*, ed. E. P. Bucy and R. L. Holbert. New York: Routledge.

—— —— Forthcoming b. Dynamic Public Opinion: Communication Effects over Time. *American Political Science Review*.

COX, G. W., and McCUBBINS, M. D. 2005. *Setting the Agenda.* New York: Cambridge University Press.

DAHL, R. A. 1971. *Polyarchy.* New Haven: Yale University Press.

DE VREESE, C. H. 2004. Primed by the Euro. *Scandinavian Political Studies*, 27/1: 45–65.

DISCH, L. 2009. Beyond Responsiveness. Unpublished paper. University of Michigan.

DRUCKMAN, D. 2003. Puzzles in Search of Researchers: Processes, Identities, and Situations. *International Journal of Conflict Management*, 14/1: 3–22.

DRUCKMAN, J. N. 2001. The Implications of Framing Effects for Citizen Competence. *Political Behavior*, 23/3: 225–56.

—— 2004. Political Preference Formation. *American Political Science Review*, 98 (Nov.), 671–86.

—— 2010. Competing Frames in a Political Campaign. In *Winning with Words*, ed. B. F. Schaffner and P. J. Sellers. New York: Routledge.

—— Forthcoming. What's It All About? In *Perspectives on Framing*, ed. G. Keren.

DRUCKMAN, J. N. and BOLSEN, T. 2009. Framing, Motivated Reasoning, and Opinions about Emergent Technologies. Paper presented at the Annual Meeting of the American Political Science Association, Toronto, Sept. 3–6.

—— and HOLMES, J. W. 2004. Does Presidential Rhetoric Matter? *Presidential Studies Quarterly*, 34: 755–78.

—— and JACOBS, L. R. 2006. Lumpers and Splitters: The Public Opinion Information that Politicians Collect and Use. *Public Opinion Quarterly*, 70: 453–76.

———— 2009. Presidential Responsiveness to Public Opinion. In *The Oxford Handbook of the American Presidency*, ed. G. C. Edwards III and W. G. Howell. Oxford: Oxford University Press.

—— and NELSON, K. R. 2003. Framing and Deliberation. *American Journal of Political Science*, 47/4: 728–44.

—— HENNESSY, C. L., ST. CHARLES, K., and WEBER, J. 2010. Competing Rhetoric over Time: Frames versus Cues. *Journal of Politics*, 72: 136–48.

—— JACOBS, L. R., and OSTERMEIER, E. 2004. Candidate Strategies to Prime Issues and Image. *Journal of Politics*, 66: 1205–27.

—— KIFER, M. J., and PARKIN, M. 2009. Campaign Communications in U.S. Congressional Elections. *American Political Science Review*, 103/3: 343–66.

—— KUKLINSKI, J. H., and SIGELMAN, L. 2009. The Unmet Potential of Interdisciplinary Research: Political Psychological Approaches to Voting and Public Opinion. *Political Behavior*, 31/4: 485–510.

EDY, J. A. 2006. *Troubled Pasts*. Philadelphia: Temple University Press.

ENELOW, J. M., and HINICH, M. J. 1984. *The Spatial Theory of Voting*. Boston: Cambridge University Press.

ENTMAN, R. M. 2004. *Projects of Power*. Chicago: University of Chicago Press.

ERIKSON, R. S., MACKUEN, M. B., and STIMSON, J. A. 2002. *The Macro Polity*. New York: Cambridge University Press.

IYENGAR, S. 1991. *Is Anyone Responsible?* Chicago: University of Chicago Press.

—— and KINDER, D. R. 1987. *News that Matters: Television and American Opinion*. Chicago: University of Chicago Press.

JACOBS, L. R., and SHAPIRO, R. Y. 2000. *Politicians Don't Pander*. Chicago: University of Chicago Press.

JACOBSON, G. 2004. *The Politics of Congressional Elections*, 6th edn. New York: Pearson Longman.

JAMIESON, K. H. 2000. *Everything You Think You Know about Politics . . . And Why You're Wrong*. New York: Basic Books.

KINDER, D. R. 1998. Communication and Opinion. *Annual Review of Political Science*, 1: 167–97.

LAKOFF, G. 2004. *Don't Think of an Elephant?* White River Junction, VT: Chelsea Green.

LAU, R. R., and REDLAWSK, D. P. 2006. *How Voters Decide*. New York: Cambridge University Press.

LECHELER, S., DE VREESE, C. H., and SLOTHUUS, R. 2009. Issue Importance as a Moderator of Framing Effects. *Communication Research*, 36/3: 400–25.

LENZ, G. 2009. Learning and Opinion Change, Not Priming. *American Journal of Political Science*, 53/4: 821–37.

LODGE, M., and TABER, C. 2000. Three Steps toward a Theory of Motivated Political Reasoning. In *Elements of Reason*, ed. A. Lupia, M. D. McCubbins, and S. L. Popkin. Cambridge: Cambridge University Press.

Lupia, A. 2006. How Elitism Undermines the Study of Voter Competence. *Critical Review*, 18: 217–32.

McCombs, M. 2004. *Setting the Agenda*. Malden, MA: Blackwell.

Matthes, J. 2008. Media Frames and Public Opinion. *Studies in Communication Studies*, 8: 101–28.

Miller, J. M., and Krosnick, J. A. 2000. News Media Impact on the Ingredients of Presidential Evaluations. *American Journal of Political Science*, 44/2: 301–15.

Mutz, D. C., and Reeves, B. 2005. The New Videomalaise. *American Political Science Review*, 99/1: 1–15.

Nelson, T. E., and Oxley, Z. M. 1999. Issue Framing Effects and Belief Importance and Opinion. *Journal of Politics*, 61: 1040–67.

—— Clawson, R. A., and Oxley, Z. M. 1997. Media Framing of a Civil Liberties Conflict and its Effect on Tolerance. *American Political Science Review*, 91/3: 567–83.

—— Oxley, Z. M., and Clawson, R. A. 1997. Toward a Psychology of Framing Effects. *Political Behavior*, 19/3: 221–46.

O'Keefe, D. J. 2002. *Persuasion*. 2nd edn. Thousand Oaks, CA: Sage.

Page, B. I., and Shapiro, R. Y. 1992. *The Rational Public*. Chicago: University of Chicago Press.

Petersen, M. B. Forthcoming. Distinct Emotions, Distinct Domains: Anger, Anxiety and Perceptions of Intentionality. *Journal of Politics*, 72/2.

Petty, R. E., and Cacioppo, J. T. 1986. *Communication and Persuasion*. New York: Springer.

Polletta, F., and Ho, M. K. 2006. Frames and their Consequences. In *The Oxford Handbook of Contextual Political Studies*, ed. R. E. Goodin and C. Tilly. New York: Oxford University Press.

Popkin, S. L. 1991. *The Reasoning Voter*. Chicago: Chicago University Press.

—— 1994. *The Reasoning Voter: Communication and Persuasion in Presidential Campaigns*, 2nd edn. Chicago: University of Chicago Press.

Price, V., and Tewksbury, D. 1997. News Values and Public Opinion. In *Progress in Communication Sciences*, xiii, ed. G. A. Barnett and F. J. Boster. Greenwich, CT: Ablex.

Riker, W. H. 1996. *The Strategy of Rhetoric*. New Haven: Yale University Press.

Schattschneider, E. E. 1960. *The Semisovereign People*. New York: Holt, Rinehart, and Winston.

Scheufele, D. A. 1999. Framing as a Theory of Media Effects. *Journal of Communication*, 49: 103–22.

—— 2000. Agenda-Setting, Priming, and Framing Revisited. *Mass Communication and Society*, 3: 297–316.

Simon, H. A. 1955. A Behavioral Model of Rational Choice. *Quarterly Journal of Economics*, 69: 99–118.

Slothuus, R. 2008. More than Weighting Cognitive Importance. *Political Psychology*, 29/1: 1–28.

—— 2009. The Political Logic of Party Cues in Opinion Formation. Unpublished paper. University of Aarhus.

Sniderman, P. M., and Levendusky, M. S. 2007. An Institutional Theory of Political Choice. In *The Oxford Handbook of Political Behavior*, ed. R. J. Dalton and H.-D. Klingeman. Oxford: Oxford University Press.

—— and Theriault, S. M. 2004. The Structure of Political Argument and the Logic of Issue Framing. In *Studies in Public Opinion*, ed. W. E. Saris and P. M. Sniderman. Princeton: Princeton University Press.

SOROKA, S. N., and WLEZIEN, C. 2009. *Degrees of Democracy*. New York: Cambridge University Press.

STONECASH, J. 2003. *Political Polling*. Lanham, MD: Rowman & Littlefield.

TOGEBY, L. 2007. The Context of Priming. *Scandinavian Political Studies*, 30/3: 345–76.

VAVRECK, L. 2009. *The Message Matters*. Princeton: Princeton University Press.

WINTER, N. J. G. 2008. *Dangerous Frames*. Chicago: University of Chicago Press.

WOOD, B. D., and VEDLITZ, A. 2007. Issue Definition, Information Processing, and the Politics of Global Warming. *American Journal of Political Science*, 51/3: 552–68.

WOOD, W. 2000. Attitude Change: Persuasion and Social Influence. *Annual Review of Psychology*, 50: 539–70.

ZALLER, J. 1992. *The Nature and Origins of Mass Opinion*. New York: Cambridge University Press.

# CHAPTER 12

......

# ISSUE FRAMING

......

## THOMAS E. NELSON

WHILE our leaders busy themselves confronting international terrorism, there is a far graver public health menace that attracts comparatively little notice. This threat kills tens of thousands of Americans every year; in fact, it is the leading cause of death among some groups. Furthermore, a simple change in the law would dramatically lessen this danger, saving hundreds or even thousands of lives without demanding great sacrifices in our way of life. That legislators have failed to enact this simple measure is scandalous enough; what's worse is that recent changes in government policy have actually increased this risk. What is this great public scourge? Automobile travel. The change in the law that would save so many lives? Lowering the speed limit (Vanderbilt 2008).

Does it seem inappropriate, not to say contrived, to call driving a "public health menace"? Does it seem perverse to state that driving is a greater threat to American welfare than terrorism? And yet the facts are plain. *Framing* automobile travel as a public health menace might be unusual, but it is not unfaithful to the facts. There are many other ways of framing automobile travel, equally faithful to the facts, but far more flattering to the peripatetic American driver. The *cost-benefit frame* depicts deaths and injuries due to driving as an unfortunate but unavoidable price we pay for the many commercial and recreational advantages that driving affords. The *libertarian* frame sees driving along the open road as the quintessential embodiment of American freedom—an informed choice that government dare not infringe (Sandel 2009).

Already we see two important qualities of issue frames. First, they include factual assertions, but go beyond the facts to offer broader interpretations and characterizations of the issue. Second, most of them are *valenced*, meaning that they support a distinct position on a (typically) controversial issue. A close analogue would be the summary statements offered at trial by plaintiffs' and defendants' counsels. Working from a common set of facts, the antagonists provide diverging interpretations of the events and points of law that suggest guilt or innocence (Pennington and Hastie 1992).

This chapter addresses two key questions about issue frames: what they *are*, and what they *do*. Framing research has rushed to pursue the latter question before really settling the former. This is probably because framing has attracted such a remarkably broad and diverse assortment of scholarly prospectors, each unearthing valuable nuggets of empirical findings, but leaving the field as a whole fragmented (Entman 1993). On balance, framing scholarship is a terrific example of strength through diversity. By taking stock of the various conceptualizations and operationalizations of framing across the traditional disciplinary centers, we learn much more than we would have if the study of framing had kept within the confines of a single discipline. This requires us, naturally, to take that stock.

## Defining Issue Framing

One widely quoted definition states that framing provides "a central organizing idea or story line that provides meaning to an unfolding strip of events, weaving a connection among them. The frame suggests what the controversy is about, the essence of the issue" (Gamson and Modigliani 1987, 140). This is a good start, but is not sufficient, because just as "framing" has been approached by different scholarly traditions, it has been applied to different phenomena. We must strive to specify clear boundaries between the different kinds of framing, while resisting the urge to call anything and everything a frame.

Imagine a debate about traffic laws that concerned itself entirely with competing predictions about the effect of lower speed limits on driving casualties (Vanderbilt 2008). Some argue, with considerable empirical backing, that the variation in casualties due to speed alone is relatively minor, and so there is little benefit to lowering speeds. Others argue, backed by their own mountain of research, that there *is* a meaningful relation between speed and risk. As with most complex human behaviors, clean tests are hard to come by; speed is hardly independent of other variables. A great deal of disagreement thus focuses exclusively on which facts one chooses to believe. Both arguments exhibit the same frame—a "casualty frame," if you will (Jerit 2008). The messages express alternative *valences* within the casualty frame (one favorable, the other unfavorable) with respect to the central question of speed limits. These alternative valences might very well influence attitudes, but it would be different from the potential effect of the casualty frame relative to, say, the libertarian frame.

Now imagine a world in which the empirical questions were actually settled to everyone's satisfaction. That is, the pro-speed and anti-speed forces agree that reducing the speed limit would significantly cut fatalities. Even in such an unlikely world, the debate would hardly end. Competing sides might remain just as entrenched, because they subscribe to competing visions, characterizations, or interpretations—*frames*, in a word—of the traffic issue. Pro-speed forces might still claim that an overbearing intrusion by the government into the freedom of the individual driver is an unacceptable price to pay for protecting the lives of people who, through their own recklessness, are doubtless partly responsible for their own fates. The only way to make the roads completely safe, after all, is to ban driving altogether. To answer the libertarian frame, anti-speed forces would be forced to go beyond the empirical predictions to offer an alternative frame, perhaps stressing that the roads are publicly owned and publicly shared, and therefore an appropriate arena for judicious government regulation. Competing factual claims, however important they are to public debate, are neither its beginning nor its end.

In the extreme, one can frame the same *facts* in different ways. Instead of talking about how many lives might be *lost* under a given scenario, for example, one could instead talk about how many lives could be *saved*. This is precisely what Kahneman and Tversky did in their experiments on prospect theory, their alternative to strict expected utility theory (Kahneman and Tversky 1984). Kahneman and Tversky demonstrated that attitudes toward risk were significantly influenced by this gain–loss framing. Subjects were more eager to take chances under the loss frame, presumably because they were willing to risk a larger loss in order to have a chance of suffering no loss at all. To present these alternative frames, the experimenters deftly manipulated the putative status quo. To establish the gain frame, a specific number of deaths was assumed; every alternative, therefore, was described as a positive change (or no change) from that reference point. To establish a loss frame, the status quo was not specified; it must therefore have been assumed to be "no change." Every prospect was therefore worse than this reference point.

These exercises are among the best-known "framing effects," but framing research stretches across an astonishingly wide range of scholarly disciplines, and many framing studies bear little resemblance to the Kahneman and Tversky experiments, nor do they relate in any obvious way to behavioral economics (Schaffner and Sellers 2009). Framing is a communal concept; perhaps alone among social science topics, it spans several layers of systemic and individual phenomena. "Frame" refers to the peculiar habits and institutional norms of news organizations; the strategic communication choices of mass movement organizers and interest group entrepreneurs; the structure and content of communication; and the mental organizations of citizens. "Frames," therefore, are static features of messages or thoughts; "framing" is the dynamic process of advocating or applying a frame to an issue.

What makes Kahneman and Tversky's demonstration so effective is that the prospects are precisely quantified and, to the fully informed observer, clearly equivalent in expected value. These features make the departures from normative decision rules obvious, but concordant with prospect theory's predictions. Druckman calls these "equivalence frames" (Druckman 2001a), and political scientists have investigated their applicability to political phenomena like strategic decision-making (Boettcher 2004). They are atypical exemplars of issue framing, however, because the *prospects*, or expected *outcomes*, are being framed, but not the issue itself (Lau and Schlesinger 2005).

Contrast these characteristics with the driving example that opened this chapter, or any of the other popular or scholarly examples of framing effects. In such cases, the issue or policy solution is subject to competing characterizations. For example, Jacoby (2000) compared opinions toward "government spending" with support for more specific programs like food stamps. Support was stronger for the narrow framing of spending than for the broader framing. Alternative frames often consist of more colorful, interpretive language than the simple quantitative expressions in Kahneman and Tversky's exercises. In a simple demonstration, Smith found greater support for "aid to the poor" than for "welfare," even though they amount to the same thing (Smith 1987).

Contestants in the health care debate disagreed strongly about its likely cost to the taxpayers, and whether citizens can choose their own doctor. When the President claimed that his health care proposal wouldn't cost the taxpayer another penny, while his opponents predicted a tax-and-spending debacle, they were debating, but not framing. An issue frame could, however, *emphasize* the cost dimension and *deemphasize* the choice dimension, or vice versa. As persuasive speech, framing is, among other things, an exercise in keeping the public's attention focused on those aspects of the issue that cast the most favorable light on one's own position (Jacobs and Shapiro 2000; Jacoby 2000).

Issue frames embody a complex semantic structure that confounds easy definition and measurement. The efforts are reminiscent of the painstaking work by international relations scholars to describe and capture the complex, synthetic world views of global leaders (Holsti 1970). They also call to mind disputes over whether the *schema* concept, also imported from cognitive psychology, provides any comparative advantage over tried and true concepts like *attitude* (Kuklinski, Luskin, and Bolland 1991). Defining issue framing remains an ongoing project (Iyengar 2009), as scholarship walks a fine line between comprehensiveness and distinctiveness.

# News Framing

Framing simplifies issues. The end of the twenty-first century's first decade will be remembered for the global credit crisis and consequent economic recession. How does the average citizen understand this labyrinthine phenomenon? Many of them don't, but that cannot be an option for all citizens, since we are expected to evaluate policies intended to rescue the world from this calamity. Rather than constructing a comprehensive mental model that incorporates all the moving parts of this crisis, we might choose a convenient frame that tells a relatively simple story about who's at fault, and what should be done (Morris 2008). One popular frame puts most of the blame on the shoulders of Wall Street hotshots, who concocted obscure financial instruments and sold them to callow investors. Another blames consumers who took on more debt than they could handle, especially home mortgages. Still another blames the lenders, brokers, and realtors who pushed houses and mortgages on those underqualified consumers, and so on.

Who especially needs compact, easily digested summaries of today's top stories? The news media, of course. News organizations can apply any number of frames to just about any kind of story (Price and Tewksbury 1997). There is the *personalization* frame, which boils down complex political–economic stories to comparatively simple narratives about individuals (Iyengar 1991). Some media stories about the economic crisis focus on detailed portraits of newly unemployed workers or homeowners facing foreclosure, while stories about health care feature disheartening tales about families enduring economic ruin over a costly illness. The *conflict* frame, by contrast, defines issues by their competing groups.

Issue frames may be reported by the media, or even supply the theme around which a news story is organized (de Vreese 2003; Nelson, Clawson, and Oxley 1997). They are not the same as news frames, however. The difference is that news frames are *generic*; they apply to just about any kind of issue. Indeed, that is their main function and appeal for news organizations. One could write a conflict-framed story about a war, of course, but also about a budget battle in Congress or a variance request placed before the local zoning commission. Issue frames are comparatively specific and ad hoc: they capture the essence of an issue, and perhaps only that issue; they do not necessarily transport to any other kind of topic. Furthermore, they are valenced, rather than neutral. They lay blame and favor particular solutions. The "pro-choice" and "pro-life" abortion frames summarize and simplify, to be sure, but they also wear their preferences plainly on their sleeves. In short, media frames are templates, whereas issue frames are themes.

There is symbiosis between media framing and issue framing, which contributes to the confusion. The news media's predilection for simple summary statements, and their reliance on skilled spokespeople for quotables, means that news organizations become the carriers of issue frames (Kellstedt 2003). This is all to the good for the creators of these issue frames, for frames acquire priceless credibility when reported by a news organization. Some tough cases have characteristics of both news frames and issue frames; for example, the *strategic game* frame that dominates news coverage of both elected leaders and political candidates. This frame assumes that leaders' explanations for their behaviors cannot be taken at face value; that some hidden venal motive provides the true energy for their actions (Cappella and Jamieson 1997; Patterson 1993). This frame, like other news frames, easily transports to all kinds of topics, but it has qualities in common with issue frames, also. Political communicators outside of the journalists' ranks rely on this frame to tarnish their opponents and the causes they represent.

## FRAME ELEMENTS AND EFFECTS

The most complete set of ideas about issue-frame substance and consequences can be found in the writings of William Gamson (for example, Gamson and Lasch 1983;

Gamson and Modigliani 1987), although reviewing his framing theory requires yet another side trip into terminology. Gamson argues that social movements wrap their positions inside holistic *issue packages*, composed of many *signature elements*, one of which is the *frame*. Other elements include *caricatures*, or exaggerated, cartoonish depictions of the opposing side (fat-cat businessmen, eco-terrorists, feminazis, etc.) In Gamson's view, frames are brief summary depictions of the entire package. We know, for example, that the "pro-choice" frame in the abortion debate conveys a lot more than a simple homage to personal choice. Frames are not to be confused with *catch-phrases*: pithy, shoutable slogans such as "keep your laws off my body." In a process of scholarly metonymy, the frame element has come to be treated as synonymous with the entire package.

Frames can be more or less comprehensive. "Whole story frames" are the broadest perspectives or points of view on an issue (Gray 2003). Environmental disputes, for example, often feature competing sides whose entire world views seem mutually alien. The groups do not represent differing interests so much as clashing cultures. Such diametrically opposed outlooks help explain why these disputes often prove intractable.

Framing happens at the sub-issue level, too. Key concepts or ideas can be subject to differing interpretations or depictions. In the perennial debate over teaching "alternatives" to evolution in public schools, disputants have wrangled over the meaning of the term "science" (Ruse 1996). Alternative framings of this household word can be more or less hospitable to theories such as intelligent design, which have more than a whiff of the supernatural about them. Evolutionists insist that real science assumes *methodological naturalism*: natural phenomena must be explicable in terms of natural forces. Intelligent designers insist on a broader definition that makes room for the deliberate actions of a super-powerful but obscure designer. This framing contest is not just an idle exercise in lay epistemology; disputants have tried to codify their preferred frame in state education policy. Everyone agrees that students should learn science; the disagreement centers around what counts as science. In this dispute, the power to frame has quite tangible policy consequences.

Contemporary communication scholarship tends to lump framing with priming and agenda-setting as examples of "subtle" communication effects (versus learning, a more overt effect). A complete understanding of issue framing thus requires disentangling it from these sister concepts. The differences are real, but people can be forgiven for scratching their heads over all these terms.

McCombs, a pioneer in agenda-setting research, sees continuity rather than divergence between framing and agenda-setting (McCombs 2004). He likens framing to "second order agenda-setting." Agenda-setting theory argues that mass media attention to a public issue begets heightened public concern about the problem. The prototype is crime coverage. Media attention to crime, especially sensational crime such as road rage or kidnapping, can raise public concern about the problem, even if the relative occurrence of such events is steady and slight (Glassner 1999). Such is first-order agenda-setting: media attention elevates concern about one type of issue (e.g., crime) relative to others competing for our interest and attention (e.g., the economy).

Second-order agenda-setting applies the same logic *within* rather than *between* issues. Issues such as the global credit crisis are usually multifaceted problems, inviting many different perspectives or approaches. Each approach isolates and elevates the prominence of one element of these complex phenomena. The consequences of second-order agenda-setting for public policy can be significant. If the credit crisis is all about reckless proliferation of investment instruments, then some regulation of the financial services industry would seem warranted; if it's all about bad mortgages, then the home lending industry would seem due for stricter oversight.

Put this way, the barriers between framing, priming, and agenda-setting seem translucent at best. Consider one of McComb's own examples: news coverage of election campaigns. Suppose that, during an election campaign, the news media lavish attention on one thorny problem (e.g., the economy) to the neglect of other, arguably equally important issues (e.g., foreign policy). The media will have thus set the agenda for the public, such that the economy becomes the number one concern for most citizens. A consequence of this agenda-setting would likely be that candidates in the upcoming election will be evaluated, first and foremost, on their economic aptitude. This is *priming*, or determining the criteria by which political actors are evaluated (Iyengar and Kinder 1987). Notice that neither of these effects depends on the media making overt connections between the economy and the upcoming election. They probably would, but the effects are presumably accomplished merely by keeping the public's thoughts occupied by the economy, rather than something else. Thus occupied, subsequent political judgments and decisions (What's the most important problem facing the nation? Whom should I vote for?) will be disproportionately affected by economics (Iyengar and Kinder 1987; Vavreck 2009).

Suppose the media *do* make overt connections between the upcoming election and the candidates' relative ability to manage the economy. This is second-order agenda-setting, or framing, according to McCombs. Elections are complex decision problems, to be sure. There are many issues that could be considered determinative, to say nothing of candidate qualities, party reputations, and so on. In second-order agenda-setting, the media don't make our decision for us, but they provide direct instruction about how to make our decision. They say, in effect, "it's the economy, stupid voter."

Second-order agenda-setting accounts nicely for many issue-framing effects, but cannot subsume them all (to be crystal clear, McCombs does not advocate abandoning the term "framing"). It works best in cases where we envision framing as an exercise in narrowing or simplifying an issue. It is less convincing when we consider the interpretive or explanatory function of frames, as in the example of alternative frames for science.

De Vreese's research on media frames for European integration provides important findings in its own right, but presents further challenges for researchers seeking coherent and consistent conceptual boundaries around all of these communication effects. Through content analysis, de Vreese found media coverage of European Union expansion dominated by an economic frame. Moreover, some stories emphasized potential economic costs of expansion, while others concentrated on benefits. Sure enough, such variations in coverage influenced audiences' attitudes. De Vreese calls these framing effects; but according to the criteria outlined above, it's not so clear. To find that economic frames of alternative valences (positive versus negative) are influential says nothing about the impact of economic frames versus some other frame (e.g., cultural, legal). Perhaps it's splitting hairs, but we could refer to de Vreese's effects as effects of frame *valence*, rather than frame.

This extended discussion of what issue frames *aren't* has, I hope, not only helped explain what they are, but also clarified sometimes maddening overlap among all these instances of the framing concept. The similarities and differences, however aggravating, tell us a lot about the origins and structure of mass communication. But this is only half of the story; what of the *consequences* of issue framing?

## COGNITIVE AND AUDIENCE FRAMES

Many cognitively oriented framing researchers conceptualize frames much like social stereotypes: they have a cultural representation outside of the individual, as well as a mental representation within the individual (Scheufele 2004). They suggest that mass communication frames correspond to a structured set of cognitions, emotions, and evaluations at the individual level. Perhaps the most obvious and straightforward "framing effect" would therefore amount to communication frames *shaping* these individual frames, or *activating* existing frames that resemble the communication frame.

As sensible as such a claim sounds, it is the rare study that has tried to demonstrate a clear communication frame–individual frame linkage (Neuman, Just, and Crigler 1992). The paucity of efforts is doubtless due to the considerable difficulties of conceptualizing, defining, and measuring a "cognitive frame." Just as with their extraindividual mates, an individual frame's holistic character defies easy description. Individual stereotypes are often conceived of as a list of traits that distinguish a social category (men are assertive, women are emotional, etc.) Frames are thought to be something more. We would not say that an individual's stereotype constitutes the totality of their attitudes toward that social category; presumably, feelings about the other group come into play, perhaps joined by a kind of ideology about intergroup relations. Likewise, individual frames have to be more than just a collection of discrete cognitions; there is a sense that the systemic interrelations among these components are also important.

This puts framing closer to the structural depictions of cognitive organization, such as *script, schema, narrative,* or *mental model.* In old-fashioned terms, it is the gestalt that establishes the frame, not its individual components. Borrowing from the "story model" of jury decision-making (Pennington and Hastie 1992), Berinsky and Kinder

(2006) argue that frames supply a plausible narrative that assembles and organizes otherwise discrete facts. In so doing, frames help citizens "make sense" of politics.

It is fascinating to pursue questions about the individual mental representation of issue frames, and about the mutual influence between such frames and mass-communicated frames. Strictly speaking, however, it is not necessary to establish frames as a viable model of cognitive representation in order to sustain the idea that framing is an important communication phenomenon in its own right. Indeed, many experimental studies of framing do not assume that there must be an isomorphic relation between communication and cognitive frames. Many studies look at framing effects on familiar constructs such as beliefs or opinions.

In examining the individual effects of frames, research has stressed three broad classes of concepts: attributions, values, and group attitudes. Attributions are paramount in the work of the social movement theorists (Gamson and Modigliani 1989; Snow and Benford 1992) as well as Iyengar's research on news frames (Iyengar 1991). To mobilize their followers, social movements must identify specific actors who are responsible for an injustice, as well as who should take responsibility for resolving the problem. In Iyengar's view, news frames do much the same thing, although far more subtly. Values are idealized conditions or behaviors that provide standards for evaluating policy solutions. Political controversies often embody several values, which might conflict. Frames can stress which value deserves the greatest recognition (Brewer and Gross 2005; Nelson 2004; Shah, Domke, and Wackman 1996). Finally, group admiration or enmity can powerfully affect political attitudes. Frames can emphasize a linkage between evaluations of a group and evaluations of a policy (Grant and Rudolph 2003; Nelson and Kinder 1996).

The common depiction of framing's simplification function puts it squarely within the bounded rationality paradigm that dominates today's cognitively oriented political psychology. The major claim of the paradigm is that citizens only think as much about politics as necessary to make judgments, formulate opinions, and reach decisions. Expending extra cognitive effort on politics, unless it's your job or your hobby, is a waste. To accomplish these tasks with minimal effort, the citizen skims the surface of his or her political memory, rather than digs deeply. What's at the surface of memory isn't necessarily the most valuable, relevant, or important fragment of information; more than likely, it simply happens to be something we heard relatively recently—say, an issue frame we just encountered. As reviewed above, such an account makes framing of a piece with priming and agenda-setting.

I've never been convinced that this is the whole story behind framing effects (Nelson, Oxley, and Clawson 1997; see also Slothuus 2008). It turns out it might not be the whole story behind agenda-setting, either (J. M. Miller 2007). More recent models of framing effects also emphasize more mindful processes such as judging the importance or relevance of different considerations (Slothuus 2008).

Cognitive psychology suggests another pair of processes that might contribute to framing effects: categorization and analogy (Holyoak and Thagard 1995; Pinker 2007). For example, the 1970s and 1980s saw many of the United States' misadventures in

research on tone, for instance), it is much less common to carefully consider the influence of the content of television advertising—issue and image content, fear vs. humor appeal, and so on. At the cutting edge of such a focus is recent research by Brader (2005) that shows advertising effects are conditional on emotional content.

## Telephone, Direct Mail, and Personal Contact

While the "air war" communications continue to receive the bulk of campaign money in most political campaigns, recent campaigns are giving renewed attention to "ground war" efforts, including direct mail, telephone calls, and personal canvassing. In recent years, there has been a decline in the efficiency and effectiveness of television advertising; with the expansion of media choice (on television and the Internet) and the widespread use of technology like remote controls and TiVo, it has become easier for the public to avoid political advertising (Prior 2007). Candidates now face a higher "cost per impression" to reach a voter with a broadcast message, so they have turned to email, direct mail, phone calls, and personal canvassing to narrowcast campaign messages to targeted audiences (Monson 2004).

Historically, research on ground war activity has focused on grassroots mobilization efforts—the targeting of core supporters to get them to the polls. One of the consistent findings in the mobilization literature is that personal contact plays a consistent role in getting out the vote (Rosenstone and Hansen 1993; Verba, Schlozman, and Brady 1995). Lower levels of voting, according to this argument, were a consequence of a less personal, increasingly mediated form of contact between parties and voters. Although an influential body of research, much of the work on party contact is also susceptible to the criticism that the observed relationship between exposure and various political outcomes is spurious, the result of campaign targeting rather than campaign effects.

Field experiments have been used as a way to address these concerns, and they come as close as possible to isolating the causal effects of personal contact. Gerber and Green's (2000a) field experiment found that face-to-face canvassing increased turnout by more than 5 percent, a finding that has been replicated in subsequent studies (Green, Gerber, and Nickerson 2003). Looking at direct mail, Gerber and Green (2000b) found that non-partisan get-out-the-vote (GOTV) postcards increased turnout among Independents by 7 percent, but had no effect on Democrats or Republicans.

Increasingly, candidates are also contacting voters directly through the Internet and email, but the effects of these sources of information are difficult to study, especially because voters tend to select exposure (Bimber and Davis 2002). In one of the few studies on the topic, Nickerson (2007) found that non-partisan email contact does not increase registration rates or lead to higher turnout, but clearly more research on the topic is needed.

Future research on the ground campaign should focus more closely on the persuasive impact of direct contact. Most of the research in the area has tended to focus on non-partisan voter mobilization efforts (for example, Green and Gerber 2004), but the reality of presidential campaign activities is that very few communications are pure GOTV messages. When a campaign sends direct mail, makes a phone call, or knocks on a door, they don't simply ask the recipient to go to the polls without also telling them who to vote for or why they should vote that way—a clear attempt to persuade. In an analysis of county-level voter behavior, for instance, Masket (2009) finds that counties that had an Obama field office in 2008 had a sharper increase in Democratic vote share relative to 2004. Future research would also benefit from studying who is responsive to which messages. In a meta-analysis, for instance, Arceneaux and Nickerson (2009) find that GOTV efforts are most effective at increasing the turnout likelihood of low-propensity voters in high-intensity elections and of high-propensity voters in low-intensity elections.

## Campaign Visits

One of the basic campaign activities in presidential elections is the simple decision by candidates to make an appearance during the campaign. Althaus, Nardulli, and Shaw (2002) found that candidates are increasing the number of appearances they make, and they are appearing in out-of-the-way places they may have avoided in years past. In an analysis of presidential campaigns between 1988 and 1996, Shaw (1999) found that candidate appearances were positively correlated with statewide vote share, particularly in states with large percentages of undecided voters. Subsequent pooled time series cross-sectional analysis by the same author for the 2000 and 2004 presidential elections concluded certain campaign appearances were associated with increased candidate favorability ratings, and changes in vote choice (Shaw 2006). Less clear is the mechanism by which candidate visits have an effect, whether through increased media coverage, direct contact with voters, or another factor.

## Campaign Events

A number of studies have also found evidence that specific campaign events can influence public opinion and behavior. Holbrook (1996) catalogued major incidents in US presidential campaigns between 1984 and 1992 and found that the relative standing of the two major-party candidates is impacted by these events. Scholars have observed that party conventions provide a "bump" for the convention candidate (Holbrook 1996; Hillygus and Jackman 2003). Campbell, Cherry, and Wink (1992) estimate the convention bump is 5 to 7 points and persists into the general election campaign.

Debates similarly offer the public unmediated exposure to the major-party presidential candidates' views and personality characteristics, at least until the talking heads begin to contribute their interpretations of the outcome. But their effects on the public may be limited by the tendency of well-prepared candidates to offer canned responses to questions and to avoid direct confrontation (Schrott 1990); presidential debates may be more like dual press conferences than an actual debate. As a consequence, we might expect the candidates' messages either to cancel one another out or simply to reinforce preexisting opinions. Certainly, debates offer evidence that the public engages in biased processing (Chaiken, Liberman, and Eagly 1989), where prior attitudes shape how people confront new information (Lanoue and Schrott 1991). Nonetheless, some scholars have found the debates do have an impact on citizens' perceptions, though the mass media again play an intervening role (Holbrook 1996; Johnston, Blais, Brady, and Crete 1992). For instance, Johnston, Hagen, and Jamieson (2004) found that debate viewers perceived Al Gore to be the winner of the first and third presidential debates, though media criticism of Gore's infamous sighs and grimaces led debate non-viewers to perceive that Bush had won.

A long series of studies also finds that debates increase viewers' knowledge of candidates' issue positions (Lanoue and Schrott 1991; but see Lanoue 1995), though there are conflicting findings about whether debates increase knowledge primarily among low-information viewers or increase the knowledge gap between different classes of viewers (Bartels 1993). Holbrook (1999) found the debates do facilitate learning, and the first debate is particularly effective in this regard. Thus, there is some evidence that the debates increase the overall level of knowledge in the electorate, though it is not clear from a normative point of view whether debates level the informational playing field among citizens from different social strata.

While the above events are known to competing candidates and their strategists well in advance, other events arise suddenly and unexpectedly, and can have consequences in the election—the so-called "October surprise." For example, some scholars have argued that the economic collapse was decisive in the 2008 election (Linn, Moody, and Asper 2009; but see Hillygus and Henderson 2010). Such research is in its relative infancy in large part because scholars have only recently had access to the data necessary for such analysis. New and emerging data collection efforts, such as the Annenberg rolling cross-sections (Johnston, Hagen, and Jamieson 2004) have increasingly made it possible to isolate the effects of specific campaign events, even those unexpected and unscheduled.

## Mediated Messages

To this point, we have focused on the consequences of active efforts by campaigns to influence election outcomes; however, many voters are influenced by information not produced by the campaigns. Indeed, since the public expects messages provided by the candidates or parties to be biased, source credibility—and thus the persuasive power—of other information sources might well be greater. For instance, scholars have found that interpersonal discussions—with friends, family, co-workers—have a large influence on candidate evaluations (for example, Beck, Dalton, Greene, and Huckfeldt 2002). Huckfeldt and Sprague (1995) report that people seek out informed and

common goal. At the same time, engaging in the democratic process can enhance feelings of political trust and efficacy. This chapter examines the key concepts of political trust and political engagement, underscoring how they are shaped by the media, and identifying fruitful avenues for research in this area.

# POLITICAL TRUST

For decades, scholars, citizens, and pundits have discussed declining levels of political trust in the United States and their implications for public life. Concerns over this crisis of confidence are grounded in the belief that without political trust, citizens will challenge their government's very existence. However, political *distrust* serves a useful role in democracy as it can motivate citizens to effect social and political change (Miller 1974).

Although there is a general consensus regarding the implications of trust in—and distrust of—government, there is some disagreement over the object and meaning of political trust. Does distrust reflect citizens' attitudes toward specific policies or the political system as a whole (Miller 1974) or does it reflect dissatisfaction with individual incumbent leaders (Citrin 1974)? Efforts to provide a conceptually grounded reply are muddied by the commonly used American National Election Studies questions that assess trust in government; some items tap respondents' trust in the institution, while others gage trust in the individuals in that institution.

Regardless of whether dissatisfaction reflects an orientation toward the system or individuals who hold office within that system, low political trust (or conversely, high political distrust or political cynicism) ultimately signals a discrepancy between citizens' expectations and governmental output, and can be related to political apathy. Further complicating matters is how political trust has been used interchangeably with "confidence," with much research focusing on the absence of such. Though trust and cynicism often are considered two sides of the same coin, they are not necessarily mirror opposites. As Hardin (2006) observed, someone who lacks cynical views is not necessarily someone who trusts. In the same vein, individuals who express low levels of trust in government are often considered high in political cynicism. However, these low levels of trust may reflect skepticism, the holding of a critical yet open stance toward government (Cappella and Jamieson 1997).

# ANTECEDENTS TO POLITICAL TRUST

## General Influences

Underlying these theoretical nuances is an overarching concern regarding the origins of low levels of trust in government. Myriad explanations include individual,

spheres is in many ways a politicizing experience" (Verba, Schlozman, and Brady 1995, 40).

The terms "political participation" and "political engagement" are sometimes used interchangeably (Bimber 2001), though some conceptual distinctions do emerge. "Political engagement" has been used to refer to more individual-level dispositions and attitudes, including citizens' levels of political interest, political knowledge, and political efficacy (Verba, Burns, and Schlozman 1997). Such research signals that in addition to participating through political actions, individuals' political cognitions are important considerations in understanding public life.

An even more inclusive term is *democratic engagement*, which Delli Carpini (2004) articulates as including attitudes, cognitions, and behaviors related to citizenship. Democratically engaged citizens presumably adhere to democratic norms and values, believe in the political system, and possess a sense of efficacy and political interest. They hold overarching views about their political and social lives as well as stable and informed opinions about specific issues. These citizens also engage in various aforementioned acts of political behavior.

The move from "political participation" to "political engagement," from "civic participation" to "civic engagement," and now "democratic engagement," reflects a shift toward more comprehensive concepts; indeed, Delli Carpini (2004) uses "democratic engagement" to include both civic and political engagement. To identify antecedents to engagement would involve casting a wide net that brings together various political attitudes, behaviors, and cognitions, a Herculean task that easily goes beyond this chapter. We therefore focus our efforts on identifying general and media-specific influences on the behavioral aspects of political engagement—namely, *behaviors* that fall under the rubrics of "political participation," "civic participation," and "civic engagement" or "social capital."

# ANTECEDENTS TO POLITICAL ENGAGEMENT

## General Influences

Early studies of political participation utilized a socioeconomic (SES) model, showing that education, income, and occupation related positively to political participation (Verba and Nie 1972). Individuals in higher socioeconomic strata tend to process political information more easily, and generally are situated in more central network positions that facilitate participation (Nie, Junn, and Stehlik-Barry 1996).

In elaborating upon the SES model, scholars have identified a host of intervening variables that would explain the process by which one becomes politically active. These variables are nicely categorized in Verba, Schlozman, and Brady's (1995) civic voluntarism model: resources such as time, money, and civic skills; psychological predispositions, including political interest, internal and external efficacy, and political knowledge; and recruitment, or requests for participation that come to a particular citizen. Still missing from recent models of political participation, however, is the potential role of the mass media in shaping behaviors.

# Media Influences

Scholarly concern over media influences on the behavioral manifestations of political engagement has implicitly and explicitly compared the effects of various media. Below we summarize the key findings relating the use of each medium to political activity.

## Newspapers

The effects of newspaper reading are positive and robust. Print news consumption directly increases citizens' engagement with civic behaviors, such as belonging to various community organizations (Beaudoin, Thorson, and Hong 2006), as well as volunteering, working on community projects, and working on behalf of social causes (Shah, Cho, Eveland, and Kwak 2005). It also is often associated with political behaviors such as being a member of a political party, being registered to vote, and voting in national and local elections (Wilkins 2000), in addition to contacting public officials, working on a political campaign, circulating petitions, and fundraising (Scheufele, Nisbet, Brossard, and Nisbet 2004), and voting (McLeod et al. 1996). As well, individuals who pay greater attention to newspaper articles are more likely to report an intention to vote (Drew and Weaver 2006).

Print media use also influences political engagement *indirectly* through a number of mechanisms. Reading newspapers not only directly increases participation, but also leads to increased knowledge (Moy and Gastil 2006), which in turn enhances participation (McLeod, Scheufele, and Moy 1999). Individuals who know more about politics tend to possess higher levels of internal efficacy and believe their actions can shape the political system (Delli Carpini and Keeter 1996), and high levels of efficacy can increase one's likelihood to take action (Gamson 1968). Newspaper articles also are more likely to convey mobilizing information that tells readers how they can actually participate (Lemert 1981).

Newspaper reading also can increase participation levels by generating interpersonal discussion. As Chaffee and Mutz put it, "mass media often provide grist for the conversation mill and stimulate informal discussions that might not otherwise take place" (1988, 21). Such discussions allow citizens to exchange information, address civic and political issues, and learn about how they can become engaged. However, interpersonal discussion can occur alongside mass media use and the two can have multiplicative effects on engagement. Individuals who read newspapers *and* discuss public affairs issues within their social networks experience differential gains; they are more likely to participate than those individuals who engage in either newspaper reading or political talk alone (Scheufele 2002).

## Television

Unlike the generally heartening effects of print media use, those of television are less conclusive and sometimes negative. This is partly due to the great variance in television's vast array of informational content and programming.

With respect to content differences, scholars typically differentiate between news and entertainment, juxtaposing "hard," "serious" news against "softer," human interest stories. Watching hard news on television correlates with participation in formal electoral politics (Wilkins 2000), and translates directly into greater attendance at political meetings, contacting public officials, working on campaigns, and writing letters to the editor (Scheufele, Nisbet, Brossard, and Nisbet 2004). However, the indirect effects of television news viewing on participation are significantly stronger. Watching television news equips citizens with knowledge regarding current events, policy issues, and political actors; armed with this knowledge and information, citizens are more likely to engage in political action (Scheufele, Nisbet, Brossard, and Nisbet 2004). The effects of television news viewing on civic participation are indirect as well, working through interpersonal political discussion (Shah, Cho, Eveland, and Kwak 2005). Unlike newspaper reading, however, which enjoys strong *direct* relationships with both civic and political participation, television hard news use is generally more likely to work *indirectly*.

Watching entertainment-oriented content has mixed effects: Keum et al. (2004) find that viewing sitcoms, dramas, and talk shows directly suppresses civic participation, but Shah, McLeod, and Yoon (2001) find that watching dramas leads to greater civic participation, while viewing situation comedies hampers it.

The picture is further complicated when one considers *infotainment*—content that is produced with entertainment values in mind, yet includes a strong political component and/or frequent references to public and political life. Watching political comedy programming can enhance *political* behaviors such as attending a campaign event, but watching late night talk shows such as the *Tonight Show* or the *Late Show with David Letterman* has mixed effects (Cao and Brewer 2008; Moy, Xenos, and Hess 2005). Infotainment can enhance *civic participation* by boosting citizens' sense of empowerment (Hoffman and Thomson 2009). However, exactly why infotainment—as opposed to more explicit public affairs news programming—has the capacity to do so needs to be addressed more closely.

## Internet

As the Internet becomes a mainstream source of information, scholars eagerly have turned to studying its impact on public life. Early studies showed meager and disparate effects: an increase in campaign contributions (Bimber 2001) and a greater likelihood to vote (Tolbert and McNeal 2003). The emergence of nuanced Internet use measures, however, generated more robust effects: frequency of use (Kim, Jung, Cohen, and Ball-Rokeach 2004) and motivations for Web use make a difference. For example, informational, social, and political uses of the Internet increased civic participation directly and indirectly via social trust, while using the medium for household or social goals undermined civic participation (Moy, Manosevitch, Stamm, and Dunsmore 2005; Shah, Kwak, and Holbert 2001).

Indeed, as new media technologies become more sophisticated, scholars have moved away from treating Web use as a single activity, opting instead to examine specific Web behaviors: commenting on political or social issues online; posting news, pictures, or videos about political or social issues; starting or joining political groups; and "friending" candidates on social networking sites (Smith, Schlozman, Verba, and Brady 2009).

As communication scholars have moved to identifying contingent media effects, so too has the research on Web effects on political and civic participation. Those who see campaign information online are more likely to be civically and politically engaged if they have high levels of political interest than if they are not too interested in politics (Xenos and Moy 2007). Also, the effects of Web use can be moderated by the quality of access (Kwak, Skoric, Williams, and Poor 2004). In general, extant data provide some evidence for claims made by optimists who believe that the Internet will draw citizens more deeply into political life (for example, Rheingold 2000), but the lack of significant trends calls for cautious optimism.

# CONCLUSION

Given the media's pervasiveness and their influence on political life, lay concern and scholarly attention to the process by which such effects occur are warranted. The corpus of literature in this domain has identified various key mechanisms by which the mass media can enhance or suppress political trust and political participation. By helping citizens understand issues, the players involved in a particular policy debate, or the ramifications of voting a particular way, the media can generate knowledge and in turn shape confidence in government and how citizens engage in politics. Media content, with its varying degrees of specificity, negativity, and accessibility to the inner sanctums of politics, also has been credited with generating attitudinal and behavioral change. Indeed, media effects are robust.

Although this chapter exclusively focused on key political outcomes of media coverage and consumption of such coverage, a richer picture would emerge from examining the multitude of forces that shape media content. After all, journalists' ideologies and beliefs, the journalist–source relationship, news values that emphasize conflict and drama, and the primacy of economic goals work in tandem to shape how citizens come to understand mediated coverage of politics (W. L. Bennett 1990; Page and Shapiro 2000; Shoemaker and Reese 1996).

Discussions of media influences on political trust and engagement also would be incomplete without taking into account the role of individual dispositions. After all, people turn to the media to fulfill specific needs and seek particular gratifications (Katz, Blumler, and Gurevitch 1974), and selective exposure processes work such that individuals gravitate toward media content that resonates with existing views and positions (Bryant and Davies 2006). In addition, the degree to which individuals process mediated information—and indeed, their motivations to process that information—can mitigate or exacerbate media effects (Eveland 2002).

Also to be considered is citizens' level of trust in the media. Greater efforts need to be taken to understand how trust in media interacts with information processing. Under what circumstances do people who distrust the media process information more thoroughly, and under what circumstances would they tune out information completely? And how does trust in one political institution relate to trust in another? There is little evidence of spillover effects related to trust (Hardin 2006), but distrust of an institution can have ripple effects (Montinola 2004). In the end, the political effects of the media may be more contingent than omnipotent, and hinge upon a number of individual-level factors.

Research illustrates the benefits of talking about politics alongside consuming political news from the media (Scheufele 2002). However, scholars need to focus not only on the frequency of discussion, but also on the heterogeneity of the discussion group and the degree of like-minded arguments encountered. Such characteristics of the group will determine whether the discussion itself is "safe" or "dangerous," and ultimately whether it will lead to political knowledge and political participation (Eveland and Hively 2009). Also, as new media technologies allow citizens to transcend geographic boundaries and redefine their sense of community, so too will the concept of political discussion change. Studying the role of interpersonal discussion, then, needs to be broadened to include discussion in non-face-to-face settings, the individuals engaged in discussion, whether the discussion is a function of or concomitant with media use, and of course, what actually transpires within these discussions.

Changes in the media landscape necessitate a careful scrutiny of media content itself. In the past half-century, the number of media outlets has proliferated and content that implicates citizens' political life can be found in a host of outlets ranging from news to entertainment and from international to local. Unfortunately, researchers' emphasis on national news has precluded investigations into the effects of local news (Friedland and McLeod 1999), which tends to be linked to community issues around which citizens can mobilize and take action. Optimistically, recognizing that political content pervades the spectrum of media outlets, researchers have begun to focus on the political effects of entertainment media (Baum and Jamison, Chapter 8 in this volume; Holbert et al. 2005; Moy, Xenos, and Hess 2005).

Alongside the proliferation of media outlets is the blurring of boundaries brought on by technological changes. As news organizations increase their online presence, the study of media effects on political life needs to be refined. Querying respondents about the number of days a week they read a newspaper is now problematic as citizens turn in droves to reading news online, and consume content that is updated not weekly, but by the hour. Scholars have illustrated differential impacts of reading print newspapers versus online newspapers (for example, Tewksbury and Althaus 2000), but their ultimate effects on political engagement have yet to be determined.

Also, as news organizations move online, they have begun to incorporate technical features that emphasize interactivity. For example, commenting has allowed readers to respond directly to journalists' content, providing direct feedback and critiquing coverage. News recommendation engines allow journalists to track audience interest and improve their coverage accordingly. And autonomous political blogging alongside newly integrated journalism blogs enable a range of civic actors—from everyday citizens to mobilized coalitions—to both compete and directly engage with mainstream media in shaping the public agenda.

Such changes ultimately raise the normative question of what it means to be a citizen. If discussing issues with other citizens via blogging, providing feedback to journalists via comments, and other related online activities can promote one's sense of horizontal engagement, will these opportunities ultimately constrain political, vertical engagement? With the blurring of mass and interpersonal communication, it remains to be seen whether citizens see engagement with the media alone as fulfilling their civic duties. For example, new genres of political activity online—adding candidates as "friends" on Facebook, or tracking their daily activities on Twitter—simulate co-presence with political elites. The novelty of these activities may raise citizen interest, but may not be as effective in conveying their needs and concerns to elected officials and the system at large. Furthermore, these activities are undertaken by a minority of citizens, almost exclusively young adults (Smith, Schlozman, Verba, and Brady 2009). Digital media may promote "deeper democracy" by improving access to political information and institutions, but this may be at the expense of promoting "thin citizenship." Citizens may feel more engaged and efficacious, but not actually participate effectively (Howard 2005). Future studies linking media use and democratic engagement will need to contend with issues of measurement as well as an evolving media landscape that generates new opportunities for citizens to engage in politics.

## REFERENCES

BEAUDOIN, C., THORSON, E., and HONG, T. 2006. Promoting Youth Health by Social Empowerment: A Media Campaign Targeting Social Capital. *Health Communication*, 19/2: 175–82.

BECKER, L. B., and WHITNEY, C. D. 1980. Effects of Media Dependencies: Audience Assessment of Government. *Communication Research*, 7/1: 95–120.

BENNETT, S. E., RHINE, S. L., FLICKINGER, R. S., and BENNETT, L. L. M. 1999. "Video Malaise" Revisited: Public Trust in the Media and Government. *Harvard International Journal of Press/Politics*, 4/4: 8–23.

BENNETT, W. L. 1990. Toward a Theory of Press–State Relations in the United States. *Journal of Communication*, 40/2: 103–25.

BIMBER, B. 2001. Information and Political Engagement in America: The Search for Effects of Information Technology at the Individual Level. *Political Research Quarterly*, 54/1: 53–67.

BREHM, J., and RAHN, W. M. 1997. Individual-Level Evidence for the Causes and Consequences of Social Capital. *American Journal of Political Science*, 41/3: 999–1023.

BRYANT, J., and DAVIES, J. 2006. Selective Exposure Processes. In *Psychology of Entertainment*, ed. J. Bryant and P. Vorderer. Mahwah, NJ: Lawrence Erlbaum.

CAO, X., and BREWER, P. R. 2008. Political Comedy Shows and Public Participation in Politics. *International Journal of Public Opinion Research*, 20/1: 90–9.

CAPPELLA, J. N., and JAMIESON, K. H. 1997. *Spiral of Cynicism: The Press and the Public Good*. New York: Oxford University Press.

CHAFFEE, S. H., and MUTZ, D. C. 1988. Comparing Mediated and Interpersonal Communication Data. In *Advancing Communication Science: Merging Mass and Interpersonal Processes*, ed. R. P. Hawkins, J. M. Wiemann, and S. Pingree. Newbury Park, CA: Sage.

CITRIN, J. 1974. Comment: The Political Relevance of Trust in Government. *American Political Science Review*, 68/3: 973–88.

COLEMAN, J. 1990. *Foundations of Social Theory*. Cambridge, MA: Harvard University Press.

CONVERSE, P. E. 1972. Change in the American Electorate. In *The Human Meaning of Social Change*, ed. A. Campbell and P. E. Converse. New York: Russell Sage Foundation.

DELLI CARPINI, M. X. 2004. Mediating Democratic Engagement: The Positive and Negative Impact of Mass Media on Citizens' Engagement in Political and Civic Life. In *The Handbook of Political Communication Research*, ed. L. L. Kaid. Mahwah, NJ: Lawrence Erlbaum.

——and KEETER, S. 1996. *What Americans Know about Politics and Why it Matters*. New Haven: Yale University Press.

DREW, D., and WEAVER, D. 2006. Voter Learning in the 2004 Presidential Election: Did the Media Matter? *Journalism and Mass Communication Quarterly*, 83/1: 25–42.

EVELAND, W. P., JR. 2002. News Information Processing as Mediator of the Relationship between Motivations and Political Knowledge. *Journalism and Mass Communication Quarterly*, 79/1: 26–40.

——and HIVELY, M. H. 2009. Political Discussion Frequency, Network Size, and Heterogeneity of Discussion as Predictors of Political Knowledge and Participation. *Journal of Communication*, 59/2: 205–24.

FALLOWS, J. 1996. *Breaking the News: How the Media Undermine American Democracy*. New York: Pantheon.

FRIEDLAND, L. A., and McLEOD, J. M. 1999. Community Integration and Mass Media: A Reconsideration. In *Mass Media, Social Control, and Social Change*, ed. D. Demers and K. Viswanath. Ames: Iowa State University Press.

FUNK, C. L. 2001. Process Performance: Public Reaction to Legislative Policy Debate. In *What Is it about Government that Americans Dislike?* ed. J. R. Hibbing and E. Thiess-Morse. New York: Cambridge University Press.

GAMSON, W. A. 1968. *Power and Discontent*. Homewood, IL: Dorsey.

GERBNER, G., GROSS, L., MORGAN, M., and SIGNORIELLI, N. 1994. Growing up with Television: The Cultivation Perspective. In *Media Effects: Advances in Theory and Research*, ed. J. Bryant and D. Zillmann. Hillsdale, NJ: Lawrence Erlbaum.

GUO, Z., and MOY, P. 1998. Medium or Message? Predicting Dimensions of Political Sophistication. *International Journal of Public Opinion Research*, 10/1: 25–50.

GUREVITCH, M., and BLUMLER, J. G. 1990. Political Communication Systems and Democratic Values. In *Democracy and the Mass Media*, ed. J. Lichtenberg. Cambridge: Cambridge University Press.

HARDIN, R. 2004. Distrust: Manifestations and Management. In *Distrust*, ed. R. Harding. New York: Russell Sage Foundation.

——2006. *Trust*. Cambridge: Polity Press.

HOCHSCHILD, J. L. 1995. *Facing Up to the American Dream: Race, Class, and the Soul of the Nation*. Princeton: Princeton University Press.

HOFFMAN, L. H., and THOMSON, T. L. 2009. The Effects of Television Viewing on Adolescents' Civic Participation: Political Efficacy as a Mediating Mechanism. *Journal of Broadcasting & Electronic Media*, 53/1: 3–21.

HOLBERT, R. L., TSCHIDA, D. A., DIXON, M., CHERRY, K., STEUBER, K., and AIRNE, D. 2005. The West Wing and Depictions of the American Presidency: Expanding the Theoretical and Empirical Domains of Framing in Political Communication. *Communication Quarterly*, 53/4: 505–22.

HOWARD, P. N. 2005. *New Media Campaigns and the Managed Citizen*. New York: Cambridge University Press.

JONES, J. M. 2008, Sept. 18. Trust in Government Remains Low. At <http://www.gallup.com/poll/110458/trust-government-remains-low.aspx>. Accessed Dec. 10, 2009.

KATZ, E., BLUMLER, J. G., and GUREVITCH, M. 1974. Uses of Mass Communication by the Individual. In *Mass Communication Research: Major Issues and Future Directions*, ed. W. P. Davison and F. T. C. Yu. New York: Praeger.

KEUM, H., DEVANATHAN, N., DESHPANDE, S., NELSON, M. R., and SHAH, D. V. 2004. The Citizen-Consumer: Media Effects at the Intersection of Consumer and Civic Culture. *Political Communication*, 21/3: 369–91.

KIM, Y.-C., and BALL-ROKEACH, S. J. 2006. Civic Engagement from a Communication Infrastructure Perspective. *Communication Theory*, 16/2: 173–97.

——JUNG, J.-Y., COHEN, E. L., and BALL-ROKEACH, S. J. 2004. Internet Connectedness before and after September 11, 2001. *New Media and Society*, 6/5: 612–32.

KWAK, N., SKORIC, M. M., WILLIAMS, A. E., and POOR, N. D. 2004. To Broadband or Not to Broadband: The Relationship between High-Speed Internet and Knowledge and Participation. *Journal of Broadcasting & Electronic Media*, 48/3: 421–45.

——WILLIAMS, A. E., WANG, X., and LEE, H. 2005. Talking Politics and Engaging Politics: An Examination of the Interactive Relationships between Structural Features of Political Talk and Discussion Engagement. *Communication Research*, 32/1: 87–111.

LEMERT, J. B. 1981. *Does Mass Communication Change Public Opinion After All? A New Approach to Effects Analysis*. Chicago: Nelson-Hall.

McLEOD, J. M., BROWN, J. D., BECKER, L. B., and ZIEMKE, D. A. 1977. Decline and Fall at the White House: A Longitudinal Analysis of Communication Effects. *Communication Research*, 4/1: 3–22.

——DAILY, K., GUO, Z., EVELAND, W. P., JR., BAYER, J., YANG, S., and WANG, H. 1996. Community Integration, Local Media Use and Democratic Processes. *Communication Research*, 23/2: 179–209.

——SCHEUFELE, D. A., and MOY, P. 1999. Community, Communication, and Participation: The Role of Mass Media and Interpersonal Discussion in Local Political Participation. *Political Communication*, 16/3: 315–36.

MANSBRIDGE, J. 1997. Social and Cultural Causes of Dissatisfaction with U.S. Government. In *Why People Don't Trust Government*, ed. J. S. Nye, Jr., P. D. Zelikow, and D. C. King. Cambridge, MA: Harvard University Press.

MILBRATH, L. W. 1965. *Political Participation: How and Why Do People Get Involved in Politics?* Chicago: Rand McNally.

MILLER, A. H. 1974. Political Issues and Trust in Government: 1964–1970. *American Political Science Review*, 68/3: 951–72.

——GOLDENBERG, E. N., and ERBRING, L. 1979. Type-Set Politics: Impact of Newspaper on Public Confidence. *American Political Science Review*, 73/1: 67–84.

MISHLER, W., and ROSE, R. 1997. Trust, Distrust and Skepticism: Popular Evaluations of Civil and Political Institutions in Post-Communist Societies. *Journal of Politics*, 59/2: 418–51.

MONTINOLA, G. R. 2004. Corruption, Distrust, and the Deterioration of the Rule of Law. In *Distrust*, ed. R. Hardin. New York: Russell Sage Foundation.

MOY, P., and GASTIL, J. 2006. Predicting Deliberative Conversation: The Impact of Discussion Networks, Media Use, and Political Cognitions. *Political Communication*, 23/4: 443–60.

——and PFAU, M. 2000. *With Malice toward All? The Media and Public Confidence in Democratic Institutions*. Westport, CT: Praeger.

——and SCHEUFELE, D. A. 2001. Media Effects on Political and Social Trust. *Journalism and Mass Communication Quarterly*, 77/4: 703–45.

——MANOSEVITCH, E., STAMM, K., and DUNSMORE, K. 2005. Linking Dimensions of Internet Use and Civic Engagement. *Journalism and Mass Communication Quarterly*, 82/3: 571–86.

——XENOS, M. A., and HESS, V. K. 2005. Communication and Citizenship: Mapping the Political Effects of Infotainment. *Mass Communication and Society*, 8/2: 111–31.

MUTZ, D. C., and REEVES, B. 2005. The New Videomalaise: Effects of Televised Incivility on Political Trust. *American Political Science Review*, 99/1: 1–15.

NIE, N. H., JUNN, J., and STEHLIK-BARRY, K. 1996. *Education and Democratic Citizenship in America*. Chicago: University of Chicago Press.

PAGE, L. R., and SHAPIRO, R. Y. 2000. *Politicians Don't Pander: Political Manipulation and the Loss of Democratic Responsiveness*. Chicago: University of Chicago Press.

PATTERSON, T. E. 1993. *Out of Order*. New York: Knopf.

PUTNAM, R. D. 1995a. Tuning In, Tuning Out: The Strange Disappearance of Social Capital in America. *PS: Political Science and Politics*, 28/4: 664–83.

——1995b. Bowling Alone: America's Declining Social Capital. *Journal of Democracy*, 6/1: 65–78.

RHEINGOLD, H. 2000. *The Virtual Community: Homesteading on the Electronic Frontier*. Boston: MIT Press.

ROBINSON, J. P., and LEVY, M. R. 1986. *The Main Source: Learning from Television News*. Beverly Hills, CA: Sage.

ROBINSON, M. J. 1976. Public Affairs Television and the Growth of Political Malaise: The Case of "The Selling of the Pentagon." *American Political Science Review*, 70/2: 409–32.

——1981. The Three Faces of Congressional Media. In *The New Congress*, ed. T. E. Mann and N. J. Ornstein. Washington, DC: American Enterprise Institute.

ROSENSTONE, S. J., and HANSEN, J. M. 1993. *Mobilization, Participation, and Democracy in America*. New York: Macmillan.

SCHEUFELE, D. A. 2002. Examining Differential Gains from Mass Media and their Implication for Participatory Behavior. *Communication Research*, 29/1: 46–65.

——and NISBET, M. C. 2002. Being a Citizen Online: New Opportunities and Dead Ends. *Harvard International Journal of Press/Politics*, 7/3: 55–75.

——BROSSARD, D., and NISBET, E. 2004. Social Structure and Citizenship: Examining the Impact of Social Setting, Network Heterogeneity, and Information Variables on Political Participation. *Political Communication*, 21/3: 315–38.

SHAH, D. V., CHO, J., EVELAND, W. P., JR., and KWAK, N. 2005. Information and Expression in a Digital Age: Modeling Internet Effects on Civic Participation. *Communication Research*, 32/5: 531–65.

——KWAK, N., and HOLBERT, R. L. 2001. "Connecting" and "Disconnecting" with Civic Life: Patterns of Internet Use and the Production of Social Capital. *Political Communication*, 18/2: 141–62.

——MCLEOD, J. M., and YOON, S.-H. 2001. Communication, Context, and Community: An Exploration of Print, Broadcast and Internet Influences. *Communication Research*, 28/4: 464–506.

SHOEMAKER, P. J., and REESE, S. D. 1996. *Mediating the Message: Theories of Influence on Mass Media Content*. White Plains, NY: Longman.

SMITH, A., SCHLOZMAN, K. L., VERBA, S., and BRADY, H. 2009. The Internet and Civic Engagement. At <http://www.pewinternet.org/Reports/2009/15--The-Internet-and-Civic-Engagement.aspx>. Accessed Dec. 10, 2009.

TEWKSBURY, D., and ALTHAUS, S. 2000. Differences in Knowledge Acquisition among Readers of the Paper and Online Versions of a National Newspaper. *Journalism and Mass Communication Quarterly*, 77/3: 457–79.

TOLBERT, C. J., and MCNEAL, R. S. 2003. Unraveling the Effects of the Internet on Political Participation. *Political Research Quarterly*, 56/2: 175–85.

USLANER, E. M., and BROWN, M. 2005. Inequality, Trust and Civic Engagement. *American Politics Research*, 33/6: 868–94.

VERBA, S., and NIE, N. H. 1972. *Participation in America: Political Democracy and Social Equality*. New York: Harper & Row.

——BURNS, N., and SCHLOZMAN, K. L. 1997. Knowing and Caring about Politics: Gender and Political Engagement. *Journal of Politics*, 59/4: 1051–72.

——SCHLOZMAN, K. L., and BRADY, H. E. 1995. *Voice and Equality: Civic Voluntarism in American Politics*. Cambridge, MA: Harvard University Press.

WILKINS, K. G. 2000. The Role of Media in Public Disengagement from Political Life. *Journal of Broadcasting & Electronic Media*, 44/4: 569–80.

XENOS, M., and MOY, P. 2007. Direct and Differential Effects of the Internet on Political and Civic Engagement. *Journal of Communication*, 57/4: 704–18.

ZUKIN, C., KEETER, S., ANDOLINA, M., JENKINS, K., and DELLI CARPINI, M. X. 2006. *A New Engagement? Political Participation, Civic Life, and the Changing American Citizen*. New York: Oxford University Press.

CHAPTER 15

......................................................................................................

# THE EFFECT OF MEDIA ON PUBLIC KNOWLEDGE

......................................................................................................

KATHLEEN HALL JAMIESON
BRUCE W. HARDY

THE founders of the United States of America considered the freedom of the press so important that they enshrined its protection in the First Amendment. The reason was simple. "[To] the press alone, chequered as it is with abuses," wrote James Madison, "the world is indebted for all the triumphs which have been gained by reason and humanity, over errors and oppression" (Madison 1799).

The role of the press in preserving democracy is based on the fact that most of us experience politics in digested mediated form. For a body politic populated with individuals preoccupied with earning a living, schooling, raising a family, spending time with friends, and the many demands of life, the press acts as a surrogate. In that role, it flags salient topics and communicates relevant information in palatable form. When the press does not focus on such important matters as the escalating presence of the US in Vietnam in 1964, the vulnerabilities of the Savings and Loan industry in 1988, the January 2001 warnings of the Hart–Rudman Commission about the probability of a terrorist attack on US soil, or the realities underlying the US war in Afghanistan in 2008, the process breaks down.

The press is often viewed as an institution of democracy or the fourth branch of government (Cater 1959). Although a free press is the idealized norm, it is not completely independent from the government as they rely on each other. Government actors depend on the news media to communicate with their constituents and the press relies on the three branches of the government for support from postal subsidies, development of new technologies, and protection of intellectual property. "The news media are an intermediary institution in Washington, DC, and a crucial one in a separation-of-powers system where action does not come easily" (Cook 2005, 164).

Although, the news media serve as the conduit between the public and government and are often indicted for their shortcomings, their failure in informing the public is sometimes the outcome of the journalistic norm to legitimize stories with official sources. Journalists "grant government officials a privileged voice in the news" and omit voices that are extreme or fall outside of the "official news gate" (Bennett 1990, 104, 106). According to scholar W. Lance Bennett, from the beat to the boardroom the press "indexes" the official debate (1990). If there is no official debate among "legitimate" voices, there will be little coverage found in mainstream news. Therefore, a failure of the press in alerting the public can be seen as a failure of public officials to stir debate.

What democracy requires is that the press wrangle with topics requiring deliberation, hold those who lead accountable, and communicate accurate information about national affairs in a venue hospitable to debate and the evaluation of alternatives. In a system of government such as ours, this function is a central one because, as Herbert Gans wrote, "The country's democracy may belong directly or indirectly to its citizens, but the democratic process can only be truly meaningful if these citizens are informed" (Gans 2003, 1).

Since US citizens vote for candidates and not policy positions, understanding candidates' stands on issues matters. During presidential elections, we should expect that those who pay reasonable attention to news in its various incarnations will grasp, if not command, the areas of candidate agreement and disagreement. Unsurprisingly, policy preferences influence how people vote (Page and Jones 1979). While the causal direction between embrace of an issue agenda and vote choice is disputed, the fact that they covary is not (Brody and Page 1972).

Although the amount of knowledge voters have about the political system and the issues being disputed in elections fails to satisfy a high ideal (Delli Carpini and Keeter 1996), confusion about candidates' position on issues is not inevitably the fault of the voters. If the media do not cover an issue or do so in ways that minimize learning, then voters must search out the details on their own. The advent of the Internet increases their capacity to do so while at the same time raising the possibility that they will fall prey to misinformation compatible with their ideological dispositions.

Scholars have found that "[although] the possession of 'facts' is related to citizens' media exposure, the correlation is weak, particularly in the case of television news. And once one controls for education level, the correlation nearly disappears" (Patterson and Seib 2005, 191). Exposure to local news actually predicts a drop in political knowledge (Jamieson and Hardy 2007; Prior 2003). Newspaper readership, however, has traditionally been a reliably positive predictor (Becker and Dunwoody 1982; Chaffee and Frank 1996, 48–58; Chaffee, Zhao, and Leshner 1994). So, too, is the use of the Internet to locate political information (Hardy, Jamieson, and Winneg 2008).

The changed media landscape calls into question findings gathered in an age when newspaper readership was more widespread, when broadcast television news, not cable opinion talk, was the audiovisual form in which most Americans got their political information and the Internet was a gleam in the eyes of a handful of defense contractors and scholars. In October 2008 a Pew survey (Pew Research Center for the People &

the Press 2008) found that television, a category that included cable, was the main source of news for 72 percent of respondents, an increase of 2 percent from 2000. Radio was also a more important source with 21 percent saying that they "got most of their news about the presidential campaign" from that source in 2008 compared with 15 percent who gave the same answer eight years earlier. Reliance on the Internet had tripled with 11 percent turning to it during the Bush–Gore contest and 33 percent reporting the same during the Obama–McCain campaign (Pew Research Center for the People & the Press 2008).

In light of the past importance of newspapers as a source of accurate information, its drop in readership raises the question we address here. In this changed media world, what is the relationship between media use and command of information useful in casting an informed vote? Some believe that the electorate needs to understand the actual distinctions between candidates. Others hold that shorthand methods are generally reliable and hence desirable in the absence of deeper knowledge. Here we ask how well the media inform about each before turning to an examination of whether, and if so how, public knowledge has been affected by two changes in the media terrain: the use of the remote control in a multichannel world and the advent of partisan media. We begin by examining the relation between media use and issue knowledge and then focus on two more telegraphic forms of information: knowledge of endorsements and awareness of elite consensus.

Overall, the altered landscape has not produced a citizenry dramatically more or less informed that it was two decades ago. "On average, today's citizens are about as able to name their leaders, and are about as aware of major news events, as was the public nearly 20 years ago," reported a Pew survey in 2007 (Pew Research Center for the People & the Press 2007). That study included "nine questions that are either identical or roughly comparable to questions asked in the late 1980s and early 1990s. In 2007 somewhat fewer were able to name their governor, the vice president, and the president of Russia, but more respondents than in the earlier era gave correct answers to questions pertaining to national politics" (Pew Research Center for the People & the Press 2007).

## Knowledge of Issue Stands of Candidates

Historically, both heading news and watching debates predicts issue knowledge. In 2004 debate-watching and newspaper-reading predicted knowing the answers to three central questions about the general election candidates' positions on issues (Jamieson and Kenski 2006). Even when education and party identification were controlled, watching a debate significantly increased a citizen's odds of knowing that Kerry was the candidate who favored reimporting drugs from Canada and favored eliminating tax breaks for overseas profits of American corporations and using the money to cut taxes for businesses that create jobs in the United States, and that Bush was the candidate who favored allowing workers to invest some of their Social Security contributions in the stock market. Although both were significant, the effect of debate watching on knowledge was stronger than that of newspaper reading.

Evidence from the 2000 National Annenberg Election Study (NAES), however, suggests that media commentary about an event can shape perceptions that differ from those one would hold as a result of actually watching the debate. After the first debate of 2000, assessments of Democratic nominee Al Gore's honesty dropped not among those who actually watched the debate but among those who obtained their information about it from media commentary that focused on putative exaggerations (Erikson 1976; Hollander 1979; Krebs 1998).

## KNOWLEDGE OF ENDORSEMENTS

Media exposure also plays a role in informing the public about who supports whom, a form of knowledge that permits voters to draw inferences about the candidates' ideological dispositions or stands on the issues. Endorsements are a useful low-information means of deducing candidate ideology and issue stands. Studies of the effects of newspaper endorsements have produced mixed results. Some have found that they may influence up to 5 percent of the vote (Erikson 1976; Hollander 1979; Krebs 1998). Others conclude that newspaper endorsements have little (Hagen and Jamieson 2000) or no effect at all on vote (Hurd and Singletary 1984; Counts 1985) or only an effect on those less engaged in politics. However, some recent studies of the role of endorsements in the nominating process found significant effects. One that examined "all publicly reported endorsements in a broad range of publications" concluded that "trial-heat" (head-to-head) poll results and endorsements "are almost equally important predictors of primary outcomes" (Cohen, Karol, Noel, and Zaller 2003, 36). A second concluded that such polls and endorsements significantly predict votes in both parties during the primaries (Steger 2007). Endorsements by groups and unions have been shown to drum up enthusiasm among their members (Gimpel 1998), and when an organization or group stands with a candidate, its members are more likely to embrace the endorsee (Burns, Francia, and Herrnson 2000; Rapoport, Stone, and Abramowitz 1991). The effects of endorsements should be more pronounced in primary campaigns in which voters confront candidates about whom they know comparatively little (Kennamer and Chaffee 1982). In intra-party contests, political communication has a unique opportunity to influence independents and party identifiers alike. These effects of course assume that the public knows who endorsed whom, an assumption that raises the question "how does the public obtain that information?"

Data from the 2008 NAES collected during the primary season show that news media consumption was significantly related to knowledge of endorsements (Jamieson and Hardy 2009). The relationship between reported television use and knowledge of endorsements was particularly strong for the endorsements that a majority of respondents could identify correctly. For example, we found that 79.2 percent of respondents knew that Oprah Winfrey supported Senator Obama and that television information seeking was positively related to knowledge of this endorsement. Similar relationships existed for knowledge of Massachusetts Senator Edward Kennedy and New Mexico Governor Bill Richardson's endorsements of Obama. More than half of respondents were familiar with each, and television news use, newspaper reading, and Internet use were all significantly and positively related to recalling that information.

*The New York Times* endorsements of Senators Hillary Clinton and John McCain were not as well known as those by Oprah Winfrey, Senator Kennedy, and Governor Richardson. Yet the three news media-use variables—television, newspaper, and Internet—were significantly and positively related to knowing the names of the candidates endorsed by the *Times*. Media use also predicted awareness of Senator Joe Lieberman's support for McCain, Dr James Dobson's for Huckabee, the United Farm Workers' for Clinton, and MoveOn.org's for Obama. By increasing voter knowledge of endorsements, media provide low-information voters in particular with a form of useful information.

Since the findings are drawn from survey data, strict causal inferences about the impact of news media on knowledge of endorsements are problematic. However, the relationships between news consumption and knowledge of endorsement, reported here, hold in the face of controls such as age, gender, race, education, and ideology, which allows us to be more confident in the relationships (Jamieson and Hardy 2009).

## WHEN CONSENSUS IS CLEAR AND COMMUNICATED BY MEDIA IT CREATES AN EFFECT: THE GAS TAX HOLIDAY

Elite consensus functions in much the same way as endorsements. For those who trust it, it minimizes the need for additional information seeking. One set of exchanges in 2008 provided a particularly apt test of the role of media in transmitting elite consensus.

As the last Form 1040s were attached to tax forms on April 15, the presumptive Republican nominee tried to harness his campaign to the news agenda by advocating suspending the federal excise tax on gasoline from Memorial Day to Labor Day. By the end of the month, Democratic contender Hillary Clinton, who remained locked in a tight contest with Barack Obama, was championing the same idea. If, as lay logic but not economic theory suggested, the reduction in the gas tax meant lower prices for consumers, the move would reduce the cost per gallon of gas by the amount of the tax, about 18.4 cents for regular unleaded and 24.4 cents for diesel.

Barack Obama opposed the gas holiday as insistently as McCain and Clinton favored it. In taking the no-tax-holiday position, the Illinois Democrat was on the side of most economists. Indeed, when pressed, Senator Clinton could not name a single one of that elite class who considered the tax holiday a good idea (ABC News 2008).

On the suspension, the views of economists were clear. "More than 200 economists, including four Nobel Prize winners, signed a letter rejecting proposals by presidential candidates Hillary Clinton and John McCain to offer a summertime gas-tax holiday," noted Brian Faler writing for Bloomberg.com. Opposition crossed party lines:

Columbia University economist Joseph Stiglitz, former Congressional Budget Office Director Alice Rivlin and 2007 Nobel winner Roger Myerson are among those who signed the letter calling proposals to temporarily lift the tax a bad idea. Another is Richard Schmalensee of the Massachusetts Institute of Technology, who was a member of President George H. W. Bush's Council of Economic Advisers. . . .

"Suspending the federal tax on gasoline this summer is a bad idea, and we oppose it," the letter says. Economist Henry Aaron of the Brookings Institution is among those circulating the letter. Aaron said that while he supports Obama, the list includes Republicans and Clinton supporters.    (Faler 2008)

Rather than taking on the economists, Senators McCain and Clinton dismissed their views. "I find people who are the wealthiest who are most dismissive of a plan to give low-income Americans a little holiday . . . Thirty dollars mean nothing to a lot of economists—I understand that. It means a lot to some low-income Americans," Senator McCain responded. When pressed by host George Stephanopoulos on ABC's May 4 *This Week* to name an economist who supported the gas tax holiday, Clinton responded, "I'm not going to put my lot in with economists."

Included in this controversy were disagreements among political elites (Senator Obama versus Senator Clinton and Senator McCain), intra-party contention (Senator Clinton versus Senator Obama), inter-party contest (Senator Obama versus Senator McCain), and a clash between expert and political elite opinion (Senators McCain and Clinton versus the economists). Put these factors together and you have a test of the scholarly consensus that: (1) expert opinion can influence public opinion; (2) citizens use elite cues to form opinions, with the most politically attentive individuals adopting elite opinion; and (3) elite opinion has the greatest impact on public opinion when there is a consensus among elites (Brody 1991; Darmofal 2005; Yin 1999; Zaller 1992).[1]

According to the 2008 NAES, media use was significantly related to knowledge of the position of the three candidates (Clinton, McCain, and Obama) on the gas tax holiday.[2] All four of our news media variables—television, talk radio, newspaper, and Internet— were positively related to knowledge of the candidates' stances.[3] Consistent with past

---

[1] Existing studies also suggest that: when elites are divided along party lines, the public becomes polarized; the influence of expert opinion on public opinion is reduced if there is disagreement between expert opinion and political elite opinion with the public following the lead of those whose ideology it shares; and citizens' level of disagreement with experts opinion is in part a function of personal attributes such as education, issue knowledge, and personal experience with the issue.

[2] Exact question wording: "Which candidate or candidates running for president supports suspending the gas tax throughout the summer months this year? (1) Does John McCain support it, or not? (2) Does Hillary Clinton support it, or not? [Deleted June 9, 2008] (3) Does Barack Obama support it, or not?"

[3] At the $p < .001$ level.

scholarship, 2008 NAES data suggest that the public accepted elite economic opinion and with it the Obama view of the gas tax holiday. The effect of media in priming the elite cue is apparent as television, newspaper, and Internet positively and significantly predicted the belief that gas tax is a bad idea. The media relationships held in the face of controls and after including knowledge of Obama's stance on the gas tax holiday in the model, which produced a significant and positive relationship with the belief that the gas tax holiday is a bad idea.

We turn next to three changes in the media environment that have affected what people know about politics by altering how they know it. First, we examine the impact of use of the remote control during news viewing; then we turn to an examination of the effects of partisan media on what people know, and close with a discussion on the effect of the Internet and viral email.

## EFFECTS OF USE OF THE REMOTE CONTROL

The few studies examining channel changing and news content (Morris and Forgette 2007; Walker, Bellamy, and Traudt 1993) used *selective avoidance* as the theoretical basis explaining motivation for using the remote control during news programs. Past studies have found that 36.5 percent to 59.4 percent of viewers often changed channels to avoid politicians and political ads that they did not like or did not agree with and changed the channel to avoid a news story that they did not like (Walker, Bellamy, and Traudt 1993). Data from a 2004 study conducted by the Pew Research Center found that 62 percent of the public agreed with the statement "I find that I often watch the news with my remote control in hand, flipping to other channels when I'm not interested" (Pew Research Center for the People & the Press 2004; Morris and Forgette 2007).

These studies focus on shifts from news to non-news content and found this news grazing to be negatively related to levels of political knowledge and positively related to cynicism (Morris and Forgette 2007). Here we are concerned instead with the viewer who switches from one news program to another mid-program.

There is debate over the level of involvement tied to remote control use (Ferguson and Perse 1993; Wang, Busemeyer, and Lang 2006). Some see channel changing as the behavior of an active viewer who is routinely evaluating what she or he is watching and making selections to satisfy certain needs (Walker and Bellamy 1991). Others believe that channel changing is an activity characteristic of the detached and uninvolved viewer, the one nonchalantly "surfing" the channels. A recent study harmonizes these views by suggesting that active and passive viewers reflect different patterns of cognitive effort in processing (Lang et al. 2005) and that remote control use can be active or passive depending on the specific situation. Regardless of level of cognitive involvement in switching channels, we add the reminder that being exposed to multiple and diverse points of views leads to greater acquisition of political knowledge (Scheufele et al. 2004, 2006).

Whatever the effect, according to NAES data collected between August 1 and November 3, 2008, surfing among news channels is common behavior. To identify channel shifters we first asked: "Thinking now about the past week how many days did you see information on broadcast or cable television about the 2008 presidential campaign? This includes seeing programs on television, on the internet, your cell-phone, iPod, or PDA." Just over 46 percent (46.6 percent—17,711 respondents) who said that they watched television news reported such switching among news programs. This level is similar to the numbers found in past research on overall levels of channel changing during any given program (Bellamy and Walker 1996). We find that the positive relationship between channel switching and knowledge of candidate issues stances becomes more robust the more times one switches among programs. These results hold in the presence of stringent controls such as level of education, overall news media use, and interest in the 2008 presidential election.

# THE EFFECTS OF PARTISAN MEDIA

Conservative radio and cable were influencing large audiences before their explicitly partisan liberal counterparts, Air America and MSNBC's *Countdown with Keith Olbermann* and *Rachel Maddow* show, launched. Rush Limbaugh made his national debut in 1988; Fox News entered the scene eight years later. In 2010 *Talkers Magazine* put Limbaugh's audience at 15 million and his fellow conservative Sean Hannity's audience at 14 million (*Talkers Magazine* 2010). A 2004 Pew Center survey found that 22 percent of those in the US get most of their news from Fox. Of those, 46 percent self-identify as conservatives, 32 percent as moderates (Pew Research Center for the People & the Press 2004).

The presence of explicitly ideological media expanded the public's range of choices and in the process opened the possibility that conservatives would seek out reinforcing information on conservative outlets and liberals would do the same on the other side. Relying on Nielsen's people meter data across sixty-two prominent television networks in the first week of February 2003, media scholar James Webster (2005) found modest evidence of polarization, defined as "the tendency of channel audiences to be composed of devotees and nonviewers." Importantly, Webster's analysis of Fox viewers concluded that "even the audience for FOX News . . . spends 92.5% of its time watching something else on television. The rest of their time is widely distributed across the channels they have available" (Webster 2005, 366, 380). "Of course," he adds, "it may be that even a little exposure to certain materials has big social effects, but if these viewers live in cloistered communities, they evidently spend a good deal of time out and about" (Webster 2005, 380). The limitation of analysis by cable network for our purposes is, of course, that where we posit a pattern of reinforcement in exposure to news and opinion talk, these data include both entertainment and non-entertainment programming.

Drawing on Webster's analysis of Nielsen data, political scientist Marcus Prior narrowed the field to focus simply on cable content on networks that program news and opinion talk and notes that "those who watched at least some Fox News spent 7.5% of their overall viewing time with the Fox News Channel, but another 6% with the other four cable networks" (CNN, CNN Headline News, CNBC, MSNBC). After analyzing these patterns, he concludes the data "offer little support for claims that the fragmentation of the cable news environment fosters political polarization by encouraging selective exposure to only one side of an issue" (Prior 2007, 157–8).

Relying on data from the Pew Research Center's 1998 to 2004 Biennial Media Consumption Survey to identify factors predicting exposure to cable and nightly news, Jonathan Morris finds that the audiences for Fox and CNN are becoming increasingly polarized, with Fox viewers less likely than CNN viewers to watch accounts critical of the Bush administration and more likely than non-watchers to underestimate the number of Americans killed in the Iraq War. The study found that "the Fox News audience prefers news that shares their own point of view on politics and issues, while CNN and network news watchers do not" (Morris 2005, 56–79). Similarly, Jamieson and Cappella found that Fox viewers and Limbaugh listeners are more likely than other conservatives to reside in a world in which their view of challenged facts coincided with those of their party (Jamieson and Cappella 2008). The same was true on the other side. CNN's viewers were more likely to accept the liberal view of contested claims.

The process by which this occurs was on display in the Republican primaries of 2008. On his radio show, Rush Limbaugh regularly argued against the candidacies of Senator John McCain and former Arkansas Governor Mike Huckabee and tepidly endorsed former Massachusetts Governor Mitt Romney. During the period between the New Hampshire primary (January 8, 2008) and Super Tuesday (February 5, 2008), Limbaugh strongly attacked McCain's conservative credentials. Those assaults coincided with listeners' perception of McCain, and those who listened to the talk show host were more likely than the non-listening population—including those who describe themselves as conservatives—to believe that McCain was a moderate. The importance of this finding is magnified by its unexpectedness. Limbaugh had vigorously opposed McCain's bid for the Republican nomination in 2000 and reiterated his disdain for the Arizona Republican in the years between 2000 and 2008. In other words, one would have assumed that any effect Limbaugh could have on his listeners had occurred long before he ratcheted up his anti-McCain rhetoric during the 2008 primaries.

The conservative talk show host escalated his attacks on the Republican contender from Arizona in the days before and immediately after McCain's victory in the New Hampshire primary on January 8. As part of his arsenal, Limbaugh repeatedly reminded his listeners that the *New York Times* had endorsed McCain. Unsurprisingly we found that Limbaugh's listeners were more likely to know about the endorsement than conservatives not in his audience. Controlling for gender, race, education, party identification, and ideology, Limbaugh listeners were 3.94 times more likely than non-listeners to know that the *New York Times* had endorsed the Arizona senator for the

Republican nomination. The *New York Times* is a frequent object of Limbaugh's attack on the "liberal media."

Controlling for sociopolitical demographic and news media use variables, we see that people's knowledge of McCain's endorsement by the liberal-leaning *New York Times* editorial page did influence perceptions of McCain's ideological dispositions. Respondents were asked to rate Senator McCain on a five-point scale ranging from "very liberal" to "very conservative." Those who knew about the *New York Times* endorsement were significantly less likely to see McCain as a conservative.

An across-time analysis of 639 Limbaugh listeners and 8,077 non-listeners surveyed by the 2008 NAES shows that Rush Limbaugh effectively defined John McCain for his listeners. Before the New Hampshire primary about half of Limbaugh's listeners said McCain was a conservative. That number dropped almost 12 percentage points after McCain won in New Hampshire. After January 8, the number of Limbaugh listeners who said McCain was a liberal jumped 9 percentage points. During this period, the political perceptions of McCain among non-Limbaugh listeners remained stable. An analysis of the differential impact of Limbaugh listening before and after the New Hampshire primaries indicated that Limbaugh had a significant impact on perceptions of McCain's ideological disposition only after the New Hampshire primary.

Immediately after the New Hampshire primary, Limbaugh listeners began to shift from their view that Senator McCain was a conservative. As mentioned above, strict causal claims should not be made. Additionally, any discussion on partisan media needs to take into account selection biases that may be at play as many people are likely to search out views that are in line with their own and don't expose themselves to diverse opinions. Therefore, attitudes, perceptions, and predispositions are likely to be simply reinforced. Yet, these results hold after controlling for gender, race, education, party identification, and respondents' own ideology, suggesting that partisan media have the capacity to increase their audience's awareness of some types of information and to shape the audience's political attitudes (Jamieson and Hardy 2009).

# INTERNET, KNOWLEDGE, AND THE VIRAL BREW

In 2004 we found that the Internet, in comparison with traditional press campaign coverage, has an informing effect similar to that of such major campaign events as conventions and debates (Hardy, Jamieson, and Winneg 2008). Following the 2004 general election, the Annenberg Public Policy Center conducted a survey of a random sample of 3,400 citizens to assess the extent to which they believed the many claims made by, or on behalf of, the Bush and Kerry campaigns. In order to test the knowledge of forty-one claims made by the major party campaigns in 2004, respondents rated the accuracy of the claims on a four-point scale ranging from very truthful to not truthful at all. All claims were offered during the course of the campaign. All were checked for accuracy by FactCheck.org, a project of the Annenberg Public Policy Center, which Jamieson and Brooks Jackson direct. We found direct evidence that accessing campaign information online significantly increases citizens' command of fact. We also found that the more respondents believe that the candidates never told the truth in the 2004 election, the more likely they were to turn to the Internet to access campaign information. The cynical voter was likely to turn to the Internet to sort fact from fiction.

The information environment found online transforms the nature of access to the mainstream in ways that increase the chance that using it will produce an effect in the offline world. At very little cost to the citizen, online one can read multiple newspapers and check multiple news sites in very short order. Information is readily and cheaply accessible, unlike, for example, the cost of subscriptions to a handful of newspapers.

Although we find evidence that citizens can seek and find factual information online, the Internet also facilitates interpersonal communication that is not bounded spatially; this capacity can accelerate the spread of misinformation among citizens quickly through email, instant messaging, and chat rooms without any vetting in the process. There is an added dimension of source heuristics at play here. Receiving a forwarded email from a trusted friend or family member may increase the likelihood of adoption of the deceptive message. The source of the email becomes, in part, the source of the message.

During the 2008 campaign, deceptions spread throughout Internet, including claims that were not extensively discussed in mainstream news or found in candidate ads. One of the more prominent viral deceptive claims of the 2008 campaign suggested that Obama was a Muslim. This notion was reinforced by another viral claim stating that Obama could not be elected president because he violated the Constitutional requirement that the president be a natural-born citizen. In our post-election deception survey we found that 19 percent believed that Obama was a Muslim. In the presence of demographic, political orientation, media-use controls we found that those who said that they received negative emails about the candidates were more likely to believe Obama is a Muslim than those who did not receive such emails.

## CONCLUSION

With the proliferation of channels, the Internet and viral email, the rise of explicitly partisan media, and the capacity to channel shift effortlessly across a medium with seven national channels of news and opinion talk, the media landscape has changed dramatically in recent decades. Although the current affairs knowledge of the public has not materially changed as a result, the sources of information contributing to that knowledge have become more varied and the potential to reside in a self-protective enclave of reinforcing information has risen as well.

As technological advances allow users to customize their news repertoire—through the use of RSS feeds, customized home pages, DVRs, mobile devices, etc.... the concept of "mainstream news" will be relegated to the history books. As we have seen in advertising, marketing strategies are shifting away from wide-ranging broadcast messages to focus on niche markets. With the rise of niche information markets, we are seeing the marketplace of ideas go through the same breakup. If these information markets subscribe to different journalistic norms, deliberation over a policy issue between groups may become more difficult as those coming to the table will have incompatible information repertoires.

Future research on the effect of media on public knowledge will need to be highly targeted. No longer will scholars be able to rely on comparing types of media (i.e., newspaper versus television). As citizens now build their own media experiences, researchers will need to focus on different communities in the social, not the geographic, sense. Information, and misinformation, flow has become malleable via emails, postings on Facebook, and tweets on Twitter. Effects researchers will need to ask who sent what information to whom in what form through what channel. Like the concept of mainstream media, our scholarly assumptions about the nature and function of media will have to be rethought.

# REFERENCES

ABC News. 2008. *This Week with George Stephanopoulos*, May 4.

BECKER, L. B., and DUNWOODY, S. 1982. Media Use, Public Affairs Knowledge and Voting in a Local Election. *Journalism Quarterly*, 59: 212–18.

BELLAMY, R. V., JR., and WALKER, J. R. 1996. *Television and the Remote Control*. New York: Guilford Press.

BENNETT, W. L. 1990. Toward a Theory of Press–State Relations in the United States. *Journal of Communication*, 40/2: 103–27.

BRODY, R. A. 1991. *Assessing the President: The Media, Elite Opinion, and Public Support.* Stanford, CA: Stanford University Press.

—— and PAGE, B. I. 1972. Comment: The Assessment of Policy Voting. *American Political Science Review*, 66/2: 450–8.

BURNS, P. F., FRANCIA, P. L., and HERRNSON, P. S. 2000. Labor at Work: Union Campaign Activities and Legislative Payoffs in the U.S. House of Representatives. *Social Science Quarterly*, 81: 507–16.

CATER, D. 1959. *The Fourth Branch of Government*. Boston: Houghton Mifflin.

CHAFFEE, S. H., and FRANK, S. 1996. How Americans Get Political Information: Print versus Broadcast News. *Annals of the American Academy of Political and Social Science*, 546/1: 48–58.

—— ZHAO, X., and LESHNER, G. 1994. Political Knowledge and the Campaign Media of 1992. *Communication Research*, 21: 305–24.

COHEN, M., KAROL, D., NOEL, H., and ZALLER, J. 2003. Polls or Pols? The Real Driving Force behind Presidential Nominations. *Brookings Review*, 3 (Summer), 36–9.

COOK, T. E. 2005. *Governing with the News: The News Media as a Political Institution.* Chicago: University of Chicago Press.

COUNTS, T. 1985. Effects of Endorsements on Presidential Vote. *Journalism Quarterly,* 62 (Autumn), 644–7.

DARMOFAL, D. 2005. Elite Cues and Citizen Disagreement with Expert Opinion. *Political Research Quarterly,* 58/3: 381–95.

DELLI CARPINI, M. X., and KEETER, S. 1996. *What Americans Know about Politics and Why it Matters.* New Haven: Yale University Press.

ERIKSON, R. S. 1976. The Influence of Newspaper Endorsements in Presidential Elections: The Case of 1964. *American Journal of Political Science,* 20: 207–33.

FALER, B. 2008. Economists Criticize Clinton, McCain Gas-Tax Plans. Bloomberg.com, 5 May. At <http://www.bloomberg.com/apps/news?pid=20601110&sid=aza2XQB.kkok>. Accessed Oct. 14, 2010.

FERGUSON, D. A., and PERSE, E. M. 1993. Media and Audience Influences on Channel Repertoire. *Journal of Broadcasting & Electronic Media,* 37/1: 31–47.

GANS, H. J. 2003. *Democracy and the News.* Oxford: Oxford University Press.

GIMPEL, J. G. 1998. Packing Heat at the Polls: Gun Ownership, Interest Group Endorsements, and Voting Behavior in Gubernatorial Elections. *Social Science Quarterly,* 79/3: 634–48.

HAGEN, M. G., and JAMIESON, K. H. 2000. Do Newspaper Endorsements Matter? Do Politicians Speak for Themselves in Newspapers and on Television? In *Everything You Think You Know about Politics . . . And Why You're Wrong,* ed. K. H. Jamieson. New York: Basic Books.

HARDY, B. W., JAMIESON, K. H., and WINNEG, K. 2008. The Role of the Internet in Identifying Deception during the 2004 U.S. Presidential Campaign. In *Routledge Handbook of Internet Politics,* ed. A. Chadwick and P. Howard. London: Taylor & Francis.

HOLLANDER, S., JR. 1979. On the Strength of a Newspaper Endorsement. *Public Opinion Quarterly,* 43: 405–7.

HURD, R. E., and SINGLETARY, M. W. 1984. Newspaper Endorsement Influence on the 1980 Presidential Election Vote. *Journalism Quarterly,* 61 (Summer), 332–8.

JAMIESON, K. H., and CAPPELLA, J. N. 2008. *Echo Chamber: Rush Limbaugh and the Conservative Media Establishment.* Oxford: Oxford University Press.

—— and HARDY, B. W. 2007. Unmasking Deception: The Capacity, Disposition, and Challenges Facing the Press. In *The Politics of News: The News of Politics,* ed. D. Graver, D. McQuail, and P. Norris. Washington, DC: CQ Press.

—— —— 2009. Media, Endorsements and the 2008 Primaries. In *Reforming the Presidential Nomination Process,* ed. S. S. Smith and M. J. Springer. Washington, DC: Brookings Press.

—— and KENSKI, K. 2006. Issue Knowledge and Perceptions of Agreement in the 2004 Presidential General Election. *Presidential Studies Quarterly,* 36/2: 243–59.

—— and WALDMAN, P. 2003. *The Press Effect: Politicians, Journalists, and the Stories that Shape the Political World.* New York: Oxford University Press.

KENNAMER, D. J., and CHAFFEE, S. H. 1982. Communication of Political Information during the Early Presidential Primaries: Cognition, Affect, and Uncertainty. *Communication Yearbook,* 5: 627–50.

KREBS, T. B. 1998. The Determinants of Candidates' Vote Share and the Advantages of Incumbency in City Council Elections. *American Journal of Political Science,* 42: 921–35.

LANG, A., SHIN, M., BRADLEY, S. D., WANG, Z., LEE, S., and POTTER, D. 2005. Wait! Don't Turn that Dial! The Effects of Story Length and Excitement and Production Pacing in Local

Television News on Channel Changing Behavior in a Free Choice Environment. *Journal of Broadcasting & Electronic Media*, 49: 3–22.

MADISON, J. 1799. *The Virginia Report of 1799*. At <http://www.constitution.org/rf/vr_1799.htm>. Accessed Oct. 14, 2010.

MORRIS, J. S. 2005. The Fox News Factor. *Harvard International Journal of Press/Politics*, 10: 56–79.

—— and FORGETTE, R. 2007. News Grazers, Television News, Political Knowledge, and Engagement. *Harvard International Journal of Press/Politics*, 12: 91–107.

PAGE, B. I., and JONES, C. C. 1979. Reciprocal Effects of Policy Preferences, Party Loyalties and the Vote. *American Political Science Review*, 73/4: 1071–89.

PATTERSON, T. E., and SEIB, P. 2005. Informing the Public. In *The Press*, ed. G. Overholser and K. H. Jamieson. New York: Oxford University Press.

Pew Research Center for the People & the Press. 2004. News Audiences Increasingly Politicized. Pew, 8 June. At <http://people-press.org/report/215/news-audiences-increasingly-politicized>. Accessed Oct. 14, 2010.

—— 2007. Public Knowledge of Current Affairs Little Changed by News and Information Revolutions. Pew, 15 Apr. At <http://people-press.org/report/319/public-knowledge-of-current-affairs-little-changed-by-news-and-information-revolutions>. Accessed Oct. 14, 2010.

—— 2008. News Interest Index. Pew, 24–7 Oct. At <http://people-press.org/reports/questionnaires/466.pdf>. Accessed Oct. 14, 2010.

PFAU, M., KENDAL, K. E., REICHERT, T., HELLWEG, S. A., LEE, W., TUSING, K. J., and PROSISE, T. O. 1997. Influence of Communication during the Distant Phase of the 1996 Republican Presidential Primary Campaign. *Journal of Communication*, 47: 6–26.

POPKIN, S. L. 1994. *The Reasoning Voter: Communication and Persuasion in Presidential Campaigns*, 2nd edn. Chicago: University of Chicago Press.

PRIOR, M. 2003. Any Good News in Soft News? The Impact of Soft News Preference on Political Knowledge. *Political Communication*, 20: 149–71.

—— 2007. *Post-Broadcast Democracy: How Media Choices Increases Inequality in Political Involvement and Polarizes Elections*. Cambridge: Cambridge University Press.

RAPOPORT, R. B., STONE, W. J., and ABRAMOWITZ, A. I. 1991. Do Endorsements Matter? Group Influence in the 1984 Democratic Caucuses. *American Political Science Review*, 85: 193–203.

SCHEUFELE, D. A., HARDY, B. W., BROSSARD, D., WAISMEL-MANOR, I. S., and NISBET, E. C. 2006. Democracy Based on Difference: Examining the Links between Structural Heterogeneity, Heterogeneity of Discussion Networks, and Democratic Citizenship. *Journal of Communication*, 56: 728–53.

—— —— NISBET, M. C., BROSSARD, D., and NISBET, E. C. 2004. Social Structure and Citizenship: Examining the Impacts of Social Setting, Network Heterogeneity and Informational Variables on Political Participation. *Political Communication*, 21: 315–38.

STEGER, W. P. 2007. Who Wins Nominations and Why? An Updated Forecast of the Presidential Primary Vote. *Political Research Quarterly*, 60: 91–9.

*Talkers Magazine*. 2010. The Top Talk Radio Audiences (Updated 9/10). At <http://talkers.com/online/?p=71>. Accessed Oct. 14, 2010.

WALKER, J. R., and BELLAMY, R. V., JR. 1991. Gratification of Grazing: An Exploratory Study of Remote Control Use. *Journalism Quarterly*, 68: 422–31.

—— —— and TRAUDT, P. J. 1993. Gratifications Derived from Remote Control Devices: A Survey of Adult RCD Use. In *The Remote Control in the New Age of Television*, ed. J. R. Walker and R. V. Bellamy, Jr. Westport, CT: Praeger.

WANG, Z., BUSEMEYER, J. R., and LANG, A. 2006. Grazing or Staying Tuned: A Stochastic Model of Channel Changing Behavior. Paper presented at the Annual Meeting of the International Communication Association, International Congress Centre, Dresden.

WEBSTER, J. G. 2005. Beneath the Veneer of Fragmentation: Television Audience Polarization in Multichannel World. *Journal of Communication*, 55: 366–82.

YIN, J. 1999. Elite Opinion and Media Diffusion: Exploring Environmental Attitudes. *Harvard International Journal of Press/Politics*, 4/3: 62–86.

ZALLER, J. R. 1992. *The Nature and Origin of Mass Opinion*. Cambridge: Cambridge University Press.

# CHAPTER 16

························································································

# NEWS POLLS

## *Constructing an Engaged Public*

························································································

## W. LANCE BENNETT*

FOR most citizens, the news is the main point of contact with issues and their framing in terms of viable political positions. Polls cue individuals about how others in the public feel about those issues and positions. They also serve as the barometer for assessing how different politicians and their backers are doing in selling their causes. The perception of winning or losing the battle for public opinion in the media often becomes the reality of political success or failure (Cook 1998; Bennett 2009). Indeed, the news, with its embedded polls, may become the symbolic public in the dramatic press construction of many public policy dialogues.

As polls become the political currency of mediated democracy, the polling industry supplies a large volume of its product to news outlets. Mark Blumenthal of the website Pollster has noted that "We live in a news environment where a combination of cable news and Web sites of every imaginable variety have an insatiable appetite for polling numbers" (Dewan 2009). Those remarks came in the context of a 2009 reprimand from the American Association of Public Opinion Research to the polling firm Strategic Vision as part of an investigation of discrepant poll results in the 2008 presidential primaries. Beyond the immediate concerns about a particular poll's sponsorship and methodology, Blumenthal (2009) noted that as media polls proliferate, "we are confronted with polls from sources we have barely heard of, including some organizations that appear to exist solely for the purpose of disseminating polls."

Although dubious methods, motives, or results occasionally make headlines, there may be deeper issues to worry about in the routine practices of even the best-known news polls. Indeed, the reporting of news polls often conveys misplaced impressions that publics are meaningfully engaged with, and hold grounded opinions on, the issues

* I would like to thank Olof Petersson of the centre for Business and Poliocy Studies (SNS) in Stockholm for encouraging me to develop this argument, and for his comments on an earlier draft. The editors of this Handbook also provided most helpful comments.

of the day. In some cases, publics are likely to be thoughtful and informed about issues that are deeply ingrained in their personal lives, as happened when Social Security reforms were proposed by George W. Bush, and his initiative to privatize the program met with strong public resistance. Similarly, when attentive publics are given a sustained look at government deliberation, grounded opinions may emerge, as when support for President Bill Clinton actually increased over the course of the impeachment proceedings led by Republican opponents.

What is curious about the reporting of news polls is that such cases of opinion formations grounded in social experience or relatively transparent and prolonged mediated debates are seldom distinguished from other, far less solid opinion formations that may occur even on crucial issues such as going to war. Consider a case in point: the widespread reporting of public support for going to war with Iraq in 2003. For example, a CNN/USA Today/Gallup poll (conducted February 17–19, 2003) reported 59 percent of Americans favoring war, 38 percent opposing, and only 3 percent saying they had no opinion (Moore 2008a, 2008b). David Moore, who was then vice-president of the Gallup Organization and managing editor of its poll, conducted a remarkable experiment around this poll (and others) by asking a follow-up question: whether or not respondents would be upset if the government did not send troops into Iraq. In effect, Moore probed Gallup samples to see if people really cared about going to war. This simple probe produced stunning shifts in the structure of opinion. Only 29 percent of those who supported the Iraq War said they would be upset if it did not happen. And only 30 percent who opposed the war said they would be upset if it did occur. This left a plurality of 41 percent who did not really care one way or another (Moore 2008a, 2008b). In light of the patriotic fervor drummed up by the White House marketing effort, it is not surprising that, when pushed by pollsters to express an opinion one way or the other, more of the "don't cares" were inclined to say they supported the war.

Despite this striking result on an issue as important as a war, the "do you care?" part of the survey was an in-house experiment, and not released at the time. Few if any news polls ask probing questions because, according to Moore, it would complicate and undermine the way in which polls are typically used in news stories to provide a "clear" sense of the public reaction to an issue (Moore 2008a). As a result, the news story from most mainstream media outlets was one of an administration marching to war against a deadly enemy with the support of the public. A news story better supported by the polls might have focused on why those impressive efforts to sell the war were deeply convincing to only 29 percent of the American people. Yet only a few feature articles told of the scripted mushroom cloud imagery chorused by administration officials on Sunday talk shows, or the reference by one White House advisor to the war as a "product" that was held for launch until after summer vacations had ended in September 2002 (Bennett, Lawrence, and Livingston 2007; Bennett 2009). The public support myth quickly became incorporated as common knowledge about the war and has been cited by politicians and pundits ever since. For example, at the time of this writing, Henry Kissinger issued a policy brief on Afghanistan in an opinion piece in which the obligatory references to Vietnam and Iraq were prefaced with the unqualified warning "Each of those wars began with widespread public support" (Kissinger 2009).

Moore concluded that the results of his experiment revealed;

[the] absurdity of much public opinion polling [if] . . . a democracy is supposed to represent, or at least take into account the "will" of the people, not the uncaring, unreflective,
top-of-the mind responses many people give to pollsters. . . . It hardly makes sense that
pollsters should treat such top-of-mind responses as a Holy Grail. Yet typically pollsters
and the media do treat those superficial results as though they represent what Americans
are really thinking, with pollsters making no distinction between those who express deeply
held views and those who have hardly, if at all, thought about an issue.    (Moore 2008b)

It is important to point out that much academic and scientific polling does examine
stability, depth, issue dimensionality, and other contextual properties of opinion.
Indeed, what is surprising about a good deal of news polling is that it ignores so
much well-established knowledge in the field (e.g., Blumer 1948; Schuman 2008). For
example, every beginning student of opinion learns that, depending on the issue, some
substantial portion of respondents will answer "no opinion" or "don't know" if given
the opportunity to do so. Schuman reports an experiment in which respondents in one
condition were asked simply whether they agreed or disagreed with the statement "The
Russian leaders are trying to get along with America." The level of "don't know" was 15
percent. In a second condition, respondents were told, "Not everyone has opinions on
these questions. If you do not have an opinion, just say so." The volume of "don't
know" or no opinion increased to 38 percent, which was equivalent to the level of
highest level of expressed opinion in the sample (Schuman 2008, 142). Schuman goes
on to note that the "don't knows" are not necessarily ignorant; many issues involve
conflicting considerations that lead knowledgeable individuals to withhold an opinion
rather than force themselves one way or another. This means that pushing respondents
to have opinions often produces artificial results (Schuman 2008, 146). Ways of
addressing top-of-head opinion measurement have been explored by Zaller and Feldman (1992) and Bishop (2005), among others.

Despite such established guidelines in scientific polling (described more fully below),
Moore (2008a) argues that news polls typically push respondents to express opinions.
He addressed a question about CNN's change of pollsters with a more general reference
to the whole news business:

It is my argument that all of the major media organizations have an unwavering commitment to a mythological public that is rational, all-knowing, and fully engaged. CNN's
search for a way to reduce even the small percentage of respondents who don't respond to
any given question is merely emblematic of the widespread view of all the major media
organizations that only a mythological public of that nature can justify their covering the
"beat" of public opinion. If a large proportion of the public, sometimes even a majority, has
no real opinion on an issue, most media organizations would dismiss the poll results as
having no news value. And if that happened on a regular basis, the whole enterprise of
media polls would be in serious jeopardy. The media don't want to tell the public the truth
about itself.    (Moore, personal communication)

This chapter explores the reasons why producing good news stories often trumps
more measured assessment of poll results. This analysis proceeds in several steps,

beginning with a brief discussion of why the construction of a mythical engaged public is an enduring media project. Then I review some well-established methodological cautions in interpreting polls, followed by an analysis of why the news media so routinely ignore those cautions. The conclusion examines the significance of constructing a news public that conveniently clusters around seemingly clear support and opposition to elite policy frames, creating a dramatic news narrative about representative democracy.

# CONSTRUCTING THE PUBLIC IN THE POLICY PROCESS

Walter Lippmann was among the most perceptive observers and influential insiders during the rise of American empire in the early twentieth century. He wrote in increasingly pessimistic terms about the engagement of the public. Lippmann concluded that most people are too busy, too poorly informed, and too removed from the realities of power to be serious participants in the decisions of the day (Lippmann 1922, 1993). At the same time, keeping the impression of democracy alive in the minds of citizens seemed of paramount importance. Lippmann witnessed and participated in grand government public relations campaigns designed to create the impression of public support for wars and domestic policies. Such campaigns introduce clear, dramatic images into the news—images that often stand in sharp contrast to the murky realities that lie beyond them. Secretary of State Dean Acheson, an architect of the cold war, once remarked that officials had to make their points "clearer than truth" (Acheson 1969, 375).

Routine journalism reports on the daily play of power, and is ill-equipped to assess the truth of competing claims—with the exception of increasingly rare instances of investigative reporting. What one might hope for in terms of bringing publics into the news conversation is accountability. While occasional news reports use polls to hold officials accountable for taking positions that run against poll trends, it is hard to establish sustainable poll-based accountability. Even in the rare cases where elite position-taking is shown repeatedly in news reports to be discrepant with public opinion, officials may ignore the tide of opinion because their political base and local constituencies line up differently, as happened when Republicans moved ahead with impeachment despite regular press reports on its growing unpopularity (Jacobs and Shapiro 2000). Unlike the Clinton impeachment, which had daily developments with news pegs hanging all over them, many other potential watchdog moments are hard to sustain because they have no ongoing political mechanism to advance them. Thus, the anemic press efforts to sort out the issue of torture policy following the Abu Ghraib incident of 2004 succumbed to Bush administration spin for lack of the institutional opposition from the Democrats needed to tell another side of the story and create a possible basis for deeper public comprehension (Bennett, Lawrence, and Livingston 2007). In the end, the more common news formula is to plug oversimplified polls into the backdrop of advancing political stories (e.g., horse-race election stories or game-framed policy stories) in ways that diminish the nuances of poll reporting in favor of creating a narrative of public engagement. These media conventions fly in the face of considerable research showing that publics are generally inattentive and uninformed about all but the most pressing and personal issues.

## How Polls Anticipate News Narratives

George Bishop opens his book called *The Illusion of Public Opinion* with an illustration of a typical polling report aimed at making headlines: a Gallup press release that said, "Americans Favor U.S. Peacekeeping Force in Liberia" (2005, p. xiii). Written like a news headline, the release shows how polling firms anticipate the news values of their product. The findings in the release are ready-made news fare, showing a solid majority (57 percent) favoring sending troops, and just 36 percent opposing the idea. Bishop then goes on to introduce an exercise that is by now familiar to most academic researchers and students of polls. He shows that other polls with differently worded questions (specifying the number of troops and the length of time they might stay) produced a majority opposing the idea. He also notes that few Americans could locate Liberia on a map, and that background polling showed that few had been following the situation closely. The moral of the story is that news organizations could have reported opinion as running either for or against sending troops. Bishop suggests that the most accurate report would be to note the shaky foundations of attention and knowledge that limited public engagement with the issue.

Bishop notes a long tradition of critical scholarship warning against facile uses of polls to create illusory publics. For example, Bourdieu (1979) argues that polls give the impression that average people have far more voice and power than elites, who often cite polls in publicizing policies and decisions. Ginsberg (1986) continues this line of thought with the idea that polling often "domesticates" mass beliefs by structuring issues, questions, and responses in line with existing elite agendas. Herbst (1993) describes the way polling can make publics seem more coherent and decisive than they are. Like Bourdieu and Ginsberg, Herbst considers the publicity surrounding polls as a mechanism of elite rule in democracies. All of these and other critiques can be traced back in one way or another to Blumer (1948), who challenged the idea that polls should give equal weight to all opinion, informed or not, organized or not, elite or mass.

In this context, the news becomes an obvious mechanism for constructing illusory images of public engagement with daily events (Lewis 2001; Bennett 2009). Lewis (2001) argues that the news is not just a passive conduit; it is an active filtering system that follows the dominant political climate by bending poll reports to fit elite issue agendas and then further shading those reports to appear more conservative than actually indicated in the data. This latter pattern may reflect the effect of long-running conservative charges of a liberal media bias, which likely makes editors anticipate the often volatile reactions to any content that hints at favoring the left. However, Lewis's main point about the polling agenda being set by the agenda of policy elites is more critical to our story of how the news constructs a seemingly engaged public around polling questions bent to the agendas of government and powerful opposition factions.

## How News Narratives Follow Elite Debate and Cue Opinion

In earlier work I have referred to this idea of writing the grand news narratives around balances of elite power in decision circles as *indexing*, meaning that news organizations weight the sources and frames they use in stories according to a situational power index: what factions journalists and their editors perceive to hold how much power in the situation being reported (Bennett 1990). This model helps explain, among other things, how such a competitive press system produces such uniform content every day, and how the news can shift from one political pole to another over time or over issues without being ideologically biased, but by merely following the flows of power. The indexing model, for example, accounts for why the quiescence of the Democrats in the debate running up to the Iraq War made the voices and views of the Bush administration so dominant (Bennett, Lawrence, and Livingston 2007).

In situations with more balance among opposing elite positions, simple cuing models of opinion (for example, Zaller 1992) might predict that, when pushed to have opinions, Moore's "don't cares" will fall evenly on both sides. By contrast, in the case of Iraq, the press filtered much of the news leading up to the war through Bush marketing frames, making it unsurprising that the "don't cares" were easily pushed by pollsters to support the war. The larger point, as demonstrated in the next section, is that for most issues, the "don't cares" form a persistent plurality, yet the news seldom reports it that way. As noted earlier, there are exceptions in terms of issues that affect people directly, often independent of media imagery: prosperity, taxes, inflation, prayer, guns, and abortion rights, among them. Even these issues seldom garner news polling that captures the nuances of public-level deliberations, resulting in other distortions of the role of the public in news reporting, as discussed below. The next section takes a closer look at news polling, raising questions about how poll topics are chosen, how questions are worded, how data are analyzed, and how results are reported.

## PUBLIC OPINION AS NEWS OUTPUT RATHER THAN DEMOCRATIC INPUT

There are at least three related issues that combine to make opinion polls more often an element of news drama than a democratic accountability mechanism.

- Decisions about the topics on which to commission and report polls are driven by implicit journalistic perceptions of power and agendas in political institutions, as opposed to other more independent assessments of the public interest. The organization of the US press system around perceptions of power in governing institutions makes the output of an otherwise free and competitive press system remarkably uniform (Bennett 1990; Cook 1998). Filtering opinion reporting through elite power balances produces often exaggerated clarity and coherence in public opinion with the aid of the related media polling practices discussed below.
- Decisions about how to ask survey questions are impacted by the close partnership and in some cases ownership of polling operations by news organizations. This often means that questions are worded to fit the most dramatic and simple news narratives. Fitting polls to predictable news plots makes polls more the products of news narratives than independent inputs in news reporting (although the quasi-scientific presentation of polls in the news may make it seem otherwise).
- Decisions about interpreting the results are often further constrained by problems of sampling, response rates, and levels of knowledge, caring, and attention. Even though pollsters may know about such problems, they tend to be ignored in news reports because they complicate the news narrative and undermine the myth that public opinion is a fully formed and credible element in the drama of democracy.

These aspects of the manufacture of public opinion in the news are explored in more detail in the following sections.

## Decisions about What Polls to Commission and Report

It is understandable that most polls in the news reflect the policy agendas and power struggles in national political institutions (Congress, the executive, and courts). The exceptions of course are a few running poll questions about presidential approval or satisfaction with the course of the nation, and the horse-race polls during elections (Lewis 2001). In addition to filtering poll reports from a top-down political perspective, there is a second filtering mechanism used by the press: the presumption that much of the domain of foreign policy is the preserve of elites and experts, and thus less relevant for reporting public opinion (historic decisions such as wars are an exception to this rule).

These selection mechanisms can be illustrated with an examination of polls reported in news stories in a sample of ten US newspapers during the 1980s and 1990s. The data revealed that news about hotly contested domestic issues contained the most poll reports. For example, poll reports appeared in 10.3 percent of the news stories on school prayer, 9 percent of gun control reports, 9 percent of abortion stories, and 5.6 percent of stories about tax reform. By contrast, news reports on pollution contained polls only 1.3 percent of the time (acid rain less than 1 percent), and school integration under 2 percent of the time (Bennett and Klockner 1996). These less-reported poll topics reflected issues that were relatively dormant institutionally during this era, but they erupted politically in later years, and climbed back up the polling agenda.

As expected, the foreign policy picture reveals relatively less public opinion in the news. A comparison of reporting on thirteen different foreign policy topics between 1980 and 1990 showed polls appearing in less than 1 percent of stories on average. Even in the most reported case, polls appeared in just 2 percent of stories on the Gulf War of 1990–1 (Bennett and Klockner 1996). In some of these cases, when the polls unaccountably ran against dominant political alignments, there was a tendency to discount opinion as uninformed, accounting for rare reports that invited academics to note that publics are generally uninformed about foreign policy matters. For example, during the US military involvements in Central America in the 1980s, polls that ran against Reagan policies of supporting proxy armies were often dismissed by experts as weakened by misinformation, such as knowledge of which side the US was backing in various wars (Bennett 1990). Although levels of knowledge about the conflicts rose over time due to repeated news exposure, reporting of opinion polls did not change substantially.

## Decisions about How to Ask Questions

As noted earlier, the effects of the wording of poll questions are legendary in the academic literature. Yet, news organizations tend to depict their polls as self-evident readings of the public mind. Consider, for example, this official statement about the ABC News Poll:

Public opinion is an integral part of the news we cover. It informs and influences political debate, the state of the economy, social trends and more. Simply put, we report what people think, along with what they do, because it is important.

At the ABCNEWS Polling Unit, we are news reporters first; we think of public opinion as our beat—like covering the Supreme Court, the White House, or the Pentagon. In many ways, the process is the same: We pick a topic, go to our best sources, ask what we need to know and report what we have learned.   (Langer 2004)

What this statement avoids discussing is the process through which questions are worded in terms of political framing based on indexing (following the trail of power) and drama (which requires simplifying and sharpening polls). There are many documented examples here, but none illustrates the point better than reporting polls on race issues. Among the most institutionally contested issues in modern American history is affirmative action, the collection of efforts to address the historic inequalities faced by women and minorities in schools, workplaces, and other public institutions. The wording of poll questions on this subject produces wildly differing readings of opinion. For example, asking whether blacks should receive preferential treatment in hiring or school admission produces far more opposition and racially polarized results than questions that mention specific conditions that might warrant such preferences. Thus, including factual information about proven discrimination or underrepresentation in an institution results in significantly higher levels of support for affirmative action from both whites and blacks. As one leading scholar concluded:

It is grossly inaccurate to conclude that racial polarization characterizes the opinions of most Americans on affirmative action and related issues. How Americans feel about affirmative action programs depends on a number of factors, including who the beneficiaries are, and whether the program was adopted to address proven discrimination... Agreement and consensus among Americans on affirmative-action related issues are detected most readily when respondents to national surveys are presented with clear-cut questions and concrete examples that allow them to decide among choices that they understand.   (Swain 2001, 344)

While social science research suggests a correspondence between public views and the historic arc of legal reasoning in matters of race, a very different impression is conveyed in the news, which often tells of polarization and public opposition to the actions of "liberal" politicians and institutions. This more dramatic news story is made credible by news polls based on asking whether unrestricted preferences or quotas should be given to women or minorities in hiring or school admissions decisions. Entman and Rojecki (2000) have shown that news stories consistently dramatized racial conflict themes and reported poll results that fit the news framing. Thus, the cover of a prominent news magazine in the mid-1990s blared the headline "RACE AND RAGE." A more reasonable story could have been written around points of racial harmony and agreement, depending on how the poll questions were worded. Such polarizing polls may have real effects on the dynamics of public policy debates by inflaming passions in so-called culture wars being waged by small numbers of elites on the extreme right wing of the political spectrum (Hochschild 1999). Those elites found news organizations eager to dramatize their polarizing efforts rather than to report more moderate and representative accounts. As Entman and Rojecki observed: "Journalists, it seems, built their frame on claims by elite sources with an interest in promoting the impression of White arousal, a goal that meshed nicely with reporters' constant search for conflict and drama. In fact, journalists appeared to confuse *elite rhetoric* with *average citizens' preferences and priorities*" (2000, 110).

This polarizing (or better put, poll-arizing) news may have inhibited moderate and left politicians from publicly supporting affirmative action or trying to lead a more moderate public consensus on policies. Entman and Rojecki conclude: "It is clear that some of the most important political leaders who set the media agenda—especially presidential hopefuls—turned more actively hostile to affirmative action.... It is far from clear that their views reflected the sentiments of ordinary White Americans" (2000, 110).

Another aspect of asking questions to create more attractive news stories involves the common tactic of pushing "don't know" responses to try to eliminate as many as possible. This often results in creating the impression of a far more opinionated public than actually exists. Despite the volume of cautionary tales from methodologists and serious pollsters (for example, Yankelovich 1991), news organizations often report lower levels of "don't know" or "no opinion responses" than would occur if polls did not push uncertain respondents to greater clarity. A study by Chang and Holland, two professional pollsters, showed that probes typically reduced uncertainty levels by half or more. For example, questions about the way President George W. Bush was handling the immigration issue produced "don't know" responses of 14 percent in a sample that did not receive a probe, while a sample that was given a hard push ended up with half that rate of "don't knows." In a Bush presidential approval question, the "don't know" rate was cut from 10 to 5 percent. In addition, there was a tendency for the pushed respondents to shift to more positive positions, although the main effect simply seemed to be to create more opinions on both sides, where none existed following the initial poll question (Chang and Holland 2007).

## Decisions about Interpreting the Results

The pressure to minimize "don't knows" leads naturally to more dramatic interpretations of poll findings than may be warranted. News polls (with the above exceptions of some foreign policy issues) are generally reported as fully formed public thinking directing the government to take action on the political alternatives that journalists and pollsters have written into the news narrative. As David Moore and Jeffrey Jones, two experts from the Gallup organization, put it: "In public opinion polling today, the results of many policy questions are interpreted by pundits and other analysts as though they constitute 'directive public opinion'—that is, as though the results constitute a mandate from the public as to what the government should do" (Moore and Jones 2002, 1).

Even independent polling organizations may be swayed to shape their products in newsworthy ways. Hyper-clarity generates buzz, attracts attention, and may increase media and scholarly citations of published poll results. For example, Moore and Jones cite an example of a poll report on the Gallup organization website:

Despite recent drops in the value of stocks, Americans continue to support the idea of investing a portion of their Social Security contributions in the stock market. A recent Gallup poll, conducted March 26–28, shows 63% favor the proposal, while 30% are opposed. The numbers are virtually unchanged from a poll conducted in June of last year, when 65% of Americans favored this particular reform proposal and 30% opposed it.   (Moore and Jones 2002, 1)

This report makes it seem that Americans favored what was at the time a leading Bush administration policy initiative favoring the privatization of the US Social Security retirement system. Yet despite a prolonged public relations campaign to sell the plan, President Bush eventually lost public support and failed to win the legislation needed to make the historic change. How could public opinion be so volatile as to swing from overwhelming support for a proposal advanced by a (then) popular president to opposition to the idea? The answer is not that opinion was so volatile, but that initial poll reporting failed to note how non-committal and weak the two to one majority was to begin with. In their in-house Gallup experiment, Moore and Jones asked a follow-up question this way:

A proposal has been made that would allow people to put a portion of their Social Security payroll taxes into personal retirement accounts that would be invested in private stocks and bonds. Do you favor or oppose this proposal?
  a. (If favor) If Congress and the President do NOT pass this proposal into law, would you be very upset, somewhat upset, not too upset, or not at all upset?
  b. (If oppose) If Congress and the President Do pass this proposal into law, would you be very upset, somewhat upset, not too upset, or not at all upset?

From these probes, a very different set of results emerged, making the strong support for Social Security reform look suddenly weak: only 27 percent favored the Bush plan and would have been upset if it did not pass. Another 36 percent said initially that they favored the plan, but in the follow-up said they would not be upset if it did not pass (Moore and Jones 2002, 3). When viewed this way, it is hard to put much stock in the earlier, seemingly strong support for privatization. In this view, there is not a solid majority either way on the issue, and there is not even a majority of combined support and opposition who care strongly about the outcome. Since it is relatively easy to collect and report such data, the failure of pollsters to do so (or at least to publicly discuss them) suggests that the reasons may have little to do with concerns for scientific and diagnostic reporting of opinion.

How common is it for majorities to collapse when survey questions are probed for levels of respondent commitment to their opinions? Very common, it would seem. Moore and Jones asked the "how upset would you be?" question to respondents in polls about a variety of issues, including drilling for oil in an Alaskan nature preserve, election campaign finance reform, gay civil unions, missile defense, and human cloning. These were among the most politically contested issues among elites at the time the polls were taken. Despite the hotly contested nature of each of these issues, what Moore and Jones call "directive majorities" (who would care if their views were not realized) collapsed on every issue except for one: human cloning, on which 53 percent favored a ban, and fully 73 percent cared whether their position prevailed (Moore and Jones 2002, 5). If opinion on many issues is as soft as these findings indicate, then it is a misrepresentation to say that publics either support or oppose particular government initiatives just to achieve dramatic clarity in news reports.

The literature on polling is filled with other concerns about scientific limitations and lapses that bear on interpretation of the results. Among the many other concerns are the notoriously low response rates in phone polls, which often fail to gain initial agreements to participate from more than 10–20 percent of those contacted. Pollsters tend to guard the actual figures, and, in any event, contend that suitable replacements are secured so that systematic bias is avoided. Nevertheless, low response rates can have varying effects on survey outcomes, with particular bias introduced into attempts to measure sensitive issues such as likelihood to vote for minority candidates (Pew 1998). Although quality polls make efforts to adjust for the refusal problem (Traugott and

Lavrakas 2000), the response rate issue in news polls is one of many methodological issues that generally remain hidden.

# Conclusion: Public Opinion as News Output

The idea that media and politicians construct a symbolic public is not new. Beginning with Lippmann (1922, 1993) and continuing through thinkers such as Murray Edelman (1977, 1988), many observers have noted that the regular invocation of the public is something of a totemic observance in democratic rituals. There is nothing inherently wrong with the ritualistic invocation of publics if, as part of the ritual, decision-makers also actively try to educate the population or invite their informed input into the daily flow of discussion and decision. While transparent public deliberations do occur on some issues (Page 1996), others are clouded by one-sided marketing efforts (e.g., the Bush administration and the selling of the Iraq War) or by hyperbolic fear campaigns from organized interests (e.g., the health care episodes of the Clinton and Obama administrations). However, for reasons involving the indexing norm used by the mainstream press to construct news reports, the spectrum of highly variable public discourse is reported much as it comes from officials, with few sustainable, independent press challenges to quality or veracity. Indeed, the companion news norm of emphasizing drama means that the more hyperbolic the claims (as long as they come from approved sources), the more newsworthy they tend to be. In this context, the similarly unqualified reporting of polls tends to smooth out the variations in the quality of mediated public deliberations and legitimize them as democratic.

It is remarkable that, despite the many highly stylized news qualities discussed above, polls have become the symbolic embodiment of the American people. There are, of course, other ways to report opinion through the many direct forms of expression such as the labor rights movement in the early twentieth century, the civil rights and anti-Vietnam War movements in mid-century, and the more recent protests against globalization and corporate power. It is ironic that from the standpoint of the news, such direct expressions of opinion are often problematic because, unlike polls, they are difficult to evaluate and report in objective or representative terms. In many cases, substantial public protests are given little media attention, at all, and when they are covered, they are often reported in negative terms as the acts of lawless and violent elements (Gitlin 1993).

It is too simple to say that such movements may not be representative of general public sentiment whereas polls are (Herbst 1993). Among other things, media reporting of polls driven by elite cuing can directly affect the political dynamics of social struggles. When elite positions and corresponding poll results appear to reject the claims of movements, opposition voices may be marginalized both in society and in the media. For example, when the Democrats made strategic electoral calculations about the costs of challenging a then popular president going to war in Iraq, the result may have been to trigger what Noelle-Neumann (1993) referred to as a spiral of silence in which people tune out social deliberations because they perceive that they are in a minority. This can become a vicious circle as news organizations avoid critical examination of ever more dominant news frames (e.g., Bush administration claims about weapons of mass destruction in Iraq), activating what Entman (2004) calls a cascade of echoing media support for otherwise dubious positions.

Although some scholars find evidence of a coherent and rational public that directs public policy (for example, Page and Shapiro 1992), others suggest a far murkier picture (Ginsberg 1986; Zaller 1992; Herbst 1993; Jacobs and Shapiro 2000). While polls could become instruments for learning and feedback between publics and politicians, they are more often used in ways that shore up Lippmann's pessimism about democratic governance (or what I have called *managerial democracy*). Many political consultants proclaim that polling and marketing represent the ultimate in empowerment for publics whose every feeling is registered and conveyed to politicians. This might be true if the common aim of strategic communication and political leadership (or journalism, for that matter) were to help publics grasp complex issues and learn new perspectives from which leaders might learn and change as well. While such moments may occur from time to time, they are at odds with the strictures of communication professionals who have inserted themselves into the heart of the political process. And insofar as journalists continue to take that process largely at face value, they are susceptible to the spin that flows from it. With official spin framing stories, polls often become the symbolic echo of public involvement in a dramatized democracy. Yet one set of polls may be enduring and grounded enough in popular experience to take seriously: the downward spiral of confidence in the political institutions most often in the news (Congress and the president) and in the press that covers them. Perhaps the public is signaling its own displeasure with politics and journalism as usual.

## REFERENCES

ACHESON, D. 1969. *Present at the Creation: My Years in the State Department*. New York: W. W. Norton.

BENNETT, W. L. 1990. Toward a Theory of Press–State Relations in the U.S. *Journal of Communication*, 40: 103–25.

—— 2009. *News: The Politics of Illusion*, 8th edn. New York: Longman.

—— and KLOCKNER, J. D. 1996. The Psychology of Mass-Mediated Publics. In *The Psychology of Political Communication*, ed. A. N. Crigler. Ann Arbor: University of Michigan Press.

—— LAWRENCE, R. G., and LIVINGSTON, S. 2007. *When the Press Fails: Political Power and the News Media from Iraq to Katrina*. Chicago: University of Chicago Press.

BISHOP, G. F. 2005. *The Illusion of Public Opinion*. Lanham, MD: Rowman & Littlefield.

BLUMENTHAL, M. 2009. Strategic Vision and the Transparency Gap. *National Journal Online*, Sept. 28. At <http://www.nationaljournal.com/njonline/print_friendly.php?ID=mp_2009 0925_5674>. Accessed Jan. 15, 2010.

BLUMER, H. 1948. Public Opinion and Public Opinion Polling. *American Sociological Review*, 13/5 (Oct.), 542–9.

BOURDIEU, P. 1979. Public Opinion Does Not Exist. In *Communication and Class Struggle*, i: *Capitalism, Imperialism*, ed. A. Mattelart and S. Sieglaub. New York: International General.

CHANG, L. C., and HOLLAND, K. 2007. Eliciting Value Responses: Follow-Up Probes to "Don't Knows" in Polls. Paper presented at the Annual Conference of the American Association for Public Opinion Research, Anaheim, California, May 17–20.

COOK, T. 1998. *Governing with the News: The News Media as a Political Institution*. Chicago: University of Chicago Press.

DEWAN, S. 2009. Polling Firm's Reprimand Rattles News Media. *New York Times*, Oct. 2. At <http://www.nytimes.com/2009/10/03/us/03survey.html>. Accessed Oct. 4, 2009.

EDELMAN, M. 1977. *Political Language: Words that Succeed and Policies that Fail*. New York: Academic Press.

——1988. *Constructing the Political Spectacle*. Chicago: University of Chicago Press.

ENTMAN, R. M. 2004. *Projections of Power: Framing News, Public Opinion, and U.S. Foreign Policy*. Chicago: University of Chicago Press.

——and ROJECKI, A. 2000. *The Black Image in the White Mind: Media and Race in America*. Chicago: University of Chicago Press.

GINSBERG, B. 1986. *The Captive Public: How Mass Opinion Promotes State Power*. New York: Basic Books.

GITLIN, T. 1993. *The Whole World Is Watching: The Mass Media in the Making and Unmaking of the New Left*. Berkeley: University of California Press.

HERBST, S. 1993. *Numbered Voices: How Opinion Polling Has Shaped American Politics*. Chicago: University of Chicago Press.

HOCHSCHILD, J. L. 1999. Affirmative Action as Culture War. In *The Cultural Territories of Race*, ed. M. Lamont. Chicago: University of Chicago Press.

JACOBS, L. R., and SHAPIRO, R. Y. 2000. *Politicians Don't Pander: Political Manipulation and the Loss of Democratic Responsiveness*. Chicago: University of Chicago Press.

KISSINGER, H. A. 2009. Deployments and Diplomacy. *Newsweek*, Oct. 3. At <http://www. newsweek.com/id/216704>. Accessed Oct. 5, 2009.

LANGER, G. 2004. ABC News' Guide to Polls & Public Opinion. At <http://abcnews.go.com/ Politics/PollVault/story?id=43943>. Accessed Oct. 8, 2009.

LEWIS, J. 2001. *Constructing Public Opinion: How Political Elites Do What They Like and Why We Seem to Go Along With It*. New York: Columbia University Press.

LIPPMANN, W. 1922. *Public Opinion*. New York: Free Press.

——1993. *The Phantom Public*. Edison, NJ: Transaction Books. First published 1925.

MOORE, D. W. 2008a. *The Opinion Makers: An Insider Exposes the Truth behind the Polls*. Boston: Beacon Press.

——2008b. The Myth of War Support. *Washington Monthly*, Aug. 12. At <http://www.washingtonmonthly.com/archives/individual/2008_08/014280.php>. Accessed Oct 23, 2010.

——and JONES, J. M. 2002. Directive vs. Permissive Public Opinion. Paper presented at the Annual Meeting of the American Association for Public Opinion Research, St Petersburg, FL, May 16–19.

Noelle-Neumann, E. 1993. *The Spiral of Silence: Public Opinion—Our Social Skin*. Chicago: University of Chicago Press.

Page, B. I. 1996. *Who Deliberates? Mass Media in Modern Democracy*. Chicago: University of Chicago Press.

——and Shapiro, R. Y. 1992. *The Rational Public: Fifty Years of Trends in Americans' Policy Preferences*. Chicago: University of Chicago Press.

Pew Research Center for the People & the Press. 1998. Possible Consequences of Non-Response for Pre-Election Surveys, May 16. At <http://people-press.org/report/89/possible-consequences-of-non-response-for-pre-election-surveys>. Accessed Jan. 17, 2010.

Schuman, H. 2008. *Method and Meaning in Polls and Surveys*. Cambridge, MA: Harvard University Press.

Swain, C. M. 2001. Affirmative Action: Legislative History, Judicial Interpretations, Public Consensus. In *America Becoming: Racial Trends and their Consequences*, vi, ed. N. J. Smelser, W. J. Wilson, and F. Mitchell. Washington, DC: National Research Council, National Academies Press.

Traugott, M. W., and Lavrakas, P. J. 2000. *The Voter's Guide to Election Polls*, 2nd edn. New York: Chatham House.

Yankelovich, D. J. 1991. *Coming to Public Judgment: Making Democracy Work in a Complex World*. Syracuse, NY: Syracuse University Press.

Zaller, J. R. 1992. *The Nature and Origins of Mass Opinion*. Cambridge: Cambridge University Press.

——and Feldman, S. 1992. A Simple Theory of the Survey Response. *American Journal of Political Science*, 35: 579–616.

# PART III

## PUBLIC OPINION

# Section Four: Foundations

# CHAPTER 17

# DEMOCRACY AND THE CONCEPT OF PUBLIC OPINION

JOHN G. GUNNELL

## INTRODUCTION

THIS chapter is limited to an intellectual history of how the term "public opinion" entered the discourse of social and political science during the nineteenth century and of how the concept to which it referred was fundamentally transformed in the early years of the twentieth century. The term "public opinion" is rooted in the origins of the American vision of democracy, but during the 1920s there was a fundamental change in democratic theory which entailed a different concept of public opinion—and of how to study it. During the nineteenth century, public opinion had been conceived as the opinion of a collective entity, but since the beginning of the twentieth century, it has been increasingly understood as an aggregation of individual and group preferences.

In his presidential address to the Seventh Annual Convention of the American Association for Public Opinion Research, Bernard Berelson (1952) famously posed the question how the study of public opinion could contribute to bringing democratic practice and democratic theory into closer harmony. The traditional image of democracy, he claimed, assumed a citizenry knowledgeable about public affairs, manifesting appropriate personality characteristics, and acting in a rational and principled manner on the basis of accurate perceptions of political reality and a dedication to the public interest. Berelson argued that although social scientific research indicated that the model did not conform very closely to the reality of American politics, this was "not necessarily a matter for disillusionment or even disappointment." As Berelson and his collaborators in the Elmira study of voting later concluded, the lack of active participation, for example, might very well represent contentment. What mattered was less the individual citizens than the "system" and its "collective properties" and the manner in which there was a symbiotic relationship between a complex of diverse "cleavages," which moved the system, and "a basic consensus," which served to "hold it together."

What was assumed in this formulation was that public opinion was not the opinion of any identifiable subject. This basic image of democracy had been articulated on the eve of the Second World War by Pendelton Herring (*The Politics of Democracy*, 1940) as both a validation of the United States as a democracy and an ideological counter-point to foreign ideologies. After the war, it was rearticulated by individuals such as David Truman (*The Governmental Process*, 1951) and Earl Latham (*The Group Basis of Politics*, 1952). It was, however, most fully elaborated by Robert Dahl and Charles Lindblom (1953) and particularly in Dahl's *Preface to Democratic Theory* (1956) and his conception of "empirical democratic theory." Dahl implied that public opinion was only a manifestation of the preferences of transient ad hoc majorities which responded to particular issues. This mid-century image of democracy was not, however, as novel as it sometimes appeared. It actually represented the re-articulation, and codification, of a theory of democracy, and a transformation in the idea of public opinion, that had been fully manifest by the end of the 1920s and which, for a generation, had informed the vision of liberal democracy embraced by political science. Lindblom (1965) recog-nized that this theory of "how people can coordinate with each other without anyone's coordinating them, without a dominant purpose, and without rules that fully prescribe their relations to each other" was an attempt to complete the "unfinished business" of an intellectual shift which had occurred a generation earlier.

## THE DEMOCRATIC STATE AND PUBLIC OPINION

The idea of popular sovereignty and republican government that informed the ideology of the American Revolution assumed that government was the virtual reflection of an organic people which was its author as well as its subject. The *Federalist Papers* stressed that the new national government was the creation and representative of what it consistently referred to as an American people and public, which transcended local attachments. Repeated references to "*the* public" and to personifications of its attri-butes and expressions were not merely metaphorical. "Public opinion" was similarly reified and described as something that could both exert and be subject to "influence." Policies could be both "justified" and "censured" by public opinion, but it was possible to "pervert," "restrain" it, and leave it in "suspense." But above all, the Constitution, once ratified by the "people," would continue to "depend on public opinion," which would also regulate such things as "legislative discretion." It was essential to the argument of *The Federalist*, and its claim that the new national government would in fact be truly republican in form and character, that there was "one united people" and that this "great body of the people" and the physical configuration of the country were "made for one another." What was paradoxical, however, was that when it came to describing political reality, a very different image emerged. Government was pointedly described as presiding over individuals, and politics, particularly in Federalist No. 10, was depicted as a divisive and contentious mixture of self-interested individuals and factions which embraced little sense of unity and common purpose.

This paradox of democracy, which suggested that the essence of democracy was at once unity and plurality, would constitute the axis of subsequent American democratic thought. There would be a consistent dialectical relationship between the belief that popular sovereignty entailed the existence of an organic people and the alternative belief that the "people" referred basically to a mass of individuals. The most immediate resolution to this paradox, and what dominated the theory and ideology of democracy during the nineteenth century, was an elaboration of the idea of the people as an autonomous entity with public opinion as its essential attribute. From the beginning, however, this idea was not free from the shadow of a worry about majorities that was quite different from that against which Madison warned.

In his *Democracy in America* (1835, 1840) Alexis de Tocqueville was among the first to speak unequivocally of America as a "democracy," and he was the first commentator on American society to speak in any extensive manner about public opinion. His work manifested some of the same ambivalence as *The Federalist*. While he consistently referred to "the American people," he also emphasized, and worried about, the extreme individualism and diversity of interests which seemed to inhibit the formation of a national community which could reach beyond the "habit of participation" that characterized various local associations and organizations. He believed that something close to a genuine community had existed at the time of the revolution, when public opinion self-consciously bound individuals together in pursuit of a common good. This, however, was lost as this sense of unity gave way to the potential for a "tyranny of the majority." This phenomenon was clearly not the numerical dominance of some particular material interest, which Madison had feared. It referred instead to the manner in which the passion for equality and the ethic of individualism created an anomic condition which, in the absence of a transcendent community, could lead to the accrual of power and authority in the form of mass sentiments.

In volume I Tocqueville noted that, in a generic sense, public opinion was the "predominant authority" in modern society—"above the head" of both the king of France and the president of the United States. The power, for example, of federal judges in the United States was really the "power of public opinion," and its "exact limits cannot be defined." This, he suggested, was where sovereignty resided and what made America a democracy, because Americans "having once admitted the doctrine of the sovereignty of the people, apply it with perfect sincerity" and bring everything before the "bar of public opinion." At times he wondered "what strength can even public opinion have retained, when no twenty persons are connected by a common tie," yet he affirmed that "inhabitants, although divided into twenty-four distinct sovereignties, still constitute a single people" and are "unanimous upon the general principles which ought to rule human society." He concluded that "the people are held to be the source of all legitimate power" and that public opinion was the "moral authority of the reason of the community" and the "political authority of the mass of the citizens" (Tocqueville 1976, 156, 191–2, 232, 238, 421, 505–6).

Although in the second volume Tocqueville approached the issue less directly, his attitude seemed even more jaded as he began to construe public opinion more pervasively as a source of democratic tyranny. He claimed that the "political omnipotence of the majority" necessarily "augments the influence that public opinion would have without it" and "faith in public opinion will become a species of religion, and the majority its ministering prophet." Even religion received its authority from public opinion, and "as public opinion grows to be more the first and most irresistible of existing powers," organized religion had no capacity to check it. While in certain countries an aristocracy "develops a public opinion of its own," there was only one opinion in America. Despite class differences in the United States, public opinion created a unity, or at least a perception of unity, despite objective differences in interest (1863, 12, 30, 56, 221, 224, 295). Although he still saw the danger of individuals becoming so isolated that "public opinion has no hold on men," his main concern was that:

Whenever social conditions are equal, public opinion presses with enormous weight upon the minds of each individual; it surrounds, directs, and oppresses him...This circumstance is extraordinarily favorable to the stability of opinions. When an opinion has taken root amongst a democratic people, and established itself in the minds of the bulk of the community, it afterwards subsists by itself and is maintained without effort.   (1863, 321)

Despite the volatility often attributed to democratic societies, Tocqueville stressed that although ideas might change when "the majority has ceased to believe what it believed before...this empty phantom of public opinion is strong enough to chill innovations, and to keep them silent and at a respectful distance" (1863, 322). The task of transforming the concept of public opinion from an amorphous aggregate will to a substantive collectivity and making it safe for the idea of democracy fell to the German émigré Francis Lieber, who can reasonably be designated the founder of American political science and who came to the United States shortly after the first visit of his acquaintance and correspondent Tocqueville.

Lieber took seriously Tocqueville's suggestion that the new world of American democracy required a "new science of politics," and he was the first both to initiate such a form of study and to present a systematic account of popular sovereignty in the United States. Lieber, who had fled the failed liberalism of Germany in 1827, was, like the American founders, wary of using the term "democracy," which still carried radical connotations and, as with Tocqueville, evoked an image of the post-revolutionary Terror in France. His preference was for the term "self-government" or his neologism "hamarchy," which referred basically to representative government. This type of regime, he believed, avoided the dangers of "democratic absolutism." In the same year that Tocqueville published the first volume of *Democracy in America*, Lieber set forth, in his *Encyclopaedia Americana*, the concept of the state as the basis of "the province of the political sciences" and their "distinctive character" (Lieber 1835), and this formulation would, for at least a half century, govern both political science as well as more popular accounts of the theory of American democracy.

Before Lieber, the term "state," apart from referring to the several states, had little currency either in the discourse of American politics or in commentary on politics. As Lieber made clear in Volume I of his first major work, the *Manual of Political Ethics*, published in 1838, what was most distinctive about this theory of the state was the fact that the word "state" did not refer to government but rather, and explicitly, to a natural and "aboriginal" sovereign community or people that was the author of, and separate from, both the Constitution and the institutions of government, which it authorized and limited. This he designated a "jural society," a "*res publica*," "*res communis*," and "*res populi*," which was the font of law and public policy. The American form of government, he claimed, was a recent development which evolved from ancient Teutonic sources and found its full expression in the "Anglican liberty" of England and, ultimately, in the United States. Despite all the social and institutional diversity, which was essential to the liberty realized in such a system, it was an "organism" in which all the parts added up to an integral whole. The voice of this people, as in the case of traditional republican theory, was that of the majority, which, in turn, spoke in the form of "public opinion." In its most "comprehensive sense," this included both the "opinion of the community" on specific issues and the general "opinion of the public, of civil society," which bound the society together and constituted the "sense and sentiment of the community, necessarily irresistible, sharing its sovereign power everywhere" and standing behind and above positive law and political leaders (1839, 238–42).

In the second volume of the *Manual of Political Ethics* and other later work, Lieber further elaborated on how the sovereign was "the political organism through which we arrive at the public opinion and public will of the whole," and "by voting on a large scale, public opinion passes into public will." He argued that it was important, however, not to mistake "coterie talk for public opinion, coterie judgment for public judgment." True public opinion was that of the "community" as a whole, which had been refined by the "modifying correction of time" and the "talent and knowledge of those who are peculiarly able to judge." Public opinion was also something different from "general opinion," which was often something of the "moment," as well as from the "aggregate opinion of many individuals singly taken," which was in many cases often "egregiously mistaken." Public opinion was "settled more or less digested opinion" which represented "the community as a connected and organized body." Lieber acknowledged that on occasion even public opinion could be "erroneous, and greatly so," but for the most part it should be respected and followed, because "it is the greatest, mightiest of all powers" and what a representative should represent even though it was only revealed through representatives and expressed in law. Majority opinions were only valid when they were the product of "true majorities" reflecting the "organically produced, well-settled" opinion of the whole society rather than a "momentary general opinion." The "public opinion which becomes public will is the well-ascertained and clearly settled opinion of the whole jural society or state, sifted and freed from the adhesions of momentary excitement, of sordid or local selfishness, and of the tyrannical dictation of one part of society over the rest." He stressed the essential importance of a free press in producing a "well-sifted and duly modified average opinion," which was subject neither to "police restrictions of government, nor the riotous procedures of mobs, nor the tyranny of associations" (1876, 137, 226, 260, 273, 275, 363; 1874, 414–18).

Two decades after Tocqueville's book was published, John Stuart Mill raised similar reservations about public opinion in his famous essay *On Liberty* (1859). He argued that in modern society tyranny was not simply a threat from government authorities but that the "moral coercion" exerted by "prevailing . . . collective opinion" in society itself had become the potential tyrant. Individuals, he claimed, had been "lost in the crowd" as "public opinion now rules the world. The only power deserving the name is that of the masses" as the "ascendancy of public opinion" and an "overruling majority" created a "general similarity among mankind." Although what constituted the source of such opinion differed in various countries, such as in the United States, in which it was "the whole white population," the "opinions of masses of merely average men are every-where become or becoming the dominant power" and generate and enforce a confor-mity based on "collective mediocrity." He claimed that the "modern regime of public opinion" was "unorganized," but this did not diminish its power and in some ways made it an elusive enemy.

The core ideas of the German-inspired democratic theory of the state were promul-gated by public intellectuals such as Orestes Brownson (*The American Republic*, 1866), the historian George Bancroft's ten-volume history of the United States (completed in 1874), political scientists such as Theodore Woolsey at Yale (*Political Science or the State, Theoretically and Practically Considered* (1877), Herbert Baxter Adams at Johns Hopkins University, and publicists such as Elisha Mulford (*The Nation*, 1887). The first comprehensive study of American government that could qualify as an empirical account was, however, that of the British statesman and scholar James Bryce, who, in *The American Commonwealth*, presented the most extended analysis up to that time of American politics and political institutions and the most effusive image of American public opinion as the foundation of American democracy.

Like Tocqueville, to whom he predicted he would be compared, Bryce took for granted the democratic character of the United States, but he pointed out that his goal was not to write a general treatise on democracy with America as an example but rather to undertake a more empirical study of American government and to "paint the institutions and people of America as they are," which included depicting "the sover-eignty of the masses." In the introduction to his work, he noted that while it might seem that political parties held the dominant power, they "are not the ultimate force in the conduct of affairs" (Bryce 1888: i. 6, 63).

Behind and above them stands the people. *Public opinion*, that is, the mind and conscience of the whole nation, is the *opinion* of persons who are included in the parties . . . Yet it stands above the parties, being cooler and larger minded than they are; it awes party leaders and holds in check party organizations. No one openly ventures to resist it. It determines the direction and the character of national policy. It is the product of a greater number of minds than in any other country, and it is more indisputably sovereign . . . nowhere is the rule of *public opinion* so complete as in America, or so direct; that is to say, so independent of the ordinary machinery of government. Now the president is deemed to represent the people no less than do the members of the legislature. *Public opinion* governs by and through him no less than them.    (Bryce 1888: i. 301)

Throughout the two volumes of his work, which were the product of several visits to the United States, Bryce repeatedly stressed the influence of public opinion on the creation of the Constitution and the actions of every institution and officer of government at every level. He maintained that "the United States, more than any other country, are governed by public opinion, that is to say, by the general sentiment of the mass of the nation" and the "ideas and feelings of the people at large." And despite the diversity of the country, it was, a generation after the Civil War, bound together by a sense of national sovereignty grounded in the unity of the people and public opinion.

In his first volume, Bryce had attested to the existence and power of public opinion, and he devoted half of the second volume to addressing its nature and forms of expression. According to Bryce, public opinion, in one form or another, was, and always had been, the foundation of political regimes, which necessarily rested on the "silent acquiescence of the numerical majority." What was unique about the United States was the highly evolved form, which was "stronger and more active than any other country" and which was not only consistently "vigilant" but, on the whole, "wholesome and upright." It was not to be confused with the organs through which it was expressed, with a numerical majority, or with some amorphous aggregation of individual opinions, and its existence should not be obscured by such defects of politics as political machines, the spoils system, and election frauds. Its "rudimentary stage" was manifest when "sentiment spontaneously arises in the mind and flows from the lips of the average man" and fuses into a "passive majority," but it later became "conscious and active" when in "free countries" people recognize that they are a "sovereign multitude" embodying the "chief and ultimate power" and "treat their rulers as their agents" over whom they exercise "constant oversight."

Bryce claimed that in the United States public opinion was more trusted than in other societies and had gained a power that made it "the master of servants who tremble before it," and, despite the absence of "direct rule," this could rightly be called "government by public opinion." The attempt of the American founders to splinter society in order to inhibit majorities had, in the end, only served to "exalt public opinion" as its expressions melded and were transformed into a "pervading and impalpable power, like the ether which, as physicists say, passes through all things. It binds all the parts of the complicated system together and gives them whatever unity of aim and action they possess." Much of this, he claimed, was facilitated by the absence of social classes and the self-conscious sense of the people as rulers. It was a "vague fluctuating complex thing . . . omnipotent yet indeterminate, a sovereign to whose voice everyone listens, yet whose words, because he speaks with as many tongues as the waves of the boisterous sea, is so hard to catch." But even though public opinion was not always clearly expressed, it was no less sovereign, and its vehicles were the press, a great variety of associations, election polls, and other elements of society. It was shaped by a wide number of American national characteristics and by social factors such as the lack of distinct upper and lower classes, but, despite great social diversity, it tended toward "homogeneity" as it evolved from the bottom up, rather than through the actions of leaders, and took residence in institutions and patterns of behavior.

Bryce was sensitive to the charge that what he claimed to be the heart of American democracy amounted to what Tocqueville had called a "tyranny of the majority," but he argued that it was a mistake to extrapolate such an image from the fact of the "fatalism of the multitude," which was characteristic of all societies. This fatalism disposed people to "acquiesce in the rule of numbers" and to believe that the majority was right and would prevail. This, however, did not necessarily "imply any exercise of power by the majority at all" but only a "loss of resisting power" which evolved from a faith in the people and, unlike a tyranny, did not involve any "wanton and improper use of strength of the stronger" to subdue and oppress a minority. Some, he claimed, had been misled by Tocqueville's analysis, but the latter's work had to some extent reflected a particular period in American history. He claimed that conditions in the United States, especially after the Civil War, had changed a great deal, and he concluded that "the tyranny of the majority is no longer a blemish on the American system, and the charges brought against democracy, from the supposed example of America, are groundless." Bryce did not claim that public opinion always judged correctly, but more often than not it "overcomes the blemishes, and maintains a high level of good feeling and well-being in the nation." It represented "a sort of atmosphere, fresh, keen, and full of sunlight, like that of American cities, and this sunlight kills many of those noxious germs which are hatched where politicians congregate," and it produces "a united and tolerably homogenous nation" (1888, ii. 230–1, 239, 247, 250–1, 255, 257, 259, 262, 332, 334, 344, 354–5).

Bryce's extravagant defense of public opinion was free from the mysticism of German philosophy, but in many respects it reinforced the core concept of the theory of the state. Although this theory had served to justify, in the case of Lieber and others, a conservative defense of limited government, it was, in principle, ideologically neutral and was also embraced by those, such as the economist Richard Ely, who favored something close to a socialist agenda. The progressively minded John Dewey responded to Henry Maine's critique of modern mass democracy by claiming that democracy was less a system of rule than an "ethical conception" which was based on the idea of a "community" constituting an "organism" in which individuals shared in the sovereignty of "a common will" of which government was only a vehicle of expression (1888). And Dewey made a similar argument when attempting to demonstrate how John Austin's theory of sovereignty had been misunderstood. Austin had claimed that moral law was above positive law, and his insistence that positive law must emanate from a "determinate source" was the only thing that distinguished his notion of sovereignty "from the force exerted by public opinion." Dewey favored Rousseau's idea of a general will and the view that governments were only "organs of expression" and that one must look for "the residence of sovereignty in the whole complex of social activities" which generate public opinion (1894).

The most elaborate historical and philosophical rendition of the theory of the state, *Political Science and Comparative Constitutional Law* (1890), was that of the conservative John W. Burgess, Lieber's successor at Columbia, who, like most of the political scientists of this generation, studied *Staatswissenschaft* in Germany and continued to adapt it to a vision of the United States. This approach was the intellectual centerpiece of his School of Political Science, which, along with Baxter's program at the Johns Hopkins University, educated a large part of the next generation of influential American political scientists such as Charles Merriam, Charles Beard, W. W. Willoughby, and Woodrow Wilson. But just as this theory, and the general identification of sovereignty with public opinion, reached its zenith in the last decade of the nineteenth century, significant inroads had begun to appear. Whether public opinion had been considered the foundation or the nemesis of democracy, its existence had not been doubted, but its reality and locus were beginning to be called into question.

## Public Opinion and the Theory of Pluralist Democracy

Willoughby and others, while still equating the domain of political science with the state, slowly but steadily began to identify the "state" with the institutions of government and to transform sovereignty into a juristic or legal concept. What had been referred to as the state was only an abstraction and "not a real thing" (Willoughby 1896). When Wilson wrote his famous essay "The Study of Administration" (1897), he complained that what inhibited efficient administration and government in modern society was that "we have enthroned public opinion" and believed that "we must instruct and persuade a multitudinous monarch called public opinion." Public opinion, he argued, really consisted of "a score of differing opinions" and had no "definite locality." In a young nation, it was volatile and consisted of little more than a mass of "prejudices" to which government must be sensitive and "responsible" but must continually attempt to "educate" (1897, 207–8, 214–17). In his influential text *The State* (1898) he continued to talk about society as an "organism" and government as an "organ," but it was clear that his concept of the state was no longer that of Lieber and Burgess. This nascent transformation in the concept of the state foreshadowed a fundamental crisis in democratic theory.

Although, by the turn of the century, increased awareness of social and cultural diversity and contentiousness did little to give credence to the traditional idea of the people and the existence of a substantive public opinion, many Progressive intellectuals, such as Herbert Croly (*The Promise of American Life*, 1910), and social scientists, such as C. H. Cooley (*Social Organization: A Study of the Larger Mind*, 1909),

# CHAPTER 18

# CONSTRUCTING PUBLIC OPINION

## A Brief History of Survey Research

### MICHAEL X. DELLI CARPINI

IN this chapter I provide an overview of what has come to define public opinion over the last seventy-five years: the aggregation of individual opinions through sampling, surveys, and quantitative analysis. This history is as complex as the concept of public opinion itself, with roots in politics, marketing, journalism, government, non-profits, and academia. To tell this story I first describe efforts to divine public opinion prior to the advent of systematic surveys. The next, most detailed section, a review of the genesis and institutionalization of scientific survey research from the 1930s through the 1950s, consists of seven subsections: social surveys; government-sponsored surveys; measuring attitudes in academia; the business of survey research; the 1936 presidential election; government, business, and academic partnerships; and the period's theoretical and methodological contributions. The final sections discuss developments since 1960, and highlight some of the challenges and opportunities facing survey research.

## READING TEA LEAVES: PUBLIC OPINION IN THE NINETEENTH AND EARLY TWENTIETH CENTURIES

A century ago Bryce wrote that the final stage of democracy could be reached "if the will of the majority were to become ascertainable at all times.... [but] the machinery for weighing and measuring the popular will from week to week or month to month has not been, and is not likely to be, invented. . . . " Without this "machinery," elites "look incessantly for manifestations of current popular opinion," and "shape their course in accordance with their readings of those manifestations" (1919, 259).

In the nineteenth and early twentieth centuries, these "manifestations of popular opinion" included many indicators, no one of which was considered definitive: conversations between elites and their constituencies; letters and editorials in newspapers; views of community representatives; reports of confidants or informants; behaviors such as rallies, strikes, protests, petitions, and votes; consumption and migration patterns; etc. (Herbst 1993). These efforts mixed rudimentary statistics (e.g., head counts or percentages) with subjective interpretations.

Among these methods were "straw votes," or "straw polls." Non-binding expressions of a group's stance on a pending decision, the first known use of a published election straw poll was by the *Harrisburg Pennsylvanian* during the 1824 presidential campaign, followed quickly by similar polls in other newspapers (Bradburn and Sudman 1988; Moon 1999). These polls were based on a hundred to several thousand people queried at public gatherings. Smith (1990) disputes the notion that the 1824 polls were "the earliest counterparts of modern opinion surveys" (Gallup and Rae 1940, 34–5), noting that gathering non-binding opinion predates 1824 and that they varied significantly from both later straw polls and scientific surveys. Nonetheless, several characteristics distinguish them from existing measures of public opinion, and presage what was to follow a century later.

One distinguishing characteristic was their context. The year 1824 marked a turning point in American politics in which control of presidential nominations was wrested from congressional caucuses, and campaigns developed a more public, democratic flavor (Hofstadter 1969). "Average" citizens were drawn into the spectacle and interest in the uncertain outcome was peaked. Indeed, most of the 1824 straw polls were conducted by organized or semi-organized citizens themselves (Smith 1990).

Newspapers, growing in circulation and transitioning from a partisan to a mass-oriented "penny press," believed that covering the election from a citizen-oriented perspective was a civic and economic benefit. Thus, in addition to their usual efforts to intuit public sentiment from endorsements, informants, or the electoral fortunes of non-presidential candidates (as well as more creative methods such as the number of toasts offered to candidates at Fourth of July celebrations or the bets placed on them), newspapers regularly reported straw-poll results (Smith 1990).

The public nature of straw polls—in origin, dissemination, and consumption—distinguished them from more elite-driven and -consumed methods. It also gave them an air of authenticity, based as they were on citizens' direct reports. None of this suggests that polls *were* accurate reflections of voters' preferences. Incorrect or dishonest counting, polling at events attended by supporters of particular candidates, the inclusion of people ineligible to vote, and the relative merits of competing polls were subjects of debate in print and conversation. As Smith notes:

The straw polls of 1824 stirred up at least as much controversy as do [contemporary] preelection polls. While the straw polls and their critics completely lacked any questionnaire design; interviewer training and quality control; interviewer effects; selection biases in mail questionnaires; the relative benefits of open- versus closed-ended questions; standardization of question wording and questionnaires; the effects of subtle differences in question wording or order; and innovative ways of asking questions (e.g., early versions of feeling thermometers).

The contribution of marketers was both individual and institutional. At the individual level, three "founding fathers" stand out: Archibald Crossley, who headed the *Literary Digest*'s market research department (1922–6) and later formed his own market research firm, which pioneered telephone interviewing; Elmo Roper, whose market research firm conducted *Fortune* magazine's national surveys on business and consumer issues starting in 1935; and George Gallup, a Ph.D. in applied psychology whose career started in market research and who in 1935 founded the American Institute of Public Opinion (later the Gallup organization) and its syndicated national polls on public issues of the day. All three were committed to the new science of survey research. All wrote extensively on the topic for general, applied, and/or academic audiences. And all were involved in the event from which systematic survey research came to be seen as *the* mechanism for determining public opinion: the 1936 presidential election.

## The 1936 Election

The story of the 1936 presidential election is a familiar one. The *Literary Digest*'s popular straw poll, based on millions of mailed ballots, showed Republican Alf Landon leading incumbent Democrat Franklin Delano Roosevelt by a substantial margin, and the magazine confidently predicted a Landon victory. At the same time, Crossley, Roper, and Gallup's polls, based on a few thousand respondents, all showed Roosevelt as the front-runner. On election day Roosevelt was indeed the winner, though by a greater margin than the three pollsters had estimated.

Adding to the drama, six weeks before the *Literary Digest* poll's release Gallup wrote a syndicated column predicting that it would wrongly show a 56 to 44 percent lead for Landon, almost exactly what the *Digest* poll eventually found. According to Gallup, the *Digest* poll suffered three fatal flaws: a sampling frame (based largely on telephone directories and car registrations) that was biased in favor of wealthier citizens; response bias to mail questionnaires that similarly favored higher-income citizens; and the emergence of class voting, which made these methodological biases especially relevant (Converse 1987, 120). The Crossley, Roper, and Gallup polls, on the other hand, "relied on relatively small numbers of respondents, selected systematically and interviewed personally by trained interviewers" (Moon 1999, 10). A key to Gallup's success was his method for selecting national quota samples, developed through extensive research during the 1934 congressional elections (Gallup 1936). This methodology was built on, but more complex than, that used in market research, and similar to Crossley and Roper's.

While its impact on survey research can be exaggerated, the 1936 election did legitimize scientific opinion polling in the public mind and increase its use in government, marketing, journalism, and academia. It also, due in part to Gallup's evangelism, raised survey research's profile as a tool in service of democracy (Gallup 1939; Gallup and Rae 1940).

## Ménage à Trois: Government, Business, and Academic Partnerships and the Institutionalization of Survey Research

The late 1930s through the 1950s saw the growth and institutionalization of survey research. State polls run or supported by newspapers, universities, and private polling firms proliferated. The federal government (centrally the Agriculture and Commerce Departments, and the Office of War Information) expanded its use of surveys, though Agriculture's involvement waned after the Second World War. Commercial polling and marketing firms grew in number and size. Survey research also spread overseas, in large part through Gallup's British (1947) and French (1948) Institutes of Public Opinion. By the 1950s institutes existed in seventeen countries under the umbrella of the International Association of Public Opinion Institutes, later renamed the Gallup International Association (Sudman and Bradburn 1987; Zetterberg 2008).

This period was also marked by often uncomfortable but important partnerships between government, business, and academia. These partnerships developed from continued concerns about national socialism, fascism, and communism; the propagandizing effects of mass media; economic issues in the aftermath of the Great Depression; increasing nationalization of the American economy; and the need to muster support for US involvement in the Second World War. For social scientists such as Paul Lazarsfeld, Hadley Cantril, and Rensis Likert these partnerships were also instrumental to refining survey research, legitimizing its claim to being "scientific," and increasing its utility and prestige in "pure" and "applied" research.

Among the many contributions of the Austrian-born Lazarsfeld was his role as founding director of the Bureau of Applied Social Research (BASR). BASR began as the Office of Radio Research (ORR) at Princeton University in 1937 under the leadership of Lazarsfeld, Cantril (a Princeton psychology professor), and Frank Stanton (research director and later president of CBS). In 1939 ORR moved to Columbia University, supported by a Rockefeller Foundation grant to study educational radio, contracts from commercial media to study radio audiences and newspaper and magazine readers, and advertising studies for products such as toothpaste, vitamins, greeting cards, and alcoholic beverages (Barton 1984; Converse 1987, 268–9). Beginning in 1944, when ORR was renamed BASR, Columbia provided limited funds for operating expenses, but the Bureau continued to depend on grants and contracts from foundations, businesses, and governments (Sudman and Bradburn 1987).

A second university-based institution was the National Opinion Research Center (NORC), founded in 1941 by Harry H. Field, with involvement from Lazarsfeld, Cantril, Gordon Allport of Harvard University, and Samuel Stouffer of the University of Chicago, as well as commercial pollsters Gallup, Roper, and Crossley. The British-born Field conceived NORC as "a non-profit research center affiliated with a university that would do no commercial research or election forecasting, but would offer its services at no cost to non-profit organizations and university researchers" (Sudman and Bradburn 1987, S69) as well as to government agencies. He also saw it (and public opinion research more broadly) as a way to increase citizens' interest in and knowledge of political, social, and economic issues of the day. And he saw it as a center for "auditing polls, conducting research into methods, and providing graduate training" (Converse 1987, 309). Financial constraints led NORC to depend more heavily on government and commercial contracts than was originally hoped. After Field's untimely death in 1947, NORC moved from the University of Denver to the University of Chicago under the directorship of Clyde Hart. The majority of NORC's expenses were covered by grants and contracts from foundations, non-profit organizations, federal agencies, and the military, as well as limited commercial contract work.

The third major institution established during this period was the University of Michigan's Survey Research Center (SRC), founded in 1946 under the leadership of Rensis Likert. Joining Likert from the Department of Agriculture's Division of Program Surveys (where he worked for ten years) were several researchers including Angus Campbell and George Katona. Most of SRC's revenue came from government grants and contracts, though over time additional funds were obtained through foundation grants and commercial contracts.

Other factors aided the institutionalization of survey research (Converse 1987, 228–32; Sheatsley and Mitofsky 1992). While marketing journals had existed for some time, established academic journals in political science, economics, sociology, and psychology increasingly published survey-based research. In 1937 *Public Opinion Quarterly* published its first issue and in 1944 expanded its editorial board to include a wider and more prestigious range of researchers from academia, business, and government. In 1945 the federal government's National Research Council and the Social Science Research Council (SSRC), with support from the Rockefeller Foundation, formed the Committee on the Measurement of Opinion, Attitudes, and Consumer Wants, chaired by Stouffer and including Cantril, Crossley, Lazarsfeld, Roper, and Stanton as members. As the name (and membership) suggests, the Committee's mission was to systematize survey research in ways that supported professional pollsters' interest in opinions, academics' interest in attitudes, and marketers' interest in consumer behavior. In 1946 NORC organized a conference bringing together researchers from academia, business, and government. The conference included panels on sampling, survey design, question wording, standards, ethics, and other technical issues. Out of this meeting the American Association for Public Opinion Research was formed (1947), adopting *Public Opinion Quarterly* as its official journal in 1948 (Sheatsley and Mitofsky 1992). The institutionalization of survey research was further advanced through the archiving of surveys, most notably at the Roper Center

(1946), originally located at Williams College and later the University of Connecticut, and the University of Michigan's Inter-University Consortium for Political Research (1961).

The value of scientific surveys was not lost on candidates and officeholders, though the institutionalization of polling into the process of campaigning and governing did not occur in earnest until the 1960s. Nonetheless, as early as 1932 Roosevelt took great interest in polls, and while this interest waned under Truman, it reemerged during the Eisenhower administration (Sudman 1982; Jacobs and Shapiro 1995).

Finally, the institutionalization of opinion polls included the public. One of the first "polls on polls," conducted by Cantril in 1944, reported that a majority of Americans were familiar with opinion polls and believed they were honest, accurate, and useful (Goldman 1944–5). This growing trust was momentarily shaken in 1948 when the major election polls showed Dewey leading Truman (Moon 1999, 12–14). A report by the SSRC identified four reasons for their failure: ending polling too early to pick up a late shift to Truman; biased sampling (due in part to the use of quotas) that favored Dewey; poor questionnaire design that improperly identified "likely voters"; and unsystematic allocation of undecided voters. In addition, the media were criticized for making too much of small leads in two of the three polls.

## Theoretical and Methodological Contributions

The 1930s to 1950s were crucial to establishing survey research as the central mechanism for understanding public opinion. This period produced seminal works whose theoretical models (e.g., the "two-step flow," "exposure–attention–reception," "selective exposure," "minimal effects," and "relative deprivation") and empirical findings continue to shape research agendas. The period also saw the genesis of several cross-sectional trend surveys, including the SRC's American National Election Studies (1948), the Survey of Consumer Finances and Index of Consumer Sentiment (both in 1947); the Census Bureau's Monthly Report on the Labor Force (1942; renamed the Current Population Survey in 1947); and later NORC's General Social Survey (1972).

Methodological advances were also extensive (see Walden 1996). During the 1930s the two competing sampling methods were quota sampling, used by commercial pollsters, and multi-stage area sampling, used by academics and government researchers (both approaches were sometimes combined with purposive sampling). By the mid-1940s quota sampling came under increasing criticism as research refined (particularly through developments in clustering) and demonstrated the advantages of probability-based area sampling (Duncan and Shelton 1978; Converse 1987, 202–11). This debate came to a head in the 1944 congressional hearings at which Gallup was asked to explain why his 1940 and 1944 presidential surveys consistently underestimated the Democrat vote. Gallup resisted calls for change and a public debate ensued in *Public Opinion Quarterly* (1944–5) between Daniel Katz and Gallup's associate Edward Benson. A year later Benson, Young, and Syze (1945–6) conceded that probability-based area sampling was preferable, but argued that commercial polls could only adopt this method if it was more cost-effective. However, continued research documenting area probability sampling's superiority eventually established it as *the* legitimate method.

Additional developments included improvements in questionnaire design; greater use of subjective measures and more detailed questions; expansion in the topics surveyed; more standardized documentation and reporting of data and methods; greater care in constructing exclusive, exhaustive, understandable, and unbiased response options; understanding the relative merits of "open-" versus "closed-ended" questions; construction of multiple-item indices and scales (e.g., Guttman scaling, Lazarsfeld's latent structure analysis); standardized interviewer training; and the inclusion of more and better questions (including demographics and media consumption) for analysis of the roots and influences of opinions and attitudes. This period also saw more concerted efforts to base survey designs on explicit hypotheses. It saw improvements in the methods used to analyze data and reject alternative explanations. And it saw the first large-scale panel surveys for gaging individual-level change and testing measurement reliability (for example, Lazarsfeld and Fiske 1938; Lazarsfeld, Berelson, and Gaudet 1944). In sum, this period was characterized by efforts to establish a science of polling that could benefit scholars, politicians, policymakers, business interests, and the public as consumers and citizens.

One non-survey innovation championed by Robert Merton of BASR was the "focused interview," progenitor to the modern focus group. According to Merton (1987) he became interested in collective interviews in 1941 while observing the questioning of a group that had just participated in an audience reaction study. The participants had been asked to "react" to a radio broadcast using the Lazarsfeld–Stanton program analyzer. This device, the forerunner of contemporary audience response technology, allowed them to register their second-by-second reactions as they listened. Using the crude polygraph-like readout as a guide, researchers then interviewed them in small groups to ascertain why they reacted as they did.

Having used depth interviews in a Works Progress Administration project, Merton saw potential in these collective interviews, and he and colleagues developed guidelines that apply well to contemporary focus groups. According to Merton and Kendall (1946) focused interviews should be *non-directed* (i.e., moderators should not dominate and should elicit opinions non-judgmentally); have *depth* (i.e., draw out "the affective and value-laden implications of the subjects' responses, to determine whether the experience had a central or peripheral significance"); put responses into a *personal context* (i.e., reveal participants' unique social and psychological makeup); explore the potential impact of a wide *range* of stimuli; and provide details about the *specific* elements of the stimuli that elicited responses.

Focused interviews seemed a promising addition for gaging public opinion. But like "social surveys," the multi-method "mass observation" approach of Harrison and Madge that competed with Gallup in Britain from 1937 to 1949 (Goot 2008), and other unobtrusive or behavioral indicators, they were marginalized. By 1960 public opinion and survey research were, for all intents and purposes, synonymous.

# SURVEY RESEARCH AFTER 1960

In some respects public opinion research since 1960 is an afterword to the story begun in the 1930s. To be sure, it has witnessed a number of theoretical, methodological, and applied developments; new, more subtle findings; and a proliferation in polling (see Walden 1990, 1996, 2002). But with few exceptions these occurred within a science of polling developed in the three prior decades.

One development was the telephone survey. Telephone surveys existed in the 1920s and studies of their strengths and weaknesses date to 1937 (Karol 1937) but not until the late 1960s, when US telephone penetration approached 90 percent, did this interviewing mode become commonplace. Despite shortcomings (e.g., their generally shorter length), they became the preferred survey mode by the 1980s, due largely to advantages in quality control, speed, and cost. Telephone surveys raised a number of methodological issues, including sampling (e.g., the use of telephone directories and, beginning in the 1970s, "random digit dialing"), interviewer effects, the trustworthiness of responses, and questionnaire design (Lavrakas 1993, 2008).

Computers led to additional developments in sampling, database management, survey design, and data analysis. Computer-assisted telephone (CATI) and personal (CAPI) interviewing increased efficiency and quality control; reduced human error; allowed for more complex, tailored surveys including embedded randomized survey experiments (e.g., the National Science Foundation funded "Time-Sharing Experiments for the Social Sciences"); and introduced unobtrusive measures such as the time taken to answer questions (Bradburn and Sudman 1988, 100–1, 108).

A more recent development is the Internet survey (Vehovar, Manfreda, and Koren 2008). Obtaining probability samples is complicated by "frame selection" (there is no equivalent to a telephone directory or RDD approach) and "coverage" (many households do not have Internet access). The former can be addressed by using different sampling modes (e.g., telephones), the latter by providing Internet access to respondents. Additional bias can be introduced by the type and mode of solicitation (e.g., personal versus general, email versus phone); respondents' comfort with computers; difficulties in monitoring who answers a survey; and difficulty in controlling what a respondent does while answering the survey (particularly problematic for questions such as those assessing knowledge). Despite these issues, Internet surveys have a number of advantages, including the use of audiovisuals and graphics.

Surveys also play a more central role in the study, practice, and coverage of politics and government, most notably through the growth in public (sponsored by news organizations, foundations, and universities) and proprietary (used by candidates, officeholders, and policy makers) polls (Jacobs and Shapiro 2000; Eisenger 2008; Steeper 2008). Regarding the latter, Kennedy, Johnson, and Nixon expanded "the institution of the presidency to include a 'public opinion apparatus'—an operation that was centralized in the White House and devoted to assembling public opinion data and conducting extensive public relations activities" (Jacobs and Shapiro 1995, 163).

One important innovation in political research are "rolling cross-sectional surveys," which allow for tracking daily or weekly opinion change, and thus better gage the influence of specific media, campaign, and/or real-world events (Johnston, Hagen, and Jamieson 2004). Another is media-sponsored "exit polls" used to capture the timely opinions of actual voters and, in conjunction with other data, predict winners in state and national elections. Exit polls led to several methodological innovations in sampling, interviewing, and data analysis, but also raise concerns regarding their impact on voter turnout and election outcomes (Delli Carpini 1984) and, following failures in 2000 and 2004, their reliability.

Another post-1960 development is the internationalization of polling. By 2004 sixty-four countries were members of the Gallup International Association. A number of cross-national surveys have been regularly conducted since the 1970s, including the Eurobarometer (since 1973), the World Values Surveys (1983), the International Social Survey Program (1985), the Comparative Study of Electoral Systems (1996), and the European Social Survey (2002), as well as periodic comparative surveys conducted by the Pew Research Center and Gallup. More recently both marketing and public interest surveys have been used in developing nations. Comparative polls raise challenges to almost every facet of the survey process, as well as new ethical and political issues (Heath, Fisher, and Smith 2005; Mattes 2008; Zetterberg 2008).

While it has roots in early attitude theory, the systematic and sometimes physiological measurement of emotions is another recent development (Marcus, Neuman, and Mackuen 2000; Lodge and Taber 2005; Brader 2006). This research has led to new survey items and scales (as well as less obtrusive measures) designed to measure respondents' affect, and has contributed to both theory development and application in marketing, health, and political communication.

One of the few non-survey developments began in the 1970s when focused interviews—now focus groups—reemerged after a two-decade absence, largely in market research. By the early 1980s they had also become a staple of campaign consulting. And while focus groups remain limited in the social sciences, several studies have used this technique (for example, Conover, Crewe, and Searing 1991; Just et al. 1996; Delli Carpini, Keeter, and Webb 1997; Delli Carpini and Williams 1994; Sigel 1996). Modern focus groups maintain the qualities of non-directedness, depth, personal context, range, and specificity (Krueger 1988; Morgan 1997). Still used largely as precursors to or explications of surveys, on occasion they serve as stimulus or response in experimental studies, and have even been used independently to provide what Krueger calls "cautious generalizations" (1988, 42–4) about the *process* of opinion formation and change.

A final innovation is "deliberative polls," in which random samples are selected, interviewed through telephone surveys, brought physically together to listen, learn, and discuss, and reinterviewed at least once following this process. While controversial methodologically, deliberative polls (and related methods such as citizen juries or focus groups) provide glimpses into what more informed, socially constructed public opinion might look like (Fishkin 2009). More generally, the role of public deliberation in opinion formation has increasingly attracted the interest of applied and scholarly empirical researchers (see Delli Carpini, Cook, and Jacobs 2004).

## FUTURE CHALLENGES AND OPPORTUNITIES

Survey research faces several challenges. The misuse of polls (e.g., polls intended to influence rather than report opinions and behaviors; "instant polls" in which biased and self-selected samples register their opinions; and "advocacy polls" that misrepresent public opinion for political gain through biased sampling or question wording) is particularly problematic. Also troubling is the lack of adequate reporting on the methods, response rates, and other technical details by survey organizations, secondary users of polls, and media outlets. Coupled with the dramatic proliferation of polls, these sins of omission and commission have weakened public trust in polls. They have also contributed to declining response rates, a problem exacerbated by answering machines and caller ID (allowing potential respondents to avoid surveyors). While to date the effect of declining response rates on polls' reliability and validity appears minimal (Keeter, Kennedy, Dimock, et al. 2006), there is no guarantee this will remain the case. Another challenge is the growing number of cellphone-only households that increase costs if they are included in sampling frames, or that bias samples and skew results (especially in terms of age) if they are not (Keeter, Kennedy, Clark, et al. 2007). While Internet surveys are potential solutions to some of these problems, their reliability and validity remain a matter of debate. For all these reasons professional associations such as the American Association of Public Opinion Research have increased efforts to enforce ethical standards, educate the public and media about surveys, lobby to protect legitimate surveys from government regulations such as "no call" lists, and increase the transparency of survey methodology.

Such challenges require adapting surveys to changing political, social, and technological environments. But these changing environments also offer opportunities. At a minimum, innovations such as deliberative polls, Internet (and cellphone) polls, rolling cross-sectional surveys, and survey-based experiments can be refined and expanded for use in both applied and academic settings. More speculatively, new information technologies offer possibilities for combining the generalizability of scientific polls with (as appropriate) the speed of "instant polls," the interactivity of deliberative polls, the richness of focus groups and depth interviews, even the authoritativeness of initiatives and referenda.

But the greatest challenge (and opportunity) facing survey research may be rethinking its hegemonic role in how public opinion is defined. Scientific polling's greatest strengths—the generalizability of results and simplification of complex attitudes and opinions through quantification—are also its greatest weaknesses. Individual and collective world views *are* complex—often too complex for the most sophisticated survey to "truly" capture. Qualitative methods that have fallen by the wayside or been relegated to the margins of opinion research—depth interviews, reports of confidants, fieldwork, open-ended questions, focus groups, participant observation, unobtrusive measures—can provide a degree of understanding that is often missed in surveys and be useful counterpoints to the sometimes reductionist conclusions drawn from them (Herbst 1993; Igo 2007).

Alternative methods have their own shortcomings of course. Nor are they immune from misuse. Ultimately, however, methodological choice is more than the weighing of relative strengths and weaknesses, inevitably reflecting fundamental differences in the ontology and epistemology of public opinion. The "public" in "public opinion" represents more than the topic in question or the summation of individual opinions. Rather, it signals both the socially constructed nature of opinion and the place where this collective opinion is constructed. Survey research can contribute to understanding this richer notion of public opinion. But doing so will require skill, creativity, and, perhaps, a willingness to relinquish its dominance in favor of a more multi-method approach.

## References

BARTON, J. 1984. *Guide to the Bureau of Applied Social Research.* New York: Clearwater.

BENIGER, J. 1983. Speaking Your Mind without Elections, Surveys, or Social Movements. *Public Opinion Quarterly,* 47: 479–84.

BENSON, E. 1944–5. Notes in Connection with Professor Katz's Article. *Public Opinion Quarterly,* 8: 482–7.

——YOUNG, C., and SYZE, C. 1945–6. Polling Lessons from the 1944 Election. *Public Opinion Quarterly,* 9: 467–84.

BOOTH, C. 1902–3. *Life and Labour of the People in London,* 17 vols. London: Macmillan. First published as separate reports, 1889–1903.

BRADBURN, N. M., and SUDMAN, S. 1988. *Polls & Surveys: Understanding What They Tell Us.* San Francisco: Jossey-Bass.

BRADER, T. 2006. *Campaigning for Hearts and Minds: How Emotional Appeals in Political Ads Work.* Chicago: University of Chicago Press.

BRYCE, J. 1919. *American Commonwealth,* ii. New York: Macmillan.

CONOVER, P., CREWE, I., and SEARING, D. 1991. The Nature of Citizenship in the United States and Great Britain: Empirical Comments on Theoretical Themes. *Journal of Politics,* 53: 800–32.

CONVERSE, J. 1987. *Survey Research in the United States.* Berkeley: University of California Press.

DELLI CARPINI, M. X. 1984. Scooping the Voter: The Consequences of the Networks' Early Call of the 1980 Presidential Race. *Journal of Politics,* 46/3: 866–85.

——and WILLIAMS, B. 1994. Methods, Metaphors, and Media Research: The Uses of Television in Political Conversation. *Communication Research,* 21: 782–812.

—— COOK, F. L., and JACOBS, L. 2004. Public Deliberation, Discursive Participation and Citizen Engagement: An Empirical Review of the Literature. *Annual Review of Political Science,* 7: 315–44.

——— KEETER, S., and WEBB, S. 1997. Effects of the "People's Presidential Debate" on Undecided Voters in the Richmond Area. In *The News Media and American Democracy*, ed. P. Norris. Boulder, CO: Lynne Rienner.

DU BOIS, W. E. B. 1899. *The Philadelphia Negro: A Social Study*. Philadelphia: University of Pennsylvania Press, 1996.

DUNCAN, J., and SHELTON, W. 1978. *Revolution in United States Government Statistics, 1926–1976*. Washington, DC: US Government Printing Office.

EATON, A. H., and HARRISON, S. M. 1930. *A Bibliography of Social Surveys*. New York: Russell Sage.

EISENGER, P. 2008. The Uses of Surveys by Governments and Politicians. In *The Sage Handbook of Public Opinion Research*, ed. W. Donsbach and M. Traugott. Los Angeles: Sage.

FISHKIN, J. 2009. *When the People Speak: Deliberative Democracy and Public Consultation*. New York: Oxford University Press.

GALLUP, G. 1936. How America Was Made to Speak. *Market Research*, 4: 6–7.

——— 1939. Public Opinion in a Democracy. Stafford Little Lecture. Princeton University.

——— and RAE, S. F. 1940. *The Pulse of Democracy*. New York: Simon & Schuster.

GOLDMAN, E. 1944–5. Poll on Polls. *Public Opinion Quarterly*, 8: 461–7.

GOOT, M. 2008. Mass-Observation and Modern Public Opinion Research. In *The Sage Handbook of Public Opinion Research*, ed. W. Donsbach and M. Traugott. Los Angeles: Sage.

HEATH, A., FISHER, S., and SMITH, S. 2005. The Globalization of Public Opinion Research. *Annual Review of Public Opinion Research*, 8: 297–333.

HERBST, S. 1993. *Numbered Voices: How Opinion Polling Has Shaped American Politics*. Chicago: University of Chicago Press.

HOFSTADTER, R. 1969. *The Idea of a Party System: The Rise of Legitimate Opposition in the United States, 1780–1840*. Berkeley: University of California Press.

Hull House. 1895. *Hull-House Maps and Papers: A Presentation of Nationalities and Wages in a Congested District of Chicago*. New York: Thomas Y. Cromwell.

IGO, S. 2007. *The Averaged American: Surveys, Citizens and the Making of a Mass Public*. Princeton: Princeton University Press.

JACOBS, L., and SHAPIRO, R. 1995. The Rise of Presidential Polling: The Nixon White House in Historical Perspective. *Public Opinion Quarterly*, 59: 163–95.

——— ——— 2000. *Politicians Don't Pander*. Chicago: University of Chicago Press.

JOHNSTON, R., HAGEN, M., and JAMIESON, K. H. 2004. *The 2000 Presidential Election and the Foundations of Party Politics*. New York: Cambridge University Press.

JUST, M., CRIGLER, A., ALGER, D., COOK, T., KERN, M., and WEST, D. 1996. *Crosstalk: Citizens, Candidates, and the Media in a Presidential Campaign*. Chicago: University of Chicago Press.

KAROL, J. 1937. Measuring Radio Audiences. *Public Opinion Quarterly*, 1: 92–6.

KATZ, D. 1944–5. In Answer to Mr. Benson's Suggested "Footnotes." *Public Opinion Quarterly*, 8: 487, 604–6.

KEETER, S., KENNEDY, C., CLARK, A., TOMPSON, T., and MOKRZYCKI, M. 2007. What's Missing from National RDD Surveys? The Impact of the Growing Cell-Only Population. *Public Opinion Quarterly*, 71: 772–92.

——— ——— DIMOCK, M., BEST, J., and CRAIGHILL, P. 2006.Gauging the Impact of Growing Nonresponse on Estimates from a National RDD Telephone Survey. *Public Opinion Quarterly*, 70: 759–79.

KRUEGER, R. 1988. *Focus Groups: A Practical Guide for Applied Research*. Newbury Park, CA: Sage.

KRUSKAL, W., and MOSTELLAR, F. 1980. Representative Sampling IV: The History of the Concept in Statistics, 1895–1939. *International Statistical Review*, 48: 169–95.

LAVRAKAS, P. 1993. *Telephone Survey Methods: Sampling, Selection and Supervision*, 2nd edn. Newbury Park, CA: Sage.

—— 2008. Surveys by Telephones. In *The Sage Handbook of Public Opinion Research*, ed. W. Donsbach and M. Traugott. Los Angeles: Sage.

LAZARSFELD, P., and FISKE, M. 1938. The "Panel" as a New Tool for Measuring Opinion. *Public Opinion Quarterly*, 2: 596–612.

—— BERELSON, B., and GAUDET, H. 1944. *The People's Choice*. New York: Columbia University Press.

LIKERT, R., ROSLOW, S., and MURPHY, G. 1934. A Simple and Reliable Method of Scoring the Thurstone Attitude Scales. *Journal of Social Psychology*, 5: 298–311.

LOCKLEY, L. 1950. Notes on the History of Marketing Research. *Journal of Marketing*, 14: 733–6.

LODGE, M., and TABER, C. 2005. The Automaticity of Affect for Political Candidates, Parties and Issues: Experimental Tests of the Hot Cognition Hypothesis. *Political Psychology*, 26: 455–82.

MARCUS, G., NEUMAN, W. R., and MACKUEN, M. 2000. *Affective Intelligence and Political Judgment*. Chicago: University of Chicago Press.

MATTES, R. 2008. Public Opinion Research in Emerging Democracies. In *The Sage Handbook of Public Opinion Research*, ed. W. Donsbach and M. Traugott. Los Angeles: Sage.

MERRIAM, C., and GOSNELL, H. 1924. *Non-Voting: Causes and Methods of Control*. Chicago: University of Chicago Press.

MERTON, R. 1987. The Focused Interview and Focus Groups: Continuities and Discontinuities. *Public Opinion Quarterly*, 51: 550–6.

—— and KENDALL, P. 1946. The Focused Interview. *American Journal of Sociology*, 51: 541–57.

MOON, N. 1999. *Opinion Polls: History, Theory and Practice*. New York: Manchester University Press.

MORGAN, D. 1997. *Focus Groups as Qualitative Research*, 2nd edn. London: Sage.

MURPHY, G., MURPHY, L., and NEWCOMB, T. 1937. *Experimental Social Psychology*. New York: Harper.

REED, V. 1936. The Census of Business as an Aid to Market Measurement. *American Marketing Journal*, 2: 68–71.

ROBINSON, C. 1932. *Straw Votes: A Study of Political Prediction*. New York: Columbia University Press.

ROPER, E. 1941. Problems and Possibilities in the Sampling Technique. *Journalism Quarterly*, 18: 1–9.

ROWNTREE, B. S. 1901. *Poverty: A Study of Town Life*. London: Macmillan.

SENG, Y. P. 1951. Historical Survey of the Development of Sampling Theories and Practice. *Journal of the Royal Statistical Society*, 114A: 214–31.

SHEATSLEY, P., and MITOFSKY, W. (eds.) 1992. *A Meeting Place: The History of the American Association for Public Opinion Research*. n.p.: American Association for Public Opinion Research.

SIGEL, R. 1996. *Ambition and Accommodation: How Women View Gender Relations*. Chicago: University of Chicago Press.

SMITH, T. 1990. The First Straw? A Study of the Origins of Election Polls. *Public Opinion Quarterly*, 54: 21–36.

STEEPER, F. 2008. The Use of Voter Research in Campaigns. In *The Sage Handbook of Public Opinion Research*, ed. W. Donsbach and M. Traugott. Los Angeles: Sage.

STOUFFER, S. 1931. Experimental Comparison of a Statistical and a Case History Technique of Attitude Research. *Publications of the American Sociological Society*, 25: 154–6.

SUDMAN, S. 1982. The Presidents and the Polls. *Public Opinion Quarterly*, 46: 301–10.

—— and BRADBURN, N. M. 1987. The Organizational Growth of Public Opinion Research in the United States. *Public Opinion Quarterly*, 51/2, S67–S78.

THURSTONE, L. L., and CHAVE, E. J. 1929. *The Measurement of Attitude*. Chicago: University of Chicago Press.

VEHOVAR, V., MANFREDA, K. L., and KOREN, G. 2008. Internet Surveys. In *The Sage Handbook of Public Opinion Research*, ed. W. Donsbach and M. Traugott. Los Angeles: Sage.

WALDEN, G. 1990. *Polling and Survey Research: A Selective Annotated Bibliography of U.S. Guides and Studies from the 1980s*. New York: Garland.

—— 1996. *Polling and Survey Research Methods 1935–1979: An Annotated Bibliography*. Westport, CT: Greenwood.

—— 2002. *Survey Research Methodology, 1990–1999: An Annotated Bibliography*. Westport, CT: Greenwood.

WHITE, W. 1936. Market Research Activities in the Department of Commerce. *American Marketing Journal*, 3: 25–31.

WILCOX, W. 1931. An Attempt to Measure Public Opinion about Repealing the Eighteenth Amendment. *Journal of the American Statistical Association*, 28: 152–63.

ZETTERBERG, H. 2008. The Start of Modern Public Opinion Research. In *The Sage Handbook of Public Opinion Research*, ed. W. Donsbach and M. Traugott. Los Angeles: Sage.

CHAPTER 19

·································································

# CRITICAL PERSPECTIVES
# ON PUBLIC OPINION

·································································

SUSAN HERBST

"PUBLIC OPINION" is one of the most nebulous concepts in democratic theory, and it is this haziness that has drawn the best scholars of many generations to it. Although the notion of public opinion dates back to the ancient Greek city states, where the popular sentiment was debated, persuaded through rhetoric, and expressed at Hellenic festivals, we typically trace its contemporary origins to the Enlightenment. It was in the heady days of literary and philosophical argument before the French Revolution that states-men and writers began to think of a distinct public, one separable in thought and feeling from the king and his court. During this period, Jürgen Habermas (1989) has argued, both public opinion and a "public sphere"—an arena for talk and critique of the Crown—were born. While not everyone agrees with the particulars of Habermas's social history, there is consensus among scholars that something profound changed during the period of the great democratic revolutions. The questions for critical theorists, typically coming from a leftist perspective, center around the nature of that eighteenth-century change, and how "the public" evolved from that period forward.

This chapter is not a comprehensive review of all critical perspectives on public opinion; that is a book-length project, or better yet, an encyclopedic website that would need constant updating. There are orthodox, Marxian views of public opinion, frozen in time and place. But there are also evolving leftist views of public opinion appearing as new governments emerge throughout the world. In fact, every new democracy or new administration, even if authoritarian, must contend with public opinion somehow. We constantly discover unique conceptions, unusual measures, and novel approaches to both opinion expression and control. In any case, my goal here is to provide students of politics with some background for understanding critical-theoretical views of public opinion, touring through the major contributions since the nineteenth century, when Karl Marx first put pen to paper. After a look at Marx's writings on public sentiment, I will introduce the signature ideas of Antonio Gramsci, the Frankfurt School, Pierre

Bourdieu, Jean Baudrillard, and Herbert Blumer, before a few concluding thoughts on the value and future of critical work in the area of public opinion, in light of the Internet.

Three notes of preface. First: critical theory is unlike many frameworks used in the area of politics and public opinion because it fuses understanding and action (praxis). Those who ascribe to critical theory, as their tool for analysis, very often interweave observation with normative judgments and even strategic argumentation—how citizens, leaders, journalists, or teachers *should* act. Theory and practice are fundamentally conflated in classical Marxism and its offspring, and while this certainly does not distinguish it from all other theoretical frameworks, it must be understood, particularly by those trained as positivists. Many contemporary critical theorists would argue that American social science also contains strong normative biases, and pushes us to certain types of action (or inaction), so is just as deeply "political" and ideological. Yet, they would note, critical theorists are at least cognizant and transparent about their normative beliefs, something other scholars should aim for as well.

Second, one of the most aggravating problems for critical theorists has been what they see as the damage to Marxist and neo-Marxist thought caused by the Soviet Union (the first nation to formally adopt Marxism as a national creed), then later by China, North Korea, and a variety of other repressive regimes. Critical theory should not be confused with dictatorships or totalitarianism, although such regimes have certainly plucked parts of Marxism for their own nefarious purposes of social control. As difficult as it may be, critical theorists ask that—in the discussion of scholarly ideas—interested students evaluate their constructs without reference to the distortion that Marxism has often undergone in international politics.

Finally, while I appreciate the tremendous contributions of critical theory to the study of public opinion, I am not a critical theorist. It is my hope that, in bringing such a rich and complex set of ideas to this volume, I have done justice to the paradigm, and have not offended the sensibilities of those who have devoted their scholarship to critical theory in its myriad forms. For those interested in a more comprehensive review, from one of the premier scholars in the area, it is best to consult David Held's introductory volume (Held 1980; or the regularly updated web resource *The Stanford Encyclopedia of Philosophy*).

# ORTHODOX MARXISM AND PUBLIC OPINION

Karl Marx and his colleague Friedrich Engels did not use the phrase "public opinion" in any sustained fashion over the decades of their collaboration in the nineteenth century. Marx certainly knew the phrase and it was in common usage, but to simply analyze his mentions—if they could be gathered systematically—would be a worthless exercise: he had complex views of public opinion that are wedded to ideas about human nature, social life, and revolution. While this may be irritating to the historian of public opinion, no understanding of classical Marxian views is possible without a broader study of his theoretical system.

Long before Marx wrote of politics, economics, and social life in the nineteenth century, it was fashionable for theorists of all stripes to opine on the fundamental characteristics of human nature. Often, the discussion was oriented around how humans might be differentiated from animals—what made them unique beings. The great political giants who preceded Marx—Machiavelli, Hobbes, Locke, Rousseau, and others—speculated on the essence of man, and how this essence is expressed in private and public settings. From Machiavelli's fearful and weak inhabitants of Florence, to Rousseau's primitives, we have a full range of possible humans, described in colorful detail. Marx wrote very much in this tradition, and felt forced to do so: how can one build a theory of society and its future without some attention to the nature of its citizens? With regard to public opinion, Marx's ideas about human nature are his guide, although he did not speak to this linkage as directly as we might hope.

Marx thought people capable of learning, of changing, and of forming opinions. But they are material beings, very closely tied to their surroundings and the networks they find themselves in. He and so many who ascribe to more conventional forms of Marxism worry most about the *control* of public opinion—indeed the squashing of public opinion—more than its formation. Marx questioned whether, in a capitalist society, with working people oppressed by industry and the need to stay alive, citizens had any voice at all. Human nature, and the opinions people *could* offer, are crushed by those who control the means and forces of production. He wrote, famously, with Engels, in *The German Ideology* in 1846:

The ideas of the ruling class are in every epoch the ruling ideas, i.e., the class which is the ruling *material* force of society, is at the same time its ruling *intellectual* force. . . . [The ruling class] rule also as thinkers, as producers of ideas, and regulate the production and distribution of the ideas of their age . . .   (Marx and Engels 1984, 64)

This notion of public opinion—as an inchoate and suppressed phenomenon—is part of the intricate model of change that Marx proposed. People are unable to express themselves; their opinions are unwanted and indeed irrelevant, given their lack of power. The ruling class—factory owners, statesmen, religious leaders—were adept at suppressing public opinion, he argued. At the least, public sentiment was an annoyance to them, and at the most, dangerous and revolutionary. In classical Marxism, the "base" is economics (the forces and relations of production) while public opinion is part of the "superstructure"—the world of ideas (art, literature, politics, law, culture) determined entirely by the base. Base and superstructure are correlated and coordinated. Put another way, public opinion—in Marx's world view—derives from economics and ownership of property, as there is no other way for it to evolve and take form.

Marx's work is complex and subtle, but is often expressed as mechanical in nature, because there are so many "moving parts" that fit together. One of the reasons his œuvre is considered a masterpiece of social theory—by theorists of all ideological persuasions—is its grandeur and precision, like the innards of a clock. It would be absurd to apply his ideas directly to contemporary Western public opinion, given the changes since he wrote (for example, the development of labor unions, of democratic rights, or the emergence of race and ethnicity as rivals to social class in personal identity), but Marx outlines the fundamental elements of "hegemonic" or critical theory of today. Contemporary neo-Marxian theorists—while they often reject significant parts of orthodox Marxism—would contend that public opinion is still very much a reflection of an elite class in American politics. The complexity and nuances associated with this reflective process, where superstructure "matches" the base, is much greater in current theory than in the nineteenth century, but the lineage to classical Marxism is clear.

# MARXISM REVISED: GRAMSCI, THE FRANKFURT SCHOOL

In the early part of the twentieth century, Antonio Gramsci, the Italian journalist and political activist, was one of many thinkers unhappy with the deterministic nature of conventional Marxism (base determines superstructure), although they shared the concerns for poverty and the effects of industrialization that inspired Marx's work. Gramsci believed that, while of course economic structure was essential in understanding law and culture, people were effective agents who could make gradual change in culture and therefore break out of repression and alienation. Revolutionary action by the proletariat, action that overthrows all social arrangements in a radical *moment* of change, was not the only way to achieve transformation. In fact, Gramsci argued, intellectuals on the left—putting aside the proletarian underclass—could themselves break the hold of class domination and free all people from oppressive conditions.

Gramsci's work is intricate, although not always consistent or disciplined in the ways that Marx's often was. He wrote under miserable conditions during the last years of his life, from an Italian prison, where he was being punished for his radical political writings. (He was jailed in 1926 and died there eleven years later, all the while suffering a variety of ailments.) The *Prison Notebooks*, a compilation of his secret writing, did not appear to the world until after the Second World War. His views on the United States, Europe, labor movements, and of course Italian fascism are worth reading, but for our purposes in understanding public opinion, it is the notion of "hegemony" that stands out as most useful.

One of the "holes" in Marx's descriptions of the ruling class's stranglehold, which Gramsci tried to fill, is public opinion itself. How, one might ask of classical Marxism, does the ruling class force its ideas upon the working class, without guns, imprisonment, and constant physical threat? Why, if proletariat workers are so unhappy, do they stay put, failing to organize or initiate the overthrow of factory owners and oppressive governments? Gramsci argued that this control of societal ideas and ideals—norms, values, approaches, attitudes—is pursued with great intentionality by a regime through hegemony: the process of generating consent of the public through persuasion, the control of information, and the framing of social problems. Hegemony is the process by which, Gramsci argues, ruling class ideology becomes the "common sense" of any age. Oft-used examples of hegemony in the United States are "Horatio Alger" (or "rags to riches") notions of how people attain personal success when they are born into poverty.

Is public opinion as gullible as Gramsci would have us believe? This is an open hypothesis, debated as fiercely in the twenty-first century as it was throughout the twentieth. Some scholars argue that media have the power to suppress ideas, and to encourage people to believe in notions that are counter to their best self-interests. Others have demonstrated that people are not Gramscian "sponges," vulnerable to subtle ideologies that keep them down: they push back at ideas they disagree with, create their own media (websites, YouTube postings, etc.), and distrust conventional journalists and politicians. In any case, it is Gramsci who ignited these debates in earnest, long before the Internet, and there is no shortage of prominent scholars who see the media as a partner with government in controlling public opinion (for example, Entman 2004).

One last set of scholars to mention in the critical tradition, even more sophisticated in their views of culture and public opinion, are the group of German theorists called the Frankfurt School. These theorists, writing during the early to mid-twentieth century, brought a tremendous interest in mass media and public opinion to their work, blending it with their neo-Marxist sensibilities. They held diverse views, but all faced very real threats as Jews during the rise of the Nazis in mid-century. (While most of the group fled to the US, one of the most distinguished members of the Frankfurt School, Walter Benjamin, committed suicide before he could be captured at the Spanish border in 1940.)

Leaders of the Frankfurt School were shaped by their experiences with fascism and Nazism, and these painful trials added a new twist to their Marxism. In particular, they lost some hope in a revolution of the underclass, seeing how workers were so easily mobilized by the Nazis. They also watched with horror as Hitler used the media—radio, newspaper, and film—to pursue his ideals and the destruction of the European Jews. But Frankfurt School theorists wrote about media and Western societies more generally, with a real interest in hegemony in the American media and within corporate capitalism. In their famous 1947 essay "The Culture Industry," Max Horkheimer and Theodor Adorno manage to discuss interlocking corporate boards, market research, and the banal, empty nature of media production simultaneously:

[The broadcasting industry, electrical industry, banks, and other industries] are in such close contact that the extreme concentration of mental forces allows demarcation lines between different firms and technical branches to be ignored. The ruthless unity in the culture industry is evidence of what will happen in politics. Marked differentiations such as those of A and B films, or of stories in magazines in different price ranges, depend not so much on subject matter as on classifying, organizing, and labeling consumers.... The public is catered for with a hierarchical range of mass-produced products of varying quality, thus advancing the rule of complete quantification.... Consumers appear as statistics on research organization charts, and are divided by income groups into red, green, and blue areas; the technique is that used for any type of propaganda.    (1987, 123)

Horkheimer and Adorno believed people to be greatly susceptible to media persuasion and therefore ruling class ideology. Their views were in keeping with general neo-Marxist thought on the lack of resistance to media or the broader "culture industry" (media, art, music, and other producers of news and entertainment).

The Frankfurt School theorists differed a bit; Benjamin in particular stood alone on some aesthetic matters, Herbert Marcuse brought sexuality into the study of capitalism, for example. But they were all concerned with the power of hegemony and the dearth of cognitive tools people have to resist it as they form opinions about politics, culture, economics, work, family, and social structure.

Jürgen Habermas, one of the few remaining descendants of the School, has argued that there was once a lively and less repressive public sphere—one that had emerged in the eighteenth century. He posits that we have seen a dramatic decline in free critical discourse since that time. In his early work, Habermas described the raucous and stimulating debate of salons and coffee houses, the appearance of independent news-papers, and in general, an electrifying and bold sensibility on the part of a rising, opinionated bourgeois class, ready to question ruling regimes. This public sphere starts to dissipate in the late nineteenth century, and the decline accelerates in the twentieth century, according to Habermas. He holds the media and attendant commercialization, particularly the formation of conglomerates and the ethic of consumerism in mass society, responsible for the decline of important, rich public debate on issues. This is very much in the spirit of his teachers, but Habermas, in his later work, did hold out some hopes for a greater spirit of public communication, one that might bring back rational and open discourse, despite the limits of the media. While debate around Habermas's public sphere decline hypothesis remains unresolved (some argue that the lively sphere of the eighteenth century was not quite as he painted), he did refocus many critical theorists on the possibilities of public opinion in a democracy, real and imagined.

# HERBERT BLUMER AND HIS CRITICAL LEGACY

The Frankfurt School made its impact largely on the study of culture, in philosophy, art history, literary criticism, and sociology, but had little effect on American political science or public opinion research. In fact, I doubt that, even today, many students of American politics are versed in critical theory beyond a surface understanding of Habermas's decline argument. In sociology, however, there has been a steady tradition of critical thinking about public opinion and opinion polling, led by Herbert Blumer in the early twentieth century.

While there was skepticism toward polls during the early decades of the twentieth century due to mis-predictions of the *Literary Digest* and then the faulty 1948 prediction that President Truman would be defeated by Thomas E. Dewey, this skepticism proved to be temporary, and the polling industry flourished. George Gallup, Sr., and other leading pollsters argued hard that survey research and polling results were synonymous with "public opinion" itself. The 1940s and 1950s were decades of great acceleration in the evolving survey research industry, within the academy and beyond. But in 1947 Herbert Blumer, a professor at the University of Chicago and one of the most distinguished sociologists in the nation, was asked to make observations at the meetings of the American Sociological Society. (This lecture was published the next year, in the premier journal, the *American Sociological Review*.) In this essay, still the most thoughtful critique of survey research we have, Blumer argued that polling simply could not serve as a measure of public opinion.

His critique was not directly rooted in Marxist theory, but came from the direction of mainstream empirical and cultural sociology. It included multiple sparring points. He worried that poll results were aggregations of individual opinions that did not map onto the existing power structure: interest groups, ethnic enclaves, and powerful people make things happen in politics, and are the *public opinion of interest* to any social scientist. Artificial publics—hundreds of anonymous, unorganized people, not related to each other in any way—have no place in social analysis. The participants in the sample survey do not "act" as bodies, and are simply a faceless American cross-section, suspended in time, never to be gathered again. How could survey results possibly be thought of as a meaningful public opinion?

Blumer saw real, empirical public opinion formation as a process driven by groups and group interests. These are "functional" groups, related to class, race, ethnicity, policy interest, religion, and other binding characteristics. Not only does polling ignore this social infrastructure, he argues; polling outright defies and crushes it, and therefore can only present us with the most unsophisticated of political analyses. Polls provide an illusion; they don't produce important, predictive data about the issue dynamics within a complex society. In addition, society is fluid, and so "sampling" it, no matter how carefully conducted, is also illusory:

In human society, particularly in modern society, we are confronted with intricate complexes of moving relations which are roughly recognizable as systems, even though loose systems. Such a loose system is too complicated, too encumbered in detail and too fast moving to be described in any one of its given "cycles" of operation adequately and faithfully. . . . to know what is going on [with a national policy issue], particularly to know what is likely to go on in the latter stages, we have to dip in here and there. The problems of where to dip in, how to dip in, and how far to dip in [are of great concern].   (1948, 549)

In the clash of opinions and groups, powerless and mighty, Blumer argues, we find the true texture of public opinion—the public opinion worth studying. Public opinion has a character, and is tethered to a nation in progress. As he famously stated it: "The formation of public opinion occurs as a function of a society in operation" (1948, 544).

Surprisingly, not long after Blumer had been pronounced intellectually dead in the 1980s by a variety of scholars (Converse 1987), the arrival of the Internet—the most important change in our communication environment since the introduction of television—led us directly back to Blumer. I would argue that Blumer is more right than ever before: public opinion is most productively defined as a phenomenon in motion, replete with power dynamics, social stratification, and most of all, conversation. If Blumer were alive today, he would view our blogs, webpages, and constant chatter as extraordinarily helpful in understanding public opinion. In fact, it is precisely the sort of textured discourse that is so superior to the aggregation of anonymous individuals gathered in our artificial "publics" produced by polls.

## POLLS AND THE EXISTENCE OF PUBLIC OPINION

Blumer likely influenced a number of cultural theorists in the field. One of these was Pierre Bourdieu, who spent his career exploring aspects of social class development, art, and culture in Western democracies. In 1979, in what is the boldest critique of public opinion polling since Blumer's 1948 article, Bourdieu goes a step further than his predecessor, arguing that "public opinion" is itself a fiction. Public opinion, Bourdieu posits, is a reification, something that seems concrete because of the ways we discuss it, write about it, and measure it. Most centrally, public opinion is an illusion created by polling and pollsters, a byproduct of an industry, but not a phenomenon that drives (or should drive) social analysis or social action.

Bourdieu makes three arguments in his essay "Public Opinion Does Not Exist," attacking the basic assumptions of polls. He asks first whether people typically have crystallized opinions, at the ready for inquiring pollsters. This is a vital point, especially given what we know about public ignorance about policy issues in American politics. It is the case that most good surveyors give respondents "don't know" or "no opinion" options. And others have developed scales to test knowledge levels on a subject, while asking opinions. These techniques help some, in determining whether people bring an appropriate understanding to the formation of their opinions. But it is also the case that most people—even those citizens who keep up with the news—have not necessarily thought through their views, or thought about them in the way that a pollster asks.

In response to this critique, many pollsters are resigned to the general problem; they survey the people as they find them. But dismissing Bourdieu in this fashion is not particularly responsible, since the results of issue polls are used—by statesmen, interest group leaders, lobbyists, and others—to argue that "the public" feels one way or another on a policy issue. Are they valid statistics, when they wrongly assume an informed and often even sophisticated respondent? Quantitative data can often feel very "factual" and authoritative, but Bourdieu wonders how steady the ground is beneath the aggregated opinions.

Acknowledging these difficulties, and they are great, we can at least speculate a bit on public opinion and the Internet, from the posture of critical theory, although it takes us to different conclusions.

One tack might be to argue that truly strong Web presence is a function of capital. The slickest, most attractive, most frequently updated websites are those owned and operated by the major media organizations, corporations, and wealthy interest groups. At any one moment, the top 100 blogs include a variety of well-established media organization sites: CNN, the Huffington Post (a conglomeration of major news outlet stories), or the *Los Angeles Times*.[1] On the other hand, websites that emerge from far less powerful organizations appear as well (for example, Thinkprogress.org, a progressive site produced by the Center for American Progress, or Michelle Malkin's conservative blog, which did not *begin* its life backed by powerful conglomerates). The presence of grassroots sites, or those that began that way, does lead one to think that the Internet might dissipate or disrupt normal power dynamics, and therefore, the hegemony that critical theorists find crushes working-class opinion. It is clear that, with some talent and perhaps not much by way of resources, a lone voice outside of the so-called "ruling class" can break through the clutter, even if temporarily.

And perhaps that is the central dynamic of worry to a critical theorist: the Internet is wide open in many ways, so all sorts of non-mainstream voices can in fact start blogs and sites without the traditionally high cost of establishing a newspaper, magazine, or television network. But, as the blog or site is discovered, it gets co-opted: a network or organization starts to support it or even buys it, taking away whatever subversive or interesting elements it may have had. Most problematic are powerful Internet providers such as Google (providing 63 percent of all Internet searches) that seem to just serve up information without bias, when they are in fact regulated:

"The idea that the user is sovereign has transformed the meaning of free speech," [Columbia Professor Tim] Wu said enthusiastically about the Internet age. But Google is not just a neutral platform for sovereign users; it is also a company in the advertising and media business. In the future, Wu said, it might slant its search results to favor its own media applications or to bury its competitors. If Google allowed its search results to be biased for economic reasons, it would transform the way we think about Google as a neutral free-speech tool. The only editor is supposed to be a neutral algorithm. But that would make it all the more insidious if the search algorithm were to become biased.   (Rosen 2008)

Critical theorists would argue, in fact, that the demise of free speech—and therefore free expression of public opinion—is inevitable. On occasion, subversive elements appear—websites that have potential to truly disrupt normal power relations in a society—but they will be either bought, crushed, or toned down, just as these elements typically have been in the mass media throughout history. The "edgy" voices—those who question and disrupt—are censored or diminished somehow, whether Howard Stern (banished

---

[1] See <http://technorati.com/blogs/top100>.

from free radio) or *The Simpsons*, where the subversive is typically undermined by a message about family values and conventionality.

As with any debate along these lines, only projects in content analysis—qualitative or quantitative—can track whether in fact content that challenges the powerful survives for very long on the Internet. Such empirical projects are far more complex than our past analyses of static media (a television show, a newspaper edition), since Internet content comes and goes, and we are all Wikipedia editors now. Without the tracking of ideas and sites, over multi-year periods, it will be impossible to support or refute the traditional critical theory hypotheses about public opinion. But it seems the only way to answer questions about the bounds of public expression at this moment.

One last intriguing note about the Internet and public opinion: it is a place where theory and praxis can meet, a vital desire of critical theorists. The Web enables more rhetorical activity than any communication technology has ever allowed in the history of human expression. Perhaps there are increasing limits to the expressive freedom we find currently on the Internet, and there is much to worry about. But at the moment, those who wish to connect with others, spread ideas, and get a sense of public opinion on any issue have a tool like no other. Facebook and other mechanisms for building community are spectacular improvements over phone calls, letter writing, and knocking on doors. Whether grassroots organizing becomes more effective, over the long run, is difficult to predict. We can hope that the Internet makes both public argument with those who oppose us, and organizing with those who think like us—across the ideological continuum—easier and more fulfilling.

Critical views of public opinion and opinion polling came most forcefully from the ideological left and from neo-Marxists in the twentieth century. But along with them, a variety of others—even many positivists—began to question the nature and value of "public opinion", as well as the methodologies for studying it. For those of us studying public opinion in the twenty-first century, some of the criticisms are more relevant and useful than others. And some neo-Marxist ideas are simply entirely outdated given the evolution of capitalism, democracies, and media technology. Nonetheless, it behooves sophisticated scholars of public opinion to understand the lengthy history of critical work, and to use it where they can, to enrich their own projects. This sort of approach makes the study of an already complex idea like public opinion even more perplexing, but democratic thought deserves no less.

# References

Avineri, S. 1978. *The Social and Political Thought of Karl Marx*. Cambridge: Cambridge University Press.

Baudrillard, J. 1988. *Selected Writings*. Stanford, CA: Stanford University Press.

BLUMER, H. 1948. Public Opinion and Public Opinion Polling. *American Sociological Review*, 13: 542–9.

BOURDIEU, P. 1979. Public Opinion Does Not Exist. In *Communication and Class Struggle*, ed. A. Mattelart and S. Siegelaub. New York: International General.

CONVERSE, P. 1987. Changing Conceptions of Public Opinion in the Political Process. *Public Opinion Quarterly*, 51: 12–24.

ENGELS, F. 1924. Engels to Eduard Bernstein in Zurich. In *Letters of Frederick Engels 1882*. Marx Engels Archives. At <http://www.marxists.org/archive/marx/works/1882/letters/82_11_02.htm#356>. Accessed July 29, 2009.

ENTMAN, R. 2004. *Projections of Power: Framing News, Public Opinion, and U.S. Foreign Policy*. Chicago: University of Chicago Press.

GLADWELL, M. 2008. *Outliers: The Story of Success*. New York: Little, Brown.

GRAMSCI, A. 1971. *Selections from the Prison Notebooks*. New York: International.

HABERMAS, J. 1989. *The Structural Transformation of the Public Sphere: An Inquiry into a Category of Bourgeois Society*. Cambridge, MA: MIT Press.

HELD, D. 1980. *Introduction to Critical Theory: From Horkheimer to Habermas*. Berkeley: University of California Press.

HORKHEIMER, M., and ADORNO, T. 1987. *The Dialectic of Enlightenment*. New York: Continuum.

MCMURTRY, J. 1978. *The Structure of Marx's World-View*. Princeton: Princeton University Press.

MARX, K., and ENGELS, F. 1984. *The German Ideology*. New York: International.

ROSEN, J. 2008. Google's Gatekeepers. *New York Times*, Nov. 28. At <http://www.nytimes.com/2008/11/30/magazine/30google-t.html?_r=1&partner=rss&emc=rss>. Accessed Dec. 1, 2009.

*Stanford Encyclopedia of Philosophy*. At <http://plato.stanford.edu>. Accessed Dec. 1, 2009.

# SECTION FIVE:
# MEASUREMENT

........................................................................................

# CHAPTER 20

# THE ACCURACY OF OPINION POLLING AND ITS RELATION TO ITS FUTURE

........................................................................................

## MICHAEL TRAUGOTT

ONE of the problems in evaluating the accuracy of the polls is that there is no agreed measure or standard for doing so. There is a small set of statistical measures that are employed and discussed among knowledgeable polling professionals, but another common measure is to see whether they showed the eventual winner ahead in the polls. When elections are not close, these two criteria will produce the same assessment; but when an election is very close, they may produce conflicting judgments. While experts can evaluate the differences in the methods and make their own judgments, the average citizen cannot. Because the public knows so little about the details of polling methodology such as sample design or weighting, they are not capable of distinguishing good polling from bad. So they are more likely to be influenced by the media discussion and debate about polling accuracy than by any more or less objective measures based upon methodology. Recent research confirms the widely held tendency for the media to discuss accuracy in terms of "the polls" rather than by discussing the quality or accuracy of estimates produced by individual firms (Frankovic 2005; Traugott, Krenz, and McClain 2008).

As the costs of data collection have declined, relatively speaking, with the advent of new technologies like the telephone, personal computer, and the availability of the Internet, new techniques for data collection have appeared. Of special note is the advent of exit polls as a feature of election night coverage by broadcast news outlets, which have not been without issues of accuracy either. And the use of Interactive Voice Response (IVR) approaches to data collection without a live interviewer and the adoption of Web-based polling have also raised accuracy-related concerns. In the 2008 campaign for the first time, a new form of estimation of election outcomes appeared that did not involve direct survey data collection at all but instead relied upon statistical models and computer simulations, forcing a reconsideration of the very term "preelection estimate" in comparison to previous election cycles. Real Clear Politics started this trend in 2000 when it began to take the average of results from polls asking essentially the same question about a well-known concept. In the case of preelection polls, this was the result from the "trial heat" question that asks people for whom they would vote if the election were held today. This methodology has its critics among knowledgeable public opinion researchers and statisticians, and it was modified during the 2004 campaign at Pollster when they adopted a regression-smoothed modeling of preferences across all of the polling that was being done. By 2008 a new website, Five Thirty Eight, was producing more sophisticated modeling of outcomes based upon computer simulations and a weighting that included the individual polling firm's accuracy record in recent elections. These websites—and others that will inevitably follow—raise new questions about the definition of election estimation and the use and meaning of polls in the process.

In this chapter, the concept of accuracy and how to measure it is addressed first. Then there is a chronology of the accuracy of presidential preelection polls through the 2008 election. This is followed by a discussion of alternative ways to estimate election outcomes that do not involve the conduct of polls by the analyst. Issues about the prospects for the impact of new technologies and changing voting procedures on the accuracy of polls are discussed in the concluding section.

# THE ROLE OF ACCURACY IN PREELECTION ESTIMATES

The 2000 presidential election was a significant civics education for a large number of Americans. It raised a number of issues about things we took for granted in the American political system, including the notion that all of the votes cast would be counted and the devices on which we cast our ballots are accurate and reliable enough to produce a generally acknowledged winner in a very close election. By 2004 further questions were raised by a few analysts and commentators about whether the elections were "stolen" in selected states or overall. These challenges to the legitimacy of the winner were based upon differences between either preelection polls or early Election Day estimates derived from exit polls and the eventual tabulation of the vote totals (Freeman and Bleifuss 2006; Miller 2005) or analyses of other polling data such as George W. Bush's approval ratings, which suggested the unlikelihood that he could be elected or reelected. In other words, if the polls were accurate, how could the vote totals—nationally or in particular states—come out the way they did?[1]

---

[1] This chapter focuses on the place of polls in American democracy, but these issues apply to other political systems as well, including the 1992 preelection polls in the United Kingdom and the unrest after the 2004 Ukrainian presidential election.

## Polls, Reporting Styles, and the Need for Accuracy

As a consequence of the symbiotic relationship between political journalists and pollsters, reporting styles have changed over time as the number of polls has proliferated (Patterson 2005; Rosenstiel 2005). Politics is often an important and newsworthy topic, and elections hold a special place in this area. Over time, the structure of news stories has changed as well. Reporting on campaigns has increasingly focused on the dynamics of the contests, including who is ahead or behind and which candidates are surging or falling farther back. Polls are such a central component of political reporting that some major news organizations have formed their own polling units or sponsored their own polls with increasing frequency. This style of reporting has clear consequences for candidates who need to raise funds, attract high-quality consultants and advisers, and recruit volunteers.

Because the consequence of polls is so significant in determining a candidate's standing, prospects, and viability, accuracy is obviously important. But using this kind of information in news stories is also potentially hazardous, as we know that most political reporters have no formal training in polling methods, and it is difficult for them to make independent judgments about data quality, including assessments about the accuracy of polls showing the relative standing of the candidates. This role for journalists is especially important because extensive research shows that most citizens know very little about the methodology of polls generally or understand specific concepts like the margin of error associated with a particular sample size.

Furthermore, the public's general impression of the polling industry is formed by what they observe about the conduct of preelection polls and the quality of their estimates, as well as journalists' commentary about the accuracy of polls in the media. Citizens use the polls' past record of accuracy to form their impressions of the business as a whole rather than by distinguishing the work of individual firms, or they rely upon media reports of how well the polls did (measured in terms of the accuracy of their preelection estimates) to make a broad assessment of the quality of their work.

Current reporting styles represent a missed opportunity for news organizations in their use of polls. If there were more of a focus on issues and policy in American campaigns and their news coverage, polls could be used to represent the voice of the electorate in terms of highlighting the issues that are most important to voters and their assessments of whether they are being addressed adequately by the candidates. In detailed form, this could include analyses of the policy interests and concerns of the total electorate as well as the interests—and differences in the interests—of politically relevant and significant subgroups in the electorate. Polls represent the only reliable way to collect such information and hence to incorporate it into campaign coverage. But as long as the emphasis remains on the dynamics of the contest and who is ahead and by how much, the prospects for this kind of expanded poll-based coverage remain dim.

## The Concept of Accuracy and How to Measure It

Evaluating the accuracy of poll-based estimates of election outcomes involves two related issues. The necessary but insufficient condition is to select the correct winning candidate, especially when there is a reasonable difference between them in their respective share of the votes cast. A second and related issue is the precision of the estimates of each major candidate's share of the vote and/or the resulting margin between the two. While these criteria apply most directly to preelection polls, recent experiences suggest that they can also be applied to exit polls and the projection of winners on Election Night as well as to the winners of primaries and caucuses in the new system for the selection of pledged delegates to the national nominating conventions. One central issue in understanding and evaluating polling accuracy is of course determining how to define and then measure it. There are different ways to calculate polling accuracy or "errors"—developed in different polling eras—which have distinct properties, and each has its advantages and disadvantages.

There are three commonly used sets of statistical measures to assess the accuracy of poll results, each developed at a point in the history of polling when concerns were raised about the accuracy of polls conducted in a particular presidential election. The first was developed by Mosteller as part of the Social Science Research Council (SSRC)'s review of the performance of the polls in the 1948 election. He discussed the relative advantages and disadvantages of eight different measures, and he proposed that two measures would be best suited to analyze what he described as the errors in "election forecasting" (Mosteller et al. 1949, 54). The first was the difference in percentage points in the estimate for either party (or both) in the poll and in the vote, and the second was the error in the estimate of the difference between the two parties (essentially the winning margin) in the poll and in the vote. This was the measure that the SSRC team employed in the bulk of its report.

Responding to Ladd's (1996) criticism of the performance of the polls in the 1996 presidential election, Mitofksy (1998) proposed using modifications to two different measures from Mosteller's list that had been dismissed in 1948: (1) the average of the absolute value of the differences between the predicted and actual vote of the two major candidates and (2) the absolute value of the difference between the two leading candidates in a poll and the difference in the vote count. These measures were adopted by the National Council on Public Polls (NCPP) and described as the Candidate Estimate Error and the Margin Error respectively.[2] He argued for the change in measures because of the relatively large number of "undecideds" in many polls and because of Ross Perot's appearance as a significant third party candidate in the 1990s. Without much further consideration, these slightly modified Mosteller measures 3 and 5 became the standard for assessing accuracy for the next few election cycles (Traugott 2001, 2005). One consequence of this shift, however, was that when

---

[2] The NCPP implemented this system in 1997 in an analysis of the 1996 results. The names and the calculation of these two statistics have changed slightly over time. The Candidate Estimate Error is actually the difference for each of the two major candidates summed and divided by two; this has the potential to reduce a potentially serious (large) estimation error for one candidate in relation to the other. And the need to take the average suggests the need to take the absolute value of the error for each. NCPP has documented all of this (NCPP 2008).

both measures encapsulated the absolute value of the differences, the ability of the accuracy assessments to capture the *direction* of the errors (whether one or both candidates' vote shares were under- or overestimated) was lost.

As a way of recapturing the directionality of estimation and providing a measure that would be standardized across elections with different outcomes or polling firms with different estimates of the outcome, Martin, Traugott, and Kennedy (2005) proposed a new measure of predictive accuracy, A, that was based on the log odds ratio of the difference in the poll estimate for the two leading candidates compared to the actual outcome of the election. Because of its derivation, this measure is not affected by the outcome of a specific election (the winner's share of the vote or margin) the way the Mosteller measures are. A popsitive sign for A indicates an estimate that favors the Republican candidate, while a negative value indicates an estimate that favors the Democrat. When the share in the poll is equivalent to the share in the election, then the value of A is 0. This measure permits analyses such as the evaluation of the relative impact of different methods that polling firms use to estimate their accuracy, assessments of how accurate a particular firm is across successive preelection estimates it produces during the campaign, or how well the polls generally performed across elections.

# THE HISTORICAL TRENDS IN ACCURACY AND ITS MEASUREMENT

The history of preelection polling in the United States is defined by a chronology of elections where significant estimation errors occurred. These major events are associated with the election of 1936, generally thought to be the key election in the development of the modern field of polling; the 1948 election, when "Dewey Beats Truman"; and the 1996 election, when Clinton beat Dole but not by as much as expected. Along the way, there were also issues associated with the increasing use of preelection polls to estimate the outcomes in primary elections, especially errors preceding the 2008 New Hampshire primary, which prompted a national review similar to the one conducted after the 1948 general election (AAPOR 2009a). Finally, there are issues associated with the accuracy of exit polls to estimate the outcome of the presidential election in each state on election night.

## The *Literary Digest* and the 1936 Election: The Advent of Modern Polling

Prior to the 1936 election, the primary public source of presidential election outcome estimates had been the *Literary Digest* poll, produced by a major circulation weekly magazine that began its polling operation in 1920 (Squire 1988). By 1936 George Gallup,

Archibald Crossley, and Elmo Roper had begun conducting preelection polls as a way to build public awareness of their nascent businesses and attract new clients. Gallup in particular understood the importance of working closely with a media client in order to increase the visibility of his American Institute of Public Opinion Research. The *Literary Digest* methodology involved mailing large numbers of straw vote ballots to lists of subscribers supplemented by names and addresses from automobile registration lists and telephone books. For the 1936 election, more than 10 million "ballots" were mailed out in late summer; by the final tabulation, more than 2.3 million were returned. The *Literary Digest* published weekly tabulations starting in September all the way through the end of the campaign; and their final unweighted totals gave Alf Landon an estimated 55 percent of the vote compared to 41 percent for Franklin Roosevelt. The actual vote totals gave Roosevelt 61 percent of the vote, while Landon got 37 percent.

There had been research on the unrepresentative nature of the *Literary Digest* (non-) sampling methodology before 1936, suggesting a variety of ways that their mailings were problematical (Robinson 1932). They relied on large mailings that often had very high coverage in some areas of the country but almost none in others; and their response rate was low overall and also highly variable by locales and population subgroups. This produced significant response bias that favored Republicans, a particularly vexing problem during the Depression. Gallup, who had the best formal training of the early pollsters, understood the potential problems that the *Literary Digest* was likely to encounter and simultaneously predicted them and their consequences. He believed strongly enough in improved sampling procedures that he offered a guarantee to his major clients, the *New York Herald Tribune* and the *Washington Post*, that he could do a better job of estimation or else forgo the annual payment for his columns. Gallup's final estimate was 54 percent for Roosevelt, satisfying the necessary condition of getting the winner right but falling significantly short of estimating his actual proportion of the vote.

## Preelection Polls and the 1948 Election

The Gallup Poll used area probability sampling to select the places where their interviewers worked, but respondent selection involved quotas that were filled by the interviewers. The use of quota sampling was the undoing of the public pollsters in the 1948 election, in conjunction with their need to stop their interviewing early enough to get their questionnaires back to headquarters and processed in time for analysis and publication. In the intervening twelve years since 1936, Gallup interviews were still being conducted face-to-face in people's homes. In order to get the data processed and analyzed and the press releases written, interviewing had to cease by mid-September. This hadn't presented problems for estimation during the Roosevelt elections, but in the open contest of 1948 it did.

For most of the next forty-eight years, the public pollsters had an enviable record of accuracy. The field of pollsters was not very crowded, especially when the capitalization of an effort required mounting a national field staff for face-to-face interviews. But in the 1960s, the penetration of telephones into American households became widespread. With the advent of personal computers in the 1970s, news organizations began to develop their own low-cost capacity to contact potential respondents through computer-assisted telephone interviewing techniques. The first operations involved combines between broadcast television networks and major metropolitan daily newspapers like the *New York Times*, the *Washington Post*, and the *Wall Street Journal*. Eventually local television stations and newspapers partnered to share the costs of data collection. This marked the beginning of a period of the proliferation of polls as they became an accepted and standard part of political reporting (Patterson 1993; Rosenstiel 2005).

## The 1996 Election and Clinton's Lead over Dole

The first source of tension about accuracy in the contemporary period came in the 1996 election, when Bill Clinton was seeking a second term running against Bob Dole. The polls showed Clinton with an early, clear lead, which increased as Election Day approached. While Clinton won by 8 percentage points, a large victory by contemporary standards, one of the preelection polls gave him an 18 percentage point advantage in their final estimate. Ladd (1996) claimed there was a pro-Democratic bias in the preelection polls as well as in the networks' use of exit-poll data on election night. Mitofsky (1998) and the NCPP (1997) prepared a defense of the polling effort in that election.

The NCPP produced two measures based upon Mosteller's measures 3 and 5: the difference between the election outcome and the estimate for each of the leading candidates divided by two (called the Candidate Error) and the difference between the poll estimates of the difference between the leading candidates and the difference in the election (called the Total Error). Mosteller specified that the value for Measure 3 should be computed "without regard to sign" but did not include any such qualification for Measure 5. Mitofsky and the NCPP proposed that both measures be computed as absolute values, and the ability to account for the partisan directionality of estimation errors was lost, although Mitofsky (1998, 245) produced a table that showed the final preelection polls favored the Democrats in both 1992 and 1996, a shift from previous elections.

## Preelection Polls and Exit Polls in the 2000 Presidential Election

In the 2000 election, another set of polling issues arose. The campaign between George W. Bush and Al Gore was hard fought among two evenly matched candidates. Most of the preelection polls indicated that Bush would win the popular vote, although by a very small margin. In the end, Gore won the popular vote by about 500,000 votes (approximately .5 percent), but a drawn-out contest in Florida ultimately decided by a US Supreme Court decision gave the Electoral College majority to Bush. Out of nineteen final preelection poll estimates, fourteen indicated Bush would win, three suggested a tie, and two indicated a Gore victory. Three of the polls showed a Bush lead as large as approximately 5 percentage points, well within sampling error, especially since the pollsters seem to have increased their sample sizes from previous elections; and the others showed smaller differences between the candidates. From a statistical perspective, all of the estimates were within a 95 percent confidence interval. But as is often the case, it also depends who was indicated as the winning candidate. This was the source of some discussion about the accuracy of the preelection polls (Traugott 2001).

There were additional issues associated with the performance of the exit polls and the networks' use of them on election night. The vote in Florida was so close that the exit poll information was used by different networks to call the state in different ways; and calls were made and then withdrawn as raw vote data entered the projection models to supplement the results based upon the interviews with voters leaving their polling places. Beyond Florida, some interest groups claimed that the discrepancy between the exit poll results and the vote totals suggested that the Republicans had stolen Ohio's electoral votes and called for a recount. After their own performance in Florida and the public debate about Ohio, network officials were called to testify before Congress after independently supporting external reviews of their performance on election night (Konner, Risser, and Wattenberg 2001; Mason, Frankovic, and Jamieson 2001).

## Preelection Polls and Exit Polls in the 2004 Presidential Election

The 2004 election between Bush and John Kerry was an easier time for the preelection pollsters as Bush established and held a lead in the general election campaign. The estimation by the preelection pollsters was very good under these conditions (Traugott 2005), but the exit polls again created tension among political cognoscenti. For several elections, early exit-poll results had been leaked and appeared on various websites in the afternoon. One of the disclosures resulting from the 2000 leaks was an acknowledgment that there was a pro-Democratic bias in the raw results of the interviews, which was corrected through successive weighting exercises during the course of Election Day. The leak of early 2004 results suggested a Kerry victory, and they actually produced a brief period when the Bush campaign became anxious and the Kerry campaign considered drafting an acceptance speech. After appropriate weighting there were no incorrect calls on election night, and the outcome was effectively decided early; but in the afternoon the stock market reacted to the possibility of a Kerry win with a sharp drop (Morin 2004).

The exit poll operation and its clients responded to the leaked preliminary results with a revision in procedures intended to prevent a recurrence. Key personnel from each network were sequestered in a "quarantine room" without any capability of communicating with the outside. Implemented for the 2006 election night coverage, it proved effective in eliminating leaked results, and it has become the standard election night procedure since. These individuals are released from their isolation chamber early in the evening and allowed to join their network's respective analysis and projection groups to support the evening's coverage.

## Preelection Polls in the Primaries and the General Election in 2008

In 2008 there was a relatively sharp disjuncture between the performance of the polls in the primary elections and in the fall campaign. In the winter, every poll before the New Hampshire primary indicated that Barack Obama would win by margins varying from 1 percentage point to a substantial 13 points. When Hillary Clinton won the actual vote by 3 percentage points, the media focused on the estimation problems of "the polls," and the American Association for Public Opinion Research appointed a committee to investigate the performance of the polls (AAPOR 2009a). A subsequent analysis by Traugott and Wlezien (2009), facilitated by the abundance of state-level polling data available in that election due to the length of the contest between Obama and Clinton, has shown that the problems of New Hampshire were not unique; the preelection polls as a group generally underestimated the winner's share of the vote for the two leading candidates in the week leading up to each election. They suggest this was due to contextual factors like the level of competition, each candidate's share of the delegates in relation to the simple majority needed to become the nominee, and the leader's actual standing in the preelection polls. Their results suggest that in a hotly contested race simply transplanting likely voter models developed in the general election to the primary context may not work; pollsters may have to rethink how they estimate the likely electorate in closely contested races.

The problems in the primaries stand in stark contrast to the high quality of the estimation in the general election, raising the question of how the pollsters could have improved their methods and subsequent accuracy so much in general elections but still be struggling in the primaries. By a variety of statistical measures, the preelection polling in the 2008 presidential contest was as good as it has ever been. For different reasons, including the division of partisanship in the electorate, the funding disparity between the two campaigns, and the candidates' debate performance, Barack Obama beat John McCain by a historically decisive margin of 6.7 percentage points. There were also issues that might have created problems for the pollsters, including concerns about a potential "Bradley effect" (Hopkins 2009), the omission of cellphones from many samples, and extensive voter registration drives by the Democrats, which added many voters to the rolls and complicated estimation of the likely electorate. In the end, every one of nineteen final estimates of the outcome suggested Obama would win by margins ranging from 2 to 11 percentage points (NCPP 2008).

In summary, there have been a series of critical election events that have periodically raised issues about the accuracy of preelection estimation in the United States across the past seventy years or so. The problems of accuracy seem worse when the preelection polls suggest the wrong winning candidate, but there are also issues of estimating the support each candidate receives as well as the winning margin. Pollsters and political commentators are still grappling with issues of how to assess the accuracy of the polls and whether and how to incorporate the direction of the errors into their evaluation. Public opinion researchers have typically responded to these incidents and the ensuing criticism with a renewed effort to improve their methods, and generally their estimation has improved as a result.

## Summarizing Polling Accuracy in Recent Elections

Given these developments, how have the pollsters done in estimating the outcome of recent elections? Table 20.1, excerpted from Traugott and Wlezien (2009), shows how the polls' performance has improved in recent general elections, with the 1948 election as a reference point. The entry in the table is the average value of A for the final preelection polls conducted in each contest. The data reveal two interesting patterns over time. First and foremost, the number of preelection polls has grown; and second, the diminishing values of A show the improvement in estimation.

The value of A for 1948 shows the large bias toward Thomas Dewey, the Republican candidate. The value for 1996 shows the overestimate of the margin for Bill Clinton, the Democratic incumbent. In the 2000 election, A shows the tendency of the polls to suggest that George W. Bush would win the popular vote, while Al Gore actually won that part of the election. In 2004 the preelection polls slightly overestimated John Kerry's estimated vote share, although all of the polls indicated that Bush would be

Table 20.1 How the performance of the preelection polls in the 2008 General Election compares historically, 1948–2008

| Election year | No. of polls | Average value of A |
| --- | --- | --- |
| 1948 | 3 | +.278 |
| 1996 | 9 | −.084 |
| 2000 | 19 | +.063 |
| 2004 | 19 | −.026 |
| 2008 | 19 | +.012 |

Note: The entry in the table is the average value of A for the final preelection polls conducted in each contest (Martin, Traugott, and Kennedy 2005).

conducting political polls, and these new voting procedures only add to concerns about how estimates are produced. No one wants to have problems in estimating the outcome of another close election be the cause for renewed concern about the entire field.

# REFERENCES

AAPOR (American Association for Public Opinion Research). 2009a. *An Evaluation of the Methodology of the 2008 Pre-Election Primary Polls.* At <http://aapor.org/uploads/AAPOR_Rept_FINAL-Rev-4-13-09.pdf>. Accessed 10/29/2010.

—— 2009b. AAPOR Transparency Initiative. At <http://www.aapor.org/AAPORNewsFall2009_AAPORTransparencyInitiative.htm>. Accessed 10/29/2010.

BARNHART, B. 2008. Primary Results Prove Prediction Market Flawed. *Chicago Tribune,* Jan. 10. At <http://articles.chicagotribune.com/2008-01-10/business/0801090783_1_prediction-markets-iowa-electronic-markets-participation>. Accessed 10/29/2010.

ERIKSON, R. S., and WLEZIEN, C. 2008. Are Political Markets Really Superior to Polls as Election Predictors? *Public Opinion Quarterly,* 72: 190–215.

FRANKOVIC, K. A. 2005. Reporting "The Polls" in 2004. *Public Opinion Quarterly,* 69: 682–97.

FREEMAN, S. F., and BLEIFUSS, J. 2006. *Was the 2004 Presidential Election Stolen? Exit Polls, Election Fraud, and the Official Count.* New York: Seven Stories Press.

HOPKINS, D. J. 2009. No More Wilder Effect, Never a Whitman Effect: When and Why Polls Mislead about Black and Female Candidates. *Journal of Politics,* 71: 769–81.

KONNER, J., RISSER, J., and WATTENBERG, B. 2001. Television's Performance on Election Night 2000: A Report for CNN. At <http://archives.cnn.com/2001/ALLPOLITICS/stories/02/02/cnn.report/cnn.pdf>. Accessed 10/29/2010.

LADD, E. C. 1996. The Election Polls: An American Waterloo. *Chronicle of Higher Education,* Nov. 22, A52.

MANSKI, C. F. 2006. "Interpreting the Predictions of Prediction Markets." Economics Letters 91, 3 (June) 425–429.

MARTIN, E. A., TRAUGOTT, M. W., and KENNEDY, C. 2005. A Review and a Proposal for a New Measure of Poll Accuracy. *Public Opinion Quarterly,* 69: 342–69.

MASON, L., FRANKOVIC, K., and JAMIESON, K. H. 2001. CBS News Coverage of Election Night 2000: Investigation, Analysis, Recommendations. At <http://www.cbsnews.com/htdocs/c2k/pdf/REPFINAL.pdf>. Accessed 10/29/2010.

MILLER, M. C. 2005. *Fooled Again: How the Right Stole the 2004 Election and Why They'll Steal the Next One Too.* New York: Basic Books.

MITOFSKY, W. J. 1998. The Polls—Review: Was 1996 a Worse Year for Polls than 1948? *Public Opinion Quarterly,* 62: 230–49.

MORIN, R. 2004. Surveying the Damage: Exit Polls Can't Always Predict Winners, So Don't Expect Them To. *Washington Post,* Nov. 21, B01.

MOSTELLER, F., HYMAN, H., McCARTHY, P. J., MARKS E. S., and TRUMAN, D.B. 1949. *The Pre-Election Polls of 1948: Report to the Committee on Analysis of Pre-election Polls and Forecasts.* New York: The Social Science Research Council.

NCPP (National Council on Public Polls). 1997. Polling Analysis Concludes Criticisms of 1996 Poll Accuracy Are Unfounded. Press release, Feb. 13. Fairfield, CT.

—— 2008. NCPP Analysis of Final Presidential Pre-Election Polls, 2008. At <http://www.ncpp. org/files/NCPP_2008_analysis_of_election_polls_121808%20pdf_0.pdf>. Accessed 10/29/2010.

PATTERSON, T. E. 1993. *Out of Order*. New York: Knopf.

—— 2005. Of Polls, Mountains: U.S. Journalists and their Use of Election Surveys. *Public Opinion Quarterly*, 69: 716–24.

Pollster. 2008. The Polls: The 2008 Presidential Election. At <http://www.pollster.com/polls/ 2008president/>. Accessed 10/29/2010.

Real Clear Politics. 2008a. Final Democratic Results. At <http://www.realclearpolitics.com/ epolls/2008/president/dem_results.html>. Accessed 10/29/2010.

—— 2008b. General Election: McCain vs. Obama. At <http://www.realclearpolitics.com/epolls/ 2008/president/us/general_election_mccain_vs_obama-225.html>. Accessed 10/29/2010.

ROBINSON, C. E. 1932. *Straw Votes*. New York: Columbia University Press.

ROSENSTIEL, T. 2005. Political Polling and the New Media Culture: A Case of More Being Less. *Public Opinion Quarterly*, 69: 698–714.

SILVER, N. 2008. Today's Polls and Final Election Projection: Obama 349, McCain 189. Five Thirty Eight, Nov. 4. At <http://www.fivethirtyeight.com/2008/11/todays-polls-and-final-election.html>. Accessed 10/29/2010.

SNEE, T. 2008a. IEM within Less than Half Percentage Point in Presidential Race Prediction. *University of Iowa News Service*, Nov. 24. At <http://www.news-releases.uiowa.edu/2008/ november/112408iem_results.html>. Accessed 10/29/2010.

—— 2008b. Obama, McCain Lead Iowa Electronic Markets on N.H. Primary Day. *University of Iowa News Service*, Jan. 8. At <http://tippie.uiowa.edu/news/story.cfm?id=1783>. Accessed 10/29/2010.

SQUIRE, P. 1988. Why the Literary Digest Poll Failed. *Public Opinion Quarterly*, 52: 125–33.

STELTER, B. 2010. *Times* to Host Blog on Politics and Polls. *New York Times*, June 3. At <http:// www.nytimes.com/2010/06/04/business/media/04silver.html?_r=1>. Accessed 10/29/2010.

STIX, G. 2008. Super Tuesday: Markets Predict Outcome Better than Polls. *Scientific American*, Feb. 4. At <http://www.scientificamerican.com/article.cfm?id=markets-predict-outcome-better-than-polls>. Accessed 10/29/2010.

TIERNEY, J. 2008a. Number-Crunching the 2008 Election. *New York Times*, Jan. 9. At <http:// tierneylab.blogs.nytimes.com/2008/01/09/number-crunching-the-2008-election/>. Accessed 10/29/2010.

—— 2008b. The Smart Money on New Hampshire. *New York Times*, Jan. 7. At <http://tierneylab. blogs.nytimes.com/2008/01/07/the-smart-money-on-new-hampshire/>. Accessed 10/29/2010.

TRAUGOTT, M. W. 2001. Assessing Poll Performance in the 2000 Campaign. *Public Opinion Quarterly*, 65: 389–419.

—— 2005. The Accuracy of the National Preelection Polls in the 2004 Presidential Election. *Public Opinion Quarterly*, 69: 642–54.

—— 2009. Changes in Media Polling in Recent Presidential Campaigns: Moving from Good to "Average" at CNN. Discussion paper R-33. Joan Shorenstein Center, Harvard Kennedy School of Government. At <http://www.hks.harvard.edu/presspol/publications/papers/research_papers/r33_traugott.pdf>. Accessed Oct. 29, 2010.

—— and WLEZIEN, C. 2009. The Dynamics of Poll Performance during the 2008 Presidential Nomination Contest. *Public Opinion Quarterly*, 73: 866–94.

—— KRENZ, B., and McCLAIN, C. 2008. Press Coverage of the Polling Surprises in the New Hampshire Primaries. Paper presented at the Annual Conference of the Midwest Association for Public Opinion Research, Chicago.

CHAPTER 21

..................................................................................................

# REPRESENTATIVE SAMPLING AND SURVEY NON-RESPONSE

..................................................................................................

ADAM J. BERINSKY

## INTRODUCTION

..................................................................................................

How can we best gage the political opinions of ordinary Americans? Conducting a census of all individuals living in the United States is not only prohibitively expensive, it is not necessary. Instead, to measure public opinion, political pollsters, media organizations, and commercial pollsters select a group of people—the sample—from the population of interest—residents of the United States.

There are many possible ways to draw such a sample. Ideally, we would select a sample through a process of simple random sampling. Simple random samples have two important properties. Each individual is chosen for inclusion in the sample by chance and each member of the population has an equal chance of being included in the sample. Under these conditions, every possible sample of a given size has the same chance of selection. Every citizen therefore has an equal chance to have their voice heard in an opinion poll.

In practice, surveys are rarely conducted through simple random sampling. Instead, other methods that ensure representative samples are employed. However, even with the best of these methods survey researchers are not always able to collect information from all potential respondents. Some people are unreachable; others refuse to answer particular questions. Under such circumstances, can opinion polls accurately measure the political predilections of the US population? This chapter explores this question.

I begin by first defining survey non-response, distinguishing between unit non-response—where we have no information about individuals selected to be in our sample—and item non-response—where we are missing some information about particular respondents. I then discuss recent trends in response rates. Over the last twenty-five years, unit non-response has become an increasing concern for survey researchers. I then discuss the causes of non-response on surveys and describe the threats non-response poses for the representativeness of surveys. Next, I discuss various methods available for dealing with non-response. I conclude by outlining directions for future research.

# Survey Non-Response

In practice, simple random sampling is difficult to implement. Consequently, modern opinion polls in the United States are conducted using other probability sampling methods—such as random digit dialing (RDD) telephone interviewing or a face-to-face multistage design.[1] For example, until recently, the phone surveys conducted by the Pew Research Center for the People & the Press used a multistage sampling technique which employed RDD to identify working banks of residential phone numbers and then randomly selected telephone numbers from those clusters. Since 2008 Pew has included cellphones in its samples as well. More recently, advances in database technology have furthered the development of large address databases which may facilitate address-based sampling for mail surveys (Link et al. 2008). While these methods are not equivalent to simple random sampling, statistical methods have been developed to account for the design components of modern survey sampling, such as clustering and stratification (Kish 1965; Lohr 1999).

However, identifying a sample of respondents is just the first step in the data collection process. What happens when we are unable to collect information from everyone in the sample on the questions we would like to ask? Here is where questions of representativeness and non-response come into play.

## Types of Non-Response

When we speak of survey non-response, we are, in fact, speaking of two distinct but related phenomena: *unit* non-response and *item* non-response. Unit non-response occurs when an entire observation unit is missing from our sample (Lohr 1999). In

---

[1] In this chapter I do not discuss Internet sampling methods. Couper (2000) provides a useful typology of these methods and the 2008 special issue of *Public Opinion Quarterly* on web survey methods is informative as well. Some Internet polls use telephone samples to identify a pool of potential respondents and therefore suffer from many of the same non-response problems discussed in this chapter. Other surveys use a convenience sample of respondents who self-select into polls. In these polls, the meaning of a "population" is not clear. Without an adequately defined population, it is difficult to address issues of non-response.

the context of survey research, unit non-response occurs when we have no information about a respondent selected to be in our sample.

Item non-response, on the other hand, occurs when some measurements are present for an observational unit, but at least one measure of interest is missing (Lohr 1999). In survey research, item non-response occurs when we have some information about the respondent, but we are missing data for a given variable or variables of interest. For instance, we may know a respondent's education level and partisanship, but not her income. These two forms of survey non-response both involve missing information, but have been dealt with separately in the literature. In this chapter, I will follow convention and take up each topic in turn.

## Unit Non-Response

Unit non-response has become an increasingly serious problem over the last forty years. Studies in the 1990s demonstrated that face-to-face surveys by academic organizations, such as the National Election Study (NES) and the General Social Survey, had response rates between 70 and 75 percent, down from 80 to 85 percent in the 1950s (Brehm 1993; Luevano 1994; Groves and Couper 1998). Telephone surveys conducted by commercial polling houses which produce the majority of polling information in circulation in the political world often have even lower response rates. For instance, in a study of polls conducted by the news media and government contractors from 1996 to 2003, Holbrook, Krosnick, and Pfent (2008) found that the mean response rate for these surveys was 30 percent.[2] Furthermore, indications are that unit non-response has become an even more serious problem since the mid-1990s (Holbrook, Krosnick, and Pfent 2008).

To understand the implications of these trends it is best to consider more closely the process of survey non-response. Non-response rates are, in fact, the product of two distinct processes: (1) some respondents cannot be found by the poll's sponsors and (2) other respondents decline to participate in the poll. In both cases potential data are lost. Unit non-response is therefore a function of both respondent contact and respondent cooperation (Groves and Couper 1998).

Conventional wisdom holds that survey response rates have been falling because potential respondents are harder to contact. For example, researchers employing telephone surveys seem to have a more difficult time reaching respondents in recent years because of the rise of caller ID and other technological innovations. However, academic studies have shown that the rise in unit non-response is as attributable to increasing refusal rates as it is to decreasing contact rates. Take, for instance, the NES.

---

[2] Holbrook, Krosnick, and Pfent (2008) report response rate 3, according to the standards codified by AAPOR (2006). To maintain consistency with the NES numbers reported above, it is better to use the RR1 calculation. In a previous version of their research, Krosnick, Holbrook, and Pfent (2005) reported that the average RR1 for the surveys was 36 percent.

In 1952, 6 percent of potential respondents refused to be interviewed by the NES. By 1986 this number had risen to 26 percent and has remained high through the present day. Similar patterns of response have been found in other face-to-face surveys (Curtin, Presser, and Singer 2005).

Moreover, the primacy of refusals as an explanation for increased rates of survey non-response extends from face-to-face academic surveys to telephone surveys. The Pew Research Center carried out surveys in 1997 and 2003 over a five-day period using polling techniques typical of professional survey houses. They found that these surveys conducted in identical manners had very different rates of response in the two time periods. While the response rate was 36 percent in 1997, by 2003 it had dropped to 27 percent. Somewhat surprisingly, the contact rate stayed roughly the same—actually increasing 1 percentage point from 69 percent to 70 percent. However, over that same time period, the refusal rate increased 20 points, from 42 percent to 62 percent. The 9 point decline in the response rate was therefore entirely a result of increasing refusal rates.

## Causes of Unit Non-Response

The increasing rates of unit non-response in surveys over the last twenty-five years are not an inevitable development. However, there are certain predictable determinants of non-response. Groves and Couper (1998) provide a seminal statement on the causes and consequences of non-response (for more recent updates, see the special issue of *Public Opinion Quarterly*, edited by Singer (2006)). Groves and Couper argue that the decision to respond to a survey is a stochastic process, and they present a unified framework representing the decision to participate in a poll, considering separately the impact of survey design, interviewer factors, and respondent characteristics on the processes of securing respondent contact and respondent cooperation. They find that contact rates are a function of the physical barriers to accessing a household (in face-to-face surveys), the patterns of times of the day when members of a household are present, and the timing and the number of attempted interviewer contacts. Refusal patterns also follow specific tendencies. Younger respondents and older respondents are more likely to cooperate with an interviewer than middle-aged respondents; respondents with low socioeconomic status are more likely to agree to be surveyed than high-status individuals. Furthermore, the socioeconomic environment of a household influences cooperation rates. They find low cooperation rates among households in high-density areas (over and above specific household characteristics). The structure of the survey and interviewer practices can also influence patterns of survey refusal. For instance, Groves and Couper find that more experienced interviewers and those who are able to establish a rapport with the respondents at first contact are more likely to secure interviews. Finally, the survey design itself can influence cooperation rates. Providing advance warning of the survey request (Groves and Couper 1998) and monetary incentives (Groves and Couper 1998; Groves 2006), and even non-monetary tokens of appreciation increase the likelihood that a respondent will agree to be interviewed, albeit modestly.

For survey practitioners, the message of this work is clear. Though some aspects of non-response are related to characteristics of the surveyed household and are beyond the control of survey researchers, response rates can be increased through the use of advance warning letters, respondent incentives, and highly trained interviewers who make multiple attempts to secure an interview. With some effort, rates of unit non-response can be held down, even in the era of increasing refusal rates.

## Cellphones

As technology changes, the process of survey research changes as well. The rise of telephones in the 1960s and 1970s permitted survey researchers to reliably conduct polls by telephone. However, with the dawn of the new century, a new source of non-response in telephone surveys has emerged—the rise of the cellphone.

An increasing number of Americans have abandoned land lines in favor of cell-phones. Since 2003 the Center for Disease Control's National Health Interview Survey (NHIS) has measured the prevalence of cellphone-only households in the US.[3] From early 2003 to the second half of 2009, the percentage of adults living in households with only wireless telephone service rose from 2.9 percent to 25.9 percent (Blumberg and Luke 2007, 2010). Telephone surveys that include only land lines therefore miss a large—and distinct—segment of the population.[4]

The rise of cellphones does not mean that land-line-only samples are inherently unreliable. Even as the proportion of cellphone-only households increased between the 2000 and 2004 presidential elections, many pollsters found that the biases induced through the failure to contact these households could be corrected by adjusting a land-line-only sample to reflect population characteristics on key variables such as age and race (Brick et al. 2006; Keeter 2006).

In 2008, however, these reassuring findings came under question. In a break from earlier work, Keeter, Dimock, and Christian (2008) found that while the addition of a cellphone-only sample to a traditional land line sample had, at most, a modest effect on the Pew estimates of candidate support, Obama's advantage over McCain was consistently slightly higher in the mixed cellphone and land line sample, even after adjusting the sample to reflect census estimates of the population characteristics.

These experiences have profoundly changed the way telephone surveys are conducted in the United States. By 2009 most media polls, including ABC/*Washington Post*, CBS News/*New York Times*, CNN/Gallup, and NBC/*Wall Street Journal*, had begun to include cellphones in their sampling schemes.

Still, the unit non-response problem caused by the rise of cellphones has not yet been fully solved. As Lavrakas, Shuttles, Steeh, and Fienberg (2007) notes, there is no widely

---

[3]  See <http://www.cdc.gov/nchs/data/nhis/earlyrelease/wireless200905.htm> for the NHIS definition of "wireless" households.

[4]  For instances, cellphone users are younger and more likely to be a member of a minority group (Keeter, Kennedy, Clark, et al. 2007). More generally, the 2007 special issue of *Public Opinion Quarterly* on cellphones provides important background information.

accepted set of cellphone surveying "best practices." Researchers have tried a variety of methods to draw samples through a "dual frame" approach that combines a land line sample and a cellphone sample. But how best to blend these samples is an open question. First, there is a basic problem related to sampling: land lines are tied to households, while cellphones are (usually) tied to individuals. Researchers need to account for these differential probabilities of respondent access. Second, respondents who have both a cellphone and a land line are different from those with just a cellphone. For instance, Brick et al. (2006) found that a dual-frame survey which combined results from a cellphone sample and a land line sample overrepresented households with cellphones, because cell-only households were more likely to respond to cellphone surveys than households with both cellphones and land lines. To adjust for this discrepancy, Brick and his colleagues suggest collecting a cellphone-only sample to combine with an RDD sample. However, even this method has its problems. Kennedy (2007) cautions that while dropping adults with land lines from a cellphone sample does not affect the coverage properties of the dual-frame survey, such procedures may affect other sources of error, such as inflating non-response bias.

In short, though the rise of the cellphone clearly threatens the representativeness of surveys, there are no obvious answers concerning how best to remedy this problem. More work in this area is needed.

## Implications of Non-Response

While reducing non-response rates is a worthy goal, achieving this goal is not without cost. High response rates often come with a high price tag. All of the methods of reducing unit non-response described above—using experienced interviewers, varying patterns of attempted contact, and employing respondent incentives—are expensive. Likewise, as of 2009 each cellphone interview is twice as expensive as a land line interview (Keeter, Dimock, and Christian 2008). Although no practitioner would disagree that efforts should be made to reduce unit non-response as much as possible, survey design decisions are never made independently of cost concerns. The salient question, then, is how much is it worth to reduce unit non-response? Here, we need to turn to questions of data quality.

Relatively high rates of non-response are potentially problematic to the representativeness of opinion polls. Those individuals who respond to polls are not perfectly representative of the mass public. I discussed above the problems created by the distinctiveness of the cellphone-only population. But similar problems have existed for years in telephone polls and face-to-face polls. In the NES, for example, non-respondents tend to be worse-off financially, are more likely to be black, and are more likely to live in rural areas than those who respond to surveys (Brehm 1993).[5]

These persistent differences have important implications for survey results. Unit non-responses can cause bias in our estimates of quantities of interest. For instance, if

---

[5] An additional problem is that surveys may attract respondents who are not representative of the particular demographic groups to which they belong. Brehm (1993) finds that those who participate in surveys are those who are most interested and most likely to participate in the political world.

respondents and non-respondents differ on particular variables of interest, estimates of the mean of those variables will be biased toward their value among respondents (Dillman, Eltinge, Groves, and Little 2002). Conventional wisdom therefore holds that low response rates are problematic. As Weisberg notes, for many researchers, "A low response rate indicates ... that there may be non-response bias, and that people will be suspicious of the study" (2005, 191). Below, I address various statistical methods to account for survey non-response, such as the weighting methods used to adjust the land-line-only surveys discussed above. But, as the Pew experience in 2008 demonstrates, these methods are not necessarily a replacement for the missing data.

Somewhat surprisingly, however, the bulk of research to date has found that the existence of significant differences between respondents and non-respondents does not seem to undermine the representativeness of polls. Brehm (1993) finds that accounting for non-response does not alter estimates of public opinion on political matters very much. Recent work yields similar conclusions. In 1997 the Pew Research Center conducted a survey experiment to assess the effects of non-response.[6] Two separate samples were drawn for parallel surveys that included the exact same questions. The first "standard" survey was conducted over a five-day period and used polling techniques typical of professional survey houses. The second survey was conducted over eight weeks, which allowed the interviewers to contact highly mobile respondents and convince some reluctant respondents to agree to be interviewed. Although, as expected, the response rates differed greatly across the two samples—42 percent in the standard sample, compared to 71 percent in the extended sample—the picture of the public's will did not differ significantly across the two surveys.[7] The average difference in the aggregate political attitudes of the two groups was just 2.7 percentage points, less than the margin of error of the surveys. Only a handful of questions differed by more than 3 or 4 percentage points. In 2003 Pew replicated this experiment (Keeter, Kennedy, Dimock, et al. 2006). Though, as noted above, overall response rates dropped over the six-year period, the researchers again found few attitudinal differences between respondents in the standard survey and those in the rigorous survey.

Altogether, the work reviewed here seems to provide a reassuring balm for pollsters. While unit non-response should, in theory, prove damaging to the ability of opinion polls to accurately measure the public's will, in practice it appears that the threat may not be serious. However, this work is not the final word on this matter for several reasons. First, there remains the question of what the existing data can tell us. The Pew study compares parallel surveys with response rates of 40 percent to those of 70 percent and finds few differences. It is not clear, though, where the tipping point lies. Is a survey with a 70 percent response rate equivalent to one with an 80 percent response rate? What about a survey with a 100 percent response rate? To draw conclusions from

---

[6] This experiment incorporated the Pew poll described above.

[7] The gain in response rate in the extended sample reflected increases in both contact and cooperation rates.

current research requires us to extrapolate well beyond the range of available data, a strategy that could lead to faulty inferences.

Second, it is not clear that representativeness on quantities we happen to measure is sufficient to ensure poll representativeness. Though respondents and non-respondents seem to hold the same views on many political questions, these two groups might differ in other important ways. For instance, the 2003 Pew survey found that respondents to the standard survey were more likely to vote than respondents in the rigorous survey. Perhaps this difference in political engagement extends to other indicators we do not measure. If these unmeasured quantities affect answers on particular survey questions, opinion polls might lead us astray.

Finally, what is true today may not be true tomorrow. During the 2004 election, pollsters were able to correct the potential bias arising from cellphone households by adjusting their samples through post-stratification weights to reflect the known characteristics of the US population. By 2008, however, this strategy was not able to fully correct for the bias induced by the distinctiveness of respondents who were not reached by land line. The experience with cellphones is important in and of itself, but it also serves as a reminder that today's received wisdom can become tomorrow's problem. Thus, on the question of whether securing a high response rate is a worthy investment, the jury is still out. Researchers should therefore continue to keep a cautious eye on response rates, especially as we move to incorporate cellphones into our sample.

# Item Non-Response

On any survey, some respondents will answer some questions and abstain from others. For instance, not a single respondent to the 2004 NES answered every question on the survey. These instances of item-non response—including "don't know" and "no opinion" responses—have been of interest to social scientists since the early days of opinion polling.

Item non-response has practical implications for the analysis of survey data: how do you analyze data in which, as is typically the case, up to 25 percent of the sample refuses to disclose their income? If you are conducting political polling for a campaign, how do you treat the "undecideds"—those respondents who fail to provide a definitive candidate choice? In this section, I review the causes and consequences of item non-response. I focus primarily on attitudinal questions. However, many of the concerns I identify here also apply to understanding item non-response on factual questions, such as measures of income and reports of church attendance (Tourangeau, Rips, and Rasinski 2000).

## Causes of Item Non-Response

The first factor to consider is the source of "don't know" responses. Just as there are predictable sources of unit non-response that can be found in the characteristics of the interviewer and the interviewed, there are regular determinants of item non-response. These determinants are often divided into three categories: respondent characteristics, questionnaire design issues, and interviewer behavior.

## Respondent Characteristics

One reason that a respondent would choose a "don't know" response is that they possess personal characteristics that lead them to such a response. Various experimental and non-experimental studies have demonstrated that increasing levels of respondent education, respondent exposure to topic-specific information, and interest in the survey topic all reduce "don't know" responses.

## Question Wording

Factors outside the immediate control of the respondent may also affect the probability that they give a "don't know" response. Some topics in the United States, such as reports of income and racial attitudes, engender item non-response because such topics are sensitive and governed by social norms (Berinsky 2004).

Beyond the particular topic of the survey, the specific wording of survey questions may affect rates of item non-response. The survey interview can be a difficult and tedious affair. Given these demands, it might be easier for respondents to "satisfice" (Krosnick 1991), and give a "don't know" response if they have difficulty readily forming a political judgment. This behavior may be exacerbated by the structure of the information conveyed from the interviewer to the respondent. Different surveys use filters of various strengths (Schuman and Presser 1981). The use of a "full filter"—where respondents are first asked if they have an opinion on a particular issue, and are then asked their opinion—or a "quasi-filter"—where the "don't know" option is presented explicitly—may serve as an implicit (if unintentional) signal that the question–answering task ahead of them is especially difficult (Schwarz 1996). The very process of asking the survey question may encourage satisficing behavior.

However, simply because people may satisfice when they answer a survey question with a "no opinion" filter does not mean they are without thought on the question. Hippler and Schwarz (1989) find that those respondents who decline to answer fully filtered questions are willing to provide substantive responses at a more general level of evaluation. In such cases, the decision to give a "don't know" response may be more a function of the specific survey instrument—such as an opinion filter—than of the respondent.

## Interviewer Behavior

Finally, the characteristics of the interviewer may affect the probability of item non-response. Just as some interviewers are more skilled than others in achieving respondent cooperation, some interviewers are especially capable of obtaining answers to specific questions on a given survey. For instance, Singer, Frankel, and Glassman (1983) find that those interviewers who believed it would be easy to administer a questionnaire were more likely to obtain responses to those items than were interviewers who thought it would be difficult to obtain a response.

## The Meaning of "Don't Know" Responses

Given that a variety of factors affect the probability that a respondent will abstain from a given survey question, what meaning should we give to the "don't know" response? Traditionally, scholars and practitioners of survey research have viewed "no opinion" responses as useful devices—a way of preventing non-attitudes (Converse 1964) from contaminating measures of public opinion. However, this view of item non-response proceeds from a particular model of the survey question–answering process as the product of individuals' attempts to reveal their fixed preference on a given policy issue. In this view, people who say "don't know" just do not have an opinion on the matter in question; a "don't know" is simply a "don't know."

In the last twenty years, however, a more fluid view of the survey response has emerged, based in part on theories of preference construction developed in cognitive psychology. This view, advanced most forcibly by Zaller, argues that "individuals do not typically possess 'true attitudes' on issues, as conventional theorizing assumes, but a series of partially independent and often inconsistent ones" (Zaller 1992, 93). According to this line of public opinion research, a survey response is not necessarily a revealed preference. Instead, answers to survey questions are, to use Zaller's (1992) turn of phrase, "opinion statements." They reflect a *sample* of the types of concerns and predispositions people bring to bear when considering issues in the realm of politics. The types of information encountered about politics in daily life, and even the wording of survey questions, can bring about systematic changes in the base of available information. Because different information may be salient at different times, the response obtained from the same person may change from interview to interview.

From this perspective, "don't know" responses are not necessarily an indication that a respondent is devoid of valid information to report on a question. Just as responses obtained from the same person may change from interview to interview, the decision to give a "don't know" response may change as well.

In *Silent Voices* (Berinsky 2004), I present a model of the survey response focused on the potential costs to the individual of answering specific questions. I argue that individuals may come to a "don't know" answer by two very different routes: either after they first attempt to form an opinion about a particular political controversy or when—if successful in coming to a judgment—they then choose the "don't know" category when expressing their answer to the survey interviewer. In the first case, the respondent fails to answer the question because of cognitive costs; in the second case, question abstention results from social costs. But in neither case does a "don't know" response indicate an absence of politically relevant considerations on the part of the respondent. Given a different set of circumstances, the same respondent might express an opinion on the same question.

Given that research has shown that "don't know" responses arise through the interaction of question wording, interviewer behavior, and respondent characteristics, it would be a mistake to attribute "don't know" responses solely to the absence of meaningful political views on the part of the survey respondent. If, as with substantive responses to survey questions, a "don't know" is a probabilistic response—dependent not only on the quality of political thought, but on the personal characteristics of the respondent and the particular circumstances of the interview, as well as other factors that we cannot fully account for—we should not take that "don't know" as the final word on the matter.

Instead, to ensure that all citizens are properly represented in opinion polls, we should incorporate information from the respondent's answers to other questions on the survey. In this way, we can come to a more complete picture of their politically relevant wants, needs, and desires. I take this position not because the decision to abstain from a survey question indicates that the respondent is consciously aware of a formed political judgment that she reserves from the interviewer. Indeed, sometimes a "don't know" response is just that: the absence of opinion. But the decision to abstain from a survey question does not mean that the respondent is devoid of politically relevant predilections. With the aid of theory and a close examination of the data—using the statistical techniques discussed in the next section—we can learn much about the political predilections of the "silent voices."

## TREATMENT OF NON-RESPONSE

Given that unit and item non-response is a fact of life for survey researchers, how should we analyze our incomplete data? The simplest way is to ignore the problem and analyze the available data. This procedure, known as "listwise deletion" of missing data, is the norm in social science analysis. While listwise deletion may be satisfactory with small amounts of missing data, under certain circumstances, as Little and Rubin (2002) note, listwise deletion of missing data can lead to serious biases.

To avoid such biases, a number of procedures have been developed to account for missing data. All methods for accounting for either item or unit non-response are by necessity model-based. As Lohr notes, "If we are to make any inference about the non-respondents, we must assume that they are related to the respondents in some way" (1999, 254). Sometimes this model is informal. For instance, many pollsters assume that voters who fail to give a candidate preference in reelection polls—the undecided voters—will break strongly against the reelection of incumbent politicians. Blumenthal (2004) terms this theory the "incumbent rule." Elections featuring an incumbent are seen as a referendum. Voters first decide if they want to fire the politician in office; only then do they decide if they wish to support the challenger. Several pollsters, in making their election night projections in 2004, followed this rule. Gallup, for instance, allocated the 3 percent of respondents who were undecided by increasing John Kerry's share by 2 percent and Ralph Nader's share by 1 percent, leading to a projected tie between Kerry and George W. Bush (Newport and Moore 2004). Only after election night was it clear that this implicit model was factually incorrect. In 2008 the picture was even more muddled as pollsters were concerned about the possibility of a "Bradley effect," where respondents who supported the white candidate would declare themselves undecided rather than voice opposition to the black candidate (Hopkins 2009).

These informal models only get us so far and, as the 2004 election example shows, they can seriously mislead us in some cases. Statisticians have developed a number of more formal methods for dealing with missing data. I first discuss those that account for unit non-response, then those that account for item non-response.

## Unit Non-Response

The statistical treatment of unit non-response depends on the availability of information. When researchers have a theory of the patterns of missing data *and* detailed information about the characteristics of non-respondents, they can employ model-based approaches, such as selection bias techniques, to account for the differences between the sample and the population. A prominent example of this research strategy in political science is Brehm's (1993) study of "phantom respondents." Brehm takes advantage of information collected in certain academic surveys about potential respondents who could not or would not be interviewed (such as the non-respondent's age, race, sex, approximate income, and the accessibility of their housing unit). With this information, he jointly models the decision to participate in a survey and the decision to engage in particular politically relevant behaviors, such as turning out in an election.

Brehm finds that in some cases the correlates of political behavior can change once we account for non-respondents. He finds, for example, that the relationship between education and turnout increases once we bring survey non-respondents into our analysis. In other cases, Brehm finds that estimates of the determinants of political behavior are unchanged. For instance, the demographic correlates of income, such as education, race, and gender, are unaffected. But these results do not give researchers license to ignore unit non-response. As Brehm notes, even though many models of individual behavior were changed only slightly with the introduction of information concerning non-respondents, there are times when non-response can greatly affect these models. Without accounting for non-response in our analyses, we will never know how biased our results might be.

Brehm's methods require rich information about non-respondents. Most times, however, we only have limited information about the population relative to the sample in the form of auxiliary information taken from the census. In these cases, weighting adjustments are typically applied to reduce the bias in survey estimates that non-response can cause (Lohr 1999). Though the use of weights to adjust for non-response is common, there is controversy about the best way to implement weighting

(Bethlehem 2002; Little 1993; Lohr 1999). One approach commonly used is raking. Raking matches cell counts to the marginal distributions of the variables used in the weighting scheme. It allows for many weighting variables to be included, an important concern for researchers and practitioners, who typically use raking to adjust samples on seven or more variables. However, it ignores information available in the joint distribution of the weighting variables. Other techniques, such as regression weighting and propensity score weighting, take advantage of this information. Lohr (1999) provides a useful overview of these different weighting methods.

## Item Non-Response

Statistical techniques can also be used to account for item non-response. If a researcher has a particular theory about the process by which individuals decide whether to answer particular survey questions, she can use an application-specific approach to model the missing data, such as the selection model that Brehm used. In my study of racial attitudes (Berinsky 1999, 2002, 2004) I used a selection model to estimate the effect of missing data on the correlates and point estimates of such attitudes. My analysis reveals that public opinion polls overstate support for government efforts to integrate schools and guarantee fair employment. Specifically, selection bias models reveal that some individuals who harbor anti-integrationist sentiments hide their socially unacceptable opinions behind a "don't know" response.

In the absence of a specific theory about particular patterns of missing data, a common solution to the problem of item non-response is imputation. Essentially imputation procedures involve using various methods to estimate a value for the missing data. With the missing values "filled in" researchers can then proceed to analyze the complete data matrix using standard methods of data analysis. Weisberg (2005) provides a detailed overview of various imputation techniques, which have become increasingly sophisticated in recent years.

## FUTURE RESEARCH

The last twenty years have seen an explosion in the study of survey non-response. Researchers have investigated the causes of unit and item non-response and have developed new ways to explore the meaning of missing data. Statisticians and applied researchers are developing and employing increasingly sophisticated methods to analyze missing data.

Though we have learned a great deal about survey non-response, there is much work to be done. To date, there has been a large divide in the study of non-response. Scholars study unit non-response and item non-response in isolation, but rarely consider the links between the two processes. However, as the work reviewed in this chapter demonstrates, similar factors—such as respondent characteristics and interviewer behavior—affect both unit non-response rates *and* item non-response rates. Furthermore, similar model-based approaches have been applied to fix the problems caused by both types of non-response. To fully consider questions of representativeness, scholars should consider these two forms of non-response together. With a common theoretic perspective on *survey* non-response, we can better understand the meaning and consequences of missing data on surveys.

Researchers should also consider new ways to draw reliable samples for surveys. As telephone interviewing becomes more difficult, scholars should further explore new methods, such as address-based sampling. The development of large computerized databases has greatly increased the coverage of households in the United States. These databases may allow researchers to draw inexpensive mail-based random samples (Link et al. 2008). Furthermore, Internet sampling, though difficult, may eventually yield reliable samples for researchers. Finally, the use of multiple modes of contact— mail, phone, and Internet—may also increase sample representativeness (Rookey, Hanway, and Dillman 2008). Each of these new technologies comes with potential drawbacks—mail surveys, for instance, take much longer to deploy and field than telephone surveys—but the potential payoffs are such that we should leave no stone unturned.

The need for a critical eye is clear. Survey non-response threatens the very foundation of the survey research enterprise. Over the course of the twentieth century, polls have emerged as an important tool to measure the public will. Surveys have become a major component of political reporting, and politicians are willing to expend large sums to conduct surveys. More importantly for present purposes, they seem to ensure that the full spectrum of political interests in the political system is heard. The reason is straightforward: surveys, if executed correctly, are conducted through random sampling. Under this system, every citizen has an equal chance of being selected for a poll, regardless of his or her personal circumstance. Furthermore, by underwriting the direct costs of participation, opinion polls ensure that disparities in politically relevant resources will not discourage the expression of politically relevant values and interests. Survey organizations, after all, contact respondents, not the other way around. In short, polls hold special appeal as a form of gaging the public's will because they appear to be free of the resource-based bias that plagues traditional forms of participation. But these attractive properties are based on representative sampling. If the representative properties of sampling are undermined by non-response, polls lose both their appeal and their purpose.

That the search for problematic results has come up empty—as it has in the Pew non-response studies—may be reassuring, but it is not a balm. The example of the *Literary Digest* debacle of 1936 stands as a warning. Before famously and disastrously picking Alf Landon to beat incumbent president Franklin D. Roosevelt in a landslide in 1936, the *Literary Digest* had correctly picked the winner in every presidential contest from 1916 to 1932 using the same flawed methods it employed in 1936. Today, as in the 1930s, we may not know that non-response is a problem until something goes spectacularly wrong with our polls.

....................................................................................

# CHAPTER 22

# INSTRUMENT DESIGN

## *Question Form, Wording, and Context Effects*

....................................................................................

GEORGE FRANKLIN BISHOP

As V. O. Key (1961) once quipped, "To speak with precision of public opinion is a task not unlike coming to grips with the Holy Ghost." Deciphering the meaning of American public opinion polls does not come easy. As any seasoned investigator knows, understanding the nature, meaning, and import of public opinion in American politics and the mass media depends upon a firm grasp of how the wording, framing, and sequencing of questions and response alternatives can affect the results of any given survey. But the art of asking survey questions has advanced considerably since the pioneering days of public opinion polling—so much so that modern scholars now feel quite comfortable in talking about the "science" of asking questions (Schaeffer and Presser 2003). The ever growing literature on question-and-response effects, however, has made the task of synthesis so much more challenging today (Schwarz, Groves, and Sudman 1998). There are lots of question design effects that have been empirically demonstrated and partially explained. But we have miles and miles to go yet in developing broad theoretical principles to tell us when such effects are likely to occur, with what magnitude, and under what conditions, so that we can know, ultimately, how to design our survey instruments to minimize and control such measurement errors as part of a "total survey error" approach to the science of survey research (Weisberg 2005). Survey rocket science does not come easy, however.

"Don't trust the 'marginals' in any absolute sense," Howard Schuman (2008, ch. 1) has repeatedly reminded us. The results of public opinion surveys do not tell us in any absolute sense about the "reality" of what the public thinks about this or that topic (Bishop 2005a; Moore 2008). What the public appears to think is very often, if not always, a function of the way in which the question is worded, the format in which it is presented, and the order and context in which the question and the response alternatives themselves are presented. As both Schuman and I would contend, the "referendum point of view"—taking univariate percentages in public opinion media polls literally—should be avoided by all, especially by those of us who are capable of designing better analytic controls to cope with the inherent ambiguity of interpreting the results of survey questions. Schuman warns us against both this "survey fundamentalism" and the equally naive belief of "survey cynicism": that no poll results can ever be trusted because they are so easily manipulated by the way in which the questions can be asked. Question "bias" is an easy charge to make and is often, like "artifacts," in the mind of the beholder.

So what do we know about question design effects, how they occur, and how they can be dealt with? Not all effects are alike. Following Schuman and Presser's typology (1981, ch. 1), I look first at question design effects on respondents' subjective judgments, attitudes, and opinions, resulting from the *form* in which the question is posed: open-ended versus closed; the presence or absence in the question of an explicit "no opinion" response category; the inclusion or omission of a "middle response alternative"; the balance or imbalance of a question, with or without a counterargument; and the perennial problem of "acquiescence bias" arising from the use and misuse of the agree-disagree response format in survey research. (See Schaeffer and Presser 2003, for a review of response effects with "factual" questions; on mode of data collection effects and their implications for instrument design, see Dillman, Smyth, and Christian 2009; also see Pasek and Krosnick 2010, on cognitive-psychological insights in instrument design for rating versus ranking scales, number of rating scale points, acquiescence response bias, social desirability attitude recall, and the dangers of asking "why.") Next, I look at how the actual *wording and content* of survey questions alters the conclusions a researcher would draw about public opinion. I then focus on how the *order and context* in which both the questions and the response alternatives themselves are presented can impact the results. Finally, I consider how question design effects of all kinds can be understood, parsimoniously, as part of a more general cognitive-psychological model of the question–answer process, and ponder the implications for the future of instrument design.

One way to get some purchase on the issue is to think of question-and-response effects as an often unintended consequence of a series of decisions that must be made in designing a survey instrument. The most fundamental of these is to decide, first, the generic form in which to pose the questions—open or closed—a decision that can produce all sorts of unintended consequences.

# QUESTION FORM EFFECTS

## Preclusion Effects of Open-and-Closed Questions

It goes nearly without saying that each of our fundamental ways of asking a survey question—open or closed—has its distinct advantages and limitations (Bradburn, Sudman, and Wansink 2004, ch. 5). Each form, as Schuman (2008, ch. 2) explains, implies a frame of reference, however subtle, that constrains the answers respondents think they can or should offer. Closed-ended questions do so more obviously by implying that respondents should essentially limit their answers to the categories explicitly presented to them, even if an "other" alternative is offered. Open-ended questions do it in a more subtle manner by suggesting a narrower, or "legitimate," frame of reference. A good example of an *open-question preclusion effect* emerged in an innovative experiment by Schuman and Presser (1981, ch. 3) with a frequently asked open-ended question in public opinion polls about the "most important problem facing the country." The problem of "crime and violence" was volunteered a lot less often, spontaneously, on the open-ended form of the question than when it was offered explicitly to respondents on the closed form. In this case, as Schuman (2008, ch. 2) keenly observed, the closed form of the question legitimized "crime and violence," which is typically viewed as more of a local, than a national, problem, whereas the open form subtly precluded it by implying that a national frame of reference is appropriate when thinking about problems "facing the country."

The preclusion effects of closed questions can be even more powerful. One profound illustration turned up in a series of experiments by Schuman and Scott (1987), in which respondents receiving the closed-ended form of the question were offered a list of four problems that were rarely mentioned (by less than 1 percent of the American public) in a prior Gallup poll as an answer to the standard open question about "the most important problem facing the country today." Though respondents receiving the closed form were told explicitly that they could name a problem other than the four "rare" ones that were presented to them, they typically did not (39 percent). Instead, the great majority (60 percent) selected one of the four extremely rare categories as "the most important problem facing the country." In contrast, just 3 percent of the respondents administered the open-ended form of the question and volunteered any such rare problems. Such is the constraining influence of closed-question forms.

And that's not all of it. Schuman and his colleagues (Schuman and Presser 1981, ch. 3; Schuman and Scott 1987, 1989) have also demonstrated significant open- and closed-question preclusion effects on such varied topics as respondents' apparent awareness of food and energy shortages during the winter of 1977; on what respondents think are the most important things to look for in a job; on what they believe are the most important values children should learn to prepare for life; and on what Americans appear to remember as the most important national or world events and changes since 1930. Using an open or closed form, however, does not invariably produce a preclusion effect. Nor have independent investigators necessarily agreed on the existence of such effects.

A case in point: the 2004 presidential election. According to polling analysts Langer and Cohen (2005), the apparent importance of "moral values" as a decisive issue in the Bush–Kerry contest was largely an artifact of a closed-ended question used in national exit polls. A post-election experiment by the Pew Research Center for the People & the Press (2004) appeared to confirm the question artifact hypothesis. But Schuman (2008, 47–54) disputed this conclusion with his own independent analysis of the same data. Whereas Bishop (2005b) finds for the defendants of the *artifact hypothesis* that the "moral values" factor in the 2004 presidential election was indeed an illusion, just like the "family values" illusion in the 1992 national election exit polls, so in this instance, causal explanations themselves become a function of how the questions are structured. Ditto for the most plausible mechanisms explaining how open- and closed-question effects occur: by the "availability" heuristic in responses to open questions, by "response constraint" in closed-ended items, and/or by the implied "frame of reference" in both such forms—another reminder of the inseparability of instrument and inference. Heisenbergian epistemologists would say as well that the presence or absence of "public opinion" does not exist apart from the measurement act of fixing it in place by asking a question: particle and wave, opinion and "no opinion."

## Effects of Offering "Don't Know" or "No Opinion"

Public opinion researchers often struggle with whether to offer respondents an explicit category that allows them to say they have "no opinion," that they're "not sure," or just "don't know" enough yet to have an opinion on a topic. Survey organizations that include such options as a standard practice have done so because of a long-standing concern about the existence of what Converse (1964, 1970) called "nonattitudes." Screening out respondents with "nonattitudes" should presumably improve the quality of measurement and minimize unintended consequences for the distribution of responses to a question and its relationship to other items. But the verdict of the literature on the response effects of offering a "don't know" or "no opinion" alternative depends upon the focus of the research. Randomized controlled experiments have certainly demonstrated that offering respondents an explicit opportunity to select a "don't know" or "no opinion" response— either as part of a list of response alternatives or in the form of a preceding filter question (e.g., "Have you heard or read anything about this?") can significantly increase the percentage of "don't know" responses over what would normally be volunteered on the standard ("volunteered" "don't know") form of the question (Schuman and Presser 1981, ch. 4). The magnitude of the incremental effect on "don't know" proportions can vary considerably, from 5 percent to as much as 47 percent, depending on the content and familiarity of the issue and how strongly the filter or "don't know" alternative is worded. So this generic *"don't know" increment effect* has been well demonstrated.

But there are other effects to worry about. When such "don't know" responses are routinely excluded from analysis, does it change the substantive conclusions about the distribution of responses on a given issue and how the responses are related to responses on other issues and to demographic characteristics such as education? The evidence is decidedly mixed. Schuman and Presser's (1981, ch. 4) experiments indicate that the univariate distributions of responses are generally unaffected (filtered versus volunteered "don't knows"), once the "don't know" responses are omitted. In other words, researchers would reach the same substantive conclusion about public opinion toward an issue regardless of question form. Bishop, Oldendick, and Tuchfarber (1983), however, found that the use of a "don't know" filter question could make a significant difference in conclusions about public opinion toward the role of the government versus the private sector in solving national problems; federal tax cut policy; and whether respondents favored or opposed the Strategic Arms Limitation Talks between the United States and the Soviet Union. So the presence or absence of these effects may depend heavily on the content of the issue and its familiarity to respondents. The less familiar and more complex an issue, the greater may be the effect of a "don't know" option.

Bivariate or multivariate response effects are even more difficult to pin down. Schuman and Presser's experiments suggest that, in most cases, the use of a "don't know" filtered form does not significantly change the magnitude of association between attitude items or between attitude items and demographics. They did, however, uncover some important exceptions, in which responses about intentions of "the Russian leaders" toward America and intentions of Arab nations with regard to Israel were strongly correlated for the standard (unfiltered) form of the question, but completely unrelated, statistically, when "don't knows" were filtered (Schuman and Presser 1981, ch. 4). There was also evidence of the opposite pattern: the association between attitude items was substantially larger for the filtered than the standard unfiltered form, as Converse's non-attitudes thesis predicted. Each of these patterns of effects uncovered by Schuman and Presser also interacted in complex and unpredictable ways with characteristics such as education, attitude strength, and a respondent's "propensity" to offer "don't know" responses. Moreover, it has been difficult to replicate such complex effects. There are therefore no easy empirical generalizations about the expected bivariate and multivariate response effects of questions with and without explicit "don't knows."

That's just part of the problem. There is growing evidence that the use of filter questions, especially strongly worded ones like those used in the American National Election Studies (e.g., "... or haven't you thought much about this?"), may discourage respondents from offering opinions that they actually do have (Schwarz 1996, ch. 5). More convincingly, experiments by Krosnick et al. (2002) have demonstrated that including a "no opinion" option encourages many respondents to "satisfice" and avoid the cognitive effort necessary to report the opinions they have; that, contrary to predictions derived from the non-attitudes thesis, eliminating a "no opinion" option from the response alternatives does not diminish the quality of the data; and that including an explicit "don't know" response alternative may, in fact, reduce empirical validity.

Krosnick et al.'s argument for omitting a "don't know" or "no opinion" option in the case of questions about fictitious or obscure issues, however, is much less convincing. Respondents can use cues from almost any part of a question or the context in which it is asked to impute a meaning—however irrelevant to the specific substance of the question—to manufacture an opinion "on the spot" about that psychological object based on some prior general attitudinal disposition. But it's not that clear whether "no opinion" response effects, non-attitudes, and the "measurement error" they generate represent mostly respondent error, instrument error, or both, as Converse (1970) observed. With this state of disarray, some might say that perhaps "deliberative polling" is the answer to this problem of non-attitudes (Fishkin 1995). But, as with other response options, it's just not that simple.

## Effects of Offering a "Middle" Response

When designing survey questions with contrasting arguments or polar positions, researchers frequently have to decide about a middle response alternative, neutral position, or mid-point on a scale, explicitly labeled or not. Many prefer to omit such a category, forcing respondents to choose one side of the issue; they believe that most people lean one way or another on most topics. Others argue that respondents with middle, ambivalent, indifferent, or neutral positions should not be forced to express opinions. For example, those who know little or nothing about a topic—therefore having "no opinion" on the specifics of an issue—may select a middle response alternative if one is explicitly offered to them and thereby create some unknown random or systematic error. Much like the potential consequences of offering a "don't know" or "no opinion" alternative, there are unintended consequences to ponder: does including a middle alternative make a significant difference in the conclusions reached about the nature of opinion on a given topic? As with other response effects, it often depends on the research question posed and on the content of the questions themselves. Offering respondents a middle option certainly has a pronounced effect on the distribution of responses on a particular topic. One Gallup poll (July 11–13, 2009), for example, found that just 32 percent of Americans thought the economy was "getting better"; 62 percent felt it was "getting worse"; and only a very small number (5 percent) volunteered that it was about "the same" (Gallup 2009).

In contrast, a CBS News/New York Times poll conducted at the same time (July 9–12, 2009) asked a similar question, with an explicit middle category. Here, however, a plurality (45 percent) believed that the economy was about the "same" (versus 5 percent in the

1992). But when presented in a visual format, as in a self-administered mail question-naire or a Web-based survey, or in a face-to-face interview using a "show card," primacy effects are generally the rule.

Even more subtle "contrast effects" can arise from an extreme anchoring stimulus in a list of response alternatives, such as a highly liked or disliked politician presented at the beginning or in the middle of a list of other political figures (Sudman, Bradburn, and Schwarz 1996, 150–3). Such contrast effects also emerge if the extreme stimulus is part of a preceding question that taps into the same underlying dimension of judgment: a possible joint question and response order effect. That is one more complexity to contend with in designing the order of questions and response alternatives.

Explaining these complex effects is challenging. Various investigators have theorized that response order effects are a function of (1) the length and complexity of survey questions—with lengthy, complex, difficult questions more likely to produce recency effects (Rugg and Cantril 1944, ch. 2; Moore and Newport 1996); (2) "uncrystallized" attitudes or opinions (McClendon 1986); and (3) memory limitations (Knauper 1999). But meta-analyses of numerous response order experiments dating back to the 1930s have provided little or no evidence for either the opinion crystallization hypothesis or its companion, the question complexity hypothesis (Bishop 1990; Krosnick and Schuman 1988). Support for the memory limitations hypothesis has been somewhat more mixed. A systematic review of the literature by Sudman, Bradburn, and Schwarz (1996, 136–7) suggests that "despite popular assumptions, sheer memory limitations are *not* the primary source of response-order effects in survey measurement." Only when response alternatives are numerous or complex and presented without visual aids are memory limitations likely to be a significant factor in generating these effects. Knauper's (1999) reanalysis of previous response order experiments by Schu-man and Presser, however, indicates that memory limitations play a major role in creating primacy and recency effects among older respondents (age 65+), for whom "working memory resources" are weaker. Individual differences in memory capacities may thus act as a moderator variable in the emergence of response order effects.

Models of the cognitive processes have done much to move beyond these more conventional accounts. Schwarz and his colleagues (Schwarz and Sudman 1992; Sud-man, Bradburn, and Schwarz 1996, ch. 6) developed a *cognitive elaboration model*, which postulates that the key mediating process underlying response order effects is the opportunity respondents have to think (elaborate) about the implications and plausi-bility of the response alternatives presented to them. Other things being equal, the cognitive elaboration model predicts largely primacy effects in visual presentation formats and mostly recency effects in auditory formats. Evidence from secondary analyses of many response order experiments (Schwarz, Hippler, and Noelle-Neumann 1992) would appear to support the cognitive elaboration model. But an extensive meta-analysis by Bishop and Smith (2001) of over 200 previous experiments conducted by the Gallup Organization in the 1930s, 1940s, and early 1950s showed that, while recency effects were more likely to occur when questions—especially longer ones—were asked in an auditory mode, the expected pattern of primacy effects with longer questions presented in a visual mode not only did not materialize; they tended to run in the opposite direction, with recency effects predominating. Though not without methodological confounds and complexities in such meta-analyses, these and other exceptions to the predictions derived from the cognitive elaboration model make it difficult to develop firm empirical generalizations about the magnitude and pattern of response order effects in large-scale national surveys, especially in an age of mixed-mode designs.

Even the more promising cognitive "satisficing" model of the survey response (Krosnick, Narayan, and Smith 1996) leaves the typical investigator without a firm sense of what types and magnitude of effects are to be expected under what conditions. Such effects are said to arise because of the tendency toward "weak satisficing" that leads respondents with more limited cognitive abilities to select the first acceptable response alternative presented to them: typically the first or second in a list administered visually; the last in a set of alternatives presented orally (Krosnick 1999, 549–52). Similarly, with choices offered in a rating-scale format, which is typically visual, primacy effects predominate presumably because of the same tendencies of weak satisficing. But such patterns, particularly for categorical questions presented in a visual format, do not invariably appear (Bishop and Smith 2001). So a simple "weak satisficing" explanation will not suffice without accounting for other moderating variables such as question length, comprehension difficulty, location within the questionnaire, linguistic complexity, and survey mode. But when, where, and with what magnitudes are such effects likely to occur? Many more complex, factorial designs are needed to sort all this out over the next generation of survey methodologists. The same applies to the most vexing effect: the influence of question order and context.

## QUESTION ORDER AND CONTEXT EFFECTS

That the response to one question can affect another is something we have long known. In the late 1930s Gallup had already begun to experiment with the order of questions about the acceptability of American citizens joining either the German or the British and French armies; involvement of the United States in the Second World War; and changing the draft age, each of which generated significant effects. Hyman and Sheatsley's (1950) classic experiment sequencing questions about letting communist and American reporters into each other's countries to "send back . . . the news as they see it" produced sizable effects that have since been replicated (Schuman and Presser 1981, ch. 2) and have also been found by Bishop, Hippler, Schwarz, and Strack (1988) and Schuman and Ludwig (1983) for questions on American–Japanese or German–Japanese trade relations. Further experiments likewise produced order and context effects on topics such as abortion rights (Schuman and Presser 1981, ch. 2); interest in politics and public affairs (Bishop 1987b); confidence in national institutions (Smith 1981); feelings of citizen duty (Abramson, Silver, and Anderson 1987); presidential and gubernatorial approval ratings (Alspach and Bishop 1991); candidate and political party preferences (Crespi and Morris 1984; Willick and Ashley 1971); racial attitudes (Schuman, Steeh, and Bobo 1985); and tax, spending, and welfare policies (Smith 1992). So we have additional empirical demonstrations of other order effects in public opinion surveys. But how well do we understand—and can we predict—their occurrence and magnitude, and under what conditions?

Relative to what we know about other response effects (e.g., question wording) we have seen significant conceptual and theoretical progress on context effects. Useful typologies for classifying different types of relations among questions, order effects, and conditions under which order effects emerge have been constructed (Schuman and Presser 1981, ch. 2; Smith 1992). Models of the cognitive-psychological processes underlying question order and context effects have also been developed and empirically tested by Sudman, Bradburn, and Schwarz (1996, chs. 4–5) and by Tourangeau, Rips, and Rasinski (2000, ch. 7). At the same time, qualitatively different types of context effects have been explained in different ways (e.g., assimilation and contrast effects, carry-over effects, conditional order effects), but none have been clearly and empirically generalized to the other. Indeed, one gets the impression that this theoretical state of affairs characterizes the entire literature on question-and-response effects in surveys: different types of effects with many types of explanations, some of which tend to cohere, but much of which does not. Qualitatively different phenomena may require qualitatively different theoretical accounts; yet we yearn for a more parsimonious account.

# Models and Theories of Survey Question Effects

A number of competing models of the question-and-answer process have emerged over the past decades, most inspired by the cognitive-psychological movement in survey research (Hippler, Schwarz, and Sudman 1987). Indeed, we have a variety of rival approaches to understanding the question-and-answer process: multistage cognitive process models (Sudman, Bradburn, and Schwarz 1996, ch. 3; Tourangeau, Rips, and Rasinski 2000, chs. 1–2); a cognitive "satisficing" model (Krosnick, Narayan, and Smith 1996); a question constraint and response–persuasion approach (Schuman and Presser 1981, ch. 12); a cognitive, logic-of-conversation perspective (Schwarz 1996); an axiomatic "considerations" model (Zaller and Feldman 1992); and a rival question ambiguity model (Bishop 2005a, ch. 6). All of these focus primarily on how individuals interpret, process, and format responses to survey questions.

The predominant consensus on the psychology of the survey response today assumes that answering questions involves distinct stages: (1) initial *comprehension*, in which the respondent first interprets the literal or semantic meaning of the question as well as its pragmatic one—i.e., inferences about the questioner's intentions; followed by (2) *retrieval,* in which the respondent accesses information from memory that is relevant to answering the question; (3) *judgment,* which utilizes information from the retrieval stage to construct an opinion or judgment required by the question; and (4) *response mapping,* in which the respondent fits his or her judgment or opinion into one or more of the categories provided by the question, with perhaps editing for self-presentation, depending on the sensitivity or social desirability of the question's content (Tourangeau, Rips, and Rasinski 2000, chs. 1–2). Plausible and useful as these cognitive models have been in providing a framework for understanding *how* respondents answer survey questions, they risk neglecting other important sources of causal variation in behavior, such as the influence of the interaction between interviewer and respondent (Schuman 2008). Such largely descriptive process models may also mislead investigators into believing they have causally explained a respondent's answering behavior. What we have now is useful, rival frameworks for understanding response effects in surveys rather than full theoretical systems for explanation and prediction. The latter, like other theories of subjective, psychological phenomena, may take generations to achieve and may well require a big assist from theoretical advances and instrumentation in the neurosciences.

# CONCLUSION AND THE FUTURE
# OF INSTRUMENT DESIGN

At this stage of development, parsimonious principles and guidance for designing survey questions are not readily available in the response effects literature. This does not mean that there are not excellent sources on question design, but rather that the often inconclusive literature leaves investigators up in the air as what to expect in the way of response effects in designing a given set of questions and how to proceed given so many complex findings on the effects of question forms, wording, order, and context. Readers digesting this review might conclude that the survey instrument suffers from so many uncertainties that one should find another way to study public opinion. That cynical reaction fails to recognize that survey researchers have increasingly come to grips with such measurement complexities in a way that allows them still to arrive at reasonably valid conclusions about aggregate-level trends in public opinion (Erikson, MacKuen, and Stimson 2002; Page and Shapiro 1992; Stimson 2004). It fails as well to comprehend Schuman's keen insight that "artifacts are in the mind of the beholder" (2008, ch. 4) and this skeptical critic's claim that, despite all these problems, there are ways to measure public opinion that can produce more than just an illusion.

Looking ahead, researchers will increasingly rely upon cognitive interviewing and other state of the art methods for pre-testing and evaluating survey questions (Presser et al. 2004; Willis 2005). Schuman (2008) has made a good case for including

KALTON, G., ROBERTS, J., and HOLT, D. T. 1980. The Effects of Offering Middle Response Option with Opinion Questions. *Journal of the Royal Statistical Society*, ser. D, 29: 65–78.

KEY, V. O., JR. 1961. *Public Opinion and American Democracy*. New York: Knopf.

KNAUPER, B. 1999. Age Differences in Question and Response Order Effects. In *Cognition, Aging, and Self-Reports*, ed. N. Schwarz, D. Park, B. Knauper, and S. Sudman. Philadelphia: Psychology Press.

KROSNICK, J. A. 1999. Survey Research. *Annual Review of Psychology*, 50: 537–67.

—— and BERENT, M. K. 1993. Comparisons of Party Identification and Policy Preferences. *American Journal of Political Science*, 37: 941–64.

—— and SCHUMAN, H. 1988. Attitude Intensity, Importance, and Certainty, and Susceptibility to Response Effects. *Journal of Personality and Social Psychology*, 54: 940–52.

——HOLBROOK, A. L., BERENT, M. K., CARSON, R. T., HANEMANN, W. M., KOPP, R. J., MITCHELL, R. C., PRESSER, S., RUUD, P. A., SMITH, V. K., MOODY, W. R., GREEN, M. C., and CONAWAY, M. 2002. The Impact of No Opinion Response Options on Data Quality. *Public Opinion Quarterly*, 66: 371–403.

—— NARAYAN, S., and SMITH, W. R. 1996. Satisficing in Surveys. In *Advances in Survey Research*, ed. M. T. Braverman and J. K. Slater. San Francisco: Jossey-Bass.

LANGER, G., and COHEN, J. 2005. Voters and Values in the 2004 Election. *Public Opinion Quarterly*, 69: 744–59.

McCLENDON, M. J. 1986. Unanticipated Effects of No Opinion Filters on Attitudes and Attitude Strength. *Sociological Perspectives*, 29: 379–95.

MacKUEN, M. B., ERIKSON, R. S., STIMSON, J. A., ABRAMSON, P. R., and OSTROM, C. W., JR. 1992. Question Wording and Macropartisanship. *American Political Science Review*, 86: 475–86.

MOORE, D. W. 2008. *The Opinion Makers*. Boston: Beacon Press.

MOORE, D. W., and NEWPORT, F. 1996. Public Policy Questions and Response Order: Prevalence of the Recency Effect. Presented at the Annual Meeting of the American Association for Public Opinion Research. Salt Lake City.

NIE, N. H., VERBA, S., and PETROCIK, J. R. 1979. *The Changing American Voter*. Cambridge, MA: Cambridge University Press.

NOELLE-NEUMANN, E. 1970. Wanted: Rules for Wording Structured Questionnaires. *Public Opinion Quarterly*, 34: 191–201.

PAGE, B. I., and SHAPIRO, R. Y. 1992. *The Rational Public*. Chicago: University of Chicago Press.

PASEK, J., and KROSNICK, J. A. 2010. Optimizing Survey Questionnaire Design in Political Science: Insights from Psychology. In *The Oxford Handbook of American Elections and Political Behavior*, ed. J. E. Leighley. New York: Oxford University Press.

PAYNE, S. 1951. *The Art of Asking Questions*. Princeton: Princeton University Press.

Pew Research Center for the People & the Press. 2004. Voters Liked Campaign 2004, But Too Much "Mud-Slinging." At <http://people-press.org/report/233/voters-liked-campaign-2004-but-too-much-mud-slinging>. Accessed Oct. 2010.

PRESSER, S., ROTHGER, J. M., COUPER, M. P., LESSLER, J. T., MARTIN, E., MARTIN, J., and SINGER, E. (eds.) 2004. *Methods for Testing and Evaluating Survey Questionnaires*. Hoboken, NJ: Wiley.

RASINSKI, K. A. 1989. The Effects of Question Wording on Public Support for Government Spending. *Public Opinion Quarterly*, 53: 388–94.

RUGG, D., and CANTRIL, H. 1944. The Wording of Questions. In *Gauging Public Opinion*, ed. H. Cantril et al. Princeton: Princeton University Press.

SCHAEFFER, N. C., and PRESSER, S. 2003. The Science of Asking Questions. *Annual Review of Sociology*, 29: 65–88.

SCHUMAN, H. 2008. *Method and Meaning in Polls and Surveys*. Cambridge, MA: Harvard University Press.

—— and HATCHETT, S. 1974. *Black Racial Attitudes: Trends and Complexities*. Ann Arbor: Institute for Social Research.

—— and KALTON, G. 1985. Survey Methods. In *Handbook of Social Psychology*, i, ed. G. Lindzey and E. Aronson. New York: Random House.

—— and LUDWIG, 1983. The Norm of Even-Handedness in Surveys as in Life. *American Sociological Review*, 48: 112–20.

—— and PRESSER, S. 1981. *Questions and Answers in Attitude Surveys*. New York: Academic Press.

—— and SCOTT, J. 1987. Problems in the Use of Survey Questions to Measure Public Opinion. *Science*, 236: 957–9.

—— —— 1989. Generations and Collective Memories. *American Sociological Review*, 54: 359–81.

—— KALTON, G., and LUDWIG, J. 1983. Context and Contiguity in Survey Questionnaires. *Public Opinion Quarterly*, 47: 112–15.

—— STEEH, C., and BOBO, L. 1985. *Racial Attitudes in America*. Cambridge, MA: Harvard University Press.

SCHWARZ, N. 1996. *Cognition and Communication*. Mahwah, NJ: Lawrence Erlbaum.

—— and SUDMAN, S. 1992. *Context Effects in Social and Psychological Research*. New York: Springer-Verlag.

—— GROVES, R. M., and SCHUMAN, H. 1998. Survey Methods. In *The Handbook of Social Psychology*, ed. D. T. Gilbert, S. T. Fiske, and G. Lindzey, 4th edn. New York: McGraw-Hill.

—— HIPPLER, H.-J., and NOELLE-NEUMANN, E. 1992. A Cognitive Model of Response-Order Effects in Survey Measurement. In *Context Effects in Survey Measurement*, ed. N. Schwarz and S. Sudman. New York: Springer-Verlag.

SMITH, T. W. 1981. Can We Have Confidence in Confidence? Revisited. In *Measurement of Subjective Phenomena*, ed. D. F. Johnston. Washington, DC: US Government Printing Office.

—— 1987. That Which We Call Welfare by Any Other Name Would Smell Sweeter. *Public Opinion Quarterly*, 51: 75–83.

—— 1992. Thoughts on the Nature of Context Effects. In *Social Information Processing and Survey Methodology*, ed. H.-J. Hippler, N. Schwarz, and S. Sudman. New York: Springer-Verlag.

—— 1995. A Review: The Holocaust Denial Controversy. *Public Opinion Quarterly*, 59: 269–95.

STIMSON, J. A. 2004. *Tides of Consent*. Cambridge: Cambridge University Press.

SUDMAN, S., BRADBURN, N. M., and SCHWARZ, N. 1996. *Thinking about Answers*. San Francisco: Jossey-Bass.

SULLIVAN, J. L., PIERESON, J. E., and MARCUS, G. E. 1978. Ideological Constraint in the Mass Public. *American Journal of Political Science*, 22: 233–49.

TOURANGEAU, R., RIPS, L. J., and RASINSKI, K. 2000. *The Psychology of Survey Response*. Cambridge: Cambridge University Press.

WANKE, M., SCHWARZ, N., and NOELLE-NEUMANN, E. 1995. Asking Comparative Questions: The Impact of the Direction of Comparison. *Public Opinion Quarterly*, 59: 347–72.

prompt a somewhat different set of recalled considerations from LTM, and these different thoughts will be integrated into different responses.

This is a *memory-based* model in that evaluations are formed at the time a judgment is needed from the likes and dislikes that citizens can recall. By contrast, *online* models of political evaluation (Lodge, McGraw, and Stroh 1989; Lodge, Steenbergen, and Brau 1995) claim that "citizens spontaneously extract the evaluative implications of political information as soon as they are exposed to it, integrate these implications into an ongoing summary counter or running tally, and then proceed to forget the nongist descriptive details of the information" (Lavine 2002: 227). The citizen in the voting booth need not reconsider pros and cons, for an evaluation has already been made.

Memory-based and online models are commonly presented as competing, with memory-based processes seen as more applicable to complex, ambivalent attitude objects (issues) and online processes more applicable to simpler, univalent objects, especially when citizens expect to be asked for a judgment (candidates). But an either–or view is theoretically flawed and empirically unfounded, with the confusion stemming from the failure to discriminate encoding from retrieval effects. Online encoding processes link affect directly to objects in memory, and this affect is retrieved automatically whenever the object is encountered. After one or two evaluations the concept is "hot," affective-charged (Lodge and Taber 2005). When asked to report an evaluation, citizens retrieve considerations and construct an attitude, but the retrieval process will be strongly influenced by the affect that was attached to the concept through an earlier online process. That is, the evidence suggests hybrid models that include both online and memory components (Hastie and Pennington 1989; Kim, Taber, and Lodge 2009; Taber 2003).

# AUTOMATICITY AND PUBLIC OPINION

With the advent of the political behavior movement in political science in the 1950s, beliefs, feelings, and behavioral dispositions were brought center-stage in the prediction and explanation of political behavior. The default presumption has been that the thoughts, feelings, and behavioral intentions that come *consciously* to mind determine our judgments, evaluations, and behavior. In accord with this assumption, we political scientists commonly ask people to voice their beliefs, report their likes and dislikes, recount feelings and past behaviors, and foretell their intended actions. As a result, virtually everything we claim to know about public opinion and electoral behavior is based on what respondents say when asked for their present, past, or future beliefs, feelings, intentions, and behavior.

Current research in the cognitive sciences posits a *dual-process model* that distinguishes between automatic and deliberative processing in the formation and expression of beliefs, attitudes, goals, and behavior (Bargh 1997; Dijksterhuis and Nordgren 2006; Lodge and Taber forthcoming). Automatic processes, in which thoughts, feelings, and intentions come to mind spontaneously, on a time scale of milliseconds, contrast with the conscious processes of deliberation or intentional reasoning. They enter the processing stream earlier than conscious considerations, and they necessarily influence what thoughts, feelings, and interpretations subsequently come consciously to mind.

Deliberative processes are cognitively effortful, demanding of attention, time-consuming, and based on an intentional memory search for relevant facts and considerations. Automatic processes are involuntary, fast, top of the head, and, unlike conscious processes, can be activated even when the individual's attention is focused elsewhere. In sum, people are frequently unaware of the specific situational and contextual factors (call them "primes") that bring to mind the thoughts, feelings, and intentions that appear to the actor to be the outcome of a deliberative evaluation of the evidence.

Priming effects are ubiquitous in everyday life, and their utility as "hidden persuaders" has been well understood by advertisers for decades (Packard 1957). Such "incidental," normatively irrelevant primes are well documented in the political domain as well as in the world of commercial advertising, as when voters' evaluations are influenced by the attractiveness of the candidate, by the amount of time ABC anchorman Peter Jennings smiled when reporting on Reagan over Mondale in the 1984 presidential race, or by the racial cues in the Willie Horton ad attacking Michael Dukakis in 1988. These effects, like the impact of a sunny day on survey respondents' evaluations of life satisfaction, are strongest when the observer is unaware of the prime's influence.

In the 2000 presidential election campaign the Republican National Committee aired a rather mundane TV ad attacking Al Gore's prescription drug plan. But when the final segment of the ad is slowed down, the word "RATS" flickers across the screen. Shown at regular speed "RATS" appears superimposed over the words "Bureaucrats Decide" for a mere 30 milliseconds. Republican strategists denied any intention to influence viewers through this subliminal message, but experimental tests of the "rats ad" do show a significant negative impact on evaluations of Gore and his drug plan (Weinberger and Weston 2008). Inside the lab and in the real world, priming effects critically influence the encoding, retrieval, interpretation, evaluation, and response to information.

A compelling test of automaticity in online processing was carried out by Tilman Betsch and his colleagues (2001). They had their subjects watch a series of thirty videotaped TV commercials, which they were told they would have to recall and evaluate. Simultaneously, these subjects performed a second, cognitively demanding distractor task: they read aloud the changing stock prices of five hypothetical companies presented on a crawler at the bottom of the TV screen. Though participants were led to believe that their ability to remember and evaluate the TV commercials under pressure of an irrelevant distraction was the primary purpose of the study (recall of the commercials proved to be very good), the researchers were actually interested in how the viewers would track the stock ticker. In a surprise test, subjects were asked their preferences for the five companies. As predicted by the online processing model, participants were unable to recall the pertinent stock information, yet their summary, rank-ordered evaluations correlated positively and strongly with the actual performance of the five companies. This result points to the automaticity of online evaluations: subjects accurately evaluated the companies' stock performances even when their attention was actively focused on an unrelated, attention-demanding task.

Verhulst, Lodge, and Taber (2009) report an experiment in which participants are presented with information about hypothetical politicians' beliefs, manipulated to be either similar to or dissimilar from each participant's previously measured attitudes. Participants were also subliminally exposed to positive or negative prime words. Not surprisingly, participants liked similar more than dissimilar candidates. More interestingly, they were also strongly influenced by the subliminal primes, such that the positive or negative incidental information led to more positive or negative evaluations of the candidate. Furthermore, thinking carefully about the candidate actually increased the impact of the primes on candidate evaluations. In the end, the people who were most affected by the incidental primes were the most politically sophisticated, who thought carefully about the candidates.

Current research has gone beyond the automaticity of evaluation processes to focus on the automatic activation of complex social behaviors. A now classic experiment primed the concept "elderly" by asking subjects to unscramble sentences that included such words as Florida, worried, old, lonely, gray, and bingo. The behavioral dependent variable was the time (measured in seconds) it took subjects to leave the lab and walk to the elevator. Those primed by the concept "elderly" took significantly longer than control subjects to walk the 30 meters to the elevator, even though none of the primes for "elderly" referenced slowness of gait and the study participants were college students, not old folks.

I see three fundamental implications of this research on unconscious thought processes for the practice of contemporary political science, which will require that we dramatically rethink our notions of how people mentally represent the world and how we go about measuring and modeling citizens' expressions of political beliefs and attitudes. The first is how automatic affect kick-starts conscious and unconscious processes that promote response biases, especially when citizens encounter incongruent information about political candidates, groups, and issues. While I do not believe even the much-maligned American voter is compelled to act contrary to her explicit beliefs and conscious choices, the evidence is strong that the monitoring and correction of unconscious biases is difficult at best. A prime example: opinions on affirmative action, it turns out, are related to unconscious race attitudes that drive the strategic application of principles for many sophisticated conservatives (Taber 2009). In these experiments, sophisticated conservatives apply principles like merit criteria when the target of an affirmative action policy program is implicitly expected to be black (through a manipulation in which the target recipient is given a traditionally African American name but is never explicitly identified as black), but *not* when the target is expected to be white.

The second implication of automaticity is that people internalize simple summary evaluations, formed spontaneously online as they encounter political information.

Once formed, such running tallies provide decision-makers with a ready-made, highly accessible heuristic to inform their beliefs and guide their behavior. Citizens need not rely on fallible memory traces of the considerations that originally informed their attitudes in order to act on their preferences. Citizens can "feel" their preferences far faster and more accurately than they can explicitly report the reasons for their beliefs and attitudes. From this vantage point, top-of-the-head judgments and evaluations may prove to be more reliable guides to the expression of attitudes and behavior than those based on the careful consideration of pros and cons.

A third implication is for the practice of survey research. This and other research strongly suggest that we cannot expect citizens to reliably and veridically access the sources of their beliefs, the reasons for their attitudes, and their past or future intentions and actions. Most of our experience takes place outside conscious awareness and is not accessible to introspection. Moreover, as our recollections fade from memory, they are replaced by rationalizations. We must be careful about the causal inferences we make based on survey research because we may unwittingly put effect before cause.

## BELIEF STRUCTURES AND IDEOLOGY

Several debates related to the structure of political knowledge have been particularly important for public opinion. Philip Converse (1964, 255) sparked one debate when he characterized American citizens as "remarkably innocent" of the liberal–conservative dimension thought to be central to Western ideology. Lacking ideological structure, mass beliefs had neither coherence nor stability, and communication between elites and ordinary citizens was greatly debilitated. Converse himself suggested one reply when he recognized the possibility that citizens might organize their political beliefs in other ways, and others have focused attention on the structural role played by core values rather than the liberal–conservative dimension (Feldman 2003; Hurwitz and Peffley 1987).

A related controversy concerns whether the political knowledge of citizens is organized in discrete attitudes and beliefs or in tightly linked sub-networks, or *schemas* (Conover and Feldman 1991; Kuklinski, Luskin, and Bolland 1991; Lodge and McGraw 1991; Taber, Lodge, and Glathar 2001). Though the term "schema" seems to have largely disappeared from the political psychology lexicon, it is clear that sophisticated citizens or those who have given much thought to a particular politician or issue do possess organized structures of knowledge, attitudes, and inferences that guide thought as schema theory suggested. In addition to providing organizational structure, schemas increase the efficiency of cognitive processing in at least two ways: they expand significantly the amount of knowledge that may be held in conscious awareness (since larger "chunks" of memory occupy the same "space" in WM as smaller memory elements); and they enrich perception by filling in details about a candidate or issue

reasoning, for automatic feelings will conspire to bias the collection and assessment of evidence, and the stronger these feelings the deeper the bias. The clear expectation is that while it may be possible for citizens, if strongly enough motivated and under favorable conditions, to search carefully and treat new information that comes to mind in an impartial manner, it is exceedingly difficult to seek out information and reappraise its implications even-handedly, all the while knowing which way you want the conclusion to come out. This is made all the more difficult because the decision to appraise or reconsider the evidence takes time, is effortful, assumes one is somehow aware of having a biased set of considerations in mind, and believes the need to be accurate is worth the effort that will be required to rethink the issue.

For better or for worse, affect and cognition are inseparable and perhaps inescapable. Where, when, and for whom this inexorable linking of feeling and thinking will facilitate good decision-making and when it will lead to systematic departures from a rational course of action are important questions that remain unanswered.

## INGREDIENTS OF OPINION

But what drives the *contents* of public opinion? What are the ingredients that simmer through the processes I have described to form individual opinion? That is, I have focused on the important questions of *how* citizens think, but have not talked at all about *what* they think. Donald Kinder (1998: 800) points to three broad types of information that have been implicated in public opinion research: *material self-interests, social identifications*, and *ideological principles*.

No organ has been more central to the anatomy of *homo economicus* than material self-interest, and psychologists also accept what they call the "law of effect," which asserts that responses "which are accompanied or closely followed by satisfaction" will become more strongly associated with a triggering stimulus while those "followed by discomfort" will become less associated with the stimulus (Thorndike 1911, 244). More generally, the principle of instrumental action has become bedrock throughout the social sciences and the most common presumption is that instrumental action is guided by self-interest. Yet, despite the prevalence of self-interest explanations for public opinion and political behavior, there are reasons to question its empirical validity (Sears and Funk 1991).

Unfortunately, though self-interest explanations for political behavior approach dogma, the concept has proven to be conceptually and empirically elusive. The most systematic empirical examination of the role of self-interest in motivating public opinion has been conducted by David Sears and colleagues. In their review of this research program, Sears and Funk (1991) suggest three criteria for defining self-interest: first, the interests involved must be tangible or material (and not amorphous psychic gratification); second, the self involved must be the individual (and not concern for others); and third, the outcomes to be evaluated for self-interest must be imminent (and not future considerations). Extending self-interest to immaterial satisfaction, group interest or altruism, or anticipation of distal consequences, they argue, would render self-interest theoretically tautological and empirically unmeasurable.

Study after study has found remarkably little connection between self-interest, so defined, and public opinion on a wide range of issues. Kinder provides a long list of examples (1998, 801), including affirmative action, unemployment, health insurance, public education, military draft, and policies targeted on women. One might expect that personal self-interest would be a powerful motivation for political behavior on economic issues, but even this has proven not to be the case (Bartels 2008; Sears and Funk 1991). Personal economic concerns, it turns out, are far less important than general concerns about the national economy in presidential voting (Kiewiet 1983). One must conclude, looking at the negative findings, that citizens are not nearly as sensitive to their own material interests as we political scientists suppose them to be. By contrast with the emphatic rejection of self-interest as a fundamental *cause* of opinion, paradoxically it turns out that material self-interest does influence what people pay attention to. That is, citizens whose interests are implicated in an issue do report that the issue is important to them (Thomsen, Borgida, and Lavine 1995), and we might presume that they are also more attentive to the issues they think are important (Krosnick 1990).

If self-interest does not drive public opinion as we commonly suppose, perhaps social and political group identifications will prove to be more potent. After all, political scientists and psychologists have long understood the importance of social identity to the development of social and political attitudes (Huddy 2003). Identifications with political, social, religious, or other groups are surely powerful orienting forces in guiding public opinion and political action. And we should not lose sight of citizens' "negative" identifications—that is, their feelings and thoughts about groups they do not belong to. Roger Brown wrote in his classic social psychology textbook (1986, 533) that group conflict "is like a sturdy three-legged stool. It is sturdy because two legs are universal ineradicable psychological processes, ethnocentrism and stereotyping, and the third leg is a state of society, unfair distribution of resources, which has always existed everywhere." This unholy mix of motivations begins with in-group and out-group identifications.

Ethnocentrism and group-based prejudice have long been thought to originate in fundamental categorization processes over which citizens may have little conscious control. Experimental research in our labs at Stony Brook finds that basic political attitudes and beliefs are strongly influenced by unconscious group categorization and identification processes (Lodge and Taber forthcoming). That is, automatic group identifications exert a strong pull on support for parties, candidates, and political issues. Labeling oneself, another person, object, or event as a member or instance of a group, be it "a robin is a bird" or a "politician is a Democrat," is critical to how citizens think and reason, as the categorized group member spontaneously inherits many of the characteristics of the group label. While categorization can and does serve important beneficial functions (we could not function intelligently without categorizing and classifying), when applied to people it has its well-documented downside in the rapid and spontaneous creation of in-groups and out-groups and the subsequent tendency to favor "us" at the expense of "them." People tend to see members of in-groups as more similar to themselves, while viewing out-group members as less similar and less individually variable. Moreover, the simple act of categorization can promote discriminatory attitudes and behavior even when there are no objective differences between the groupings (Perdue, Dovidio, Gurtman, and Tyler 1990). In short, the act of categorization involves both cognitive and affective processes that are difficult if not impossible to disentangle. From this "hot identifications" perspective the categorization of self, in-groups, and out-groups is an affectively charged process.

What conditions promote the influence of group identifications on public opinion? Three factors, corresponding neatly to Brown's three-legged stool, emerge from various areas of research. Most famously, a large literature in political psychology emphasizes individual differences (for example, Adorno, Frenkel-Brunswik, Levinson, and Sanford 1950). Group identifications are more central motivators for some people than for others. A second literature has focused on the ways the information environment may frame or prime widely shared group stereotypes (Kinder and Sanders 1996). That is, the way information is presented by elites or the media will influence how group orientations are brought to bear on a given issue. Finally, group conflict is surely responsive to genuine conflicts of interest (Huddy 2003). Greater intergroup conflict or issues that highlight conflicting group interests should increase the importance of group identifications in individual information processing.

For some citizens, politics is all about principles. Abortion, national health care, gun control, capital punishment, welfare, and an ever-changing mix of other particular political issues all align to at least some degree on the central axes of the American ethos: individualism, equality, opposition to intrusive government (Kinder 1998). Politics brings values into conflict (Feldman 2003; Tetlock 1986), and these principles help structure political knowledge, provide constraint across issues, and motivate persistence of political attitudes, at least for some citizens (Feldman 2003). Given this centrality of principles in theory, it may be surprising that the impacts of individualism, egalitarianism, tolerance, and opposition to government power have generally been weak and contingent. Consider briefly research on individualism.

Hardy individualism, the notion that people are and should be responsible for their own lot in life, has been found to contribute to opposition to government assistance programs as well as the inclination to blame the poor for their poverty (Feldman 2003). White Americans' attitudes toward blacks and especially toward race-conscious policies like affirmative action could be understood in terms of this same principled logic: blacks are poor because they do not work hard enough (Sniderman and Carmines 1997). On the other hand, racial group identifications also powerfully drive the same policy attitudes (Kinder and Sanders 1996).

My own recent research finds that white Americans regardless of ideology associate affirmative action with race and not ideology (Taber 2009). When consciously thinking about affirmative action, conservatives think mostly about race, and only bring individualism or opposition to government intrusion to mind when they expect to have to defend their beliefs—that is, *strategically*. Liberals draw upon a mix of race and egalitarianism when thinking about affirmative action. Moreover, white Americans, and in particular conservatives, strongly associate race and principle in their automatic (uncontrolled) thoughts. Contrary to the expectations of principled conservatism (Feldman and Huddy 2005; Sniderman and Carmines 1997), most white Americans cannot construct purely ideological thoughts without also bringing to mind racial considerations and feelings. Enough effort and motivation may allow citizens to control the influence of such racial concerns on conscious thoughts and behaviors, but pure ideological thinking is highly unlikely. Finally, the conservative white respondents in my adult sample harbor substantial racial antipathy that they are unwilling or unable to report, and these implicit negative feelings help explain their opposition to affirmative action.

# CONCLUSION

In theory, rational public opinion underwrites the fair and efficient working of modern representative democracy. This chapter has examined work on the individual construction of public opinion, the rising interest in automaticity and control in political cognition, the structures of beliefs and how these may give rise to political ideology, the persistence or persuasion of political attitudes, and the thematic sources of political opinions. In each area there are difficult controversies as well as emerging answers. Perhaps most troubling from a normative perspective are the questions that arise about the capacity of citizens to respond rationally to an increasingly complex political environment.

Political scientist and Nobel laureate Herbert Simon first raised the implications of the limitations of human cognitive capacity for political information processing (summarized in 1985). His notion of bounded rationality is a direct consequence of the limitations on conscious thought. Today, cognitive scientists (Norretranders 1998) estimate the total human capacity for processing sensory experience to be about 11 million bits per second, about 90 percent of which is visual. By contrast, the conscious processing of visual information can only handle about 40 bits per second, or about 1/250,000 of what we actually see and respond to. This bottleneck on processing provides the theoretical micro-foundations for citizen incompetence or irrationality. By the same token, the much greater capacity for non-conscious processing offers hope that we humans may be built to overcome our conscious limitations.

Perhaps the most influential contemporary solution to the problem of bounded rationality is the idea that citizens may use heuristic cues to guide their behavior. Such "low information rationality" (Popkin 1991) will operate largely out of awareness, allowing citizens to cue their political behavior on widely available heuristics, including party identification and interest groups (Kuklinski and Quirk 2000; Lupia 1994). In this way, ill-informed citizens can behave as if they were fully informed. On the other hand, heuristic processes may be a source of inferential biases, and cue sources may be wrong or misperceived (Kuklinski and Quirk 2000). There is no question that citizens use heuristics to simplify their information processing; there is considerable uncertainty, however, about whether such shortcuts allow them to behave competently.

A second solution to the problem of bounded rationality rests on a citizen's ability to process most information online (that is, at the time the information is encountered), extracting the affective implications of that information (Lodge, McGraw, and Stroh 1989; Lodge, Steenbergen, and Brau 1995). Much easier to update a running tally for one's candidate evaluation than to store detailed campaign information about that candidate. As long as this updating process is relatively unbiased, online processing can be quite responsive to the information environment, allowing citizens to behave reasonably. This, along with our considerable capacity for unconscious information processing, raises the possibility of "high information rationality" even for citizens who appear in surveys to be rather unsophisticated.

Unfortunately for this comforting story, research suggests that unbiased online processing is very unlikely, and automatic information processing may also encounter the dangers of bias and manipulation. Research on motivated reasoning finds that citizens are unable to treat new information even-handedly; rather, they find agreeable information more convincing and actively counterargue what they disagree with, especially sophisticates and those with strong priors (for example, Taber and Lodge 2006). More generally, it seems that one's feelings, which become activated very early in the stream of information processing, systematically bias the sample of considerations that subsequently come to mind. These considerations seem subjectively to citizens to cause their political behavior (as when someone reports they voted for candidate X because she supports abortion rights), but they might more accurately be seen as justifications of behavior that is actually caused by earlier affective processes. Moreover, these early affective responses may be manipulated by environmental cues (e.g., flags or other symbols; candidate appearance; background music; or other manipulations of affect). In this sense, the citizen might be described more as a rationalizing than rational voter (Lodge and Taber forthcoming). In short, while automaticity and online processing offer hope of lifting some of the limits on human cognitive capacity, they also impose a strong likelihood of bias and susceptibility to manipulation that undermine their normative benefits.

# REFERENCES

ACHEN, C. H. 1975. Mass Political Attitudes and the Survey Response. *American Political Science Review*, 69: 1218–31.

ADORNO, T. W., FRENKEL-BRUNSWIK, E., LEVINSON, D., and SANFORD, N. 1950. *The Authoritarian Personality*. New York: Harper & Row.

ANDERSON, J. R. 1983. *The Architecture of Cognition*. Cambridge, MA: Harvard University Press.

BARGH, J. A. 1997. The Automaticity of Everyday Life. In *The Automaticity of Everyday Life: Advances in Social Cognition*, x, ed. R. S. Wyer. Mahwah, NJ: Lawrence Erlbaum.

BARTELS, L. M. 2008. *Unequal Democracy: The Political Economy of the New Gilded Age*. Princeton: Princeton.

BETSCH, T., PLESSNER, H., SCHWIEREN, C., and GUTIG, R. 2001. I Like It but I Don't Know Why: A Value Account Approach to Implied Attitude Formation. *Personality and Social Psychology Bulletin*, 27: 242–53.

BROWN, R. 1986. *Social Psychology*, 2nd edn. New York: Free Press.

CONOVER, P. J., and FELDMAN, S. 1991. Where Is the Schema? Critiques. *American Political Science Review*, 85: 1364–9.

CONVERSE, P. E. 1964. The Nature of Belief Systems in Mass Publics. In *Ideology and Discontent*, ed. D. E. Apter. New York: Free Press.

DIJKSTERHUIS, A., and NORDGREN, L. F. 2006. A Theory of Unconscious Thought. *Perspectives on Psychological Science*, 1: 95–109.

EDWARDS, K., and SMITH, E. A. 1996. A Disconfirmation Bias in the Evaluation of Arguments. *Journal of Personality and Social Psychology*, 71: 5–24.

EYSENCK, M. W., and KEANE, M. T. 2010. *Cognitive Psychology: A Student's Handbook*, 6th edn. London: Psychology Press.

FELDMAN, S. 2003. Values, Ideology, and the Structure of Political Attitudes. In *The Oxford Handbook of Political Psychology*, ed. D. O. Sears, L. Huddy, and R. Jervis. Oxford: Oxford University Press.

——and HUDDY, L. 2005. Racial Resentment and White Opposition to Race-Conscious Programs: Principles or Prejudice? *American Journal of Political Science*, 49: 168–83.

FESTINGER, L. 1957. *A Theory of Cognitive Dissonance*. Palo Alto, CA: Stanford University Press.

FORGAS, J. 2000. *Feeling and Thinking: The Role of Affect in Social Cognition*. New York: Cambridge University Press.

HASTIE, R. 1986. A Primer of Information-Processing Theory for the Political Scientist. In *Political Cognition*, ed. R. R. Lau and D. O. Sears. Hillsdale, NJ: Erlbaum.

——and PENNINGTON, N. 1989. Notes on the Distinction between Memory-Based and On-Line Judgment. In *On-Line Cognition in Person Perception*, ed. J. Bassili. Hillsdale, NJ: Lawrence Erlbaum.

HEIDER, F. 1958. *The Psychology of Interpersonal Relations*. New York: Wiley.

HUDDY, L. 2003. Group Identity and Political Cohesion. In *The Oxford Handbook of Political Psychology*, ed. D. O. Sears, L. Huddy, and R. Jervis. Oxford: Oxford University Press.

HURWITZ, J., and PEFFLEY, M. 1987. How Are Foreign Policy Attitudes Structured? A Hierarchical Model. *American Political Science Review*, 81: 1099–110.

KIEWIET, D. R. 1983. *Macroeconomics and Micropolitics*. Chicago: University of Chicago Press.

KIM, S.-Y., TABER, C. S., and LODGE, M. 2009. A Computational Model of the Citizen as Motivated Reasoner: Modeling the Dynamics of the 2000 Presidential Election. *Political Behavior*, 32: 1–28.

KINDER, D. 1998. Opinion and Action in the Realm of Politics. In *The Handbook of Social Psychology*, 4th edn., ed. D. T. Gilbert, S. T. Fiske, and G. Lindzey, i. Boston: McGraw-Hill.

——and SANDERS, L. 1996. *Divided by Color: Racial Politics and Democratic Ideals*. Chicago: University of Chicago Press.

Krosnick, J. A. 1990. Government Policy and Citizen Passion: A Study of Issue Publics in Contemporary America. *Political Behavior*, 12: 59–92.

Kuklinski, J. H., and Quirk, P. J. 2000. Reconsidering the Rational Public: Cognition, Heuristics, and Mass Opinion. In *Elements of Reason: Cognition, Choice, and the Bounds of Rationality*, ed. A. Lupia, M. D. McCubbins, and S. L. Popkin. Cambridge: Cambridge University Press.

——Luskin, R., and Bolland, J. 1991. Where Is the Schema? Going beyond the "S" Word in Political Psychology. *American Political Science Review*, 85: 1341–56.

Kunda, Z. 1990. The Case for Motivated Reasoning. *Psychological Bulletin*, 1083: 480–98.

Lavine, H. 2002. On-Line vs. Memory-Based Process Models of Political Evaluation. In *Political Psychology*, ed. K. Monroe. Mahwah, NJ: Lawrence Erlbaum.

Lazarus, R. 1995. Vexing Research Problems Inherent in Cognitive-Mediational Theories of Emotion and Some Solutions. *Psychological Inquiry*, 6/3: 183–96.

Lodge, M., and McGraw, K. 1991. Where Is the Schema? Critiques. *American Political Science Review*, 85: 1357–64.

——and Taber, C. 2000. Three Steps toward a Theory of Motivated Political Reasoning. In *Elements of Reason: Cognition, Choice, and the Bounds of Rationality*, ed. A. Lupia, M. McCubbins, and S. Popkin. New York: Cambridge University Press.

————2005. The Primacy of Affect for Political Candidates, Groups, and Issues: An Experimental Test of the Hot Cognition Hypothesis. *Political Psychology*, 26/3: 333–87.

————Forthcoming. *The Rationalizing Voter*. Cambridge: Cambridge University Press.

——McGraw, K., and Stroh, P. 1989. An Impression Driven Model of Candidate Preference Formation. *American Political Science Review*, 83/2: 399–420.

——Steenbergen, M., and Brau, S. 1995. The Responsive Voter: Campaign Information and the Dynamics of Candidate Evaluation. *American Political Science Review*, 89/2: 309–26.

Lupia, A. 1994. Shortcuts versus Encyclopedias: Information and Voting Behavior in California Insurance Reform Elections. *American Political Science Review*, 88: 63–76.

Marcus, G., Neuman, W. R., and MacKuen, M. 2000. *Affective Intelligence and Political Judgment*. Chicago: University of Chicago Press.

Matheson, K., and Durson, S. 2001. Social Identity Precursors to the Hostile Media Phenomenon: Partisan Perceptions of Coverage of the Bosnian Conflict. *Group Processes & Intergroup Relations*, 4/2: 116–25.

Meffert, M. F., Chung, S., Joiner, A., Waks, L., and Garst, J. 2006. The Effects of Negativity and Motivated Information Processing during a Political Campaign. *Journal of Communication*, 56: 27–51.

Norretranders, T. 1998. *The User Illusion: Cutting Consciousness down to Size*. New York: Penguin.

Packard, V. 1957. *The Hidden Persuaders*. New York: D. Mackay.

Perdue, C., Dovidio, J., Gurtman, M., and Tyler, R. 1990. Us and Them: Social Categorization and the Process of Intergroup Bias. *Journal of Personality and Social Psychology*, 59/3: 475–86.

Popkin, S. L. 1991. *The Reasoning Voter: Communication and Persuasion in Presidential Campaigns*. Chicago: University of Chicago Press.

Redlawsk, D. 2001. Hot Cognition or Cool Consideration: Testing the Effects of Motivated Reasoning on Political Decision Making. *Journal of Politics*, 64/4: 1021–44.

Sears, D. O., and Funk, C. 1991. The Role of Self-Interest in Social and Political Attitudes. In *Advances in Experimental Social Psychology*, xxiv, ed. M. P. Zanna. New York: Academic Press.

Simon, H. A. 1985. Human Nature in Politics: The Dialogue of Psychology and Political Science. *American Political Science Review*, 79: 293–304.

Sniderman, P. M., and Carmines, E. G. 1997. *Reaching beyond Race*. New Haven: Harvard University Press.

Taber, C. S. 2003. Information Processing and Public Opinion. In *The Oxford Handbook of Political Psychology*, ed. D. Sears, L. Huddy, and R. Jervis. New York: Oxford University Press.

——2009. Principles of Color: Implicit Race, Ideology, and Opposition to Racial Policies. Unpublished paper. Stony Brook University.

——and Lodge, M. 2006. Motivated Skepticism in the Evaluation of Political Beliefs. *American Journal of Political Science*, 50/3: 755–69.

——Cann, D., and Kucsova, S. 2009. The Motivated Processing of Political Arguments. *Political Behavior*, 31/2: 137–55.

——Lodge, M., and Glathar, J. 2001. The Motivated Construction of Political Judgments. In *Citizens and Politics: Perspectives from Political Psychology*, ed. J. H. Kuklinski. Cambridge: Cambridge University Press.

Tetlock, P. E. 1986. A Value Pluralism Model of Ideological Reasoning. *Journal of Personality and Social Psychology: Personality Processes and Individual Differences*, 50: 819–27.

Thomsen, C. J., Borgida, E., and Lavine, H. 1995. The Causes and Consequences of Personal Involvement. In *Attitude Strength: Antecedents and Consequences*, ed. R. E. Petty and J. A. Krosnick. Hillsdale, NJ: Lawrence Erlbaum.

Thorndike, E. L. 1911. *Animal Learning*. New York: Macmillan.

Tourangeau, R., Rips, L., and Rasinski, K. 2000. *The Psychology of the Survey Response*. New York: Cambridge University Press.

Verhulst, B., Lodge, M., and Taber, C. S. 2009. The Effect of Unnoticed Affective Cues and Cognitive Deliberation on Candidate Evaluation. Unpublished manuscript. Stony Brook University.

Weinberger, J., and Westen, D. 2008. RATS, We Should Have Used Clinton: Subliminal Priming in Political Campaigns. *Political Psychology*, 29/5: 631–51.

Zaller, J. R. 1992. *The Nature and Origins of Mass Opinion*. Cambridge: Cambridge University Press.

——and Feldman, S. 1992. A Simple Theory of the Survey Response. *American Journal of Political Science*, 36: 579–616.

CHAPTER 24

........................................................................

# EMOTION AND PUBLIC
# OPINION

........................................................................

TED BRADER
GEORGE E. MARCUS
KRISTYN L. MILLER

TWENTY years ago, a volume such as this would have been unlikely to include a chapter on emotion and public opinion. That is so for two reasons. First, although there were sporadic publications on emotion in that period (for example, see Abelson, Kinder, Peters, and Fiske 1982; Conover and Feldman 1986; Marcus 1988; Sullivan and Masters 1988), political science and psychology were largely under the sway of the "cognitive revolution" and this was reflected in research on opinion. Second, the social sciences were then, as now, guided by Enlightenment precepts that hypothesized an emergent world in which reason would increasingly hold sway and ancient practices of faith and emotionally entrenched tradition would retreat. Enlightenment formulations frequently cast emotion into an old, familiar role as normatively destructive and dysfunctional (Marcus 2008). But emotions have proved to be of enduring relevance to human life, even critical to reasoned action, and so, in the intervening years, the study of emotion has been resurgent throughout the academy (Damasio 1994; Ledoux 1996). Thus, scholarship on the role of emotion in politics, though recent, has appeared at an accelerating rate.

Much of this new work challenges older formulations, but a mature theoretical grounding has not yet been achieved. There is no settled definition of "affect," and as a consequence, the term "cognition" has become equally problematic. Though publications frequently invoke the phrase "affective and cognitive" or "affect and cognition" to convey this new-found interest in emotion, usage of these terms often reflects the vagaries of everyday language, with the multiple meanings and imprecision that scientific terminology is meant to resolve. Although attempts have been made to review the multiplicity of meanings (Neuman, Marcus, Crigler, and MacKuen 2007), much remains to be resolved before the field has all the tools, theoretical and methodological, to reach a mature stage.

Nonetheless, the field has seen progress in moving from the haphazard toward a more fully specified state wherein agreed theoretical definitions, criteria for measurement, and substantive theoretical propositions mutually reinforce and shape the work of all scholars.

Early research seems to fall into one of two perspectives. First, some undertook research on emotion with a dependent variable focus: that is to say, what can these new emotion variables add to our understanding of the topic of interest? Second, other scholars began with an independent variable focus. Here the interest has been on the emotion itself, with the hope that something systematic can be said about the impact a specific emotion, say anger, or a group of emotions, say positive emotions, or, more globally, all emotion, has across all manifestations of public opinion and political behavior.

We begin with discussions of how emotion has been variously understood and theorized by scholars. Then we take a broadly integrated view of current research on the consequences of emotion for public opinion and political behavior. Lastly, we review what emotions have contributed to the study of particular substantive domains.[1]

# WHAT IS EMOTION?

Research on emotion requires an agreed definition of "emotion." The scientific concept of emotion ought to be based on two features: a coherent definition and clarity on processes that are affective as distinct from cognitive. The field of political science, drawing on psychology and neuroscience, has utilized three sometimes overlapping ideas of what "emotion" means. The existence of these different conceptions becomes especially problematic when authors are unclear as to which meaning they have in mind.

One tradition harkens back through William James (1884) to Aristotle (1954). In this view, different emotions are specific physical states each joined with a specific conscious understanding. Hence, to use a well-known example from James, one sees a bear charging and feels fear, thus linking the physiological state of sweating, heightened pulse rate, and so on with the perception of a chasing bear. That tradition has more recently broken into two distinct conceptions: (1) cognitive appraisal theories (emotion is generated as a consequence of how a situation is understood); or (2) theories asserting that "discrete" emotions are each defined by a distinct pattern of physiological changes (Ekman, Levenson, and Friesen 1983). This leaves a residual category of "mood," a state of emotion without a clear understanding that resides alongside feelings that do have clear physical markers *and* conceptual attributes. The physiological approach has been slowed because there is no clear evidence that specific physiological markers are tied to discrete emotions (Cacioppo, Berntson, and Klein 1992; Fowles 1982). This has left the Jamesian approach with cognitive appraisal as the principal explanation of the subjective experience of feeling states (Lazarus 1991).

---

[1] In this chapter we focus primarily on peer-reviewed research published since 2000. For a more complete review of the field prior to this period, see Marcus (2000).

A third conception turns away from bodily feelings and states of mind to neural processes, conceiving of affect as pre-conscious processes that provide ongoing appraisals essential to pre-conscious evaluations and to enacting behavioral routines (Damasio 1994; Gray 1987; Ledoux 1996).[2] It follows from this conception that affective states vary along functionally defined dimensions rather than occurring as differentiated discrete states. Pre-conscious processes and conscious reflective assessments can, and most likely do, coexist and interplay so that each may have separate and coordinated dynamic influences on the way the mind and behavior are enacted. At this stage of theoretical development there is no candidate theory that attempts to integrate all of these attributes of affect. Hence, the dynamic role of time in the unfolding of upstream and downstream affective processes has been largely ignored.

Beyond definitional concerns, measurement issues also need to be addressed more fully before the field of emotion and public opinion can be considered mature. Specifically, the field needs measures that meet psychometric standards of reliability and validity. In sum, a developed theory of emotion ought to be comprehensive, in that it identifies each aspect of emotion, the variants, and their relationships to one another. And it ought to account for the antecedents and consequences of emotion in its various guises. Although considerable progress has been made in the empirical study of emotions and politics, much less progress has been made in meeting these theoretical and methodological goals.

# THEORIES OF EMOTION

Scholars studying emotion and public opinion in recent years have been guided by at least three fairly broad theories of emotion. First, a few studies have drawn on the cognitive appraisal approach already discussed. Appraisal theories predict that each emotion has both specific antecedents, rooted in how an individual (consciously or subconsciously) makes sense of her situation, and specific response tendencies adapted for dealing with that situation (Lazarus 1991). Appraisal tendency theory is a variant that emphasizes the ability of emotions to generate the same sorts of appraisals that gave rise to them. Recent studies have drawn on appraisal theories to test expectations about perceptions of risk and blame following terrorist attacks (Lerner, Gonzalez, Small, and Fischhoff 2003; Small, Lerner, and Fischhoff 2006), media-framing effects (Gross 2008), policy opinions (Brader, Groenendyk, and Valentino 2010; Nabi 2003; Small and Lerner 2008), candidate evaluations (Just, Crigler, and Belt 2007; Steenbergen and Ellis 2006), and political participation (Valentino, Brader, et al. 2011). Despite

---

[2] The term "pre-conscious" will strike most as curious as conscious awareness offers the subjective sense of immediacy. But neuroscience research has found that the brain requires 500 milliseconds to constitute conscious awareness, leaving ample time for pre-conscious neural processes to execute within the 500 milliseconds that begin with the arrival of sensory and somatosensory signals. These neural processes have robust "downstream" effects on affective and cognitive states.

the expanding usage of this approach, there has been little effort to construct a broader appraisal theory of emotions and public opinion.

Another line of research in recent years is rooted in the concepts of "motivated reasoning" and "hot cognition." The hot cognition hypothesis suggests that learned sociopolitical concepts are affectively charged and that this charge is automatically activated upon reexposure to the concept. The emphasis is on positive and negative affect, rather than distinctions between specific emotions. A number of studies find support for the "automaticity" and primacy of affect in cognitive judgments (Cassino and Lodge 2007; Lodge and Taber 2005; Morris, Squires, Taber, and Lodge 2003). Beyond demonstrating the ubiquitous involvement of affect, however, these studies do not offer more fine-grained analyses.

At this juncture, the theory of affective intelligence (AI) represents the broadest and best-known model of emotion and politics. Developed by Marcus, Neuman, and MacKuen (2000), it suggests that there are two basic emotional systems that monitor an individual's environment and allocate neural resources in accordance with situational needs. The disposition system relies on learned routines to translate feedback about current endeavors, generating affective states that range from enthusiasm to depression for habits that obtain rewarding goals, and varying states of aversion (anger) when habits engage familiar punishing circumstances. The surveillance system redirects attention and thoughts based on the novelty of the environment, with the primary emotions ranging along a dimension from calm to anxiety. Studies testing and finding support for the predictions of AI theory include work on candidate evaluations and electoral behavior (Brader 2006; Hutchings, Valentino, Philpot, and White 2006; Marcus, Neuman, and MacKuen 2000), political learning (MacKuen, Wolak, Keele, and Marcus 2010; Redlawsk, Civettini, and Lau 2007; Valentino, Hutchings, Banks, and Davis 2008; Valentino, Banks, Hutchings, and Davis 2009), policy opinions (Brader, Valentino, and Suhay 2008), and framing effects (Druckman and McDermott 2008; Marcus, Sullivan, Theiss-Morse, and Stevens 2005).

Recently, studies attempting to compare broad models of emotion also have presented evidence conflicting with AI theory. One team of researchers examined which of three models of emotion—bipolar, two-dimensional, or discrete—predicted best the relationship between candidate emotions and candidate evaluations following a presidential debate (Hullet, Louden, and Mitra 2003). Their factor analyses suggested the valence of reactions is sufficient to explain attitudes, which would support the bipolar model. Another set of researchers claims strongest support for the contention, dubbed endogenous affect, that emotional reactions are simply rationalizations of candidate evaluations (Ladd and Lenz 2008).[3] Taken together, these conflicting results draw attention to the need for conceptual clarity and the development of a more fully theorized basis for future research, one in which there are testable propositions for competing theories and in which more scholars test those competing propositions head-to-head.

---

[3] But see Marcus, MacKuen, and Neuman (forthcoming) and Brader (forthcoming).

# OVERVIEW OF THE EFFECTS OF EMOTION

## Opinion Formation

Most of the early research in this field focused on emotions as predictors of public opinion (Abelson, Kinder, Peters, and Fiske 1982; Conover and Feldman 1986; Kinder 1994; Marcus and MacKuen 1993; Sullivan and Masters 1988). Scholars tend to treat emotions as having either a direct or an indirect influence on opinion. We take up each approach in turn.

Many studies treat emotional reactions (to candidates, issues, etc.) as direct determinants of opinion. Models of opinion incorporate emotions as one more set of considerations that citizens weigh in their judgments. Regardless of whether researchers group measures into negative and positive affect (Lodge and Taber 2005) or into discrete emotions (Gross, Brewer, and Aday 2009), studies of direct effects often do not emphasize distinctions among emotions. The general expectation and finding is that emotions have a large, directionally consistent impact (i.e., negative emotions lead to more negative evaluations, positive emotions to positive evaluations). Research has generally uncovered large direct effects beyond what can be explained by other "key ingredients" such as values, identities, and interests. This suggests that emotions represent a significant part of opinion formation not otherwise captured in traditional models. However, one important question raised by survey studies in this domain is whether the observed relationships reflect the impact of episodic emotions on opinions or, alternatively, merely pick up the affective dimensions of the attitude under investigation (Isbell and Ottati 2002).

Some recent work, while largely focusing on direct effects, pushes further by demonstrating the distinctive impact of particular emotions on risk perceptions, causal attributions, and policy preferences. Shortly after the September 11 (9/11) attacks, Lerner, Gonzalez, Small, and Fischhoff (2003) found that fearful citizens perceived greater risks (of both future terrorism and unrelated dangers) and foresaw a greater need for precautionary actions, while angry citizens saw fewer risks and less need for precautions (cf., Huddy, Feldman, and Cassese 2007). Relative to either fear or sadness, anger also leads citizens to call to mind more causes or sources of blame (Small, Lerner, and Fischhoff 2006). Druckman and McDermott (2008) come to similar conclusions, finding that enthusiasm and anger generated greater confidence and support for risky policy options, but "distress" (conceived as analogous to anxiety, or fear[4]) diminished confidence and support for risky policies. Fear also causes citizens to prefer protective and conciliatory policies, while anger causes them to prefer punitive policies (Lerner,

---

[4] Researchers generally use "anxiety" or "fear" to refer to the same underlying emotion. Though some theories treat them as distinct, there is little evidence to date that citizens use the terms (and cognates) differently in the self-reported feelings that form the basis for most analyses in this field.

Gonzalez, Small, and Fischhoff 2003; Nabi 2003). Similarly, MacKuen, Wolak, Keele, and Marcus (2010) found that anxiety increases, but anger decreases, willingness to consider policy compromises.

Studies of indirect effects, in many respects, illustrate potentially powerful and more distinctive contributions of emotions to public opinion. For example, emotions can influence the *process* of opinion formation by altering the weight citizens give to various considerations. Research in this vein has applied AI theory to electoral judgments, suggesting that anxiety serves as a trigger that switches a citizen between two classical modes of citizenship: the habitual partisan voter versus something closer to the progressive ideal of the rational citizen who weighs policies, current conditions, and leadership qualities in light of available information. Both survey analyses of reactions to presidential candidates and experiments on the impact of campaign ads find that anxiety awakens the rational citizen (Brader 2005; Marcus, Neuman, and MacKuen 2000). There is also evidence that enthusiasm and aversion (anger) amplify the partisan voter's reliance on habit (Brader 2006; MacKuen, Wolak, Keele, and Marcus 2010).

Scholars have also shown that emotions moderate the impact of message frames: anxiety attunes people to their environment, thus enhancing framing effects, while both enthusiasm and anger lessen attention to the environment, thereby tempering framing effects (Druckman and McDermott 2008; Marcus, Sullivan, Theiss-Morse, and Stevens 2005). Similar findings emerge for the effects of sadness and anger on policy judgments (Small and Lerner 2008): sadness and anger, even when incidental (i.e., unrelated to policy or politics), trigger systematic or heuristic processing of information, respectively, which in turn cause divergent judgments about welfare assistance. Finally, another study took a different tack, focusing on the *strength* of emotional responses (to the Hurricane Katrina disaster) rather than on distinctions among emotions, and found that stronger (negative) emotions were associated with heuristic processing and weaker emotions associated with systematic processing (Malhotra and Kuo 2009).

## Attention and Learning

Public opinion research includes not just the study of opinions, but also the closely related domain of political knowledge. On what information do citizens base their preferences and choices? Are citizens passive or active learners? How well do they pay attention to sources of political information? Recent research suggests that emotions can profoundly influence processes of engagement (interest), attention, information seeking, and memory—in short, what citizens are exposed to and what they learn.[5]

---

[5] Much of the work on emotions and politics, like the study of political knowledge in general, focuses on evidence of learning that may implicate memory but has not directly studied memory processes (e.g., encoding versus recall of information).

Early work on AI theory suggested that enthusiasm and anxiety initiate attention to and interest in politics (Marcus, Neuman, and MacKuen 2000). Enthusiasm about candidates spurred interest in the campaign and caring about the election outcome, whereas anxiety increased attention to news sources and learning about the candidates. Rudolph, Gangl, and Stevens (2000) proposed that internal political efficacy modulates the relationship between anxiety and interest, such that anxiety causes only efficacious citizens to become more engaged. Experimental research found that fear-inducing campaign ads trigger a desire to learn more about issues, greater interest in the news, and enhanced recall of news stories (Brader 2005, 2006). Moreover, fear directed attention specifically toward issues and news relevant to the threat mentioned by the ads. In contrast, enthusiasm-eliciting ads had none of these effects, but instead simply stimulated broad interest in the campaign; fear also stimulated interest, but only among the politically sophisticated.

A recent spate of studies is pushing research on emotions and on political learning generally to new frontiers. First, many of them incorporate measures of actual information seeking by tracking behavior in a simulated campaign (Redlawsk, Civettini, and Lau 2007), offering respondents opportunities to request information (Brader, Valentino, and Suhay 2008), or monitoring searches in a controlled Web environment (MacKuen, Wolak, Keele, and Marcus 2010; Valentino, Hutchings, Banks, and Davis 2008; Valentino, Banks, Hutchings, and Davis 2009). Second, recent work draws finer distinctions among emotions in terms of the nature of searches they instigate and their consequences for learning. These studies have found evidence that any of the high arousal emotions—enthusiasm (Redlawsk, Civettini, and Lau 2007; Valentino, Hutchings, Banks, and Davis 2008; but cf. MacKuen, Wolak, Keele, and Marcus 2010), hope (Just, Crigler, and Belt 2007), anger (Huddy, Feldman, and Cassese 2007; Valentino, Hutchings, Banks, and Davis 2008), and anxiety or fear (Feldman and Huddy n.d.; Valentino, Hutchings, Banks, and Davis 2008)—initiated attention to sources of political information.

Much of the new focus, however, is on the distinctive impacts of anger and fear. Anger appears to reduce the amount of time actually spent visiting political websites (Valentino, Hutchings, Banks, and Davis 2008), shrink the number of webpages visited and narrow searches to opinion-confirming sources (MacKuen, Wolak, Keele, and Marcus 2010), produce less thoughtful opinions (Huddy, Feldman, and Cassese 2007), and inhibit accurate recall of information (Geva and Skorick 2006; Redlawsk, Civettini, and Lau 2007). In contrast, anxiety mediates the positive impact of threats on actual information seeking (Brader, Valentino, and Suhay 2008; MacKuen, Wolak, Keele, and Marcus 2010; Redlawsk, Civettini, and Lau 2007; Valentino, Hutchings, Banks, and Davis 2008). Anxious citizens are also more likely to conduct balanced searches for available information, including or especially disagreeable points of view (MacKuen, Wolak, Keele, and Marcus 2010; Valentino, Banks, Hutchings, and Davis 2009). According to most of the evidence to date, the end result is that anxious citizens learn more and thus demonstrate gains in political knowledge (Hutchings, Valentino, Philpot, and White 2006; Redlawsk, Civettini, and Lau 2007; Valentino, Hutchings,

Banks, and Davis 2008; Valentino, Banks, Hutchings, and Davis 2009), but one new study suggests that anxiety—perhaps when particularly acute or personal—can diminish learning even while making citizens more attentive (Feldman and Huddy n.d.). Finally, a couple of studies suggest that the impact of anxiety is conditional on the relevance of the information, for example when people know it affects a view they must defend (Redlawsk, Civettini, and Lau 2007; Valentino, Banks, Hutchings, and Davis 2009).

## Political Action

Of the myriad ways in which emotions may affect citizens, the least well explored is their impact on political participation. This is surprising given that a defining feature of emotions is that they are motivational impulses (Damasio 1994), impelling us to run, fight, hide, shout, embrace, look away, or extend a hand. In politics, of course, actions flow mostly through institutionalized channels. Thus, emotions—whether aggressive, defensive, or something else—will largely find a common outlet in voting, volunteering, donating, attending, contacting, and so forth.[6] Incorporating emotion into future research should help scholars address a critical and venerable weakness in the study of public opinion: the gap between opinions and behavior. Emotions likely play a central role in explaining when, and in what way, citizens act on their opinions and beliefs.

Early work on emotions and politics said little about participation, except to note that strong emotions may indeed distinguish those who claim an opinion from those who hold the opinion with conviction enough to act on it (Kinder 1994). More recent research has found effects for all of the high-arousal emotions commonly studied. Initial tests of AI theory found that both enthusiasm and anxiety increase political participation beyond voting, though the impact of anxiety appeared stronger (Marcus, Neuman, and MacKuen 2000). Similarly, advertisements eliciting fear or enthusiasm spurred an increased willingness to vote and volunteer (Brader 2006); these effects were broader, however, for enthusiasm, with the positive impact of fear evident primarily among sophisticated citizens and even a negative impact emerging among the less sophisticated. In one study that examines actual participation decisions during experiments, anxiety triggered by news stories caused citizens to contact their members of Congress to voice their opinion (Brader, Valentino, and Suhay 2008). Finally, other studies have found that, while enthusiasm and fear can boost participation, anger has a powerful mobilization effect, albeit one that may be more conditional on the internal efficacy, or more generally the level of material, social, and psychological resources

---

[6] Future research may wish to test for distinctive effects of particular emotions by examining types of activity that have a more focused directional goal (e.g., protests, relief work) or by measuring the self-conscious goals of participation (e.g., protect, punish, celebrate).

available to the citizen (Valentino, Brader, et al. 2011; Valentino, Gregorowicz, and Groenendyk 2009).

# Major Substantive Applications

We next turn to a set of substantive topics for which researchers have relied on emotion to explain some facet of public opinion or the media.

## Terrorism and War

Not surprisingly, research on terrorism and war has grown rapidly in recent years. Work in this area addresses a wide range of emotions that are thought to shape public opinion on terror and war-related policy choices. A number of scholars have found evidence of distinct effects within the domain of negative emotions. For instance, anxiety has consistently been shown to lead to more risk-averse or isolationist policy preferences, whereas anger predicts support for more confrontational policies (Huddy, Feldman, Taber, and Lahav 2005; Skitka, Bauman, Aramovich, and Morgan 2006). These findings are echoed in work that addresses risk estimates: fear increased and anger decreased perceived risks from terrorism (Fischhoff, Gonzalez, Lerner, and Small 2005; Lerner, Gonzalez, Small, and Fischhoff 2003). Moreover, anger has been found to trigger more attributions of blame for terrorism (Small, Lerner, and Fischhoff 2006). Thus, across a range of behaviors, anger seems to promote a more confident, aggressive response during crises, while fear causes individuals to draw inward. The inclusion of a wide variety of other emotions, from hope and pride (Gross, Brewer, and Aday 2009) to sadness, empathy, and guilt (Small, Lerner, and Fischhoff 2006; Pagano and Huo 2007; Zebel, Zimmermann, Viki, and Doosje 2008), suggests that scholars in this field have begun to evaluate the causes and effects of emotion on public opinion from a broader emotional foundation. For example, studies of post-conflict regions such as Bosnia and Iraq have demonstrated that guilt motivates support for reparative policies aimed at compensating for past harms (Pagano and Huo 2007; Zebel, Zimmermann, Viki, and Doosje 2008).

Terror management theory (TMT) suggests that terror arising from "mortality salience" intensifies efforts to maintain a cultural world view. For example, researchers have shown that reminders of death and the 9/11 attacks both increased support for President Bush (Landau et al. 2004). Evidence so far suggests that these findings are driven not by changes in emotional states, but rather by "death-related cognitions." That said, TMT claims that reactions are motivated by *terror* at the prospect of one's own death and induces this condition experimentally by asking subjects to write down what it will *feel like* when they die.

In general, content analyses have shown clear evidence of the "politics of fear," wherein politicians attempt to utilize emotion as a tool to stir public opinion (Burkitt 2005; De Castella, McGarty, and Musgrove 2009). Despite the common belief that the public can be manipulated by the use of emotion (cf. Brader 2006), there are few studies that attempt to test this presumption explicitly. That is, politicians have been shown to use fear as a tool, but researchers have not ascertained whether it has worked, or even exactly what it means to be "manipulated." Recent work exploring the effectiveness of politicians' scare tactics integrates game-theoretic modeling into the study of emotion and politics. The authors suggest that the strategic use of fear is constrained by a competitive information environment; politicians ought to be less likely to use fear as a manipulative tool when citizens are likely to receive feedback about the credibility of claims (Lupia and Menning 2009).

## Election Campaigns and Mass Media

Researchers also have explored the role of emotions in election campaigns and mass-mediated communication. Several studies focus on the relationship between emotions and the framing of political issues in the news. In addition to work already discussed on how emotions moderate framing effects, new research explores how framing of news stories affects emotions, drawing on appraisal theory to predict the triggers of specific emotions. In one experiment, news emphasizing situational explanations for the 1992 Los Angeles riots was more likely to elicit anger at racism and sympathy for rioters, while dispositional accounts provoked greater anger at the violence and sympathy for innocent victims (Gross and D'Ambrosio 2004). Another study found that news on globalization and viral outbreaks caused anxiety when stories stressed uncontrollable, unintentional threats, but also triggered anger when stories stressed controllable, intentional, and thus blameworthy threats (Brader, Groenendyk, and Valentino 2010).

Other work explores how emotions influence which news stories capture public attention. For example, episodically framed news is more emotionally engaging than thematically framed news (Gross 2008). Moreover, a new line of research suggests that emotions mediate the agenda-setting power of news. Accessibility in memory is necessary but not sufficient for agenda-setting; instead, problems are assessed as important to the extent the news arouses negative emotions (Miller 2007).

Several studies on war and terrorism in the past decade reinforce notions of the emotional power of television and imagery. Television coverage of the 9/11 attacks used more emotional language than print sources and, in turn, had a larger impact on the negative emotions of viewers (Cho et al. 2003). In news about 9/11, the intensity of attack images and strength of emotional expressions displayed by President Bush combined to produce stronger feelings of either anxiety or reassurance (Bucy 2003). When newspaper articles about a British engineer kidnapped during the Iraq War were combined with photos of the victim, readers experienced increased fear (but not anger or sympathy) and this boosted support for negotiations (Iyer and Oldmeadow 2006).

Elections are high tides of political passion, so it is unsurprising that scholars have focused heavily on the role of emotions in campaigns. As noted earlier, emotions appear to play a critical role in determining which of two classic profiles a voter resembles at any moment. Enthusiasm, and sometimes anger, give rise to the loyal partisan, while anxiety awakens the "reasoning good citizen" (Marcus, Neuman, and MacKuen 2000). Defection from political loyalties occurs, therefore, when campaigns successfully induce anxiety in an opposing partisan base, thereby enabling the campaign to use issues or candidate attractiveness to recruit crossover voters (MacKuen, Marcus, Neuman, and Keele 2007). In contrast to work on voting behavior, however, there has been comparably little rigorous research on how campaign media elicit emotions. A few studies have begun to examine how campaign ads in selected elections attempt to elicit emotions (Brader 2006; Richardson 2008; Scammell and Langer 2006). Others, building on earlier research into the emotional displays of politicians (Sullivan and Masters 1988), have explored how the intensity and appropriateness of candidates' emotional expressions affect TV audiences (Bucy and Bradley 2004; Stroud, Glaser, and Salovey 2005–6).

## Group-Based Emotions

Groups are central features of human existence, and as such they evoke powerful feelings. Group-based emotions are presumed to be affective responses uniformly evoked within a group, based on shared identities, and often evoked by and directed toward some out-group. These emotions are thought to arise from collective experience, real or imagined. Research tends to be highly situationally specific, with scholars studying particular regions or conflicts, such as Israel, Bosnia, and the US invasion of Iraq.

Many studies have focused on collective emotions defined by national groups. For example, research on Israeli attitudes toward Palestinians found hatred—as distinct from other emotions (i.e., anger, fear) and perceptions of threat—was the most important predictor of political intolerance (Halperin, Canetti-Nisim, and Hirsch-Hoefler 2009). In another study, Americans were more forgiving of harm committed against Iraqis by fellow Americans to the extent that they felt anxious about the future of their in-group (Wohl and Branscombe 2009). Research in South Africa (Klandermans, Werner, and Van Doorn 2008) and the Netherlands (Zebel, Zimmermann, Viki, and Doosje 2008) has suggested that collective feelings of guilt about in-group behavior strongly mediate support for reparations or affirmative action policies.

Not all studies focus on national groups, however. A number of scholars have examined how emotions shape the internal and external politics of social movements (see Goodwin, Jasper, and Polletta 2001). For example, in an in-depth study of AIDS activism, Gould (2009) argues that activists in the late 1980s and early 1990s cultivated an "emotional common sense" that drew on grief and anger to redirect the gay rights movement toward more open and confrontational action.

Emotions may prove particularly important when examining in-group/out-group distinctions. Recently, scholars have argued for moving beyond the simple focus on in-group pride and out-group prejudice that has dominated past research and focusing instead on specific emotions arising from distinct situational appraisals (most of this work is grounded explicitly in appraisal theories of emotion). Cottrell and Neuberg (2005), for example, found that white Americans expressed a distinct "profile" of emotions—anger, fear, disgust, pity, and envy—toward groups in society (e.g., racial minorities, fundamentalist Christians, feminists, gays) that was not captured by general measures of prejudice. Although many such studies have been carried out in social psychology, often under the heading of intergroup emotions theory (MacKie and Smith 2003), few studies have extended this line of work to the political domain. Nonetheless, these yield promising results. In the wake of the 9/11 attacks, Dutch and Belgian citizens felt greater fear when cued experimentally to think of Americans as part of a common group rather than as a distinct group (Dumont, Yzerbyt, Wigboldus, and Gordijn 2003). Comparable effects for sadness and anger did not emerge, because only fear-relevant appraisals (e.g., future risk of being harmed) were altered by the shift in whether participants saw themselves linked to Americans. Similarly, Democrats and Republicans were more likely to report feelings of pleasure at others' misfortunes (*schadenfreude*) when those others were from the opposing party (Combs, Powell, Schurtz, and Smith 2009). Finally, new research on whites' racial attitudes has found that priming anger, not fear, activates racial resentment, thereby increasing opposition to affirmative action (Banks and Valentino 2007), and that anti-Hispanic prejudice has stronger links to anger about immigration than to emotions like fear and enthusiasm (Brader and Valentino 2007).

## CONCLUDING THOUGHTS

In sum, the study of emotion and public opinion is a young but rapidly growing field. Recent years have witnessed a steady stream of publications and an expanding, increasingly diverse set of contributors from several disciplines. Already this fresh line of inquiry promises to make major contributions to our understanding of politics. Three stand out to us. First, emotions help to reconcile competing theoretical accounts by explaining individual and situational heterogeneity in the process of opinion formation and political choice. Second, emotions, as motivational impulses, provide scholars with a way to make the often elusive connection between public opinion and political action. Third, cognizance of emotions and their functions allows us to make better sense of parts of the media and political environment that have been previously ignored or taken for granted.

All of that said, there remains much growing to do. The literature contains a mix of different approaches and few full theories. Empirical scholarship has focused on the effects of emotions, while saying comparably little about their situational and individual antecedents. Few scholars attempt to consider both the antecedents and consequences of emotion within the confines of a single study, thus leaving a patchwork of findings with little to connect them. More complicated theoretical issues also await, such as the need to integrate pre-conscious and post-awareness affective processes. Furthermore, this body of research has yet to integrate the role of personality, for one way of understanding personality is an array of baseline responsiveness of emotional systems. Finally, the field would greatly benefit from more work on measurement. Few publications address the reliability or validity of their measures, let alone consider whether their methodological approach is suited to the theoretical focus.

The "dependent variable" approach many studies adopt makes it a challenge to determine whether relationships are narrow (specific to the outcome under examination) or broad (applicable across a broad class of phenomena). The dependent variable focus also tends to balkanize the research as scholars contributing or consuming research with a given focus may not attend to parallel work focused on other outcomes. Thus, this pattern of research will retard a broader understanding of the central roles that emotion plays in politics and public opinion.

Despite these concerns, we have seen material progress in understanding what role emotions play in political life. We need but repeat here that the presumption of an executive and insulated cognition protected from the despoliations of passion has largely been set aside for a reformulation of mutually interactive and dependent affective and cognitive processes. Moreover, as work on emotion has proceeded from a simple valence, approach avoidance conception to one of multiple dimensions, this has import for the lay and academic interest in "negative" politics. The concept of negativity is likely confounded inasmuch as research on emotion has identified at least three distinct "negative" states, each with distinct antecedents and downstream effects: anxiety, depression, and anger.[7]

Finally, the findings of this field have clear normative import for our view of emotions and their "place" in politics. Much of the early research, echoing work in psychology, focused on rehabilitating emotions such that they are understood as essential, adaptive, functional elements of human reason and behavior. This is, in our view, a necessary and proper corrective to centuries-old misunderstandings about emotions that persist in popular culture and scholarship today. But the pendulum is wont to swing too far. Whatever their adaptive evolutionary benefits, emotions can also, *at times*, live up to their reputation for being disruptive, destructive, and overwhelming. The lesson of contemporary research is that emotions are neither inherently inferior nor inherently superior, but rather essential to both carrying out and understanding human behavior.

---

[7] According to AI theory, these emotions lead to deliberative citizenship, abandonment of citizen action, and steadfast reliance on extant convictions, respectively (MacKuen, Wolak, Keele, and Marcus 2010).

# REFERENCES

ABELSON, R., KINDER, D., PETERS, M., and FISKE, S. 1982. Affective and Semantic Components in Political Personal Perception. *Journal of Personality and Social Psychology*, 42: 619–30.

ARISTOTLE. 1954. *Rhetoric*. New York: Modern Library.

BANKS, A., and VALENTINO, N. 2007. Those Darn Blacks: Anger, Fear and Whites' Racial Policy Preferences. Paper presented at the Annual Meeting of the International Society of Political Psychology, Portland, OR.

BRADER, T. 2005. Striking a Responsive Chord: How Political Ads Motivate and Persuade Voters by Appealing to Emotions. *American Journal of Political Science*, 49: 388–405.

—— 2006. *Campaigning for Hearts and Minds*. Chicago: University of Chicago Press.

—— Forthcoming. The Political Relevance of Emotions: "Reassessing" Revisited. *Political Psychology*.

—— and VALENTINO, N. 2007. Identities, Interests, and Emotions: Symbolic versus Material Wellsprings of Fear, Anger, and Enthusiasm. In *The Affect Effect: Dynamics of Emotion in Political Thinking and Behavior*, ed. W. R. Neuman, G. Marcus, A. Crigler, and M. MacKuen. Chicago: University of Chicago Press.

—— GROENENDYK, E., and VALENTINO, N. 2010. Fight or Flight? When Political Threats Arouse Public Anger and Fear. Paper presented at the Annual Meeting of the International Society of Political Psychology, San Francisco, July 7–10.

—— VALENTINO, N., and SUHAY, E. 2008. What Triggers Public Opposition to Immigration? Anxiety, Group Cues, and Immigration Threat. *American Journal of Political Science*, 52: 959–78.

BUCY, E. 2003. Emotion, Presidential Communication, and Traumatic News. *Harvard International Journal of Press/Politics*, 8: 76–96.

—— and BRADLEY, S. 2004. Presidential Expressions and Viewer Emotion. *Social Science Information*, 43: 59.

BURKITT, I. 2005. Powerful Emotions: Power, Government and Opposition in the "War on Terror." *Sociology*, 39: 679–95.

CACIOPPO, J., BERNTSON, G., and KLEIN, D. 1992. What Is an Emotion? The Role of Somatovisceral Afference, with a Special Emphasis on Somatovisceral Illusions. *Review of Personality and Social Psychology*, 14: 63–98.

CASSINO, D., and LODGE, M. 2007. The Primacy of Affect in Political Evaluations. In *The Affect Effect: Dynamics of Emotion in Political Thinking and Behavior*, ed. W. R. Neuman, G. Marcus, A. Crigler, and M. MacKuen. Chicago: University of Chicago Press.

CHO, J., BOYLE, M., KEUM, H., SHEVY, M., MCLEOD, D., SHAH, D., and PAN, Z. 2003. Media, Terrorism, and Emotionality. *Journal of Broadcasting & Electronic Media*, 47: 309–27.

COMBS, D., POWELL, C., SCHURTZ, D., and SMITH, R. 2009. Politics, *Schadenfreude*, and Ingroup Identification. *Journal of Experimental Social Psychology*, 45: 635–46.

CONOVER, P., and FELDMAN, S. 1986. Emotional Reactions to the Economy. *American Journal of Political Science*, 30: 30–78.

COTTRELL, C., and NEUBERG, S. 2005. Different Emotional Reactions to Different Groups: A Sociofunctional Threat-Based Approach to "Prejudice." *Journal of Personality and Social Psychology*, 88: 770–89.

DAMASIO, A. R. 1994. *Descartes' Error: Emotion, Reason and the Human Brain*. New York: Putnam.

DE CASTELLA, K., MCGARTY, C., and MUSGROVE, L. 2009. Fear Appeals in Political Rhetoric about Terrorism. *Political Psychology*, 30: 1–26.

DRUCKMAN, J., and MCDERMOTT, R. 2008. Emotion and the Framing of Risky Choice. *Political Behavior*, 30: 297–321.

DUMONT, M., YZERBYT, V., WIGBOLDUS, D., and GORDIJN, E. 2003. Social Categorization and Fear Reactions to the September 11th Terrorist Attacks. *Personality and Social Psychology Bulletin*, 29: 1509–20.

EKMAN, P., LEVENSON, R., and FRIESEN, W. 1983. Autonomic Nervous System Activity Distinguishes among Emotions. *Science*, 221: 1208–10.

FELDMAN, S., and HUDDY, L. n.d. The Paradoxical Effects of Anxiety on Political Learning. Unpublished manuscript. Stony Brook University.

FISCHHOFF, B., GONZALEZ, R., LERNER, J., and SMALL, D. 2005. Evolving Judgments of Terror Risks: Foresight, Hindsight, and Emotion. *Journal of Experimental Psychology: Applied*, 11: 124–39.

FOWLES, D. 1982. Heart Rate as an Index of Anxiety: Failure of a Hypothesis. In *Perspectives in Cardiovascular Psychophysiology*, ed. J. Cacioppo and R. Petty. New York: Guilford Press.

GEVA, N., and SKORICK, J. M. 2006. The Emotional Calculus of Foreign Policy Decisions. In *Feeling Politics: Emotion in Political Information Processing*, ed. D. Redlawsk. New York: Palgrave Macmillan.

GOODWIN, J., JASPER, J., and POLLETTA, F. (eds.) 2001. *Passionate Politics: Emotions and Social Movements*. Chicago: University of Chicago Press.

GOULD, D. 2009. *Moving Politics: Emotion and ACT UP's Fight against AIDS*. Chicago: University of Chicago Press.

GRAY, J. 1987. *The Psychology of Fear and Stress*. Cambridge: Cambridge University Press.

GROSS, K. 2008. Framing Persuasive Appeals: Episodic and Thematic Framing, Emotional Response, and Policy Opinion. *Political Psychology*, 29: 169–92.

—— and D'AMBROSIO, L. 2004. Framing Emotional Response. *Political Psychology*, 25: 1–29.

—— BREWER, P., and ADAY, S. 2009. Confidence in Government and Emotional Responses to Terrorism after September 11, 2001. *American Politics Research*, 37: 107–28.

HALPERIN, E., CANETTI-NISIM, D., and HIRSCH-HOEFLER, S. 2009. The Central Role of Group-Based Hatred as an Emotional Antecedent of Political Intolerance. *Political Psychology*, 30: 93–123.

HUDDY, L., FELDMAN, S., and CASSESE, E. 2007. On the Distinct Political Effects of Anxiety and Anger. In *The Affect Effect: Dynamics of Emotion in Political Thinking and Behavior*, ed. W. R. Neuman, G. Marcus, A. Crigler, and M. MacKuen. Chicago: University of Chicago Press.

—— —— TABER, C., and LAHAV, G. 2005. Threat, Anxiety, and Support for Antiterrorism Policies. *American Journal of Political Science*, 4: 593–608.

HULLETT, C., LOUDEN, A., and MITRA, A. 2003. Emotion and Political Cognition. *Communication Monographs*, 70: 250–63.

HUTCHINGS, V., VALENTINO, N., PHILPOT, T., and WHITE, I. 2006. Racial Cues in Campaign News: The Effects of Candidate Strategies on Group Activation and Political Attentiveness among African Americans. In *Feeling Politics: Emotion in Political Information Processing*, ed. D. Redlawsk. New York: Palgrave Macmillan.

ISBELL, L., and OTTATI, V. 2002. The Emotional Voter. In *The Social Psychology of Politics*, ed. V. Ottati, S. Tindale, et al. New York: Kluwer.

IYER, A., and OLDMEADOW, J. 2006. Picture This: Emotional and Political Responses to Photographs of the Kenneth Bigley Kidnapping. *European Journal of Social Psychology*, 36/5: 635–47.

JAMES, W. 1884. What Is an Emotion? *Mind*, 9: 188–205.

JUST, M., CRIGLER, A., and BELT, T. 2007. Don't Give Up Hope: Emotions, Candidate Appraisals, and Votes. In *The Affect Effect: Dynamics of Emotion in Political Thinking and Behavior*, ed. W. R. Neuman, G. Marcus, A. Crigler, and M. MacKuen. Chicago: University of Chicago Press.

KINDER, D. 1994. Reason and Emotion in American Political Life. In *Beliefs, Reasoning, and Decision Making*, ed. R. C. Schank and E. Langer. Hillsdale, NJ: Lawrence Erlbaum.

KLANDERMANS, B., WERNER, M., and VAN DOORN, M. 2008. Redeeming Apartheid's Legacy: Collective Guilt, Political Ideology, and Compensation. *Political Psychology*, 29: 331–49.

LADD, J., and LENZ, G. 2008. Reassessing the Role of Anxiety in Vote Choice. *Political Psychology*, 29: 275–96.

LANDAU, M., SOLOMON, S., GREENBERG, J., COHEN, F., PYSZCZYNSKI, T., ARNDT, J., MILLER, C., OGILVIE, D., and COOK, A. 2004. Deliver Us from Evil: The Effects of Mortality Salience and Reminders of 9/11 on Support for President George W. Bush. *Personality and Social Psychology Bulletin*, 30: 1136–50.

LAZARUS, R. 1991. *Emotion and Adaptation*. New York: Oxford University Press.

LEDOUX, J. 1996. *The Emotional Brain*. New York: Simon & Schuster.

LERNER, J., GONZALEZ, R., SMALL, D., and FISCHHOFF, B. 2003. Effects of Fear and Anger on Perceived Risks of Terrorism: A National Field Experiment. *Psychological Science*, 14: 144–50.

LODGE, M., and TABER, C. 2005. The Automaticity of Affect for Political Leaders, Groups, and Issues. *Political Psychology*, 26: 455–82.

LUPIA, A., and MENNING, J. 2009. When Can Politicians Scare Citizens into Supporting Bad Policies? *American Journal of Political Science*, 53: 90–106.

MACKIE, D., and SMITH, E. (eds.) 2003. *From Prejudice to Intergroup Emotions*. New York: Psychology Press.

MACKUEN, M., MARCUS, G., NEUMAN, W. R., and KEELE, L. 2007. The Third Way: The Theory of Affective Intelligence and American Democracy. In *The Affect Effect: Dynamics of Emotion in Political Thinking and Behavior*, ed. W. R. Neuman, G. Marcus, A. Crigler, and M. MacKuen. Chicago: University of Chicago Press.

——WOLAK, J., KEELE, L., and MARCUS, G. 2010. Civic Engagements: Resolute Partisanship or Reflective Deliberation. *American Journal of Political Science*, 54: 440–58.

MALHOTRA, N., and KUO, A. 2009. Emotions as Moderators of Information Cue Use. *American Politics Research*, 37: 301–26.

MARCUS, G. 1988. The Structure of Emotional Response: 1984 Presidential Candidates. *American Political Science Review*, 82: 735–61.

—— 2000. Emotions in Politics. *Annual Review of Political Science*, 3: 221–50.

—— 2008. Presidential Address—Blinded by the Light: Aspiration and Inspiration in Political Psychology. *Political Psychology*, 29: 313–30.

—— and MACKUEN, M. 1993. Anxiety, Enthusiasm, and the Vote: The Emotional Underpinnings of Learning and Involvement during Presidential Campaigns. *American Political Science Review*, 87: 672–85.

—— —— and NEUMAN, W. R. Forthcoming. Parsimony and Complexity: Developing and Testing Theories of Affective Intelligence. *Political Psychology*.

MARCUS, G., NEUMAN, W. R., and MacKUEN, M. 2000. *Affective Intelligence and Political Judgment*. Chicago: University of Chicago Press.

—— SULLIVAN, J., THEISS-MORSE, E., and STEVENS, D. 2005. The Emotional Foundation of Political Cognition. *Political Psychology*, 26: 949–63.

MILLER, J. 2007. Examining the Mediators of Agenda Setting: A New Experimental Paradigm Reveals the Role of Emotions. *Political Psychology*, 28/6: 689–717.

MORRIS, J., SQUIRES, N., TABER, C., and LODGE, M. 2003. Activation of Political Attitudes: A Psychophysiological Examination of the Hot Cognition Hypothesis. *Political Psychology*, 24/4: 727–45.

NABI, R. 2003. Exploring the Framing Effects of Emotion. *Communication Research*, 30/2: 224–47.

NEUMAN, W. R., MARCUS, G., CRIGLER, A., and MacKUEN, M. (eds.) 2007. *The Affect Effect: Dynamics of Emotion in Political Thinking and Behavior*. Chicago: University of Chicago Press.

PAGANO, S., and HUO, Y. 2007. The Role of Moral Emotions in Predicting Support for Political Actions in Post-War Iraq. *Political Psychology*, 28/2: 227–55.

REDLAWSK, D. (ed.) 2006. *Feeling Politics: Emotion in Political Information Processing*. New York: Palgrave Macmillan.

—— CIVETTINI, A., and LAU, R. 2007. Affective Intelligence and Voting. In *The Affect Effect: Dynamics of Emotion in Political Thinking and Behavior*, ed. W. R. Neuman, G. Marcus, A. Crigler, and M. MacKuen. Chicago: University of Chicago Press.

RICHARDSON, G., JR. 2008. *Pulp Politics*. Lanham, MD: Rowman & Littlefield.

RUDOLPH, T., GANGL, A., and STEVENS, D. 2000. The Effects of Efficacy and Emotions on Campaign Involvement. *Journal of Politics*, 62: 1189–97.

SCAMMELL, M., and LANGER, A. I. 2006. Political Advertising: Why Is It So Boring? *Media, Culture, & Society*, 28: 763–84.

SKITKA, L., BAUMAN, C., ARAMOVICH, N., and MORGAN, G. S. 2006. Confrontational and Preventative Policy Responses to Terrorism: Anger Wants a Fight and Fear Wants "Them" to Go Away. *Basic and Applied Social Psychology*, 28: 375–84.

SMALL, D., and LERNER, J. 2008. Emotional Policy: Personal Sadness and Anger Shape Judgments about a Welfare Case. *Political Psychology*, 29: 149–68.

—— —— and FISCHHOFF, B. 2006. Emotion Priming and Attributions for Terrorism. *Political Psychology*, 27: 289–98.

STEENBERGEN, M., and ELLIS, C. 2006. Fear and Loathing in American Elections. In *Feeling Politics: Emotion in Political Information Processing*, ed. D. Redlawsk. New York: Palgrave Macmillan.

STROUD, L., GLASER, J., and SALOVEY, P. 2005-6. The Effects of Partisanship and Candidate Emotionality on Voter Preference. *Imagination, Cognition, and Personality*, 25: 25–44.

SULLIVAN, D., and MASTERS, R. 1988. Happy Warriors: Leaders' Facial Displays, Viewers Emotions, and Political Support. *American Journal of Political Science*, 32: 345–68.

VALENTINO, N., BANKS, A., HUTCHINGS, V., and DAVIS, A. 2009. Selective Exposure in the Internet Age: The Interaction between Anxiety and Information Utility. *Political Psychology*, 30: 591–613.

—— BRADER, T., GROENENDYK, E., GREGOROWICZ, K., and HUTCHINGS, V. 2011. Election Night's Alright for Fighting: The Role of Emotions in Political Participation. *Journal of Politics*, 73: 156–70.

—— GREGOROWICZ, K., and GROENENDYK, E. 2009. Efficacy, Emotions and the Habit of Participation. *Political Behavior*, 31: 307–30.

—— HUTCHINGS, V., BANKS, A., and DAVIS, A. 2008. Is a Worried Citizen a Good Citizen? Emotions, Political Information Seeking, and Learning via the Internet. *Political Psychology*, 29: 247–73.

WOHL, M., and BRANSCOMBE, N. 2009. Group Threat, Collective Angst, and Ingroup Forgiveness for the War in Iraq. *Political Psychology*, 30: 193–217.

ZEBEL, S., ZIMMERMANN, A., VIKI, G. T., and DOOSJE, B. 2008. Dehumanization and Guilt as Distinct but Related Predictors of Support for Reparation Policies. *Political Psychology*, 29: 193–219.

CHAPTER 25

........................................................................................

# PROSPECT THEORY AND RISK ASSESSMENT

........................................................................................

ROSE McDERMOTT

ANY discussion of public opinion, democratic governance, and deliberation involves the possibility of risk for some group of citizens. When one interest group succeeds in captivating the forces of government to serve their needs and goals, another group with conflicting or contrasting aims may suffer, if only as a result of the diversion of resources from their constituency. But obviously some risks constitute greater threats to more people than others, and various ways of assessing and responding to the relative allocation of risk exist. Individuals perceive and respond to various risks differently, finding some more threatening and problematic than others, and governments face tremendous challenges in interpreting, communicating, and managing these dangers in a way the public finds responsive and appropriate.

Traditional economic models conceptualize risk in terms of cost-benefit analyses, calculating the relative cost and probability across various choices, and advocating for the options that present the highest likelihood of achieving the greatest good for the most people, or, more cynically, best serve the needs and interests of those who have the ability, power, wealth, and influence to substantively affect the nature of the choice. Such models, although largely based on theories developed exclusively in the context of financial risk, dominate the analysis of risk and offer parsimonious normative guides for human decision-making. However, they often fail to adequately represent the way people actually make decisions, particularly when confronting non-monetary choices.

In fact, the concept of risk and its assessment and evaluation can be measured and analyzed in more descriptively accurate, empirically valid ways, including the psychological model prospect theory (Kahneman and Tversky 1979, 1984). Kahneman won the Nobel Prize for economics for this work in 2004; although Tversky had died in 1996 and thus was denied this honor, Kahneman accepted the award in both their names. This model examines the nature of decision-making under conditions of risk. More recent developments in the areas of psychology, cognitive neuroscience, and behavioral economics have also demonstrated the importance of incorporating emotion into comprehensive models of risk assessment.

This chapter proceeds in four parts. First, prospect theory and its contributions to the literature will be defined and described in more depth. This overview situates prospect theory within a broader context of reaction to more traditional economic approaches to risk-taking. The second section addresses more recent developments in the psychological literature on risk, which attempts to incorporate notions of affect and emotion into risk perception and management. Third, opportunities for theoretical development in this area, including promising avenues of application to topics in public opinion research, will be addressed. Less fruitful paths in the development of future research will be noted as well. The final section provides an overview of the ways in which these enduring debates and controversies can inform our understanding of the processes of public opinion and democratic governance.

## PROSPECT THEORY AND RISK-TAKING

As noted, traditional economic models approach risk, like anything else, from the assumption of rational actors seeking to maximize their utility. But actual human risk perception, assessment, and propensity, particularly outside the domain of finances and in the realm of life and death, often fail to comply with such assumptions.[1]

Prospect theory was developed in explicit opposition to standard economic theories of expected utility whose assumptions of rational behavior on the part of individual actors met with serious empirical compromises in the experimental literature in both psychology and behavioral economics. Aware of these limitations, Kahneman and Tversky developed a more empirically based approach to decision-making under conditions of risk, which they called prospect theory (1979, 1984). This model demonstrated that individuals respond to risk differently depending on whether they are confronting gains or losses. Specifically, people tend to respond cautiously in the face of gains and take risks to recoup losses. Importantly, losses matter more to people psychologically when making decisions about risk than gains. Prospect theory has been well described and characterized in political science, and interested readers are referred for greater detail and applications to those previous discussions (Levy 1997a, 1997b; McDermott 1998, 2004).

Prospect theory has two parts. First comes the editing phase, which allows for the introduction of the now famous "framing" effects, whereby options can be presented or manipulated in ways that allow the method, order, or wording of choices to

---

[1] For examples of psychometric assessment of risk with regard to evaluations of nuclear power, see Slovic (1987). For work on the influence of emotion on risky decision-making, including references to differences in assessments based on life and death issues versus financial ones, see Druckman and McDermott (2008).

substantively affect the content of the decision reached. This is followed by the evaluation phase, which itself consists of two distinct aspects which roughly correspond in purpose, if not in function, to the economic concepts of utility and probability. These are referred to as the "value" and the "weighting" functions, respectively.

The value function describes the way in which people attach value, or what economists might call "utility," to options. But such assessments take place in ways which radically diverge from the processes that undergird rational theories. The value function reflects three important characteristics about the way in which people make choices concerning risk. First, marginal changes matter. In other words, while classical economic theory argues that absolute outcomes drive behavior, and more is always better, prospect theory allows for the recognition that relative outcomes sometimes matter more. This provides insight into why a poor person might value a small reduction in his taxes more than a rich person might appreciate a larger one.

Second, people act differently when confronting gains as opposed to losses. People tend to be risk-averse when they are doing well, or contemplate gains, but demonstrate risk-seeking when confronting losses. These judgments are evaluated relative to a so-called "reference point." While most observers typically treat the reference point as synonymous with the status quo, or current position of the decision-maker, the reference point can refer to some point of expectation, aspiration, or social comparison held by the individual.

Third, loss hurts more than concomitant gains please. On average, losses hurt about two and a half times more than gains (Tversky and Kahneman 1991; Kahneman, Knetsch, and Thaler 1991; Shefrin and Statman 1985). In other words, in order to induce someone to risk a loss of $1, a potential benefit of $2.50 would need to be offered to make that person indifferent across the gamble. More than any other aspect of prospect theory, loss aversion has provided the most robust and versatile experimental result; across many issues and measures, it proves close to impossible to eliminate.

The second aspect of the evaluation phase of prospect theory involves the weighting function, which provides the psychological representation of how individuals calibrate the importance of likelihood, as opposed to probability itself. Two important features of the weighting function deserve mention. First, people have a hard time with outcomes they perceive to be either impossible or certain. Importantly, an outcome does not *actually* have to be certain or impossible to be psychologically treated as such; "close enough for company work" evaluations become collapsed into extreme judgments in ways which economists would find normatively unjustified. In short, people will pay more to decrease the chance of an undesired outcome from 1 percent to absolute zero than they will pay to reduce it an equal amount in another part of the distribution, from, say, 40 percent to 39 percent.

Second, people tend to overweight the importance of unlikely events while simultaneously underweighting the influence of moderate- to high-probability events. So, for example, people find it easy to be terrified of terrorism, although the overall base rate probability of being killed in a terrorist act in the United States remains vanishingly small. Simultaneously, changing very common negative lifestyle habits such as smoking, unsafe sex, overeating, or being sedentary remains a perpetually excruciating challenge for public health officials, although the probability of death, much less huge and escalating public health costs, resulting from such activities in fact remains much higher than as a consequence of terrorism.

# ADDITIONAL PSYCHOLOGICAL PERSPECTIVES ON RISK

Prospect theory does not offer the only conceptualization of risk in the psychological literature any more than expected utility models present the only approach to risk within economics. Before moving on to a discussion of recent developments in risk analysis from a more affective perspective, at least one perspective emerging from an older tradition deserves mention.

## Personality Approaches

Prior to the cognitive revolution in psychology, which arguably reached its apex with the work of Tversky and Kahneman in the late 1980s and early 1990s, research in personality and clinical psychology posited that risk-taking emerged as a function of individual personality. Some people, whether by temperament or by socialization, simply seem more comfortable taking risks than others. Note the important difference in putative causal mechanism between these models and prospect theory. Personality models locate the cause of risk in internal, relatively stable aspects of character, while prospect theory locates the motive for action within the external situational environment. The relative advantage of prospect theory in this regard, which no doubt accounts, at least in part, for its appeal and accessibility, thus lies in its straightforward parsimony and elegance. Observers do not need to know anything about the individual person in order to predict her risk propensity when confronting particular classes of risk; such causal models held familiarity from standard economic theories such as the laws of supply and demand that allowed aggregation of choice across individuals without having to know anything outside a simple economic indicator such as income.

For many years, personality theory floundered because of its inability to predict behavior across situations at a level that was any greater than about .3 (Mischel and Peake 1982). The development of the so-called Big Five personality typing system (Costa and McCrae 2003) revolutionized the field and gave it a new lease of life by providing an empirically based consensus of the fundamental dimensions of personality, providing a series of five dimensions along which any individual can be characterized and compared with others. These basic dimensions encompass extroversion, neuroticism, openness to experience, agreeableness, and conscientiousness. Note that none of these categories, nor any of their subtypes, specifically assess or categorize risk-taking per se.

Work on leadership in political science has begun to use the Big Five and other personality instruments to explore how individual differences in risk propensity might drive variance in outcome (Kowert and Hermann 1997). Byman and Pollack (2001) also suggest that individual character provides an important component in analyzing political leaders and their behavior; indeed, those who rise to high levels of political power may in fact be more risk-taking than most. Personality authors suggest that the character of the person as well as the context of choice may influence the nature of risky decision-making in important ways.

## Risk as Feelings

An alternative model of risk-taking which has emerged more recently represents a swing in the theoretical pendulum from the more cognitive approach presented by prospect theory to the more affectively focused perspective currently favored by many psychologists and other neuroscientists.

Slovic and his colleagues, among others, helped elucidate some of the emotional factors which influence decision-making, but which often run contrary to more normative economic notions of how such decisions should be made (Slovic, Finucane, Peters, and MacGregor 2004; Peters and Slovic 2006). Other scholars, building on this insight, contrast risk as analysis with risk as feelings (Loewenstein, Weber, Hsee, and Welch 2001). These two systems operate simultaneously and in interaction to assess risk using different strategies of evaluation. At root, these two mechanisms reflect the distinction between automatic and controlled processes first delineated by Schneider and Shiffrin (1977) and characterized in many similar ways since by various others, including rational and experiential (Kirkpatrick and Epstein 1992) and reflective and reflexive (Lieberman, Gaunt, and Gilbert 2002), or Kahneman and Tversky's notion of System 1 and System 2 (Kahneman and Tversky 1982).

The controlled processes refer to those that rely on normative rules, such as logic, probability, and other abstract concepts in order to assess risk. The automatic processes rest on intuitive, affective, instinctive reactions that often remain inaccessible to conscious reflection or deliberation. This system depends heavily on images and the way in which experience becomes associated with an intuitive feeling that something is good or bad; in this way, the model appears synchronous with the one posited by Damasio's (1994) somatic marker hypothesis, which also suggests an association between such emotional experiences and physical feelings in the body.

The automatic system has often been referred to as the "affect heuristic" (Slovic, Finucane, Peters, and MacGregor 2004), indicating the way in which affect can serve as a rule of thumb upon which people base decisions; like any other heuristic, it typically operates with incredible speed, accuracy, and efficiency, but remains prone to particular systematic biases in certain contexts. Slovic, Finucane, Peters, and MacGregor

(2004) suggest an evolutionary basis for the development of this rapid and efficient automatic system, explaining why such a means of risk assessment remains the most natural and automatic for most people to employ when confronting new dangers. However, many advocates of normative risk analysis would consider assessments based on emotion to rest on faulty, irrational grounds.

In reality, while each system manifests particular limits and biases, both are required to produce rational decision-making. Indeed, these two systems may find expression in the distinction between expert and lay risk assessment. Experts, who tend to assess risk in terms of expected annual mortality rates as a function of population (e.g., one in a million risk of contracting cancer given exposure to a particular environmental toxin), clearly rely disproportionately on abstract data to reach their conclusions (Slovic, Fischhoff, and Lichtenstein 1979). Such strategies depend on more controlled processes. Lay people, on the other hand, tend to react to many threats instinctually, displaying automatic responses to such dangers, particularly when those threats seem to incorporate some dread component. This disparity in the mechanisms upon which experts and the mass public rely when perceiving and responding to risk may help explain the difficulty in developing effective public policies precisely because experts and lay people approach these problems from differing perspectives, employing often disparate value systems based on quite divergent bases of evaluation.

Depending on the problem, either automatic or controlled processes can potentiate effective decision-making. However, optimal choice requires both systems working in concert. Without emotional guidance, rational judgment as it is typically understood fails to exist (Bechara, Damasio, Tranel, and Damasio 1997). And calculated deliberation, without sufficient consideration of how people actually feel, think about, and respond to risk, will likely result in counterproductive forms of public policy by breeding mistrust between policy-makers, government regulators, and citizens in precisely those domains where success may depend on public acquiescence. Imagine, for example, an anti-terrorism policy which required public participation in reporting unusual incidents, or a public health campaign where citizens needed to stay home when they became infected to reduce the spread of a disease. If the public did not believe the instructions given by the government, because of either lack of understanding or skepticism about manipulation, compliance would suffer, strategies would fail, and any subsequent negative consequences would only serve to fuel the flames of future mistrust.

One of the interesting aspects of risk perception relates to the often-found inverse relationship between perceived risk and benefit. In other words, in contemplating a potential risk such as nuclear power, those who believe it will prove beneficial also tend to simultaneously expect few problems to result, while those who fear the risks expect little benefit. Logically, these factors of risk and benefit need not be related in such a fashion, and yet public reactions tend to occur in this way with great regularity (Alhakami and Slovic 1994; Finucane, Alhakami, Slovic, and Johnson 2000). This observed pattern recalls Jervis's (1976) mention of a similar phenomenon, whereby those who advocated a policy envisioned fewer downsides and saw many more potential benefits than those who opposed it, and vice versa.

Finucane, Alhakami, Slovic, and Johnson (2000) suggest that these responses inter-twine under the rubric of the affect heuristic, which provides a unified emotional foundation upon which individuals rest their evaluation of both risks and benefits. Obviously this linked relationship between risks and benefits raises the question of whether manipulating one component, for example by highlighting perceived benefits, might shift people's responses to the expected risks in a concomitant fashion as well (Alhakami and Slovic 1994).

In some sense, what a two-system approach suggests is that the contrast between affect and cognition, at least with regard to risk, but likely in response to many other stimuli as well, remains an utterly false dichotomy. It is not that one or the other guides decisions about risk exclusively. Rather, each operates independently but simulta-neously, and each can be overridden by the other depending on context and situation.

In truth, these automatic and controlled systems operate in concert as well as in contrast, depending on the specific challenge. Problems tend to emerge when a conflict develops between these two systems in terms of our behavioral intentions. This conundrum will be familiar to anyone who has ever been on a diet, or struggled with an addiction of any kind. The conscious, deliberative process can tell us that we should not eat that cookie, that we should go take a walk instead, and that if we eat the cookie, we will regret it later and sabotage our earlier good efforts, while all the while the automatic system simply wants to eat the cookie because it tastes good and makes us feel better because of past positive associations and current physiological reinforce-ments. Camerer, Loewenstein, and Prelec (2005, 43) depict this conflict between the deliberative and visceral responses to risk in less pedestrian fashion when they note the many ways "our deliberative self uses diverse tactics to get us to take risks, or to perform in the face of risks, that our visceral self would much prefer to avoid."

Neuro-imaging evidence shows that a great deal of risk-averse behavior results from the fear that such risks generate in the mind of the decision-maker. Anatomically, this activation occurs in the area of the amygdala, the part of the limbic system in the brain that processes many of our emotions, but appears particularly implicated in the experience and expression of fear. The amygdala receives information from both the automatic and controlled systems (Ledoux 1996; Vuilleumier, Armony, Driver, and Dolan 2001).

Moreover, the brain appears to process risk and uncertainty in different places (McCabe et al. 2001). Risk typically incorporates known odds, while uncertain or ambiguous choices involve some lack of clarity about the probabilities confronted. Hsu et al. (2005) found activation in the insula as well as the amygdala when subjects confronted ambiguous problems. The insula has most typically been associated with disgust responses in past research.

Emotion can also help explain risk-taking as well, as when the pleasures associated with an addiction incentivize costly behavior (for a nice review, see Camerer, Loewen-stein, and Prelec 2005). It increasingly appears that, at least in some cases, genetic predisposition can play a role in susceptibility to risk-taking. For example, a genetic polymorphism on the dopamine allele (D2A1), which has been associated with thrill-seeking, appears more commonly in compulsive gamblers (Comings 1998). Drugs developed to block the action of opiates in the brain, such as naltrexone, seem to block this compulsion (Moreyra et al. 2000) and have been shown to have some success in reducing the propensity to engage in compulsive shopping as well (McElroy et al. 1991).

Importantly, different discrete emotions can affect risk assessment and risk propensity in various ways as well. For example, sadness appears to make people ruminate more, which can increase the time they take to make decisions, enhancing the probability that controlled processes become engaged in decision-making despite the overall mood state (Bodenhausen, Sheppard, and Kramer 1994). Sadness also heightens bottom-up processing, while anger induces exactly the opposite, top-down kinds of processing (Schwarz and Clore 1983).

Anger, on the other hand, tends to increase optimism and confidence, such that people become more likely to believe that their enterprises will achieve success, raising prospects for risk-taking in the face of challenge (Lerner and Keltner 2000). Since the propensity for anger and fear differs by sex, with men displaying greater anger and women showing a higher tendency to experience fear, hormonal processes may be implicated in the expression and manifestation of these emotions as well. It would not be surprising, for example, if testosterone potentiated both anger and optimism at higher levels in men than in women.

What all these models suggest is that an essential component of comprehensive risk analysis must involve the incorporation of affective elements. Models of risk perception or management which fail to encompass the role of emotion fall dramatically short of providing an accurately integrated perspective on the human reaction to threat. As Camerer, Loewenstein, and Prelec (2005, 46) state: "We are skeptical of whether any theory that fails to incorporate the affective dimension of risk will be capable of shedding much light on such important phenomena as stock market booms and busts, the ubiquity of gambling . . . and the vicissitudes of public responses to threats as diverse as terrorism and global warming." Public opinion itself intrinsically incorporates important elements of emotion in assessments of risk, judgments concerning the acceptability of different kinds of risk, and prospects for their appropriate management.

## RISK AND DEMOCRACY

In proposing two alternative solutions for improving risk management, Slovic (1993) presents one model, based on the French system, which increases centralized government control, and a second one, more in keeping with American political culture, which encourages enhanced citizen participation. Slovic comes down on the side of the second model precisely because Americans display less trust in the government agencies that regulate risk than the French do.

Just as risk can be understood in terms of analysis or feelings, it can also be examined in terms of politics (Slovic 1999). As Slovic (1999, 689) eloquently argues, "Defining risk is . . . an exercise in power." Because risk is in many ways both socially created in reality, as well as socially constructed in perception, the people who control the agenda possess tremendous ability to skew the debate toward preferred solutions through the strategic or incidental manipulation of how risks are presented.

Slovic (1999) notes the central role that trust plays in the relationship between government and citizens surrounding the communication and reduction of risk. Yet little trust exists in this arena between these groups. Unfortunately, psychological tendencies tend to exacerbate the difficulty of establishing trust between individuals and the government charged with protecting them. As anyone knows from their personal relationships, trust takes a long time to establish and can be permanently eviscerated in a heartbeat. Negative events which can compromise trust both receive more attention in public debate and hold more power in personal psychology than the positive events which might more slowly create, build, foster, and sustain more positive relationships. And of course, distrust breeds on itself, since it precipitates exactly the kind of avoidance and detachment that prevent the reestablishment of trust.

Significantly, interest groups are no doubt well aware of these processes, and work to communicate frightening risks to the public in attempts to further more parochial political interests and enhance public distrust of the government in order to substitute their political agenda in its place. An adversarial legal system only exacerbates the sense of public distrust as observers see experts for hire prostitute themselves in battles where integrity emerges the biggest loser.

Yet, as with alcoholism, recognizing the problem provides the first step toward its resolution. Experts and lay people need not exist in opposition to each other in a conflictual political dynamic. Rather, each can join forces in a democratic system to encourage greater public participation and government accountability and transparency; after all, such processes aggregate into the measures we construe as public opinion. Each group brings distinct and important skills and perspectives to any informed debate on properly managing the nature of the public risks that confront us all daily.

Paul Slovic provides the most eloquent statement concerning the nature of the two systems, automatic and controlled, expert and lay, in directing and guiding appropriate risk assessment and management in a democratic system through increased deliberation and negotiation:

Risk assessment is inherently subjective and represents a blending of science and judgment with important psychological, social, cultural and political factors. . . . The public is not irrational. Their judgments about risk are influenced by emotion and affect in a way that is both simple and sophisticated. The same holds true for scientists. Public views are also influenced by worldviews, ideologies and values; so are scientists' views . . . The limitations of risk science, the importance and difficulty of maintaining trust, and the complex, sociopolitical nature of risk point to the need for . . . more public participation into both risk assessment and risk decision-making in order to make the decision process more democratic . . . and increase the legitimacy and public acceptance of the resulting decisions.   (Slovic 1999, 699)

# OPPORTUNITIES AND ROADBLOCKS

Several opportunities exist to further the research on risk perception and management in ways which can advance the debate. Three of these avenues are discussed below. However, some additional areas appear unlikely to bear fruit, and continued efforts in these areas may not prove warranted. These are mentioned briefly at the end of this section as well.

First, one continually intriguing aspect of risk research relates to the association between certain demographic characteristics and risk propensity. Rather than attributing such findings to personality, risk researchers tend to discuss these links in aggregate group terms. Most prominently, sex differences consistently emerge which show that men tend to assess lower risk than women in general. Moreover, white people similarly judge risks to be less than people of color on average. Controlling for education and income does not measurably diminish this sex difference effect (Slovic 1999), although each factor is inversely related to perception of risk.

With respect to the sex difference, the findings appear to be driven by about 30 percent of the white male population, who consistently estimate the risks they confront to be extremely low (Finucane, Slovic, et al. 2000). The authors attribute these findings to various social and political factors because these men tend to display quite divergent attitudes in other areas as well, including world views and trust measures. Associations between world views and risk perception show that egalitarians tend to remain more sensitive to risk than those who espouse fatalist, hierarchical, or individualist views (Peters and Slovic 2006; Slovic and Peters 1998).

It may be the case that some of these demographic differences might have roots in genetic variance. This certainly is not the case for all such differences, especially those involving racial groups. But the obvious question about whether biological or genetic differences play a role in sex-linked variance remains. Such divergence in perspective would make evolutionary sense if women show greater caution in service of protecting children, while men demonstrate greater risk in hope of achieving status and the reproductive advantage such dominance affords. The broader implications for mass public opinion remain clear. Elite manipulation of affect in service of support for particular policy positions will find differential traction based on the specific emotion elicited. Spawning anger will increase support for war among men, and fear will enhance opposition for war among women, for example.

Exploring the nature of these demographic differences more closely not only may help reveal some of the essential reasons why different people perceive and respond to risk in conflicting ways, but may also help inform public policy debates by suggesting ways in which risks, whether real or perceived, can be more effectively communicated to the public. As suggested above, since the majority of variance is accounted for by one subpopulation, namely white men, it is worth questioning whether the risks they confront in their lives actually are lower because of their privileged status in society.

Since white men have historically controlled a majority of resources, perhaps the 30 percent who perceive less risk actually confront less risk by being less exposed to crime, poverty, and inadequate health care.

Indeed, in at least one survey, the men who reported the lowest risk assessment were in fact more educated, richer, and more politically conservative than those who expressed higher risk sensitivity. Moreover, these men displayed systematically different attitudes on important social and political values than white women or people of color. Specifically, these men were more likely to: agree that future generations should take care of themselves when confronting risks posed by current technology; judge it acceptable to impose small risks on society without consent; believe that government can be trusted to make good decisions about risk; feel that the country has gone too far in supporting civil rights; support capital punishment; disagree that technology is hurting the environment; reject the notion that they have little control over risks to their health; and argue against the idea that the world needs a more equitable distribution of wealth (Flynn, Slovic, and Mertz 1994).

Examining the sources of such inoculation against risk perception should prove a productive avenue of inquiry to discover what distinguishes the accurate perception of risk, which may induce appropriate precautionary actions, from callous disregard for one's fate or the fate of others. Demographic factors offer a window for potential theoretical exploration into the nature of these phenomena.

A second area of inquiry that some scholars have begun to explore, and certainly seems worthy of further exploration, concerns the interaction between the two processes described above in communicating and managing risk at a public level. Since experts often rely on abstract data to prove their points, and such information largely does not find resonance among the mass public, little overlap for effective communication of important risk information exists as scholars denigrate a public consumed by the latest celebrity misstep and lay people roll their eyes at experts who appear impervious to the feelings that guide daily behavior.

Yet communication of such issues in effective and realistic ways remains central to critical public debates surrounding such issues as nuclear waste disposal, and also absolutely central to the widespread control of certain public health threats such as influenza epidemics. When threat is overblown by public officials, or not properly or accurately explained or calibrated, as many argue occurred in response to the 9/11 terrorist attacks, public vigilance may wane, and mistrust between the government and public can build. And yet when dangers are not adequately addressed, as when public events and movements are not minimized during times of epidemic disease, devastation can result. Supreme Court Justice Breyer argues that excessive regulation results precisely from public misunderstanding of risk in combination with high levels of mathematical illiteracy among the public; he proposes a government agency, similar to the French Conseil d'État, to centralize technical aspects of risk management (Breyer 1993). While important to improve technical skill and expert oversight, such a proposal would not adequately reassure the emotional concerns people often possess about the risks they confront unless they already trusted the government to be truthful concerning the risks they face.

From the perspective of research, the key question becomes how to effectively combine large-scale numerical information with personal experiential content in such a way as to effectively communicate the real nature of risk to the mass public. This mutual interaction between automatic and controlled systems offers at least two potential avenues of attack. First, work on psychic numbing seeks to address how to infuse dry statistics about famine, genocide, or other natural disasters, which seem both large and impersonal, with enough emotional content to motivate effective action in response to such tragedies (Peters and Slovic 2006). Clearly humanitarian fatigue emerges in the wake of sequential tragedies such as large tsunamis, earthquakes, or other natural disasters which hurt many people or devastate a wide area. However, sometimes it is easier for people to concentrate on a single child killed by a neighbor, or a boy in a balloon, than to worry about the half a million people killed across the globe, precisely because the single child presents a clear emotional image, with resonant affective attachments to family, friends, and place. For effective public policy to respond to large-scale challenges affecting numerous faceless and nameless others, officials must find a way to instill these statistics with personal emotional information.

The flip side of this conundrum appears obvious. To the extent that the mass public ignore dry, abstract, statistical data, they may remain impervious, and thus vulnerable, to real risks they encounter in their daily lives, from radon poisoning in their house to the dangers that result from unsafe sexual practices. Again, scientific practitioners should explore ways to communicate such information in effective ways to inform lay people about how to understand and reduce the nature of the real risks they confront. The affect heuristic may prove a largely effective and efficient mechanism for under-standing and responding to risk, but it can also lead individuals astray when it privileges pictures, stories, and symbols over more normatively appropriate numerical information in assessing the actual probabilities or frequencies of particular dangers, especially low-level dangers that occur over time as a result of long-term exposure, as in how smoking leads to lung cancer.

A third area which offers prospects for advancing research in the area of risk incorporates the tools of neuroscience to further investigate the nature of brain activity, and supporting genetic factors, under particular conditions of risk and uncertainty. Such studies can explore a wide variety of phenomena using a diversity of methodo-logical tools. Studies with patients who have brain lesions have shown how people with damage to the orbital frontal cortex, the part of the brain involved in abstract reasoning, and who cannot receive information from the amygdala, or emotional part of the brain, behave more in keeping with rational expected utility models by treating ambiguity and risk in identical fashion (Hsu et al. 2005). Such findings illustrate how logical rationality and affective rationality can operate in fundamental contradistinction (Shiv et al. 2005).

Some of this work can prove quite instructive about the nature of risk-taking within a political context. Additional imaging work has shown that Republicans show greater

political attitudes such as party identification and ideology. For each, I highlight what is known, what is largely speculative, and what needs to be addressed in future research. Future research will need to focus on identifying the mechanisms through which biological, especially genetic, and environmental factors interact. To do so, the field also needs more theoretical development to help identify the most fruitful avenues for study.

# NEW RESEARCH TOOLS FOR UNDERSTANDING PUBLIC OPINION

Empirical research using a biological approach to the study of public opinion can be roughly divided into that focused on the role of genes and that focused on the role of neurological systems in the brain. Each has adopted a set of methodological tools from existing disciplines. A good deal of what is new about biological approaches to the study of public opinion stems from the new methodological tools that are helping to uncover new insights. Many of these methods are still unfamiliar to social scientists. Before detailing the recent research findings, I briefly describe the main methodological approaches used in each area and a few of the benefits and limitations of these methods.

## Twin Studies: The Building Blocks for Genetic Research

Twin studies are a mainstay of genetic research. The twin study design is used as a first step to establish whether or not there is a substantial genetic component for a given phenotype (i.e., any observable characteristic or "trait"). Twin studies estimate the amount of variance in a phenotype that can be attributed to either genetic or environmental sources. The environment is used in the broadest sense, to encompass all variation attributable to the social environment, namely, anything that cannot be attributed to genetics. This partitioning of variance is possible because monozygotic (MZ) twins are genetically identical (sharing 100 percent of their genes), whereas dizygotic (DZ) twins (and other siblings) share on average 50 percent of their segregating genes (because these siblings arise from two different ova fertilized by different sperm). For any trait that is partly heritable, the tendency for MZ twins to share that characteristic should be stronger than the tendency for DZ twins to share that characteristic. If a characteristic comes solely from the environment, there should be no difference between the degree of similarity between MZ twin pairs and DZ twin pairs on that characteristic. Thus, the combination of MZ and DZ twin pairs, raised by the same parents in the same home environment, provides a natural experiment which can separate the effects of familial background and socialization from genetic effects.

Typically, the analysis partitions the variance into one of three sources: additive genetic (A), common or shared environment (C), and unique or unshared environment (E). The A factor reflects the combination of all additive genetic influences.[1] C reflects all environmental factors that make family members similar; this is typically thought of as the extent to which family and parental socialization makes members of the same family more similar than would be predicted solely from their genetic relationships. E reflects the unique or unshared environmental influences that make members of the same family different; it reflects the unique experiences of an individual or unique reactions to the environment.

Variants of the twin design include twins reared apart in different households and extended family designs that make use of both twin similarity and similarity with parents and non-twin siblings. Adoption studies follow a similar logic to that of twin studies in making use of the known genetic similarity between biological relatives and adoptive relatives to partition the variance into additive genetic and environmental components.

The twin design is widely used in the behavioral genetics, psychology, and medical literatures. The design requires a special sample, making it time-consuming and costly to identify twins for potential study and then to collect data from them on the desired attributes. There are a handful of twin registries in the US and in other countries (e.g., Australia, Sweden, Denmark) that are used to facilitate the process. Each of these samples is essentially a convenience sample of twins; as such, variance estimates from twin studies are considered specific to a given twin population. It is helpful when the results from twin studies can be replicated across multiple samples. The method is an important first step in identifying phenotypes with substantial genetic variance; such evidence supports the need for follow-up research.

The most common critique of twin studies stems from concerns about the equal environments assumption (EEA). If MZ twins share not only more of their genetic code but also more of their environmental experiences for reasons that extend beyond their genetic similarity, relative to DZ twins, then variance attributed to genetics may actually be the result of environmental forces. The concern is that heritability estimates will be inflated while the effect of shared environment will be underestimated if this assumption is violated. Concerns about the EEA are specific to the phenotype under study, however; if there is a greater similarity of environments between MZ twins relative to DZ twins, this similarity must be relevant to the phenotype of interest for it to jeopardize estimates of heritability in the study. The EEA is problematic for some traits but not others. There have been a number of approaches to addressing the EEA. Studies with twins reared apart provide one powerful approach to controlling for possible violations of the EEA. Another approach analyzes (mis)perceptions of zygosity to determine whether actual or perceived zygosity explains concordance between twin pairs. Other approaches involve controls for environmental factors that are plausibly

---

[1] If there is evidence of a genetic effect that does not tend to run in families, observed when DZ twin pairs are not similar on a characteristic while MZ pairs are highly similar, the analysis can include non-additive genetic effects (D).

related to the phenotype (for example, Fowler, Baker, and Dawes 2008; Smith, Alford, et al. 2010) and some have controlled for the extent of contact between twins when estimating heritability in an extended family design that includes parents and other, non-twin siblings (Hatemi, Hibbing, et al. 2010). The extended-family design makes it possible to test many of the concerns surrounding the EEA since non-twin siblings share roughly similar environments as their twin siblings. Visscher et al. (2006) derived heritability estimates for height similar to those produced by twin analyses based on genotyping a large sample of non-twin siblings; future research may no longer need the natural experiment provided by samples of twins, rendering concerns about the EEA moot.

A related critique of twin studies stems from concerns that partitioning the variance into A, C, and E components does not capture the likely complexity of genetic influences as they interact with environmental factors, overemphasizing genetic effects while underplaying environmental effects. This concern stems, in part, from the definition of additive genetic effects to include gene × environment interactions. Others are concerned about underestimating heritability if assortative mating is present for the phenotype.[2] Both critiques can be addressed with more sophisticated theory testing using structural equation modeling. The ACE models are considered first steps that can support further, more complex analyses. Twin studies and extended-family designs can be used to test directly for more complex patterns such as correlations between genetic propensities and exposure to particular environments (i.e., gene–environment correlation, rGE) and differential sensitivity to experiences or environments depending on genetic propensities (i.e., gene × environment interactions, G × E). Multivariate genetic analysis can also be used to estimate the extent to which genetic and environmental factors that affect one trait also affect another trait or set of other traits. One example of this approach has led to the concept of "generalist genes" that affect an array of different learning disabilities (Plomin and Kovas 2005).

Genetic research related to political phenomena is still in the beginning stages. Only a handful of studies using these more complex analyses on phenotypes relevant to public opinion exit to date. Such analyses will most likely dominate future research as the field begins to think seriously about how to integrate genetic influences into models of public opinion.

## Molecular Genetic Research: Connecting Specific Genes with Phenotypes

Molecular genetic research seeks to connect phenotypes with specific genes. The term references the application of a set of laboratory techniques that can identify and manipulate DNA segments. Research of this sort uses genome-wide linkage and

---

[2] Assortative mating refers here to a tendency to choose mates, such as spouses, that are more similar to the self on the phenotype of interest than would be expected by chance.

genome-wide association studies to identify correlations between specific genetic variations and phenotypes. One of the hurdles for this type of research stems from the size and complexity of the human genome; with thousands of genetic markers, it is difficult to know which associations are worth testing without a strong theoretical rationale. Such studies are also limited by the genetic markers available in a dataset typically developed for applications rather far afield from traditional public opinion research purposes. The application of molecular genetic research techniques to studies of public opinion are quite scarce but likely increase over time. Ultimately, this line of research promises a much finer-grained understanding of how inherent genetic differences across individuals are linked with differences in social and political behavior.

## Neuroscience Methods: Looking Inside the Black Box

Neuroscientific and psychophysiological techniques for the study of behavior are multiplying at a rapid pace across a number of social scientific disciplines. Genetic and neuroscientific research dovetail nicely since most believe that the paths from genes to attitudes, values, and other phenotypes operate through the physiological variations in brain structure and function. The methods used in this research require specialized knowledge to measure and interpret appropriately. The best-known method involves brain-imaging techniques using functional magnetic resonance imaging; other measures include electroencephalography (EEG), facial electromyographs, and hormonal measures such as cortisol and testosterone levels. Brain imaging techniques used to map the neural correlates of social processes lead to a long list of functions associated with each region of the brain. These lists can, in turn, generate new insights and ideas for theory testing but, like most scientific research, the theoretical benefit from this approach tends to involve a longer, iterative process before a new understanding takes hold (see Cacioppo, Tassinary, and Berntson 2007; Harmon-Jones and Winkielman 2007).

Psychology has a long history of research connecting the biological organism and a range of behaviors. Others are now applying neuroscientific techniques to the study of behaviors that could be relevant for public opinion and political participation such as altruism, cooperation, trust, and risk-taking. Research focused on understanding the role of emotion in judgment and decision-making has been particularly promising for lending new insights into opinion of political candidates (for example, Kaplan, Freedman, and Iacoboni 2007; Lodge and Taber 2005; Marcus, Neuman, and MacKuen 2000; Westen et al. 2006; Winkielman, Knutson, Paulus, and Trujillo 2007).

## GENETIC INFLUENCES ON PUBLIC OPINION

Attitudes on social and political issues are the key component of the most common model of public opinion. For some, attitudes relevant to public opinion are limited to evaluations about social and political issues of the day. Psychologists often treat attitudes in a broader sense referring to any evaluation of a person, thing, event, or idea. And some make no particular distinction between attitudes and other internal constructs such as values. There is clear evidence that individual differences on at least some attitudes can be attributed to genetic factors. And, there is converging evidence from smaller-scale studies that the degree of heritability is associated with attitude strength.

Current thinking argues that the role of genetics on the direction of attitude positions is likely to be indirect. Much work remains to test whether genetic influences on attitudes operate through value orientations as key antecedents of attitudes (Alford, Funk, and Hibbing 2005; Funk et al. 2009), through partisan and other group identifications, or perhaps through other constructs such as intelligence or personality temperaments (Tesser 1993; Olson, Vernon, Harris, and Lang 2001). Some have speculated that physiological and biochemical differences in behavioral reactions may explain the link between genes and some sorts of attitudes (Oxley et al. 2008; Tesser 1993). Beyond looking at the direction of attitude positions, a limited number of studies have begun to look at the potential heritability of holding opinions, and new studies are under way to test the heritability of attitude intensity and extremity (Alford, Funk, and Hibbing 2005; Funk et al. 2010).

## Attitude Position

Much of the empirical evidence about the heritability of attitude positions stems from twin studies in Great Britain, Australia, and the US that included a series of three-point attitude ratings on a wide variety of issues.[3] Eaves and colleagues (Eaves, Eysenck, and Martin 1989; Martin et al. 1986) report sizeable heritability coefficients across the individual issues and when combining the attitude items into an index of conservatism. Their study with British twins also included five-point attitude evaluations on a wide-ranging set of statements known as the Public Opinion Inventory, developed by Eysenck. They report strong heritability coefficients for the individual items and when combining items into scales of toughmindedness and radicalism.

In a detailed analysis of twins and their family members in the US, Eaves, Heath, et al. (1999) found similar evidence of heritability for attitudes in a twenty-eight-item version of the issue index, whether considered as individual items, as one of five subscales, or as a single index of conservatism. They found strong correlations between twin and spouse attitudes on these items, a pattern not found for personality traits; consequently, assortative mating was controlled in the analysis. (If ignored, assortative mating leads to underestimates of heritability.) Their findings provided strong evidence for the heritability of these attitudes, with a large percentage of the variance on these

---

[3] Known as the Wilson–Patterson Index of ideology or sometimes labeled "conservatism."

attitudes attributed to unique environmental factors and relatively little attributed to shared environment.

Alford, Funk, and Hibbing (2005) replicated and extended their analysis using the same attitude items. While they, too, show heritability estimates for individual attitude items in the scale, their treatment of this material is focused on the overall index of ideological orientations. They consider the heritability of attitudes on specific issues as likely to be indirectly influenced by genes through key antecedents of attitudes, namely, core value orientations that relate to how society is organized and functions.

Olson, Vernon, Harris, and Lang (2001) tested a wide-ranging set of attitude measures with a sample of twins from British Columbia, Canada. Their measures tapped seven-point evaluations related to engaging in exercise and athletics; public speaking and being a group leader; views about euthanasia, abortion, and religion; engaging in "sensory experiences" such as smoking, big parties, and roller-coaster rides; attitudes toward education and intellectual pursuits such as reading and crossword puzzles; attitudes toward equality, race, gender, and immigration; sociability and appearance; and attitudes about the death penalty. While heritability coefficients were calculated for each of the thirty items, the theoretical assumption of this work is that any genetic influence on attitudes will be indirect through one of several potential mediators.

Olson et al. tested several potential mediators of heritability including personality, physical athleticism, attractiveness, and academic achievement (based on grade point average). This array of tests is difficult to neatly summarize. Using multivariate genetic analysis, they report a number of attitude factors showing a substantial correlation in shared genetic variance with one or more personality traits. A personality trait of sociability, for example, shared significant genetic variance with five of the six attitude factors tested. Findings of shared genetic variance are consistent with the notion that one variable mediates the other, although the direction of causality is not clear from this finding alone. Cross-correlation techniques were used to test the causal direction between attitude factors and mediator variables, but these tests were largely inconclusive. For six of the nine tests, neither model of causal direction was conclusive. Their findings supported the idea that self-reported athletic ability, itself strongly heritable, causes attitudes about engaging in athletics and exercise. This is consistent with the idea that, in some cases, an inherited behavioral tendency, such as athleticism, can lead individuals to develop more favorable attitudes about those kinds of behaviors. Contrary to expectations, the cross-correlations data suggested that attitudes toward sensory experiences cause personality traits of aggressiveness and sociability, rather than the reverse. Looking across the set of thirty attitudes, they also find that attitudes which are correlated with academic achievement, itself a strongly heritable construct, tend to be more heritable. They speculate that academic achievement may contribute to the heritable component of individual differences in many attitudes.

Other kinds of attitudes, though not typically considered highly relevant for public opinion on social and political issues, also show substantial genetic influences. Attitudes about the workplace, job satisfaction, and vocational interests are, in part, transmitted genetically. And some have found evidence of a genetic component in attitudes about alcohol use and smaller effects in attitudes about cigarette and coffee use (see Bouchard and McGue 2003).

Individual differences in expressed attitudes across a wide range of topics are partly determined by genetic factors. Current thinking hypothesizes an indirect role between genes and attitudes, although much remains unclear about exactly what the mediators entail. Two findings are particularly important to bear in mind. First, not all attitudes are equally heritable. The degree to which genetic factors influence attitudes varies along a continuum across attitude constructs. Second, even when a substantial genetic component for attitudes is present, a similarly sized or often larger percentage of variance in attitudes tends to be attributed to unique environmental factors. As Olson, Vernon, Harris, and Lang (2001) expressed it,

To be sure, the environment is necessary for the development of attitudes. But the hypothesis that attitudes are learned is not incompatible with the notion that biological and genetic factors also influence attitudes. That is, there is a second necessary component to the development of attitudes: the biological organism within which events are subjectively experienced and mnemonically recorded. Biological factors presumably mediate and moderate the impact of personal experiences, in that events are experienced through our sensory structures, and memories and evaluations are stored in our brains.   (2001, 845)

Thus, future research needs to take a more integrative approach linking genetics and biological processes with the expression, formation, and modification of attitudes.

## Attitude Strength

A few studies suggest that attitude strength coincides with the degree of heritability. Tesser (1993) used estimates of heritability[4] for specific items in the Wilson–Patterson Index and the Public Opinion Inventory to test the implications of heritability for theories of attitudes. He finds that attitudes with higher heritability estimates show shorter response latencies, consistent with the hypothesis that such attitudes are stronger. In an experimental study, he finds that attitudes lower in heritability are more easily influenced by social conformity norms than are more strongly heritable attitudes. And he finds some support for the notion that similarity on more heritable attitudes is more consequential for interpersonal attraction.

Olson, Vernon, Harris, and Lang (2001) also find evidence of a link between attitude strength and the heritability of attitudes. They find self-reports of attitude strength correlated with attitude heritability; mean strength ratings for factors of attitudes also correlated at about .5 with heritability estimates for those factors. Roughly 25 percent of the variation in the strength scores was attributable to variation in the heritability of

---

[4] These estimates were drawn from Martin et al. (1986) and Eaves, Eysenck, and Martin (1989).

factors. Thus, there is converging evidence that highly heritable attitudes also tend to be held more strongly than less heritable attitudes.

## Political Expertise and Opinionation

Recent neuroscientific studies suggest that differences between political sophisticates and novices arise from use of different neural substrates (Fowler and Schreiber 2009; Schreiber 2007). Alford, Funk, and Hibbing (2005) also found a moderate role of genetics in the likelihood of holding opinions across a set of twenty-eight items on diverse issues. There was virtually no role of shared environmental factors in opiniona-tion; the largest proportion of variance was attributed to unique environmental factors. These findings have implications for our understanding of political sophistication, expertise, and knowledge differences among citizens. Until recently, there have been no data available to test these ideas more directly, but new data collected with a sample of US twins will allow such tests in the near future.

## Partisanship, Party Strength, and Independence

Research to date on the heritability of party identification paints a different picture from that on attitude positions and value orientations. Alford, Funk, and Hibbing (2005) report a relatively low heritability coefficient for party identification in a sample of US twins from the Virginia 30,000; shared environmental factors explained a much larger share of the variance for party identification.[5] Hatemi, Alford, et al. (2009) replicated this finding with different modeling strategies. They find a large effect of shared environment for party; a model with no genetic effects fit the data better than one including both genetic and unique environmental variance.

An analysis of Australian twins by Hatemi, Medland, et al. (2007) found a similar pattern. This study asked whether respondents "think of themselves" according to one of several party labels; the analysis looked at the probability of identifying as Labor Party or one of the more conservative parties (e.g., the Conservative, Liberal, or National party).[6] Consistent with analysis of US twins from the Virginia 30,000 study, they found only small additive genetic effects for partisanship and large effects for shared environmental factors. Further analyses showed that the small genetic influences on partisanship stem from indirect influence through attitudes toward the issue of socialism.

Other concepts tell a different story. Individual differences in the strength of partisanship (treated, in this case, as a dichotomous measure that contrasts those with weak or no partisanship to strong partisans) were explained by a combination

---

[5] Party identification is based on a five-point measure with those not able or not willing to make a choice on the scale omitted from the analysis.

[6] The authors treat this measure as reflecting vote choice.

of genetic and unique environmental factors with little influence of the shared environment (Hatemi, Alford, et al. 2009).[7] Analysis on a separate sample of US twins by Settle, Dawes, and Fowler (2009) lends further support for this pattern; they found, at best, a small role for genetic factors in the direction of partisanship and a sizable role for genetics and unique environmental factors for strength of partisanship.[8]

One study tested how specific genes may operate to influence partisanship. Dawes and Fowler (2009) used allele association tests on a representative sample of adolescents and young adults in the US and find an association between the DRD2 dopamine receptor gene and the likelihood of identifying with either political party (regardless of direction). The dopamine system is associated with a number of different regulatory functions; the D2 receptor has been associated with differences in cognitive functioning and the formation of social attachments. Those with two A2 alleles of the DRD2 were more likely to identify with a party than those with either one or no A2 alleles. This pattern holds for both Democrats and Republicans, suggesting that the likelihood of forming a political attachment is influenced by genetic factors even if the direction of partisanship is largely influenced by shared environmental factors such as parental socialization.

Research to date reinforces the need for conceptual distinctions when it comes to studying the genetics of partisanship. The direction of partisan identification appears to be largely explained by shared environmental factors, consistent with a model of partisan affiliation based largely on family socialization. A larger role for genetics is found for partisan strength. Some caution is needed, however, until more studies replicate these patterns with different samples of twins and measures of partisanship. A key limitation of research in this area is the reliance on twin studies in the US and Australia; thus, we do not yet know how well these findings will hold in other political systems.

## Ideology and Other Value Orientations

Public opinion on issues of the day is often thought to be determined by underlying values held by the individual. Values, or subsets of values, are sometimes referred to as predispositions or core values—labels which reflect the theoretical assumption that values precede the development of social and political attitudes and are important determinants for a wide range of attitudes. Such values reflect abstract normative beliefs about society and are thought to apply across different cultural contexts and specific situations (Schwartz 1992). Research to date shows a substantial genetic

---

[7] The party identification question asked on the Virginia 30,000 twin survey is different from other surveys. The question stem asks for party affiliation; the response options combine a party label with a frequency of support for the party. Non-partisans are classified as those selecting the mid-point on the scale. Those answering some other party and preferring not to answer or not answering are omitted from analyses.

[8] Partisan identification is based on a seven-point scale that ranges from strong Democrat to strong Republican. Strength of partisanship is based on a four-point scale that "folds" identification at the mid-point with independents at one end of the scale and strong partisans at the other end.

component in the transmission of value orientations, particularly liberal or conservative ideology. Research on other values is now under way. As with attitude positions, the degree of heritability is likely to vary across specific values and that variation could have important consequences.

## Liberal or Conservative Political Ideology

Several twin studies have used the Wilson–Patterson Index of attitude positions across a large number of social and political issues to gage an overall direction of liberal or conservative beliefs. While this index is not particularly common in political behavior or public opinion literatures, it reflects a conceptualization of ideology as a coherent belief system (Converse 1964; Jost 2006). Several studies have shown a substantial genetic influence on ideology using this index including samples of twins from Australia (Martin et al. 1986), twins reared apart (Bouchard, Segal, et al. 2002), a large-scale sample of twins in the US (Alford, Funk, and Hibbing 2005; Eaves, Heath, et al. 1999), and a recent survey of US twins (Funk et al. 2009). The overall pattern of findings suggests a sizable influence of both genetic and unique environmental influences with a smaller effect from the shared environment. These findings were replicated with a sample of US twins using a self-classification of ideology along a seven-point liberal to conservative continuum (Funk et al. 2009). The pattern of genetic and environmental influences appears to hold regardless of whether ideology is treated as a single dimension of liberal–conservative beliefs or treated as separate subfactors of beliefs in domains such as militarism and size of government.

Genetic factors underlying political ideology are not expressed until young adulthood. Hatemi, Funk, et al. (2009) analyzed a longitudinal sample of US twins in childhood and adolescence along with a cross-sectional sample of adult twins, aged 18 to 60 years and older. They found no evidence of genetic influences on liberal–conservative ideological orientations[9] until early adulthood. Between the ages of 9 and 17, individual differences in ideological orientations were accounted for by a mix of shared and unique environmental influences; the role of shared influences accumulated strongly throughout adolescence. Starting in early adulthood and coinciding with leaving the parental home, however, there was a sizable genetic influence explaining individual differences in ideological orientations that remained stable across adults of all ages. These findings raise intriguing questions about the interplay between genes and the environment in the expression of genetic influences and the underlying mechanisms at work.

## Strength of Ideology

Not all ideological concepts demonstrate the same patterns, however. Settle, Dawes, and Fowler (2009) report a minimal effect of genetics in explaining individual differences in the strength of self-identified ideology; for this sample of US twins, strength of

---

[9] Measured by the Wilson–Patterson Index.

ideology was largely explained by unique environmental factors.[10] Note that the pattern differs from that found for strength of party identification. Such variations caution against generalizing patterns of findings to other constructs. It also argues for more replication across different samples and measures as well as greater theoretical clarity in future work.

## Other Approaches to Understanding Ideology

The mechanisms through which genes operate to influence ideology (and other value orientations) are likely to be complex and involve dozens of genes and at least some interactions between genetic makeup and environmental conditions or experiences. One molecular genetic study has started down the path of trying to identify specific gene × environment interactions influencing political ideology. Settle, Dawes, Christakis, and Fowler (2010) conducted allele association tests on a representative sample of adolescents and young adults in the US. They focused on the 7R variant of the dopamine receptor D4 gene, a gene associated with risk-taking and novelty seeking. They find that teenagers who report larger social networks *and* have the DRD4 7R variant are more likely to self-identify as liberals (about six years later) than do those without this gene or with smaller social networks during their teenage years. Their findings point to an interaction between a particular gene, the DRD4, and a particular social environment, the social network size of adolescents, influencing the direction of self-identified ideology.

A different approach can be found in physiological and neurological studies of differences between self-identified liberals and conservatives. Oxley et al. (2008) found that conservatives are more likely than liberals to exhibit startle reflexes when presented with visual and auditory fear stimuli. This finding is consistent with the idea that conservatism is associated with a need to maintain order (Jost, Glaser, Kruglanski, and Sulloway 2003). Amodio, Jost, Master, and Yee (2007) used EEG to measure brain activity in response to situational cues that conflict with habitual responses. They hypothesized that differences between liberals and conservatives in response to self-regulation mechanisms are associated with differences in neural activity in the anterior cingulated cortex. Liberals showed more conflict-related neural activity and more behavioral accuracy than did conservatives during the condition requiring an inhibition of the habitual response. More research along these lines is in development and promises a deeper understanding of the processes connecting genes, neurological reactions, and ideology.

## Other Values: Authoritarianism, Social Orientations, Egalitarianism

A handful of studies have tested the heritability of other value orientations. A few studies have found a sizable genetic component to authoritarianism. McCourt et al. 1999 found a substantial role for genetics in an analysis of twins reared apart on Altemeyer's right-wing authoritarianism scale. Their findings were consistent with an adoption study by

---

[10] Strength of ideology refers to a four-point measure created by "folding" ideological self-placement at the mid-point, thus ranging from moderate to either very liberal or very conservative.

Scarr and Weinberg (1981) using the F-scale. And a recent US twin study replicated these findings using a variant of the authoritarianism scale (Funk et al. 2009).

Smith, Hibbing, et al. (2008) hypothesized that individual dispositions toward social rules, order, and behavioral conduct are the psychological foundation for political ideology. They developed a measure to capture these "bedrock social orientations" called the Society Works Best Index. In a first test of this measure, results support the idea that there is a sizable genetic component to social orientations (Funk et al. 2009). The same study also found a sizable genetic influence on a multi-item index of egalitarianism. Across the five measures of value orientations in the Funk et al. (2009) study, the results supported a sizable influence of both genetic and unique environmental influences with a smaller effect from the shared environment. Future analyses are likely to tell us more about the degree to which the genetic effects across these values stem from shared genetic variance. Multivariate genetic analyses sometimes suggest that the same genetic influences affect a range of related phenotypes (as for the class of phenotypes related to cognitive ability) or that the heritability of one variable mediates some or all of the heritability of another variable due to its genetic overlap.

## Religiosity and Other Constructs

There have been a number of genetic studies related to religiosity. Past studies by genetic researchers sometimes measure religiosity with indicators of the psychological importance of religion but others treat church attendance as well as religious attitude, beliefs, and values as indicators of religiosity. Given the importance of religiosity for predicting public opinion on a range of social issues and voting behavior, especially in the US, it is important to review what we know about genetic influences on these concepts.

Research suggests that religiosity is partly heritable. Koenig, McGue, Krueger, and Bouchard (2007) found that heritability explains about 40 percent of the variance on a nine-item index of religiosity in a sample of male twins from the US. Bouchard, McGue, Lykken, and Tellegen (1999) estimated the heritability of religiousness at about the same level in their sample of twins reared apart. Waller et al. 1990 estimated the heritability of a set of religious values, interests, and beliefs including fundamentalism at about .4 to .5; although some report a smaller role for genetics on measures of church attendance (D'Onofrio, Eaves, et al. 1999; Kirk et al. 1999; Truett et al. 1992).[11]

As was the case with political ideology, genetic factors are not expressed for religiosity until later in life. A number of twin studies have found only a small role for genetics in religiosity during childhood and adolescence (Abrahamson, Baker, and Caspi 2002; Boomsma, DeGeus, van Baal, and Koopmans 1999; D'Onofrio, Murrelle, et al. 1999). And Eaves, Hatemi, et al. (2008) found that shared environmental factors

---

[11] There are a number of multivariate genetic studies looking at the relationship between religiousness and other characteristics such as helping behavior, antisocial behavior, and substance abuse (for example, Koenig, McGue, Krueger, and Bouchard 2007; Truett et al. 1992).

accounted for the vast majority of variance in church attendance for children and adolescents, but shared environment decreased in importance during late adolescence and young adulthood, while genetic influences on church attendance increased over the same period.

When it comes to religious affiliation (as Catholic, Protestant, or specific Protestant denominations), research suggests a minimal role for genetics. Individual differences in religious affiliation are largely explained by shared environmental influences (D'Onofrio, Eaves, et al. 1999; Eaves, Martin, and Heath 1990). Religious affiliation shows evidence of strong assortative mating effects.

The degree to which genetics and environmental influences explain the transmission of concepts relevant to public opinion including social and political attitudes, partisanship, values, and religiosity can vary widely. While genetic influences are sizable for a number of attitudes and values, the contribution of genes is quite limited for concepts such as partisan and religious affiliation. Such findings require researchers to think more deeply about the differences among phenotypes. Beyond asking about the relative contribution of genes and environmental influences, genetic research can address a number of other questions. Research using extended-family designs can demonstrate the relative importance of assortative mating influences; longitudinal studies show the expression of genetic and environmental influences over the life course; and more complex models can test whether the expression of genetic influences depends on specific environmental conditions. The tools for addressing these more complex questions about the role of genetics in public opinion are already available. Thus, future research needs to focus on developing clear theoretical models that can better illuminate the relationship among this disparate set of phenotypes and the potential mediating role of phenotypes known to be influenced by genetic factors on these phenomena.

## Implications and Challenges for Future Research

The idea that genetic factors could (and do) account for some of the individual differences in intelligence or cognitive abilities, psychiatric diseases such as schizophrenia, and personality is widely accepted (for example, Bouchard and McGue 2003; Eaves, Eysenck, and Martin 1989). The same idea when applied to social and political attitudes has long been considered counterintuitive. Fully accepting the empirical evidence that these kinds of political phenotypes are, in part, stemming from genetic factors will require an adjustment to our assumptions and models about the development of public opinion.

Past evidence of a correlation between parent and offspring political attitudes, values, and behaviors has often been interpreted as evidence of the importance of pre-adult socialization. Such findings are also consistent with the notion that genetic similarity between parents and their offspring contribute to that similarity. Evidence of the stability of partisanship and political orientations over the life course has often been interpreted as underscoring the importance of early political learning in the family environment. But more heritable attitudes are also likely to be stronger and possibly more resistant to change; thus, genetic influences could also account for attitude stability over time.

Research on the heritability of attitudes, partisanship, values, and other beliefs makes it clear that the degree to which genetics and environmental factors are at work can vary widely depending on the construct. The degree to which genetic factors influence attitude positions ranges along a continuum. These differences are consequential; attitudes higher in heritability tend to be expressed more quickly, are more resistant to social conformity pressures, and are more influential in social reactions. A number of studies have shown a sizable role for genetic (and unique environmental) factors in ideological orientations along a liberal–conservative continuum. The relative contribution of genetic factors is much more varied when looking across constructs such as party affiliation, independence, and strength of partisanship. These findings challenge researchers to think more clearly about the differences among these constructs and to ground further explorations in theoretical expectations about which constructs are likely to be strongly and weakly transmitted through genetic factors.

Once you accept the empirical evidence that *any* of these kinds of political phenotypes are, in part, stemming from genetic factors, the primary intellectual question centers around how it works. It would be extremely easy to throw up our hands and say simply that political phenotypes stem from a complex interaction of genes and the environment (see Macoby 2000). But we cannot leave it at that. We need to be much more specific about the nature of the interaction, the environments, and the genes in order to gain any leverage in understanding. Some have speculated that the underlying process connecting genetic factors to differences in adult attitudes are likely to operate through iterative behavioral preferences. Eaves, Heath, et al. (1999) suggest that small initial genetic differences may encourage people to seek out particular kinds of experiences; these, in turn, are "augmented over time by the incorporation into the phenotype of environmental information, correlated with the genotype, in a continual process of sifting and evaluation" (1999, 79; also see Scarr and McCartney 1983).

Several researchers have speculated about an indirect relationship between genes and attitude positions through value orientations, partisan and other group identifications, intelligence, personality temperaments, or specific biochemical differences in behavioral reactions. Much work remains to thoroughly test these potential mediating factors.

Genetic association studies that can link specific genes to specific opinions and behaviors are promising, especially where other known correlates of the allele can help point the way to specifying the mechanisms at work. Some have begun down this path but much more work of this sort is needed. Similarly, neuroscientific methods for studying social behavior are allowing new linkages to be drawn between genes and neurological processes with the expression, formation, and modification of attitudes. The challenge for public opinion researchers is twofold: (1) to select areas of study that are theoretically grounded and thus hold the most promise, and (2) to fully integrate the findings across these different techniques into our theoretical models and understanding of public opinion.

Public opinion research already draws scholars from a number of different disciplines. For the most part, however, those disciplines share a broad set of social scientific research skills (though not always theoretical assumptions and values). This line of research stretches the notion of multidisciplinary research to a much wider stance, drawing on highly specialized research skills of the behavioral geneticist, molecular geneticist, and the neuroscientist. Researchers cannot expect to follow the Renaissance man approach of many social science fields. Instead, social scientists need to team up with experts in other fields. Carrying out this research requires larger research teams working together with a more delegated set of responsibilities. Beyond the practical requirements, it also requires an active attempt to bring the insights of a broader range of disciplines together. It is difficult and it can be messy and inefficient, but the ultimate rewards are promising.

# References

ABRAHAMSON, A. C., BAKER, L. A., and CASPI, A. 2002. Rebellious Teens? Genetic and Environmental Influences on the Social Attitudes of Adolescents. *Journal of Personality and Social Psychology*, 83: 1392–408.

ALFORD, J. R., FUNK, C. L., and HIBBING, J. R. 2005. Are Political Orientations Genetically Transmitted? *American Political Science Review*, 99/2: 153–68.

AMODIO, D. M., JOST, J. T., MASTER, S. L., and YEE, C. M. 2007. Neurocognitive Correlates of Liberalism and Conservatism. *Nature Neuroscience*, 10/10: 1246–7.

BOOMSMA, D. I., DEGEUS, E. J. C., VAN BAAL, G. C. M., and KOOPMANS, J. R. 1999. A Religious Upbringing Reduces the Influence of Genetic Factors on Disinhibition: Evidence for Interaction between Genotype and Environment on Personality. *Twin Research*, 2: 115–25.

BOUCHARD, T. J., JR., and MCGUE, M. 2003. Genetic and Environmental Influences on Human Psychological Differences. *Journal of Neurobiology*, 54: 4–45.

——— LYKKEN, D. T., and TELLEGEN, A. 1999. Intrinsic and Extrinsic Religiousness: Genetic and Environmental Influences on Personality Correlates. *Twin Research*, 2: 88–98.

—— SEGAL, N. L., TELLEGEN, A., MCGUE, M., KEYES, M., and KRUEGER, R. 2002. Evidence for the Construct Validity and Heritability of the Wilson–Patterson Conservatism Scale: A Reared-Apart Twins Study of Social Attitudes. *Personality and Individual Differences*, 34/2003: 959–69.

CACIOPPO, J. T., TASSINARY, L. G., and BERNTSON, G. G. (eds.) 2007. *Handbook of Psychophysiology*, 3rd edn. Cambridge: Cambridge University Press.

CONVERSE, P. E. 1964. The Nature of Belief Systems in Mass Publics. In *Ideology and Discontent*, ed. D. Apter. New York: Free Press.

DAWES, C. T., and FOWLER, J. H. 2009. Partisanship, Voting, and the Dopamine D2 Receptor Gene. *Journal of Politics*, 71/3: 1157–71.

D'ONOFRIO, B. M., EAVES, L. J., MURELLE, L., MAES, H. H., and SPILKA, B. 1999. Understanding Biological and Social Influences on Religious Affiliation, Attitudes, and Behaviors: A Behavior Genetic Perspective. *Journal of Personality*, 67: 953–84.

——MURRELLE, L., EAVES, L. J., McCULLOUGH, M. E., LANDIS, J. L., and MAES, H. H. 1999. Adolescent Religiousness and its Influence on Substance Use: Preliminary Findings from the Mid-Atlantic School Age Twin Study. *Twin Research*, 2: 156–68.

EAVES, L. J., EYSENCK, H. J., and MARTIN, N. G. 1989. *Genes, Culture and Personality: An Empirical Approach*. London: Academic Press.

——HATEMI, P. K., PROM-WOMLEY, E. C., and MURRELLE, L. 2008. Social and Genetic Influences on Adolescent Religious Attitudes and Practices. *Social Forces*, 86/4: 1621–46.

——HEATH, A. C., MARTIN, N. G., MAES, H. H., NEALE, M. C., KENDLER, K. S., KIRK, K. M., and COREY, L. 1999. Comparing the Biological and Cultural Inheritance of Personality and Social Attitudes in the Virginia 30,000 Study of Twins and Their Relatives. *Twin Research*, 2 (June), 62–80.

——MARTIN, N. G., and HEATH, A. C. 1990. Religious Affiliation in Twins and Their Parents: Testing a Model of Cultural Inheritance. *Behavior Genetics*, 20/1: 1–22.

FOWLER, J. H., and SCHREIBER, D. 2009. Biology, Politics, and the Emerging Science of Human Nature. *Science*, 322: 912–14.

——BAKER, L. A., and DAWES, C. T. 2008. The Genetic Basis of Political Participation. *American Political Science Review*, 102/2: 233–48.

FUNK, C. L., SMITH, K. B., ALFORD, J. R., HIBBING, M. V., HATEMI, P. K., and HIBBING, J. R. 2010. Toward a Modern View of Political Man: Genetic and Environmental Sources of Political Orientations and Participation. Paper presented at the Annual Meeting of the American Political Science Association, Washington, DC, Sept. 2–5.

——————KRUEGER, R. F., EAVES, L. J., and HIBBING, J. R. 2009. Genetic and Environmental Transmission of Value Orientations: A New Twin Study of Political Attitudes. Paper presented at the Annual Meeting of the American Political Science Association, Toronto, Sept. 3–6.

HARMON-JONES, E., and WINKIELMAN, P. (eds.) 2007. *Social Neuroscience: Integrating Biological and Psychological Explanations of Social Behavior*. New York: Guilford Press.

HATEMI, P. K., ALFORD, J. R., HIBBING, J. R., MARTIN, N. G., and EAVES, L. J. 2009. Is There a Party in Your Genes? *Political Research Quarterly*, 62/3: 584–600.

——FUNK, C. L., MEDLAND, S. E., MAES, H. H., SILBERG, J. L., MARTIN, N. G., and EAVES, L. J. 2009. Genetic and Environmental Transmission of Political Attitudes over a Life Time. *Journal of Politics*, 71/3: 1141–56.

——HIBBING, J. R., MEDLAND, S. E., KELLER, M. C., ALFORD, J. R., SMITH, K. B., MARTIN, N. G., and EAVES, L. J. 2010. Not by Twins Alone: Using the Extended Family Design to Investigate Genetic Influence on Political Beliefs. *American Journal of Political Science*, 54/3: 798–814.

——MEDLAND, S. E., MORLEY, K. I., HEATH, A. C., and MARTIN, N. G. 2007. The Genetics of Voting: An Australian Twin Study. *Behavior Genetics*, 37/3: 435–48.

JOST, J. T. 2006. The End of the End of Ideology. *American Psychologist*, 61: 651–70.

——GLASER, J., KRUGLANSKI, A. W., and SULLOWAY, F. J. 2003. Political Conservatism as Motivated Social Cognition. *Psychological Bulletin*, 129/3: 339–75.

KAPLAN, J., FREEDMAN, J., and IACOBONI, M. 2007. Us versus Them: Political Attitudes and Party Affiliation Influence Neural Response to Faces of Presidential Candidates. *Neuropsychologica*, 45: 55–64.

KIRK, K. M., MAES, H. H., NEALE, M. C., HEATH, A. C., MARTIN, N. G., and EAVES, L. J. 1999. Frequency of Church Attendance in Australia and the United States: Models of Family Resemblance. *Twin Research*, 2: 99–107.

KOENIG, L. B., McGUE, M., KRUEGER, R. F., and BOUCHARD, T. J., JR. 2007. Religiousness, Antisocial Behavior, and Altruism: Genetic and Environmental Mediation. *Journal of Personality*, 75/2: 265–90.

LODGE, M., and TABER, C. S. 2005. The Automaticity of Affect for Political Leaders, Groups and Issues: An Experimental Test of the Hot Cognition Hypothesis. *Political Psychology*, 26: 455–82.

MACCOBY, E. E. 2000. Parenting and its Effects on Children: On Reading and Misreading Behavior Genetics. *Annual Review of Psychology*, 51: 1–27.

McCOURT, K., BOUCHARD, T. J., JR., LYKKEN, D. T., TELLEGAN, A., and KEYES, M. 1999. Authoritarianism Revisited: Genetic and Environmental Influence Examined in Twins Reared Apart and Together. *Personality and Individual Differences*, 27: 985–1014.

MARCUS, G. E., NEUMAN, W. R., and MACKUEN, M. 2000. *Affective Intelligence and Political Judgment*. Chicago: University of Chicago Press.

MARTIN, N. G., EAVES, L. J., HEATH, A. C., JARDINE, R., FEINGOLD, L. M., and EYSENCK, H. J. 1986. Transmission of Social Attitudes. *Proceedings of the National Academy of Sciences* (15 June), 4364–8.

OLSON, J. M., VERNON, P. A., HARRIS, J. A., and LANG, K. L. 2001. The Heritability of Attitudes: A Study of Twins. *Journal of Personality and Social Psychology*, 80/6: 845–60.

OXLEY, D. R., SMITH, K. B., HIBBING, M. V., MILLER, J. L., ALFORD, J. R., HATEMI, P. K., and HIBBING, J. R. 2008. Political Attitudes Are Predicted by Physiological Traits. *Science*, 321/5896: 1667–70.

PLOMIN, R., and KOVAS, Y. 2005. Generalist Genes and Learning Disabilities. *Psychological Bulletin*, 131/4: 592–617.

SCARR, S., and McCARTNEY, K. 1983. How People Make Their Own Environments: A Theory of Genotype→Environment Effects. *Child Development*, 54: 424–35.

—— and WEINBERG, R. A. 1981. The Transmission of Authoritarianism in Families: Genetic Resemblance in Social–Political Attitudes? In *Race, Social Class, and Individual Differences in IQ*, ed. S. Scarr. Hillsdale, NJ: Lawrence Erlbaum.

SCHREIBER, D. 2007. Political Cognition as Social Cognition: Are We All Political Sophisticates? In *The Affect Effect: Dynamics of Emotion in Political Thinking and Behavior*, ed. W. R. Neuman, G. E. Marcus, M. MacKuen, and A. Crigler. Chicago: University of Chicago Press.

SCHWARTZ, S. H. 1992. Universals in the Content and Structure of Values: Theoretical Advances and Empirical Tests in 20 Countries. *Advances in Experimental Social Psychology*, 25: 1–65.

SETTLE, J. E., DAWES, C. T., CHRISTAKIS, N. A., and FOWLER, J. H. 2010. Friendships Moderate an Association between a Dopamine Gene Variant and Political Ideology. *Journal of Politics*, 72/4: 1189–98.

—— —— and FOWLER, J. H. 2009. The Heritability of Partisan Attachment. *Political Research Quarterly*, 62/3: 601–13.

SMITH, K. B., ALFORD, J. R., HATEMI, P. K., FUNK, C. L., and HIBBING, J. R. 2010. Biology, Ideology and Epistemology: How Do We Know Political Attitudes Are Inherited? Paper presented at the Annual Meeting of the Midwest Political Science Association, Chicago, Apr. 22–5.

—— HIBBING, J. R., OXLEY, D., HIBBING, M., and ALFORD, J. R. 2008. The Ideological Animal: The Origins and Implications of Ideology. Paper presented at the Annual Meeting of the American Political Science Association, Boston, Aug. 28–31.

TESSER, A. 1993. The Importance of Heritability in Psychological Research: The Case of Attitudes. *Psychological Review*, 100/1: 129–42.

TRUETT, K. R., EAVES, L. J., MEYER, J. M., HEATH, A. C., and MARTIN, N. G. 1992. Religion and Education as Mediators of Attitudes: A Multivariate Analysis. *Behavior Genetics*, 22/1: 43–62.

VISSCHER, P. M., MEDLAND, S. E., FERREIRA, M. A. R., MORLEY, K. I., ZHU, G., CORNES, B. K., MONTGOMERY, G. W., and MARTIN, N. G. 2006. Assumption-Free Estimation of Heritability from Genome-wide Identity-by-Descent Sharing between Full Siblings. *PLoS Genetics*, 2/3: 316–24.

WALLER, N. G., KOJETIN, B. A., BOUCHARD, T. J., JR., LYKKEN, D. T., and TELLEGEN, A. 1990. Genetic and Environmental Influences on Religious Interests, Attitudes, and Values: A Study of Twins Reared Apart and Together. *Psychological Science*, 1: 138–42.

WESTEN, D., BLAGOV, P. S., HARENSKI, K., KILTS, C., and HAMANN, S. 2006. Neural Basis of Motivated Reasoning: An fMRI Study of Emotional Constraints on Political Judgment during the U.S. Presidential Election of 2004. *Journal of Cognitive Neuroscience*, 18: 1947–57.

WINKIELMAN, P., KNUTSON, B., PAULUS, M., and TRUJILLO, J. L. 2007. Affective Influence on Judgments and Decisions: Moving towards Core Mechanisms. *Review of General Psychology*, 11/2: 179–92.

# CHAPTER 27

........................................................................

# ATTITUDE ORGANIZATION
# IN THE MASS PUBLIC

*The Impact of Ideology and Partisanship*

........................................................................

WILLIAM G. JACOBY

THE American public is continuously confronted by a political world composed of multiple stimuli: at any point in time, there are a number of issues on the public agenda; in modern presidential elections, there are usually several candidates within each of the parties; and the modern mass media provide multiple sources of information. Presumably, most citizens react to the external environment by developing beliefs and attitudes about the various political objects that catch their attention. So this immediately raises questions about the ways that people organize their reactions into belief systems or attitude structures.

The organizational structures underlying mass opinions are important for several reasons. For one thing, well-structured attitudes are frequently interpreted as an indicator of coherence, clarity, and sophistication in political thinking (Converse 1964; Luskin 1987). Closely related to this, the structure of attitudes and beliefs can have an important impact on the ways that people process new, incoming information (Campbell, Converse, Miller, and Stokes 1960, chs. 9 and 10; Hastie 1986).

The preceding factors involve the psychology of individual citizens. But democratic theory provides additional motivation for focusing on the nature of belief systems and attitude structures. Communication of mass preferences to governmental officials will be facilitated if these two sets of actors think about social problems and political issues in comparable ways (Delli Carpini and Keeter 1996). Therefore, if people organize their thinking along the lines of the policy "packages" that are offered by political parties (which are themselves generated by the ideologies to which the leaders of the respective parties adhere), it should enhance the chances of democratic responsiveness with public policies that are generally consistent with mass preferences (Erikson, MacKuen, and Stimson 2002).

This chapter will examine attitude structure within American public opinion, paying particular attention to three broad questions from the research literature. First, how can attitude structure be discerned and measured? Second, how do ideology and partisanship contribute to individual attitude structures? Third, are there alternative mechanisms that serve to organize citizens' feelings about the various elements of the political world?

# ATTITUDE STRUCTURE AND THE ORGANIZATION OF OPINIONS

Political scientists typically define attitude structures in terms of connections between discrete opinions. For example, *The American Voter* states, "We speak of an 'attitude structure' when two or more beliefs or opinions held by an individual are in some way or another functionally related" (Campbell, Converse, Miller, and Stokes 1960, 189). More recently, *The American Voter Revisited* provides a similar definition: "For our purposes, an attitude structure exists when a common element underlies the ways that an individual reacts to different political issues" (Lewis-Beck, Jacoby, Norpoth, and Weisberg 2008, 203).

A closely related term is *belief system*, which Luskin (1987) has defined as the collection of constrained political cognitions that a person holds. In this case, "constraint" refers to the degree of coherent organization that exists among the individual's idea elements. The level of belief system constraint is a variable, which differs from one person to the next, depending upon the scope of the organizational principles that provide the basis for the attitudinal consistency in the first place (Campbell, Converse, Miller, and Stokes 1960, ch. 9; Converse 1964). There are several different sources of constraint, including ideology (Converse 1964), partisan alignments (Baldassarri and Gelman 2008), and perhaps even idiosyncratic principles that vary from one person to the next (Lane 1962; Conover and Feldman 1984).

Regardless of the terminology or precise conceptualization that is employed, the emphasis is on the existence of a relatively broad psychological element that provides general guidance for the development of opinions toward specific issues. Since the same judgmental criterion is being applied to multiple stimuli, the resultant attitude structures are usually expected to produce consistent opinions across a range of discrete and substantively distinct issues. Thus, attitude structures and belief systems are both concepts referring to the source of organization among an individual's political orientations. For the remainder of this chapter, these terms are used interchangeably.

## Measurement Strategies for Attitude Structures

Attitude structures and belief systems necessarily imply the existence of connections between distinct psychological elements (e.g., beliefs and attitudes about political issues). Empirically, beliefs and attitudes are usually measured using responses to questions on public opinion surveys. So, for example, a survey instrument might include a battery of items asking people about their stands across a range of specific issues. Responses to the individual items are interpreted as empirical indicators of the separate attitudes. But attitude structures are typically assessed using scaling methods, which seek to combine information from the separate responses in order to produce a new variable, or "scale," summarizing the common characteristics that exist across the original set of survey responses.[1]

In empirical investigations of individual attitude structures, the main questions are usually: (1) to what extent do attitude structures actually exist in public opinion? and (2) what is the organizational basis of any such structures that are found? In order to answer these kinds of questions, the researcher would typically apply a scaling technique to survey responses on questions about policy issues. If the analysis reveals non-random patterns in the data, it is taken as evidence of constraint, emanating from an underlying attitude structure. The substantive nature of the structure, and the sources of the constraint, are inferred from the content of the items that are combined in the scale.

A number of scaling techniques have been employed in the political science literature to examine issue attitude structures. One of the earliest methodologies was Guttman scaling, which assumes that survey questions vary systematically in the degree to which they reflect some underlying evaluative criterion, such as liberal (or conservative) ideology.[2] Guttman scaling was employed to measure attitude structures in some of the classic studies of political behavior, such as *The American Voter* (Campbell, Converse, Miller, and Stokes 1960). It was also used more recently in *The American Voter Revisited* (Lewis-Beck, Jacoby, Norpoth, and Weisberg 2008).

For the most part, Guttman scaling has fallen out of use in the public opinion literature because its methodology is considered a bit primitive. However, it is closely related to a family of newer techniques based upon item response theory (Andrich 1985; Baker and Kim 2004). These latter methods are quite new in the political behavior literature, but they have already been employed to measure structured attitudes toward government spending (Jacoby 2000) and ideological configurations of issue attitudes (Treier and Hillygus 2009).

Another common approach for measuring individual-level attitude structures relies upon the related (but different) methodologies of principal components analysis (PCA) and factor analysis (FA).[3] The composite variables generated by PCA and FA are interpreted as empirical reflections of the underlying sources of constraint in individual attitude structures. Some representative applications of PCA and FA to belief system

---

[1] Dawes (1972) provides a useful—although somewhat dated—introduction to the logic and practice of scaling methodology, with particular emphasis on attitude measurement.

[2] Guttman scaling is covered in Dawes (1972) and McIver and Carmines (1981).

[3] Bartholomew, Steele, Moustaki, and Galbraith (2008) provide a concise introduction to principal components and factor analysis.

measurement include Stimson 1975; Nie, Verba, and Petrocik 1979; Judd and Milburn 1980; and Layman and Carsey 2002.

Perhaps the best-known strategy for measuring attitude constraint, first used by Philip E. Converse (1964) in his seminal paper "The Nature of Belief Systems in Mass Publics," uses pairwise correlations between separate issue questions. Again, constraint is defined as the use of broad evaluative standards to guide responses toward specific stimuli (such as issues). If constraint actually exists in public opinion, then people should tend to take similar positions across distinct issues. That, in turn, generates correlations across the responses to separate survey items measuring attitudes on those issues. Alternatively, low correlations would signal that people are not using a consistent criterion to determine their positions on issues. And such findings would be taken as evidence for low levels of constraint and limited attitude structures.

Converse (1964) used intercorrelations to compare the degree of attitude constraint in the mass public to that exhibited by a sample of congressional candidates. Later Nie, Verba, and Petrocik (1979) used correlations to study changes in constraint over time. Apart from these highly influential works, empirical analyses based on intercorrelations between survey items have largely disappeared from the research literature, due to several methodological and theoretical critiques (for example, Barton and Parsons 1977; Wray 1979; Wyckoff 1987).

While the preceding methodological approaches have dominated the literature, there have been a variety of other measurement strategies that have been employed from time to time to measure attitude structuring. These include cluster analysis (Fleishman 1986), multidimensional scaling (Marcus, Tabb, and Sullivan 1974), and simply counting the number of issues on which a person adopts a given ideological position (for example, Jacoby 1991) or places political stimuli (e.g., parties) in the ideologically "correct" positions (Hamill, Lodge, and Blake 1985; Luskin 1987). Fortunately, the empirical results obtained using these various methods generally have been quite consistent with each other, although the substantive interpretations of those results have sometimes gone in very different directions. For example, Marcus, Tabb, and Sullivan (1974) and Hamill, Lodge, and Blake (1985) both emphasize that multiple dimensions can be used to organize political thinking, while Luskin (1987) and Jacoby (1991) show that active ideological thinking occurs primarily among the most sophisticated strata of the general public.

# Attitude Structuring Over Time in American Public Opinion

The authors of *The American Voter* were the first to consider explicitly the question of attitude structure (Campbell, Converse, Miller, and Stokes 1960, ch. 9), although earlier research actually anticipated some of their findings (Berelson, Lazarsfeld, and McPhee 1954). Like their predecessors, Campbell et al.'s findings suggest that, to the extent attitude structures did exist within the electorate of the 1950s, their scope was quite limited. For one thing, attitudes were organized separately around issues of domestic and foreign policy, respectively. At the same time, each attitude structure encompassed only a subset of the available issues within each policy domain. There was no evidence that individuals organized their attitudes in the broad and encompassing ways that might be characterized meaningfully as ideologies. Converse's subsequent analysis (1964) produced a stark picture, showing that attitude constraint within the mass public was very low, both in absolute terms and relative to the levels of constraint illustrated by political elites.

The preceding, rather pessimistic, view characterized American public opinion through about 1960. However, beginning in 1964, the coherence and organization of citizens' political attitudes seemed to increase markedly. For example, Nie, Verba, and Petrocik (1979) showed that the intercorrelations among survey responses to issue questions shot upward that year, and remained quite high throughout the 1970s. These authors also demonstrated that other measures of constraint showed similar patterns over the same period.

For a time, the predominant interpretation of these results was that attitude constraint was responsive to stimuli within the external political environment. Hence, the issues that emerged during the 1960s (e.g., welfare, civil rights, different lifestyles, etc.) impinged more directly on people's lives than the remote foreign policy concerns that dominated the 1950s, leading citizens to develop broader and more coherent attitude structures with respect to these newer policy controversies. There was always some degree of skepticism about the existence of such broad changes in the mass public (for example, Margolis 1977; Smith 1989; Bishop and Frankovic 1981). But major criticism of the "revisionist" view really arose during the late 1970s, when several teams of researchers showed that the larger correlations used to signal higher levels of attitude constraint were almost certainly due to changes in the survey questions that were used to measure the separate issue attitudes (Bishop, Tuchfarber, and Oldendick 1978; Brunk 1978; Sullivan, Piereson, and Marcus 1978).

There was sharp disagreement among the protagonists and other interested parties about the appropriate interpretation of the evidence regarding attitude constraint (Nie and Rabjohn 1979; Bishop, Tuchfarber, Oldendick, and Bennett 1979; Sullivan, Piereson, Marcus, and Feldman 1979; Judd and Milburn 1980; Converse 1980). But it is probably safe to say that the revisionists' critics dominate the current scholarly consensus about temporal changes in attitude structuring within the mass public (for example, Bishop 2005). On the other hand, Jacoby points out that several "other measures which are not dependent upon the wording of survey issue questions . . . also signal increases in ideological awareness during this same time period" (2002, 108). For example, the active use of liberal–conservative abstractions to organize individual political orientations became much more prevalent from the mid-1960s (Hagner and Pierce 1982a, 1982b). So it appears likely that American public opinion does contain a discernible amount of attitude structure giving coherence to the ways that individual citizens think about a variety of political issues (Ansolabehere, Rodden, and Snyder 2008).

# ORGANIZATIONAL FOUNDATIONS OF
# ATTITUDE STRUCTURE

The early research on attitude structure in public opinion focused almost exclusively on determining the *amount* of systematic organization that seemed to exist within individual citizens' political orientations (Luskin 1987). But the conflicting interpretations of the empirical evidence and apparent lack of theoretical progress led to some overt frustration and calls to abandon non-productive lines of research (W. L. Bennett 1977; Kinder 1983). Such critiques had a pronounced effect on the field and led to two closely related shifts in focus.

First, scholarly attention shifted away from questions about the *prevalence* of attitude structures within the mass public and toward the *impact* that attitudinal organization has on subsequent political orientations. Second, recent scholarship has returned to the original conceptual definition of constraint, as articulated in *The American Voter* and "The Nature of Belief Systems in Mass Publics," by emphasizing the dependence of specific issue attitudes on more general underlying principles (Peffley and Hurwitz 1985; Jacoby 1991; W. E. Miller and Shanks 1996). While the substantive content of these psychological organizing mechanisms is in principle infinitely variable, there are two specific structural foundations that stand out due to their widespread use in American public opinion and their obvious relevance to the political world: ideology and party identification.

## Liberal–Conservative Ideology and Attitude Organization

Ideology is often defined as a view of the ideal society along with the means of achieving it (for example, Downs 1957; Hinich and Munger 1994; Jacoby 2009). So ideological labels like "liberal" and "conservative" summarize different ideas about appropriate governmental institutions and responsibilities for addressing social problems. Many scholars also regard ideology as a set of assumptions about basic human nature (for example, Barker and Tinnick 2006). In either case, the traditional bipolar ideological continuum provides a useful source of attitude structure, precisely because it involves broad abstractions that can readily encompass a wide variety of more specific phenomena (Jacoby 1995).[4]

There is a massive amount of evidence showing that ideological self-placements along the liberal–conservative continuum exert a pronounced influence on the

---

[4] Liberal–conservative self-placements can also be used in "non-ideological" ways, to guide individual orientations toward political stimuli like presidential candidates (Levitin and Miller 1979) and policy issues (Sears 1993). When they operate in this manner, ideological identifications are more important as a source of affective cues than as a foundation for organizing separate attitudes (Sniderman, Brody, and Tetlock 1991).

There are some differences of scholarly opinion regarding the exact psychological processes that are involved. Some researchers argue that partisan influence can be best understood as an example of reference groups (Jacoby 1988). Others emphasize social identity theory (Green, Palmquist, and Schickler 2002). And it can also be viewed as a straightforward manifestation of attitude theory (Weisberg and Greene 2003). In any case, political parties serve as tangible sources of guidance for the development and organization of personal opinions (for example, Bartels 2002; Tomz and Sniderman 2005).

## Alternative Sources of Attitude Organization

Of course, ideology and partisanship are not the only possible sources of attitude organization within the American public. But it is striking that many of the other alternatives only display very limited effects on citizens' opinions. For example, there are clear socioeconomic cleavages in modern society, with immediate political implications (Bartels 2008). And while there is evidence that some people rely upon class considerations to organize their political thinking (Hamill, Lodge, and Blake 1985), the effects are generally quite limited (Kuklinski, Metlay, and Kay 1982) and largely funneled through the political parties (Manza and Brooks 1999).

On a related, but more general, point, self-interest has very little impact on the content or structure of political attitudes (Sears and Funk 1990). This finding stands in marked contrast to the predictions of rational actor models, which hold that people should adopt political positions in order to maximize their personal utilities (Downs 1957). But a very long research program carried out by David Sears and his colleagues has shown that tangible personal considerations are far less potent predictors of issue attitudes than are symbolic orientations like ideology and party identification (Lau and Heldman 2009).

Still another possible foundation for attitude structures lies in people's feelings about core values; that is, their abstract conceptions about the desirable and undesirable end states of human life (Rokeach 1973). Values are easily accessible and they could very easily function as a set of general evaluative standards for structuring reactions to political issues (Schwartz 1992). But at least one recent study has shown that value choices have no more influence on issue attitudes than ideology and partisanship (Jacoby 2006). And there is even evidence that individual feelings about values are affected by party identification, which raises further questions about their theoretical status as a foundation for attitude structures (Goren 2005; Goren, Federico, and Kittilson 2009).

Finally, the mass media are another potential influence on attitude structures. However, while there is an enormous amount of research on how the media affect the *content* of political orientations, there has been relatively little work aimed at explicating media effects on the *organization* of individual beliefs and attitudes. And the existing research on related topics could lead to varying interpretations. For example, several recent studies indicate that individuals are selective in their exposure to the mass media, focusing on sources providing information that is consistent with prior beliefs (Lavine, Lodge, and Fratas 2005; Stroud 2008); these findings provide some contrast to earlier research which suggested that selective exposure to media content was not a widespread phenomenon (Sears and Freedman 1967). But such selectivity is probably on the increase, as the growing number of media outlets provides new opportunities for people to focus on the kinds of information to which they are already predisposed and avoid dissonant messages (Prior 2005). To the extent that selective exposure to information occurs, the media content to which citizens are exposed will reinforce existing attitude structures.

From a different perspective, the content of the mass media is also relevant to individual attitude structures. Jerit (2009) has shown that, when the media provide contextual information in news stories (i.e., covering the background and implications of particular events), it contributes to citizens' political knowledge, even among less-sophisticated strata within the public. Knowledge is generally believed to be highly correlated with coherent belief systems (for example, Zaller 1992), so this could be taken as indirect evidence for a media effect on attitude structure. But contextual information in the news is probably fairly rare (for example, Mutz and Martin 2001). In a similar vein, Iyengar (1991) shows that the media often frame news stories in episodic, rather than thematic, terms (e.g., showing specific poor families, rather than the systemic sources of poverty in American society). Such episodic coverage does not encourage news consumers to make the kinds of broad connections that would exist in a constrained belief system. Thus, the role of the mass media in attitude organization is not entirely clear.

# Conclusion

One of the major findings from modern political science research is that ideology and political parties play important roles in American public opinion. In this context, the focus is not really on the notion of ideology as a broad philosophical system, or on parties as formal organizations. Instead, ideology and political parties provide the organizational foundations for many individuals' political beliefs and attitudes. In this manner, they comprise an integral element of public opinion, effectively linking the broader political system to citizens' psychological orientations.

The inherently political nature of mass belief systems means that the latter will almost certainly vary in interesting ways over time. The clarity and dominant organizational structures underlying citizens' attitudes will be affected by the salient political divisions that exist within the external environment. For example, the emergence of potent new issues and intra-party conflicts during the 1960s and early 1970s contributed to liberal–conservative structure in political attitudes, but simultaneously diminished the impact of party identification on citizens' orientations (for example, A. H. Miller,

Miller, Raine, and Brown 1976; W. E. Miller and Levitin 1976). In contrast, the recent sharp polarization in American politics has proceeded along clear partisan lines (McCarty, Poole, and Rosenthal 2006). Accordingly, the public's reactions to a broad array of issues are also organized in ways that are consistent with individual attachments to the respective parties—self-identified Democrats are taking consistently liberal stands on issues, while Republican identifiers adhere to conservative policy positions (Hetherington 2001; Abramowitz and Saunders 2008; Bafumi and Shapiro 2009). But the increasing polarization in public opinion appears to be almost entirely due to the enhanced clarity in the parties' respective policy positions, rather than to increases in sophistication or ideological awareness among individual citizens (Fiorina, Abrams, and Pope 2006; Baldassarri and Gelman 2008).

The ongoing interplay between political leadership on the one hand and the organization of public opinion on the other hand guarantees that there is no "final word" on individual attitude structures and belief systems. And there are several lines of inquiry that clearly deserve further attention. For example, there is renewed interest in the psychological sources of ideology (Jost, Nosek, and Gosling 2008), as liberal and conservative stands appear to be linked to fundamental elements of personality, such as authoritarianism (Stenner 2005; Hetherington and Weiler 2009) and need for cognitive closure (Jost, Glaser, Kruglanski, and Sulloway 2003). Furthermore, the emergence of new issues, such as the environment, globalization, illegal immigration, and the war on terror, raises questions about how the resultant policy controversies (and others as yet unforeseen) will be incorporated into existing partisan and ideological "packages." And, as mentioned earlier, there is very little known about the impact of the mass media on the ways people make connections across different issues. For all of these reasons, the structure of political beliefs and attitudes undoubtedly will continue to be an important focus of political science research on into the future.

# REFERENCES

ABRAMOWITZ, A. I., and SAUNDERS, K. L. 2008. Is Polarization a Myth? *Journal of Politics*, 70: 542–55.

ANDRICH, D. 1985. An Elaboration of Guttman Scaling with Rasch Models for Measurement. In *Sociological Methodology*, ed. N. Brandon-Tuma. San Francisco: Jossey-Bass.

ANSOLABEHERE, S., RODDEN, J., and SNYDER, J. M., JR. 2008. The Strength of Issues: Using Multiple Measures to Gauge Preference Stability, Ideological Constraint, and Issue Voting. *American Political Science Review*, 102: 215–32.

BAFUMI, J., and SHAPIRO, R. Y. 2009. A New Partisan Voter. *Journal of Politics*, 71: 1–24.

BAKER, F. B., and KIM, S.-H. 2004. *Item Response Theory: Parameter Estimation Techniques*, 2nd edn., rev. and expanded. New York: Marcel Dekker.

BALDASSARRI, D., and GELMAN, A. 2008. Partisans without Constraint: Political Polarization and Trends in American Public Opinion. *American Journal of Sociology*, 114: 408–46.

BARKER, D. C., and TINNICK, J. D. 2006. Competing Visions of Parental Roles and Ideological Constraint. *American Political Science Review*, 100: 249–63.

BARTELS, L. M. 2000. Partisanship and Voting Behavior, 1952–1996. *American Journal of Political Science*, 44: 35–50.

—— 2002. Beyond the Running Tally: Partisan Bias in Political Perceptions. *Political Behavior*, 24: 117–50.

—— 2008. *Unequal Democracy: The Political Economy of the New Gilded Age*. Princeton: Princeton University Press.

BARTHOLOMEW, D. J., STEELE, F., MOUSTAKI, I., and GALBRAITH, J. I. 2008. *Analysis of Multivariate Social Science Data*, 2nd edn. Boca Raton, FL: CRC Press.

BARTON, A. H., and PARSONS, R. W. 1977. Measuring Belief System Structure. *Public Opinion Quarterly*, 41: 159–80.

BAUM, M. A., and GROELING, T. 2009. Shot by the Messenger: Partisan Cues and Public Opinion regarding National Security and War. *Political Behavior*, 31: 157–86.

BENNETT, L. M., and BENNETT, S. E. 1990. *Living with Leviathan: Americans Coming to Terms with Big Government*. Lawrence: University of Kansas Press.

BENNETT, W. L. 1977. The Growth of Knowledge in Mass Belief Systems: An Epistemological Critique. *American Journal of Political Science*, 21: 465–500.

BERELSON, B. R., LAZARSFELD, P. F., and McPHEE, W. N. 1954. *Voting*. Chicago: University of Chicago Press.

BERINSKY, A. J. 2007. Assuming the Costs of War: Events, Elites, and American Public Support for Military Conflict. *Journal of Politics*, 69: 975–97.

BISHOP, G. F. 2005. *The Illusion of Public Opinion: Fact and Artifact in American Public Opinion Polls*. Lanham, MD: Rowman & Littlefield.

—— and FRANKOVIC, K. A. 1981. Ideological Consensus and Constraint among Party Leaders and Followers in the 1978 Election. *Micropolitics*, 1: 87–111.

—— TUCHFARBER, A. J., and OLDENDICK, R. W. 1978. Change in the Structure of American Political Attitudes: The Nagging Question of Question Wording. *American Journal of Political Science*, 22: 250–69.

—— —— —— and BENNETT, S. E. 1979. Questions about Question Wording: A Rejoinder to Revisiting Mass Belief Systems Revisited. *American Journal of Political Science*, 23: 187–92.

BRUNK, G. G. 1978. The 1964 Attitude Consistency Leap Reconsidered. *Political Methodology*, 5: 347–60.

CAMPBELL, A. E., CONVERSE, P. E., MILLER, W. E., and STOKES, D. 1960. *The American Voter*. Chicago: University of Chicago Press.

—— GURIN, G., and MILLER, W. E. 1954. *The Voter Decides*. Evanston, IL: Row, Peterson.

CARMINES, E. G., and STIMSON, J. A. 1989. *Issue Evolution: Race and the Transformation of American Politics*. Princeton: Princeton University Press.

CONOVER, P. J., and FELDMAN, S. 1984. How People Organize the Political World: A Schematic Model. *American Journal of Political Science*, 28: 95–126.

CONVERSE, P. E. 1964. The Nature of Belief Systems in Mass Publics. In *Ideology and Discontent*, ed. D. E. Apter. New York: Free Press.

—— 1980. Comment: Rejoinder to Judd and Milburn. *American Sociological Review*, 45: 644–6.

DAWES, R. M. 1972. *Fundamentals of Attitude Measurement*. New York: Wiley.

DELLI CARPINI, M. X., and KEETER, S. 1996. *What Americans Know about Politics and Why it Matters*. New Haven: Yale University Press.

DOWNS, A. 1957. *An Economic Theory of Democracy*. New York: Harper & Row.

ERIKSON, R. S., MACKUEN, M. B., and STIMSON, J. A. 2002. *The Macro Polity*. Cambridge: Cambridge University Press.

FEDERICO, C. M. 2006. Race, Education, and Individualism Revisited. *Journal of Politics*, 68: 600–10.

FIELD, J. O., and ANDERSON, R. A. 1969. Ideology in the Public's Conceptualization of the 1964 Election. *Public Opinion Quarterly*, 33: 380–98.

FIORINA, M. P., ABRAMS, S. J., and POPE, J. C. 2006. *Culture War? The Myth of a Polarized America*, 2nd edn. New York: Pearson Longman.

FLEISHMAN, J. A. 1986. Types of Political Attitude Structure: Results of a Cluster Analysis. *Public Opinion Quarterly*, 50: 371–86.

FREE, L. A., and CANTRIL, H. 1967. *The Political Beliefs of Americans*. New Brunswick, NJ: Rutgers University Press.

GARTNER, S. S. 2008. The Multiple Effects of Casualties on Public Support for War: An Experimental Approach. *American Political Science Review*, 102: 95–106.

GILENS, M. 1999. *Why Americans Hate Welfare*. Chicago: University of Chicago Press.

GOREN, P. 2005. Party Identification and Core Political Attitudes. *American Journal of Political Science*, 49: 881–96.

—— FEDERICO, C. M., and KITTILSON, M. C. 2009. Source Cues, Partisan Identities, and Political Value Expression. *American Journal of Political Science*, 53: 805–20.

GREEN, D., PALMQUIST, B., and SCHICKLER, E. 2002. *Partisan Hearts and Minds: Political Parties and the Social Identities of Voters*. New Haven: Yale University Press.

HAGNER, P., and PIERCE, J. C. 1982a. Conceptualization and Party Identification: 1956–1976. *American Journal of Political Science*, 26: 377–87.

—— —— 1982b. Correlative Characteristics of the Levels of Conceptualization in the American Public, 1956–1976. *Journal of Politics*, 44: 779–807.

HAMILL, R., LODGE, M., and BLAKE, F. 1985. The Breadth, Depth, and Utility of Class, Partisan, and Ideological Schemata. *American Journal of Political Science*, 29: 850–70.

HASTIE, R. 1986. A Primer of Information Processing Theory for the Political Scientist. In *Political Cognition: The 19th Annual Carnegie Symposium on Cognition*, ed. R. R. Lau and D. O. Sears. Hillsdale, NJ: Lawrence Erlbaum.

HETHERINGTON, M. J. 2001. Resurgent Mass Partisanship: The Role of Elite Polarization. *American Political Science Review*, 95: 619–31.

—— and WEILER, J. D. 2009. *Authoritarianism and Polarization in American Politics*. Cambridge: Cambridge University Press.

HINICH, M. J., and MUNGER, M. C. 1994. *Ideology and the Theory of Political Choice*. Ann Arbor: University of Michigan Press.

IYENGAR, S. 1991. *Is Anyone Responsible? How Television Frames Political Issues*. Chicago: University of Chicago Press.

JACKSON, J. E. 1975. Issues, Party Choice, and Presidential Votes. *American Journal of Political Science*, 19: 161–85.

JACOBY, W. G. 1988. The Impact of Party Identification on Issue Attitudes. *American Journal of Political Science*, 32: 643–80.

—— 1991. Ideological Identification and Issue Attitudes. *American Journal of Political Science*, 35: 178–205.

—— 1995. The Structure of Ideological Thinking in the American Electorate. *American Journal of Political Science*, 39: 314–35.

—— 2000. Issue Framing and Public Opinion on Government Spending. *American Journal of Political Science*, 44: 750–67.

—— 2002. Liberal–Conservative Thinking in the American Electorate. In *Research in Micropolitics: Political Decision Making, Participation, and Deliberation*, vi, ed. M. X. Delli Carpini, L. Huddy, and R. Y. Shapiro. Greenwich, CT: Jai Press.

—— 2006. Value Choices and American Public Opinion. *American Journal of Political Science*, 50: 706–23.

—— 2009. Is a Liberal–Conservative Identification an Ideology? In *Understanding Public Opinion*, ed. B. Norrander and C. Wilcox, 3rd edn. Washington, DC: CQ Press.

JERIT, J. 2009. Understanding the Knowledge Gap: The Role of Experts and Journalists. *Journal of Politics*, 71: 442–56.

JOST, J. T., GLASER, J., KRUGLANSKI, A. W., and SULLOWAY, F. J. 2003. Political Conservatism as Motivated Social Cognition. *Psychological Bulletin*, 129: 339–75.

—— NOSEK, B. A., and GOSLING, S. D. 2008. Ideology: Its Resurgence in Social, Personality, and Political Psychology. *Perspectives on Psychological Science*, 3/2: 126–36.

JUDD, C. M., and MILBURN, M. A. 1980. The Structure of Attitude Systems in the General Public: Comparisons of a Structural Equation Model. *American Sociological Review*, 45: 627–43.

KINDER, D. R. 1983. Diversity and Complexity in American Public Opinion. In *Political Science: The State of the Discipline*, ed. A. W. Finifter. Washington, DC: American Political Science Association.

KUKLINSKI, J. H., METLAY, D. S., and KAY, W. D. 1982. Citizen Knowledge and Choices on the Complex Issue of Nuclear Energy. *American Journal of Political Science*, 26: 615–42.

LANE, R. E. 1962. *Political Ideology: Why the American Common Man Believes What He Does*. New York: Free Press.

LAU, R. R. 1986. Political Schemata, Candidate Evaluations, and Voting Behavior. In *Political Cognition*, ed. R. R. Lau and D. O. Sears. Hillsdale, NJ: Lawrence Erlbaum.

—— and HELDMAN, C. 2009. Self-Interest, Symbolic Attitudes, and Support for Public Policy: A Multilevel Analysis. *Political Psychology*, 30: 513–37.

—— BROWN, T. A., and SEARS, D. O. 1978. Self-Interest and Civilians' Attitudes toward the Vietnam War. *Public Opinion Quarterly*, 42: 464–83.

LAVINE, H., LODGE, M., and FRATAS, K. 2005. Threat, Authoritarianism, and Selective Exposure to Information. *Political Psychology*, 26: 219–44.

LAYMAN, G. C., and CARSEY, T. M. 2002. Policy Polarization and "Conflict Extension" in the American Electorate. *American Journal of Political Science*, 46: 786–802.

LEVITIN, T. E., and MILLER, W. E. 1979. Ideological Interpretations of Presidential Elections. *American Political Science Review*, 73: 751–71.

LEWIS-BECK, M. S., JACOBY, W. G., NORPOTH, H., and WEISBERG, H. F. 2008. *The American Voter Revisited*. Ann Arbor: University of Michigan Press.

LUSKIN, R. C. 1987. Measuring Political Sophistication. *American Journal of Political Science*, 31: 856–99.

MCCARTY, N., POOLE, K., and ROSENTHAL, H. 2006. *Polarized America: The Dance of Ideology and Unequal Riches*. Cambridge, MA: MIT Press.

MCIVER, J. P., and CARMINES, E. G. 1981. *Unidimensional Scaling*. Beverly Hills, CA: Sage.

MANZA, J., and BROOKS, C. 1999. *Social Cleavages and Political Change: Voter Alignments and US Party Coalitions*. Oxford: Oxford University Press.

Marcus, G., Tabb, D., and Sullivan, J. L. 1974. The Application of Individual Differences Scaling to the Measurement of Political Ideologies. *American Journal of Political Science*, 18: 405–20.

Margolis, M. 1977. From Confusion to Confusion: Issues and the American Voter (1956–1972). *American Political Science Review*, 71: 31–43.

Miller, A. H., Miller, W. E., Raine, A. S., and Brown, T. H. 1976. A Majority Party in Disarray: Policy Polarization in the 1972 Election. *American Political Science Review*, 70: 753–78.

Miller, W. E., and Levitin, T. E. 1976. *Leadership and Change: Presidential Elections from 1952 to 1976*. Cambridge, MA: Winthrop.

—— and Shanks, J. M. 1996. *The New American Voter*. Cambridge, MA: Harvard University Press.

Mutz, D., and Martin, P. S. 2001. Facilitating Communication across Lines of Political Difference: The Role of the Mass Media. *American Political Science Review*, 95: 97–114.

Nie, N. H., and Rabjohn, J. N. 1979. Revisiting Mass Belief Systems Revisited, or, Doing Research Is Like Watching a Tennis Match. *American Journal of Political Science*, 23: 139–75.

—— Verba, S., and Petrocik, J. R. 1979. *The Changing American Voter*, enlarged edn. Cambridge, MA: Harvard University Press.

Page, B. I., and Jones, C. 1979. Reciprocal Effects of Policy Preferences, Party Loyalties, and the Vote. *American Political Science Review*, 73: 1071–89.

Peffley, M., and Hurwitz, J. 1985. A Hierarchical Model of Attitude Constraint. *American Journal of Political Science*, 29: 379–406.

Prior, M. 2005. News vs. Entertainment: How Increasing Media Choice Widens Gaps in Political Knowledge and Turnout. *American Journal of Political Science*, 49: 577–92.

Rahn, W., Aldrich, J., Borgida, E., and Sullivan, J. L. 1990. A Social-Cognitive Model of Candidate Appraisal. In *Information and Democratic Processes*, ed. J. Ferejohn and J. Kuklinski. Urbana: University of Illinois Press.

Rokeach, M. 1973. *The Nature of Human Values*. New York: Free Press.

Schneider, S. K., and Jacoby, W. G. 2005. Elite Discourse and American Public Opinion: The Case of Welfare Spending. *Political Research Quarterly*, 58: 367–79.

Schulman, M. A., and Pomper, G. M. 1975. Variability in Electoral Behavior: Longitudinal Perspectives from Causal Modeling. *American Journal of Political Science*, 19: 1–118.

Schwartz, S. H. 1992. Universals in the Content and Structure of Values: Theoretical Advances and Empirical Tests in 20 Countries. In *Advances in Experimental Social Psychology*, ed. M. P. Zanna. Orlando, FL: Academic Press.

Sears, D. O. 1993. Symbolic Politics: A Socio-Psychological Theory. In *Explorations in Political Psychology*, ed. S. Iyengar and W. J. McGuire. Durham, NC: Duke University Press.

—— and Freedman, J. L. 1967. Selective Exposure to Information: A Critical Review. *Public Opinion Quarterly*, 31: 194–213.

—— and Funk, C. L. 1990. Self-Interest in Americans' Political Opinions. In *Beyond Self-Interest*, ed. J. J. Mansbridge. Chicago: University of Chicago Press.

—— Hensler, C. P., and Speer, L. K. 1979. Whites' Opposition to "Busing": Self-Interest or Symbolic Politics? *American Political Science Review*, 73: 369–84.

—— Huddy, L., and Shaffer, L. G. 1986. A Schematic Variant of Symbolic Politics Theory, as Applied to Racial and Gender Equality. In *Political Cognition*, ed. R. R. Lau and D. O. Sears. Hillsdale, NJ: Lawrence Erlbaum.

—— Lau, R., Tyler, T. R., and Allen, H. 1980. Self-Interest versus Symbolic Politics in Policy Attitudes and Presidential Voting. *American Political Science Review*, 74: 670–84.

—— Tyler, T. R., Citrin, J., and Kinder, D. 1978. Political System Support and Public Response to the Energy Crisis. *American Journal of Political Science*, 22: 56–82.

Shapiro, R. Y., and Bloch-Elkon, Y. 2008. Foreign Policy, Meet the People. *National Interest*, 97: 37–42.

Smith, E. R. A. N. 1989. *The Unchanging American Voter*. Berkeley: University of California Press.

Sniderman, P. M., Brody, R. A., and Kuklinski, J. H. 1984. Policy Reasoning and Political Values: The Problem of Racial Equality. *American Journal of Political Science*, 28: 75–94.

—— —— and Tetlock, P. E. 1991. *Reasoning and Choice: Explorations in Political Psychology*. New York: Cambridge University Press.

Snyder, J., Shapiro, R. Y., and Bloch-Elkon, Y. 2009. Free Hand Abroad, Divide and Rule at Home. *World Politics*, 61: 155–87.

Stenner, K. 2005. *The Authoritarian Dynamic*. Cambridge: Cambridge University Press.

Stimson, J. A. 1975. Belief Systems: Constraint, Complexity, and the 1972 Election. *American Journal of Political Science*, 19: 393–418.

—— 2004. *Tides of Consent: How Public Opinion Shapes American Politics*. Cambridge: Cambridge University Press.

Stokes, D. E. 1966. Some Dynamic Elements of Contests for the Presidency. *American Political Science Review*, 60: 19–28.

Stroud, N. J. 2008. Media Use and Political Predispositions: Revisiting the Concept of Selective Exposure. *Political Behavior*, 30: 341–66.

Sullivan, J. L., Piereson, J. E., and Marcus, G. E. 1978. Ideological Constraint in the Mass Public: A Methodological Critique and Some New Findings. *American Journal of Political Science*, 22: 223–49.

—— —— —— and Feldman, S. 1979. The More Things Change, the More They Stay the Same. *American Journal of Political Science*, 23: 176–86.

Tomz, M., and Sniderman, P. M. 2005. Brand Names and the Organization of Mass Belief Systems. Unpublished paper.

Treier, S., and Hillygus, D. S. 2009. The Nature of Political Ideology in the Contemporary Electorate. *Public Opinion Quarterly*, 73: 679–703.

Weisberg, H. F., and Greene, S. H. 2003. The Political Psychology of Party Identification. In *Electoral Democracy*, ed. M. B. MacKuen and G. Rabinowitz. Ann Arbor: University of Michigan Press.

Wray, J. H. 1979. Comment on Interpretation of Early Research into Mass Belief Systems. *Journal of Politics*, 41: 1173–81.

Wyckoff, M. L. 1987. Issues of Measuring Ideological Sophistication: Level of Conceptualization, Attitude Consistency, and Attitude Stability. *Political Behavior*, 9: 193–224.

Zaller, J. 1992. *The Nature and Origins of Mass Opinion*. Cambridge: Cambridge University Press.

# SECTION SEVEN: THE PLURALISM OF PUBLIC OPINION

CHAPTER 28

........................................................................................................

# POLITICAL SOCIALIZATION

*Ongoing Questions and New Directions*

........................................................................................................

LAURA STOKER
JACKIE BASS

## INTRODUCTION

........................................................................................................

LIKE other work on public opinion and political behavior, political socialization research strives to understand where citizens' political views and actions come from and what causes them to change. What makes a socialization perspective on these questions unique is that it considers them with reference to the human life span. In thinking about the origins of political attributes socialization researchers look first to childhood and adolescence, when family, peers, and school loom as influential. Change in later years is judged against baselines set down (or, sometimes, not) earlier in life. Whether political views formed in the pre-adult years persist as individuals move into and through adulthood is a question of the first order. Also important is whether there are general age-related developments in political views or behavior—developments tied to the accumulation of political experience or to life events that come with age.

Another defining feature of political socialization research is its focus on the macro-level implications of micro-level socialization dynamics. Early research emphasized how political stability is fostered when children acquire attitudes that are supportive of the existing system, how aggregate continuity in opinion is heightened by high rates of parent–child transmission, and how class inequalities in political involvement are perpetuated by socialization processes. Scholars have looked to socialization dynamics within families as sources of aggregate gender gaps in political involvement and attitudes. Innumerable studies have sought to better understand aggregate shifts in behavior or opinion by decomposing them into period, life cycle, and generation effects.

The field of political socialization has changed considerably over time, in focus as well as in levels of scholarly interest and enthusiasm. Comprehensive reviews chart this history and provide a more detailed account of approaches, controversies, and findings in the field than is possible to provide here (for example, Niemi and Hepburn 1995; Niemi and Sobieszek 1977; Sapiro 2004; Sears and Levy 2003). This chapter will outline some of the main research threads in the field and consider at greater length several topics on which research is booming: (*a*) the civic orientations and political attitudes of today's young Americans, which distinguish them from previous generations, (*b*) the transformative potential of new media, and (*c*) the influence of genetics and biology on political attitudes and behavior.[1] It concludes by considering directions for future research.

# PRE-ADULT POLITICAL SOCIALIZATION

Early work in the field assumed that political orientations would be formed in childhood and adolescence under the influence of family, first and foremost, but with other agents—schools and teachers, churches, peers, and mass media—also playing a role. As research progressed, scholars began to question the importance of the pre-adult years for understanding the political behavior of adults. Modest levels of parent–child similarity in political attributes suggested that not much socialization was taking place in many American homes (for example, Jennings and Niemi 1974). Analysis of repeated cross-sectional surveys cast doubt on whether orientations acquired early in life affected political views developed later (for example, Searing, Schwartz, and Lind 1973). Panel studies covering the pre-adult and early adult years revealed a significant amount of instability in political views (for example, Jennings and Niemi 1981).

Current thinking holds that the pre-adult years are important for the development of some political orientations, especially party identification, ideological leaning, and attitudes on social issues such as abortion (for example, Jennings, Stoker, and Bowers 2009). Childhood is also a crucial period in the development of racial and ethnic identity and prejudice (Sears and Levy 2003) and attitudes concerning gender roles (Cunningham 2001). Predispositions formed early in life may not persist unchanged through adulthood, but they do shape later development. The party identification of the adolescent predicts the partisanship and voting behavior of the young adult (for example, C. H. Franklin and Jackson 1983). Racial attitudes formed in childhood both resemble those held much later in life and shape the response to new race-related issues that arise in the adult years (Sears and Funk 1999).

The pre-adult years become even more important to political attitude development if parents are highly engaged politically and provide frequent and consistent political cues. Children from such homes are more likely to develop political views that mirror

---

[1] See Jennings (2007) for a discussion of other recent developments in the field, including a renewed interest in political socialization in comparative politics research.

those of their parents and to retain them as they move through early and mid-adulthood (Jennings, Stoker, and Bowers 2009). Similarly, the adult party identification of children who grew up with highly politically engaged parents is more likely to be bolstered by beliefs about party differences, connected to issue attitudes and ideology, and to shape candidate evaluations and voting (Stoker 2007; see also Kroh and Selb 2009). Moreover, parents who are involved in the civic life of their communities and active in politics tend to produce children who exhibit these same attributes as adults, with the offspring tendencies shaped both directly through social learning processes and indirectly through status inheritance (for example, Verba, Schlozman, and Burns 2005).

Although parents have tended to be the focus in studies of pre-adults, a burgeoning literature on the socialization of citizenship orientations has turned its eye to the character of the communities in which children grow up and on what they experience in high school. Being raised in an environment beset by poverty and other social ills has deleterious consequences for civic engagement levels (Pacheco and Plutzer 2008), whereas the opposite occurs in environments "where partisanship thrives, participation is high, and where elections for major offices are regularly contested" (Gimpel and Lay 2005, 226). Adolescents will grow into more civically competent and engaged adults if they spend time discussing current events in high-school civic education courses (Niemi and Junn 1998), participate in extracurricular organizations and activities (McFarland and Thomas 2006), work collaboratively with adults and share decision-making within schools (Mitra and Gross 2009), and undertake community service work (Hart, Donnelly, Youniss, and Atkins 2007). Positive citizenship outcomes in adulthood are especially likely if civic development activity is sustained across adolescence (Zaff, Malanchuk, and Eccles 2008).

More attention is also being given to how children, parents, peers, schools, and mass media interact during the pre-adult years. In contrast to the traditional (but oft-criticized) view that treats children as passively acquiring political orientations from parents, this work portrays youth as active learners who bring into the home political experiences from outside of it. Sears and Valentino (1997), for example, have called attention to how vivid, sustained, and information-rich political events like presidential elections influence how and when adolescents develop politically. For events to play this catalytic socializing role the adolescents need to be both exposed to the event-driven communications via schools and the media and to discuss them with parents, friends, and teachers. Others have argued that reciprocal, or "trickle-up," influence occurs within the home, where children exposed to non-familial political influences can end up changing family dynamics and even altering parents' political beliefs (McDevitt and Chaffee 2002). For example, participation in service learning programs may lead students to initiate political discussions with their parents, which can alter political communication patterns within the home and cause parents to rethink their own views.[2]

---

[2] Parents are also thought to be influenced by simply having or raising children. For example, having school-age children leads parents (especially mothers) into school-related community involvement

Studies of immigrants offer the strongest examples of reciprocal political socialization. Immigrant parents are usually less familiar with US politics than their children, who quickly become proficient in English and are exposed to US culture through schooling. Because of these proficiencies, second-generation children often play a critical role in helping their families adapt to US society (Tseng 2004). They are more likely than native-born children to communicate what they have learned in school about politics and offer advice about voting to their parents. Immigrant parents do still contribute to their children's political socialization by, for example, passing on information about politics in the country of origin or discussing challenges they face within the workplace (Wong and Tseng 2008). Moreover, mobilization efforts flow both ways, so much so that the 2006 protests for immigrant rights in California have been characterized as "family affairs," where both children and parents were integral in drawing other family members in (Bloemraad and Trost 2008).

## DEVELOPMENTS OVER THE ADULT LIFE CYCLE

If there is one period of the life cycle to be singled out as key to the development of the political self, it is not adolescence but the "impressionable years" of early adulthood—roughly the late teens to the mid- or late twenties. Many strands of research lend support to this conclusion. Long-term panel studies have found attitudes to be fairly unstable from adolescence to early adulthood but to stabilize subsequently (for example, Alwin, Cohen, and Newcomb 1991; Sears and Funk 1999). Similar findings have emerged in short-term panel studies that break the sample down by age (for example, Alwin and Krosnick 1991). Early adulthood provides individuals with their first opportunity to embrace their citizenship through voting; whether they actually turn out or not in those early years sets down patterns or habits that tend to be followed later in life (Plutzer 2002). Major political events are more likely to be remembered and judged important if experienced in young adulthood (Schuman and Rogers 2004) and to be cited as influential to one's political development (Jennings and Stoker 2006).

The idea that the late teens and twenties are formative years for political development is also central to the vast literature that considers political variation across birth cohorts, generations, and generation units.[3] The political views of young people are

---

(Jennings 1979), while parenting daughters appears to prompt more liberal attitudes on gender-related issues (Washington 2008).

[3] People use these terms in different ways. Some treat "generation" and "birth cohort" as synonyms, denoting groups defined by the conjunction of age and year of birth. Karl Mannheim's (1952) treatment of "generation" also depicted members of a generation as having a collective identity that distinguished them from others. "Generation units" are subgroups who develop similar reactions to political events by virtue of a shared social location. "Generation" is also used to describe groups related biologically, as in parent and filial generations. Alwin and McCammon (2003) provide a useful discussion of these variations.

thought to be shaped strongly by the political character of the time during which they came of age, and to persist in later years. If so, then as the political environment changes, a stable pattern of inter-cohort differences will appear. And as population replacement proceeds, the exit of old cohorts and entrance of new ones will transform the aggregate profile of the polity (so-called "generation effects").

The literature is replete with findings of cohort differences and generational effects. Illustratively, women who attained adulthood before the Nineteenth Amendment extended the franchise were never as likely to vote as those who entered the electorate in later years; the erosion of the gender gap in turnout across the mid- to late 1900s was largely driven by the dwindling numbers of the former cohort (Firebaugh and Chen 1995). African Americans going through their "impressionable years" during the Warren Court era still held highly favorable attitudes toward the Supreme Court many years later, more so than did those who came of age earlier or later (Gibson and Caldeira 1992). Young adults today are more likely to form partisan attitudes tied to issue preferences and ideology than those socialized in previous periods, which both reflects the growing polarization of party elites and is fueling overall partisan polarization in the mass electorate (Stoker and Jennings 2008). Because youth tend to develop voting or non-voting habits in early adulthood, high-stimulus elections leave a "footprint" in the form of higher turnout subsequently (M. Franklin, Lyons, and Marsh 2004). The party identification and voting choices of young adults are typically most responsive to prevailing national tides; young cohorts were more Democratic during the New Deal era, more Republican during the Reagan era, and lined up strongly behind Obama in 2008.

Why is early adulthood so politically formative? The answer is at least threefold (see, for example, Sears 1983). A first reason is simply that for many youth the pre-adult years have not been formative; they find themselves on the cusp of adulthood with political views that are weakly held, poorly integrated, and resting on fragmentary knowledge bases. A second is that early adulthood is a life stage in which young people are striving to develop new adult identities and objectives, both personal and political, as they shed their dependence on their parents and move into new adult roles—including that of citizen. A third reason is that the early adult years are dense with significant personal life events that also have important political consequences.

Scholars have studied these issues with an eye to the typical developmental trajectories that accompany the aging process. As individuals move through adulthood and gain experience with the political system, they tend to develop greater political knowledge (Delli Carpini and Keeter 1997, ch. 5), a stronger sense of party identification (Converse 1976), a richer set of party images, and a more consistent set of partisan and ideological orientations (Stoker and Jennings 2008). They become more likely to hold political attitudes with certainty, to profess to know a lot about the issues on which they express attitudes, and to maintain their original views in the face of counter-arguments (Visser and Krosnick 1998). As political orientations crystallize in this fashion, they also tend to stabilize, to be more resistant to potential change-inducing experiences—whether because of motivational processes (e.g., biased information processing) or the diminishing effects of new information as the base of prior knowledge expands. All of these socialization gains tend to be front-loaded during early adulthood though continue in later years.

Researchers have also sought to understand developments across early adulthood by directly studying the political effects of major life experiences and transitions. Of those, one of the most common, seemingly significant, and closely researched is the acquisition of higher education. A college education appears have effects on political attitudes and behavior[4] that flow through exposure to new references groups (Alwin, Cohen, and Newcomb 1991), through protest activity centered on college campuses (Jennings 1987), through its effects on cognitive development as well as on how it positions one in the social status hierarchy (Nie, Junn, and Stehlik-Barry 1996), through the kind of curriculum one is exposed to (Hillygus 2005), through involvement in college-sponsored multicultural programs (Gurin, Nagda, and Lopez 2004), and through service learning and civic education experiences (Colby, Ehrich, Beaumont, and Stephens 2003).

Young adulthood is also a life stage in which people move around a lot, get married and sometimes become parents, begin a career, and face their first elections as voters. All of these experiences have been examined for their effects on political attitudes and behavior, sometimes together (for example, Highton and Wolfinger 2001). As with higher education, their effects are both direct and contingent. Moving will reduce one's likelihood of voting because one must re-register. But each move will place the individual into a new social context, producing effects on partisan attitudes that depend upon the partisan makeup of the community (Brown 1989, ch. 6). Similarly, a new marriage may bring personal preoccupations that tend to crowd out political involvement in the short run, but it also opens one up to social learning and influence from the new spouse (Jennings and Stoker 1995). Votes cast in elections tend to reinforce and strengthen partisan leanings, but elections may prompt a change in party identification depending upon how one reacts to issues that are salient at the time (for example, C. H. Franklin 1984).

In sum, early adulthood is a period of great political flux in part because it contains a panoply of new and change-inducing life experiences, but also because it is a time of much learning and development, even if more is yet to come. With age comes a settling down process that yields more continuity in the individual's contexts and networks. Age also enables the accumulation of political experience that helps people to better understand politics and to develop a stronger, more stable, and more consistent set of political attitudes as a result. These dynamics spur further age-related political developments, most notably the tendency for civic and political involvement levels to climb with age (for example, Strate, Parrish, Elder, and Ford 1989).

---

[4] Scholars are increasingly questioning whether obtaining a college education has the causal effects long supposed (for example, Kam and Palmer 2008). Strong selection effects are operating here, an issue we return to in the conclusion.

# TODAY'S YOUNGER GENERATIONS

Young Americans today are often collected into two groups, with those born from about the mid-1960s through the late 1970s or 1980 often referred to as "Gen X," and those born later classified under various titles including the "Millenials" and "Gen Y." Although the two cohorts are distinguishable from each other in some respects, and not so distinguishable from their elders in others, one often finds clear political differences between them and older cohorts examined at comparable life stages.

A major focus of the research is on the younger generations' civic inclinations. They are significantly less likely to vote, to view voting as an important civic duty, to express interest in politics, and to be knowledgeable about public affairs. While they do participate in politics, they tend to do so in more individuated and non-traditional ways (e.g., boycotting). They are less likely to read newspapers at all, let alone follow politics in the medium, and to view news broadcasts on television. They are less likely to join civic organizations as adults and were less likely to do so as adolescents. When they do get involved in their communities, they participate in a more sporadic fashion. They are more materialist in their aspirations—increasingly focused on attaining their own economic goals—and yet also more post-materialistic in their values—increasingly likely to value self-expression and quality of life over physical and economic security. They are less trusting of other people, government, and the media.[5]

It is easy to draw these developments together into a bleak portrayal of the character of the youngest generations—as populated by politically disengaged, disinterested, self-centered cynics—and, given population replacement dynamics, into a bleak outlook for the nation's future. But the youngest cohorts are also different from older cohorts in a number of more salutary ways. They are at least as likely or even more likely to engage in volunteer work (for example, Levine 2007). New cohorts of college freshman are more likely than older cohorts to cite "becoming a community leader" as very important and to express an intention to participate in community service (*Higher Education Research Brief* 2008). Voting rates may be comparatively low for the young cohorts, but the age gap diminished in the most recent presidential elections as youth turnout rebounded from its 2000 low. Presumably because of candidate Obama's targeting of youth through grass-roots mobilization, participation gains among young adults were even more pronounced in the 2008 caucuses and primaries (Dalton 2009). In light of these disparate trends, scholars have suggested that the norms and styles of citizenship

[5] Support for most of these statements can be found in Bennett (1998), Dalton (2009), Delli Carpini (2000), Levine (2007), Putnam (2000), and Zukin et al. (2006). See also Rahn and Transue (1998) on social trust and materialism, Mindich (2004) on media usage, Wuthnow (1998) on sporadic civic involvement, Inglehart (2007) on post-materialism, and Delli Carpini and Keeter (1996, ch. 4) on political knowledge. Not all of the evidence extends to both Gen X and Gen Y. Some of the findings taken as evidence of generation gaps are based on cross-sectional analyses, in which case differences may be due to age as well as generation.

are changing, with younger generations still concerned about the American society and polity, but expressing their citizenship in new ways (Bennett 2008; Dalton 2009).

Generations X and (especially) Y are also distinctive in their political attitudes. Compared to older generations, they hold more liberal attitudes on cultural issues involving gender roles, homosexuality, and gay rights, and to a lesser extent, abortion. They are stronger advocates of civil liberties and hold more egalitarian or progressive attitudes on questions involving immigration and racial equality. Environmental conservation and clean energy are a higher priority. Compared to older Americans, though perhaps not older generations, their views on foreign policy are more anti-war and more supportive of cooperative, multilateral efforts. And, while distrusting of politicians and the government, they are nevertheless even more supportive than their elders of a strong governmental role in solving economic and social problems, including national health care. Not surprisingly in light of this configuration, they are more Democratic in their party identification and voting.[6]

Because of the thought that what is true of America's youth may, because of population replacement, soon be true of America, scholarly interest in this topic is extremely strong. Will apathy, distrust, and disengagement be the norm among citizens of the future? With the help of aging Gen Xers and Gen Yers, will the Democratic Party's partisanship advantage persist or even grow in the future? Moreover, we are nowhere close to understanding what has produced these developments, although potential explanations abound. Compared to their elders, the younger generations are demographically different—more educated, less likely to be married, less religious, and more ethnically diverse. They were more likely to have grown up with a mother in the workforce, as children of immigrants, and in families marked by divorce. They are children of the digital age, with ready access to video games and the Internet. And, of course, they have grown up in a social and political milieu that in many ways is unlike what previous generations experienced. All of these characteristics and more are likely relevant to understanding Gen X and Y's political distinctiveness. Explaining the generational divides, not just mapping and tracking them, is the major scholarly challenge that lies ahead.

## YOUTH AND THE NEW MEDIA

Each year, more young people are turning to the Internet as their primary source of political information (Xenos and Foot 2008). Some scholars are cautiously optimistic about the potential of the Internet to positively influence the civic and political engagement of young people (for example, Delli Carpini 2000; Lupia and Philpot 2005). Observers cite Internet features (e.g., that it is interactive, easy to use, and low in cost

---

[6] For evidence of these developments, see Madland and Teixeira (2009), Smith (2005), and Zukin et al. (2006).

to access) and Internet innovations (e.g., blogs, YouTube, and social networking sites) as capable of reinvigorating flagging rates of youth political involvement. Against the argument that Internet use might be substituting for and driving down civic engagement, scholars have found that young adults who use the Internet for email and information searches are more, not less, likely to be civically involved (Shah, McLeod, and Yoon 2001). Members of the young cohorts have also turned to the Internet as a resource for political action, for example in online campaigns against errant corporations (Scammell 2000) and for mobilizing peers during elections (for example, Rainie and Smith 2008).

At the same time, however, most research suggests that the Internet is not reshaping the demographic profile of the politically active. Individuals of high socioeconomic status are most likely to have the resources, skills, and interest that lead to use of the Internet for political purposes (for example, Jennings and Zeitner 2003; Krueger 2006). Even when young people are drawn into politics through an Internet campaign, it appears that they are not, then, more likely to remain active in other ways (Krueger 2002). Furthermore, while politicians are starting to utilize the Internet in their electoral campaigns, most continue to present information in traditional ways, rather than using interactive formats that are more effective in mobilizing young voters (Iyengar and Jackman 2004; Xenos and Foot 2008). The Dean and Obama presidential bids offered hope of campaigns effectively utilizing new media to mobilize youth participation—through email, texting, online social networking, and online fundraising—but it is too early to tell if this was the start of a permanent transformation.

The picture is not much brighter when one considers alternative news sources. Entertainment "news" shows such as the *Daily Show* have become increasingly popular among younger voters, as have high-conflict shows like the *O'Reilly Factor*. Although there is some evidence that such non-traditional news sources increase viewers' level of political knowledge (for example, Baek and Wojcieszak 2009), viewership has also been associated with more cynical views about politicians, elections, and the media (Baumgartner and Morris 2006).

As scholars have frequently argued, the principal challenge facing political scientists is to break through generalizations about the Internet to isolate the effects of specific media forms and innovations. There is much more to be learned as well about how media developments in the realm of popular culture (e.g., hip-hop, video games, reality television) are affecting youth political socialization (see Jackson 2009).

## GENETICS, BIOLOGY, AND PERSONALITY

The past decade has brought an explosion of work finding genetic effects on political attitudes and behavior. Studies comparing the similarity of dizygotic (DZ, fraternal) and monozygotic (MZ, so called "identical") twins have found sizable genetic effects for political ideology and attitudes, especially attitudes on cultural issues, strength of partisanship but not its direction, social trust, and political participation.[7] Scholars have even begun to carry out work that ties specific genes to specific political outcomes (for example, Fowler and Dawes 2008; McDermott et al. 2009).

Almost all of this research focuses on adults and does not consider variation over the life cycle. One important exception is Hatemi, Funk, et al. (2009), which found sizable socialization effects and almost no genetic effects among adolescents and young adults who were still living at home, but the reverse among the rest of the adult sample. Studies of religious orientations that distinguish adolescents and adults have yielded similar findings (Eaves, Hatemi, Prom, and Murrelle 2008). The researchers conclude from this that parents, by what they say and do, have at best temporary effects on their children's political views. Once children leave home and enter adulthood, their political views adjust in a fashion that suits their genetic makeup.

The genetics and politics literature presents a strong challenge to traditional inter-pretations of many (but certainly not all) political socialization findings. Parent–(adult) offspring political similarity, in general, is laid at the genetic doorstep (the exception of party leaning set aside). The fact that similarity between a child and any one parent is heightened when the second parent agrees with the first is considered an outcome of genetic similarity wrought by assortative mating not social learning processes: spouses who are politically similar are likely to be genetically similar, producing a child that is more genetically similar to each of them. The fact that adolescent attitudes are susceptible to revision in early adulthood and achieve higher levels of stability in later years is a function of the genetic sorting process that kicks in when children are no longer under a parent's thumb. The higher stability of attitudes on social and moral issues is due not to the centrality of those issues in parental socialization practices, but instead to their strong genetic basis: attitudes higher in heritability are expressed more quickly and are less changeable in response to experimentally varied peer opinion (Tesser 1993).

The studies yielding such strong conclusions are not without their critics (for example, Beckwith and Morris 2008; Charney 2008). Higher heritability rates will tend to be found if MZ twins are more similar in their attitudes than are DZ twins, which is taken as evidence of genetic influence. But such higher rates of similarity might also be due to greater similarity in the way that MZ twins are treated by others, to a greater incidence of shared experiences, or to stronger mutual influence, since MZ twins tend to spend more time together than do DZ twins. In the rejoinders one finds skepticism about whether these rivals are plausible based on studies that have tried to take them into account. But one also finds the argument that genetic factors may be behind social influence processes—that people who are genetically similar would, *ipso facto*, be led to share more experiences, to be treated more similarly, and to want to spend more time together. If so, it is genetics, ultimately, that stands as a root cause.

---

[7] See Funk (Chapter 26 in this volume) and Alford and Hibbing (2008) for reviews.

Research is also growing on how political characteristics relate to biological attributes and personality traits. Self-identified political conservatives have a stronger startle response when shown threatening images (Oxley et al. 2008), have a greater tendency to persist in a habitual response pattern when prompted to change (Amodio, Jost, Master, and Yee 2008), and are more prone to feeling disgust in situations involving feces, cockroaches, and the like (Inbar, Pizarro, and Bloom 2009). Social trust is diminished among those who find themselves in stressful environments, because such environments inhibit the release of hormones that help us trust others (Zak 2008). Democrats and liberals tend to be high on the personality trait of openness and low on conscientiousness (Gerber et al. 2010), while political participation rates are higher among extroverts, though only with respect to acts that have a social component (Mondak et al. 2010). Personality traits themselves have high levels of genetic heritability, though they develop also under the influence of parents and life experiences and do not fully stabilize until mid-adulthood (Caspi, Roberts, and Shiner 2005). None of the work in these research streams directly challenges prior political socialization findings as does the genetics research reviewed above. But these studies do converge in support of the contention that political attitudes and behaviors have genetic foundations, mediated by biological processes and personality traits that influence how people think, feel, and act in non-political as well as political spheres.

It might be tempting to think of genetic, biological, and even personality traits as so far back in the funnel of causality that they can be safely set aside until we better understand more proximate dynamics. The temptation is even greater given the likely complexity of the causal pathways involved, frequently described in terms like these: "[the genetics–political behavior connection] involves the interaction of thousands of genes, not to mention further interactions of those genes with environmental triggers and modifiers" (Alford and Hibbing 2008, 190). But for the field of political socialization, at least, the challenges posed are direct and must be engaged. Building a better understanding of the pre-adult origins of political orientations and their subsequent development over the life span requires that genetic and biological traits be considered alongside mechanisms of social learning and influence.

# REFLECTIONS ON THE FUTURE

Political socialization research has always been hampered by the long time frame it considers, both with respect to individual lives and with respect to intergenerational comparisons. Further complicating matters are the number of influences operating on individuals as they develop politically—including the traditional collection of socialization agents and the Zeitgeist, now extended to include genes and biology. Making progress at all has required large, ambitious, and long-ranging projects such as the classic study initiated in 1965 by M. Kent Jennings, which gathered data independently from parents, children, and the children's classmates beginning when the child was a senior in high school, then reinterviewed the parent and filial generations on several occasions over the ensuing decades, adding data on spouses and the younger generation's children along the way.

One way to make progress is to launch another, albeit new and improved, version of the Jennings project. In order to gain more purchase on the developmental processes, more survey waves at shorter intervals carried out over decades would be ideal. Shorter intervals would also place the research in a better position to understand the role of major political events, like elections, in political development over the life span. It is important that such a project be designed so to situate the child within the realm of influences that, in current thinking, he or she is not just "shaped by" but actively engages. For example, one could select as a starting sample adolescents in schools where, through random assignment, a civic engagement initiative is or is not introduced. Youth use of new media, and all of the civic and political attributes that appear to be distinguishing Gen X and Gen Y from older cohorts, would be essential to assess. Genetic testing, personality assessment, and perhaps even "disgust sensitivity" and "startle response" measures would be essential as well.

There are other areas where innovation would be welcome. Despite the attention that has been given to pre-adult socialization, we still have an impoverished view of the socialization practices of families, and of how what is happening within the family relates to what is happening outside of it. This stands in stark contrast to research in the field of ethnic and racial socialization. Parents' socialization practices in that domain have taken center stage, with research showing how some parents strive to inculcate a sense of ethnic or racial pride in their children, prepare them to cope with discrimination, and foster distrust of out-groups (Hughes et al. 2006). In the political socialization literature, there is no such inventory of socialization practices relevant to citizenship, and few attempts to tie ethnic–racial socialization practices to political outcomes (but see Nunnally 2003). Thus, in the dream (perhaps pipe dream) study these topics would need to be incorporated anew.

Existing research has also given us little purchase on the dynamics underlying the formation of unique political generations. The analysis of repeated cross-sections helps scholars identify and track cohorts that vary in their political attitudes and behaviors, but are of little help in identifying what produces such variations. Projects like the Bennington study (Alwin, Cohen, and Newcomb 1991) or the Jennings study give insights only into the one or two generations they consider, exclusively. Thus, any new large-scale panel study would ideally incorporate a rolling design, continually adding new cohorts and following each one over time.

Although we did not emphasize the issue, selection threats loom large in much of the socialization research. They particularly bedevil cross-sectional work, but also pose barriers to causal inference when working with panel data that traverse the pre-adult to adult years. Consider, for example, the question of whether adolescent participation in extracurricular activities fosters political involvement in later years. Adolescents who participate in such activities tend to have better grades, lower dropout rates, and lower rates of drinking and drug use (Eccles, Barber, Stone, and Hunt 2003). Any or all of these could be part of a selection mechanism producing the observed "effects" of adolescent civic engagement on adult political behavior. Selection effects are routinely addressed, usually through statistical control, but are rarely ruled out.

Experimentation is the ideal method for overcoming the threat to causal inference from selection threats. Although it would not be feasible to randomly assign some kids to, say, the "must participate in debate club" group and others to the "barred from participating in debate club" group, we must hope that clever researchers nonetheless find ways to find or introduce the relevant experimental variations. More generally, we need fewer studies of how this is correlated with that and more that utilize designs permitting strong causal inference (see, for example, Dinas 2010). Even in a replication and extension of the Jennings study, however, it would help to begin interviews even before the child hits high school and to expand the set of characteristics measured in order to get more purchase on selection effects.

# REFERENCES

ALFORD, J. R., and HIBBING, J. R. 2008. The New Empirical Biopolitics. *Annual Review of Political Science*, 11: 183–203.

ALWIN, D. F., and KROSNICK, J. A. 1991. Aging, Cohorts, and the Stability of Sociopolitical Orientations over the Life Span. *American Journal of Sociology*, 97: 169–95.

—— and MCCAMMON, R. J. 2003. Generations, Cohorts, and Social Change. In *Handbook of the Life Course*, ed. J. T. Mortimer and M. J. Shanahan. New York: Kluwer Academic, Plenum.

—— COHEN, R. L., and NEWCOMB, T. M. 1991. *Political Attitudes over the Life Span*. Madison: University of Wisconsin Press.

AMODIO, D. M., JOST, J. T., MASTER, S. L., and YEE, C. M. 2008. Neurocognitive Correlates of Liberalism and Conservatism. *Nature Neuroscience*, 10: 1246–7.

BAEK, Y. M., and WOJCIESZAK, M. E. 2009. Don't Expect Too Much! Learning from Late-Night Comedy and Knowledge Item Difficulty. *Communication Research*, 36: 783–809.

BAUMGARTNER, J., and MORRIS, J. S. 2006. The *Daily Show* Effect: Candidate Evaluations, Efficacy, and American Youth. *American Politics Research*, 34: 341–67.

BECKWITH, J., and MORRIS, C. A. 2008. Twin Studies of Political Behavior: Untenable Assumptions? *Perspectives on Politics*, 6: 785–90.

BENNETT, W. L. 1998. The Uncivic Culture: Communication, Identity, and the Rise of Lifestyle Politics. *PS: Political Science and Politics*, 31: 741–61.

—— 2008. Changing Citizenship in the Digital Age. In *Civic Life Online*, ed. W. L. Bennett. Cambridge, MA: MIT Press.

BLOEMRAAD, I., and TROST, C. 2008. It's a Family Affair: Intergenerational Mobilization in the Spring 2006 Protests. *American Behavioral Scientist*, 52: 507–32.

BROWN, T. 1989. *Migration and Politics*. Chapel Hill: University of North Carolina Press.

CASPI, A., ROBERTS, B. W., and SHINER, R. L. 2005. Personality Development: Stability and Change. *Annual Review of Psychology*, 56: 453–84.

CHARNEY, E. 2008. Genes and Ideologies. *Perspectives on Politics*, 5: 299–319.

COLBY, A., EHRICH, T., BEAUMONT, E., and STEPHENS, J. 2003. *Educating Citizens*. San Francisco: Jossey-Bass.

CONVERSE, P. E. 1976. *The Dynamics of Party Support*. Beverly Hills: Sage.

CUNNINGHAM, M. 2001. The Influence of Parental Attitudes and Behaviors on Children's Attitudes toward Gender and Household Labor in Early Adulthood. *Journal of Marriage and Family*, 63: 111–22.

DALTON, R. J. 2009. *The Good Citizen*. Washington, DC: CQ Press.

DELLI CARPINI, M. X. 2000. Gen.com: Youth, Civic Engagement, and the New Information Environment. *Political Communication*, 17: 341–9.

—— and KEETER, S. 1996. *What Americans Know about Politics and Why it Matters*. New Haven: Yale University Press.

DINAS, E. 2010. The Impressionable Years: The Formative Role of Family, Vote, and Political Events during Early Adulthood. Ph.D. thesis, European University Institute Department of Political and Social Sciences.

EAVES, L. J., and HATEMI, P. K. 2008. Transmission of Attitudes toward Abortion and Gay Rights: Effects of Genes, Social Learning and Mate Selection. *Behavior Genetics*, 38: 247–5.

—— —— PROM, E. C., and MURRELLE, E. L. 2008. Social and Genetic Influences on Adolescent Religious Attitudes and Practices. *Social Forces*, 86: 1621–46.

ECCLES, J. S., BARBER, B. L., STONE, M., and HUNT, J. 2003. Extracurricular Activities and Adolescent Development. *Journal of Social Issues*, 59: 865–89.

FIREBAUGH, G., and CHEN, K. 1995. Vote Turnout of Nineteenth Amendment Women: The Enduring Effect of Disenfranchisement. *American Journal of Sociology*, 100: 972–96.

FOWLER, J. H., and DAWES, C. T. 2008. Two Genes Predict Voter Turnout. *Journal of Politics*, 70: 579–94.

FRANKLIN, C. H. 1984. Issue Preferences, Socialization, and the Evolution of Party Identification. *American Journal of Political Science*, 28: 459–78.

—— and JACKSON, J. E. 1983. The Dynamics of Party Identification. *American Political Science Review*, 77: 957–73.

FRANKLIN, M., LYONS, P., and MARSH, M. 2004. Generational Basis of Turnout Decline in Established Democracies. *Acta Politica*, 39: 115–51.

GERBER, A. S., HUBER, G. A., DOHERTY, D., DOWLING, C. M., and HA, S. E. 2010. Personality and Political Attitudes: Relationships across Issue Domains and Political Contexts. *American Political Science Review*, 104: 111–33.

GIBSON, J. L., and CALDEIRA, G. A. 1992. Blacks and the United States Supreme Court: Models of Diffuse Support. *Journal of Politics*, 54: 1120–45.

GIMPEL, G. J., and LAY, J. C. 2005. Party Identification, Local Partisan Contexts, and the Acquisition of Participatory Attitudes. In *The Social Logic of Politics*, ed. A. S. Zuckerman. Philadelphia: Temple University Press.

GREENSTEIN, FRED I. 1965. *Children and Politics*. New Haven: Yale University Press.

GURIN, P., NAGDA, B. A., and LOPEZ, G. E. 2004. The Benefits of Diversity in Education for Democratic Citizenship. *Journal of Social Issues*, 60: 17–34.

HART, D., DONNELLY, T. M., YOUNISS, J., and ATKINS, R. 2007. High School Community Service as a Predictor of Adult Voting and Volunteering. *American Education Research*, 44: 197–219.

HATEMI, P. K., ALFORD, J. R., HIBBING, J. R., MARTIN, N. G., and EAVES, L. J. 2008. Is There a "Party" in Your Genes? *Political Research Quarterly*, 62: 584–600.

—— FUNK, C. L., MEDLAND, S. E., MAES, H. M., SILBERG, J. L., MARTIN, N. G., and EAVES, L. J. 2009. Genetic and Environmental Transmission of Political Attitudes over a Life Time. *Journal of Politics*, 71: 1141–56.

*Higher Education Research Brief.* 2008. The American Freshman: Forty-Year Trends: 1966–2006, Jan. At <http://www.heri.ucla.edu/PDFs/pubs/briefs/40yrTrendsResearchBrief.pdf>. Accessed Jan. 10, 2010.

HIGHTON, B., and WOLFINGER, R. E. 2001. The First Seven Years of the Political Life Cycle. *American Journal of Political Science*, 45: 202–9.

HILLYGUS, D. S. 2005. The Missing Link: Exploring the Relationship between Higher Education and Political Engagement. *Political Behavior*, 27: 25–47.

HUGHES, D., RODRIGUEZ, J., SMITH, E. P., JOHNSON, D. J., STEVENSON, H. C., and SPICER, P. 2006. Parents' Ethnic–Racial Socialization Practices: A Review of Research and Directions for Future Study. *Developmental Psychology*, 42: 747–7.

INBAR, Y., PIZARRO, D. A., and BLOOM, P. 2009. Conservatives Are More Easily Disgusted than Liberals. *Cognition and Emotion*, 23: 714–25.

INGLEHART, R. 2007. Postmaterialist Values and the Shift from Survival to Self-Expressive Values. In *The Oxford Handbook of Political Behavior*, ed. R. J. Dalton and H.-D. Klingemann. New York: Oxford University Press.

IYENGAR, S., and JACKMAN, S. 2004. *Technology and Politics: Incentives for Youth Participation.* CIRCLE Working Paper No. 24. At <http://www.civicyouth.org/circle-working-paper-24-technology-and-politics-incentives-for-youth-participation>. Accessed Nov. 14, 2009.

JACKSON, D. J. 2009. *Entertainment and Politics.* New York: Peter Lang.

JENNINGS, M. K. 1979. Another Look at the Life Cycle and Political Participation. *American Journal of Political Science*, 23: 755–71.

—— 1987. Residues of a Movement: The Aging of the American Protest Generation. *American Political Science Review*, 81: 367–81.

—— 2007. Political Socialization. In *The Oxford Handbook of Political Behavior*, ed. R. J. Dalton and H.-D. Klingemann. New York: Oxford University Press.

—— and NIEMI, R. G. 1974. *The Political Character of Adolescence.* Princeton: Princeton University Press.

—— —— 1981. *Generations and Politics.* Princeton: Princeton University Press.

—— and STOKER, L. 1995. Life-Cycle Transitions and Political Participation: The Case of Marriage. *American Political Science Review*, 89: 421–33.

—— —— 2006. Evaluating Dramatic Events during the Formative Years: A Longitudinal Approach. Paper presented at the Midwest Political Science Association Convention, Chicago.

—— and ZEITNER, V. 2003. Internet Use and Civic Engagement: A Longitudinal Analysis. *Public Opinion Quarterly*, 67: 311–34.

—— STOKER, L., and BOWERS, J. 2009. Politics across Generations: Family Transmission Reconsidered. *Journal of Politics*, 71: 782–99.

KAM, C. D., and PALMER, C. L. 2008. Reconsidering the Effects of Education on Political Participation. *Journal of Politics*, 70: 612–31.

KROH, M., and SELB, P. 2009. Inheritance and the Dynamics of Party Identification. *Political Behavior*, 31: 559–74.

KRUEGER, B. S. 2002. Assessing the Potential of Internet Political Participation in the United States: A Resource Approach. *American Politics Research*, 30: 476–98.

—— 2006. A Comparison of Conventional and Internet Political Mobilization. *American Politics Research*, 34: 759–76.

LEVINE, P. 2007. *The Future of Democracy.* Medford, MA: Tufts University Press.

LUPIA, A., and PHILPOT, T. S. 2005. Views from Inside the Net: How Websites Affect Young Adults' Political Interest. *Journal of Politics*, 67: 1122–42.

MCDERMOTT, R., TINGLEY, D., COWDEN, J., FRAZZETTO, G., and JOHNSON, D. D. P. 2009. Monoamine Oxidase A Gene (MAOA) Predicts Behavioral Aggression Following Provocation. *Proceedings of the National Academy of Sciences*, 106: 2118–23.

MCDEVITT, M., and CHAFFEE, S. 2002. From Top-Down to Trickle-Up Influence: Revisiting Assumptions about the Family in Political Socialization. *Political Communication*, 19: 281–301.

MCFARLAND, D. A., and THOMAS, R. J. 2006. Bowling Young: How Youth Voluntary Associations Influence Adult Political Participations. *American Sociological Review*, 71: 401–25.

MADLAND, D., and TEIXEIRA, R. 2009. New Progressive America: The Millennial Generation. Center for American Progress. At <http://www.americanprogress.org/issues/2009/05/millennial_generation.html>. Accessed Feb. 1, 2010.

MANNHEIM, K. 1952. *Essays on the Sociology of Knowledge*. London: Routledge & Kegan Paul. First published 1926.

MINDICH, D. T. Z. 2004. *Tuned Out*. New York: Oxford University Press.

MITRA, D. L., and GROSS, S. J. 2009. Increasing Student Voice in High School Reform: Building Partnerships, Improving Outcomes. *Educational Management Administration & Leadership*, 37: 522–43.

MONDAK, J. J., HIBBING, M. V., CANACHE, D., SELIGSON, M. A., and ANDERSON, M. R. 2010. Personality and Civic Engagement: An Integrative Framework for the Study of Trait Effects on Political Behavior. *American Political Science Review*, 104: 85–110.

NIE, N. H., JUNN, J., and STEHLIK-BARRY, K. 1996. *Education and Democratic Citizenship in America*. Chicago: University of Chicago Press.

NIEMI, R. G., and HEPBURN, M. A. 1995. The Rebirth of Political Socialization. *Perspectives on Political Science*, 24: 7–16.

—— and JUNN, J. 1998. *Civic Education*. New Haven: Yale University Press.

—— and SOBIESZEK, B. L. 1977. Political Socialization. *Annual Review of Sociology*, 3: 209–33.

NUNNALLY, S. C. 2003. Racial Socialization as Political Socialization? The Effect of Racial Socialization on African Americans' Perceptions of Trust in Government. Paper presented at the American Political Science Association Annual Convention, Philadelphia.

OXLEY, D. R., SMITH, K. B., ALFORD, J. R., HIBBING, M. V., MILLER, J. L., SCALORA, M., HATEMI, P. K., and HIBBING, J. R. 2008. Political Attitudes Vary with Physiological Traits. *Science*, 321: 1667–70.

PACHECO, J. S., and PLUTZER, E. 2008. Political Participation and Cumulative Disadvantage: The Impact of Economic and Social Hardship on Young Citizens. *Journal of Social Issues*, 64: 571–93.

PLUTZER, E. 2002. Becoming a Habitual Voter, Inertia, Resources, and Growth in Young Adulthood. *American Political Science Review*, 96: 41–56.

PUTNAM, R. D. 2000. *Bowling Alone*. New York: Simon & Schuster.

RAHN, W. M., and TRANSUE, J. E. 1998. Social Trust and Value Change: The Decline of Social Capital in American Youth, 1976–1995. *Political Psychology*, 19: 545–65.

RAINIE, L., and SMITH, A. 2008. The Internet and the 2008 Election. Pew Internet & American Life Project. At <http://www.pewinternet.org/Reports/2008/The-Internet-and-the-2008-Election.aspx>. Accessed Feb. 1, 2010.

SAPIRO, Virginia. 2004. Not Your Parents' Political Socialization: Introduction for a New Generation. *Annual Review of Political Science*, 7: 1–23.

SCAMMELL, M. 2000. The Internet and Civic Engagement: The Age of the Citizen–Consumer. *Political Communication*, 17: 351–5.

SCHUMAN, H., and RODGERS, W. L. 2004. Cohorts, Chronology, and Collective Memories. *Public Opinion Quarterly*, 68: 217–54.

SEARING, D. D., SCHWARTZ, J. J., and LIND, A. E. 1973. The Structuring Principle: Political Socialization and Belief Systems. *American Political Science Review*, 67: 415–32.

SEARS, D. O. 1983. The Persistence of Early Political Predispositions: The Roles of Attitude Object and Life Stage. In *Review of Personality and Social Psychology*, iv, ed. L. Wheeler and P. Shaver. Beverly Hills: Sage.

—— and FUNK, C. 1999. Evidence of the Long-Term Persistence of Adults' Political Predispositions. *Journal of Politics*, 61: 1–28.

—— and LEVY, S. 2003. Childhood and Adult Political Development. In *Oxford Handbook of Political Psychology*, ed. D. O. Sears, L. Huddy, and R. Jervis. Oxford: Oxford University Press.

—— and VALENTINO, N. A. 1997. Politics Matters: Political Events as Catalysts for Preadult Socialization. *American Political Science Review*, 91: 45–65.

SHAH, D. V., MCLEOD, J. M., and YOON, S.-H. 2001. Communication, Context, and Community: An Exploration of Print, Broadcast, and Internet Influences. *Communication Research*, 28: 464–506.

SMITH, T. W. 2005. Generation Gaps in Attitudes and Values from the 1970s to the 1990s. In *On the Frontier of Adulthood*, ed. R. A. Settersten, Jr., F. F. Furstenberg, Jr., and R. G. Rumbaut. Chicago: University of Chicago Press.

STOKER, L. 2007. Growing up with Politics. Paper prepared for the Festschrift honoring David O. Sears, presented at the American Political Science Association Annual Convention, Chicago.

—— and JENNINGS, M. K. 2008. Of Time and the Development of Partisan Polarization. *American Journal of Political Science*, 52: 619–35.

STRATE, J. M., PARRISH, C. J., ELDER, C. D., and FORD, C. 1989. Life Span Civic Development and Voting Participation. *American Political Science Review*, 83: 443–64.

TESSER, A. 1993. The Importance of Heritability in Psychological Research: The Case of Attitudes. *Psychological Review*, 100: 129–42.

TSENG, V. 2004. Family Interdependence and Academic Adjustment in College: Youth from Immigrant and U.S.-Born Families. *Child Development*, 75: 966–83.

VERBA, S., SCHLOZMAN, K. L., and BURNS, N. 2005. Family Ties: Understanding the Intergenerational Transmission of Political Participation. In *The Social Logic of Politics*, ed. A. S. Zuckerman. Philadelphia: Temple University Press.

VISSER, P. S., and KROSNICK, J. A. 1998. The Development of Attitude Strength over the Life Cycle: Surge and Decline. *Journal of Personality and Social Psychology*, 75: 1388–409.

WASHINGTON, E. L. 2008. Female Socialization: How Daughters Affect their Legislator Fathers' Voting on Women's Issues. *American Economic Review*, 98/1: 311–32.

WONG, J., and TSENG, V. 2008. Political Socialisation in Immigrant Families: Challenging Top-Down Parental Socialisation Models. *Journal of Ethnic and Migration Studies*, 34: 151–68.

WUTHNOW, R. 1998. *Loose Connections*. Cambridge, MA: Harvard University Press.

XENOS, M., and FOOT, K. 2008. Not Your Father's Internet: The Generation Gap in Online Politics. In *Civic Life Online*, ed. W. L. Bennett. Cambridge, MA: MIT Press.

diminished support for aggressive foreign policy as a response to terrorism. Despite women's heightened sensitivity to terror threat, women are less supportive than men of the use of harsh interrogation techniques on suspected enemy combatants (Haider-Markel and Vieux 2008).

Women's reluctance to endorse governmental use of force also extends to domestic contexts, including the criminal justice system. They are much less likely than men to support capital punishment, though majorities of both men and women support it (Stack 2000). Women are also less likely to condone the use of police violence in a variety of scenarios (Halim and Stiles 2001). They are more likely than men to oppose harsh punishment for criminals, although this difference depends on the nature of the crime and disappears for crimes such as rape and the sale of drugs to children (Hurwitz and Smithey 1998; Smith 1984). Women are also more likely than men to favor government restrictions on access to firearms, expressing greater support of gun control measures, including assault weapons bans, seven-day waiting periods, and door-to-door searches for illegal weapons (Wolpert and Gimpel 1998). Many attribute these differences to women's greater fear of crime and personal victimization (Hurwitz and Smithey 1998; Schafer, Hubner, and Bynam 2006).

## Morality Issues

On average, women are more religious than men, and religiosity is associated with moral traditionalism, resulting in a third politically distinct gender gap on morality issues (with women leaning toward the right). Women report higher levels of religiosity and religious fundamentalism than men and a stronger commitment to religion and religious institutions (Tolleson-Rinehart and Perkins 1989). Women are less supportive than men of behaviors and policies that violate conventional moral norms, such as casual sex, drug use, and suicide (Eagly, Mitchell, and Paludi 2004). Eagly and colleagues find that marital status and parenthood are strong predictors of such attitudes, and argue that women with children are more likely to endorse morally traditional behavior because it protects children and the family unit. Women are also more supportive than men of school prayer and greater governmental restrictions on access to pornography, and are more opposed to the legalization of marijuana. Such gender differences are moderate in size, ranging from 7 percent on school prayer to 18 percent on pornography (Clark and Clark 1993).

Differences between men and women on moral issues are not fully consistent, however, when it comes to gay rights. On average, women report higher levels of tolerance toward homosexuals than men, more positive affect, and fewer negative feelings. This difference is associated with women's stronger support of gays in the military and greater support of gay civil rights (Herek 2002). In the end, it may be heterosexual men's intolerance toward gay men that drives this difference in attitudes toward gays overall, though women's greater egalitarianism may also play a role (Kite and Whitley 1996).

# Women's Issues

Despite expectations of pervasive gender differences in support of women's issues, men and women equally support government action on most women's issues—policies that either explicitly affect women's rights or have a disproportionate impact on women (Sapiro 2003). There are also few gender differences in attitudes toward women's roles outside the home (Bolzendahl and Myers 2004). The Equal Rights Amendment, which explicitly promoted women's collective interests, was supported to the same degree by men and women in the late 1970s and early 1980s (Sears and Huddy 1990). And there are few differences on other women's issues, including abortion (Chaney, Alvarez, and Nagler 1998; Shapiro and Mahajan 1986). Women and men do differ, however, in their attitudes and beliefs about sexual harassment. Women define a wider range of behaviors as harassment, feel it is more pervasive, have less tolerance for it, and are less likely to attribute responsibility for harassment to the victim (Kenig and Ryan 1986).

# Vote Choice and Partisanship

Finally, there is a politically important gender gap in vote choice and partisanship. Since the early 1980s, women have consistently voted in greater numbers than men for Democratic presidential and congressional candidates (Manza and Brooks 1998). They have also expressed greater identification with the Democratic Party (Chaney, Alvarez, and Nagler 1998; Box-Steffensmeier, De Bouf, and Lin 2004). In pooled ANES data, Ronald Reagan is the only Republican presidential candidate favored by a majority of women since 1980. In contrast, Bill Clinton was the only Democrat to obtain majority support from men (in 1992 and 1996). Overall, roughly 6 to 12 percent more women than men have supported the Democratic candidate in the past seven presidential elections based on ANES data. Moreover, the gender gap is of uniform size across a broad array of demographic groups including race, age, education, and religiosity (Huddy, Cassese, and Lizotte 2008b).

The gender gap in vote choice and partisanship is typically driven by women's greater support of government social welfare spending (Gilens 1988; Manza and Brooks 1998). Defense and military issues can also elicit a gender gap in support of political candidates, as was observed for presidential elections in the early 1980s (Gilens 1988; Frankovic 1982). For the most part women and men weigh similar factors such as social welfare and foreign policy issues in making their vote choice. The one exception may be economic matters. Women are typically more pessimistic than men about the nation's economy and are more inclined to vote on that basis, whereas men rely more on personal finances. This suggests that women may be more inclined to punish an incumbent president in times of national economic hardship regardless of party (Chaney, Alvarez, and Nagler 1998; Welch and Hibbing 1992).

# GENDERED SUPPORT FOR FEMALE POLITICIANS

The political effects of gender extend to an assessment of women candidates and politicians (Huddy and Capelos 2002). Public opinion data suggest a steady decline in support for statements such as "a woman's place is in the home" and "men are better emotionally suited for politics" (Eagly and Carli 2007). Despite this liberalizing trend in attitudes toward gender roles, gender stereotypes continue to play a significant role in the evaluation of political leaders. Experimental studies provide compelling evidence that voters use gender stereotypes to assess a male and female politician's respective areas of issue expertise. Such candidate experiments demonstrate that female politicians are commonly portrayed as better able to handle "compassion" issues, such as education, health care, and poverty, but are seen as less able to deal with big business, the military, defense issues, and crime (Sanbonmatsu 2003). When a candidate's personality traits are manipulated directly, candidates with feminine personality traits are rated as more competent to handle compassion issues regardless of their gender, whereas candidates with masculine personality traits are seen as more competent to handle the military (Huddy and Terkildsen 1993a).

## Gender Stereotypes

Differences in male and female politicians' perceived areas of issue competence stem from pervasive gender stereotypes in which a typical woman is seen as having communal traits such as warmth, gentleness, kindness, and passivity, whereas a typical man is viewed as having agentic or instrumental traits such as toughness, aggression, and assertiveness (Williams and Best 1982). Communal traits are more stereotypically feminine, whereas agentic traits reflect more masculine qualities. At the same time, agentic traits are closely linked to popular notions of strong, effective leadership. Eagly and Carli (2007) and Jost and Kay (2005) both argue that there is an implicit preference for male leadership based on the automatic activation of gender stereotypes which produces a spontaneous association between masculine qualities and leadership.

Communal traits such as warmth and kindness give women politicians a perceived advantage in handling social welfare and other compassion issues, but they are not regarded as the most desirable traits for political officeholders more generally. This distinction extends to instrumental traits such as rationality and toughness, which are typically rated as more important for a political figure than typical feminine traits. This is consistent with Cejka and Eagly's (1999) finding that masculine traits are considered desirable for male-dominated occupations. Thus, presidential popularity rests on perceived masculine traits such as strength, determination, and confidence (Funk 1999). Moreover, the perceived importance of masculine qualities extends beyond the presidency to include legislative positions, state and local offices, and the military (Huddy and Terkildsen 1993b; Fox and Oxley 2003).

In contrast, typical feminine personality traits such as warmth and compassion are considered less crucial, especially for higher levels of office such as the presidency. Of the four key dimensions of presidential personality—leadership, competence, empathy, and integrity—empathy, the dimension containing the most typically feminine traits, has the least impact on assessments of actual and ideal presidents (Funk 1999). Chaio, Bowman, and Gill (2008) find that raters judge male congressional candidates as more competent and female candidates as more approachable on the basis of their photos. Attractive women candidates may be seen as even less competent than the typical female politician. In a study by Heflick and Goldenberg (2009), former Republican vice-presidential candidate Sarah Palin's perceived competence decreased when raters were instructed to focus on her appearance (a similar effect was observed for ratings of actor Angelina Jolie). And a number of experimental studies demonstrate that competence is more critical to vote choice than warm and expressive qualities (Chaio, Bowman, and Gill 2008; Huddy and Terkildsen 1993a).

There are also differences in how well women and men are expected to handle different kinds of policy issues, a judgment linked to stereotypes that portray women and men as having different personality traits. Competence on typical "male" issues, which are derived in part from masculine traits, is more beneficial to candidates, especially those running for higher executive office (Mueller 1986; Rosenwasser and Seale 1988; Huddy and Terkildsen 1993b). Dolan (2009), drawing on a survey conducted just prior to the Democratic primaries in 2007, also found that male issues such as defense loomed larger in the minds of voters than typical female issues such as social welfare policy.

A male advantage in perceived competence on military and security affairs has had particularly strong political effects in the aftermath of the terrorist attacks of September 11, 2001. Falk and Kenski (2006) found Americans who rated terrorism, the Iraq War, or homeland security as the most important problem facing the nation were less supportive of a female president and less confident in a woman's ability to handle security issues than those for whom security issues were less salient. Similarly, Lawless (2004) found that Americans viewed men as more competent than women to manage security issues, and were less supportive of a possible female president after 9/11. This preference may work at an implicit level under conditions of threat. Working from a terror management perspective, Cohen and colleagues (2004) demonstrate that mortality salience (e.g., asking someone to write about their own death) strongly increased preferences for leaders who demonstrated stereotypically masculine qualities, and depressed evaluations of leaders whose strengths were more relational or communal in nature. Little, Burris, Jones, and Robert (2007) found a preference for more masculine than feminine facial features in a presidential candidate when the vote choice task included the words "in a time of war."

The media also plays a role in reinforcing gender stereotypes. Female candidates attract more superficial coverage than do men (Bystrom, Robertson, and Banwart 2001; Kahn 1996). They are also more likely than men to be described in feminine terms, a finding that extends beyond the United States (Kittilson and Fridkin 2008). Women tend to receive more negative horse-race coverage, indicating they are less viable than their male competitor (Kahn 1996). And in mixed-gender campaigns, women receive more media coverage on social issues and men receive more coverage on economic matters (Smith 1997).

Finally, women politicians are seen as more liberal and Democratic than their male counterparts in the absence of specific or detailed information about their political views (Huddy and Terkildsen 1993a; Matland and King 2002). These expectations are consistent with political reality. Female politicians support more liberal and feminist positions than male politicians (Dodson and Carroll 1991) and write more legislation on women's issues (Thomas and Welch 1991). But voters' expectations are probably not derived from detailed knowledge of an individual candidate's issue positions, which is notoriously meager. Indeed, McDermott (1997) found that women congressional candidates were seen as more liberal regardless of their party but only by voters with little knowledge of the candidate. And Koch (2002) discovered that female Republican and Democratic Senate candidates were rated by citizens as more liberal than their actual ideology (as reflected in their roll-call votes).

There is some evidence that gender stereotypes that portray women as more liberal than men hurt female Republican candidates, making it harder for them to gain endorsement from voters in their own party (Lawless and Pearson 2008). Dolan (2004) suggests this disadvantage arises from stereotypes that portray women politicians as more liberal than men regardless of party. The existence of visible and vocal women Republican candidates such as Sarah Palin might seem to contradict this view. But in reality, the number of female Republican candidates and politicians has increased little over the past twenty years, whereas the number of female Democrats has increased markedly. For example, seventy female Democrats ran for a seat in the US House of Representatives in 1992 and ninety-six ran in 2008, representing a 37 percent increase. In contrast, thirty-six Republican women ran in 1992 and thirty-seven in 2008 (CAWP 2008), representing little or no increase over time.

Research on gender stereotypes thus holds potentially bad news for women political candidates, suggesting a crucial mismatch between the characteristics of a "good" politician and a typical woman that places them at a potential disadvantage. A female candidate stereotyped as a typical *feminine* woman might well lose electoral support because she is seen to lack typical male traits and expertise in policy areas thought most necessary for effective national leadership. Nonetheless, there are elections in which typical female characteristics work to a woman candidate's advantage (Lawless and Pearson 2008). Dolan (2004) concludes that women gubernatorial candidates who ran for office in the 1980s received more positive media coverage and were at a significant electoral advantage compared to women running for the Senate in the same period. This advantage arose because state-wide races featured issues that benefit women such as education and social welfare policy. In contrast, Senate races in this era were dominated by the military, foreign policy, and other cold war issues that advantaged men. Issue context can thus help to explain women politician's electoral successes.

## Women Voting for Women?

Finally, we turn to consider whether women are more likely than men to support women candidates. This question takes on new urgency in the aftermath of the 2008 presidential primaries, in which Hillary Clinton received especially strong support from women Democrats. Can women candidates increasingly count on the support of women voters? Research evidence indicates that the answer is complex and conditional. Female voters who support anti-sexual harassment policy, take a pro-choice position on abortion, and favor parental leave policies are especially likely to support female Democratic candidates, creating a gender gap in their favor. Moreover, this gap is most pronounced in elections in which women's issues are salient (Dolan 2008). The gender gap in support of female candidates also rests heavily on women's stronger support of the government provision of social services, and their greater emphasis on social welfare issues in deciding for whom to vote (Huddy, Cassese, and Lizotte 2008a). Women's support of women candidates is, therefore, especially pronounced when a female candidate takes a liberal position on social welfare spending and is most prominent in elections that involve a woman Democratic candidate (Dolan 2008).

Women candidates need not support expanded social welfare spending, however, to elicit stronger support from female than male voters. In low-stimulus elections, such as Congressional House races, the gender gap in support of women candidates stems from gender stereotypes, which portray women candidates as more liberal, supportive of women's issues, and pro-government than men even when they are not (McDermott 1997; Koch 2002; Sanbonmatsu 2002). This gender gap can evaporate once women voters learn something about a female candidate's ideology and political views. Thus, a conservative candidate such as Sarah Palin is extremely unlikely to elicit a gender gap in her favor because she will not attract liberal women voters, who typically provide a boost to female Democrats.

# CONCLUSION

In sum, gender permeates politics in complex ways with varying effects. There is a series of moderately sized gender gaps in support of social welfare issues, the governmental use of force, and issues linked to traditional morality that likely have differing origins and dynamics. Moreover, the electoral impact of a given issue gap further varies by election, lending a dynamic quality to the gender gap in vote choice. A gender gap in support of social welfare issues has played a consistent and prominent role in driving electoral behavior in recent years. But women are unlikely to provide greater support than men for Democratic candidates in an election dominated by concerns over pornography, drug usage, and morality. The gender gap on force which propelled women's greater opposition to Ronald Reagan in the early 1980s is further complicated by recent concerns about terrorism and national security that can reduce the gender gap in the post-9/11 era. More research is needed on how temporal fluctuations in issue salience influence the emergence and size of the gender gap in partisanship and vote choice.

Gender has similarly complex effects on political involvement. There is a persistent and small gender gap in political engagement with women being less interested, knowledgeable, and active than men in political campaigns. Yet women turn out to vote at greater rates than men, presenting political behavior researchers with an interesting puzzle with which they are only beginning to grapple. The persistent gender gap in political interest and knowledge is especially perplexing given women's increasing levels of educational attainment and movement into professional occupations. Moreover, the gap is not confined to older generations or less-educated individuals.

The political effects of gender stereotypes evince similar complexity. Despite the appealingly straightforward notion that voters are responsible for the paucity of women in national politics, there is no evidence that voters' gender stereotypes prevent women candidates from attaining political office once they are on the ballot. Admittedly, gender stereotypes that portray women as warm and nurturing are at odds with the profile of a typical tough and aggressive politician. This suggests a potential disadvantage for women candidates. But women candidates work diligently to evade voters' stereotypes, and voters, when exposed to sufficient information about a candidate, view women candidates as unique individuals. Furthermore, female attributes and areas of issue competence can prove advantageous to women candidates in certain electoral contexts.

We have not delved deeply into the origins of gender differences in this review. But more comprehensive and theoretically grounded research on the origins of political gender differences is sorely needed (see Huddy, Cassese, and Lizotte 2008a). Explanations can be classified into three broad categories. First, some researchers focus on the divergent socialization of boys and girls into specific personality traits, value priorities, behaviors, and adult roles to explain why women are more supportive than men of social welfare spending, less enthusiastic about overseas military engagement, or less interested in politics (Eagly 1987). Second, others gravitate toward reasons based on men and women's differing tangible interests that result in women being more dependent on the welfare state or more likely to work in the public sector to explain their greater support of social welfare programs and lesser support for military spending (Box-Steffensmeier, De Bouf, and Lin 2004; Carroll 2006). Third, others rely on gendered identities (e.g., feminist consciousness) and symbolic concerns about women's status to account for women's greater support of Democratic and female candidates (Conover and Sapiro 1993).

The three approaches hold differing implications for the development and persistence of various gender gaps. From a socialization perspective the movement of women away from the helping professions and into careers such as the law that require assertiveness and rational decision-making (considered stereotypically male qualities) could minimize compassion-based support of social welfare policies. On the other hand, feminist consciousness linked to women's greater education and movement into formerly male professions might enhance women's awareness of their shared interests and increase support for social welfare policies that disproportionately benefit women as a group. All three approaches must grapple with the relatively modest size of political gender differences, a fact that poses an especially tough challenge to a fourth set of biological and genetic explanations for gender differences that are gaining renewed traction but are difficult to reconcile with subtle differences in political attitudes and behavior (Hatemi et al. 2009). At present, there is little evidence in support of self-interest as a basis for pervasive gender differences. But the socialization and personality explanations have not received very extensive empirical attention, and the gender consciousness approach, while promising, obviously falls short in explaining why women are not more supportive than men of numerous women's issues.

In the end, pressing questions remain on all sides. What beliefs account for women's greater opposition to the use of force? Why are women more supportive than men of social welfare spending? What role does women's greater self-rated compassion play in accounting for differences in electoral choice? How easily can women candidates overcome cultural stereotypes that portray them as warm but insufficiently competent, and will such judgments subside over time? Research on gender and politics provides a rich domain for extensive research on these and other questions at a time when women are advancing quickly into the highest ranks of politics, have more electoral power than men because of their greater numbers at the polls, and continue to sway elections through their small but persistently greater support of Democratic candidates. For better or worse, gendered politics is here to stay and will continue to surface in myriad complex ways, presenting political behavior researchers with an ongoing and suitably challenging set of research topics.

# REFERENCES

BELENKY, M., CLINCHY, B., GOLDBERGER, N., and TARULE, J. 1986. *Women's Ways of Knowing*. New York: Basic Books.

BENNETT, L., and BENNETT, S. E. 1989. Enduring Gender Differences in Political Interest: The Impact of Socialization and Political Dispositions. *American Politics Quarterly*, 17: 105–22.

BOLZENDAHL, C. I., and MYERS, D. J. 2004. Feminist Attitudes and Support for Gender Equality: Change in Women and Men 1974–1998. *Social Forces*, 83/2: 758–90.

BOX-STEFFENSMEIER, J., DE BOUF, S., and LIN, T.-M. 2004. The Dynamics of the Partisan Gender Gap. *American Political Science Review*, 98/3: 515–28.

BURNS, N., SCHLOZMAN, K. L., and VERBA, S. 2001. *The Private Roots of Public Action: Gender, Equality, and Political Participation*. Cambridge, MA: Harvard University Press.

BYSTROM, D. G., ROBERTSON, T. A., and BANWART, M. C. 2001. Framing the Fight: An Analysis of Media Coverage of Male and Female Candidates in Primary Races for Governor and U.S. Senate in 2000. *American Behavioral Scientist*, 44/12: 1999–2013.

CARROLL, S. 2006. Voting Choices: Meet You at the Gender Gap. In *Gender and Elections: Shaping the Future of American Politics*, ed. S. J. Carroll and R. Fox. Cambridge: Cambridge University Press.

CAWP (CENTER FOR AMERICAN WOMEN AND POLITICS). 2008. Gender Differences in Voter Turnout. Fact sheet. At <http://www.cawp.rutgers.edu/fast_facts/voters/documents/gender-diff.pdf>. Accessed Aug. 1, 2010.

CEJKA, M. A., and EAGLY, A. H. 1999. Gender-Stereotypic Images of Occupations Correspond to the Sex Segregation of Employment. *Personality and Social Psychology Bulletin*, 25/4: 413–23.

CHAIO, J. Y., BOWMAN, N. E., and GILL, H. 2008. The Political Gender Gap: Gender Bias in the Facial Inferences that Predict Voting Behavior. *PLoS One*, 3/10: e3666.

CHANEY, C. K., ALVAREZ, R. M., and NAGLER, J. 1998. Explaining the Gender Gap in U.S. Presidential Elections, 1980–1992. *Political Research Quarterly*, 51/2: 311–39.

CLARK, J., and CLARK, C. 1993. The Gender Gap 1988: Compassion, Pacifism, and Indirect Feminism. In *Women in Politics: Insiders or Outsiders? A Collection of Readings*, ed. L. L. Duke. Englewood Cliffs, NJ: Prentice-Hall.

COHEN, F., SOLOMON, S., MAXFIELD, M., PYSZCZYNSKI, T., and GREENBERG, J. 2004. Fatal Attraction: The Effects of Mortality Salience on Evaluations of Charismatic, Task-Oriented, and Relationship Oriented Leaders. *Psychological Science*, 15/12: 846–51.

CONOVER, P. J., and SAPIRO, V. 1993. Gender, Feminist Consciousness, and War. *American Journal of Political Science*, 37/4: 1079–99.

CONWAY, M. M., STEURNAGEL, G. A., and AHERN, D. W. 2005. *Women and Political Participation: Cultural Change in the Political Arena*, 2nd edn. Washington, DC: CQ Press.

DELLI CARPINI, M., and KEETER, S. 2005. Gender and Political Knowledge. In *Gender and American Politics: Women, Men, and the Political Process*, ed. S. T. Rinehart and J. J. Josephson. Armonk, NY: M. E. Sharpe.

DODSON, D. L., and CARROLL, S. J. 1991. *Reshaping the Agenda: Women in State Legislatures*. Center for the American Woman and Politics (CAWP), Eagleton Institute of Politics, State University of New Jersey—Rutgers. At <http://www.cawp.rutgers.edu/research/topics/documents/reshapingtheagenda.pdf>. Accessed Aug. 1, 2010.

DOLAN, K. 2004. *Voting for Women: How the Public Evaluates Female Candidates*. Boulder, CO: Westview Press.

—— 2008. Is There a Gender Affinity Effect in American Politics? Information, Affect, and Candidate Sex in U.S. House Elections. *Political Research Quarterly*, 61: 79–89.

—— 2009. The Impact of Gender Stereotyped Evaluations on Support for Women Candidates. *Political Behavior*, 32/1: 69–88.

EAGLY, A. H. 1987. *Sex Differences in Social Behavior: A Social-Role Interpretation*. Hillsdale, NJ: Lawrence Erlbaum.

—— and CARLI, L. L. 2007. *Through the Labyrinth: The Truth about How Women Become Leaders*. Boston: Harvard Business School Press.

—— MITCHELL, A. A., and PALUDI, M. A. 2004. Social Role Theory of Sex Differences and Similarities: Implications for the Sociopolitical Attitudes of Women and Men. In *Guide to the Psychology of Gender*, ed. M. A. Paludi. Westport, CT: Praeger, Greenwood.

EICHENBERG, R. C. 2003. Gender Differences in Public Attitudes towards the Use of Force by the United States, 1990–2003. *International Security*, 28/1: 110–41.

FALK, E., and KENSKI, K. 2006. Issue Saliency and Gender Stereotypes: Support for Women as President in Times of War and Terrorism. *Social Science Quarterly*, 87/1: 1–18.

Fox, R. L., and Lawless, J. 2004. Entering the Arena? Gender and the Decision to Run for Office. *American Journal of Political Science*, 48/2: 264–80.

—— and Oxley, Z. M. 2003. Gender Stereotyping in State Executive Elections: Candidate Selection and Success. *Journal of Politics*, 65/3: 833–50.

Frankovic, K. A. 1982. Sex and Politics: New Alignments, Old Issues. *PS: Political Science and Politics*, 15/3: 439–48.

Funk, C. L. 1999. Bringing the Candidate into Models of Candidate Evaluation. *Journal of Politics*, 61/3: 700–20.

Gilens, M. 1988. Gender and Support for Reagan: A Comprehensive Model of Presidential Approval. *American Journal of Political Science*, 32/1: 19–49.

Haider-Markel, D. P., and Vieux, A. 2008. Gender and Conditional Support for Torture in the War on Terror. *Politics and Gender*, 4: 5–33.

Halim, S., and Stiles, B. L. 2001. Differential Support for Police Use of Force, the Death Penalty, and Perceived Harshness of the Courts: Effects of Race, Gender, and Region. *Criminal Justice and Behavior*, 28/1: 3–23.

Hatemi, P. K., Medland, S. E., Morley, K. I., Heath, A. C., and Martin, N. G. 2009. The Genetics of Voting: An Australian Twin Study. *Behavior Genetics*, 37/3: 435–48.

Heflick, N. A., and Goldenberg, J. L. 2009. Objectifying Sarah Palin: Evidence that Objectification Causes Women to Be Perceived as Less Competent and Less Fully Human. *Journal of Experimental Social Psychology*, 45/3: 598–601.

Herek, G. M. 2002. Heterosexuals' Attitudes toward Bisexual Men and Women in the United States. *Journal of Sex Research*, 39/4: 264–74.

Howell, S. E., and Day, C. L. 2000. Complexities of the Gender Gap. *Journal of Politics*, 62/3: 858–74.

Huddy, L., and Capelos, T. 2002. The Impact of Gender Stereotypes on Voters' Assessment of Women Candidates. In *Social Psychological Applications to Social Issues: Developments in Political Psychology*, v, ed. V. Ottati. New York: Kluwer Academic, Plenum.

—— and Terkildsen, N. 1993a. Gender Stereotypes and the Perception of Male and Female Candidates. *American Journal of Political Science*, 37/1: 119–47.

—— —— 1993b. The Consequences of Gender Stereotypes for Women Candidates at Different Levels and Types of Office. *Political Research Quarterly*, 46/3: 503–25.

—— Cassese, E., and Lizotte, M.-K. 2008a. Gender, Public Opinion, and Political Reasoning. In *Political Women and American Democracy*, ed. C. Wolbrecht, K. Beckwith, and L. Baldez. Cambridge: Cambridge University Press.

—— —— —— 2008b. Sources of Political Unity and Disunity among Women: Placing the Gender Gap in Perspective. In *Voting the Gender Gap*, ed. L. D. Whitaker. Champaign: University of Illinois Press.

—— Feldman, S., and Cassese, E. 2009. Terrorism, Anxiety, and War. In *Terrorism and Torture: An Interdisciplinary Perspective*, ed. W. G. Stritzke, S. Lewandowsky, D. Denmark, J. Clare, and F. Morgan. Cambridge: Cambridge University Press.

—— —— Taber, C., and Lahav, G. 2005. Threat, Anxiety, and Support of Antiterrorism Policies. *American Journal of Political Science*, 49/3: 593–608.

Hughes, M., and Tuch, S. A. 2003. Gender Differences in Whites' Racial Attitudes: Are Women's Attitudes Really More Favorable? *Social Psychology Quarterly*, 66/4: 384–401.

Hurwitz, J., and Smithey, S. 1998. Gender Differences on Crime and Punishment. *Political Research Quarterly*, 51/1: 89–115.

HUTCHINGS, V. L. 2001. Political Context, Issue Salience, and Selective Attentiveness: Constituent Knowledge of the Clarence Thomas Confirmation Vote. *Journal of Politics*, 63/1: 846–68.

JOST, J. T., and KAY, A. C. 2005. Exposure to Benevolent Sexism and Complementary Gender Stereotypes: Consequences for Specific and Diffuse Forms of System Justification. *Journal of Personality and Social Psychology*, 88/3: 498–509.

KAHN, K. F. 1996. *The Political Consequences of Being a Woman*. New York: Columbia University Press.

KAUFMANN, K. M., and PETROCIK, J. R. 1999. The Changing Politics of American Men: Understanding the Sources of the Gender Gap. *American Journal of Political Science*, 43/3: 864–87.

KENIG, S., and RYAN, J. 1986. Sex Differences in Levels of Tolerance and Attribution of Blame for Sexual Harassment on a University Campus. *Sex Roles*, 15/9–10: 535–49.

KENSKI, K., and JAMIESON, K. H. 2000. The Gender Gap in Political Knowledge: Are Women Less Knowledgeable than Men about Politics? In *Everything You Think You Know About Politics...And Why You're Wrong*, ed. K. H. Jamieson. New York: Basic Books.

KITE, M. E., and WHITLEY, B. E. 1996. Sex Differences in Attitudes towards Homosexual Persons, Behaviour, and Civil Rights: A Meta-Analysis. *Personality and Social Psychology Bulletin*, 22: 336–53.

KITTILSON, M. C., and FRIDKIN, K. 2008. Gender, Candidate Portrayals, and Election Campaigns: A Comparative Perspective. *Politics & Gender*, 4/3: 371–92.

KOCH, J. W. 2002. Gender Stereotypes and Citizens' Impressions of House Candidates' Ideological Orientations. *American Journal of Political Science*, 46/2: 453–62.

KOHUT, A., and PARKER, K. 1997. Talk Radio and Gender Politics. In *Women, Media, and Politics*, ed. P. Norris. New York: Oxford University Press.

LAWLESS, J. L. 2004. Women, War, and Winning Elections: Gender Stereotyping in the Post-September 11th Era. *Political Research Quarterly*, 57/3: 479–90.

—— and PEARSON, K. 2008. The Primary Reason for Women's Underrepresentation? Reevaluating the Conventional Wisdom. *Journal of Politics*, 70/1: 67–82.

LERNER, J., GONZALEZ, R., SMALL, D., and FISCHHOFF, B. 2003. Effects of Fear and Anger on Perceived Risks of Terrorism: A National Field Experiment. *Psychological Science*, 14/2: 144–50.

LITTLE, A. C., BURRIS, R. P., JONES, B. C., and ROBERT, S. C. 2007. Facial Appearance Affects Voting Decisions. *Evolution and Human Behavior*, 28/1: 18–27.

LIZOTTE, M.-K., and SIDMAN, A. 2009. Explaining the Gender Gap in Political Knowledge. *Politics and Gender*, 5/2: 127–51.

McDERMOTT, M. L. 1997. Race and Gender Cues in Low-Information Elections. *Political Research Quarterly*, 51/4: 895–918.

MANZA, J., and BROOKS, C. 1998. The Gender Gap in US Presidential Elections: When, Why, Implications? *American Journal of Sociology*, 103/5: 1235–66.

MARGOLIS, J. 1992. Piranhas, Monsters, and Jugglers: The Psychology of Gender and Academic Discourse. *On Teaching and Learning*, 4: 5–26.

MATLAND, R., and KING, D. 2002. Women as Candidates in Congressional Elections. In *Women Transforming Congress*, ed. C. S. Rosenthal and R. F. Fenno, Jr. Norman: Oklahoma University Press.

MONDAK, J. J., and ANDERSON, M. R. 2008. The Knowledge Gap: A Reexamination of Gender-Based Differences in Political Knowledge. *Journal of Politics*, 66/2: 492–512.

MUELLER, C. M. 1986. The Empowerment of Women: Polling and the Women's Voting Bloc. In *The Politics of the Gender Gap: The Social Construction of Political Influence*, ed. C. M. Mueller. Newbury Park, CA: Sage.

ROSENWASSER, S., and SEALE, J. 1988. Attitudes towards a Hypothetical Male or Female Presidential Candidate: A Research Note. *Political Psychology*, 9/4: 591–8.

SANBONMATSU, K. 2002. Gender Stereotypes and Vote Choice. *American Journal of Political Science*, 46/1: 20–34.

—— 2003. Political Knowledge and Gender Stereotypes. *American Politics Research*, 31/6: 575–94.

SAPIRO, V. 2003. Theorizing Gender in Political Psychology Research. In *The Oxford Handbook of Political Psychology*, ed. D. O. Sears, L. Huddy, and R. Jervis. New York: Oxford University Press.

SCHAFER, J. A., HUBNER, B. M., and BYNAM, T. S. 2006. Fear of Crime and Criminal Victimization: Gender Based Contrasts. *Journal of Criminal Justice*, 34/3: 285–301.

SCHLESINGER, M., and HELDMAN, C. 2001. Gender Gap or Gender Gaps? New Perspectives on Support for Government Action and Policies. *Journal of Politics*, 63/1: 59–92.

SEARS, D. O., and HUDDY, L. 1990. On the Origins of the Political Disunity of Women. In *Women, Politics, and Change*, ed. L. A. Tilly and P. Gurin. New York: Russell Sage.

SHAPIRO, R., and MAJAHAN, H. 1986. Gender Differences in Policy Preferences: A Summary of Trends from the 1960s to the 1980s. *Public Opinion Quarterly*, 50: 42–61.

SMITH, K. B. 1997. When All's Fair: Signs of Parity in Media Coverage of Female Candidates. *Political Communication*, 14/1: 71–82.

SMITH, T. W. 1984. The Polls: Gender and Attitudes toward Violence. *Public Opinion Quarterly*, 48/1: 384–96.

STACK, S. 2000. Support for the Death Penalty: A Gender Specific Model. *Sex Roles*, 43/3: 163–79.

THOMAS, S., and WELCH, S. 1991. The Impact of Gender on Activities and Priorities of State Legislators. *Western Political Quarterly*, 44/2: 445–56.

TOLLESON-RINEHART, S., and PERKINS, J. 1989. The Intersection of Gender Politics and Religious Beliefs. *Political Behavior*, 11/1: 33–55.

VERBA, S., BURNS, N., and SCHLOZMAN, K. 1997. Knowing and Caring about Politics: Gender and Political Engagement. *Journal of Politics*, 59/4: 1051–72.

WELCH, S., and HIBBING, J. 1992. Financial Conditions, Gender, and Voting in American National Elections. *Journal of Politics*, 54/1: 197–213.

WILLIAMS, J. E., and BEST, D. L. 1982. *Measuring Sex Stereotypes: A Multination Study*. Beverly Hills: Sage.

WOLPERT, R. M., and GIMPEL, J. G. 1998. Self-Interest, Symbolic Politics, and Public Attitudes toward Gun Control. *Political Behavior*, 20/3: 241–62.

......................................................................................

# CHAPTER 30

# THE CONTOURS OF BLACK PUBLIC OPINION

......................................................................................

FREDRICK C. HARRIS

THE study of black public opinion has focused on understanding how black Americans think about social and political issues that affect them as a group. Decades of research have shown that black Americans' political attitudes have been shaped by their shared history and experiences and by the influence of indigenous leaders, media, and community institutions. These combined forces serve as a foundation for the formation and stability of black public opinion. Despite breakthroughs in the study of black public opinion in the past decade, black public opinion has only recently become a serious academic field of study. This is mainly due to the complicated history of race and survey research and the paucity of opinion surveys that have large samples of black respondents for intra-racial group analysis. Consequently, theoretical developments in the field of black public opinion have lagged behind, and have indeed been isolated from, research developments in the study of white racial attitudes and American public opinion writ large.

Black public opinion as a field of study evolved from the American public's interest in and concern about the civil rights and black power movements of the 1960s and 1970s. As black Americans' demand for civil rights began to be placed at the top of the nation's policy agenda, a crop of academic and media-sponsored opinion surveys that focused on black political attitudes and behavior were developed. Prior to the development of these surveys, few black respondents were represented in surveys that analyzed American public opinion, again mainly because of the relatively small percentage of blacks in national samples. Rarely did these national surveys ask questions about race relations or civil rights.

Most of the first surveys on black opinion, several of which were produced by Louis Harris for *Newsweek Magazine*, were designed to probe blacks' attitudes toward political protest. Given the temporal nature of the reasons behind designing surveys that gaged black opinion, surveys in this era did not think about using black opinion as

the Civil Rights Act, and his support for government policies to address poverty, consolidated the black vote for the Democratic Party. The Republican Party's presidential nominee, Barry Goldwater, campaigned against the Civil Rights Act and opposed social welfare programs for the poor. More than whites, Latinos, and other minorities, African Americans have the strongest—and most durable—partisan attachments, a pattern that has been relatively stable for the past forty years. Blacks are more likely to report that they are "strong" rather than "weak" Democrats and are less likely than whites to report that they are Independents. In analyzing black partisanship since 1952, Tate (1994) documents how blacks' attachment as strong Democrats has hovered around 40 percent while their attachment as weak Democrats has been between 20 and 40 percent. The proportion of blacks who identify as Independent Democrats, Independents, or Republicans has been less than 20 percent.

The distribution of partisan attachments for whites differs: whites are less likely to be Democrats and are more likely to be Republicans or Independents. Even when considering the proportion of whites who identify as strong Democrats and Republicans, blacks' attachment as strong Democrats still outweighs whites' combined strong attachment to both political parties. Thus, blacks are not only overwhelmingly Democrats, they have a rock-solid commitment to their party of choice.

However, Hajnal and Lee's most recent study (2007) shows that since 1970 there has been a considerable decline in blacks' strong attachment to the Democratic Party. They show that over 40 percent of blacks now identify as Independent or Republican, a shift in party attachment that has received little notice in the literature. Instead of the traditional way of estimating partisan choice, the authors argue that for blacks the choice should not be structured along a continuum between strong Democrats and strong Republicans but between being Democrats—strong or weak—and Independents, or being Republicans—strong or weak—and Independents. This choice should also be estimated by evaluations of how hard the Democratic and Republican parties work on issues that are important to the black community as well as beliefs in various black nationalists ideologies. They find this approach provides more explanation for black partisanship than conventional models that are used to explain partisan attachments in the United States.

Similarly, the effects of political ideology on partisan attachments also differ between blacks and whites. While for whites the partisan continuum parallels the liberal–moderate–conservative ideological dimension, it does not work when explaining the effects of ideology on blacks' partisan attachments. Blacks tend to be more liberal than whites in their support of government social policies, but are more conservative than whites on social issues such as gay marriage, prayer in schools, and abortion rights (Tate 1994). Indeed, some evidence suggests that on policy issues on which blacks have traditionally held liberal positions—guaranteed jobs for all Americans, support for government aid to blacks, reduced spending on social services—there has been moderation in opinion over time (Tate 2004). In order to understand the partisan and the ideological preferences of African Americans—and why they differ from whites—scholars need to focus their attention on the ideological traditions that are indigenous to the history and politics of black communities.

# THE NATURE OF BLACK POLITICAL
# BELIEF SYSTEMS

More recent scholarship on black public opinion has located what can be described as a black belief system that assists African Americans in evaluating and cognitively navigating the political environment (Shingles 1981; Allen, Dawson, and Brown 1989; Simpson 1998; Harris-Lacewell 2004). Allen, Dawson, and Brown (1989) find that a black belief system includes, at the very least, blacks' feelings of group solidarity, their positive and negative evaluations of blacks as a group, and blacks' desire for social and political autonomy from whites. These feelings and desires are mediated through political socialization processes such as black media, the black Church, and black cultural practices (also see Harris-Lacewell 2004).

The role that racial identity plays in the formation, direction, and maintenance of black public opinion is not clear. Scholars have used related but different measures to analyze the role of racial identity on black political behavior. These different but interconnected constructs are group membership, group identity, and group consciousness (McClain, Carew, Walton, and Watts 2009). The distinction between identity—how one describes oneself—and group membership—how others, particularly the state, define you—has influenced how students of black opinion approach the field. While how one identifies oneself is based on individual preferences, group membership is "based on the subjective assignment of people, particularly in the case of racial membership, that is arbitrary, and, at times, flexible" (2009, 473). In contrast, identity—including racial identity—is based on the awareness that individuals have of their identity. This awareness is reflected in the psychological attachments individuals have to a group, which are manifested through shared beliefs, memories, ideas, and preferences (Dawson 1994; McClain, Carew, Walton, and Watts 2009; Harris 2006). Additionally, racial identity is different than racial consciousness. Racial group consciousness involves a sense of psychological attachment to a group but is an "in-group identification politicized by a set of ideological beliefs about one's social standing, as well as a view that collective action is the best means by which the group can improve its status and realize its interests" (McClain, Carew, Walton, and Watts 2009). It is this aspect of identity—a politicized group consciousness—that has implications for how scholars of black public opinion approach, analyze, and interpret black public opinion.

Scholarship on black opinion has focused more on the ideology of black nationalism and its relationship to black belief structures than any other ideological tradition in black communities (Davis and Davenport 1997; Brown and Shaw 2002; Davis and Brown 2002; Price 2009). While black consciousness does not explicitly measure ideological dispositions, black nationalism, as an ideology, is intertwined with black consciousness. In his analysis of the 1992–3 National Black Politics Survey (NBPS), Michael Dawson identifies black nationalism as "support for African-American autonomy and various degrees of cultural, social, economic, and political separation from white America" (Dawson 2001, 21). He finds solid empirical support for black nationalism as well as the other traditions of black thought in his analysis.

Using the NBPS, Brown and Shaw (2002) identify two strands of black nationalism: what they describe as community-focused black nationalism and separatist black nationalism. The community variant of black nationalism is based on the premise that blacks should politically and economically control the communities where blacks are the dominant racial group. Traditionalist views of separatist black nationalism adhere to the idea that blacks should develop a separate territory either within or outside the United States. In this study, Brown and Shaw use four questions from the NBPS to measure community activism. These questions ask whether blacks should shop at black-owned stores whenever possible, should control the government in mostly black neighborhoods, should control the economy in mostly black neighborhoods, or should rely on themselves as blacks and not on others. Four questions are used to measure the separatist dimensions of black nationalism. These questions ask whether black people should always vote for black candidates when they run for public office, form their own political party, have their own separate nation, and whether they believe in the idea of blacks as a "nation within a nation."

In contrast to the studies on black political attitudes in the 1960s, Brown and Shaw find social class differences in their analysis of nationalism in black public opinion. They find that more affluent blacks support the more community-oriented variant of nationalism than less affluent blacks, while young blacks and black males are more likely to support the separatist variant of black nationalism. Though they identify two strands of black nationalism in their study, the authors acknowledge that both measures have similar effects on some black attitudes. They observe, for instance, that both community nationalists and separatist nationalists are "more likely to be suspicious of whites' motives toward blacks, to believe Africa is a special homeland for all blacks, and to regard [black nationalist Louis] Farrakhan positively" (2002, 40). Thus, they conclude, these similar effects show that the "points of agreement speak to a common desire for autonomy and group independence, which are the core ideals of a Black Nationalist worldview" (2002, 40).

Other scholars have a different interpretation of black nationalism and its effects on black political attitudes. Several scholars argue that black nationalism actually breeds racial conflict and intolerance toward whites and Jews (Davis and Brown 2002; Sniderman and Piazza 2002). Echoing the research that Gary Marx began in the 1960s, these scholars of black opinion argue that strong black nationalist sentiments among blacks are linked to anti-white and anti-Semitic attitudes and a general intolerance toward people who are different from black people. Directly challenging the work of Brown and Shaw (2002), Davis and Brown (2002) argue that their demarcation of black nationalism into community and separatist variants is flawed. Davis and Brown make a distinction between social identity and the ideology of black nationalism and argue that Brown and Shaw's two measures of black nationalism give a distorted interpretation of the effects of black nationalism on black attitudes. Using the data set (NBPS), Davis and Brown include additional questions in their analysis to probe black nationalist sentiment; they also employ a more rigorous test to sort out the difference between blackness as identity and blackness as ideology. Questions added to the analysis are: "should blacks participate in all-black organizations?", "should black males attend all-black schools?", and "should black children learn an African language?"

Davis and Brown exclude one item from their analysis that was included in the Brown and Shaw study, the question whether blacks "form a nation within a nation." The authors exclude this question because they believe that it is similar to another question that asks respondents whether they think blacks should form a separate nation. The authors also include in their analysis of survey items a battery of questions that measure the intensity of blacks' closeness to other blacks, what the authors describe as "social identity." Social identity is measured by respondents' affirmative responses to three questions that ask whether what happens to (1) black women, (2) black men, and (3) blacks in general will affect what happens in their own lives. (Note that these questions are normally used to measure the concept of linked fate but Davis and Brown use the concept of "social identity." The concept of "linked fate" is discussed in the next section.)

The authors use a confirmatory factor analysis that produces two constructs: a Social Identity Index, which combines all three questions on closeness to blacks, and a Black Nationalism Index, which includes Brown and Shaw's measures of community and separatist definitions of nationalism (excluding the question that asks blacks whether they believe blacks are part of a "nation within a nation"). Davis and Brown add three questions to the analysis: "should blacks participate in all-black organizations?", "should black males attend all-black schools?", and "should black children learn an African language?" Their measure of black nationalism predicts a "greater affection toward blacks in general and poor blacks, but not toward middle-class blacks and black conservatives" (2002, 247). But they also find that black nationalism and social identity serve different functions in the structure of black beliefs. Black nationalist sentiments, they argue, lead to "greater antipathy toward whites," while "a stronger black social identity leads to greater affection toward whites" (2002, 247).

Sniderman and Piazza (2002) come to somewhat similar conclusions in their analysis of black nationalist ideologies and their impact on social intolerance. Their survey of Chicago blacks shows that pride in being black does not necessarily produce prejudice against whites. However, they do argue that a cultural variant of black nationalism—Afrocentrism—is linked to prejudicial feelings toward whites and to acceptance of negative stereotypes of Jews. Sniderman and Piazza gage Afrocentrism through respondents' positive responses to two statements: "African wise men who lived hundreds of years ago do not get enough credit for their contributions to modern science" and "ancient Greek philosophers copied many ideas from black philosophers who lived in Egypt." Though they do not find a direct relationship between

Afrocentrism and social identity (or rather, strong feelings of linked fate), the authors suggest that blacks' social identity might be indirectly linked to social intolerance. Sniderman and Piazza note that "Blacks who feel they share a common fate with other blacks are more likely to support Afrocentrism than are blacks who do not feel that what happens to other blacks has a large impact on what happens to them" (2002, 171).

Their analysis also shows—despite Sniderman and Piazza's assertion of the negative side of black social identity—strong support for egalitarian values among African Americans. Using survey experiments that ask two sets of respondents slightly altered questions on race-based affirmative action, the authors are able to estimate how blacks respond to the policy in different contexts. In the experiment respondents are asked to evaluate whether a black applicant or a white applicant should be admitted to college based on their credentials. One group of respondents is presented with a scenario in which there is a small gap in SAT scores between a hypothetical black and a hypothetical white applicant. The other group is presented with a scenario in which there is a wide gap between the scores of a black and a white applicant. In both scenarios the white applicant has the highest score. A majority of respondents in both groups agreed that the white applicant should be admitted, regardless of whether the differences in the scores were small or great. To Sniderman and Piazza's surprise, an overwhelming majority of blacks hold principled positions on educational achievement. Not only do blacks favor this achievement in the abstract, the authors argue, but blacks "make it the decisive principle even when doing so comes at the expense of fellow blacks" (2002, 179).

While black nationalism and its influence on black political beliefs has been the focus of scholarship in the field, less attention has been given to the intersection of black racial identity and other social identities that blacks inhabit. Some research has centered on the intersection of gender and racial identity on black women's political attitudes (but not black men's), but clearly not enough given the importance of both identities to the experiences of black women (Mansbridge and Tate 1992; Gay and Tate 1998; Simien 2006). The research that does exist has examined whether either race or gender is salient to black women's political consciousness and preferences. Like the literature on whether race or class is a more salient feature of black public opinion (Dawson 1994; Hochschild 1995), research on the intersection of race and gender explores potentially competing identities among African-American women.

In the case of gender, scholars have attempted to estimate whether gender consciousness or racial group consciousness or a combination of both these politicized social identities influence black public opinion. Most of this research has found that race trumps gender. Gay and Tate found that although black women strongly identify politically with women more generally (as measured by a question that measures a sense of shared fate with other women), black solidarity had overall a greater effect than gender solidarity or the interaction of both identities. Gay and Tate estimated the effects of strong racial and gender identifiers on support for race-specific public policies and support for universal social policies. They found that both social identities are strongly linked: women who identified strongly with their gender also identified strongly with their race. However, when considered together, the impact of racial identification was greater than the gender identification of black women in predicting liberal support for policy issues.

Gay and Tate also found that on race-specific public policy issues the effect of liberal support for those policies was greater among strong race identifiers than for strong race and gender identifiers (when estimating the interactive effects of both race and gender). The authors conclude that the impact of these two potentially competing identities is complex when it comes to the policy preferences of black women. "Race remains the dominant political screen through which black women view politics," Gay and Tate conclude, "not only because most consider racism a greater evil than sexism, but because gender is simply a weak vehicle for political identification" (1998, 182).

## PARADIGM SHIFT: A THEORY OF LINKED FATE

A theoretical perspective that has reshaped the study of black public opinion in the past decade is the theory of shared, or linked, fate (Dawson 1994; Tate 1994). Adopting a variant of rational choice theory, this perspective on black public opinion states that blacks' individual decision-making in forming their political preferences is determined by how individual blacks evaluate how candidates and policies will affect blacks as a group. As Dawson explains the concept, it is "far more efficient for African-Americans to determine what [is] good for the racial group than to determine what [is] good for themselves individually, and more efficient for them to use the status of the group, both relative and absolute, as a proxy for individual utility." Dawson refers to this cognitive processing as the "black utility heuristic" (1994, 10). According to Dawson, linked fate is sustained through various processes that guide African Americans' commitment to racial group solidarity. These processes include "media outlets, kinship networks, community and civil rights organizations, and especially the preeminent institution in the black community, the black church" (1994, 11). The concept of linked fate has been measured mostly by one survey instrument: "Do you think that what happens generally to black people in this country will have something to do with what happens in your life?" The category values for the question are "a lot," "some," "not much," and "not at all."

Roughly a third of respondents have consistently reported in surveys that what happens to black people affects them "a lot" (31 percent in 1984; 34 percent in 1988), another third regularly report that it affects them some (32 percent in both 1984 and 1988), about one in ten report "not much" (11 percent in 1984 and 12 percent in 1988), and about a quarter report "not at all" (26 percent in 1984 and 22 percent in 1988) (Dawson 1994, 78). This measure of racial group solidarity goes beyond the black consciousness measures on black solidarity, which asked respondents how close they felt to other blacks or how often respondents mentioned racial issues when discussing policy issues in surveys. This one survey instrument has captured the essence of racial group solidarity better than other survey questions on black solidarity.

As Dawson argues in his book *Behind the Mule: Race and Class in African-American Politics* (1994), the sense of linked fate among blacks helps to explain the homogeneity in most domains of black public opinion. Indeed, when it comes to political preferences such as partisanship or support for policies that remedy racial discrimination such as affirmative action, there are few differences among blacks across education and income. Though some research has shown that middle class blacks are more pessimistic about achieving racial equality than less affluent African Americans (Hochschild 1995), Dawson finds that education did not predict support for linked fate. Indeed, he finds that middle-class blacks are more likely than less affluent blacks to believe that blacks as a group are "economically subordinated" and consequently "more likely to believe that one's fate was linked to that of the race" (1994, 82). Thus, he finds, "education... had the opposite effect from the one predicted by those who believe that increased opportunities for blacks should lead to a weakening of perceived attachment to race" (1994, 82).

Again, using the status of the group as a proxy for individual evaluations of political preferences, black Americans are able to calculate the costs and the benefits of policies that would affect them individually. These calculations are based on the assumption that all blacks—even those who are involved in black organizations or receive information about the status of the group through black media—have available to them perfect information about the status of the community. What we do not know from this line of reasoning is how black decision-making operates in situations where information about policies or candidates is imperfect or when indigenous media, institutions, and leaders are weak purveyors of information about group interest. And as other research has argued, the theory of linked fate does not account for diversity within black populations—along the lines of gender, class, ethnicity, sexuality—that is masked, at least implicitly, by symbolic support for black racial solidarity (Cohen 1999). Since other identities are not accounted for in estimating the support for linked fate, we do not know the extent of competing identities' impact on linked fate among blacks.

Nevertheless, the theoretical insights that the theory of linked fate has brought to the study of black public opinion have been far-reaching. Scholars employing the theory of linked fate have produced important scholarship on the political socialization of black youth (Simpson 1998); the role of black media, the black Church, and other indigenous social institutions in shaping black opinion formation (Harris-Lacewell 2004; Harris 1999); gender differences in black political attitudes (Simien 2006); black nationalism and its influence on political attitudes (Brown and Shaw 2002; Price 2009); collective memory and black activism (Harris 2006); and the importance of neighborhood context in understanding the dynamics of racial group solidarity among blacks (Gay 2004). There are virtually no rival conceptual frameworks to compete with the theory of linked fate that explain how black public opinion is formed or understood. Though the theory of linked fate has dominated the field of black public opinion, scholars of race and politics are beginning to adopt the theory to understand the public opinion behavior of other racial and ethnic groups (Masuoka 2006; Junn and Masuoka 2008).

Indeed, it has become standard practice to include a question on linked fate on surveys devoted to analyzing racial and ethnic politics in the United States.

## RACE OF INTERVIEWER EFFECTS
## ON BLACK OPINION

In addition to understanding the nature of black belief systems and incorporating a framework to analyze black public opinion, research in the field has also been concerned with methodological issues. These issues have primarily centered around race of interviewer effects on blacks' responses to racially sensitive questions (Davis 1997; Davis and Silver 2003). Various studies have found that blacks give different responses to specific types of questions based on whom they perceive to be the interviewer. When looking at responses to questions dealing with race and the evaluation of political elites and institutions in the 1984 pre- and post- National Black Election Study, Davis (1997) found that blacks who were interviewed by whites in that survey were more likely to give contradictory evaluations of both the Democratic and Republican parties and to Ronald Reagan and Jesse Jackson when compared to responses given by blacks who were interviewed by other blacks.

Davis also estimates shifts in attitudes when the racial identity of interviewers is evaluated from the first wave of respondents (preelection survey) to the second wave of respondents (post-election). He discovers that "the most dramatic adjustment in African Americans' political beliefs occurs when the interviewer changes from African American to white, when there is a different white interviewer, and when the interviewer is the same white interviewer from the first wave." The contradictory findings in black attitudes that Davis finds when blacks perceive that whites are interviewing them are the result of African Americans being "pressured by white interviewers to conceal their true political beliefs to the extent that they would disassociate themselves from black issues, and alternatively, appear more docile and accommodating" (1997, 320).

## FUTURE RESEARCH: LINKED FATE AND THE
## EMERGING FLUIDITY OF BLACK IDENTITIES

The election of the nation's first black president will shape black public opinion for years to come. Obama's campaign style and his campaign's theme of national unity over racial, ethnic, and religious differences resonated with blacks, as it did for most Americans. Obama's diverse background—being the son of a man from Kenya and a (white) woman from Kansas—symbolizes the fluidity of black identities in contemporary

American life. These emerging differences will have implications for understanding black public opinion in the future.

Thus, innovative research on black public opinion must confront the changing demographics of the black population and the multiplicity of ways in which people of African ancestry in the United States have choice in defining themselves. Immigration of people of African descent from the continent of Africa, the Caribbean, and from South America is beginning to redefine what it means to be an African American in the twenty-first century. Similarly, a black identity is increasingly not the only self-described primary identity that people of African descent embrace. For many black women, both gender and race stand at the intersection of their primary identities and researchers have still not empirically untangled whether a black identity or a gender identity or a combination of both identities has implications for black women's political behavior.

Few surveys on black public opinion allow black respondents to state the choice of their primary identity in opinion surveys. The approach of survey research on the black experience oftentimes assumes that respondents' self-described social identity is primarily black. Not only do blacks have a racial identity, they also have other social identities that might relate to their religion, sexuality, social class, or sense of national identity. Though these social identities might be less politically salient than racial identities given the history and the continuation of racial conflict in the United States, for some segments of the black population other social identities may have primacy over racial identities. Asking respondents about their commitments or attachments to non-black social identities would provide a more contextual perspective on the theory and the measurement of linked fate as well as other measures of group solidarity.

Findings from the ABC News Polling Unit/Columbia University's Center on African-American Politics 2008 Black Politics Survey provide a glimpse into the complexity of blacks' commitment to linked fate and the social identities and values that might compete, collide, or counter blacks' commitment to a sense of linked fate. In addition to the standard question on linked fate, the survey asked the following questions:

1. Do you feel you have more in common with other [people in self-described social class] or more in common with other blacks no matter your social class?
2. Do you agree or disagree with the following statement?: Blacks should stop thinking of themselves as a group and think more of themselves as individuals.
3. In your own personal identity do you think of yourself as Black first, as an American first, what?

As has been documented in other surveys, about 64 percent of blacks in the ABC/Columbia University Black Politics Survey report that what happens to other blacks will also affect them, an indication that the bonds of linked fate among blacks remain strong.

However, responses from the other three questions indicate complexity in the concept of linked fate. When asked the question about commonality with people of their race or social class, a majority reported being connected more with their social class (60 percent) than fellow blacks (36 percent). Thus, nearly the same percentage of blacks that felt that their fates were linked to other blacks also felt that they had more in common with people of their social class than their racial group.

Another counterintuitive finding is the proportion of blacks who think blacks as a group should think of themselves as a group or as individuals. Nearly half—49 percent—of blacks in the survey agree that blacks should think of themselves as individuals rather than as part of a group (48 percent disagree). Thus, a large portion of the black population thinks that its destiny is linked with other blacks but nearly half think that blacks should think of themselves as individuals. This suggests that linked fate might be more than a measure of group solidarity; it might also reflect what many respondents see as the realities of racial discrimination that links them to other blacks as well as believing in the values of individualism that are so prevalent in American society. Lastly, the question of which personal identity comes first—being black or being American—reveals that African Americans are divided on which matters most. Forty-six percent of blacks answered that they saw themselves as American first, 45 percent viewed themselves as black first, and 5 percent volunteered to report that both identities mattered equally in thinking about their personal identity. Unraveling the primacy of various social identities beyond race that are important to blacks' social identities would provide more nuance to the role that linked fate plays in black public opinion.

New developments in this aspect of research in black public opinion will depend on scholars in the field developing new survey instruments. Developing new survey instruments also means that there need to be more academic surveys devoted to black and/or minority political attitudes. Though the University of Michigan's Program on Black America produced some path-breaking surveys during the presidential election years of 1984, 1988, and 1996, national surveys that focus on the political values, beliefs, and behaviors of blacks are few and far between. If the field of black public opinion is to sustain its vibrancy, this problem will have to be remedied.

## References

ABERBACH, J. D., and WALKER, J. 1970. The Meaning of Black Power: A Comparison of White and Black Interpretations of a Political Slogan. *American Political Science Review*, 64 (June), 367–88.

ALLEN, R. L., DAWSON, M. C., and BROWN, R. E. 1989. A Schema-Based Approach to Modeling an African-American Racial Belief System. *American Political Science Review*, 83/2 (June), 421–41.

BRINK, W., and HARRIS, L. 1964. *The Negro Revolution in America*. New York: Simon & Schuster.

BROWN, R. A., and SHAW, T. C. 2002. Separate Nations: Two Attitudinal Dimensions of Black Nationalism. *Journal of Politics*, 64 (Feb.), 22–44.

CALHOUN-BROWN, A. 1996. African American Churches and Political Mobilization: The Psychological Impact of Organizational Resources. *Journal of Politics*, 58: 935–53.

COHEN, C. 1999. *The Boundaries of Black Politics: AIDS and the Breakdown of Black Politics.* Chicago: University of Chicago Press.

DAVIS, D. W. 1997. The Direction of Race of Interviewer Effects among African-Americans: Donning the Black Mask. *American Journal of Political Science,* 41: 309–22.

—— and BROWN, R. E. 2002. The Antipathy of Black Nationalism: Behavioral and Attitudinal Consequences of an African American Ideology. *American Journal of Political Science,* 46: 239–53.

—— and DAVENPORT, C. 1997. The Political and Social Relevancy of Malcolm X: The Stability of Black Political Attitudes. *Journal of Politics,* 59: 550–64.

—— and SILVER, B. D. 2003. Stereotype Threat and Race of Interviewer Effects in a Survey on Political Knowledge. *American Journal of Political Science,* 47: 33–45.

DAWSON, M. C. 1994. *Behind the Mule: Race and Class in African-American Politics.* Princeton: Princeton University Press.

—— 2001. *Black Visions: The Roots of Contemporary African-American Political Ideologies.* Chicago: University of Chicago Press.

—— BROWN, R. E., and ALLEN, R. E. 1990. Racial Belief Systems, Religious Guidance, and African American Political Participation. *National Review of Political Science,* 2: 22–44.

GAY, C. 2004. Putting Race in Context: Identifying the Environmental Determinants of Black Racial Attitudes. *American Political Science Review,* 98: 547–62.

—— and TATE, K. 1998. Doubly Bound: The Impact of Gender and Race on the Politics of Black Women. *Political Psychology,* 19: 169–84.

GOLDMAN, P. 1970. *Report from Black America.* Simon & Schuster.

HAJNAL, Z. L., and LEE, T. 2007. When and Why Do African Americans Not Identify as Democrats? (Sept.). At ⟨http://ssrn.com/abstract=1012638⟩. Accessed Nov. 5, 2010.

HARRIS, F. C. 1999. *Something Within: Religion in African-American Political Activism.* New York: Oxford University Press.

—— 2006. It Takes a Tragedy to Arouse Them: Collective Memory and Collective Action during the Civil Rights Movement. *Social Movement Studies,* 5 (May), 19–43.

HARRIS-LACEWELL, M. 2004. *Barbershops, Bibles, and BET: Everyday Talk and Black Political Thought.* Princeton: Princeton University Press.

HENRY, P. J., and SEARS, D. O. 2002. The 2000 Symbolic Racism Scale. *Political Psychology,* 23 (June), 253–83.

HOCHSCHILD, J. 1995. *Facing Up to the American Dream: Race, Class, and the Soul of a Nation.* Princeton: Princeton University Press.

JUNN, J., and MASUOKA, N. 2008. Asian American Identity: Shared Racial Status and Political Context. *Perspectives on Politics,* 6: 729–40.

KINDER, D. R., and SANDERS, L. M. 1996. *Divided by Color: Racial Politics and Democratic Ideals.* Chicago: University of Chicago Press.

McCLAIN, P. D., CAREW, J. J., WALTON, E., JR., and WATTS, C. A. 2009. Group Membership, Group Identity and Group Consciousness: Evolving Racial Identity in American Politics. *Annual Review of Political Science,* 12 (June), 471–85.

MANSBRIDGE, J., and TATE, K. 1992. Race Trumps Gender: The Thomas Nomination in the Black Community. *PS: Political Science and Politics,* 25: 488–92.

MARX, G. T. 1967. *Protest and Prejudice: A Study of Belief in the Black Community.* New York: Harper & Row.

Masuoka, N. 2006. Together They Become One: Examining the Predictors of Panethnic Group Consciousness among Asian Americans and Latinos. *Social Science Quarterly*, 87/5: 993–1011.

Matthews, D. R., and Prothro, J. W. 1966. *Negroes and the New Southern Politics*. New York: Harcourt, Brace, and World.

National Advisory Commission on Civil Disorders. 1968. *Report*. New York: Bantam Books.

Price, M. T. 2009. *Dreaming Blackness: Black Nationalism and African-American Public Opinion*. New York: New York University Press.

Reed, A. 1986. *The Jesse Jackson Phenomenon: The Crisis of Purpose in Afro-American Politics*. New Haven: Yale University Press.

Schuman, H., Steeh, C., Bobo, L., and Krysan, M. 1997. *Racial Attitudes in America: Trends and Interpretations*. Cambridge, MA: Harvard University Press.

Sears, D. O., and Henry, P. J. 2003. The Origins of Symbolic Racism. *Journal of Personality and Social Psychology*, 85: 259–75.

Sigelman, L., and Welch, S. 1991. *Black Americans' View of Racial Inequality: The Dream Deferred*. New York: Cambridge University Press.

Shingles, R. D. 1981. Black Consciousness and Political Participation: The Missing Link. *American Political Science Review*, 75: 76–81.

Simien, E. M. 2006. *Black Feminist Voices in Politics*. Albany: State University of New York Press.

Simpson, A. 1998. *The Tie that Binds: Identity and Political Attitudes in the Post-Civil Rights Generation*. New York: New York University Press.

Sniderman, P. M., and Piazza, T. 1993. *The Scar of Race*. Cambridge, MA: Harvard University Press.

—— —— 2002. *Black Pride and Black Prejudice*. Princeton: Princeton University Press.

Tate, K. 1994. *From Protest to Politics: The New Black Voters in American Elections*. Cambridge, MA: Harvard University Press, Russell Sage Foundation.

—— 2004. Political Incorporation and Critical Transformation of Black Public Opinion. *Du Bois Review*, 1: 345–59.

CHAPTER 31

·····································································

# LATINO PUBLIC OPINION

·····································································

RODOLFO O. DE LA GARZA
SEUNG-JIN JANG

SINCE the 1990s there has been a continuing increase in the study of Latino public opinion. Rapid population growth fueled by immigration has led many to expect that Latinos would soon constitute a significant voting bloc with distinct preferences, which in turn made closely monitoring their opinions an important staple in both academic and practical worlds. Successive large-scale opinion polls since the 1990s have helped scholars to accumulate a good deal of knowledge on their opinions on public issues. Among others, two nationally representative surveys of Latinos stand out as important watersheds in understanding Latino public opinion. The Latino National Political Survey (LNPS) 1989–90 was the first comprehensive effort to collect basic data describing Latino political values, attitudes, and behavior. The LNPS was succeeded by the Latino National Survey (LNS) of 2006, which was modeled on the LNPS with noteworthy methodological advances and included respondents from more diverse nationalities. In this respect, a close examination of changes and continuities between the LNPS and the LNS, along with other national surveys of Latinos since the late 1990s (Kaiser Family Foundation and Pew Hispanic Center 2002; Pew Hispanic Center 2006; *Washington Post*, Kaiser, and Harvard 1999), offers a valuable insight into understanding the components and evolution of recent Latino public opinion.

## THE GENERAL CONTOUR OF
## LATINO PUBLIC OPINION

·····································································

The LNPS revealed two important patterns that characterize Latino public opinion. First, though Latinos from different countries of origin may not constitute a single cohesive political community, they have much in common regarding their views of key political issues. Regardless of national origin, Latinos tend to place similar issues on the national and local public agendas. And significant majorities of each group call for increased government involvement to address those issues, even at the cost of higher taxes on themselves. Second, despite their general liberal position on a broad range of policy issues, the majority of respondents, regardless of national origin, identify themselves as moderate to conservative (de la Garza, DeSipio, et al. 1992).

What is especially striking from findings of the LNPS is how stable they have been over time. The Latino population is in constant transformation because of continuous inflows of immigrants. For instance, 54.3 percent of all respondents in the LNS are new immigrants who first arrived to live in the US after the LNPS was completed. In addition, the ethnic composition of the Latino population has increasingly diversified: whereas the LNPS's sample of three ethnic groups—Mexicans, Cubans, and Puerto Ricans—was representative of more than 90 percent of the nation's Latino population at the time, the LNS sample includes respondents from the Dominican Republic, El Salvador, and other Central American countries yet it is representative only of 87.5 percent of the Latino population. In spite of the rapid expansion of the Latino population, however, the LNS and other surveys subsequent to the LNPS closely replicate the basic findings of the LNPS.

All available data sources since the LNPS have repeatedly confirmed Latinos' generally liberal stance on the government's role on many issues. In 1999 two out of every three Latinos preferred a larger government with many services to a smaller one with fewer services, and believed that the government should do everything possible to improve the standard of living of all Americans (*Washington Post*, Kaiser, and Harvard 1999). As recently as 2006, 90.8 percent of the LNS respondents supported the government's intervention in health care, and 87 percent were in favor of governmental income support. Overall, education, economic security, and health care are particularly salient issues for Latinos, and Latinos are significantly more supportive than whites of increased government spending on these issues (Griffin and Newman 2008).

In terms of protecting minority groups, Latino opinions fall in between whites and blacks. In general, blacks are the most supportive of affirmative action; Latino views tend to be similar to those of blacks, but more moderate; and whites often see many of the same problems but are generally less willing to support spending to alleviate those problems. The most vivid example can be found in California. In 1996, 62 percent of whites, compared to 27 percent of blacks and 32 percent of Latinos, supported Proposition 209, which targeted the ethnic and gender preferences embedded in California's affirmative action programs for public employment (Cain, Citrin, and Wong 2000). Latinos were significantly less likely than whites to support the initiative after differences in party affiliation and ideology were controlled for. When Proposition 209 passed, it was replaced by special outreach programs that sought to identify qualified minority applicants and encourage them to apply to colleges and public employment. These outreach programs generated the same pattern of racial divide: the overwhelming majority of blacks (87 percent) supported them, followed closely by Latinos (79 percent); on the other hand, only 54 percent of whites supported them (Hajnal and Baldassare 2001).

The pattern in the LNPS regarding ideological self-placement also remains intact after the influx of millions of new immigrants. In LNPS 40.7 percent of Mexicans, 47.7 percent of Puerto Ricans, and 54.1 percent of Cubans identified as ideologically conservative, while the proportion of self-professed liberals was less than 30 percent regardless of ethnic origin (de la Garza, DeSipio, et al. 1992); and this ideological distribution among different ethnic groups had hardly changed in LNS. In addition, Latinos from Central American countries, who were not included in the LNPS, also report a very strong conservative ideological stance. In comparison, the General Social Survey in 2006 shows that among blacks, who also register a generally liberal stance on the government's role on many issues, self-professed liberals outnumber conservatives by the ratio of 1.4 to 1.

These patterns raise two important questions about Latino public opinion. First, why, in spite of a generally liberal stance on the government's role, do many Latinos identify as moderates or conservatives? The second question is how this basic structure in Latino public opinion persists over time in spite of rapid changes in the demographic composition. In other words, why do new Latino immigrants quickly develop political and ideological preferences that closely resemble those of earlier immigrants and US-born Latinos?

In addressing these questions, one should first note that Latino public opinion does not seem to reflect something inherently "Latino." As a result of acculturation, Latino immigrants quickly absorb core American political values and are often more likely to endorse them than are Anglos (De La Garza, Falcon, and Garcia 1996). With respect to Spanish language retention, we observe the rapid linguistic assimilation of Latino immigrants from one generation to the next, regardless of age, educational attainment, or ethnic makeup of their residential environment (Citrin, Lerman, Murakami, and Pearson 2007). Nor is it the case that Latinos are exceptionally trustful of the government: though the foreign-born tend to be more trusting, Latinos become increasingly cynical about the government as they are incorporated into, or are exposed to, American society (Michelson 2003; Wenzel 2006).

Moreover, we cannot attribute Latino public opinion solely to their socioeconomic characteristics. Given that lower socioeconomic status is generally associated with higher levels of support for the expansion of governmental intervention, Latino support for an active governmental role can partly be explained by the socioeconomic disadvantages they face in the US; and continuous inflows of new immigrants keep the overall socioeconomic status of the Latino population at a lower level than that of the general population. However, research shows that the difference between Latino and Anglo support for an activist government does not disappear even after individual-level socioeconomic status is controlled for (Leal 2004; Griffin and Newman 2008). Income and education, the most prominent indicators of individual socioeconomic status, often do not have the expected effects on Latino policy views (Branton 2007).

Instead, Latino policy preferences seem to reflect their structural placement in American society, which is closely correlated with, but cannot necessarily be reduced to, traditional measures of socioeconomic status. For instance, variability in attitudes among Latinos exists as a function of generational status and acculturation. Support for government spending on services and policies that distribute benefits to immigrants, the needy, and minority groups is notably stronger among more recent immigrants and less acculturated Latinos (Branton 2007). Sanchez (2006) finds that group conscious-ness tends to have significant effects on Latino political attitudes, especially when the issue is closely tied to ethnicity. On the other hand, English-speaking Latinos, i.e., the more acculturated, show political attitudes and policy views that place them closer to Anglos than Spanish-speaking Latinos are (Hill and Moreno 2001).

If structural and socioeconomic conditions make Latinos generally liberal on the government's role and spending, then why do they not have a similar effect on Latinos' ideological self-placement? There is no evidence that this is because Latinos inter-pret ideology differently from non-Latinos. To the contrary, existing evidence indicates that ideological positions relate to issue preferences in ways that are quite similar in the Latino population and the rest of the public, and the same is true for subpopulations of Latinos (Uhlaner and Garcia 2002, 99).

Some argue that Latinos are conservative on moral and family-related issues, abortion being the most often cited example, and thus reluctant to identify themselves as ideologically liberal in spite of their support for strong government. However, although Latinos generally appear to oppose abortion, divorce, and homosexuality, the difference between Latinos and non-Latinos on these issues often disappears once individuals' socioeconomic status and other demographic factors are controlled for (Leal 2004). Not only do Latino attitudes toward abortion resemble those of the general population, they are influenced by the same variables as the general population (Bolks, Evans, Polinard, and Wrinkle 2000). In addition, while a large proportion of Catholics among Latinos often leads to the expectation of their strong pro-life position, it is committed Protestants, rather than Catholics, who are the staunchest opponents of abortion among the Latino population (Ellison, Echevarria, and Smith 2005). In short, while Latino attitudes toward moral and family-related issues may contribute to their self-professed conservatism, their effects seem to be limited.

One explanation for the mismatch between policy preferences and the liberal–conservative ideology, and for its persistence across generations of immigrants, is related to the way Latino immigrants are socialized into US politics. Many Latino immigrants experience their primary political socialization outside the US; after immi-gration, they are incorporated into US society through social and informational net-works in the ethnic communities (Portes and Rumbaut 2001). On the one hand, this implies that, even after a significant length of residence, many Latinos may not be knowledgeable about the political consequences of different ideological positions in the American political system. Consequently, in contrast to their policy preferences on concrete issues that directly affect them, Latinos' self-placement on a general ideologi-cal spectrum may reflect a high degree of uncertainty and ambivalence and is likely to show a weak correlation with their position on other concrete policy issues. On the other hand, the difference in the channel of political socialization implies that the prevailing attitudes and values of ethnic communities and other primary contacts have significant repercussions in the formation of political attitudes and values of new Latino immigrants (Uhlaner and Garcia 2005). In other words, the basic structure of Latino public opinion has been stable over time because new immigrants are constrained to learn and adapt to policy preferences and the overall ideological leaning of their more established co-ethnics.

# TRANSNATIONALISM AND LATINO VIEWS ON FOREIGN POLICIES

There is widespread suspicion that Latinos retain political loyalty to their country of origin, which impedes their political incorporation into the United States and undermines American national unity (for example, Huntington 2004). Such suspicion is supported by high rates of dual citizenship among Latino immigrants as well as extensive interaction between immigrants and their home country. According to the LNS, between 30 and 50 percent of Latinos frequently contact and regularly visit friends and family members in their country of origin, send money back, and even own land, a house, or a business there; and they maintain these relationships in spite of the fact that only a small number of them plan to move back to their country of origin permanently.

Such patterns notwithstanding, there is little evidence that transnational ties impede political incorporation and civic engagement among Latino immigrants. To the contrary, naturalization rates are higher among immigrants from countries that recognize dual nationality than among those from countries that do not: dual nationality lowers the psychological costs associated with choosing a new political identity by allowing immigrants to have legal rights as nationals in their country of origin while exercising political rights in their new country of residence (Jones-Correa 1998, 2001). Beyond naturalization, some studies find that dual nationals are significantly less likely than their US national counterparts to be proficient in English and to be registered or to have voted in a US election (Cain and Doherty 2006; Staton, Jackson, and Canache 2007); however, these negative relationships seem to reflect the fact that dual nationals are generally concentrated in older and first-generation immigrants. In addition, there is evidence that home country ties, particularly transnational organizational involvements, offer an opportunity for political socialization and civic engagement among Latino immigrants in the US (Desipio 2006; DeSipio, Pachón, de la Garza, and Lee 2003).

Likewise, there is no evidence that Latinos maintain political loyalty to their country of origin and become an "ethnic lobby" mobilized around policy issues affecting their country of origin (De La Garza and Desipio 1998; de la Garza, Pachón, Orozco, and Pantoja 2000). While between one third and almost half of Latinos follow homeland politics to some degree, only a very small number are concerned primarily about politics in their home country rather than politics in the US (de la Garza,

Hernandez, et al. 1997) or are actually engaged in electoral or partisan activities in their home country (DeSipio, Pachón, de la Garza, and Lee 2003). Even the activities of Latino political and civic organizations whose agenda is focused mostly toward their homeland help develop the social and leadership capital that facilitate the incorporation of Latino immigrants into the American political system, rather than leading to a denial of loyalty to the host country (De La Garza and Hazan 2003).

Regarding specific issues related to US policy vis-à-vis Latin-American countries, Latinos from the target country may show slightly distinctive attitudes compared to other Latino ethnic groups or to non-Latinos, but the differences generally indicate that they are more supportive of, rather than opposed to, US foreign policies toward Latin America. For instance, when the LNPS asked about Mexican economic problems, 85 percent of Mexican Americans, 90 percent of other Latinos, and 86 percent of Anglos agreed that government corruption and inefficiency in Mexico was the main cause of its crisis. Regarding policy issues toward Puerto Rico and Cuba, Puerto Ricans are the least likely group to support the complete independence of Puerto Rico, and Cubans are the most strongly opposed to reestablishing diplomatic relations with Cuba, while opinions among Latinos closely resemble those of non-Latinos (de la Garza, DeSipio, et al. 1992); in addition, it is noteworthy that changes in attitudes toward both issues since the LNPS have moved both Latinos and non-Latinos in the same direction (*Washington Post*, Kaiser, and Harvard 1999).

Like Anglos, the majority of Latinos oppose relaxing restrictions on immigration in general and to special treatment for immigrants from Latin America (de la Garza, DeSipio, et al. 1992; Kaiser Family Foundation and Pew Hispanic Center 2002). However, the fact that many Latinos seem to oppose increased immigration does not mean they are unfavorable toward immigrants (De La Garza and Desipio 1998). While Latinos may resemble Anglos in their opposition to more immigration and support for stricter border control, a majority of Latinos support the extension of amnesty and government assistance to undocumented immigrants. For instance, when asked about the preferred policy on undocumented immigration, 42 percent of LNS respondents supported the immediate legalization of all undocumented immigrants and 31.7 percent supported a guest worker program leading eventually to legalization. Similarly, most Latinos agreed that undocumented immigrants should be allowed to stay in the US permanently and have a chance to become citizens if they meet a certain residency requirement (Pew Hispanic Center 2006). In general, Latinos support policies that facilitate the social and political incorporation of Latino immigrants, including the expansion of government assistance for immigrants, the provision of government services in Spanish, and bilingual education programs (de la Garza, DeSipio, et al. 1992; Schmidt 1997; Uhlaner and Garcia 2002).

Overall, Latinos do not seem to hold distinctive views about US policies toward Latin-American countries or about its foreign agenda in general.[1] In fact, foreign policy

---

[1] Regarding the latter point, Latino views on the most important foreign policy issue at this time—the Iraq War—are very similar to those of blacks. For instance, in the 2008 National Election Study, 73.6

perspectives of Latino opinion leaders in the US are not congruent with the official perspectives of most Latin American governments; and, while Latino opinion leaders show a greater interest in elevating the importance of Latin-American countries, most of them believe they must work within the framework and bounds of official US foreign policy (Pachón, De La Garza, and Pantoja 2000). Simply put, Latinos may influence policies that concern their countries of origin, but this influence will be shaped not out of a loyalty to their country of origin but instead out of their own interests in US policy (De La Garza and Desipio 1998).

## EFFECTS OF LATINO PUBLIC OPINION: PARTISANSHIP AND VOTE CHOICES

The majority of Latinos identify with the Democratic Party, with the notable exception of Cubans, who have historically preferred the Republican Party. This pattern of partisanship among Latinos is generally attributed to the perception that the Democratic Party is more supportive of policies favoring minorities and other disadvantaged groups and to the Republican Party's strong anti-communist stance, which is especially salient to Cubans but not to other Latinos (Cain, Kiewiet, and Uhlaner 1991; de la Garza, DeSipio, et al. 1992). Although the LNS and other national surveys of Latinos since the LNPS we considered show that the proportion of Democratic identifiers has somewhat decreased, with corresponding increases in the number of Independents, Latino Democrats consistently outnumber Latino Republicans except among Cubans. Latinos from Central American countries, who were not included in the LNPS, also strongly identify themselves with the Democratic Party.

Alvarez and García Bedolla (2003) argue that Latino partisanship is more explicitly political than that of Anglos. From a national survey of Latino likely voters in 2000, they find that political ideology and issue preferences strongly predict Latino partisanship; in contrast, economic factors such as income generally have a weak impact on Latino partisanship. Many Latinos perceive the Democratic Party as more credible and supportive of their interests on issues that matter to Latinos (Nicholson and Segura 2005). More education leads to higher support for the Democratic Party as it helps Latinos to understand which party is better for their group (Alvarez and Bedolla 2003; Uhlaner and Garcia 2005). In this respect, the strong presence of the Republican Party among Cubans can be attributed to the fact that their status as refugees has insulated them from various policies directed against immigrants and offered them certain benefits independently of affirmative action programs (Uhlaner and Garcia 2005, 80).

percent of Latinos say the number of troops in Iraq should be decreased, compared to 71.2 percent of blacks and 67 percent of whites. Similarly, 65.4 percent of Latinos favor setting a deadline for withdrawing all US troops from Iraq, compared to 67.6 percent of blacks and 45.2 percent of whites.

The political nature of Latino partisanship is particularly notable when they feel threatened by the political environment surrounding the issues salient to the Latino community. For instance, in California during the mid-1990s, debates on affirmative action, immigration, and welfare reform drove a great number of new Latino voters to the Democratic side, which overwhelmed the effect of changing levels of income and the relative religiosity of the Latino community that might potentially have benefited Republicans (Barreto and Woods 2005; Segura, Falcón, and Pachón 1997).

Nevertheless, most empirical models of Latino partisanship find that the effect of national origin still persists even after a series of political, social, and demographic characteristics of an individual are controlled for. However, one should not attribute independent status to national origin, which easily leads to making ethnicity an unchanging attribute rather than a fluid characteristic (De La Garza 2004, 103). Rather, national origin may be acting as a proxy for each group's historically unique migration and settlement experiences (Alvarez and Bedolla 2003). Distinctive patterns of partisanship across different Latino ethnic groups are continuously reproduced as new immigrants learn the political experience of their group over time from the prevailing partisanship of their neighbors and other primary contacts (Uhlaner and Garcia 2005), which makes Latino partisanship less variable over time and across generations.

A number of empirical findings in fact support the intergenerational transmission of Latino partisanship. For instance, length of residence in the United States is associated with a greater propensity to identify as a Democrat, controlling for other changes in social and demographic characteristics (Cain, Kiewiet, and Uhlaner 1991; Uhlaner and Garcia 2005). A survey of Cuban Americans in south Florida shows that those who are outside of the region's ethnic "enclave" and who receive news primarily from English-language media are significantly less likely to support the exile ideology and anti-Castro ideology, both of which are important in the support for the Republican Party among Cuban Americans (Girard and Grenier 2008). In each ethnic group, Latinos whose social interactions stay more within the group are more likely to share the dominant partisanship, whereas those whose social interactions move outside of the group are more likely to identify with the minority party (Uhlaner and Garcia 2005).

In line with their partisanship, Latinos have voted for the Democratic candidate in most recent elections. However, this does not imply that Latino voters cast their ballots blindly for one party over the other. Research shows that Latino vote choices in national elections are significantly influenced by policy preferences (Abrajano, Alvarez, and Nagler 2008; Barreto et al. 2002). A survey of Latino registered voters prior to the 2000 presidential election found that respondents who ranked education, race relations, or economy as the most important issue facing the Latino community were much more likely to support Gore, while Bush garnered large support from those concerned about moral issues (Barreto et al. 2002). Similarly, analysis of exit polls after the 2004 presidential election found that Latino voters who listed health care, the economy, and education as their most important issue were more likely to vote for Kerry, but those who ranked moral issues or terrorism as their most important issue were more likely to vote for Bush controlling for other factors (Abrajano, Alvarez, and Nagler 2008). In other words, the salience of specific issues to individual Latino voters frames their vote choice.

Meanwhile, issue-based voting is not universal among Latino voters. Nicholson, Pantoja, and Segura (2006) show that policy issues play an important role in shaping voting preferences among politically knowledgeable voters, while among uninformed voters, symbolism and long-standing partisan preferences matter most. In the 2000 presidential election, a significant majority of those Latinos with a presidential preference articulated issue preferences that were consistent with the beliefs of their preferred candidate, and the level of issue agreement greatly increased among better-informed voters (Nicholson, Pantoja, and Segura 2006). Abrajano (2005) similarly finds that Latinos with lower levels of education are more likely to evaluate a candidate using personalistic or non-policy campaign messages, while better-educated Latino voters are more likely to use informationally demanding factors such as candidates' issue positions and ideology.

What do these studies on Latino partisanship and vote choice suggest with respect to the Republican efforts to attract Latino voters? In past elections, Republicans have made significant efforts to create inroads into the Latino electorate. However, there is little evidence that the Latino electorate has abandoned its historic attachment to the Democratic Party. In most recent elections, Latino voters have remained remarkably stable in their partisan preferences, preferring Democrats over Republicans by a margin of two to one or greater, both nationally and in most states. The Democratic advantage in partisanship remains strong across all nationality groups except Cubans, and even Cubans show signs of drifting into the Democratic column as the generation that came of age in opposition to the Castro revolution is gradually replaced by younger cohorts (Gimpel and Kaufmann 2001). Occasional improvements in the Latino GOP vote with the Bush candidacy seem to have more to do with low turnout and demobilization but not with political conversion (De La Garza and Cortina 2007; Leal, Nuño, et al. 2008).

Republican strategists have claimed that Latinos are ready for conversion because of their socioeconomic mobility and religiosity. However, as in the case of Latino partisanship, upward mobility in terms of income does not have a statistically significant effect on the odds of voting for the Republican candidate (Abrajano, Alvarez, and Nagler 2008; De La Garza and Cortina 2007). Although some studies find that better-educated Latinos are more likely to vote for Republicans, this is not necessarily welcome news for Republicans: it suggests that as the Latino electorate grows because of new young voters and naturalized immigrants, the pool of uneducated voters will expand much more rapidly than will the ranks of the better-educated (De La Garza and Cortina 2007, 217). On the other hand, there is some evidence of a religious gap within the Latino electorate. Latino non-Catholic Christians, especially those who are evangelical or born-again, are part of a Republican coalition of religious voters (Kelly and Kelly 2005; Leal, Barreto, et al. 2005; Lee and Pachón 2007; McDaniel and Ellison 2008). However, one should note that non-Catholic Christians constitute less than 20 percent of the Latino electorate as a great majority of Latino voters are Catholic, who are more

newcomers, which in turn may strongly influence the subsequent development of their political attitudes and preferences. However, in contrast to recent attention devoted to how racial contexts influence the political participation of Latinos (for example, Jang 2009; Leighley 2001), most studies on Latino public opinion have focused on individual-level demographic and political characteristics and have paid little attention to how they interact with contextual factors in influencing Latino public opinion.

In conclusion, Latino public opinion shares much with the national mainstream while retaining salient ethnic distinctions. The balance between the two will reflect the societal contexts within which Latinos are socialized. The evidence to date suggests they will continue to learn and share the values and preferences of the mainstream, but the pace and extent of this process will depend on how the mainstream welcomes them. In our judgment, thanks in part to the fact that many Latinos have already become part of the mainstream, this process of incorporation will continue even as Latinos maintain distinctive ethnic, cultural, and political characteristics.

# REFERENCES

ABRAJANO, M. A. 2005. Who Evaluates a Presidential Candidate by Using Non-Policy Campaign Messages? *Political Research Quarterly*, 58/1: 55–67.

—— ALVAREZ, R. M., and NAGLER, J. 2008. The Hispanic Vote in the 2004 Presidential Election: Insecurity and Moral Concerns. *Journal of Politics*, 70/2: 368–82.

ALVAREZ, R. M., and BEDOLLA, L. G. 2003. The Foundations of Latino Voter Partisanship: Evidence from the 2000 Election. *Journal of Politics*, 65/1: 31–49.

BARRETO, M. A., and WOODS, N. D. 2005. Latino Voting Behavior in an Anti-Latino Political Context: The Case of Los Angeles County. In *Diversity in Democracy: Minority Representation in the United States*, ed. G. M. Segura and S. Bowler. Charlottesville: University of Virginia Press.

—— DE LA GARZA, R. O., LEE, J., RYU, J., and PACHÓN, H. P. 2002. *Latino Voter Mobilization in 2000: A Glimpse into Latino Policy and Voting Preferences*. Report No. 2. Claremont, CA: Tomás Rivera Policy Institute.

BOLKS, S. M., EVANS, D., POLINARD, J. L., and WRINKLE, R. D. 2000. Core Beliefs and Abortion Attitudes: A Look at Latinos. *Social Science Quarterly*, 81/3: 253–60.

BRANTON, R. 2007. Latino Attitudes toward Various Areas of Public Policy: The Importance of Acculturation. *Political Research Quarterly*, 60/2: 293–303.

CAIN, B. E., and DOHERTY, B. 2006. The Impact of Dual Nationality on Political Participation. In *Transforming Politics, Transforming America: The Political and Civic Incorporation of Immigrants in the United States*, ed. T. Lee, S. K. Ramakrishnan, and R. Ramírez. Charlottesville: University of Virginia Press.

—— CITRIN, J., and WONG, C. 2000. *Ethnic Context, Race Relations, and California Politics*. San Francisco: Public Policy Institute of California.

—— KIEWIET, D. R., and UHLANER, C. J. 1991. The Acquisition of Partisanship by Latinos and Asian Americans. *American Journal of Political Science*, 35/2: 390–422.

CITRIN, J., LERMAN, A., MURAKAMI, M., and PEARSON, K. 2007. Testing Huntington: Is Hispanic Immigration a Threat to American Identity? *Perspectives on Politics*, 5/1: 31–48.

DE LA GARZA, R. O. 2004. Latino Politics. *Annual Review of Political Science*, 7: 91–123.

—— and CORTINA, J. 2007. Are Latinos Republicans But Just Don't Know It? The Latino Vote in the 2000 and 2004 Presidential Elections. *American Politics Research*, 35/2: 202–23.

—— and DESIPIO, L. 1998. Interests Not Passions: Mexican-American Attitudes toward Mexico, Immigration from Mexico, and Other Issues Shaping US–Mexico Relations. *International Migration Review*, 32/2: 401–22.

—— and HAZAN, M. 2003. *Looking Backward, Moving Forward: Mexican Organizations in the U.S. as Agents of Incorporation and Dissociation*. Claremont, CA: Tomás Rivera Policy Institute.

—— DESIPIO, L., GARCIA, F. C., GARCIA, J., and FALCON, A. 1992. *Latino Voices: Mexican, Puerto Rican, and Cuban Perspectives on American Politics*. Boulder, CO: Westview Press.

—— FALCON, A., and GARCIA, F. C. 1996. Will the Real Americans Please Stand Up: Anglo and Mexican-American Support of Core American Political Values. *American Journal of Political Science*, 40/2: 335–51.

—— HERNANDEZ, J., FALCON, A., GARCIA, F. C., and GARCIA, J. 1997. Mexican, Puerto Rican, and Cuban Foreign Policy Perspectives: A Test of Competing Explanations. In *Pursuing Power: Latinos and the Political System*, ed. F. C. Garcia. Notre Dame, IN: University of Notre Dame Press.

—— PACHÓN, H. P., OROZCO, M., and PANTOJA, A. D. 2000. Family Ties and Ethnic Lobbies. In *Latinos and U.S. Foreign Policy: Representing the Homeland?* ed. R. O. de la Garza and H. P. Pachón. Lanham, MD: Rowman & Littlefield.

DESIPIO, L. 2006. Transnational Politics and Civic Engagement: Do Home-Country Political Ties Limit Latino Immigrant Pursuit of U.S. Civic Engagement and Citizenship? In *Transforming Politics, Transforming America: The Political and Civic Incorporation of Immigrants in the United States*, ed. T. Lee, S. K. Ramakrishnan, and R. Ramírez. Charlottesville: University of Virginia Press.

—— PACHÓN, H. P., DE LA GARZA, R. O., and LEE, J. 2003. *Immigrant Politics at Home and Abroad: How Latino Immigrants Engage the Politics of their Home Communities and the United States*. Claremont, CA: Tomás Rivera Policy Institute.

ELLISON, C. G., ECHEVARRIA, S., and SMITH, B. 2005. Religion and Abortion Attitudes among U.S. Hispanics: Findings from the 1990 Latino National Political Survey. *Social Science Quarterly*, 86/1: 192–208.

FLORES, M., and MCCOMBS, M. E. 2008. Latino Agenda-Setting Effect on the 2004 Presidential Election. In *The Mass Media and Latino Politics: Studies of U.S. Media Content, Campaign Strategies and Survey Research 1984–2004*, ed. F. A. Subervi-Vélez. New York: Routledge.

GIMPEL, J. G., and KAUFMANN, K. 2001. *Impossible Dream or Distant Reality? Republican Efforts to Attract Latino Voters*. Washington, DC: Center for Immigration Studies.

GIRARD, C., and GRENIER, G. J. 2008. Insulating an Ideology: The Enclave Effect on South Florida's Cuban Americans. *Hispanic Journal of Behavioral Sciences*, 30/4: 530–43.

GRIFFIN, J. D., and NEWMAN, B. 2008. *Minority Report: Evaluating Political Equality in America*. Chicago: University of Chicago Press.

HAJNAL, Z., and BALDASSARE, M. 2001. *Finding Common Ground: Racial and Ethnic Attitudes in California*. San Francisco: Public Policy Institute of California.

election. All data reported here are weighted to represent the national population of Asian Americans.

# ASIAN-AMERICAN PARTISANSHIP

When we turn to the 2008 NAAS, the findings mostly confirm the general patterns highlighted in voting behavior from exit poll data. Party identification here is defined in the conventional manner, in seven categories ranging from strong Democrats on one end of the spectrum to strong Republicans on the other. A disproportionate number of Asian Americans who can place themselves on the conventional seven-point party identification scale identify as Democrats. Combining self-identified Democrats together with Independents who report leaning Democrat, our initial estimate suggests that fully 61 percent of our sample can be classified as Democrats. By contrast, 28 percent are classifiable as Republicans and only 11 percent as pure Independents.

In addition, there are also interesting and important ethnic group differences in party identification. Most groups identify as Democrats, with Asian Indians as the most heavily Democratic among the groups in our sample (the split between self-identified Democrats and Democrat leaners and self-identified Republicans and Republican leaners for Asian Indians is 72 percent to 18 percent). Other groups are also unmistakably, if less strongly, Democratic: 70 percent of Japanese, 68 percent of Koreans, 62 percent of Chinese, and 58 percent of Filipinos are Democrats or Democrat leaners; the proportion of Republicans and Republican leaners for these ethnic subgroups, respectively, is 22 percent, 31 percent, 19 percent, and 33 percent. The one group that stands out here is Vietnamese. Fully 54 percent of Vietnamese identify as Republicans or Republican leaners, with only 34 percent identifying as Democrats or Democrat leaners.

We have thus far highlighted two defining features of Asian-American partisanship: its contingency across time and data sources and its partiality for the Democratic Party in the dyadic choice between identifying with the Republican or Democratic parties. But these features, important as they are, mask another important feature: the tendency of large segments of the population to remain outside the traditional US partisanship scale. While party identification is a mainstay among the native-born, for immigrants there is a critical prior question and they must first ponder what it means to be a partisan. The willingness to think in partisan terms—by which we mean the willingness to place oneself on a party identification spectrum at all—is a separate and important prior factor to the specific self-placement on the spectrum from strong Democratic to Independent to strong Republican identification.

This decision is relatively inconsequential when we consider the white or African-American populations. In the American National Election Study cumulative file from 1948 to 2004, less than 7 percent of the black and white sample across these years chose one of the following non-partisan responses—"no preference," "none," "neither," "other," "don't know"—or otherwise refused to answer questions. Thus, it is not surprising to find that most studies of partisanship simply dismiss this group as an anomaly, code them as missing, and drop them from analysis altogether.[5]

While the phenomenon of uncommitted and non-identifiers may be rare enough among whites and African Americans to treat as a residual response category, for immigrant-laden groups like Latinos and Asian Americans, defining oneself in terms of the two-party system is a challenging cognitive task (Lee and Hajnal forthcoming). In the 2006 LNS, fully 38 percent of respondents were uncommitted to a partisan category and non-partisans (non-identifiers and Independents, taken together) made up 55 percent of all responses.

These numbers are closely mirrored in the 2008 NAAS. Thus, perhaps the most pronounced finding on partisanship in the 2008 NAAS is that the modal respondent in our survey simply did not make head or tails of the conventional party identification question. As Table 32.1 shows, fully 34 percent of NAAS respondents indicated that they "do not think in these terms," where the terms of partisanship are self-identifying as a Republican, Democrat, or Independent. When "non-identifiers" are combined with those Asian Americans who identify as Independents, 55 percent of NAAS respondents did not identify as either a Democrat or a Republican. This tendency not to identify with a major party is quite pervasive across ethnic subgroups, moreover. The range of non-identifiers in the 2008 NAAS was between 28 percent among Japanese Americans and 40 percent among Chinese Americans, and the range of non-partisans ("non-identifiers" and Independents, together) was between 43 percent among Japanese Americans and 68 percent among Chinese Americans.

Table 32.1 Party identification, four categories, by ethnic origin group, 2008 (%)

| Category | Asian Indian | Chinese | Filipino | Japanese | Korean | Vietnamese | Total |
|---|---|---|---|---|---|---|---|
| Republican | 9 | 8 | 16 | 13 | 17 | 31 | 14 |
| Democrat | 35 | 25 | 34 | 40 | 38 | 19 | 31 |
| Independent | 22 | 28 | 18 | 16 | 11 | 18 | 20 |
| Non-identifier | 34 | 39 | 32 | 31 | 34 | 31 | 35 |

Source: 2008 National Asian American Survey.

[5] We refer interchangeably to those who opt for these "non-compliant" response categories— "no preference," "none," "neither," "other," "don't know," or some other mode of refusal to self-identify as "Democrat," "Republican," or "Independent"—as "uncommitteds" and "non-identifiers." We further refer to "non-partisans" as the larger set of individuals who are either non-identifiers or self-identify as Independents.

# ASIAN-AMERICAN OPINION
## ON POLITICAL ISSUES

There are few existing studies of Asian-American opinion on public issues in part because of the absence of reliable data sources, but also because until recently there was not substantial interest in the attitudes of this relatively small and geographically concentrated group of Americans. The racial and ethnic diversity of the US population is changing rapidly, however, and there is growing interest in the extent to which members of minority groups hold distinctive opinions on political issues. While we cannot answer these questions in comparison to other racial and ethnic groups, we can outline the basic contours of Asian-American opinion by examining data from the 2008 NAAS on the issues of health care, abortion, immigration policy, and US involvement in the war in Iraq.

Before proceeding with a discussion of the data, it is important to note two important characteristics about Asian Americans. Not only is the population growing rapidly and moving to geographic locations outside of traditional immigrant gateways, but barring any significant change to federal immigration policy in the US, the size and dispersion of the Asian-American population will grow exponentially. Opinion on political issues in the US might therefore vary systematically by generation of immigration or years in the United States for Asian Americans. Second, English is a second language for most Asian Americans, and fully 80 percent of adults are foreign-born. Many survey respondents may struggle with questions posed to them in English and, in addition, may be unfamiliar with political terms commonly used in public opinion surveys, such as "liberal" and "conservative." Thus, while mirroring the time-in-the-US distinction made above, there could be systematic differences in issue opinions when the questions are asked in the respondent's native language rather than in English.

The 2008 NAAS asked respondents whether or not they agreed or disagreed with a series of statements representing five policy issues. The first issue was US military involvement in the war in Iraq. Asked to say whether they agreed strongly, agreed somewhat, neither agreed nor disagreed, disagreed somewhat, or disagreed strongly, respondents answered about the statement: "The U.S. should get our military troops out of Iraq as soon as possible." Taken during the heat of the general election campaign in 2008, when the Iraq war was an important issue, Asian Americans responded with overwhelmingly strong support to end American involvement with 54 percent agreeing strongly and another 19 percent saying they agreed somewhat with this policy statement. In contrast, only 16 percent of Asian Americans said they disagreed somewhat or strongly with the statement that the US should remove military troops from Iraq as soon as possible. Just under 10 percent of the population refused or replied that they did not know in response to this question.

In terms of differences in responses by language of interview and years in the United States, those completing the survey in English were more likely (75 percent) to say they agreed strongly or somewhat with the policy position to remove American troops from Iraq than those who were asked in their native language (70 percent). The differences for native-born and years in the US, however, do not show variation across opinion on US military policy in Iraq.

In terms of support for universal health care, Asian Americans display strong positive sentiment toward this policy. We asked respondents the extent to which they agreed or disagreed with the statement "The federal government should guarantee health coverage for everyone." We found even stronger levels of support among Asian Americans for universal health care compared with the troop withdrawal question. More than eight in ten Asian Americans (60 percent agreed strongly and 23 percent agreed somewhat) supported this statement. Only 11 percent said they disagreed with the statement on universal health care, while 6 percent were uncommitted, and 3 percent refused or said they did not know. Just the reverse was true in terms of language of interview for this policy issue, and 88 percent of those completing the interview in an Asian language supported universal health care compared with 81 percent of respondents interviewed in English. There were also differences in terms of years in the US and native-born status, with second-generation respondents the least likely to support universal health care (77 percent)—while still overwhelmingly in support—than the 90 percent of respondents who had been in the US five years or less or 88 percent support among those in the US between five and fourteen years.

While Asian Americans may be "liberal" on issues such as health care, they are divided on whether abortion should be legal in all cases. Twenty percent agreed strongly with the statement, 19 percent agreed somewhat, while 18 percent said they neither agreed or disagreed. A substantial proportion of Asian Americans are opposed to abortion rights and 27 percent said they disagreed strongly with the statement that abortion should be legal in all cases while 17 percent said they disagreed somewhat. Eight percent of the population either refused to answer the question or said they did not know. Japanese Americans and Indian Americans were most strongly in favor, while Filipino Americans and Vietnamese Americans were most strongly opposed. In addition, among those who took the interview in English, 41 percent responded in favor of abortion rights in all cases, while a third (32 percent) of those interviewed in an Asian language replied favorably. Similarly, support for abortion rights was strongest among the native-born (50 percent) and weaker among the foreign-born, with little relationship to how many years they had been in the US.

Asian Americans are also divided on questions of immigration policy. Even though many Asian-American advocacy organizations are strongly in favor of a path to citizenship for unauthorized immigrants, more Asian Americans oppose the policy than support it. When they read the statement "The U.S. should provide a path to citizenship for people in this country illegally," 15 percent of Asian Americans said they agreed strongly and another 20 percent said they agreed somewhat. Ten percent refused to answer the question or said they did not know, while 15 percent replied by saying they neither agreed nor disagreed with the policy statement. There is strong opposition to this policy among Asian Americans, and 21 percent disagreed somewhat

MASUOKA, N. 2006. Together they Become One: Examining the Predictors of Panethnic Group Consciousness among Asian Americans and Latinos. *Social Science Quarterly*, 87/5: 993–1011.

NAKANISHI, D. T. 1991. The Next Swing Vote? Asian Pacific Americans and California Politics. In *Racial and Ethnic Politics in California*, ed. B. O. Jackson and M. B. Preston. Berkeley: Institute of Governmental Studies Press, University of California.

OKAMOTO, D. 2003. Toward a Theory of Panethnicity: Explaining Asian American Collective Action. *American Sociological Review*, 68: 811–42.

ONG, P., and NAKANISHI, D. T. 1996. Becoming Citizens, Becoming Voters. In *Reframing the Immigration Debate*, ed. B. O. Hing and R. Lee. Los Angeles: LEAP Asian Pacific American Public Policy Institute and UCLA Asian American Studies Center.

RAMAKRISHNAN, S. K. 2005. *Democracy in Immigrant America: Changing Demographics and Political Participation*. Stanford, CA: Stanford University Press.

—— WONG, J. S., LEE, T., and JUNN, J. 2009. Race-Based Considerations and the Obama Vote: Evidence from the 2008 National Asian American Survey. *Du Bois Review*, 6/1: 219–38.

RIM, K. H. 2009. Racial Context Effects and the Political Participation of Asian Americans. *American Politics Research*, 37/4: 569–92.

TAM, W. 1995. Asians—A Monolithic Voting Bloc? *Political Behavior*, 17: 223–49.

TUAN, M. 1996. *Forever Foreigners or Honorary Whites? The Asian Ethnic Experience Today*. New Brunswick, NJ: Rutgers University Press.

WONG, J. S. 2000. The Effects of Age and Political Exposure on the Development of Party Identification among Asian American and Latino Immigrants in the United States. *Political Behavior*, 22/4: 341–71.

—— 2006. *Democracy's Promise: Immigrant and American Civic Institutions*. Ann Arbor: University of Michigan Press.

—— RAMAKRISHNAN, S. K., LEE, T., and JUNN, J. 2010. *Asian American Political Participation: Emerging Constituents and their Political Identities*. Unpublished manuscript.

WU, F. H. 2002. *Yellow: Race in America beyond Black and White*. New York: Basic Books.

CHAPTER 33

.............................................................................................................

# A VINE WITH MANY BRANCHES

## Religion and Public Opinion Research

.............................................................................................................

AIMEE E. BARBEAU
CARIN ROBINSON
CLYDE WILCOX

It is clear that political leaders and parties believe that religion influences public opinion. The 2008 presidential candidates debated the theory of evolution, made speeches detailing their faith and its implications for policy, mounted massive outreach efforts toward particular religious constituencies, and worried as videos of a sermon circulated on YouTube (Smidt, den Dulk, Froehle, and Penning 2010). In 2010 politicians and activists used religious language and arguments in debates over health insurance and the war in Afghanistan, testing this approach with focus groups and surveys.[1]

But had this Handbook been assembled in the 1960s or 1970s, it would probably not have included a chapter on religion and public opinion. Churches and religious leaders played a visible role in the civil rights and anti-war movements, but political scientists largely ignored religion as a source of political attitudes and behaviors. In 1978 *Public Opinion Quarterly*, the *Journal of Politics*, and *Social Science Quarterly* did not publish a single article on religion and public opinion; thirty years later, in 2008, they published thirteen articles on the topic. In spite of a long history in America of religion influencing politics, it was the formation of the Christian Right in the 1980s that prompted

---

[1] For example, one poll by the Public Religion Research Institute tested arguments to persuade southern white evangelicals to oppose torture. <http://www.publicreligion.org/research/published/?id=136>, accessed Nov. 8, 2010.

scholars to begin seriously studying the relationship between faith and politics (Smidt, Kellstedt, and Guth 2009; Wald and Wilcox 2006).

There is ample reason to take religion seriously in American politics. A large majority of Americans profess a belief in God and proclaim that religion is important to their lives, and a sizable minority claims to attend religious services at least once a week. More Americans are members of churches than of political parties. A majority of Americans say that religion is "very important" in their lives, and for a smaller subset, religious experiences are transformative and central to their identities (Wald and Calhoun-Brown 2010; Mitchell 2007).

In recent years, new data on and measures of religion have multiplied. Once academics distinguished only between Protestants, Catholics, and Jews; today surveys identify small denominations such as the Church of God of Anderson, Indiana, the Church of God of Cleveland, Tennessee, and the Church of God in Christ. Surveys ask about beliefs in demons and angels, in reincarnation, and in transubstantiation (that the wafer and wine in the Christian communion actually become the body and blood of Christ), and they probe attitudes concerning the nature of God and whether Christ will come back before or after the millennium of perfect peace. Scholars study the interaction between clergy and their congregations, tracking changes in the attitudes of both religious leaders and members.

We have learned a great deal about the connections between religion and public opinion, but gaps in our knowledge remain. Because much of the early research focused on white evangelicals, our measures of religious belief and practice fit that community but are less appropriate for other traditions (Mockabee, Wald, and Leege 2009). We know a great deal about the relationship between religious attributes and political attitudes, but less about how the meaning of religion is constructed and mobilized (Wald, Silverman, and Fridy 2005). Moreover, although most studies assume that religion is exogenous, more recent research suggests that the relationship between religion and politics is reciprocal: religion influences political attitudes, but political debates influence religion as well (Patrikios 2008; Putnam and Campbell 2010). Finally, demographic changes in the religious landscape raise important questions about the future of religion and public opinion. In this chapter we will review basic models of religion and public opinion, and then address some of the most common ways that religion has been conceptualized and measured. We then highlight some of the complexity of religious effects on public attitudes. We will conclude with avenues for further research.

## MODELS OF RELIGION AND PUBLIC OPINION: THE ONE, THE TWO, THE FEW, THE MANY

Scholars have implicitly drawn on four models of religion and American politics, with implications for the way that religion and politics interact.[2] First, some scholars have

---

[2] These models are drawn from Huntington (1974).

focused on shared religious values and identities as a source of cohesion and support for democratic politics. Tocqueville remarked that the innumerable religious communities in the United States preached the same moral law, and that Americans of all classes and parties saw religion as indispensable for republican government. Today scholars similarly speak of the Judeo-Christian values that underpin the country, and of a civil religion that blends nationalism and faith (Reichley 1985; Bellah 1986).

Other scholars and especially political pundits describe a broad culture war between secular and religious citizens, reflecting deep disagreements on political issues and resulting in a "God gap" in partisanship and voting (Guth, Smidt, Kellstedt, and Green 1996; Hunter 1991; Layman 2006). Religious and secular citizens are described as holding different core values, which have resulted in conflicts around sexuality and the family roles such as abortion and GLBT (gay, lesbian, bisexual, and transgender) issues and also debates over the public role of religion and the separation of Church and State. The language of the culture war sounds loudly in political mobilization today, from candidates and political organizations to journalists.

Two additional, related models describe the US as a religiously pluralist culture where religious groups disagree on important issues and none are able to consistently define public morality. Some scholars describe different political coalitions among a few large contending ethno-religious traditions: white evangelicals, mainline Protestants, African-American Protestants, and Catholics, along with less numerous but politically important groups such as Jews and Mormons (Campbell and Robinson 2007). Others describe a far more diverse pluralist system, with religious and political divisions within religious traditions that have important political consequences. This more diverse model highlights the uniqueness of distinctive denominations and of congregations, but also the way that religious effects may vary by context (Campbell 2006; Guth, Green, Smidt, et al. 1997).

These four models are all useful in understanding the relationship between religion and public opinion, but in different ways. The "one" explains why surveys show that a majority of Americans would vote for a presidential candidate from many faith traditions but not an atheist. The "two" helps us understand the language of political mobilization, and the central nature of issues such as abortion and gay rights in American politics. The "few" focuses our attention on large groups that can affect electoral outcomes and help to pass public policy, and on the different religious coalitions that form on different sets of issues.

But to fully understand the relationship between religion and public opinion, it is necessary to consider the religious "many." There are important differences between denominations within broader religious families, and between congregations within a particular denomination (Guth, Green, Smidt, et al. 1997; Djupe and Gilbert 2009). Within a congregation, individuals may hold different doctrinal beliefs and disagree on the political implications of their doctrine. Religion effects vary with social and political contexts (Campbell 2006; Cook, Jelen, and Wilcox 1993). In the next section we will discuss the most common measures of politically relevant elements of religion.

# CONCEPTUALIZING AND MEASURING
# RELIGION

The great diversity of religious experience and belief has inspired great poetry, from the ninety-nine names of Allah to the varieties of praise of God described in Psalms 150, but it poses problems for scholars who seek to identify the elements of religion that affect and are affected by politics. Social scientists have spent a great deal of effort determining which aspects of religion influence public opinion and debating the best way to measure religion in surveys. Communities of scholars have improved religious measurement in national surveys such as the General Social Survey (GSS) and the National Election Studies (NES), and many specialized surveys have been conducted using new measures (Leege and Kellstedt 1993; Putnam and Campbell 2010).

Scholars have primarily sought to measure membership in religious institutions, theological beliefs, and religious behaviors. In some cases these measures provide alternative measures of a given religious community: in some studies evangelicals are identified by their denomination, in others by their doctrinal beliefs, and in still others by their self-identification.[3] But many studies explore different religious effects in additive or interactive models.

## Belonging: Denominations and Congregations

In most national surveys, around 85 percent of Americans claim an affiliation with a religious tradition or denomination. There are more than 1,200 religious denominations in the United States (Melton 1989), but in the combined 1990–2000 NES surveys 120 denominations had at least one respondent, and a large majority of those respondents were members of one of the largest twelve traditions. Questions on religious affiliation have been asked by academic and commercial surveys for decades, but improvement in instrumentation complicates longitudinal comparisons.

Those who list a denomination in a survey may not be signaling a deep or abiding affiliation. Some who claim an affiliation seldom if ever attend services, while some who do not list an affiliation do attend. Moreover, there is surprising flux in religious affiliation both within and even across religious families: the Pew Forum on Religion and Public Life reported in 2009 that nearly half of all Americans change their religious affiliation at least once in adulthood.

Denominations espouse theological positions which may have political implications (Guth, Green, Smidt, et al. 1997). They may also take positions on political issues, as the US Catholic bishops have done on matters of nuclear weapons and abortion, or the

---

[3] The consequences of these operational definitions can be substantial (Wilcox 1986; Hackett and Lindsay 2008).

Southern Baptist Convention has done opposing national health insurance (Wald 1992). But the effects of denominations on their members are limited by internal battles over theological and political questions (Djupe and Gilbert 2002; Ammerman 1990). Moreover, congregations and individual members may ignore or be unaware of the official positions of national religious bodies (Wilson 2009).

Many scholars have combined individual denominations into larger religious traditions based on theological similarity and shared history (Kellstedt and Green 1993; Steensland et al. 2000). Studies commonly divide Christians into mainline Protestants, evangelical Protestants, Catholics, and African-American Protestants, often with an "other Christian" category that captures smaller denominations that do not fit neatly into any of the categories.[4] Larger or specialized surveys allow scholars to identify theological subgroups (e.g. Pentecostals) and to study the attitudes of members of less numerous traditions, such as Jews, Mormons, and Muslims (Djupe and Green 2007; Sigelman 1991; Campbell and Monson 2007b; Jamal 2010).

Many Americans belong to a specific congregation, regardless of whether they identify with a denomination. Congregations constitute political communities that may have more influence on their members than the parent denomination (Ammerman 1987; Wald, Owen, and Hill 1988; Djupe and Gilbert 2009). Within denominations, congregations may vary in their doctrine, and even more in the world view through which they interpret doctrine. For example, Rick Warren's Saddleback Church in California is affiliated with the Southern Baptist Convention, but it is very different from Southern Baptist congregations in, for instance, Mississippi. Congregations vary in their degree of politicization, and in the way that members and religious leaders influence one another. Religious leaders may try to shape political opinions of congregations, but they are often constrained by anticipated congregational reaction (Jelen 1993; Smith 2008). Congregations are frequently a nexus for strong friendship networks which stimulate civic and political participation (Putnam and Campbell 2010).

# Believing

Religion involves countless beliefs about theological, social, and political issues, and seemingly minor theological differences can matter greatly to those involved in the dispute. Doctrinal differences between fundamentalist and Pentecostal evangelicals limited cooperation in the early Christian Right (Bendyna, Green, Rozell, and Wilcox

---

[4] Studies differ in how they code Protestants who attend non-denominational churches, with most scholars assigning them to the evangelical category. Scholars differ also in how they measure the unaffiliated (Dougherty, Johnson, and Polson 2007; Hout and Fiser 2002; Wald and Calhoun-Brown 2007; Steensland et al. 2000). Finally, the "African-American Protestant" category in some cases identifies all African Americans who attend Protestant churches and in other cases citizens of all races who attend congregations in historically black denominations (Wald and Calhoun Brown 2010; Steensland et al. 2000).

2001), and differences between evangelicals and Mormons limited Mitt Romney's presidential prospects in 2008.

But doctrinal differences are muted in the US by two factors. First, substantial majorities of Americans believe that "there are basic truths in many religions" and that a person "who is not of your faith can go to heaven or attain salvation" (Campbell 2009). Moreover, many people hold apparently inconsistent theological beliefs; for example, that the Bible is literally true and that souls are reincarnated after death.[5] The combination of deep religiosity and shallow theology may dampen the divisive effects of religion (Wald and Calhoun-Brown 2010).

The most frequently asked doctrinal question in national surveys concerns biblical authority. Surveys offer somewhat different options: NES in 2008 offered a literalist option, "The Bible is the actual Word of God and is to be taken literally, word for word," but the NES in 1988 offered instead an inerrancy option, "the Bible is God's word and all it says is true."[6] Other surveys have incorporated multiple measures of evangelical orthodoxy, including questions about belief in the divinity of Christ, his virgin birth, his resurrection, in Satan and hell—all combined into a measure that better differentiates evangelicals from other Christians (Guth, Green, Kellstedt, and Smidt 1995b). Studies have shown that some of these beliefs have special political implications: for instance, the belief in Satan is a strong predictor of low levels of political tolerance (Nunn, Crockett, and Williams 1978).

There has been less research on beliefs central to other faith traditions. Scattered research has focused on the impact of Mariology on Catholic gender role attitudes, and the impact that the belief in transubstantiation might have on attitudes and behavior (Mockabee, Wald, and Leege 2009; Jelen 1989). There has been surprisingly little research on the impact of Calvinist beliefs on economic attitudes, despite the long pedigree of this question (but see Patrikos 2008). Other issues, such as the debate within Protestantism concerning human free will and God's sovereignty, have been neglected. Similarly, there have been only a small number of surveys that measure theological differences among Jews, Muslims, Hindus, and others.

Studies have also explored the impact of images of God on political attitudes. The image of a judging, authoritarian God has been linked to political intolerance (Froese, Bader, and Smith 2008). Among African Americans, differing images of Christ have been linked to whether the Church preaches a liberation theology that includes support for government actions to redress racism and poverty, or a "prosperity gospel" that takes opposing positions on these issues (Harris-Lacewell 2006; Harris 2010).

[5] In the 2008 GSS survey, one quarter of those who proclaimed the Bible to be literally true professed a belief in reincarnation.

[6] The difference between a literal interpretation of sacred religious texts and the view that these texts are meant to provide spiritual guidance but not to be read literally is an important one. For a discussion of the difference, and ethnographic detail of literalism in a congregation, see Ammerman (1987).

# Religiosity

Americans vary in the types and frequency of their public and private religious behavior, and in the importance accorded to faith in their lives. They differ in how religious they are, and how they are religious. Studies frequently measure how often Americans engage in a variety of religious behaviors, including attending worship services, other activities in their congregations, private devotions, reading of Scriptures, and subjective religious salience.

The most common survey measure of religiosity is frequency of church attendance. Over time, attendance measures have been improved to allow better estimates of those who attend seldom and of those who attend more than once a week. Regular attendance results in greater exposure to political cues from religious leaders and from other members of the congregation. For this reason it is often combined with denominational affiliation to sort out committed members and less committed members of religious traditions (Layman 1997). Some surveys measure a variety of activities in congregations, including small group attendance, worship attendance, and volunteering. Other specialized surveys have asked about particular behaviors during worship services, including Pentecostal practices such as speaking in tongues. More recently, scholars have begun to explore participation in religious friendship networks (Putnam and Campbell 2010).

Other studies have measured a variety of private religious behaviors: prayer, Bible reading, devotions, and meditation, and subjective religious salience. Public and private religiosity are correlated, but they may have different political effects. For example, African Americans who have high levels of private religiosity but who attend church less frequently are more conservative but less likely to be mobilized into politics than those with higher levels of public religiosity (Harris 1999).

Evangelical congregations emphasize regular church attendance, and many offer services several times a week. But other faith traditions place less emphasis on regular attendance, and scholars have sought to develop measures of religious behavior separate from attendance. One recent study asked Christians if they tried to be a good Christian, and if so, whether this was primarily by trying to avoid sin, or by helping others. The authors suggested that this more communal form of religiosity was relevant for the study of mainline Protestants (Mockabee, Wald, and Leege 2009).

## RELIGION AND PUBLIC ATTITUDE DOMAINS

There is a large and growing literature that explores the relationship between religion and public attitudes in a variety of attitude domains (Guth 2009; Wilson 2009). Because studies employ different measures and models, it is not easy to compare results. Many studies acknowledge but do not measure the indirect role of religion on attitudes through its influence on partisanship and general ideology. Some model religious effects as additive; others explore interactions between religious attributes.

Across many different attitudinal domains, there is a common simple "culture wars" story: white evangelical Protestants are distinctly more conservative than other Americans on social, economic, and foreign policy issues, and less tolerant of those with whom they disagree, and this distinctiveness is largely attributable to religious beliefs. This is not surprising, since white evangelicals have been the target of substantial political mobilization by social movement organizations and political parties (Wilcox and Robinson 2010). But studies have also revealed more subtle and complex religious effects in explaining each of these sets of attitudes. We cannot fully review these substantial literatures here, but instead point to some results that demonstrate the complex relationships between religion and public opinion.

## Sexuality and Gender Roles

In the last twenty years, cultural conflict over abortion, gay rights, sex education, and gender roles have been central to politics (Abramowitz 1995; Campbell and Monson 2007a). On each of these issues, white evangelicals are distinctly more conservative, and this is especially so for those who accept a literal interpretation of the Bible. But the effects of doctrine are more subtle: a "high" view of scripture increases opposition to abortion among both whites and blacks, but among African Americans this doctrine increases support for gender equality. Many African-American evangelical churches focus on biblical passages that emphasize equality, which appears to generalize from racial and class issues to gender (Thomas and Wilcox 1992).

The complexity of religious effects is evident among Catholics: the most committed Catholics are less supportive of legal abortion than mainline Protestants, but also more supportive of gender equality. Recent studies have shown that even controlling for other religious and political variables Catholics are more likely than mainline Protestants to support same-sex marriage, despite the unified and strong condemnation of the Catholic hierarchy (Jelen 2010).

American Jews are more liberal on abortion and gay rights than other Americans, but their liberalism on abortion is entirely explained by demographic variables such as education, religious variables such as public religiosity, and political variables such as partisanship. Yet Jews remain statistically more supportive of same-sex marriage even after incorporating controls. Jews may view same-sex marriage as an issue of full citizenship and inclusion, thus drawing on a unique cultural history to interpret their faith (Wald 2010).

The simple story of an emerging culture war on sexuality issues also does not explain societal shifts in attitudes. Americans of all religious traditions hold more egalitarian attitudes toward women and toward gays and lesbians in 2010 than they did in 1980, and they are also somewhat less pro-choice on abortion. Moreover, there are today generational differences across all religious traditions, with younger citizens more supportive of GLBT rights but less supportive of abortion. These generational differences also hold for the most devout evangelicals—even those who believe that the Bible is literally true (Wilcox and Robinson 2010).

## Economic Policy

On economic issues such as taxation and spending for social welfare programs, white evangelicals are again distinctively conservative, a finding that has been linked to the individualism preached in evangelical congregations (Barker and Carman 2000). But once again there is a more complex story of religious effects. There are evangelical groups seeking to reshape attitudes in their community on economic policy and on the environment (Wallis 1996).

Among mainline Protestant and Catholic religious elites and activists, there is strong support for redistributive economic programs (Kellstedt, Smidt, Green, and Guth 2007). But there are only faint echoes of this economic liberalism in the pews (Wilson 2009). Although African-American churches have been a source of progressive attitudes on economic issues, a growing number of large suburban churches preach a "prosperity gospel" that deemphasizes racial solidarity and instead focuses on individual behaviors that lead to prosperity. Studies suggest that those who attend such congregations are less supportive of redistributive policies (Harris 2010), although it is not clear whether membership in these congregations affects attitudes or whether they merely attract those seeking validation of their economic views.

## Foreign Policy

Most studies of public attitudes on foreign policy ignore the role of religion, but religious organizations have been quite active in foreign policy debates, from foreign aid to involvement in the United Nations to the Iraq War. Religious doctrine on foreign policy can be complex: there is substantial debate over the applicability of Catholic "just war" doctrine to specific conflicts, for example. Ethnic ties can interact with religious identities: eastern European Catholics held strong anti-communist attitudes during the cold war.

White evangelicals are the most supportive of unilateral US military engagement, high levels of military spending, limits on immigration, and minimal US involvement in international institutions such as the United Nations (Guth 2009). They are also strongly supportive of Israel, although there is diversity of opinion on the best solution for Middle Eastern problems (Mayer 2004). But once again there is a more complex story. Younger evangelical leaders have staked positions on global poverty, global warming, and international cooperation to fights AIDS. Evangelicals have entered into diverse alliances to elevate religious freedom as a foreign policy goal (Hertzke 2004). And more recently the National Association of Evangelicals issued a strongly worded condemnation of the use of torture.

Catholics have moved from strong anti-communism and support for military involvement to a more moderate position. American bishops issued a pastoral letter on nuclear weapons in 1983, and there is some evidence that this helped increase Catholic support for cuts in defense spending (Wald 1992). Catholics have been more supportive of allowing immigrants to earn citizenship, even after controls for ethnicity, and Catholic leaders have engaged evangelicals in a discussion of the issue.

## Democratic Values, Tolerance, and Deliberation

Political theorists have engaged in a vigorous debate about whether religious citizens are likely to be good democrats, and whether religious certainty is consistent with deliberation and tolerance (Conger and McGraw 2008; Rosenblum 2003). Most research has shown that religiosity per se is not associated with greater levels of intolerance, but rather certain religious traditions and beliefs might lead to intolerance via other intermediary variables (Gibson 2010; Eisenstein 2008). Once again, studies show that evangelicals are distinctive in their relatively low levels of political tolerance (Beatty and Walter 1984; Guth and Green 1991).

But the strongest predictors of intolerance are doctrinal beliefs. Those who believe the Bible is literally true are less likely to believe that alternative views should be welcome in the public square (Wilcox and Jelen 1990). Second, those who believe in a wrathful God and in the active role in the world of the Devil and/or demons are markedly less tolerant (Froese, Bader, and Smith 2008; Nunn, Crockett, and Williams 1978). These doctrinal beliefs increase intolerance among all Christian religious traditions, perhaps because they lower the benefits and raise the perceived price of tolerance: the marketplace of ideas is less valuable, with one certain truth and a host of counterfeits peddled by evil forces seeking the soul's damnation. Among Catholics, there is evidence that the Church's history of banning books has led them to structure tolerance attitudes differently (Jelen and Wilcox 1990). More recently, studies have pointed to churches as locations of public deliberation on key issues (Neiheisel, Djupe, and Sokhey 2009). Interfaith deliberation may lead to increased tolerance. Some political groups that mobilize religious citizens may also teach deliberative skills, although other groups may reduce tolerance (Robinson 2008; Shields 2008; Wilcox 2010). And joining a congregation helps lead to increases in civic voluntarism among those who form close friendships within the congregation (Putnam and Campbell 2010).

## NEW DIRECTIONS FOR FURTHER RESEARCH

There is now a substantial body of research that demonstrates that many facets of religion influence political attitudes. Yet there are many questions left to explore. We know the most about the beliefs and behaviors of white evangelical Protestants, but in recent years there has been a flourishing of scholarship on other religious traditions. Today there is a rich body of public and private survey data that includes a variety of religious measures but which remains underexplored. The Pew Forum on Religion and Public Life has conducted cross-national surveys of religious renewalists (Pentecostal or Charismatic Christians), and surveyed Muslims in the US and other countries. Denominations conduct their own surveys, and some non-profits specialize in surveys of religious constituencies. There is data aplenty from which young scholars can work.

Perhaps the most important question for future research is how religion takes on political meaning. Many religious practices, such as Buddhist meditation or being slain in the Spirit in an African-American Pentecostal service, have no obvious political meaning. Similarly, the core texts of most faith traditions do not discuss cap and trade policies, or single-payer national health plans. Furthermore, many Americans simply segment their religious beliefs and behaviors from politics, but others draw broader connections (Wilcox 1988). How these connections are drawn is open to contention and revision.

It would seem that elites play a role in forging connections between religion and politics by offering interpretive frames. These elites may contest the meaning of doctrine, and political arguments can change the content of religious belief. For example, pre-millennial dispensationalism—the belief that the world must inevitably worsen before the imminent second coming of Jesus—was in the 1980s interpreted to imply that there was little need to protect the environment, since the world would soon end (Guth, Green, Kellstedt, and Smidt 1995a). But more recently, a new group of activists who favor "Creation Care" has conversely argued that there is little need to tear up the Arctic to drill for oil if Christ's return is imminent (Dewitt 2006).[7]

Today it seems evident that evangelicals oppose abortion, but this has not always been true. The Southern Baptist Convention endorsed liberalized abortion laws in the early 1970s, but in 1976 they voted to condemn abortion as a form of contraception. In 1980 the Convention adopted a resolution endorsing a national constitutional amendment to ban all abortions except to save the life of the mother. This dramatic change was the result of internal theological and political debates within the denomination (Ammerman 1990). As evangelical and political elites debated abortion, some came to interpret Exodus 21: 22–5 as proscribing abortion, altering a much older interpretation that the verses referred to miscarriage.[8]

Thus, there are a number of potential sites where the connection between religion and political attitudes can be framed, challenged, and reforged. From the level of national denominational and movement leaders to local clergy to friendship networks within congregations to political activists, many forces are involved in shaping the political meaning of religion. For instance, national religious leaders may develop teaching documents to share with clergy in an effort to help shape opinions of their members.

---

[7] "Creation Care" is a label coined by environmentally conscious evangelicals to separate themselves from environmentalists, whom they perceive as liberal.

[8] For the earlier interpretation, see the classic Matthew Henry commentary, now online at <http://www.ccel.org/ccel/henry/mhc1.html>, accessed Nov. 8, 2010.

But clergy who agree with these positions may be constrained by their desire not to divide their congregations, and thus may restrain from a prophetic stance. Or clergy may disagree with their denominational leaders and lead their congregants in breaking away, as a number of Episcopal congregations have done over the issue of ordination of sexual minorities. Such dissent is common not only within denominations, but also within broader religious movements, as competing leaders can offer competing political visions. During the 1990s, National Association of Evangelicals Vice-President Richard Cizik led a faction that favored religious mobilization to protect the environment, but faced strong opposition from then president of Focus on the Family James Dobson.

Within congregations, political meaning can emerge from the deliberation among individual congregants (Djupe and Gilbert 2009) or among friendship networks (Putnam and Campbell 2010). As individuals deliberate and share religious and political views, they may construct new linkages and interpretations. Some members may reject some of their community's interpretations, constructing their own "everyday theology" to incorporate personal experiences (Moon 2004; Harris-Lacewell 2006), often with the help of friends within and outside the congregation (Bates 1993; Andersen 1988). There is evidence that building friendships with someone outside a faith tradition leads to more tolerance of the new friend's faith, and this tolerance may generalize to other religious groups (Campbell 2009). Recent research highlighting the importance of religious friendship networks suggests that additional research on deliberation within these networks and within congregations will be a fertile area for future research.

Religious actors are not the only ones to offer cues; political parties, candidates, and interest groups do so as well. Republican political actors helped form the Moral Majority and the Christian Coalition, primarily to increase turnout and GOP vote share among white evangelicals. These organizations made theological arguments for policies, and also sought to counter theological justifications for political inaction. There is some evidence that these efforts led to some modest change in theology among fundamentalists and Pentecostals (Ingersoll 2009). In 2010 Christian Right organizations rallied quickly to oppose the Democratic national health insurance plan, using both theological and political arguments—including the charge that it would lead to forced abortions. Political parties and candidates also use religious rhetoric or phrases in their mobilization efforts.

Clearly, many individuals receive conflicting religious and political cues about the political implications of their faith. They may receive messages from their imam or rabbi, another on televised religious broadcasts, and another set through political networks (Welch and Leege 1991; Andersen 1988). Experimental work to unravel the way that contested frames influence the connection between religion and politics seems likely to yield promising results. Untangling the processes behind the social construction of religion will require a shift away from cross-sectional surveys toward panel studies, experiments, and contextual studies. There has been increased interest in these methods in recent years, but to fully understand the dynamics of the interaction between religion and politics, more of this type of work will be required.

Furthermore, key to parsing out the ways in which religion becomes political is a closer attention to the reciprocal relationship between religion and political attitudes. Religious values shape political attitudes, but politics also helps influence religious doctrine and practice. In the 2008 presidential election, some Catholic bishops denied communion to pro-choice Catholic politicians, but in other parishes progressive Catholics organized lay discussions to highlight Church teachings on economic justice, compassion, the death penalty, and just war. Individual Catholics in different parishes heard different messages, and this may have affected both their politics and their enthusiasm for the local parish. There is some evidence that younger Americans may attend church less often because they associate organized religion with anti-GLBT policies and the Christian Right (Hout and Fiser 2002). Many studies show that these younger unaffiliated citizens retain religious and spiritual beliefs and identities, and this seems a fertile area for additional research. But we need better panel data to sort out these reciprocal linkages. In a one-year panel study, Putnam and Campbell (2010) found church attendance by liberals declined while that of conservatives increased. It may be that congregations have come to have an overtly political stance. In these congregations, dissenters may stop attending, while the most partisan may become more involved. Additional longer panel studies may help us sort out the ways that doctrine shapes political views, and that political views shape religious doctrine. American religion appears to be entering a time of flux, and those who are able to trace the interactions between politics and religion will be best equipped to understand the implications of this change.

America has been an overwhelmingly religious nation since its inception, a fact that many from Tocqueville to Robert Bella have well noted. However, the political mobilization of white evangelicals in the 1980s prompted modern political science to take notice of the influence of religion on politics, and of the influence of one particular group as against the others. Thus, results motivated by this focus are historically contingent. In the 1960s mainline Protestants, liberal Catholics, and Jews marched with African Americans against segregation, hunger, and the Vietnam War. Consequently, we need better theoretical understanding of what resources and opportunities lead to political mobilization of religion (Wald, Silverman, and Fridy 2005). Comparative studies, historical studies, and studies of regional or state political mobilization may prove useful in theory building, as well as longitudinal and contextual studies. Ultimately, scholars must use methods to move beyond solely identifying the generically religious "one," the divisive dichotomy of "two," and the major coalitions of the "few" to fully exploring the various "many" of the American religious landscape.

# REFERENCES

ABRAMOWITZ, A. I. 1995. It's Abortion, Stupid: Policy Voting in the 1992 Presidential Election. *Journal of Politics*, 57/1: 176–86.

AMMERMAN, N. T. 1987. *Bible Believers: Fundamentalists in the Modern World*. New Brunswick: Rutgers University Press.

AMMERMAN, N. T. 1990. *Baptist Battles: Social Change and Religious Conflict in the Southern Baptist Convention*. New Brunswick, NJ: Rutgers University Press.

ANDERSEN, K. 1988. Sources of Pro-Family Beliefs: A Cognitive Approach. *Political Psychology*, 9/2: 229–43.

BARKER, D. C., and CARMAN, C. J. 2000. The Spirit of Capitalism? Religious Doctrine, Values, and Economic Attitude Constructs. *Political Behavior*, 22/1: 1–27.

BATES, S. 1993. *Battleground: One Mother's Crusade, the Religious Right, and the Struggle for Control of our Classrooms*. New York: Poseidon.

BEATTY, K. M., and WALTER, O. 1984. Religious Preference and Practice: Reevaluating their Impact on Political Tolerance. *Public Opinion Quarterly*, 48/1: 318–29.

BELLAH, R. N. 1986. *Habits of the Heart: Individualism and Commitment in American Life*. First Perennial Library. New York: Harper & Row.

BENDYNA, M. E., GREEN, J. C., ROZELL, M. J., and WILCOX, C. 2001. Uneasy Alliance: Conservative Catholics and the Christian Right. *Sociology of Religion*, 62/1: 51–64.

CAMPBELL, D. 2006. Religious "Threat" in Contemporary Presidential Elections. *Journal of Politics*, 68/1: 104–15.

——2009. The Puzzle of Religious Pluralism in the United States. Paper presented at the Diversity and Democratic Politics: Canada in Comparative Perspective conference, Queen's University, Kingston, Ontario, May 8.

——and MONSON, J. Q. 2007a. The Case of Bush's Re-election: Did Gay Marriage Do It? In *A Matter of Faith: Religion and the 2004 Presidential Election*, ed. D. E. Campbell. Washington, DC: Brookings Institution.

————2007b. Dry Kindling: A Political Profile of American Mormons. In *From Pews to Polling Places: Faith and Politics in the American Religious Mosaic*, ed. J. M. Wilson. Washington, DC: Georgetown University Press.

——and ROBINSON, C. 2007. Religious Coalitions For and Against Gay Marriage: The Culture War Rages On. In *The Politics of Same-Sex Marriage*, ed. C. Rimmerman and C. Wilcox. Chicago: University of Chicago Press.

CONGER, K. H., and McGRAW, B. T. 2008. Religious Conservatives and the Requirements of Citizenship: Political Autonomy. *Perspectives on Politics*, 6/2: 253–66.

COOK, E. A., JELEN, T. G., and WILCOX, C. 1993. Catholicism and Abortion Attitudes in the American States: A Contextual Analysis. *Journal for the Scientific Study of Religion*, 32/3: 223–30.

DEWITT, C. B. 2006. The Scientist and the Shepherd: The Emergence of Evangelical Environmentalism. In *The Oxford Handbook of Religion and Ecology*, ed. R. S. Gottlieb. Oxford: Oxford University Press.

DJUPE, P. A., and GILBERT, C. P. 2002. The Political Voice of Clergy. *Journal of Politics*, 64/2: 596–609.

————2009. *The Political Influence of Churches*. Cambridge Studies in Social Theory, Religion, and Politics. Cambridge: Cambridge University Press.

——and GREEN, J. C. 2007. The Politics of American Muslims. In *Religion and Political Mobilization in the United States*, ed. M. J. Wilson. Washington, DC: Georgetown University Press.

DOUGHERTY, K. D., JOHNSON, B. R., and POLSON, E. C. 2007. Recovering the Lost: Remeasuring U.S. Religious Affiliation. *Journal for the Scientific Study of Religion*, 46/4: 483–99.

EISENSTEIN, M. A. 2008. *Religion and the Politics of Tolerance*. Waco, TX: Baylor University Press.

FROESE, P., BADER, C., and SMITH, B. 2008. Political Tolerance and God's Wrath in the United States. *Sociology of Religion*, 69/1: 29–44.

GIBSON, J. L. 2010. The Political Consequences of Religiosity: Does Religion Always Cause Political Intolerance? In *Religion and Democracy in the United States: Danger and Opportunity?* ed. A. Wolfe and I. Katznelson. Princeton: Princeton University Press.

GUTH, J. L. 2009. Religion and American Public Opinion: Foreign Policy. In *The Oxford Handbook of Religion and American Politics*, ed. C. E. Smidt, L. A. Kellstedt, and J. L. Guth. New York: Oxford University Press.

—— and GREEN, J. C. 1991. An Ideology of Rights: Support for Civil Liberties among Political Activists. *Political Behavior*, 13/4: 321–44.

—— GREEN, J. C., KELLSTEDT, L. A., and SMIDT, C. E. 1995a. Faith and the Environment: Religious Beliefs and Attitudes on Environmental Policy. *American Journal of Political Science*, 39/2: 364–82.

—— —— —— —— 1995b. Onward Christian Soldiers: Religious Activist Groups in American Politics. In *Interest Group Politics*, 4th edn, ed. A. J. Cigler and B. A. Loomis. Washington, DC: CQ Press.

—— —— SMIDT, C. E., KELLSTEDT, L. A., and POLOMA, M. 1997. *The Bully Pulpit: The Politics of Protestant Clergy*. Lawrence: University of Kansas Press.

—— SMIDT, C. E., KELLSTEDT, L. A., and GREEN, J. C. (eds.) 1996. *Religion and the Culture War: Dispatches from the Front*. Lanham, MD: Rowman & Littlefield.

HACKETT, C., and LINDSAY, D. M. 2008. Measuring Evangelicalism: Consequences of Different Operational Strategies. *Journal for the Scientific Study of Religion*, 47/3: 499–514.

HARRIS, F. C. 1999. *Something Within: Religion in African-American Political Activism*. New York: Oxford University Press.

—— 2010. Entering the Promised Land? The Rise of Prosperity Gospel and Post Civil Rights Black Politics. In *Religion and Democracy in the United States: Danger or Opportunity?* ed. A. Wolfe and I. Katznelson. Princeton: Princeton University Press.

HARRIS-LACEWELL, M. V. 2006. *Barbershops, Bibles, and BET: Everyday Talk and Black Political Thought*. Princeton: Princeton University Press.

HERTZKE, A. D. 2004. *Freeing God's Children: The Unlikely Alliance for Global Human Rights*. Lanham, MD: Rowman & Littlefield.

HOUT, M., and FISER, C. S. 2002. Why More Americans Have No Religious Preference: Politics and Generations. *American Sociological Review*, 67/2: 165–90.

HUNTER, J. D. 1991. *Culture Wars: The Struggle to Define America*. New York: Basic Books.

HUNTINGTON, S. P. 1974. Paradigms of American Politics. *Political Science Quarterly*, 89: 1–26.

INGERSOLL, J. 2009. Mobilizing Evangelicals: Christian Reconstructionism and the Roots of the Religious Right. In *Evangelicals and Democracy in America*, ii: *Religion and Politics*, ed. S. Brint and J. R. Schroedel. New York: Russell Sage.

JAMAL, A. 2010. Muslim Americans: Enriching or Deleting American Democracy? In *Religion and Democracy in the United States: Danger or Opportunity?* ed. A. Wolfe and I. Katznelson. Princeton: Princeton University Press.

JELEN, T. G. 1989. Helpmeets and Weaker Vessels: Gender Role Stereotypes and Attitudes toward Female Ordination. *Social Science Quarterly*, 70: 575–85.

—— 1993. *The Political World of the Clergy*. New York: Praeger.

—— 2010. Catholicism, Homosexuality, and Same-Sex Marriage in the United States. In *Religious Faith, Sexual Diversity, and Political Conflict in Canada and the United States*, ed. D. Rayside and C. Wilcox. Vancouver: University of British Columbia Press.

JELEN, T. G., and WILCOX, C. 1990. Denominational Preference and the Dimensions of Political Tolerance. *Sociological Analysis*, 51: 69–80.

KELLSTEDT, L. A., and GREEN, J. C. 1993. Knowing God's Many People: Denominational Preference and Political Behavior. In *Rediscovering the Religious Factor in American Politics*, ed. D. C. Leege and L. A. Kellstedt. Armonk, NY: M. E. Sharpe.

——SMIDT, C. E., GREEN, J. C., and GUTH, J. L. 2007. A Gentle Stream or a River Glorious? The Religious Left in the 2004 Election. In *A Matter of Faith: Religion in the 2004 Presidential Election*, ed. D. E. Campbell. Washington, DC: Brookings Institution.

LAYMAN, G. C. 1997. Religion and Political Behavior in the United States: The Impact of Beliefs, Affiliations, and Commitment from 1980 to 1994. *Public Opinion Quarterly*, 61/2: 288–316.

——2006. Religion, Culture Wars, and American Democracy: Party Activists from 1972 to 2004. In *APSA Task Force on Religion and Politics*. Washington, DC: American Political Science Association.

LEEGE, D. C., and KELLSTEDT, L. A. 1993. *Rediscovering the Religious Factor in American Politics*. Armonk, NY: M. E. Sharpe.

MAYER, J. 2004. Christian Fundamentalists and Public Opinion toward the Middle East: Israel's New Best Friends? *Social Science Quarterly*, 85/3: 695–712.

MELTON, G. J. 1989. *The Encyclopedia of American Religions*. Detroit: Gale Research.

MITCHELL, J. 2007. Religion Is Not a Preference. *Journal of Politics*, 69/1: 349–60.

MOCKABEE, S. T., WALD, K. D., and LEEGE, D. C. 2009. Is There a Religious Left? Evidence from the 2006 and 2008 ANES. Paper presented at the Annual Meeting and Exhibition of the American Political Science Association, Toronto, Sept. 3–6.

MOON, D. 2004. *God, Sex, and Politics: Homosexuality and Everyday Theologies*. Chicago: University of Chicago Press.

NEIHEISEL, J., DJUPE, P. A., and SOKHEY, A. 2009. Veni, Vidi, Disseri: Churches and the Promise of Democratic Deliberation. *American Politics Research*, 37/4: 614–43.

NUNN, C. Z., CROCKETT, H. J., JR., and WILLIAMS, J. A. 1978. *Tolerance for Nonconformity*. San Francisco: Jossey-Bass.

PATRIKIOS, S. 2008. American Republican Religion? Disentangling the Causal Link between Religion and Politics in the U.S. *Political Behaviour*, 30: 367–89.

PUTNAM, R. D., and CAMPBELL, D. E. 2010. *American Grace: The Changing Role of Religion in America*. New York: Simon & Schuster.

REICHLEY, J. 1985. *Religion in American Public Life*. Washington, DC: Brookings Institution.

ROBINSON, C. 2008. Doctrine, Discussion and Disagreement: Evangelicals and Catholics together in American Politics. Dissertation, Georgetown University.

ROSENBLUM, N. L. 2003. Religious Parties, Religious Political Identity, and the Cold Shoulder of Liberal Democratic Thought. *Ethical Theory and Moral Practice*, 6: 25–53.

SHIELDS, J. A. 2008. *The Democratic Virtues of the Christian Right*. Princeton: Princeton University Press.

SIGELMAN, L. 1991. If You Prick Us, Do We Not Bleed? If You Tickle Us, Do We Not Laugh? Jews and Pocketbook Voting. *Journal of Politics*, 53/4: 977–92.

SMIDT, C. E., DEN DULK, K., FROEHLE, B., and PENNING, J. 2010. *The Disappearing God Gap? Religion in the 2008 Presidential Election*. New York: Oxford University Press.

——KELLSTEDT, L. A., and GUTH, J. L. (eds.) 2009. *The Oxford Handbook of Religion and American Politics*. New York: Oxford University Press.

SMITH, G. A. 2008. *Politics in the Parish: The Political Influence of Catholic Priests.* Washington, DC: Georgetown University Press.

STEENSLAND, B., PARK, J. Z., REGNERUS, M. D., ROBINSON, L. D., WILCOX, W. B., and WOODBERRY, R. 2000. The Measure of American Religion: Toward Improving the State of the Art. *Social Forces,* 79/1: 291–318.

THOMAS, S., and WILCOX, C. 1992. Religion and Feminist Attitudes among African-American Women: A View from the Nation's Capitol. *Women & Politics,* 12/1: 19–40.

WALD, K. D. 1992. Religious Elites and Public Opinion: The Impact of the Bishops' Peace Pastoral. *Review of Politics,* 54/1: 112–43.

—— 2010. Paths from Emancipation: American Jews and Same-Sex Marriage. In *Religious Faith, Sexual Diversity, and Political Conflict in Canada and the United States,* ed. D. Rayside and C. Wilcox. Vancouver: University of British Columbia Press.

—— and CALHOUN-BROWN, A. 2007. *Religion and Politics in the United States,* 5th edn. Lanham, MD: Rowman & Littlefield.

—— —— 2010. *Religion and Politics in the United States,* 5th edn. Lanham, MD: Rowman & Littlefield.

—— and WILCOX, C. 2006. Getting Religion: Has Political Science Rediscovered the Faith Factor? *American Political Science Review,* 100/4: 523–9.

—— OWEN, D. E., and HILL, S. S. 1988. Churches as Political Communities. *American Political Science Review,* 82/2: 531–48.

—— SILVERMAN, A. L., and FRIDY, K. 2005. Making Sense of Religion in Political Life. *Annual Review of Political Science,* 8: 121–43.

WALLIS, J. 1996. *Who Speaks for God? An Alternative to the Religious Right—a New Politics of Compassion, Community, and Civility.* New York: Delacorte.

WELCH, M. R., and LEEGE, D. C. 1991. Dual Reference Groups and Political Orientations: An Examination of Evangelically Oriented Catholics. *American Journal of Political Science,* 35/1: 28–56.

WILCOX, C. 1986. Fundamentalists and Politics: An Analysis of the Effects of Differing Operational Definitions. *Journal of Politics,* 48/4: 1041–51.

—— 1988. Seeing the Connection: Religion and Politics in the Ohio Moral Majority. *Review of Religious Research,* 30/1: 47–58.

—— 2010. The Christian Right and Civic Virtue. In *Religion and Democracy in the United States: Danger or Opportunity?* ed. A. Wolfe and I. Katznelson. Princeton: Princeton University Press.

—— and JELEN, T. G. 1990. Evangelicals and Political Tolerance. *American Politics Quarterly,* 18: 25–46.

—— and ROBINSON, C. 2010. *Onward Christian Soldiers: The Christian Right in American Politics,* 4th edn. Boulder, CO: Westview Press.

WILSON, J. M. 2009. Religion and American Public Opinion: Economic Issues. In *The Oxford Handbook of Religion and American Politics,* ed. C. E. Smidt, L. A. Kellstedt, and J. L. Guth. New York: Oxford University Press.

# CHAPTER 34

························································

# CLASS DIFFERENCES IN SOCIAL AND POLITICAL ATTITUDES IN THE UNITED STATES

························································

LESLIE McCALL

JEFF MANZA

POLICY attitudes and preferences have long been thought to vary widely between citizens with different levels of income or wealth, and indeed to provide one key to understanding public opinion at both the individual and aggregate level. The "class" thesis in public opinion research has, however, proven to be one of the more vexing questions in the field. The basic idea is deceptively simple. Citizens will think differently about many social and political issues depending on where they sit in the stratification order. Poor people have a strong material interest in redistributive public policies. Rich people, by contrast, will resist such policies (and in particular the taxes they inevitably require). Because inequality is rooted in the relative differences between individuals and groups, such attitudinal gaps can be expected to persist even in the face of rising affluence, and should further strengthen in periods when inequality widens.

While seemingly straightforward, the class thesis has generated theoretical controversy and conflicting empirical evidence from the very start. Since the advent of modern public opinion surveys, debates over whether there are meaningful differences to be found along class lines, and if so on what specific issues, have been plentiful. A major source of confusion in these debates arises from the fact that analysts have employed varying ways of conceptualizing class, and these different conceptualizations produce different empirical results. We review and reconsider these debates and the analytical and empirical puzzles they have generated in the context of contemporary American public opinion. Our discussion is in three parts. We begin with a brief description of some of the classical and contemporary controversies about class differences in public opinion. We then consider some definitional issues that have plagued work in this area. Next we offer some illustrative examples of variation in social and political attitudes across different specifications of class. A brief conclusion summarizes where things stand and where future research might go.

# CLASSICAL POSITIONS AND CONTEMPORARY CONTROVERSIES

## The Classical Debate: Theoretical Sources of Class Influence on Citizens' Attitudes

Class differences in social and political preferences were, for many decades, one of the central research questions in the field of public opinion research. The claim that individuals and groups with different levels of income and wealth should be expected to have different attitudes appears in many different places. Werner Sombart's *Why Is there No Socialism in the United States?* (1906) posed the question sharply in his famous essay on what would come to be known as the "American exceptionalism" thesis. For Sombart, the relative affluence of American workers meant that "all socialist utopias come to nothing on roast beef and apple pie" (for later examples of the "embourgeoisement thesis," see, for example, Kerr, Dunlop, Harbison, and Myers 1960). By contrast, Selig Perlman (1928) argued in his institutional account that class consciousness among American workers never took hold because of the absence of feudal legacies, the early extension of the franchise, and successive waves of immigration which undermined class-wide solidarity. Generations of scholarship on American exceptionalism have periodically reiterated these claims (see, for example, Hartz 1955; Bell 1960; Lipset and Marks 2000).

Although it suggests the absence of strong class divides, the American exceptionalism thesis stimulated rather than ended debate about class divisions in public opinion. Indeed, some of the earliest efforts at systematic research on public preferences, using voting behavior as a proxy for "public opinion," sought to explore the link between class location and political preferences and test the exceptionalism thesis. In the era before the advent of modern survey research, for example, early ecological analyses by W. F. Ogburn (Ogburn and Peterson 1916) and Stuart Rice (1928) used voting data as a proxy to analyze the underlying beliefs of different class segments (see also Ogburn and Coombs 1940 and Anderson and Davidson 1943 on class differences in politics in the New Deal era).

In the post-Second World War era, Seymour Martin Lipset probably did as much as anyone to focus attention on the role of class divisions in structuring political preferences (Lipset 1960; Lipset and Rokkan 1967; see also Alford 1963). In the essays gathered together in his widely read 1960 book *Political Man*, for example, Lipset developed what he would later characterize—in the 1981 postscript to the reissue of the book—as an "apolitical Marxist" approach to explaining the social origins of democracy, fascism, communism, and the social bases of modern political parties. The values that sustain democratic societies were said to be more prevalent in societies with a large and stable bloc of middle-class citizens, especially where education levels were relatively high. Authoritarian preferences, by contrast, could be traced to marginalized groups or classes, including workers (Lipset's famous formulation of the thesis of "working class authoritarianism"), small business owners, and other economically vulnerable class segments.

Lipset's early work implied both a rational foundation to class-based public opinion, in which class location normally gives rise to an orientation toward social and political issues, and an "irrational" attraction to left- or right-wing extremism. Anthony Downs's (1957) landmark work on an economic model of political behavior pushed much further in developing a rational model of class-based preferences. For Downs, "groups" of voters are simply aggregates of self-interested actors (albeit with similar calculations of utility), and group-based voting or attitudes can be explained in terms of calculations of individuals within the group. Influential extensions of this approach can be seen in Meltzer and Richard's (1981) model of median voter support for redistribution and Hibbs's (1982, 1987) model of vote choice determined by working-class preferences for low unemployment and middle-class preferences for low inflation. Brustein (1998) even provided an answer to Lipset's irrational account of fascism in his study of National Socialism's appeal, finding evidence that early party members were drawn from class segments potentially benefiting economically from the Nazi platform.

The interest-based account of class preferences was long predominant, indeed the default model of class influence on public opinion. But it presumes high information on the part of citizens; they have to reliably connect their economic situation to other social and political attitudes. Not surprisingly, alternative and less demanding models of the links between class and attitudes developed in the post-war era as well. The most influential work came out of the Columbia School and its panel survey of voters in the 1940 and 1948 elections, which found voter preferences to be surprisingly stable (Lazarsfeld, Berelson, and Gaudet 1948; Berelson, Lazarsfeld, and McPhee 1954). This led the authors to identify a simple "index of political predisposition," rooted in socioeconomic status, and attribute both stability and class bias to the influence of social networks of friends, family members, and co-workers in guiding and reinforcing political preferences (even in the face of the noise of the campaign and low levels of information). After a flurry of interest, however, contextual models fell out of fashion; their relatively recent rediscovery as a source of class influence on political preferences remains very much a work in progress (cf. Weakliem and Heath 1994; Kohler 2006; Zuckerman 2006).

The social psychological approach of the Michigan School of Angus Campbell and his colleagues provides yet another possible source of understanding how class membership may shape attitudes through partisanship (A. Campbell, Converse, Miller, and

Stokes 1960). The idea is that partisan and socioeconomic influences from individual families create enduring attitudes and behaviors in adulthood (cf. Green, Palmquist, and Schickler 2002). Later extensions of the model argued that "group identity," or a sense of "linked fate," becomes the source of strength of class politics (cf. Conover 1988; Gurin, Hatchett, and Jackson 1989; Dawson 2003 introduces the concept of "linked fate" in analyzing African Americans' high levels of Democratic partisanship). Powerful evidence of the importance of childhood inheritance has also come from studies of socially mobile individuals who often retain preferences as close to their class origin as to their class destination (for example, De Graaf, Nieuwbeerta, and Heath 1995; Kohler 2006). The social mobility thesis remains one of the more powerful sources of evidence of the relevance of class as a background factor in shaping citizens' attitudes.

In spite of these theoretical insights, however, it is fair to say that the classical tradition produced no consensus about why social attitudes should be linked to class, or, for that matter, to any coherent and consistent system of thought (Converse 1964; cf. Svallfors 2006, 7; Kohler 2006, 117). Where mechanisms rooted in class relations have been systematically tested, it has primarily been voting behavior—not attitudes—that is of primary interest (cf. Hout, Brooks, and Manza 1995; Gelman 2008). Yet it is hardly unreasonable to expect that social and political attitudes may invoke different class (and non-class) factors, or that class may have different consequences for attitude formation than for vote choice.

## Recent Controversies

If class divisions in public opinion were for a long time a staple of debate and investigation in research in public opinion and political behavior, there has been somewhat less attention in recent decades. Indeed, something of a popular and scholarly backlash against the view that class remains a relevant factor shaping individual attitudes has emerged. For example, while Seymour Martin Lipset was once associated with a strong view of the enduring importance of class, toward the end of his long scholarly career he came to adopt the view that class divisions were of declining importance (see, for example, Clark and Lipset 1991). A flurry of works published in the 1990s asserted "the death of class politics" in a variety of manifestations, including class differences in public opinion (Inglehart 1990; Pakulski and Waters 1996; Kingston 2000, ch. 6).

One widely discussed recent set of controversies has arisen in relation to Thomas Frank's best-selling book *What's the Matter with Kansas?* (2004). Frank asserts that traditional patterns of class politics in the United States have declined, with white working-class voters increasingly influenced by the conservative framing of electoral contests around social issues such as abortion, gun control, and family values, encouraging them to overlook (or misunderstand) their own economic interests (see also Roemer 1998). A more general variant of Frank's "cultural turn" argument can be found in claims that the contemporary political landscape is defined more by ideological polarization on cultural and social issues than on economic ones. Here, the role of education (one component of class in the broadest conceptualization) appears to be the driving factor between those with liberal and conservative views on social and cultural matters (Van Der Waal, Achterberg, and Houtman 2007; see also Gelman 2008).

The class thesis has also been controversial outside the electoral context, where it is not uncommon to find relatively modest differences between higher-class and lower-class groups across a range of attitudes. Studies of attitudes toward rising inequality, for example, do not appear to have generated the expected class divisions in response and, moreover, show responses to be sensitive to income and education in different ways (Bartels 2008; McCall and Kenworthy 2009b; Page and Jacobs 2009). On related issues, comparative research shows Americans to be much less divided on questions of worker–management relations, the role of economic markets, and attitudes toward the welfare state than Europeans (Svallfors 2006; Wright 1997). Casting the net still wider, several recent studies of the responsiveness of politicians and policy to public opinion on a variety of issues conclude that even if policy is more reflective of the views of upper-income constituents (see Bartels 2008; Gilens 2005; and Jacobs and Page 2005), underlying differences in views among income groups are small (R. S. Erikson and Bhatti forthcoming; Ura and Ellis 2008). Changes in aggregate "policy mood" correlate well with both changes in policy outcomes and changes in opinion among lower-income groups (Enns and Kellstedt 2008; Page and Shapiro 1992; Soroka and Wlezien 2009).

Pronouncements about the declining significance of class and economic self-interest have not gone unanswered, however. While the responses have been forceful, they have also been reflective of what might be called an emerging middle ground in class analysis. In this view, the potential for wide variation in the political importance of class is acknowledged and the growing salience of non-economic issues, and the complexity this introduces, is appreciated. On the subject of cultural polarization, for instance, an extensive analysis by Ansolabehere, Rodden, and Snyder (2006) affirmed the sense that many political and social commentators have that social issues are more prominent in politics than they once were. Yet it also revealed a rise in the salience of economic issues such that these issues continue to dominate partisanship and vote choice for all demographic groups, as they have in the past (cf. the cross-national evidence presented in Van Der Waal, Achterberg, and Houtman 2007).

Similarly, while scholars have challenged the thesis that class position no longer guides political behavior by showing in a variety of ways that income significantly shapes electoral outcomes (for example, McCarty, Poole, and Rosenthal 2006; Stonecash and Brewer 2006; Bartels 2008), these scholars have also demonstrated that the income effect varies by time period and by region. In a state-level analysis, for example, Gelman (2008) finds widening income divides in vote choice throughout much of the country, especially in the South, but narrowing divides in affluent states, particularly on the two coasts. Likewise, Gilens's (2009) analysis of policy preferences spanning perhaps the widest range of issues yet considered suggests that preference gaps by income and education vary across both policy domains and specific policy options within such domains. Such gaps can be substantial (20–30 percentage points) not only for economic issues but for cultural and foreign policy issues as well (see also Jacobs and Page 2005).

As these findings naturally demand further explanation, the contextual and multidimensional nature of preference and attitude formation will no doubt continue to preoccupy scholars of public opinion for some time to come. Two avenues of research are particularly relevant in this respect. The first combines the insights of political psychology and political institutions to understand how asymmetries in information processing and political motivation are connected to economic inequalities and exploited or crafted by political elites and the media (for example, Jacobs and Shapiro 2000; Hacker and Pierson 2005; see also (Chong and Druckman 2007)). Studies of both public opinion and elite discourse on single issues can be especially revealing of the conditions under which policy preferences do and do not conform to rational expectations, particularly when studied over time (Bartels 2005; A. L. Campbell 2009). Because public opinion data typically come in aggregate form, however, "average" public opinion is often confounded with that of the "middle class" and then opposed to the views of political and economic "elites." While this seems reasonable, much further research is needed to discern the true extent of class differences in both information and opinion.

Second, research that more tightly controls for the informational context of opinion formation can have important explanatory value even if it is limited to narrow groups and contexts or to experimental settings (Chong and Druckman 2007). Scheve and Slaughter (2007), for instance, home in on the threat of job loss among low-skill workers in sectors exposed to import competition to show how this leads to their greater support for immigration and trade restrictions even relative to high-skill workers in the same sectors (whose jobs are less substitutable). Incorporating the influence of organizational contexts and selection bias in their frameworks, a number of scholars demonstrate that employment in the public sector corresponds with distinctive attitudes toward government spending, individual programs, and aid recipients, which in turn affect the political views of recipients themselves in a policy feedback chain of relations (Lipsky 1983; Mettler and Soss 2004; Kumlin 2007). More generally, Weeden and Grusky (2005) identify narrow occupations as the key source of class influence, with individuals more absorbed by their specific occupation than the bigger class groupings ("working class," "middle class," "managers," etc.) that most class analysts of public opinion have employed.

## DEFINITIONS AND EXTENSIONS

Thus far we have ignored a frequent point of contention in classical and contemporary debates: whether analysts should conceptualize classes in terms of education, occupation, or income, and whether to break the distribution into smaller or larger members of classes. The multiplicity of definitions suggests that before any firm conclusions about trends in the class–attitude relationship are drawn, analysts should consider a wider range of definitions of socioeconomic status than is typical in most studies. In the rest of this chapter, we first provide some brief commentary on the underlying logic of the major approaches using definitions other than income, such as those based on occupations, subjective social class identification, social mobility, and intersecting identities. We then provide, in the next section, an illustrative analysis of four major areas of public opinion across five major definitions of class.

For sociologists, the predominant approach to identifying individuals' class locations has long centered on occupation, for two main reasons. First, occupations are intended to capture the multidimensionality of work (Hauser and Warren 1997; Ganzeboom and Treiman 2003). In socioeconomic indices or scales, detailed occupations are scored according to an occupation's human capital requirements and monetary rewards, thus taking both education and earnings into account (with education typically weighted more than earnings). Similarly, several categorical typologies mix occupational and organizational characteristics to create a multidimensional class map (Wright 1997). Based on a combination of factors such as work content (routine or non-routine), working conditions (office or factory), and especially employment relations (owner or non-owner, supervisor or non-supervisor, secure or insecure) (Goldthorpe 2000), such typologies are common in the large literature on class voting, where they show divergences among groups with similar incomes and educations, such as managers and business owners (more Republican or right-wing) versus professionals (more Democratic or left-wing) (Manza and Brooks 1999).

Second, occupation-based measures are intended to capture the social and collective aspects of economic life. Individuals communicate with co-workers in their same line of work to a greater extent than with all but family members (cf. Weeden and Grusky 2005). Some research suggests that such co-worker networks are also more diverse than friend, family, and neighborhood networks, which in turn fosters the political goods of knowledge and tolerance (Mutz and Mondak 2006). Furthermore, as compared to income, occupation may represent a more stable indicator of socioeconomic status and ideological views over the life course (Goldthorpe 2000; Hauser and Warren 1997). Occupational niches with concentrations of like-minded individuals are especially likely both to select certain kinds of people in, and to reinforce their underlying world views through, their occupational networks (Brint 1994). The influence of occupation-based associations and business and labor organizations in shaping social policy legislation is also richly documented (for example, Starr 1983).

If one of the virtues of occupations is that they combine education and earnings in a parsimonious way, this may tend to confuse truly "class" effects with educational effects (see, for example, Van Der Waal, Achterberg, and Houtman 2007). Particularly when assessing class differences in social attitudes, a long line of research suggests the importance of the independent role of education. For example, Lipset's working class authoritarian thesis drew from research on the timely subject of social and political tolerance, especially concerning the civil liberties of free speech and association (but also racial inclusion), which was found to be greater among those with higher education and occupational status and in positions of community leadership (Stouffer 1955).

Later analyses in the same vein would emphasize the importance of education over occupational status in fostering more liberal values and attitudes (Davis 1982).

As an alternative to occupation measures, some analysts have focused on "subjective" measures of class identity (i.e., the social class category respondents place themselves in). Although subjective measures are sometimes viewed with skepticism, several studies provide evidence of their reliability and usefulness (Jackman and Jackman 1983; Vanneman and Cannon 1987). For example, about a third of Americans will say they do *not* think of themselves as belonging to the working or even middle class when given the chance to abstain (as in a National Election Study screening question on class identity), yet when presented with a forced-choice question on class identity such as on the General Social Survey (i.e., lower, working, middle, or upper), nearly half identify as lower or working class, a share that has barely budged over several decades of growing real incomes (Hout 2008). This suggests a tendency to view economic status in relative terms, which in turn is useful in assessing trends over time in class-based attitudes and political behavior (Walsh, Jennings, and Stoker 2004).

The strength and consistency of the signal provided by subjective measures of class identity depend on a number of factors, however. The correlation of subjective class identity with education, income, and occupation is strongest at the extremes of the distribution while those in the middle exhibit greater heterogeneity in status (e.g., lower than average income and higher than average education) and therefore class identity (Jackman and Jackman 1983; Hout 2008). Political sophistication, interest, participation, and partisanship also have the potential to accentuate the degree to which subjective class distinctions affect vote choices (A. Campbell, Converse, Miller, and Stokes 1960; Lewis-Beck, Weisberg, Norpoth, and Jacoby 2008). Conversely, the strength and substance of class identity influence political efficacy and participation, with middle class identifiers more likely to feel efficacious and to engage in politics, net of objective indicators of class (Walsh, Jennings, and Stoker 2004).

Yet another step beyond measuring social class as one of the "big three" objective indicators (i.e., education, income, and occupation) is to more explicitly cast it as a function of future rather than current economic well-being. In Max Weber's classic conception, class is distinct from other forms of social stratification because it is meant to capture an individual's "life chances." Thus, expectations of upward social mobility, however modest (Lane 1962), may help explain why those at the bottom or in the middle might not fully embrace redistribution despite their objective economic interests in doing so, especially as income inequality rises (Benabou and Ok 2001; Piketty 1995). But while broadly sympathetic to this approach, other scholars find that Americans' tolerance of inequality and opposition to redistribution is heterogeneous *within* income groups. This suggests that values of fairness and reciprocity may be more important than narrow economic self-interest (Ansolabehere, Rodden, and Snyder 2006; Fong, Bowles, and Gintis 2004). This perspective converges with those in political science who emphasize the psychological importance of values such as deservingness and need, and not egalitarianism per se, in shaping support for social policy (Feldman and Steenbergen 2001; Hochschild 2001).

Finally, we note the potential significance in shaping public opinion of intersections of class with gender, race–ethnicity, region, and nation. On the one hand, this hardly needs stating. Particularly in studies of partisan identification and presidential voting, the centrality of race and the South to shifts in trends over time is incontrovertible. Cross-national comparative research also recognizes that class structures and ideologies are enduringly embedded in national political, economic, racial, and social institutions (Brooks and Manza 2007; Svallfors 2006; Alesina and Glaeser 2004). On the other hand, Hochschild (2009) argues that recent concerns about the adverse impact of income inequality on democratic representation have led to studies focused exclusively on class. Similarly, the important literature on the gender gap in voting and preferences for government spending generally speaks little of class differences among women (but see Brady, Sosnaud, and Frenk 2009; Edlund and Pande 2002). Not all intersections need be explored nor should they be expected to result in substantive differences, but the recent trend toward intersectional approaches has been productive and should be encouraged further.

# ISSUE- AND INDICATOR-SPECIFIC PATTERNS

Since it is rare for scholars to include a full gamut of indicators of class in their analyses of public opinion, with earlier scholars more partial to occupation and subjective class and later scholars more partial to income and education, we provide a simple illustrative analysis here using data from the General Social Survey. As shown in Figures 34.1–4, we examine the effects of five different indicators of socioeconomic status on four different indices of public opinion. The indicators of socioeconomic status are coded as categorical variables, each with between four and six categories, and entered as a set of dummy variables to capture potential non-linear effects. The indicators are family income (roughly in quintiles), education (less than high school, high school, some college, college, and postgraduate), the Erikson–Goldthorpe class schema (six categories based on occupation and self-employment; see R. Erikson and Goldthorpe 1992), subjective social class (lower, working, middle, and upper class), and optimism about future economic mobility, measured in levels of agreement to the statement that "people like me and my family have a good chance of improving our standard of living" (five categories from strong disagreement to strong agreement). Detailed information about the data and analysis are available in the appendix to this chapter.

Following from the discussion in previous sections, the outcomes were selected to cover both economic and non-economic issues and policies that do and do not require government spending. The four outcomes map onto the cells in a two-by-two table of attitudes involving government spending (yes/no) and economic issues (yes/no). To maximize coverage of topics and facilitate the presentation of results, we also selected outcomes that could be constructed from multiple items into a continuous index with a mean of zero and a standard deviation of one. We chart gross effects only in order to make simple, baseline comparisons of strength and direction across indicators and

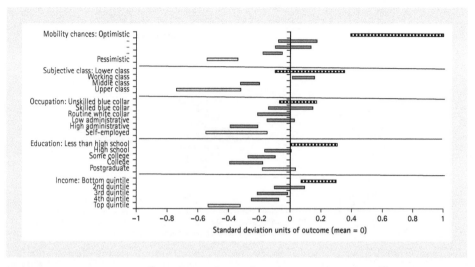

**Figure 34.1** Socioeconomic effects (95% CI) on index of support for redistribution

Same sample for all models (N = 1,100) and separate models for each indicator; no controls added. Outcome is average of *helppoor, eqwlth,* and *goveqinc.* Vertical striped bars refer to lowest-class group and two-tone bars refer to highest-class group. See text and appendix to this chapter for further details.

*Source:* General Social Survey 1996, 2000, 2008.

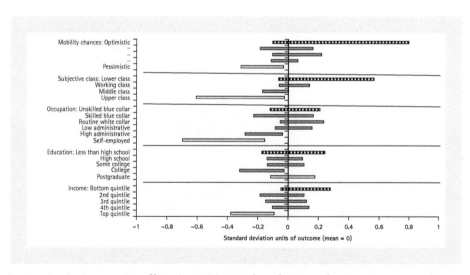

**Figure 34.2** Socioeconomic effects (95% CI) on index of support for government spending

Same sample for all models (N = 1,100) and separate models for each indicator; no controls added. Outcome is index of ten questions about government spending (*nat\** questions). Vertical striped bars refer to lowest-class group and two-tone bars refer to highest-class group. See text and appendix to this chapter for further details.

*Source:* General Social Survey 1996, 2000, 2008.

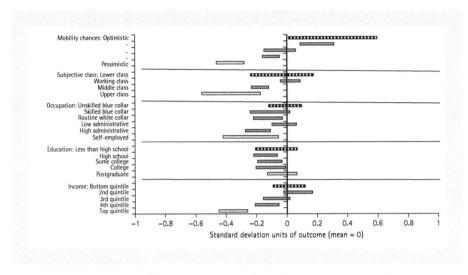

**Figure 34.3** Socioeconomic effects (95% CI) on index of opposition to inequality

Same sample for all models (N = 1,100) and separate models for each indicator; no controls added. Outcome is average of *incgap, inequal3, inequal5*. Vertical striped bars refer to lowest-class group and two-tone bars refer to highest-class group. See text and appendix to this chapter for further details.

*Source*: General Social Survey 1996, 2000, 2008.

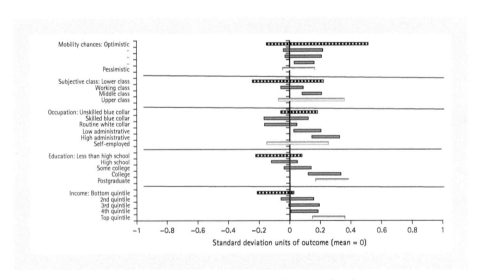

**Figure 34.4** Socioeconomic effects (95% CI) on index of support for abortion

Same sample for all models (N = 1,100) and separate models for each indicator; no controls added. Outcome is average of seven questions about abortion (*ab** questions). Vertical striped bars refer to lowest-class group and two-tone bars refer to highest-class group. See text and appendix to this chapter for further details.

*Sources*: General Social Survey 1996, 2000, 2008.

outcomes (higher values are coded in the liberal direction). We also examine and discuss other outcomes—such as capital punishment, happiness, trust, ideological views, and partisan identification—as well as full models that are not presented in the figures.

The results are consistent with the "middle ground" view about the significance of class differences in public opinion that we suggested above. Class differences are more evident in support of a three-item index of redistribution in Figure 34.1 than in support of a ten-item index of support for government spending across economic and other domains in Figure 34.2. Individuals in the lowest-class group (vertically striped bars) are significantly more supportive of government redistribution than those in the highest-class group (the two-tone bars) for four out of the five indicators of class. Education is the exception but only partially so because of non-linear effects: postgraduates have more liberal views on redistribution than college graduates but college graduates have more conservative views than those with a high-school education or less. Class differences in support of government spending more broadly are in the same direction but are much weaker, with significant differences for only two of the five indicators of class.

Much the same general pattern, albeit more muted, is found in public opinion on economic and social issues unrelated to government spending. Attitudes about income inequality (a three-item index) and abortion (a seven-item index) are shown in Figures 34.3 and 34.4, respectively. For two of the five indicators (family income and mobility optimism) individuals in the lowest class are significantly more likely to oppose income inequality than are those in the top class. For a third indicator, differences are significant between the second lowest and top groups (i.e., between the working and upper classes). The range of variation in support of abortion is much smaller across all indicators of class. Where class matters, the difference runs in the opposite direction, with higher education, income, and occupation groups significantly more likely to support the liberal position. We find analogous patterns for other outcomes. For example, indicators of class were much weaker in their effects on ideological views than on partisan identification, and a postgraduate education resulted in the most liberal ideology but not the most liberal partisanship. If ideological views are considered more representative of public opinion on a wide range of social and economic issues, relative to partisan identification, these results suggest, along with those in Figures 34.1–4, that the farther the outcome is from measuring preferences related to narrow economic issues or formal political practices, the weaker the class effect.[1]

Taken as a whole, several other notable patterns emerge from Figures 34.1–4. First, income has the broadest impact across outcomes; it is the only indicator of class that resulted in significant differences between the bottom and top groups for all four outcomes. This may reflect the fact that the income measure does not confound education and material well-being. Second, differences in outcomes are weak among middle groups; this suggests that finer and more disaggregated measures will yield

---

[1] We examined opposition to capital punishment (a binary variable) and also found postgraduate education and lower administrative occupations to be associated with greater opposition, the liberal view. We found less of an effect for income.

greater variation and illuminate potentially important divergences between groups at the extremes. Third, non-linear effects are common, most especially with occupational groups (as expected, of course, since it is a non-ordinal variable) but also with education because of the tendency for postgraduates to be more liberal than college graduates on government programs. Fourth, and related, education is the least correlated with other indicators of class and ought to be entered separately to capture the multidimensionality of socioeconomic status. Fifth, the subjective indicator of optimism about upward mobility is of clear and substantial significance in models predicting preferences regarding redistribution and income inequality.[2] Sixth, as noted by other scholars, preferences among lower-class groups are measured less precisely than preferences among higher-class groups. And finally, the overall range of variation in outcomes as a result of differences in socioeconomic status is modest but not trivial in most cases (e.g., a third of a standard deviation) but in some instances is substantively large (e.g., two thirds to a full standard deviation).

# CONCLUSION

In this chapter, we have endeavored to present both an overview of classical and contemporary theoretical debates about class differences in social and political attitudes and an empirical investigation of class effects across multiple specifications. Two questions have dominated research on class and public opinion: (1) how large are class differences in public opinion? and (2) what are the trends? Are "classes dying," as some have suggested, or does class remain a robust force in contemporary public opinion? Our dissection of the scholarly literature suggests that these continue to be vexed questions. Analysts have deployed multiple specifications of class in their work, producing results that either speak past one another or fail to capture the full extent of economic stratification. This could also be said of other related areas of research that we have not discussed. Most important, perhaps, is the subject of class asymmetries in the information and knowledge upon which public opinion is often formed. Such asymmetries stem from several potential sources, from differences in education and family background to class biases in political participation and media framing. But whatever their origin, a better understanding of their extent and nature could help explain some of the patterns we observe, such as the absence of strong class differences in public opinion where we might otherwise expect them.

The analyses we have presented in this chapter are meant to demonstrate the need to study these questions with multiple measures of class and across a range of social, economic, and political issues. They are primarily illustrative and not intended to

---

[2] To explore the broader influence of this indicator, we ran ordered probit models with trust and happiness as outcomes and found sizable positive effects of mobility optimism on both (again, also in models with controls).

resolve existing debates. Nevertheless, we are confident that the results we have presented are supportive of an argument emerging from recent research, albeit one in need of further exploration. This argument holds that socioeconomic differences matter in the formation of public opinion but their impact varies across issue area (Gilens 2009) and across indicators of socioeconomic status. Moreover, indicators other than those commonly included in public opinion research are of potentially large import. Finally, preferences formed in proximity to or directly within the formal political sphere—regarding economic policy, partisanship, turnout, and vote choice— are among the most susceptible to the influence of class background, perhaps justifying the classical literature's emphasis on voting behavior instead of public opinion more broadly. Overall, then, the domains in which class seems to matter the most are domains of considerable consequence in democratic, capitalist societies.

# REFERENCES

ALESINA, A., and GLAESER, E. L. 2004. *Fighting Poverty in the US and Europe: A World of Difference*. New York: Oxford University Press.

ALFORD, R. R. 1963. *Party and Society*. Chicago: Rand McNally.

ANDERSON, D, and DAVIDSON, P. 1943. *Ballots and the Democratic Class Struggle*. Stanford, CA: Stanford University Press.

ANSOLABEHERE, S., RODDEN, J., and SNYDER, J. M. 2006. Purple America. *Journal of Economic Perspectives*, 20/2: 97–118.

BARTELS, L. M. 2005. Homer Gets a Tax Cut. *Perspectives on Politics*, 3: 15–31.

—— 2008. *Unequal Democracy: The Political Economy of the New Gilded Age*. Princeton: Princeton University Press.

BELL, D. 1960. *The End of Ideology*. Glencoe, IL: Free Press.

BENABOU, R., and OK, E. A. 2001. Social Mobility and the Demand for Redistribution: The POUM Hypothesis. *Quarterly Journal of Economics*, 16: 447–87.

BERELSON, B. R., LAZARSFELD, P. F., and MCPHEE, W. 1954. *Voting: A Study of Opinion Formation in a Presidential Campaign*. Chicago: University of Chicago Press.

BRADY, D., SOSNAUD, B., and FRENK, S. M. 2009. The Shifting and Diverging White Working Class in U.S. Presidential Elections, 1972–2004. *Social Science Research*, 38: 118–33.

BRINT, S. 1994. *In an Age of Experts*. Princeton: Princeton University Press.

BROOKS, C., and MANZA, J. 2007. *Why Welfare States Persist: The Importance of Public Opinion in Democracies*. Chicago: University of Chicago Press.

BRUSTEIN, W. 1998. *The Logic of Evil: The Social Origins of the Nazi Party, 1925–1933*. New Haven: Yale University Press.

CAMPBELL, A., CONVERSE, P., MILLER, W., and STOKES, D. 1960. *The American Voter*. New York: Wiley.

CAMPBELL, A. L. 2009. What Americans Think of Taxes. In *The New Fiscal Sociology: Taxation in Historical and Comparative Perspective*, ed. I. Martin, A. Mehrotra, and M. Prasad. New York: Cambridge University Press.

CHONG, D., and DRUCKMAN, J. N. 2007. Framing Public Opinion in Competitive Democracies. *American Political Science Review*, 101: 637–55.

CLARK, T. N., and LIPSET, S. M. 1991. Are Social Classes Dying? *International Sociology*, 6: 397–410.

CONOVER, P. J. 1988. The Role of Social Groups in Political Thinking. *British Journal of Political Science*, 18: 51–76.

CONVERSE, PHILIP. 1964. The Nature of Belief Systems in Mass Publics. In *Ideology and Discontent*, ed. D. Apter. Glencoe, IL: Free Press.

DAVIS, J. A. 1982. Achievement Variables and Class Cultures: Family, Schooling, Job, and Forty-Nine Dependent Variables in the Cumulative GSS. *American Sociological Review*, 47: 569–86.

DAWSON, M. 2003. *Black Visions: The Roots of Contemporary African-American Political Ideologies*. Chicago: University of Chicago Press.

DE GRAAF, N. D., NIEUWBEERTA, P., and HEATH, A. 1995. Class Mobility and Political Preferences: Individual and Contextual Effects. *American Journal of Sociology*, 100: 997–1027.

DOWNS, A. 1957. *An Economic Theory of Democracy*. New York: Harper.

EDLUND, L., and PANDE, R. 2002. Why Have Women Become Left-Wing? The Political Gender Gap and the Decline in Marriage. *Quarterly Journal of Economics*, 117: 917–61.

ENNS, P. K., and KELLSTEDT, P. M. 2008. Policy Mood and Political Sophistication: Why Everybody Moves Mood. *British Journal of Political Science*, 38: 433–54.

ERIKSON, R., and GOLDTHORPE, J. 1992. *The Constant Flux*. New York: Oxford University Press.

ERIKSON, R. S., and BHATTI, Y. Forthcoming. How Poorly Are the Poor Represented in the U.S. Senate? In *Who Gets Represented?* ed. P. K. Enns and C. Wlezien. New York: Russell Sage.

—— MacKUEN, M., and STIMSON, J. 2002. *The Macropolity*. New York: Cambridge University Press.

EVANS, G. (ed.) 1999. *The End of Class Politics?* New York: Oxford University Press.

FELDMAN, S., and STEENBERGEN, M. 2001. Social Welfare Attitudes and the Humanitarian Sensibility. In *Citizens and Politics: Perspectives from Political Psychology*, ed. J. H. Kuklinski. New York: Cambridge University Press.

FONG, C. M., BOWLES, S., and GINTIS, H. 2004. Strong Reciprocity and the Welfare State. *Handbook on the Economics of Giving, Reciprocity and Altruism*, ed. S.-C. Kolm and J. M. Ythier. Amsterdam: Elsevier.

FRANK, T. 2004. *What's the Matter with Kansas?* New York: Metropolitan Books.

GANZEBOOM, H. B. G., and TREIMAN, D. J. 2003. Three Internationally Standardized Measures for Comparative Research on Occupational Status. In *Advances in Cross-National Comparison*, ed. J. H. P. Hoffmeyer-Zlotnick and C. Wolf. New York: Kluwer Academic Press.

GELMAN, A. 2008. *Red State, Blue State, Rich State, Poor State: Why Americans Vote the Way They Do*. Princeton: Princeton University Press.

GILENS, M. 2005. Inequality and Democratic Responsiveness. *Public Opinion Quarterly*, 69: 778–96.

—— 2009. Preference Gaps and Inequality in Representation. Unpublished manuscript. Department of Politics, Princeton University.

GOLDTHORPE, J. H. 2000. Rent, Class Conflict, and Class Structure: A Commentary on Sorensen. *American Journal of Sociology*, 105: 1572–82.

—— 2006. *On Sociology*, ii: *Illustrations and Retrospect*. Oxford: Oxford University Press.

GREEN, D., PALMQUIST, B., and SCHICKLER, E. 2002. *Partisan Hearts and Minds*. New Haven: Yale University Press.

GURIN, P., HATCHETT, S., and JACKSON, J. S. 1989. *Hope and Independence: Blacks' Response to Electoral and Party Politics*. New York: Russell Sage Foundation.

HACKER, J., and PIERSON, P. 2005. Abandoning the Middle: The Bush Tax Cuts and the Limits of Democratic Control. *Perspectives on Politics*, 3: 33–53.

HARTZ, L. 1955. *The Liberal Tradition in America*. New York: Harcourt Brace.

HAUSER, R. M., and WARREN, J. R. 1997. Socioeconomic Indexes for Occupations: A Review, Update, and Critique. *Sociological Methodology*, 27: 177–298.

HIBBS, D. 1982. The Dynamics of Political Support for American Presidents among Occupational and Partisan Groups. *American Journal of Political Science*, 26: 313–32.

—— 1987. *The American Political Economy*. Cambridge, MA: Harvard University Press.

HOCHSCHILD, J. 2001. Where You Stand Depends on What You See: Connections among Values, Perceptions of Fact, and Political Prescriptions. In *Citizens and Politics*, ed. J. H. Kuklinski. New York: Cambridge University Press.

—— 2009. Perspectives on Unequal Democracy: The Political Economy of the New Gilded Age. *Perspectives on Politics*, 7: 145–7.

HOUT, M. 2008. How Class Works: Objective and Subjective Aspects of Class since the 1970s. In *Social Class: How Does It Work?* ed. A. Lareau and D. Conley. New York: Russell Sage.

—— BROOKS, C., and MANZA, J. 1995. The Democratic Class Struggle in the United States, 1948–1992. *American Sociological Review*, 60: 805–28.

INGLEHART, R. 1990. *Culture Shift in Advanced Industrial Society*. Princeton: Princeton University Press.

JACKMAN, M. R., and JACKMAN, R. W. 1983. *Class Awareness in the United States*. Berkeley: University of California Press.

JACOBS, L. R., and PAGE, B. I. 2005. Who Influences U.S. Foreign Policy? *American Political Science Review*, 99: 107–23.

—— and SHAPIRO, R. 2000. *Politicians Don't Pander: Political Manipulation and the Loss of Democratic Responsiveness*. Chicago: University of Chicago Press.

KERR, C., DUNLOP, J. T., HARBISON, F. H., and C. H. MYERS. 1960. *Industrialism and Industrial Man*. Cambridge, MA: Harvard University Press.

KINGSTON, P. 2000. *The Classless Society*. Stanford, CA: Stanford University Press.

KNUTSEN, O. 2007. The Decline of Social Class? In *The Oxford Handbook of Political Behavior*, ed. R. J. Dalton and H.-D. Klingmann. New York: Oxford University Press.

KOHLER, U. 2006. Changing Class Locations and Partisanship in Germany. In *The Social Logics of Politics*, ed. A. Zuckerman. Philadelphia: Temple University Press.

KUMLIN, S. 2007. The Welfare State: Values, Policy Preferences, and Performance Evaluations. In *The Oxford Handbook of Political Behavior*, ed. R. J. Dalton and H.-D. Klingmann. New York: Oxford University Press.

LANE, R. E. 1962. *Political Ideology: Why the American Common Man Believes What He Does*. Glencoe, IL: Free Press.

LAZARSFELD, P. F., BERELSON, B. R., and GAUDET, H. 1948. *The People's Choice*. New York: Columbia University Press.

LEWIS-BECK, M. S., WEISBERG, H. F., NORPOTH, H., and JACOBY, W. G. 2008. *The American Voter Revisited*. Ann Arbor: University of Michigan Press.

LIPSET, S. M. 1960. *Political Man*, expanded edn. Baltimore: Johns Hopkins University Press, 1981.

—— and MARKS, G. 2000. *It Didn't Happen Here: The Failure of Socialism in America*. New York: Norton.

—— and ROKKAN, S. 1967. Cleavage Structures, Party Systems, and Voter Alignments: An Introduction. In *Party Systems and Voter Alignments*, ed. S. M. Lipset and S. Rokkan. New York: Free Press.

LIPSKY, M. 1983. *Street-Level Bureaucracy*. New York: Russell Sage.

McCALL, L., and KENWORTHY, L. 2009a. Americans' Social Policy Preferences in the Era of Rising Inequality. *Perspectives on Politics*, 7: 459–84.

—— —— 2009b. Explaining Americans' Beliefs about Income Inequality. Unpublished manuscript. Department of Sociology, Northwestern University.

McCARTY, N., POOLE, K. T., and ROSENTHAL, H. 2006. *Polarized America: The Dance of Ideology and Unequal Riches*. Cambridge, MA: MIT Press.

MANZA, J., and BROOKS, C. 1999. *Social Cleavages and Political Change: Voter Alignments and U.S. Party Coalitions*. Chicago: University of Chicago Press.

MELTZER, A. H., and RICHARD, S. F. 1981. A Rational Theory of the Size of Government. *Journal of Political Economy*, 89: 914–27.

METTLER, S., and SOSS, J. 2004. The Consequences of Public Policy for Democratic Citizenship: Bridging Policy Studies and Mass Politics. *Perspectives on Politics*, 2: 55–73.

MUTZ, D. C., and MONDAK, J. J. 2006. The Workplace as Context for Cross-Cutting Political Discourse. *Journal of Politics*, 68: 140–55.

OGBURN, W. F., and COOMBS, L. 1940. The Economic Factor in the Roosevelt Elections. *American Political Science Review*, 34: 719–27.

—— and HILL, E. 1935. Income Classes and the Roosevelt Vote in 1932. *Political Science Quarterly*, 50: 186–93.

—— and PETERSON, D. 1916. Political Thought of Social Classes. *Political Science Quarterly*, 31: 300–17.

PAGE, B. I., and JACOBS, L. R. 2009. *Class War: What Americans Really Think about Class War*. Chicago: University of Chicago Press.

—— and SHAPIRO, R. Y. 1992. *The Rational Public*. Chicago: University of Chicago Press.

PAKULSKI, J., and WATERS, M. 1996. *The Death of Class*. Newbury Park, CA: Sage.

PERLMAN, S. 1928. *A Theory of the Labor Movement*. New York: Macmillan.

PIKETTY, T. 1995. Social Mobility and Redistributive Politics. *Quarterly Journal of Economics*, 110: 551–84.

RICE, S. A. 1928. *Quantitative Methods in Politics*. New York: Russell and Russell, 1969.

ROEMER, J. 1998. Why the Poor Do Not Expropriate the Rich: An Old Argument in New Garb. *Journal of Public Economics*, 70: 399–424.

SCHEVE, K., and SLAUGHTER, M. 2007. Public Opinion, International Economic Integration, and the Welfare State. In *Globalization and Egalitarian Redistribution*, ed. S. Bowles, P. Bardhan, and M. Wallerstein. Princeton: Princeton University Press.

SOMBART, W. 1906. *Why Is there No Socialism in the United States?* White Plains, NY: M. E. Sharpe, 1976.

SOROKA, S., and WLEZIEN, C. 2009. *Degrees of Democracy*. New York: Cambridge University Press.

STARR, P. 1983. *The Social Transformation of American Medicine*. New York: Basic Books.

STONECASH, J., and BREWER, M. 2006. *Split: Class and Cultural Divides in American Politics*. Washington, DC: CQ Press.

STOUFFER, S. A. 1955. *Communism, Conformity, and Civil Liberties*. New York: Doubleday.

SVALLFORS, S. 2006. *The Moral Economy of Class*. Stanford, CA: Stanford University Press.

URA, J. D., and ELLIS, C. R. 2008. Income, Preferences, and the Dynamics of Policy Responsiveness. *PS: Political Science and Politics*, 41: 785–94.

VAN DER WAAL, J., ACHTERBERG, P., and HOUTMAN, D. 2007. Class is Not Dead—It Has Been Buried Alive: Class Voting and Cultural Voting in Postwar Western Societies (1956–1990). *Politics and Society*, 35: 403–26.

VANNEMAN, R., and CANNON, L. W. 1987. *The American Perception of Class*. Philadelphia: Temple University Press.

WALSH, K. C., JENNINGS, M. K., and STOKER, L. 2004. The Effects of Social Class Identification on Participatory Orientations toward Government. *British Journal of Political Science*, 34: 469–95.

WEAKLIEM, D. L., and HEATH, A. 1994. Rational Choice and Class Voting. *Rationality and Society*, 6: 243–70.

—— 1999. The Secret Life of Class Voting: Britain, France, and the United States since the 1930s. In *The End of Class Politics? Class Voting in Comparative Context*, ed. G. Evans. New York: Oxford University Press.

WEEDEN, K. A., and GRUSKY, D. B. 2005. The Case for a New Class Map. *American Journal of Sociology*, 111: 141–212.

WRIGHT, E. O. 1997. *Class Counts*. New York: Cambridge University Press.

ZUCKERMAN, A. (ed.) 2006. *The Social Logics of Politics: Personal Networks as Contexts for Political Behavior*. Philadelphia: Temple University Press.

# APPENDIX 34.1

## DATA

All data are from the General Social Surveys (GSS) for 1996, 2000, and 2008.

### Views about Redistribution

The three items for the index on views about redistribution are averaged for each respondent (McCall and Kenworthy 2009a). The items are: "Should the government do everything possible to improve the standard of living of all poor Americans, or should each person take care of himself?" (*helppoor*, 5 categories); "Should the government reduce income differences between the rich and poor, perhaps by raising taxes of wealthy families or by giving income assistance to the poor, or should the government not concern itself with reducing differences?" (*eqwlth*, 7 categories); and "Do you agree or disagree that it is the responsibility of the government to reduce differences in income between people with high incomes and those with low incomes?" (*goveqinc*, 1 = strongly agree to 5 = strongly disagree). All items and the average are coded so that positive values indicate the liberal position.

### Views about Government Spending

The ten-item index on government spending is taken from Ura and Ellis (2008) and is based on the national spending questions (*nat**): "We are faced with many problems in this country, none of which can be solved easily or inexpensively. Are we spending too much money, too little money, or about the right amount on" (1) "welfare," (2) "improving and protecting the nation's health," (3) "improving the nation's education system," (4) "improving the condition of blacks," (5) "improving and protecting the environment," (6) "solving the problems of big cities," (7) "dealing with drug addiction," (8) "halting the rising crime rate," (9) "foreign aid," and (10) "military/armaments/defense?" All items and the index are coded so that positive values indicate the liberal position.

## Views about Income Inequality

The three items for the index of views about income inequality are taken from McCall and Kenworthy (2009a) and are averaged for each respondent: "Do you agree or disagree: Differences in income in America are too large?" (*incgap*, 5 categories); "Do you agree or disagree: Large differences in income are necessary for America's prosperity?" (*inequal5*, 5 categories); and "Do you agree or disagree: Inequality continues to exist because it benefits the rich and powerful?" (*inequal3*, 5 categories). All items and the average are coded so that positive values indicate the liberal position.

## Views about Abortion

The seven items for the index of abortion attitudes is an average for each respondent and is based on a battery of questions on abortion (*ab\**): "Please tell me whether or not you think it should be possible for a pregnant woman to obtain a legal abortion (yes or no) if " (1) "there is a strong chance of a serious defect in the baby," (2) "she is married and does not want any more children," (3) "the woman's own health is seriously endangered by the pregnancy," (4) "the family has a very low income and cannot afford any more children," (5) "the woman became pregnant as a result of rape," (6) "the woman is not married and does not want to marry the man," or (7) "the woman wants it for any reason." All items and the average are coded so that positive values indicate the liberal position.

## The Sample Size and Controls in the Full Models

All class indicators are included in the full models, but they are measured as continuous or ordinal variables instead of as dummy variables. Controls include views about the role of hard work in getting ahead, ideological views, party identification, church attendance, dummies for Jewish, Protestant, and Catholic denominations, marital status, age, age squared, household size, and dummies each for being white and male. Inclusion of these variables reduces the sample size to 1,100 observations across three years, and this same sample is used for all analyses. These three years were selected because they are the most recent years containing each of the outcome measures.

## Other Coding Issues

The GSS occupational categories were converted to the Erikson–Goldthorpe schema using Stata routines developed by John Hendrickx (*ssc isco* and *ssc isko*) and based on Ganzeboom and Treiman (2003).

The income quintiles are inexact due to changes across General Social Surveys in the measurement of family income categories.

CHAPTER 35

................................................................

# KNOWLEDGE, SOPHISTICATION, AND ISSUE PUBLICS

................................................................

VINCENT HUTCHINGS
SPENCER PISTON

## INTRODUCTION

................................................................

POLITICAL information is an important commodity in a democracy. This is because the chief responsibility of citizens in democratic systems is to monitor elected representatives and evaluate their performance at election time. It is difficult to envision how citizens can carry out this duty without some information about the activities of government officials.

We begin this chapter by reviewing research showing that American citizens have quite low levels of general knowledge compared to political elites or to citizens from other Western nations. Given that scholars are still in the process of refining measures of political knowledge, we then discuss ways in which our current measures might be improved. We next review literature on ideological sophistication. Scholars have argued not just that Americans are ignorant but also that they are not ideologically sophisticated. We examine this contention, and then review scholars' views of the consequences of a lack of knowledge and sophistication. Finally, we discuss research on issue publics. Even if Americans are mostly inattentive to politics in general, some are attentive to the issues they care about most, with consequences for the political opinions they hold. We conclude by suggesting directions for future research.

## ASSESSING LEVELS OF POLITICAL KNOWLEDGE

................................................................

Michael Delli Carpini and Scott Keeter provide a comprehensive overview of the levels of political knowledge in the mass public in their book entitled *What Americans Know about Politics and Why it Matters* (1996). They rely on data from over fifty years' (1940–94) worth of surveys to lay out what Americans know about politics. This research establishes that the American public is not totally uninformed about political matters. It is also clear, however, that the information levels for the average citizen fall far below elite standards. For example, virtually all Americans know the length of a presidential term in office (93 percent), can provide a definition of a presidential veto (89 percent), and recognize that the US is a democracy (88 percent). However, less than half of Americans can define the Bill of Rights (41 percent), understand the substance of the *Roe* v. *Wade* court decision (30 percent), or know the length of term served by US senators (25 percent). More sobering still, *only slightly more than half* (59 percent) are aware of the party affiliation of their state governor, how their representative voted on the first Gulf War (57 percent), or that the Republican Party is the more conservative of the two major parties (57 percent). Given that virtually all respondents know that there are only two major parties, there is actually a 50 percent chance that a respondent could guess the right answer to these questions.

It is clear from the data compiled by Delli Carpini and Keeter that most Americans are not very informed about politics, although they are not entirely uninformed. Still, how does the average American compare to citizens in other countries? It might be reassuring if Americans were about as informed as one could expect given international levels of political sophistication. This is not, however, the case. Delli Carpini and Keeter report that Americans typically rank near or at the bottom when compared to other Western democracies. For example, when responding to a range of questions asking to identify the secretary general of the UN or the president of Russia, Americans only answered 31 percent accurately. In contrast, the Germans were correct 71 percent of the time and the Italians were correct 50 percent of the time. Canadians (38 percent), the French (43 percent), and the British (40 percent) also scored higher than Americans, with only the Spanish scoring lower on this measure.

Why is it that Americans tend to score lower on measures of political knowledge relative to citizens in other Western democracies? One explanation involves the different roles played by the mass media in the US as compared to various European countries. Curran, Iyengar, Lund, and Salovaara-Moring (2009) argue that the increasingly market-driven, and thus entertainment-centered, news media in the US provide less information than the more public service oriented approach adopted in some European nations. In order to test this hypothesis, Curran and his colleagues content analyzed major newspapers and television news programs in four countries, the United Kingdom, Finland, Denmark, and the US, in the winter and early spring of 2007. Their aim was to identify trends in coverage of "hard news," or issues that were discussed in the context of their more general implications for public policy, and "soft news" as well as domestic and international news. Additionally, they surveyed respondents in each of the four countries on their knowledge of hard and soft news as well as domestic and international issues. They found that the focus on hard news and international issues was generally much higher in European television news programs, although the reverse was generally true with respect to newspaper coverage. In terms of information levels, Americans were typically much less knowledgeable about international issues, and to a lesser extent domestic hard news, than were European respondents. Consistent with their expectations, Curran and his co-authors also found that the amount of media coverage devoted to an issue was strongly correlated with levels of political knowledge. They conclude that Americans are less knowledgeable than their European counterparts at least in part because they receive less information from their mass media.

## MEASUREMENT OF POLITICAL KNOWLEDGE

Scholars following Delli Carpini and Keeter are working to refine measurements of political knowledge. In this section we review some of the problems previous measures have encountered. The first problem is the need to account for the social context surrounding the measurement of political knowledge. Previous measures indicated that women in the United States know less about politics than men (Delli Carpini and Keeter 1996; Jamieson and Kenski 2000). McGlone, Aronson, and Kobrynowicz (2006) provide some suggestive evidence questioning this conclusion in their survey of 141 undergraduates at Lafayette College. The authors found that this gender gap was nearly eliminated among those respondents whose interviewer was female. They argue that the presence of a male interviewer causes the female respondent to fear confirming the stereotype that females have less political acumen than males, and that this fear has debilitating consequences. It is not clear, however, whether McGlone, Aronson, and Kobrynowicz's results would translate to a nationally representative sample of adults.

Survey designs that include a "don't know" response may contribute to the gender gap, since such designs contaminate knowledge scores with personality factors associated with guessing, such as self-confidence and risk-taking (Mondak 2001). Indeed, analyses of survey responses of national samples of adults indicate that men's increased propensity to guess may account for over a third (Lizotte and Sidman 2009) or even one half (Mondak and Anderson 2004) of the gender gap in performance on political knowledge tests.

In a similar vein, Davis and Silver (2003) argue that "stereotype threat," or the fear of confirming a derogatory stereotype, leads blacks to perform worse on political knowledge tests. They surveyed a random digit dialing (RDD) sample of Michigan adults, including an oversample of 212 black respondents, and found that black respondents performed worse than whites on a political knowledge test, answering about 0.5 fewer questions out of a total of 7 correctly, after controlling for education. This gap, however, may have been moderated by perceived race of interviewer. The authors found that those black respondents who perceived their interviewer to be black answered correctly about 0.4 questions more than those who perceived their interviewer to be white and 0.7 questions more than those who perceived their interviewer's race to be ambiguous. We cannot be certain that stereotype threat accounts for the entirety of the racial gap identified by Davis and Silver since the authors do not explicitly compare the effect of perceived interviewer race on blacks to that on whites as many white respondents were either unable or unwilling to identify what they perceived their interviewer's race to be. It is also worth noting that the authors find no effect for the interviewer's self-identified race.

Finally, survey design and coding of responses may result in systematic underestimates of political knowledge, although it is not yet clear that the magnitude of these underestimates is large. First, surveys do not typically offer respondents incentives to provide correct answers, which may lead to a lack of effort on the part of the respondent. Second, respondents are typically asked to demonstrate political knowledge without warning, and thus are forced to rely on top of the head responses. What if citizens were given either incentive or opportunity to come up with the correct answer to a political knowledge test? Prior and Lupia randomly assign a national sample of adults to conditions that vary in two respects: (1) whether or not the subjects receive a small payment of $1 per correct answer, and (2) whether the subjects have one minute or twenty-four hours to answer each question. They find that either increased incentive or increased time results in higher performance on the political knowledge tests, although the size of the effect is at most about one additional question out of fourteen answered correctly.

Third, overly stringent standards are sometimes applied to the coding of open-ended responses. Gibson and Caldeira (2009) find that in the 2004 American National Election Study (ANES) time series survey, interviewers were instructed to code as correct only those responses to the question "Who is William Rehnquist?" that included *both* the phrase "Chief Justice" and "Supreme Court." "Chief Justice of the Court" would therefore be coded as incorrect, as would "Supreme Court judge who is the head honcho." Gibson and Caldeira apply a more forgiving standard to the 2000 ANES, since the verbatim responses to the 2004 ANES were not recorded. They find that a full 71.8 percent of those coded by ANES interviewers as giving incorrect answers could be considered to have given "nearly correct" answers, such as "a Supreme Court justice."

## Levels of Political Sophistication: Converse and His Critics

The view that the American voter is guided by ideological principles is something many of us learned in our high school civics class. However enduring this perspective may be at the popular or journalistic level, scholars have known for some time that this is not an accurate view of the public. Perhaps more than any other scholar, Phil Converse, in his 1964 article "The Nature of Belief Systems in Mass Publics," is responsible for undermining the reassuring idea that Americans are ideologically motivated. This controversial article set much of the research agenda in public opinion for some time, attracting many critics and supporters. Although some of its conclusions have been modified over time, it remains the cornerstone of what we understand about political sophistication.

In this article, Converse sought to explain how citizens organize their perceptions of the political world. These perceptions might be organized in ideological terms (i.e., "left," "right") but Converse cast a somewhat broader net by focusing on *belief systems*. By "belief systems" he meant ideas and attitudes about the political world that are "bound together by some form of *constraint* or functional interdependence." By "constraint," he meant an ostensibly logical framework in which knowing someone's position on one policy matter meant that you could reasonably predict how this person felt about a related matter. For example, if one knows that a person favors a significant reduction in taxes, then (presumably) one can infer that person is a conservative and probably also favors cutbacks in social welfare spending generally.

In order to test his claims about constraint, Converse relied upon two kinds of evidence. The first was drawn from his earlier work *The American Voter* (Campbell, Converse, Miller, and Stokes 1960), which coded open-ended responses to survey questions concerning the good and bad points of the two political parties and two presidential candidates in the 1956, 1958, and 1960 ANES surveys. Based on his coding of the responses on these items, he concluded that the constraint or internal logic present in the belief systems of elites is extremely rare in the mass public. He found that only about 2.5 percent of respondents in the 1956 sample had a strong command of ideological terms. Another 9 percent of the sample made occasional use of the terms but it was not always clear that they understood them. Thus, about 88 percent of the respondents seemed to have no grasp of ideological terms.[1] The second source of evidence relied on the panel study design of the 1956, 1958, and 1960 ANES surveys. Converse reported that respondent attitudes on a variety of issues were wildly unstable over time. On average, only slightly more than half of respondents came down on the same side of a policy dispute over a two-year period. Half could be expected to do so by chance.[2] Converse concluded that this response instability indicated that many Americans had "non-attitudes" on most policy matters: they selected issue positions as if they were flipping a coin.

A number of scholars were less than persuaded by Converse's devastating critique of the American electorate. Much of their criticism centered on the political environment of the 1950s and how this purportedly uninteresting political era may have artificially depressed levels of political engagement (for example, Nie, Verba, and Petrocik 1979). Although some subsequent work did show increased levels of constraint and

---

[1] The plurality of respondents provided answers suggesting that they view the parties and candidates in terms of "Group Benefits" (42 percent). The other two categories are "Nature of the Times" (24 percent), and "No Issue Content" (22 percent).

[2] Some attitudes were more stable than others. Party identification was found to be highly stable over time and issues relating to African Americans and federal job guarantees somewhat less so. Of course, the parties and blacks involve well-known groups in society, whereas jobs involve an issue close to home for most Americans.

sophistication (i.e., issue voting) in the 1960s and 1970s, it turned out that much of this was due to changes in question wording (Sullivan, Piereson, and Marcus 1978) or the rise in prominence of so-called "easy issues" such as race, drugs, or abortion (Carmines and Stimson 1980; Converse and Markus 1979). In support of Converse, Jennings (1992) also uncovered results suggesting that levels of political sophistication in the mass public were generally low. Drawing on survey data from the mid-1970s to the late 1980s, he compared levels of constraint among ordinary citizens with delegates to the major party conventions. Jennings found that constraint across a variety of policy questions was remarkably low for the general public especially when compared to party elites.

Converse's research on response instability, and the resulting "non-attitudes" thesis, has fared less well over time than some other elements of his work. Zaller (1992) argues that there is another, more compelling, explanation for the tendency for survey respondents to adopt different issue positions over time. According to his Receive–Accept–Sample (RAS) model, citizens do not have fixed opinions or a single attitude toward a political issue. Instead, they have multiple, and often conflicting, attitudes on any given political issue. This is due to their exposure to a number of conflicting elite messages which citizens, especially those who are not politically sophisticated, internalize indiscriminately. When confronted with survey questions, respondents simply provide answers that are based on whatever considerations happen to be most salient at the moment based in part on whatever political talking point they may have been exposed to most recently. When confronted some time later with the same question, they may draw on a different consideration and thus view it from a different perspective and provide a different response. With this model, response instability indicates only that people are often ambivalent on matters of public policy, even if they do possess some true underlying position. Zaller develops a series of tests for his RAS model, and generally finds evidence in support of his explanation, rather than the non-attitudes thesis.

## WHAT ARE THE CONSEQUENCES OF LIMITED CITIZEN KNOWLEDGE AND SOPHISTICATION?

Since the initial wave of research on political sophistication tapered off in the 1990s, scholars have begun to revisit some of the issues in this debate. Most of this newer literature does not focus on whether average citizens are as politically informed or sophisticated as elites, as the field has generally concluded that they are not (Kinder 2003). Instead, scholars have explored a variety of topics such as the consequences of political ignorance, the circumstances under which citizens can become more informed, appropriate ways to measure information, and explanations for subgroup differences in political knowledge. Below we address each of these subjects and some of the recent research published in this area.

One of the questions scholars of political information have sought to answer is whether or not the informed tend to have different preferences than the uninformed. That is, would the policy or candidate preferences of the voters differ significantly if they were more knowledgeable about politics? In order to answer this question, Bartels (2005) examines support for the 2001 tax cuts proposed by President Bush. He notes that, of those respondents in the 2002 ANES offering an opinion on the subject (about 40 percent did not), supporters outnumbered opponents by 2 to 1. As Bartels points out, the Bush tax cuts were heavily skewed toward the wealthy, which might suggest that they would be less popular among low-income Americans or respondents who believed the rich paid too little in taxes. In fact, neither variable had a statistically significant effect on support for the tax cut. Along with party identification and political ideology, the most important determinant of support for the 2001 tax cut was whether the respondent thought that their own tax burden was too heavy. Moreover, the more politically informed the respondent, the more likely they were to oppose the Bush tax cuts.[3] Bartels concludes that these results indicate that "Public opinion in this instance was ill informed, insensitive to some of the most important implications of the tax cuts, and largely disconnected from (or misconnected to) a variety of relevant values and material interests" (2005, 15).

Lupia, Levine, Menning, and Sin (2007) take issue with Bartels's conclusions. In particular, they show that Bartels's finding that political knowledge is associated with greater opposition to the Bush tax cuts only applies to Democrats or political liberals. Increases in political information have no effect among Republicans or conservatives, as these respondents were almost uniformly supportive of the 2001 tax cuts. Lupia and his colleagues argue that it is premature to conclude that citizens who supported the tax cuts were unenlightened as the data are insufficient to allow for any definitive conclusions. That is, there is no direct measure in the 2002 ANES as to whether the tax cuts would affect respondents' relative tax burden. Instead, Bartels relies on respondents' more general assessments of their tax burden. Bartels (2007) concedes that Lupia and his co-authors provide an important elaboration on his earlier work, but views their findings as reconcilable with his larger argument.

This exchange was useful, both because it confirms much of what we have learned about political sophistication from other studies and because it highlights some important qualifications of conventional wisdom. Bartels's (2005) examination of the factors influencing support for the Bush tax cuts is consistent with other studies showing limited public understanding of salient public policy disputes (for example, see Converse 1964; Hutchings 2003; Kuklinski et al. 2000; Kuklinski and Quirk 2000). However, by showing in this instance that the information effects were localized among Democrats, Lupia and his colleagues draw our attention to the role that contextual and political factors can play in mitigating the importance of general political sophistication. That is, for Republicans and conservatives, adopting a position on the tax cuts that

---

[3] Levels of political information were measured with interviewer ratings.

was consistent with their party identification or ideology did not require high levels of political knowledge. On the other hand, in the absence of political knowledge many Democrats were inclined to support a policy that some conceivably would have opposed if they were more informed.

## THE REVISIONIST VIEW, MISINFORMATION, AND THE ROLE OF MEDIA

Very soon after researchers identified the limited knowledge and political sophistication in the mass public, other scholars would offer a very different view. One of the earliest critics of this increasingly dominant view was V. O. Key, who argued in his posthumously published book *The Responsible Electorate* that "voters are not fools" (1966, 7). By this he meant that the lack of information in the electorate was due, at least in part, to the purposefully vague and inconsistent pronouncements from political elites. In short, sometimes elites have an incentive to cultivate an ignorant public in order to further their political objectives. However, when candidates offer the voters stark choices, they are much more inclined to bring their ideological views to bear on their voter choice (Page and Brody 1972). Some more recent scholarship has also offered a revisionist view suggesting that citizens sometimes have the information they need to form coherent, stable political preferences (NB Bartels 2003) or to hold politicians accountable to those preferences.

For example, in a study of voting on five insurance initiatives in California, Lupia (1994) finds that those citizens who were uninformed about the content of a given initiative but were able to identify that initiative's sponsor supported that initiative at similar rates to those citizens who were informed about the initiative's content. Such citizens were able to act "as if" they were fully informed. Lupia is careful to acknowledge, however, that a substantial proportion of citizens lacked even knowledge of the initiative's sponsor.

As a general rule, then, under what conditions is knowledge necessary? Lupia and McCubbins (1998) concede that many citizens are ignorant about a wide slew of political issues, but argue that this does not necessarily lead to political incompetence. Rather, given that people lack the informational resources to reason through the ins and outs of every political issue, it may be more efficient to rely on the advice of others. The most important thing for citizens to know, therefore, is whom they can trust. Another way in which citizens may be able to bypass more comprehensive knowledge is through the "likability heuristic" (Sniderman, Brody, and Tetlock 1993). This is the tendency for people to infer the preferences of social groups based on how much they like those groups. For example, a Democrat might infer the policy positions of a Republican candidate by reasoning that she does not like Republicans so their beliefs probably differ from her own. Citizens may not need to know the details of a candidate's platform, therefore, in order to make educated guesses about their stance on public policy. In a similar vein, Popkin (1991) argues that the high-profile (and sometimes low-profile) events associated with presidential campaigns can also provide the voters with sufficient, if not comprehensive, information to evaluate the candidates on policy grounds.

A somewhat different assault on the conclusion of Converse and his supporters comes from Benjamin Page and Robert Shapiro in *The Rational Public* (1992). Page and Shapiro are troubled most by Converse's finding that citizens typically possess "non-attitudes" and consequently their opinions fluctuate wildly and in a random fashion. Implicit in the "non-attitudes" argument as well is the notion that citizens are largely uninformed about important aspects of the policy debates taking place at the elite level. Page and Shapiro advance a simple yet powerful response to these charges based primarily on the principle of aggregation. They argue that while attitude stability and information levels may be low among most voters individually, collectively the public is remarkably rational. By rational they mean that aggregate public opinion is frequently stable (although not fixed); is able to make distinctions; is coherently organized; takes into account the best available information; and changes in predictable and reasonable ways. Page and Shapiro support this view by examining evidence from over 1,000 repeated survey questions dating from the 1930s until the 1990s.

The revisionist view's main contribution has been to bring scholars' attention to circumstances under which the consequences of citizen ignorance may not be as dire as some had thought. However, other recent scholarship gives reason for pessimism as well.

For one thing, *misinformation* (rather than the lack of information) may be widespread. Kuklinski and colleagues (2000) find evidence of systematic bias in factual beliefs in their survey experiment on 1,160 Illinois residents. Respondents greatly overestimated the percentage of welfare recipients that are African American, the amount of money welfare recipients receive, and the percentage of the federal budget that welfare payments constitute. These inaccurate beliefs were strongly associated with opposition to welfare. Furthermore, those who held the least accurate beliefs expressed the most confidence in them, which might indicate that the preferences based on these inaccurate beliefs are unlikely to change. Indeed, the authors find evidence of resistance to change in preferences even when the correct facts about welfare are presented, though they also find that a more obtrusive presentation results in some movement.

Consistent with other work in this literature, Bobo and Johnson (2004) also find that opinions about the death penalty are resistant to information pointing out a racial double standard in its application. In their survey experiment of a nationally representative sample of 724 whites and 831 blacks, the authors find that informing respondents that blacks are overrepresented on Death Row had no effect on support for the death penalty among either black or white respondents, relative to a control group. However, informing respondents that homicidal offenders are more likely to be sentenced to death when the victim is white reduced support for the death penalty among black but not white respondents. Bobo and Johnson also find that attitudes about drug sentencing policies are somewhat more receptive to elite issue frames for both racial groups.

Misleading statements in the media may be one cause of misinformation among citizens. Jerit and Barabas (2006) find that the proportion of statements that were inaccurate in Associated Press stories about Social Security correlates with the tendency to incorrectly answer questions about Social Security in public opinion surveys. Similarly, Gilliam and Iyengar (2000) find that violent crime committed by blacks is overreported in local television news, leading to increased racial animus and support for punitive anti-crime policies among white (but not black) viewers.

Even when citizens are presented with correct information, they may not choose to attend to it. Zaller (1992) argues that only those who are moderately attentive to politics are susceptible to elite influence. On the low end of the political awareness spectrum, many citizens do not pay attention to political messages or are not sophisticated enough to process them. On the high end of the spectrum, those who are most exposed to information may also have formed an opinion on an issue. As a result they may have become "motivated skeptics" (Taber and Lodge 2006), ignoring information that is inconsistent with their opinion and subjecting arguments opposed to their position to increased scrutiny and counterargument. Many citizens are overly confident in their beliefs, which may inhibit learning and opinion change (Druckman 2004).

What is the role of the media in communicating knowledge? As stated above, the media can serve as a source of both valid and invalid information. They can also shape what information citizens attend to, as is demonstrated by Iyengar and Kinder's (1989) study of television news. Experimental participants were randomly assigned to groups that watched newscasts with varying levels of discussion of different policy issues. The participants then were asked to evaluate the president both on a number of different policy issues and overall. Iyengar and Kinder found that the participant's evaluation of the president on a given policy issue had a greater influence on the participant's overall evaluation of the president if the participant had been assigned to watch a newscast that spent more time discussing that policy issue. Iyengar and Kinder's research design is impressive. The authors went to great lengths to simulate a realistic environment, allowing participants to bring their families into the laboratory, embedding the newscasts in other television programming, and allowing twenty-four hours to pass before asking participants to evaluate the president. Finally, the authors found similar results using national surveys, leading to a compelling finding that the media exert substantial agenda-setting power.

## POLITICAL KNOWLEDGE AND ISSUE PUBLICS

The evidence that citizens are typically uninformed about politics relative to political elites is difficult to dispute. However, an important caveat to this finding is the possibility that segments of the population can become relatively more informed on matters that they regard as important. That is, although there can be little doubt that most individuals are generally uninformed about politics, if portions of the electorate are at least somewhat more knowledgeable on those subjects that implicate their values or perceived interests, then the electorate might be more competent than we suspect. This view has been offered by a number of scholars over the years, perhaps most prominently by V. O. Key (1961), Converse (1964), and Neuman (1986). Key referred to these individuals as "special publics," whereas Converse dubbed them "issue publics." Neuman argued that although about 75 percent of the public follow only one or two issues, even this level of interest, in combination with tolerably high levels of voting, is enough to keep the system afloat, given that another 5 percent are actively involved and well informed.

The evidence that citizens tend to be information specialists rather than information generalists has traditionally been mixed. Supporting the idea that people are information-specialists, Iyengar (1990), in a telephone survey of about 150 respondents in New York, found that blacks were more likely than whites to possess factual information about civil rights issues and Jewish Americans were more likely than other Americans to know more about the Middle East. Furthermore, Aldrich, Sullivan, and Borgida (1989) found from national survey data that a substantial proportion of the public have clear attitudes about foreign policy and use these attitudes to make voting decisions. However, Price and Zaller (1993) find only limited evidence that respondents in the 1989 ANES were typically information specialists. They examined information about sixteen news stories and found that specialists, respondents identified with demographic or attitudinal measures, were more informed in only a handful of cases. Respondents with more general knowledge about politics were more likely than those scoring low on this scale to learn about each story (also see Delli Carpini and Keeter 1996).

Hutchings (2003) takes issue with previous efforts to test whether issue publics are more knowledgeable on relevant matters of public policy. He notes that some scholars have identified issue publics with imprecise demographic categories and have failed to take into account the impact of contextual factors. For example, with the confirmation vote for Clarence Thomas to the Supreme Court, some scholars assumed that women should have been more likely than men to learn how their senator voted and more likely to use this information when casting their ballot in the 1992 senate elections. However, Hutchings argues that citizens have multiple group memberships and these multiple identities may have suppressed or enhanced the attentiveness of issue publics. When the identities are reinforcing, issue publics should be distinctively informed, but when they are in conflict we would not expect this outcome. In the case of the sexual harassment allegations surrounding the Thomas vote, Hutchings theorizes that liberal women and conservative men should have been most attentive but liberal men and conservative women, owing to their conflicted gender and ideological identities, should not be especially attentive. Similarly, African Americans residing in states represented by moderate Democratic senators, who represented the center of gravity in the confirmation vote because they publicly wavered on their position, should have been more informed of their senators' votes than whites residing in these same states.

Examining survey data drawn from the 1992 Senate Election Study, Hutchings finds that his expectations are confirmed.[4] This suggests that more precise measures, coupled with a greater appreciation of context effects, might show more widespread effects of issue public attentiveness.

Is information acquired about a given issue area useful? Gilens (2001) finds that information about a specific policy area is influential to the formation of political judgments. Through analysis of survey data and randomized experiments, he finds first that policy-specific information influences public opinion even after general political knowledge is taken into account. Indeed, in five of the seven issue areas Gilens examines, policy-specific information has a greater effect on public opinion than does general political knowledge. Furthermore, the impact of policy-specific information is greatest among those with the highest levels of political knowledge. In sum, scholars following Key and Converse have found that issue publics exist: groups whose members care more about particular issues, learn more about these issues as a result, and base their opinions on this knowledge.

# Conclusion

Scholarship on political knowledge, sophistication, and issue publics has yielded rich findings. Here we present recommendations for future research.

Our first recommendation concerns measurement. We urge scholars to do their best to take into account the many obstacles that knowledge measures face, including the possibility that response option effects bias results against certain subgroups (Davis and Silver 2003; McGlone, Aronson, and Kobrynowicz 2006). Additionally, researchers should be mindful of the role that incentives play in motivating levels of political knowledge (Prior and Lupia 2008), as well as the overly stringent standards often applied to measures of political information (Gibson and Caldeira 2009).

Second, we encourage scholars to move past the overly general debate over whether widespread ignorance is woeful or not all that bad. Clearly, previous research has demonstrated both that citizens are quite ignorant about many political matters and that citizens sometimes function quite well despite such ignorance. Future research would therefore do well to tackle such questions as the following: under what conditions is ignorance harmful? What kinds of knowledge are necessary, and for which specific tasks?

Finally, we regard as positive the growing trend to bring experimental methods to bear on questions of political knowledge. Some of the work highlighted above (for example, Bobo and Johnson 2004; Prior and Lupia 2008; Kuklinski et al. 2000) illustrates the (albeit limited) role that incentives and elite cues can play in spurring

---

[4] He also found that respondents with more general knowledge of politics were more likely to correctly identify how their senators voted on the nomination.

greater levels of sophistication and political attentiveness. For example, although Kuklinski and his colleagues (2000) found that presenting survey respondents with accurate information about welfare does not influence their attitudes on this policy, in a separate study of Iowa State University students they uncovered more reassuring results. Participants in this study were asked their view about how much of the federal budget was allocated to welfare followed by how much this amount should be. A random half of this sample was then provided with accurate information on this subject and, compared to the control group, respondents who had previously over-stated this estimate were much less critical of the policy after learning the true (and comparatively low) figure. In short, sometimes even misinformed citizens can become enlightened. We would urge scholars to continue to rely on experimental designs, and other tools, to extend our understanding of the circumstances that lead to heightened levels of information and greater incentives to seek out political knowledge.

## References

ALDRICH, J. H., SULLIVAN, J. L., and BORGIDA, E. 1989. Foreign Affairs and Issue Voting. *American Political Science Review*, 83/1: 123–41.

BARTELS, L. M. 2003. Democracy with Attitudes. In *Electoral Democracy*, ed. M. B. MacKuen and G. Rabinowitz. Ann Arbor: University of Michigan Press.

—— 2005. Homer Gets a Tax Cut. *Perspectives on Politics*, 3/1: 15–31.

—— 2007. Homer Gets a Warm Hug. *Perspectives on Politics*, 5/4: 785–90.

BOBO, L. M., and JOHNSON, D. 2004. A Taste for Punishment. *Du Bois Review*, 1/1: 151–80.

CAMPBELL, A., CONVERSE, P., MILLER, W., and STOKES, D. 1960. *The American Voter*. New York: Wiley.

CARMINES, E. G., and STIMSON, J. A. 1980. The Two Faces of Issue Voting. *American Political Science Review*, 74/1: 78–91.

CONVERSE, P. E. 1964. The Nature of Belief Systems in Mass Publics. In *Ideology and its Discontents*, ed. D. E. Apter. New York: Free Press of Glencoe.

—— and MARKUS, G. B. 1979. A Dynamic Simultaneous Equation Model of Electoral Choice. *American Political Science Review*, 73/4: 1055–70.

CURRAN, J., IYENGAR, S., LUND, A. B., and SALOVAARA-MORING, I. 2009. Media System, Public Knowledge and Democracy: A Comparative Study. *European Journal of Communication*, 24/1: 5–26.

DAVIS, D. W., and SILVER, B. D. 2003. Stereotype Threat and Race of Interviewer Effects in a Survey of Political Knowledge. *American Journal of Political Science*, 47/1: 33–45.

DELLI CARPINI, M. X., and KEETER, S. 1991. Stability and Change in the U.S. Public's Knowledge of Politics. *Public Opinion Quarterly*, 55/4: 583–612.

—— —— 1996. *What Americans Know about Politics and Why it Matters*. New Haven: Yale University Press.

DRUCKMAN, J. 2004. Political Preference Formation. *American Political Science Review*, 98/4: 671–86.

GIBSON, J. L., and CALDEIRA, G. A. 2009. Knowing the Supreme Court? A Reconsideration of Public Ignorance of the High Court. *Journal of Politics*, 71/2: 429–41.

GILENS, M. 2001. Political Ignorance and Collective Policy Preferences. *American Political Science Review*, 95/2: 379–96.

GILLIAM, F. G., JR., and IYENGAR, S. 2000. Prime Suspects: The Influence of Local Television News on the Viewing Public. *American Journal of Political Science*, 44/3: 560–73.

HUTCHINGS, V. L. 2003. *Public Opinion and Democratic Accountability*. Princeton: Princeton University Press.

IYENGAR, S. 1990. Shortcuts to Political Knowledge: The Role of Selective Attention and Accessibility. In *Information and Democratic Processes*, ed. J. A. Ferejohn and J. H. Kuklinski. Urbana: University of Illinois Press.

—— and KINDER, D. R. 1989. *News that Matters: Television and American Opinion*. Chicago: University of Chicago Press.

JAMIESON, K. H., and KENSKI, K. 2000. The Gender Gap in Political Knowledge: Are Women Less Knowledgeable than Men about Politics? In *Everything You Think You Know about Politics and Why You're Wrong*, ed. K. H. Jamieson. New York: Basic Books.

JENNINGS, M. K. 1992. Ideological Thinking among Mass Publics and Political Elites. *Public Opinion Quarterly*, 56/4: 419–41.

JERIT, J., and BARABAS, J. 2006. Bankrupt Rhetoric: How Misleading Information Affects Knowledge about Social Security. *Public Opinion Quarterly*, 70/3: 278–303.

KEY, V. O., JR. 1961. *Public Opinion and American Democracy*. Knopf.

—— 1966. *The Responsible Electorate: Rationality in Presidential Voting, 1936–1960*. Cambridge, MA: Harvard University Press.

KINDER, D. R. 2003. Belief Systems after Converse. In *Electoral Democracy*, ed. M. B. MacKuen and G. Rabinowitz. Ann Arbor: University of Michigan Press.

KUKLINISKI, J. H., and QUIRK, P. J. 2000. Reconsidering the Rational Public: Cognition, Heuristics, and Mass Opinion. In *Elements of Reason: Cognition, Choice, and the Bounds of Rationality*, ed. A. Lupia, M. D. McCubbins, and S. L. Popkin. New York: Cambridge University Press.

—— —— JERIT, J., SCHWIEDER, D., and RICH, R. F. 2000. Misinformation and the Currency of Democratic Citizenship. *Journal of Politics*, 62/3: 790–816.

LIZOTTE, M.-K., and SIDMAN, A. H. 2009. Explaining the Gender Gap in Political Knowledge. *Politics and Gender*, 5/2: 127–51.

LUPIA, A. 1994. Shortcuts versus Encyclopedias. *American Political Science Review*, 88/1: 63–76.

—— and MCCUBBINS, M. D. 1998. *The Democratic Dilemma*. Cambridge: Cambridge University Press.

—— LEVINE, A. S., MENNING, J. O., and SIN, G. 2007. Were Bush Tax Cut Supporters Simply Ignorant? *Perspectives on Politics*, 5/4: 773–84.

McGLONE, M. S., ARONSON, J., and KOBRYNOWICZ, D. 2006. Stereotype Threat and the Gender Gap in Political Knowledge. *Psychology of Women Quarterly*, 30/4: 392–8.

MONDAK, J. J. 2001. Developing Valid Knowledge Scales. *American Journal of Political Science*, 45/1: 224–38.

—— and ANDERSON, M. R. 2004. The Knowledge Gap: A Reexamination of Gender-Based Differences in Political Knowledge. *Journal of Politics*, 66/2: 492–512.

NEUMAN, W. R. 1986. *The Paradox of Mass Politics*. Cambridge, MA: Harvard University Press.

NIE, N., VERBA, S., and PETROCIK, J. R. 1979. *The Changing American Voter*. Cambridge, MA: Harvard University Press.

PAGE, B. I., and BRODY, R. A. 1972. Policy Voting and the Electoral Process: The Vietnam War Issue. *American Political Science Review*, 66/3: 979–95.

—— and SHAPIRO, R. Y. 1992. *The Rational Public*. Chicago: University of Chicago Press.

POPKIN, S. L. 1991. *The Reasoning Voter: Communication and Persuasion in Presidential Campaigns*. Chicago: University of Chicago Press.

PRICE, V., and ZALLER, J. 1993. Who Gets the News? *Public Opinion Quarterly*, 57/2: 133–64.

PRIOR, M., and LUPIA, A. 2008. Money, Time, and Political Knowledge: Distinguishing Quick Recall and Political Learning Skills. *American Journal of Political Science*, 52/1: 169–83.

SNIDERMAN, P. M., BRODY, R. A., and TETLOCK, P. 1993. *Reasoning and Choice: Explorations in Political Psychology*. Cambridge: Cambridge University Press.

SULLIVAN, J. L., PIERESON, J. E., and MARCUS, G. E. 1978. Ideological Constraint in the Mass Public: A Methodological Critique and Some New Findings. *American Journal of Political Science*, 22/2: 233–49.

TABER, C. S., and LODGE, M. 2006. Motivated Skepticism in the Evaluation of Political Beliefs. *American Journal of Political Science*, 50/3: 755–69.

ZALLER, J. 1992. *The Nature and Origins of Mass Opinion*. Cambridge: Cambridge University Press.

# PART IV

················································································

# ISSUES AND POLITICS

················································································

# SECTION EIGHT: DOMESTIC

......................................................................................

# CHAPTER 36

# PUBLIC OPINION, THE MEDIA, AND ECONOMIC WELL-BEING

......................................................................................

## JASON BARABAS

THERE have been profound economic changes around the world in recent years. To what extent are citizens aware of important developments that influence their economic well-being and does that awareness have political ramifications? Scholars devote considerable attention to studying the relationship between variations in leading economic indicators (e.g., inflation, unemployment, gross domestic product) and political outcomes such as electoral support or executive branch approval. By one count there have been almost 400 studies documenting linkages between the economy and voting (Lewis-Beck and Stegmaier 2007). However, there are lingering disputes about the level at which this occurs—i.e., personal ("egocentric," "pocketbook," or "egotropic") versus national ("sociotropic")—as well as the degree to which citizens look forward or backward (for example, Clarke and Stewart 1994; Duch, Palmer, and Anderson 2000; MacKuen, Erikson, and Stimson 1992; Evans and Andersen 2006).

The heterogeneous effects of the economy on political behavior could signal that individuals are basing their impressions upon different pieces of information or that they process the same information differently. In other words, perceived economic experience may matter as much if not more than objective changes, especially when economic perceptions deviate from reality (for example, Conover, Feldman, and Knight 1986; Duch, Palmer, and Anderson 2000; Hetherington 1996; Goidel and Langley 1995). Findings like these underscore the role of the news media. Whether by radio, newspapers, television, or the Internet, information about economic affairs often originates in the mass media even though the news is sometimes disseminated through interpersonal contacts (Katz and Lazarsfeld 1955; Mutz 1992).

This chapter is primarily concerned with economic welfare as it relates to public opinion and the mass media. The term "economic welfare" refers to the financial well-

information magnifies partisan differences in perceptions of income inequality. Yet these findings, while certainly provocative, do not directly implicate the mass media and they leave several questions. Do partisan subgroups use different media? Do various media sources treat the topic differently? And finally, does the public receive and comprehend information about economic inequality? Regrettably, we do not know much about the system that created such opposing views of inequality, although it would be logical to suspect that the mass media play an important role (see Shapiro and Bloch-Elkon 2008 for more).

## Political Economy

Many studies fall under the rubric of political economy, but arguably the ones with the most relevance to economic welfare concern the partisan differences in economic outcomes. That is, if political control of the government produces differences in economic performance, then that process is worth considering from the perspective of the mass media and public opinion. Here, again, there are some provocative scholarly findings but little when it comes to studies of mass media coverage or public awareness.

For example, Bartels states unequivocally that "Economic inequality is, in substantial part, a political phenomenon." He adopts this view because, "On average, the real incomes of middle-class families have grown twice as fast under Democrats as they have under Republicans, while the real incomes of working poor families have grown six times as fast under Democrats as they have under Republicans" (2008, 3). In other words, the changes in income inequality—in the direction of increasing concentration— have been concentrated under Republican administrations. Bartels discovers that under Republican administrations, real income growth for the lower- and middle-income classes has consistently lagged behind the income growth rate for the rich, and well behind the income growth rate for the lower and middle classes under Democratic administrations (Bartels 2008, 30; also see Smith 2007, 185, and Hibbs 1987).

Despite scholarly findings like these over the last few decades, it is unclear whether these extraordinary data patterns make it into the media and, in turn, register in the consciousness of Americans. It could be that the trends are simply too one-sided for mainstream journalists who are trying to present "both" sides of the story. Assuming news audiences did not get lost in the statistical techniques used to generate these facts, Republicans probably would not appreciate stories documenting the subpar economic experience during periods of Republican control. Allegations of "liberal bias" would likely ensue. Nevertheless, these findings, to the extent that citizens encounter them with an open mind, might have a persuasive effect.

## Macroeconomic Changes

Given the strong relationship between inequality and which party holds political power, it seems logical to explore the degree to which media coverage of economic experience affects voting behavior or related forms of public support. After all, if unemployment goes up, then it is typically the case that general economic welfare declines. The same may be said of other macroeconomic indicators, such as changes in the overall indicator of economic activity—the gross domestic product—or measures of inflation and consumer sentiment. Aggregate economic indicators like these have been used in studies relating economic changes to voting, presidential approval, or other political variables (for example, Monroe 1984; Nadeau and Lewis-Beck 2001). Yet studies explicitly incorporating the media are much less common.

For example, the title of one prominent media effects article by Larry Bartels, "Messages Received: The Political Impact of Media Exposure" (1993), conveys his main point succinctly. Individuals who report using the media have different opinions on a range of attitudinal measures compared to people who do not use the media or at least those who use it less. The irony, though, is that there is no explicit consideration of the messages that were reportedly received. Instead, Bartels uses a sophisticated modeling approach, one designed to correct for error-prone media measures, to infer the presumed distinctiveness of the media messages over a six-month period of the 1980 presidential campaign (i.e., between February and September). Given that the study uses panelists, in theory all changes can be attributed to what transpired between surveys (i.e., the media and other campaign-relevant information). This provides some of the most compelling evidence that exposure to the mass media influences opinions, especially for candidate perceptions (e.g., where Reagan or Carter stood on issues as well as how well they would handle economic affairs). However, the effects are much smaller or insignificant in the domain of economic and ideology-based policy attitudes.

All of that might lead some to wonder whether the media have an effect on politics in the realm of macroeconomic changes, but evidence of the mass media's role typically takes one of two paths. First, Iyengar and Kinder (1987) demonstrated in laboratory experiments as well as in analyses of survey opinion data that media content influences which problems are rated as most important. Beyond setting the agenda, Iyengar and Kinder found that media coverage also "primes" individuals when it sets the basis for political evaluation. For example, when people see stories on inflation or unemployment, they are more likely to evaluate political leaders on those issues.

Second, the strong evidence of a link between economic experience and politics (Lewis-Beck and Stegmaier 2007) leads to the question of how citizens learn of the changes. Many studies hint that the media influences economic opinions. In one of the earliest works, Shapiro and Conforto (1980) found that changes in consumer prices and the percentage of the workforce unemployed affect the public's perception and evaluation of economic conditions, and that this popular assessment in turn affects disapproval of presidential performance. However, they make a common assumption that is shared by many others: that information about the economy is obtained from the news (MacKuen, Erikson, and Stimson 1992, 605; Shapiro and Conforto 1980, 52). In other words, the media connection was implicit—which is not unreasonable, especially in an era when media content databases were not widely available.

Later works added the media explicitly. For example, Mutz (1992) finds that individual perceptions of unemployment are related to the amount of newspaper coverage devoted to the unemployment issue. To the extent that media coverage influences individuals, it typically means that the mass personal economic experiences play less of a role. Thus, in contrast to the literatures on inequality and political economy, the mass media now factor regularly into studies of the macroeconomy and politics (for example, Shah et al. 1999). Probably more so than in any other area of economic welfare, there appears to be a firm connection between the media and politics in the sphere of macroeconomics.

However, reality is largely filtered through the media. Sometimes the filtering process mirrors reality, and sometimes it does not. One of the more stark cases of the latter occurred in the 1992 presidential election. Hetherington (1996) showed that overly negative coverage of the economy helped contribute to the defeat of President George H. W. Bush in 1992 (also see Dalton, Beck, and Huckfeldt 1998 or Holbrook and Garand 1996). Similarly, Goidel and Langley (1995) studied the same 1992 election and showed that news coverage affects economic perceptions even after controlling for actual economic conditions. They also discovered that journalists tend to cover negative economic conditions more closely than positive economic conditions, particularly in non-election years. Moreover, citizens respond asymmetrically to economic information in the news by overweighting bad economic information (Soroka 2006). All of this further elevates the role of the mass media in structuring beliefs and attitudes about how the nation is faring economically.

## Economic Policy

Economic welfare, in the form of inequality or macroeconomic changes, is related to public policy decisions. In other words, government actions affect the financial well-being of citizens (Page and Simmons 2000). As such, it is helpful to work on the issue from the other direction. Instead of considering forms of economic awareness, one could look at levels of knowledge or opinions pertaining to the governmental programs or policies that are among the most responsible for the economic welfare of the public.

Many observers argue that one of the most important economic welfare programs in the United States is Social Security. In the years following the creation and implementation of Social Security, the 1950 elderly poverty rate was above 30 percent. In the following decades, seniors experienced dramatic gains in their economic standing. By 1965 the poverty rate for Americans over age 65 was cut nearly in half to 17 percent (Gilens 1999). These trends continued to the point where seniors are much less likely to be poor than adults under age 65; decades ago, older citizens were twice as likely to be economically impoverished.

While these poverty reduction statistics are a success from a policy point of view, journalists and politicians regularly raise the specter of Social Security bankruptcy. An example appeared in the writings of a columnist for *U.S. News & World Report*, Emily

Brandon, who started an article on Social Security with the following: "Retirees often sign up for Social Security payments as soon as possible, at age 62. And who can blame them? In just seven years, program costs will exceed tax revenues, according to the most recent Social Security Board of Trustees report. And the trust fund is expected to be exhausted in 2037" (Brandon 2009). Statements like these are ubiquitous in the Social Security debate (Jerit 2006), but they are also misleading, especially when taken out of context.

The key issue concerns what happens when the "bankruptcy" year arrives. According to the estimates of the trustees who run it, the Social Security program will have the ability to pay roughly three quarters of benefits even after the financial doomsday arrives. Most people, however, believe "bankrupt" means the program will be in financial ruins, which is inaccurate. As it turns out, these perceptions are shaped by media coverage, particularly the type of words used. Experiments confirm that some synonyms that journalists use to describe the financial condition, including "bankrupt," "exhausted," or "run out of money," as well as dozens of other terms used widely, cause people to overestimate the severity of the problem (Jerit and Barabas 2006). All of this means that media coverage plays an important role in shaping perceptions, in this case misperceptions, of a major program central to economic welfare.

There are other programs that influence economic welfare, most notably a collection of means-tested benefits for able-bodied adults commonly thought of as "welfare." Programs thought to fall under the banner include Temporary Assistance to Needy Families, which replaced Aid to Families with Dependent Children as well as food stamps and Medicaid. Welfare is not especially politically popular and it is racially charged (Weaver, Shapiro, and Jacobs 1995). In a review of more than forty years of news coverage, Gilens (1999) argues that the mass media contribute to public opposition by depicting the poor as atypically black and undeserving, especially since the late 1960s (also see Clawson and Trice 2000; Kellstedt 2003). The notion that media coverage drives support for welfare also enjoys support in a study by Schneider and Jacoby (2005), although welfare attitudes did not seem to moderate much after the much publicized welfare reform efforts of the Clinton administration (Soss and Schram 2007). While the links between media and attitudes are somewhat indirect, these studies generally support the idea that the media shape public opinion, at least in regard to welfare.

Social Security and related welfare programs are examples of government spending programs, but fiscal revenue policies, such as taxes, also influence economic welfare. Many assume Americans hate taxes, but they display a surprising degree of support for using tax money to pay for specific policies such as job training, health care for children, food stamps, or retirement security (for example, Cook and Barrett 1992; Page and Jacobs 2009). Furthermore, there is heterogeneity with respect to types of taxation. Attitudes toward taxes—income, sales, and property—are related to actual tax rates in the states (Bowler and Donovan 1995; see Hibbs and Madsen 1981 for cross-national patterns), although scholars have not said whether these patterns reflect media coverage of tax policies in each locale (but see Campbell 2009 for data on variations in campaign ads mentioning taxes).

However, elite rhetoric, particularly on the political right, shifted in the US toward an increasing focus on economic policy and tax cuts (Smith 2007; also see Campbell 2009). Some of the most dramatic changes in tax law were detailed by Bartels (2008), who studied the Bush tax cuts of 2001 and 2003 as well as the repeal of the estate tax (also see Rudolph 2009). The cost to the federal treasury of the tax cuts was estimated at $4.6 trillion. The benefits were also concentrated on the upper-income tier (Bartels 2008, 163). Amazingly, though, in the years following the tax cut enactment, 40 percent of the public had not thought about the tax cuts. Bartels (2005, 23) attributes tax cut support to "unenlightened self-interest," and he states, "Most of the people who recognized and regretted the fact that economic inequality has been increasing nevertheless supported President Bush's tax cuts" (Bartels 2008, 163).

In his analyses, Bartels focuses on the role of political information, indirectly implicating the mass media. He found that better-informed people were more likely to express an opinion and they attached more importance to the 2001 tax cut. Better-informed people were also more likely to recognize the party positions on the issue. Overall, support for tax cuts drops as levels of information rise for all respondents. However, Republicans at any information level support tax cuts while Democratic support drops off as they know more (Bartels 2008, 183; Lupia, Levin, Menning, and Sin 2007). Bartels continues, "As in the case of the Bush tax cuts more generally, this pattern of support leads one to wonder what considerations have led so many people to embrace policies that are so clearly contrary to their material interests" (2008, 202). Lower-income people mistakenly believe that the estate tax will apply to them. In reality, it is concentrated on people in the upper-income tiers, but we do not know whether this fact was publicized widely in the media.

However, in the case of the estate tax, there is reason to suspect that information from the mass media may not matter. Bartels found that better-informed people were slightly more likely to favor the estate tax repeal (2008, 208–13; but see Rudolph 2009). Thus, making citizens more informed does not alter opinions in this instance. Yet the information measures that Bartels relies upon—a range of facts unrelated to the policy in question as well as subjective interviewer ratings—leave open the possibility that a different combination of the facts, presented in a compelling format, might alter preferences.

# FUTURE RESEARCH

At this point it might be helpful to transition from the existing literature on economic welfare, opinions, and the media to relatively uncharted territory. A common theme so far has been the need to add explicit measures of media content in an effort to study media effects. This topic is covered in depth elsewhere in this volume (see Chapter 9, by

Jerit and Barabas). However, there are several other paths that seem ripe for researchers to pursue. In each, scholars should rethink how the topic has been studied and whether the assumptions, methods, or approaches of the past have limited what is known or what is possible to know.

## Biased Information Processing

In studying public opinion about economic affairs, it is important to establish a firm factual basis for financial conditions. The problem, though, is that political preferences may shape perceptions of reality rather than the opposite. This is an issue that has recently vexed scholars working in the field of economics and politics.

The problem was summarized by Lewis-Beck, Nadeau, and Elias (2008) with the following hypothetical example. Before an election, Republican identifiers will tend to favor the candidate from their party. If a Republican occupies the presidency, they will tend to see the economy as better than it is, presumably because they credit the Republican management style. As a result, there should be a robust correlation between economic perception and vote choice. The relationship, while certainly strong, is not necessarily causal. A variety of studies have proposed this basic criticism (Anderson, Mendes, Tverdova, and Kim 2004; Evans and Andersen 2006; Wlezien, Franklin, and Twiggs 1997).

The logic behind the causality critique is that instead of moving from facts to opinions, it could be that people do the opposite. That is, political preferences tend to shape how people look at the world. Within political psychology, the phenomenon is called "motivated reasoning" (for example, Kunda 1990; Redlawsk 2002; Rudolph 2006; Taber and Lodge 2006), and it occurs when affective judgments lead individuals to reject information inconsistent with their prior preferences. Such findings contradict the claims of scholars who steadfastly maintain that economic perceptions are unbiased and highly accurate (for example, Anderson and O'Connor 2000; Haller and Norpoth 1997; Nadeau and Lewis-Beck 2001). However, others disagree since individuals display little factual knowledge about real economic conditions (Holbrook and Garand 1996; Conover, Feldman, and Knight 1986, 1987). Such discrepancies remind us of how public opinion in the aggregate can seem reasonable or rational even with individual-level errors (Page and Shapiro 1992). Nevertheless, since the existing linkages are largely associational, it is hard to determine the causal ordering between opinions and economic experience. It may be that the relationship flows from experience to opinions, but often scholars lack conclusive evidence.

To get around this problem, one potential solution is to use panel data. The idea is that if one can pin down partisan impressions before the moment of evaluation, or at least hold them constant, then it should be possible to clarify the causal orderings. Unfortunately, though, teams of scholars have tried panel data and their studies point to different conclusions. One group, headed by Lewis-Beck, Nadeau, and Elias (2008), suggests that endogeneity is not a problem; that is, once the reciprocal influence of party identification is purged with panel data, economic perceptions are even stronger predictors of voting behavior. The other camp, led by Larry Bartels (2002), shows that Democrats and Republicans arrive at starkly different conclusions about the same objective macroeconomic trends such as whether unemployment or inflation improved during the Reagan administration. Partisanship, it seems, strongly colors incumbent evaluations. Thus, there is some ambiguity in the literature on this point even in the panel studies.

To adjudicate these differences, it might be possible to combine panel surveys with media content data. Another possibility would be to construct "within-survey/within-subjects" estimates of media effects by comparing the responses of individuals on several questions covering the same topic in the same survey, some of which receive media coverage and others of which do not (Barabas and Jerit 2009). In either case, however, it will be helpful to include meta-attitudinal measures of opinion strength and uncertainty. For example, under a Bayesian updating framework (for example, Gerber and Green 1999; Barabas 2004), we would not expect factual beliefs or opinions to change much in the face of media messages if the new information lacks precision or if the prior beliefs are held with conviction. Thus, it may seem as if members of the public are not responding to messages in the mass media even when they are actually quite sensitive to it. Importantly, though, it is wise to measure the uncertainty of the media messages as well as individual-level uncertainty. That means, once again, that theoretical clarification depends in large part on isolating the media messages in the information environment.

## Which Economic Activities, Facts, or Policies?

Thus far the discussion has centered on prominent economic outcomes as well as the policies that lead to them, but what about understudied aspects of economic welfare? In particular, the stock market is a major source of economic activity that shapes economic welfare. However, studies of financial markets are, relative to the voluminous literature on economics and politics, fairly uncommon. As one might guess, then, studies integrating media coverage are even rarer. Some articles rely on market disruptions that were highly publicized, such as the effects of the 1998 Russian currency crisis and how stock market volatility altered public support for Social Security privatization (Barabas 2006), but again there is no explicit media component.

At any rate, most studies using macroeconomic variables tend to show that people react to changes in national economics rather than their own pocketbook. However, it could be that people politicize more personal forms of economic activity, such as stock market participation. The logic here is that much more so today than in the past, citizens are expected to be financially savvy. Written into public policy are programs like Flexible Spending Accounts (FSAs), which require individuals to accurately forecast how much health-care spending they will incur over the next year. Similarly, Health Savings Accounts (HSAs) and Individual Retirement Accounts (IRAs) demand individual decisions about where to allocate investments (Barabas 2009). Of course, many citizens delegate this task to investment professionals. However, scholars need to probe the degree to which the mass media convey basic financial information that will help citizens navigate the economic world.

## Connecting Economic Facts, Beliefs, and Policy

Can citizens make linkages between their values and beliefs on the one hand and their policy opinions or voting decisions on the other? In other words, can citizens make enlightened decisions in a modern democracy? The extent to which they do will likely affect the quality of political representation and their economic welfare. For example, some of the macro-level statistics on economic inequality presented earlier are a product of differential patterns of earnings in the economy. To what degree is the public aware of this? Page and Jacobs (2009) conclude from a national survey that Americans are relatively accurate about the annual incomes of factory workers, sales clerks, and small shop owners, but they regularly underestimate the annual incomes of doctors, surgeons, and corporate executives.

The question from a mass media perspective is whether individuals are encouraged to connect the dots. That is, to what extent are Americans told that income inequality is growing, that there are huge differences in pay rates, and that public policies like tax cuts exacerbate those trends? To the extent that any of these are covered at all, a story about CEO compensation might appear in the business section while inequality trends could be buried in the national section and a piece on tax cut proposals might appear on the front page. Moreover, each of these stories could be scattered across publications or media. In short, citizens probably get isolated doses of economic information, but whether they can link the various pieces together to inform political opinions remains uncertain. Political advertisements sometimes fill this void, connecting facts, or at least innuendos, to persuade voters about candidates. Campaign ads may be emotionally or visually compelling, but one might question whether this is the best way for individuals to receive political information. If ads reinforce existing opinions or fail to provide diverse perspectives, they are unlikely to stimulate high-quality policy debate.

# CONCLUSION

Deliberation in modern democracies takes place from time to time in issue forums or town hall meetings (Barabas 2004; Mansbridge 1980; Jacobs, Cook, and Delli Carpini 2009). However, we delegate a lot of serious policy discussion to the mass media (Page 1996). While it is too early to generalize about how much news is devoted to economic welfare, it is probably fair to say that it is not as much as, say, coverage of entertainment or sports. One might argue that to help citizens make informed political choices, the nation needs more coverage of economic trends and the policies are responsible for these changes. Moreover, scholars also need to continue their efforts to document the degree to which the mass media alter opinions in the arena of economic welfare.

Over a decade ago there was a call for a more citizen-oriented form of journalism, also known as "civic journalism" or "public journalism" (Glasser 1999; Merritt 1997; Rosen 1999). Perhaps the time is right for "public policy journalism." Public policies are more complex and far-reaching than ever before. There needs to be more consciousness-raising on the part of journalists, not only by including the public in the debate, but also through press coverage that places a premium on factual presentation as well as linking public concerns, beliefs, or preferences to policy outcomes. Government policy dramatically alters economic fortunes. Do the media help citizens make connections between their values, beliefs, facts, and preferences? In particular, there is a need to look for times when the media highlights a pressing problem and the best solution. Of course, "best" is in the eye of the beholder and proposals for more policy-oriented media coverage are likely to bump up against two countervailing journalistic trends.

The first set of impediments to having journalists take a more active role in policy-oriented news coverage is that of norms of media objectivity. The term "objectivity," outside of the media, is usually thought to mean focusing on the facts without impressions, personal emotions, or prejudicing normative statements about what should take place. Within the media profession, objectivity typically means presenting both or multiple sides (Graber 2010; Bennett 1996). But is it possible to always have two sides of the story, even when the preponderance of the factual evidence points overwhelmingly to one side? For example, a media story reporting on the vast differentials in economic growth under Democrats or Republicans will likely lead to charges of media bias, presumably by the Republicans given the empirical evidence reviewed earlier. In that sense, media objectivity norms are probably well suited for preferences or policy solutions rather than factual descriptions of the status quo. Of course, strong partisans will undoubtedly argue about what constitutes reality, but in the end it would be helpful from the standpoint of democracy to have a common set of basic economic welfare facts.

A second impediment concerns audience dynamics and ownership. News is driven by audience tastes, and it is increasingly the case that citizens can change the channel to more entertaining formats (Prior 2007). Since many news providers are for-profit corporations, there are incentives to eschew public policy minutiae in favor of tantalizing coverage (Bagdikian 1997; Bennett 1996; Graber 2010). It is also the case that audiences seek out news channels that tend to confirm their preexisting beliefs (for example, Morris 2005; Stroud 2008). Thus, it may be hard to bring about the kind of news coverage that promotes public deliberation on topics like economic welfare.

## References

Anderson, C. J., and O'Connor, K. 2000. System Change, Learning, and Public Opinion about the Economy. *British Journal of Political Science*, 30: 147–72.

—— MENDES, S. M., TVERDOVA, Y. V., and KIM, H. 2004. Endogenous Economic Voting: Evidence from the 1997 British Election. *Electoral Studies*, 23/4: 683–708.

BAGDIKIAN, B. H. 1997. *The Media Monopoly*, 5th edn. Boston: Beacon Press.

BARABAS, J. 2004. How Deliberation Affects Policy Preferences. *American Political Science Review*, 98: 687–701.

—— 2006. Rational Exuberance: The Stock Market and Public Support for Social Security Privatization. *Journal of Politics*, 68: 50–61.

—— 2009. Not the Next IRA: How Health Savings Accounts Shape Public Opinion. *Journal of Health Politics, Policy and Law*, 34/2: 181–217.

—— and JERIT, J. 2009. Estimating the Causal Effect of Media Coverage on Policy-Specific Knowledge. *American Journal of Political Science*, 53: 73–89.

BARTELS, L. M. 1993. Messages Received: The Political Impact of Media Exposure. *American Political Science Review*, 87: 267–85.

—— 2002. Beyond the Running Tally: Partisan Bias in Political Perceptions. *Political Behavior*, 24: 117–50.

—— 2005. Homer Gets a Tax Cut: Inequality and Public Policy in the American Mind. *Perspectives on Politics*, 3: 15–31.

—— 2008. *Unequal Democracy: The Political Economy of the New Gilded Age*. Princeton: Princeton University Press.

BENNETT, W. L. 1996. *News: The Politics of Illusion*, 3rd edn. White Plains, NY: Longman. First published 1983.

BOWLER, S., and DONOVAN, T. 1995. Popular Responsiveness to Taxation. *Political Research Quarterly*, 48: 79–99.

BRANDON, E. 2009. 5 Ways to Maximize Your Social Security Payout. *U.S. News & World Report*, Aug. 6.

CAMPBELL, A. L. 2009. What Americans Think of Taxes. In *The New Fiscal Sociology: Taxation in Comparative and Historical Perspective*, ed. I. W. Martin, A. K. Mehrotra, and M. Prasad. New York: Cambridge University Press.

CLARKE, H. D., and STEWART, M. C. 1994. Prospections, Retrospections, and Rationality: The Bankers' Model of Presidential Approval Reconsidered. *American Journal of Political Science*, 38: 1104–23.

CLAWSON, R. A., and TRICE, R. 2000. Poverty as We Know It: Media Portrayals of the Poor. *Public Opinion Quarterly*, 64: 53–64.

CONOVER, P. J., FELDMAN, S., and KNIGHT, K. 1986. Judging Inflation and Unemployment: The Origins of Retrospective Evaluations. *Journal of Politics*, 48: 565–88.

—— —— —— 1987. The Personal and Political Underpinnings of Economic Forecasts. *American Journal of Political Science*, 31: 559–83.

COOK, F. L., and BARRETT, E. J. 1992. *Support for the American Welfare State*. New York: Columbia University Press.

DALTON, R. J., BECK, P. A., and HUCKFELDT, R. 1998. Partisan Cues and the Media: Information Flows in the 1992 Presidential Election. *American Political Science Review*, 92: 111–26.

DANZIGER, S. 1994. *Uneven Tides: Rising Inequality in America*. New York: Russell Sage.

DUCH, R. M., PALMER, H. D., and ANDERSON, C. J. 2000. Heterogeneity in Perceptions of National Economic Conditions. *American Journal of Political Science*, 44: 635–52.

EVANS, G., and ANDERSEN, R. 2006. The Political Conditioning of Economic Perceptions. *Journal of Politics*, 68: 194–207.

GERBER, A., and GREEN, D. 1999. Misperceptions about Perceptual Bias. *Annual Review of Political Science*, 2: 189–210.

GILENS, M. 1999. *Why Americans Hate Welfare*. Chicago: University of Chicago Press.

GLASSER, T. L. 1999. *The Idea of Public Journalism*. New York: Guilford Press.

GOIDEL, R. K., and LANGLEY, R. E. 1995. Media Coverage of the Economy and Aggregate Economic Evaluations: Uncovering Evidence of Indirect Media Effects. *Political Research Quarterly*, 48: 313–28.

GRABER, D. A. 2010. *Mass Media and American Politics*, 8th edn. Washington, DC: CQ Press.

HAAS-WILSON, D. 1993. The Economic Impact of State Restrictions on Abortion: Parental Consent and Notification Laws and Medicaid Funding Restrictions. *Journal of Policy Analysis and Management*, 12 (Summer), 498–511.

HALLER, H. B., and NORPOTH, H. 1997. Reality Bites: News Exposure and Economic Opinion. *Public Opinion Quarterly*, 61: 555–75.

HETHERINGTON, M. 1996. The Media's Role in Forming Voters' National Economic Evaluations in 1992. *American Journal of Political Science*, 40: 372–95.

HIBBS, D. A. 1987. *The American Political Economy: Macroeconomics and Electoral Politics*. Cambridge, MA: Harvard University Press.

—— and MADSEN, H. J. 1981. Public Reactions to the Growth of Taxation and Government Expenditure. *World Politics*, 33: 413–35.

HOLBROOK, T., and GARAND, J. C. 1996. Homo Economus? Economic Information and Economic Voting. *Political Research Quarterly*, 49: 351–75.

IYENGAR, S., and KINDER, D. 1987. *News that Matters: Television and American Opinion*. Chicago: Chicago University Press.

JACOBS, L. R., COOK, F. L., and DELLI CARPINI, M. X. 2009. *Talking Together: Public Deliberation and Political Participation in America*. Chicago: University of Chicago Press.

JERIT, J. 2006. Reform, Rescue, or Run Out of Money: Problem Definition in the Social Security Reform Debate. *Harvard International Journal of Press/Politics*, 11/1: 9–28.

—— and BARABAS, J. 2006. Bankrupt Rhetoric: How Misleading Information Affects Knowledge about Social Security. *Public Opinion Quarterly*, 70: 278–303.

KATZ, E., and LAZARSFELD, P. F. 1955. *Personal Influence: The Part Played by People in the Flow of Mass Communications*. Glencoe, IL: Free Press.

KELLSTEDT, P. M. 2003. *The Mass Media and the Dynamics of American Racial Attitudes*. New York: Cambridge University Press.

KLAPPER, J. 1960. *The Effects of Mass Communication*. Glencoe, IL: Free Press.

KUNDA, Z. 1990. The Case for Motivated Reasoning. *Psychological Bulletin*, 108: 480–98.

LEWIS-BECK, M. S., and STEGMAIER, M. 2007. Economic Models of the Vote. In *The Oxford Handbook of Political Behavior*, ed. R. Dalton and H.-D. Klingemann. Oxford: Oxford University Press.

—— NADEAU, R., and ELIAS, A. 2008. Economics, Party, and the Vote: Causality Issues and Panel Data. *American Journal of Political Science*, 52: 84–95.

LUPIA, A., LEVINE, A. S., MENNING, J. O., and SIN, G. 2007. Were Bush Tax Cut Supports "Simply Ignorant?" A Second Look at Conservatives and Liberals in "Homer Gets a Tax Cut." *Perspectives on Politics*, 5: 773–84.

McCOMBS, M. E., and SHAW, D. 1972. The Agenda-Setting Function of the Mass Media. *Public Opinion Quarterly*, 36: 176–87.

MACKUEN, M. B., ERIKSON, R. S., and STIMSON, J. A. 1992. Peasants or Bankers? The American Electorate and the U.S. Economy. *American Political Science Review*, 86: 597–611.

MANSBRIDGE, J. 1980. *Beyond Adversary Democracy*. New York: Basic Books.

MERRITT, D. 1997. *Public Journalism and Public Life: Why Telling the News Is Not Enough*. Mahwah, NJ: Lawrence Erlbaum.

MONROE, K. R. 1984. *Presidential Popularity and the Economy*. New York: Praeger.

MORRIS, J. S. 2005. The Fox News Factor. *Harvard International Journal of Press/Politics*, 10/3: 56–79.

MUTZ, D. C. 1992. Mass Media and the Depoliticization of Personal Experience. *American Journal of Political Science*, 36: 483–508.

NADEAU, R., and LEWIS-BECK, M. S. 2001. National Economic Voting in U.S. Presidential Elections. *Journal of Politics*, 63: 159–81.

PAGE, B. I. 1996. *Who Deliberates? Mass Media in Modern Democracy*. Chicago: University of Chicago Press.

—— and JACOBS, L. R. 2009. *Class War? What Americans Really Think about Economic Inequality*. Chicago: University of Chicago Press.

—— and SHAPIRO, R. Y. 1992. *The Rational Public: Fifty Years of Trends in Americans' Policy Preferences*. Chicago: University of Chicago Press.

—— and SIMMONS, J. R. 2000. *What Government Can Do: Dealing with Poverty and Inequality*. Chicago: University of Chicago Press.

PRIOR, M. 2007. *Post-Broadcast Democracy: How Media Choice Increases Inequality in Political Involvement and Polarizes Elections*. New York: Cambridge University Press.

REDLAWSK, D. P. 2002. Hot Cognition or Cool Consideration? Testing the Effects of Motivated Reasoning on Political Decision Making. *Journal of Politics*, 64: 1021–44.

ROSEN, J. 1999. *What Are Journalists For?* New Haven: Yale University Press.

RUDOLPH, T. J. 2006. Triangulating Political Responsibility: The Motivated Formation of Responsibility Judgments. *Political Psychology*, 27/1: 99–122.

—— 2009. Political Trust, Ideology, and Public Support for Tax Cuts. *Public Opinion Quarterly*, 73: 144–58.

SCHNEIDER, S., and JACOBY, W. G. 2005. Elite Discourse and American Public Opinion: The Case of Welfare Spending. *Political Research Quarterly*, 58: 367–79.

SHAH, D. V., WATTS, M. D., DOMKE, D., FAN, D. P., and FIBISON, M. 1999. News Coverage, Economic Cues, and the Public's Presidential Preferences, 1984–1996. *Journal of Politics*, 61: 914–43.

SHAPIRO, R. Y., and BLOCH-ELKON, Y. 2008. Do the Facts Speak for Themselves? Partisan Disagreement as a Challenge to Democratic Competence. *Critical Review*, 20/1–2: 115–39.

—— and CONFORTO, B. M. 1980. Presidential Performance, the Economy, and the Public's Evaluation of Economic Conditions. *Journal of Politics*, 42: 49–67.

SMITH, M. A. 2007. *The Right Talk: How Conservatives Transformed the Great Society into the Economic Society*. Princeton: Princeton University Press.

SOROKA, S. N. 2006. Good News, Bad News: Asymmetric Responses to Economic Information. *Journal of Politics*, 68: 372–85.

SOSS, J., and SCHRAM, A. 2007. A Public Transformed? Welfare Reform as Policy Feedback. *American Political Science Review*, 101: 111–27.

STROUD, N. J. 2008. Media Use and Political Predispositions: Revisiting the Concept of Selective Exposure. *Political Behavior*, 30: 341–66.

TABER, C., and LODGE, M. 2006. Motivated Skepticism in the Evaluation of Political Beliefs. *American Journal of Political Science*, 50: 755–69.

WEAVER, R. K., SHAPIRO, R. Y., and JACOBS, L. R. 1995. The Polls—Trends: Welfare. *Public Opinion Quarterly*, 59: 606–27.

WLEZIEN, C., FRANKLIN, M., and TWIGGS, D. 1997. Economic Perceptions and the Vote Choice: Disentangling the Endogeneity. *Political Behavior*, 19/1: 7–17.

ZALLER, J. R. 1996. The Myth of Massive Media Impact Revived: New Support for a Discredited Idea. In *Political Persuasion and Attitude Change*, ed. D. C. Mutz, P. M. Sniderman, and R. A. Brody. Ann Arbor: University of Michigan Press.

# CHAPTER 37

................................................................

# RACE, PUBLIC OPINION,
# THE MEDIA

................................................................

TAEKU LEE
NICOLE WILLCOXON

ON Tuesday, November 3rd, 2008, American voters did what very few would have thought possible even a year before. The nation elected to the highest office in the land a 47-year-old junior senator from Illinois, the first American of African heritage to carry this distinction. Barack Obama, in his acceptance speech, took note of the historical moment: "It's been a long time coming, but tonight, because of what we did on this date in this election at this defining moment, change has come to America." That same night John McCain, his Republican challenger, also recognized, "This is a historic election, and I recognize the significance it has for African Americans and for the special pride that must be theirs tonight. We both realize that we have come a long way from the injustices that once stained our nation's reputation."

Many observers echoed this sense that America had reached a watershed in its history of race relations. In two *Los Angeles Times* opinion pieces following the election (November 5th, 2008), two African-American public intellectuals at opposite ends of the ideological spectrum shared a common sentiment about the possibility of a turning point. Thus, Shelby Steele reflected, "Does his victory mean that America is now officially beyond racism? . . . Doesn't a black in the Oval Office put the lie to both black inferiority and white racism? Doesn't it imply a 'post-racial' America?" And Michael Eric Dyson declared, "The distance from King's assassination to Obama's inauguration is a quantum leap of racial progress whose timeline neither cynics nor boosters could predict. Today is a benchmark that helps to fulfill—and rescue—America's democratic reputation."

If these buoyant remarks were to be taken seriously, one might worry about the relevance of this chapter or, more broadly, the prospects for social science research on race in the wake of Obama's successful election. Why study a phenomenon that is obsolete? The answer, simply put, is that the rosy blush of public discourse on Obama's "post-racialism" has paled in the continuing and unremitting light of deeply racial events and experiences. The 2008 election season was replete with signs of racial schism—from ex-President Bill Clinton's alleged race baiting in South Carolina to the Reverend Jeremiah Wright's firebrand sermons, Obama's "A More Perfect Union" speech to the McCain–Palin campaign's "America First" sloganeering. Since Obama's election, mass media outlets have lingered over episodic coverage of the grievances of fringe political elements like the "Birthers" and "Tea Party Patriots," often forgoing more substantive and thematic coverage of key policy initiatives on health-care reform, home mortgage markets, America's continued military presence in Afghanistan and Iraq, and working the country's way out of the worst economic crisis in eight decades.

Far from rendering research into public opinion, race, and the media obsolete, the events of the 2008 presidential election and those since have spawned a renewed, reinvigorated body of research on the significance of race in American electoral politics. Some of this work has analyzed aggregate-level correlates of Obama's vote share, with mixed assessments about whether Obama succeeded in transcending deep-rooted voter prejudices (Ansolabehere, Persily, and Stewart 2010; Hill, Herron, and Lewis 2009; Mas and Moretti 2009). Some of this research has also followed the more conventional route of using individual-level measures like the "racial resentment scale" and the "affect misattribution procedures," work that concludes that prejudice continues to be a robust determinant of vote choice in American electoral politics (for example, Greenwald et al. 2009; Hutchings 2009; Jackman and Vavreck 2009; Pasek et al. 2009). Yet other works examine the primary contest between Obama and Hillary Clinton to consider the intersecting effects of race and gender (Jackman and Vavreck 2009; McConnaughy and White 2010) and the support (or lack thereof) for Obama among Latinos and Asian Americans (Barreto, Fraga, et al. 2008; Barreto and Segura 2009; Ramakrishnan, Wong, Lee, and Junn 2009).

Taken together, these studies imply that—far from shifting to a transcendent, post-racial "Age of Obama"—racial conflicts and competition have a renewed, if reconfigured, vigor in American political life and, with it, the potential for a reinvigorated scholarly focus on race, public opinion, and the mass media. We begin this chapter with a review of the existing literature on race and media in electoral and non-electoral contexts. The ramifications of this review are that racial considerations continue to play a significant, at times defining, role in shaping public opinion across a broad array of politics. We then shift to a discussion of recent trends in the scholarship, with special attention paid to respective "cognitive" and "contextual" turns in research. The review here is less a comprehensive exposition on the field than it is a whirlwind tour in the service of foregrounding key developments and important avenues for progress. The chapter thus closes with gaps in our knowledge and future directions.

# DEBATING THE PERSISTENCE OF RACISM

The dialectics of race in 2008—between a racial and a post-racial state of affairs—mirrors a central line demarcating many scholars of race and public opinion. Descriptively, there has been a tide shift in the racial attitudes of white Americans from majority support of decidedly negative stereotypes about the intelligence, industry, and criminality of African Americans to majority rejection of such stereotypes (Schuman, Steeh, Bobo, and Krysan 1997). Furthermore, shifts in attitudes are reflected in the transformation of societal norms since the civil rights era. Majorities of whites now favor the principle of equality for blacks, express negative attitudes toward segregation, and are more in favor of busing. Yet, this majoritarian shift toward racial egalitarianism has not yet been coupled to an equal degree of support for policies like affirmative action that aim to ameliorate racial disparities. Attitudes toward the application of policy starkly diverge from attitudes toward principles; in the case of desegregation, opposition becomes more apparent as whites are faced with a majority of blacks rather than generic integration (Schuman, Steeh, Bobo, and Krysan 1997). Whites also seem to hold negative attitudes toward government involvement in issues that are not explicitly racial. Do white attitudes merely reflect shifting norms rather than reveal their true opinions? The continued disapproval of policies to close the gap of inequality manifested in white public opinion reveals the complexity of progress made since the end of Jim Crow. Explaining this "principle-implementation gap" has for a long time been a defining debate among scholars of racial attitudes (see Sears, Sidanius, and Bobo 2000).

One point of view is that while "old-fashioned," or "Jim Crow," racism no longer permeates society, a new symbolic form of racism has taken hold (Kinder and Sears 1981). Under "modern" or "symbolic" variants of racism, overt racism and stereotypes of racial inferiority have been replaced by negative affect toward African Americans (and other racial minority groups) founded on socialized beliefs that minority groups violate cherished norms of individualism and self-reliance. Under "laissez-faire racism," these socialized beliefs are coupled to a rejection of structural explanations of inequality, and a repudiation of active government intervention (Bobo, Kluegel, and Smith 1997). Under "racial resentment," this new variant of racism is measured using an index of statements like "Irish, Italians, Jewish and many other minorities overcame prejudice and worked their way up. Blacks should do the same without any special favors" and "It's really a matter of some people not trying hard enough; if blacks would only try harder they could be just as well off as whites" (Kinder and Sanders 1996).

A second point of view debates whether survey-based symbolic racism items actually tap into anti-black affect and racially resentful preferences per se, rather than tapping into an individual's principled ideological commitments. The specific objection is that these items measure individuals' considered views about the proper role of government in society, untarnished by negative sentiments toward the targeted beneficiaries of government policy (Sniderman and Tetlock 1986; cf. Tarman and Sears 2005). Whites, or so the "principled conservatism" viewpoint argues, are merely expressing opposition to race-based policies because they adhere to principles of ideological conservatism that emphasize limited government and individual self-reliance (for example, Sniderman and Piazza 1993).

A third standpoint is that racial attitudes are shaped by the relative position of groups in society vis-à-vis each other. One variant of this view builds on Blumer's (1958) symbolic interactionist account of prejudice as a "sense of group position" and posits whites and blacks as engaged in "realistic group conflict" (Bobo 1983). Whites, by this account, oppose policies that aim to address racial inequality because they feel threatened at the prospect of blacks obtaining equal economic footing in society. By another variant of a group conflict theory, immanent to the morphology of societies is a "social dominance orientation" (Sidanius and Pratto 2001) that insists on the maintenance of group-based hierarchies that stratify by sex, race, nation, class, and so on.

# The Continuing Significance of Race in Electoral Politics

Volleys continue to be fired in this debate, evolving into ever more textured claims about whether Democrats or Republicans are more prejudiced toward African Americans (Sniderman and Carmines 1997); whether individualism and anti-black resentment are inextricable (Kinder and Sanders 1996); whether realistic group conflict is really *realistic* and really about *groups* (Bobo and Tuan 2006); and whether the difference is less about rightful truths than about "lumping" or "splitting" the social world (Hochschild 2000). Notwithstanding these disagreements, there is a steady and growing body of evidence from survey experimental studies that shows a continuing and central role of racial considerations in differentiating candidate choice and policy preferences. For example, Terkildsen (1993) shows that whites not only were more likely to support white candidates than blacks, but were also more likely to support *lighter-skinned* blacks over darker-skinned blacks. Peffley and his colleagues (1997) find that whites are more likely to support welfare policy when the targeted beneficiaries are identified as European immigrants, rather than African Americans. Berinsky (1999) further suggests that we may actually *underestimate* the extent to which whites express negative racial attitudes because those who actually harbor racial resentments often choose to opt for "don't know" or some other non-compliant response category, rather than reveal their underlying sentiments. Still others argue that we have buried overt racism prematurely (for example, Feldman and Huddy 2009).

Where do these racial effects come from? What role do the mass media play in structuring the political messages that we receive and in sustaining racial biases? Political messages are always ubiquitous, often polysemous, sometimes contradictory, and occasionally indigestible and confusing. How do even the most attentive, civic-minded of us make sense of it all? Other chapters in this volume detail the many ways the mass media shape public opinion by setting the agenda on which issues and individuals to cover, framing and priming which aspects of those issues or individuals to highlight, and reducing complexity through the use of heuristics. Because race is an "easy" issue for voters to understand, it is a powerful and exploitable cue for politicians and candidates (Carmines and Stimson 1989). Deploying racial cues can reinforce elites' "racial coding" of policies (Gilens 1999); these messages can sometimes become central, decisive features of a campaign (Jamieson 1992).

There is perhaps no more thoroughly studied case of racial cuing in campaigns than the 1988 presidential election and the linkage of the Democratic candidate Michael Dukakis to a furloughed felon, William Horton. Horton, a convicted murderer and serving a life sentence in Massachusetts, received a weekend furlough while under Dukakis's gubernatorial watch, whereupon he committed assault, armed robbery, and rape. An infamous series of advertisements on Horton, followed by media coverage of those ads, came to signify Dukakis's stance on crime and incite race-based fears among segments of the electorate (Dawson 1994; Jamieson 1992; Mendelberg 1997). The Horton ads, and the swirl of controversy that surrounded them, epitomize the media's penchant for high drama, conflict, and the misrepresentation of key facts in lieu of symbolic, simplified framing of issues (Entman and Rojecki 2000; Jamieson 1992).

The Horton ads also demonstrated to scholars the power of implicit cues and racial priming. Racial priming works by activating or reinforcing existing stereotypes and making certain racial schemas more accessible in memory and thus automatically retrieved during subsequent decision-making (see Devine 1989). The mechanism here is key. According to one influential account, whites are likely to reject *explicit* cues because they violate societal norms, but are likely to be more vulnerable to accepting *implicit* cues that more effectively activate anti-black predispositions (Mendelberg 1997, 2001). If true, candidates who are the targets of "the race card" need to call out the implicit associations that are being deployed against them in order to defuse the effects of racial priming. Conversely, politicians who seek to exploit such associations need to prime racial considerations without making them explicit and, as Valentino (1999) shows, perhaps even without making politics explicit. Racial priming notably works best when (a) implicit cues conform to preexisting stereotypes and (b) the priming of racial considerations is suppressed when counter-stereotypic cues are deployed (Valentino, Hutchings, and White 2002). The implicit associations that accompany racial cues, furthermore, can be evoked not just through visual images, but also through the use of racially coded words and phrases such as "inner city" (Hurwitz and Peffley 2005).

The idea that the effects of implicit racial cues are more profound than explicit ones—and in turn render explicit cues less effective—has not gone unchallenged, however. Using national surveys with embedded experiments, one study finds that with the exception of poorly educated voters, who are receptive to *explicit* cues, racial primes appear to have no effect on public opinion (Huber and Lapinski 2006; but see Mendelberg 2008 for a response). Yet another study confirms the power of oblique references to race among whites, but finds a fundamentally different dynamic for

African Americans. For African Americans both implicit and explicit cues work, but through different mechanisms: explicit cues activate in-group identification while implicit cues only prime opinion when mediated by the activation of negative representations of African Americans (White 2007).

While research over the balance of implicit and explicit cues continues, there is an equally important and growing body of work on the specific effect of media coverage in bringing racial considerations to the foreground of the American public's mind. Some findings are straightforward and unsurprising: media coverage of an election will mention race more often if one of the candidates is African-American than if both candidates are white (Caliendo and McIlwain 2006). More expressly, the media may act as "racial arbitrators" who adjudicate how often and in what contexts race is emphasized in an electoral contest (Terkildsen and Damore 1999). Advocates of the "racial dualism hypothesis" contend that when African Americans compete in biracial elections (involving a black candidate and a white candidate), their race is always mentioned; when whites run for office, their race is never mentioned, regardless of the race of their competitor (Terkildsen and Damore 1999).

Voters are thus cued by the racial content of media coverage, with potentially important consequences for electoral outcomes. In survey experiments, for example, merely manipulating the race of a fictional mayoral candidate affects appeal of that candidate, especially when the candidate is tied to stereotype-consistent public policy positions—like a hypothesized African-American candidate running against a hypothesized white candidate, both of whom support affirmative action (Reeves 1997). These effects are also compounded by a common tendency of media entities to favor conflict in stories and focus on the simplicity of stories and incorporation of iconic visuals (Jamieson 1992), a dynamic that results in the reinforcement of racial animus and the portrayal of African-American candidates as "alien and threatening" and an out-group vis-à-vis policies such as affirmative action (Entman and Rojecki 2000).

## MEDIATING RACE BEYOND ELECTIONS

The continued, evolving salience of racial considerations on public opinion is not limited to electoral politics. A significant body of work shows its pervasive role across a broad range of public policy domains. Here, too, scholars have debated the extent to which opposition to social policies such as crime, welfare, affirmative action, and immigration are opposed because of the "coded" nature of these policies, lending opposition to racial animosity; or whether race plays a benign role in public opinion toward these policies. Many studies show that whites' opinions on welfare are heavily influenced by racial resentment, even controlling for beliefs about individualism (Bobo and Kluegel 1993; Gilens 1996; Kinder and Sanders 1996). Yet others contend that political differences, not racial prejudice, are at the root of white opposition to race-based policy, especially among more highly educated voters (Federico and Sidanius 2002; Jacoby 1994; Sniderman and Piazza 1993).

Notwithstanding these bones of contention, there is a consistent "racial divide" between the opinions on whites and African Americans across a broad range of policy areas, both race-targeted and non-targeted (Kinder and Winter 2001). This racial divide is perhaps nowhere more pointedly and poignantly felt than in the views of whites and African Americans in the aftermath of Hurricane Katrina; for instance, while an overwhelming majority of African Americans felt that the government's response would have been faster if those stranded in New Orleans were white, only a small minority of whites agreed (see Dawson 2006; Huddy and Feldman 2006).

Evidence is also clear that the media's coverage of issues—electoral or non-electoral— plays a defining role in shaping the public's views on an issue. One very well-studied issue domain here is social welfare or anti-poverty policies. Media coverage disproportionately represents African Americans in their stories about poverty and the "undeserving poor," an association which in turn reinforces prevailing stereotypes among white Americans that all African Americans are poor and that anti-poverty policies are, de facto, race-targeted programs and thus less worthy of public support (Gilens 1999).

This racial cast to media coverage is equally salient and striking in issue domains other than welfare and poverty. Media coverage on crime, for instance, is much likelier to portray violent crime with African Americans and Latinos as perpetrators (Gilliam and Iyengar 2000). These representations in turn heighten the sense of psychological discomfort felt by whites and the accessibility of crime stories (Dixon and Maddox 2005). They also activate more negative stereotypes of African Americans (Akalis, Banaji, and Kosslyn 2008) and lead to greater support for punitive crime policy (Gilliam and Iyengar 2000). With crime, the associations are bidirectional, with racial cues (of blacks) effectively cuing crime (Eberhardt, Goff, Purdie, and Davies 2004). Media cues that link race to social policies have also been shown with Social Security (Winter 2006) and health care reform (Valentino, Hutchings, and White 2002).

## New Trends in Scholarship

In our review of the field thus far, it is clear that the role of racial considerations in media coverage and public opinion continues to remain significant, with perhaps more debate over whether and by how much racism and racial prejudice undergird these considerations. The field has not remained still, however, or affixed to just one question about whether race and racism still matter. As with any other area of active innovation, there are some identifiable substantive and methodological directions in which the state of the art is moving and future research will grow. To a large extent, these recent shifts in substantive areas of interest reflect the discipline's response to three key developments: (1) the dramatic demographic transformation in the United States since the mid-twentieth century; (2) technological innovations and shifting methodological practices; (3) evolving substantive interests in identity, institutions, and the boundaries of the political.

The first of these developments has spurred a trend toward greater inclusiveness in the groups that are studied. As others have observed, there have been several discernibly distinct shifts in whose opinions have been studied over time (Fraga et al. 2006; McClain and Garcia 1993; A. W. Smith 1987). First, an initial wave of survey-based research focused primarily on the attitudes of white Americans about race, especially pertaining to their views on blacks and racial segregation. This emphasis exemplified the prevailing perspective of the period that if invidious and stereotyped views of African Americans would only loosen their stranglehold on majority whites, the "American dilemma" would be resolved (Myrdal 1944). Next came a second wave of scholarship—roughly coterminous with the civil rights movement—that extended the sampling frame by interviewing oversamples of African-American respondents and broadened the range of racial attitude items correspondingly. The most recent wave of surveys has broadened the reach even further with a robust mix of some surveys, like the Multi-City Study of Urban Inequality that oversamples multiple racial minority groups, and others that target the study of single minority groups (see Bobo and Hutchings 1996; O'connor, Tilly, and Bobo 2001). These surveys of single groups like the 1984–8 National Black Election Studies, the 1994 National Black Politics Study, the 1989–90 Latino National Politics Study, the 2001 Pilot National Asian American Survey, the 2006 Latino National Survey, and the 2008 National Asian American Survey have produced research that probes patterns of public opinion and political behavior of each group (see Abrajano and Alvarez 2010; Dawson 1994; Fraga et al. 2010; Ramakrishnan, Wong, Lee, and Junn 2009; Tate 1993).

The research here, however, has developed beyond merely augmenting the sampling frame. Along with a consideration of groups beyond blacks and whites, the wellspring of new data sources has also cultivated a ripening field of scholarship that examines across-group comparisons, including laterally between racial minority groups (see Bobo 2000; Bobo and Tuan 2006; Chong and Kim 2006; Oliver 2010; C. J. Wong 2010). Furthermore, the shift away from a primary focus on the racial attitudes of white Americans has sparked a boom in theoretical innovation and substantive range. In this section, we mention just a few such growth areas. The discussion here is for illustrative purposes rather than with the aim of comprehensively dissecting the literature.

One trajectory has been to more fully theorize "groupness" and the underlying mechanisms and dynamics of racial attitudes among minority groups. The progress here starts with a cognitive turn to the study of African-American political behavior, where the salience of race is located in an "African-American racial belief system" and in the centrality of a "linked fate heuristic" (Allen, Dawson, and Brown 1989; Dawson 1994; Tate 1993). This focus on individual-level psychological mechanisms has developed further into research that differentiates the role of racial priming (implicit and explicit) among African Americans (see Valentino, Hutchings, and White 2002; White 2007), extends tests of the salience of linked fate to other racial minority groups (see Masuoka

2006; Sanchez 2006), and examines the salience of group identity to the political attitudes and behavior of Latinos and Asian Americans (Fraga et al. 2010; Lee 2008).

Following on the heels of this cognitive turn, recent studies have also doubled back to a "contextual turn" toward more fully understanding the dynamics of group behavior within ideological, historical, organizational, institutional, and spatial contexts. One strand here is a body of work that pushes beyond the conventions of a unidimensional liberal-to-conservative spectrum and argues for a consideration of *racially* conditioned ideological belief systems. Dawson (2001), for instance, argues for at least six distinct ideological traditions within the African-American community: radical egalitarianism, disillusioned liberalism, black conservatism, black nationalism, black Marxism, and black feminism. Harris-Lacewell (2004) homes in on a subset of these and examines how they are sustained by "everyday talk" and locally embedded institutions of civil society. Sawyer (2006) further considers the role of the state in constructing ideologies of racial harmony and color-blindness, while Parker (2009) inverts this lens by detailing the power and agency of African-American soldiers and veterans to contest regnant views of citizenship, democracy, and equality in a bundle of beliefs and behavior the author terms "black republicanism." Hajnal and Lee (forthcoming) and Fraga et al. (2010) further extend this line of work to the fit (or lack thereof) between ideological traditions in the US and emerging minority groups like Latinos and Asian Americans.

Beyond ideology and history as contextual influences on race relations and racial attitudes, a related strand of research studies the defining role of historical moments and social movements that activate particular identities and demobilize others. Focal events like the civil rights movement and more recent collective action over immigration (e.g., California's Proposition 187 and the spring 2006 protest marches) can awaken an otherwise quiescent and dispossessed minority group politically (Barreto, Manzano, Ramirez, and Rim 2009; Lee 2002; Pantoja, Ramirez, and Segura 2001; Ramakrishnan 2005), while other phenomena like the AIDS epidemic in the African-American community can deter a requisite community response to threat as a result of destabilizing "cross-cutting issues" and forms of "secondary marginalization" (Cohen 1999).

The presence and strength of a mobilized group response, furthermore, is often prefigured by the presence and strength of a strong civil society and a rich amalgam of social networks, community organizations, and organized advocacy groups. Along these lines, a further promising and productive direction is the study of the specific communities and organizational contexts that condition race relations and group mobilization (see Cohen 1999; García Bedolla 2005; McClain et al. 2006; J. S. Wong 2006). These studies hark back to the Elmira, New York, and Erie, Pennsylvania, of Paul Lazarsfeld and his colleagues, (Berelson, Lazarsfeld, and Gaudet 1948; Berelson, Lazarsfeld, and McPhee 1954) albeit with an improved understanding of the limits of cross-sectional survey data and firmer commitments to the use of multiple methodologies. An important variant here is studies of civil society organizations—especially religious institutions—and their role in shaping racial and immigrant politics (see Harris 1994; Harris-Lacewell 2004; McDaniel 2008; J. S. Wong 2006).

A final area of current research that could (with some nudging) be squeezed into this broad contextual turn is research into the electoral contexts and political institutions that define racial attitudes. Extant works here identify a key role of minority empowerment and majority–minority districts (see Barreto, Segura, and Woods 2004; Barreto 2007; Bobo and Gilliam 1990; Gay 2001, 2002; Hajnal 2001) in electoral mobilization (and demobilization) and in altering perceptions of political efficacy and trust. The literature also keys on the role of institutions like political parties and the mass media on racial attitudes and political participation (see Abrajano 2010; Hajnal and Lee forthcoming; Kellstedt 2003; Philpot 2007), and a particular state or local jurisdiction's racial and ethnic composition (Hajnal and Trounstine 2005; Hero and Tolbert 1996). One of the more highly prized, if sometimes controversial, variants is studies that adopt a field experimental research design (see below).

Accompanying these cognitive and contextual turns are several notable methodological advances used to probe racial attitudes. In the psychological realm, perhaps the most pervasive change has been the seemingly ubiquitous use of survey experiments, enabled by technological innovations like computer-assisted telephone interviewing, audio computer-assisted self-interview, and the emergence of online surveys, as well as the availability of pooled resources for experimentation like the Time Sharing Experiments for the Social Sciences and the Cooperative Congressional Election Studies. Additionally, scholars have more recently started to turn away from studying expressed responses to experimental treatments toward implicit responses, as reflected in the racial priming literature and in the growing use of methodologies like implicit association tests (Greenwald et al. 2009; Greenwald and Banaji 1995) and affect misattribution procedures (Pasek et al. 2009). These methods often appear to reveal a deeper attitudinal structure. At the same time, they have also been called into question for bearing only weakly on choice and behavior, for reifying response time into racism, and for measuring a meta-level of extra-personal associations and cultural competence (see Arkes and Tetlock 2004).

The burning desire to draw causal inferences through well-designed experiments is a methodological fever that has spread beyond treatments of question wording or visual cues and has not left the field of racial attitudes untouched. In rare cases, natural experiments in the field are available to be exploited, such as the exogenous resettlement of Hurricane Katrina survivors (Hopkins 2009) or having a survey in the field during the 1992 Los Angeles riots (Bobo, Zubrinsky, Johnson, and Oliver 1994). In other cases, field experiments are expressly designed through treatments to the course of political and social events itself (Gerber and Green 2000). Field experiments have generated important new findings into the efficacy of different strategies for voter mobilization, findings that have clear implications for the proper functioning of a participatory democracy given the underrepresentation of many racial minority groups at the polls (García Bedolla and Michelson, forthcoming; Green 2004; Ramirez 2005; J. S. Wong 2005). While clearly an area for future interest, field experimental methods, too, are not without their own limitations such as cost, proper statistical tests, and the general inability (as with lab experiments) of isolating a treatment effect while taking into account other environmental factors that are apt to condition the result (Imai 2005). Here a more explicit consideration of the media environment and social networks of communication and persuasion is essential to the interests of a cumulative social science, as voters receive multiple messages and cross-cutting pressures from various sources as a general, if inconvenient, fact of social life.

# CONCLUDING THOUGHTS

The study of race, public opinion, and the media has been and will likely continue to be fertile ground for scholars. This final section might well be reserved for our views on seeds for future research that we find especially likely to yield a bumper crop of compelling findings. While the previous sections of this chapter have largely summarized and synthesized extant work in a relatively straightforward manner, with (hopefully) limited possible variation among capable judges, proposing future directions for research is much likelier to provoke a varied reaction. It is an opportunity for an idiosyncratic and fleeting itemization of "dos" and "don'ts."

To give this chapter some hope of longevity, we avoid recommending greater emphasis on an especially favored group, methodology, or substantive topic. Future work in this area is likely to continue its current duality: the turn inward by some toward more clearly specifying the psychological bases of racial attitudes and behavior; the shift outward by others toward more fully situating these individual-level determinants within multiple contexts and constraints—historical, ideological, organizational, spatial, and political. Future work is also likely to fix on better understanding racial identity—its activation, salience, and intersection with other activated and salient identities. One key challenge, in this regard, is to answer Smith's (2004) recent claim that "identity" is at the center of the study of political science and that existing "abstract, ahistorical" methods of studying political behavior are ill-suited to generate durable knowledge about the role of identity in politics.

To a large extent, much of the current and promising trends in political behavior research into racial attitudes and mass media have already taken up this challenge by situating our understanding of public opinion more firmly in history and in the specificity of spatial, institutional, and ideological contexts. As a result, current work is increasingly diversifying beyond an exclusive reliance on survey data and moving closer to answering Jacobs and Shapiro's (1996) call for a more "integrated" field of study of political communications that uses mixed methodologies and multiple measurement approaches. The "essential tension," however, between innovation and conservatism in our frameworks of inquiry remains in this field as in any other. To that end, the greatest challenges awaiting current and future scholars in this field lie in how they will negotiate emerging and evolving changes in real-world events—from the election of Barack Obama to the growing traces of a reinscription of biological approaches to the study of race—and changes in the instruments we deploy to study those events—from methodologies that exploit the seemingly ubiquitous reach of online connectivity to diagnostic tools used in the medical and cognitive sciences.

# REFERENCES

ABRAJANO, M. A. 2010. *Campaigning to the New American Electorate: Television Advertising to Latinos.* Stanford, CA: Stanford University Press.

—— and ALVAREZ, R. M. 2010. *New Faces, New Voices: The Hispanic Electorate in America.* Princeton: Princeton University Press.

AKALIS, S. A., BANAJI, M. R., and KOSSLYN, S. M. 2008. Crime Alert! How Thinking about a Single Suspect Automatically Shifts Stereotypes toward an Entire Group. *Du Bois Review,* 5/2: 217–33.

ALLEN, R. L., DAWSON, M. C., and BROWN, R. E. 1989. A Schema-Based Approach to Modeling an African-American Racial Belief System. *American Political Science Review,* 83/2: 421–41.

ANSOLABEHERE, S., PERSILY, N., and STEWART, C., III. 2010. Race, Region, and Vote Choice in the 2008 Election: Implications for the Future of the Voting Rights Act. *Harvard Law Review,* 123/6: 1385–436.

ARKES, H. R., and TETLOCK, P. E. 2004. Attributions of Implicit Prejudice, or, Would Jesse Jackson "Fail" the Implicit Association Test? *Psychological Inquiry,* 15/4: 257–78.

BARRETO, M. 2007. *¡Si se puede!* Latino Candidates and the Mobilization of Latino Voters. *American Political Science Review,* 101/3: 425–41.

—— and SEGURA, G. M. 2009. Estimating the Effects of Traditional Predictors, Group Specific Forces, and Anti-Black Affect on 2008 Presidential Vote among Latinos and Non-Hispanic Whites. Paper presented at the Transformative Election of 200 Conference, Columbus, OH.

—— FRAGA, L. R., MANZANO, S., MARTINEZ-EBERS, V., and SEGURA, G. M. 2008. Should they "Dance with the One Who Brung 'Em?" Latinos and the 2008 Presidential Election. *PS: Political Science and Politics,* 41/4: 753–60.

—— MANZANO, S., RAMIREZ, R., and RIM, K. 2009. Mobilization, Participation, and *Solidaridad*: Latinos during the 2006 Immigration Protest Rallies. *Urban Affairs Review,* 44/5: 736–64.

—— SEGURA, G. M., and WOODS, N. 2004. The Effects of Overlapping Majority–Minority Districts on Latino Turnout. *American Political Science Review,* 98 (Feb.), 65–75.

BERELSON, B. R., LAZARSFELD, P. F., and McPHEE, W. N. 1954. *Voting: A Study of Opinion Formation in a Presidential Campaign.* Chicago: University of Chicago Press.

BERINSKY, A. J. 1999. The Two Faces of Public Opinion. *American Journal of Political Science,* 43/4: 1209–30.

BLUMER, H. 1958. Race Prejudice as a Sense of Group Position. *Pacific Sociological Review,* 1/1: 3–7.

BOBO, L. 1983. Whites' Opposition to Busing: Symbolic Racism or Realistic Group Conflict? *Journal of Personality and Social Psychology,* 45/6: 1195–210.

—— and GILLIAM, F. D., JR. 1990. Race, Sociopolitical Participation, and Black Empowerment. *American Political Science Review,* 84/2: 377–93.

—— and HUTCHINGS, V. L. 1996. Perceptions of Racial Group Competition: Extending Blumer's Theory of Group Position to a Multiracial Social Context. *American Sociological Review,* 61/6: 951–72.

—— and KLUEGEL, J. R. 1993. Opposition to Race-Targeting: Self-Interest, Stratification Ideology, or Racial Attitudes? *American Sociological Review*, 58/4: 443–64.

—— and TUAN, T. 2006. *Prejudice in Politics*. Cambridge, MA: Harvard University Press.

—— KLUEGEL, J. R., and SMITH, R. A. 1997. Laissez-Faire Racism: The Crystallization of a Kinder, Gentler, Anti-Black Ideology. In *Racial Attitudes in the 1990s: Continuity and Change*, ed. S. A. Tuch and J. K. Martin. Westport, CT: Praeger.

—— ZUBRINSKY, C. L., JOHNSON, J. H., JR., and OLIVER, M. L. 1994. Public Opinion before and after a Spring of Discontent. In *The Los Angeles Riots: Lessons for the Urban Future*, ed. M. Baldassarre. Boulder, CO: Westview Press.

CALIENDO, S. M., and MCILWAIN, C. D. 2006. Minority Candidates, Media Framing, and Racial Cues in the 2004 Election. *Harvard International Journal of Press/Politics*, 11: 45–69.

CARMINES, E. G., and STIMSON, J. A. 1989. *Issue Evolution: Race and the Transformation of American Politics*. Princeton: Princeton University Press.

CHONG, D., and KIM, D. 2006. The Experiences and Effects of Economic Status among Racial and Ethnic Minorities. *American Political Science Review*, 100/3: 335–51.

COHEN, C. J. 1999. *The Boundaries of Blackness: AIDS and the Breakdown of Black Politics*. Chicago: University of Chicago Press.

DAWSON, M. C. 1994. *Behind the Mule: Race and Class in African-American Politics*. Princeton: Princeton University Press.

—— 2001. *Black Visions: The Roots of Contemporary African-American Political Ideologies*. Chicago: University of Chicago Press.

—— 2006. After the Deluge: Publics and Publicity in Katrina's Wake. *Du Bois Review*, 3/1: 239–49.

DEVINE, P. 1989. Stereotypes and Prejudice: Their Automatic and Controlled Components. *Journal of Personality and Social Psychology*, 56/1: 5–18.

DIXON, T. L., and MADDOX, K. B. 2005. Skin Tone, Crime News, and Social Reality Judgments: Priming the Stereotype of the Dark and Dangerous Black Criminal. *Journal of Applied Social Psychology*, 35/8: 1555–70.

DYSON, M. E. 2008. Race, Post Race. *Los Angeles Times*, Nov. 5. At <http://www.latimes.com/news/opinion/la-oe-dyson5-2008nov05,0,5307282.story>. Accessed Jan. 25, 2010.

EBERHARDT, J. L., GOFF, P. A., PURDIE, V. J., and DAVIES, P. G. 2004. Seeing Black: Race, Crime, and Visual Processing. *Journal of Personality and Social Psychology*, 87/6: 876–93.

ENTMAN, R. M., and ROJECKI, A. 2000. *The Black Image in the White Mind: Media and Race in America*. Chicago: University of Chicago Press.

FEDERICO, C. M., and SIDANIUS, J. 2002. Sophistication and the Antecedents of Whites' Racial Policy Attitudes: Racism, Ideology, and Affirmative Action in America. *Public Opinion Quarterly*, 66: 145–76.

FELDMAN, S., and HUDDY, L. 2009. On Assessing the Political Effects of Racial Prejudice. *Annual Review of Political Science*, 12: 423–47.

FRAGA, L. R., GARCIA, J. A., HERO, R. E., JONES-CORREA, M., MARTINEZ-EBERS, V., and SEGURA, G. M. 2006. *Su casa es nuestra casa*: Latino Politics Research and the Development of American Political Science. *American Political Science Review*, 100/4: 515–21.

—— —— —— —— —— —— 2010. *Latino Lives in America: Making it Home*. Philadelphia: Temple University Press.

GARCÍA BEDOLLA, L. 2005. *Fluid Borders: Latino Power, Identity, and Politics in Los Angeles*. Berkeley: University of California Press.

García Bedolla, L., and Michelson, M. R. Forthcoming. *Mobilizing Inclusion: Getting Out the Vote among Low-Propensity Voters.* New Haven: Yale University Press.

Gay, C. 2001. The Effect of Black Congressional Representation on Political Participation. *American Political Science Review,* 95/3: 589–602.

—— 2002. Spirals of Trust: The Effect of Descriptive Representation on the Relationship between Citizens and their Government. *American Journal of Political Science,* 46/4: 717–32.

Gerber, A. S., and Green, D. P. 2000. The Effects of Canvassing, Telephone Calls, and Direct Mail on Voter Turnout: A Field Experiment. *American Political Science Review,* 94/3: 653–63.

Gilens, M. 1996. "Race Coding" and White Opposition to Welfare. *American Political Science Review,* 90 (Sept.), 593–604.

—— 1999. *Why Americans Hate Welfare: Race, Media, and the Politics of Antipoverty Policy.* Chicago: University of Chicago Press.

Gilliam, F. D., Jr., and Iyengar, S. 2000. Prime Suspects: The Influence of Local Television News on the Viewing Public. *American Journal of Political Science,* 44/3: 560–73.

Green, D. P. 2004. Mobilizing African-American Voters Using Direct Mail and Commercial Phone Banks: A Field Experiment. *Political Research Quarterly,* 57/2: 245–55.

Greenwald, A. G., and Banaji, M. R. 1995. Implicit Social Cognition: Attitudes, Self-esteem, and Stereotypes. *Psychological Review,* 102/1: 4–27.

—— Tucker Smith, C., Sriram, N., Bar-Anan, Y., and Nosek, B. A. 2009. Implicit Race Attitudes Predicted Vote in the 2008 U.S. Presidential Election. *Analyses of Social Issues and Public Policy,* 9/1: 241–53.

Hajnal, Z. L. 2001. White Residents, Black Incumbents, and a Declining Racial Divide. *American Political Science Review,* 95/3: 603–17.

—— and Lee, T. Forthcoming. *Why Americans Don't Join the Party: Race, Immigration, and the Failure (of Political Parties) to Engage the Electorate.* Princeton: Princeton University Press.

—— and Trounstine, J. 2005. Where Turnout Matters: The Consequences of Uneven Turnout in City Politics. *Journal of Politics,* 67: 515–35.

Harris, F. C. 1994. Something Within: Religion as a Mobilizer of African-American Political Activism. *Journal of Politics,* 56: 42–68.

Harris-Lacewell, M. K. 2004. *Barbershops, Bibles, and BET: Everyday Talk and Black Political Thought.* Princeton: Princeton University Press.

Hero, R. E., and Tolbert, C. J. 1996. A Racial/Ethnic Diversity Interpretation of Politics and Policy in the States of the U.S. *American Journal of Political Science,* 40/3: 851–71.

Hill, S. J., Herron, M. C., and Lewis, J. B. 2009. Economic Crisis, Iraq, and Race: A Study of the 2008 Presidential Election. *Election Law Journal: Rules, Politics, and Policy,* 9/1: 41–62.

Hochschild, J. L. 2000. Lumpers and Splitters, Individuals and Structures. In *Racialized Politics: The Debate about Racism in America,* ed. D. O. Sears, J. Sidanius, and L. Bobo. Chicago: University of Chicago Press.

Hopkins, D. J. 2009. *Flooded Communities: Explaining Local Reactions to the Post-Katrina Migrants.* Social Science Research Network Working Paper. At <http://papers.ssrn.com/sol3/papers.cfm?abstract_id=1508426>. Accessed Oct. 2010.

Huber, G. A., and Lapinski, J. S. 2006. The "Race Card" Revisited: Assessing Racial Priming in Policy Contests. *American Journal of Political Science,* 50/2: 421–40.

Huddy, L., and Feldman, S. 2006. Worlds Apart: Blacks and Whites React to Hurricane Katrina. *Du Bois Review,* 3/1: 97–114.

HURWITZ, M., and PEFFLEY, J. 2005. Playing the Race Card in the Post-Willie Horton Era: The Impact of Racialized Code Words on Support for Punitive Crime Policy. *Public Opinion Quarterly*, 69: 99–112.

HUTCHINGS, V. L. 2009. Change or More of the Same? Evaluating Racial Attitudes in the Obama Era. *Public Opinion Quarterly*, 73/5: 917–42.

IMAI, K. 2005. Do Get-Out-the-Vote Calls Reduce Turnout? The Importance of Statistical Methods for Field Experiments. *American Political Science Review*, 99/2: 283–300.

JACKMAN, S., and VAVRECK, L. 2009. Meaning beyond Measure: Separating the Effects of Obama's Race from the Effects of Racial Prejudice. Unpublished working paper. Stanford University.

JACOBS, L. R., and SHAPIRO, R. Y. 1996. Toward the Integrated Study of Political Communications, Public Opinion, and the Policy-Making Process. *Political Science and Politics*, 29/1: 10–13.

JACOBY, W. G. 1994. Public Attitudes toward Government Spending. *American Journal of Political Science*, 38/2: 336–61.

JAMIESON, K. H. 1992. *Dirty Politics: Deception, Distraction, and Democracy*. New York: Oxford University Press.

KELLSTEDT, P. M. 2003. *The Mass Media and the Dynamics of American Racial Attitudes*. New York: Cambridge University Press.

KINDER, D. R., and SANDERS, L. M. 1996. *Divided by Color: Racial Politics and Democratic Ideals*. Chicago: University of Chicago Press.

—— and SEARS, D. O. 1981. Prejudice and Politics: Symbolic Racism versus Racial Threats to the Good Life. *Journal of Personality and Social Psychology*, 40/3: 414–31.

—— and WINTER, N. 2001. Exploring the Racial Divide: Blacks, Whites, and Opinion on National Policy. *American Journal of Political Science*, 45/2: 439–56.

LAZARSFELD, P. F., BERELSON, B., and GAUDET, H. 1948. *The People's Choice: How the Voter Makes up his Mind in a Presidential Campaign*, 2nd edn. New York: Columbia University Press.

LEE, T. 2002. *Mobilizing Public Opinion*. Chicago: University of Chicago Press.

—— 2008. Race, Immigration, and the Identity-to-Politics Link. *Annual Review of Political Science*, 11: 457–78.

McCLAIN, P. D., and GARCIA, J. A. 1993. Expanding Disciplinary Boundaries: Black, Latino, and Racial Minority Group Politics in Political Science. In *Political Science: The State of the Discipline II*, ed. A. W. Finifter. Washington, DC: American Political Science Association.

—— CARTER, N. M., DEFRANCESCO SOTO, V. M., LYLE, M. L., GYNAVISKI, J. D., NUNNALLY, S. C., SCOTTO, T. J., KENDRICK, J. A., LACKEY, G. F., and COTTON, K. D. 2006. Racial Distancing in a Southern City: Latino Immigrants' Views of Black Americans. *Journal of Politics*, 68/3: 285–304.

McCONNAUGHY, C. M., and WHITE, I. K. 2010. Identity Politics Complicated: Race, Gender, and Election 2008. Unpublished manuscript. Ohio State University.

McDANIEL, E. L. 2008. *Politics in the Pews: The Political Mobilization of Black Churches*. Ann Arbor: University of Michigan Press.

MAS, A., and MORETTI, E. 2009. Racial Bias in the 2008 Presidential Election. *American Economic Review: Papers and Proceedings*, 99/2: 323–9.

MASUOKA, N. 2006. Together they Become One: Examining the Predictors of Panethnic Group Consciousness among Asian Americans and Latinos. *Social Science Quarterly*, 87/5: 993–1011.

MENDELBERG, T. 1997. Executing Hortons: Racial Crime in the 1988 Presidential Campaign. *Public Opinion Quarterly*, 61/1: 134–57.

—— 2001. *The Race Card: Campaign Strategy, Implicit Messages, and the Norm of Equality.* Princeton: Princeton University Press.

—— 2008. Racial Priming Revived. *Perspectives on Politics*, 6/1: 109–23.

MYRDAL, G. 1944. *An American Dilemma: The Negro Problem and Modern Democracy.* New York: Pantheon.

O'CONNOR, A., TILLY, C., and BOBO, L. D. (eds.) 2001. *Urban Inequality: Evidence from Four Cities.* Multi-City Study of Urban Inequality. New York: Russell Sage Foundation.

OLIVER, J. E. 2010. *The Paradoxes of Integration: Race, Neighborhood, and Civic Life in Muliethnic America.* Chicago: University of Chicago Press.

PANTOJA, A. D., RAMIREZ, R., and SEGURA, G. M. 2001. Citizens by Choice, Voters by Necessity. *Political Research Quarterly*, 54/4: 729–50.

PARKER, C. S. 2009. *Fighting for Democracy: Black Veterans and the Struggle against White Supremacy in the Postwar South.* Princeton: Princeton University Press.

PASEK, J., TAHK, A., LELKES, Y., KROSNICK, J. A., PAYNE, B. K., AKHTAR, O., and THOMPSON, T. 2009. Determinants of Turnout and Candidate Choice in the 2008 U.S. Presidential Election. *Public Opinion Quarterly*, 73/5: 943–94.

PEFFLEY, M., HURWITZ, J., and SNIDERMAN, P. M. 1997. Racial Stereotypes and Whites' Political Views of Blacks in the Context of Welfare and Crime. *American Journal of Political Science*, 41/1: 30–60.

PHILPOT, T. S. 2007. *Race, Republicans and the Return of the Party of Lincoln.* Ann Arbor: University of Michigan Press.

RAMAKRISHNAN, S. K. 2005. *Democracy in Immigrant America: Changing Demographics and Political Participation.* Stanford, CA: Stanford University Press.

—— WONG, J., LEE, T., and JUNN, J. 2009. Race-Based Considerations and the Obama Vote. *Du Bois Review*, 6: 219–38.

RAMIREZ, R. 2005. Giving Voice to Latino Voters: A Field Experiment on the Effectiveness of a National Nonpartisan Mobilization Effort. *Annals of the American Academy of Political and Social Sciences*, 601: 66–84.

REEVES, K. 1997. *Voting Hopes or Fears: White Voters, Black Candidates, and Racial Politics in America.* New York: Oxford University Press.

SAWYER, M. Q. 2006. *Racial Politics in Post-Revolutionary Cuba.* New York: Cambridge University Press.

SANCHEZ, G. 2006. The Role of Group Consciousness in Latino Public Opinion. *Political Research Quarterly*, 59/3: 435–46.

SCHUMAN, H., STEEH, C., BOBO, L., and KRYSAN, M. 1997. *Racial Attitudes in America: Trends and Interpretations*, rev. edn. Cambridge, MA: Harvard University Press.

SEARS, D. O., SIDANIUS, J., and BOBO, L. (eds.) 2000. *Racialized Politics: The Debate about Racism in America.* Chicago: University of Chicago Press.

SIDANIUS, J., and PRATTO, F. 2001. *Social Dominance: An Intergroup Theory of Social Hierarchy and Oppression.* New York: Cambridge University Press.

SMITH, A. W. 1987. Problems and Progress in the Measurement of Black Public Opinion. *American Behavioral Scientist*, 30: 441–55.

SMITH, R. M. 2004. Identities, Interests, and the Future of Political Science. *Perspectives on Politics*, 2/2: 301–12.

SNIDERMAN, P. M., and CARMINES, E. G. 1997. *Reaching beyond Race*. Cambridge, MA: Harvard University Press.

—— and PIAZZA, T. 1993. *The Scar of Race*. Cambridge, MA: Belknap/Harvard University Press.

—— and TETLOCK, P. E. 1986. Symbolic Racism: Problems of Motive Attribution in Political Debate. *Journal of Social Issues*, 42 (Summer), 129–50.

STEELE, S. 2008. Obama's Post-Racial Promise. *Los Angeles Times*, Nov. 5. At <http://www.latimes.com/news/opinion/commentary/la-oe-steele5-2008nov05,0,6553798.story>. Accessed Jan. 25, 2010.

TARMAN, C., and SEARS, D. O. 2005. The Conceptualization and Measurement of Symbolic Racism. *Journal of Politics*, 67/3: 731–61.

TATE, K. 1993. *From Protest to Politics: The New Black Voters in American Elections*. Cambridge, MA: Harvard University Press.

TERKILDSEN, N. 1993. When White Voters Evaluate Black Candidates: The Processing Implications of Candidate Skin Color, Prejudice, and Self-Monitoring. *American Journal of Political Science*, 37/4: 1032–53.

—— and DAMORE, D. F. 1999. The Dynamics of Racialized Media Coverage in Congressional Elections. *Journal of Politics*, 61: 680–99.

VALENTINO, N. A. 1999. Crime News and the Priming of Racial Attitudes during Evaluations of the President. *Public Opinion Quarterly*, 63: 293–320.

—— HUTCHINGS, V. L., and WHITE, I. K. 2002. Cues that Matter: How Political Ads Prime Racial Attitudes during Campaigns. *American Political Science Review*, 96/1: 75–90.

WHITE, I. K. 2007. When Race Matters and When it Doesn't: Racial Group Differences in Response to Racial Cues. *American Political Science Review*, 101/2: 339–54.

WINTER, N. J. G. 2006. Beyond Welfare: Framing and the Racialization of White Opinion on Social Security. *American Journal of Political Science*, 50/2: 400–20.

WONG, C. J. 2010. *Boundaries of Obligation in American Politics: Geographic, National, and Racial Communities*. New York: Cambridge University Press.

WONG, J. S. 2005. Mobilizing Asian American Voters: A Field Experiment. *Annals of the American Academy of Political and Social Sciences*, 601/1: 102–14.

—— 2006. *Democracy's Promise: Immigrants and America's Civic Institutions*. Ann Arbor: University of Michigan Press.

CHAPTER 38

..............................................................................................................

# PUBLIC OPINION, THE MEDIA, AND SOCIAL ISSUES

..............................................................................................................

## PATRICK J. EGAN*

In demarcating the set of salient controversies in American politics that should be called "social issues," scholars have cast a wide net and employed varying labels. In this chapter, I consider the characteristics that social issues have in common and their implications for public opinion. I then turn to empirical efforts to delineate the set of political debates that should be called social issues, paying special attention to efforts made to cast opinion on these issues as a second dimension of political conflict that is separate from the primary axis of debate over economic policies in the United States. The chapter proceeds by examining broad trends in opinion on social issues and considering how media coverage of these issues has changed with public opinion. It then discusses three explanations regarding the sources of attitudes on social issues—authoritarianism, core values, and elite opinion leadership—and considers the strengths of these explanations, the extent to which they suggest that the etiology of public opinion on social issues is particularly unusual or distinctive from that of other issues, and the research frontier on these questions.

## WHAT IS A "SOCIAL ISSUE"?
..............................................................................................................

There can be a fair amount of disagreement among scholars about just what should be considered a social issue, but at the core of most typologies are those controversies that fall under the aegis of "religious and cultural conflict" (Layman 2001): issues such as

* I thank Henry Brady and this volume's editors for extensive helpful comments on previous drafts of this chapter, and Christopher Bowman for research assistance.

abortion, gay rights, the role of religion in public schools, and euthanasia. Other scholars also include additional battles over freedom of speech and the public regulation of private behavior—such as use of recreational drugs and the availability of pornography—on a longer register of what they call "moral issues" (for example, Ansolabehere, Rodden, and Snyder 2008). An even further expansion of the list is promoted by those who locate the origins of opinion in the extent of one's predisposition toward authoritarianism, which they view as a cause of what one scholar calls the "familiar triad of racial, political and moral intolerance" (Stenner 2005: 1). Within this framework, added to the list of issues are those involving race and ethnicity, such as educational and residential desegregation, affirmative action, and immigration. Other scholars take a different approach by setting forth criteria that can be used to separate social issues from others. Leege and his collaborators define what they call "cultural politics" as "less a set of issues than a style of argumentation that invokes fundamental social values and emphasizes group differences" (Leege, Wald, Krueger, and Mueller 2002: 27–8). Thus elaborated, this approach justifies including—in certain contexts— issues such as crime (including the death penalty, punishment of criminals, and gun control) and national security as subjects of research.

# THE DISTINCTIVENESS OF SOCIAL ISSUES: SHARED CHARACTERISTICS

Some important similarities are shared by many of the policy domains scholars have identified as social issues. For one, debates about social issues are usually about ends, rather than means: should gay people be allowed to serve openly in the military? Should abortion be legal? Should patients with incurable diseases be allowed to seek a doctor's assistance to end their lives? In Donald Stokes's terminology, they are thus generally *position* rather than *valence* issues (1963, 373). Typically there is much more disagreement over the desired end state in social issue domains than on valence issues like schools, the environment, or foreign policy—where most Americans agree that, all things being equal, they'd like a well-educated citizenry, clean air and water, and a nation safe from its enemies. A second distinction is that the social issues identified here are generally associated with policies whose implementations require little in the way of resources. In fact, we might consider social issues to be distinguished from others by the fact that they are attempts to redistribute values rather than resources (Gusfield 1963). While most welfare state issues involve taxing and spending and thus inevitably require the consideration of tradeoffs among them, for the most part social issues are not subject to a similar budget constraint. Third, scholars have noted how social issues are generally "easy" rather than "hard" issues according to the distinction made first by Carmines and Stimson (1980). Easy issues are symbolic rather than technical, deal with policy ends rather than means, and have been on the political agenda for a relatively long time—all criteria often associated with social issues. The characteristic feature of easy issues is that voters at all levels of sophistication are equally able to translate their issue attitudes into votes—and thus empirically we see little difference among the least and best-informed in the relationship between preferences on easy issues and voting. A related feature is that voters' opinions on social issues tend to be more stable over time than on other issues (Converse and Markus 1979; Erikson and Tedin 2007). Social issues are arguably easier for lawmakers as well: information barriers are low, and thus little expertise is required to change policy in a definitive way on social issues (Haider-Markel and Meier 1996).

These three attributes that many social issues have in common—they are about ends, not means; they are less affected by resource constraints; and they are easy for both citizens and policymakers—bring us to a final characteristic that distinguishes social issues from others in the American context: the strong role courts have played in their recent political trajectory. It is not inconceivable that one of the reasons courts have been so active in this realm is that a change in policy on these issues can be accomplished with relatively little cost and expertise, making court rulings credible and enforceable. On many of the most salient social issues, the United States Supreme Court has issued highly consequential rulings striking down democratically enacted laws and policies between the mid-1950s and the present day. These include decisions on abortion, gay rights, school prayer, interracial marriage, racial segregation, and pornography. In each of these cases, the court changed policy in an unmistakably liberal direction. Public opinion on these issues has not necessarily followed suit (Persily, Citrin, and Egan 2008), and some rulings have polarized—rather than led—public opinion (Brickman and Peterson 2006; Franklin and Kosaki 1989; Johnson and Martin 1998). All told, in the post-New Deal era, federal courts have played a much larger role in adjudicating disputes on social issues than on economic issues.

## SOCIAL ISSUES AS A SECOND DIMENSION OF CONFLICT IN AMERICAN POLITICS

A complementary approach adopted by scholars seeking to circumscribe the set of issues properly considered "social" has been to conduct some sort of data reduction process designed to identify underlying factors, dimensions, or latent variables. Many of these analyses have uncovered a dimension consisting of social issues that is distinct from the primary left–right conflict over the role of government in economic matters in the United States. Depending on the survey questions being analyzed, the dimension typically includes a tightly interrelated set of controversies over morality, the role of the state in regulating private behavior, and the rights of disadvantaged groups, including women, racial minorities, and gays (for example, Ansolabehere, Rodden, and Snyder 2006; Fleishman 1988; Layman and Carsey 2002a; Stimson 1975; Treier and Hillygus 2009). Analyses like these find much less frequently that debates about crime, welfare, or guns belong distinctly to the family of social issues. To be clear, attitudes on the social issues dimension are not entirely unrelated to those regarding the welfare state: preferences on the two dimensions tend to covary to a substantial degree with one another and with survey respondents' placements of themselves on the generic liberal-to-conservative scale.

The distinctiveness of social issues as a separate dimension of conflict in American politics has been found to varying degrees in other arenas, including congressional roll-call votes (Poole and Rosenthal 1997), congressional constituency opinion (Fleck and Kilby 2002), and interest groups (Poole and Rosenthal 1998). Overarching ideologies stitch voters located in different areas of this policy space into political coalitions (Hinich and Munger 1994). Although the chief lines of battle in contemporary American politics are drawn between liberals (those who favor expansion of the welfare state, but less state promotion of traditional morality) and conservatives (those who favor more state promotion of traditional morality, but a smaller welfare state), there is nothing particularly natural about these coalitions. The primary conflict in American politics at the turn of the twentieth century pitted social liberals and economic conservatives on one side against social conservatives and economic liberals on the other (Brady 2001; G. Miller and Schofield 2003). Currently, however, in advanced industrial democracies it is generally the case that parties that support expansion of the welfare state also advocate less traditional positions on social issues (Benoit and Laver 2006).

## TRENDS IN OPINION ON SOCIAL ISSUES

In the very long term, trends in American opinion on most leading social issues have moved in an unmistakably liberal direction—that is, away from support for government regulation of private behavior and toward less traditional views of morality and intergroup relations. For example, where survey data are available, scholars have found that current attitudes are substantially more liberal than in the 1960s on social issues as diverse as abortion, school prayer, the right to die, gay rights, desegregation, and women's roles (see, generally, Persily, Citrin, and Egan 2008). Trends like these—and similar opinion change around the world that has coincided with industrialization and prosperity—are cited by Ronald Inglehart in support of his "post-materialism" thesis (Inglehart 1977, 1990, 1997; Inglehart and Welzel 2005). Inglehart's explanation for liberalizing opinion trends is simple: economic security makes humans cognitively and socially more autonomous. It thus leads us to turn away from traditional, religious values toward the rational and secular—and to prize self-expression over conformity. Global opinion data provide substantial cross-national evidence for the theory.

However, Inglehart's human development sequence is less helpful in explaining opinion on social issues over the past four decades in the United States, where many liberalizing trends have flattened out in ways that the theory would not predict. Figure 38.1 plots American public opinion on leading social issues, separating these

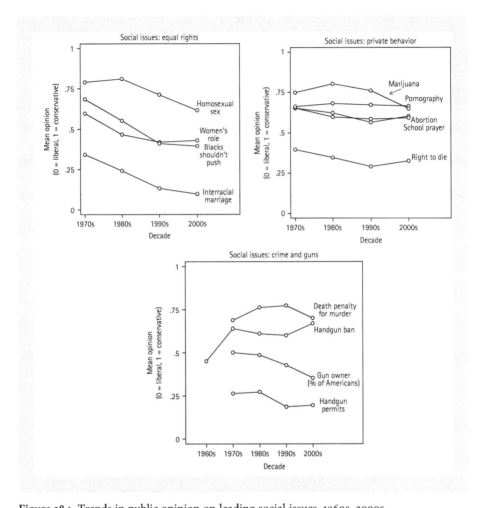

**Figure 38.1** Trends in public opinion on leading social issues, 1960s–2000s

Source: All data come from the General Social Survey Cumulative File, except for
opinion on banning handguns, which comes from the Gallup Poll.

issues into three groups: those that many Americans currently associate with some
notion of equal rights (controversies dealing with race, gender, and sexual orientation),
those that have remained distinctly in the realm of private behavior, and those having
to do with crime and guns. The differences among these trends are striking. Attitudes
on social issues that can be viewed through an egalitarian lens have generally moved in
a liberal direction since the 1970s, but attitudes on social issues regarding private
behavior have remained relatively stable over the past forty years. The data suggest
that Americans are increasingly uncomfortable with the idea of unequal treatment of
their fellow citizens, even as they continue to frown upon behavior they view as
immoral or licentious. Nowhere is this distinction more important than in the battle
over gay rights, where advocates have pinned their hopes on—and become increasingly
successful at—framing homosexuality as an issue of ascriptive identity rather than

discretionary sexual behavior (for example, D'Emilio 1998; Haider-Markel and Joslyn 2008). Finally, attitudes on crime and guns have changed over time—but not in any reliable fashion. Support for requiring handgun permits has moved in a slightly liberal direction, while support for a handgun ban has moved in a decidedly conservative one—even as the proportion of Americans reporting that they keep a gun in their home has fallen sharply over the past four decades. Americans' support for capital punishment for convicted murderers remains consistently high, but it has tended to fluctuate with the murder rate (Baumgartner, De Boef, and Boydstun 2008; Hanley 2008). The lack of consistency in these trends provides further confirmation that attitudes on crime and guns do not fit quite as squarely as do the other controversies discussed in this chapter in the category of issues considered "social."

Two other notable trends in opinion shared by most social issues in the United States over the past fifty years are increased salience and increased partisan conflict. The space occupied by most of the leading social issues on the current landscape of American politics was minimal until the second half of the twentieth century, and the partisan divisions we take for granted on these issues have arisen relatively recently compared to those that have long accompanied Americans' views on the welfare state. Democratic and Republican elites actually switched sides on race relations in the 1960s (Carmines and Stimson 1989) and on abortion in the 1970s (Adams 1997). Significant differences between rank-and-file Democrats and Republicans in attitudes on women's rights, abortion, and gay rights did not emerge in full force until the 1990s (Layman and Carsey 2002b). Over the past few decades, the association between partisanship and attitudes on social issues has grown across all birth cohorts (Stoker and Jennings 2008), but faster among those with college degrees (Bartels 2006), women (Kaufmann 2002), and whites in the South (Knuckey 2006).

Analysts have found that attitudes on social issues—notably, abortion—are significantly associated with vote choice (Abramowitz 1995; Alvarez and Nagler 1995, 1998; Ansolabehere, Rodden, and Snyder 2008; Domke, Shah, and Wackman 2000; Highton 2004). This has inspired a lively debate in both popular and academic literatures about the extent to which the issues have split the parties' coalitions. Pundits and pollsters have reacted to the Democratic Party's recent decline among white voters by asserting that those of lower socioeconomic status have been persuaded to vote against their economic interests by a Republican Party that takes a conservative position on issues like abortion and gay rights (Frank 2004; Greenberg 2004). But political scientists have countered with analyses showing these claims to be incorrect, or—at best—lacking proper nuance. Support for the Democrats among low-income white voters has actually remained steady over time (Bartels 2006; Stonecash 2000), and income and class remain strong predictors of party identification and vote choice (McCarty, Poole, and Rosenthal 2006; Manza and Brooks 1999). While it is true that lower-income whites are less supportive of abortion rights and gay rights than those with high incomes (M. D. Brewer and Stonecash 2007), it is generally the case that attitudes on economic issues continue to more strongly affect vote choice and partisanship than social issues (Ansolabehere, Rodden, and Snyder 2006). If anything, social issues drive the votes of rich whites more than of poor whites (Gelman 2008) and those of whites with college degrees more than of whites without college degrees (Bartels 2006).

What explains the recent emergence of social issues as highly salient controversies on which Democrats and Republicans increasingly take opposing sides? And why hasn't American opinion on social issues moved in the unambiguously liberal direction predicted by post-materialism theory? The most persuasive answers to these questions lie in America's distinct political culture, which has remained tied to religious tradition even as the country has attained nearly unparalleled prosperity. The United States is truly an outlier, standing virtually alone as a highly religious society among the world's advanced industrial democracies (Pew Research Center 2002, 2003). Americans' persistent embrace of religion in the face of rising living standards presents fertile ground for the highly salient debates on school prayer, abortion, gay rights, and euthanasia seen across the nation over the past few decades. Religious communities—and in particular, evangelical Christian churches—have found themselves in conflict with emerging post-materialist values in America, producing "both a demand for political action and thousands of activists dedicated to supplying it" (J. C. Green 1995, 5).

## Media Coverage of Social Issues

Trends in media coverage of individual social issues have largely tracked the degree of their importance in American politics. For example, the media paid little attention to segregation until the mid-1950s (Murakami 2008); abortion until the late 1960s (Luks and Salamone 2008); the right to die controversy until the late 1980s (J. A. Green and Jarvis 2008); and same-sex marriage until the mid-1990s (Egan, Persily, and Wallsten 2008). As an illustration of these patterns, Figure 38.2 plots trends in network television news coverage over the past four decades. The top panel graphs the average number of stories per year on leading social issues appearing on each of the three major networks' evening news programs. The graph shows that racial issues, once the clear leader in terms of news coverage, were eclipsed by abortion in the 1990s—and then homosexuality in the 2000s—as the leading social issues of the day. The share of Americans naming these sorts of cultural issues as the nation's most important problem has risen significantly over the past few decades (M. D. Brewer and Stonecash 2007). But all of this is put in perspective in the bottom panel of Figure 38.2, where the average number of stories per year per network about any social issue is plotted alongside the number of stories on education, the economy, and taxes. In this graph it is clear that news coverage of social issues is relatively light compared to the number of stories devoted to issues aligned firmly on the first dimension of conflict in American politics. Furthermore, coverage of social issues displays no upward trend over time, either in absolute numbers of stories or relative to trends in coverage of other issues.

Little is known about what distinctiveness, if any, characterizes the way media cover social issues and the extent of media effects on public opinion regarding these issues.

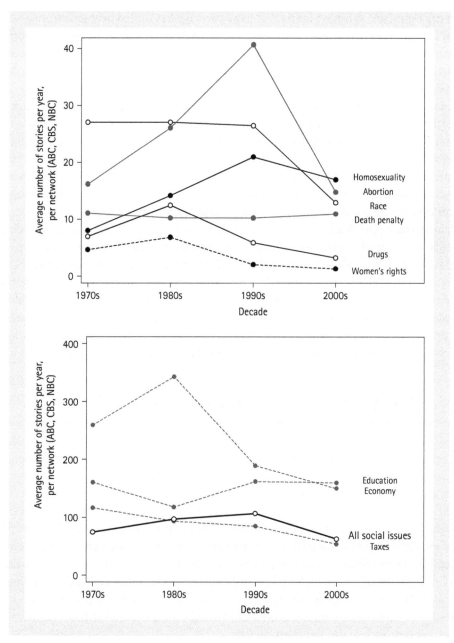

**Figure 38.2** Trends in television news coverage of leading social issues, 1970–2009

Search terms for trends (*indicates Boolean "wild-card" operator):
Abortion: "abortion"
Death Penalty: "death penalty" or "capital punishment"
Drugs: "drug control" or "drug abuse" or "drug problem"
Economy: "unemployment" or "inflation" or "economy"
Education: "education" or "schools"
Homosexuality: "gay" or "homosexual*"
Race: "civil rights" or "affirmative action" or "race relations"
Taxes: "tax*"
Women's rights: "equal rights amendment" or "feminism" or "women's rights" or "sex discrimination"

*Source*: Vanderbilt Television News Archive.

On gay rights, analysts have found that news coverage has shifted over time from a tone that is unambiguously negative (for example, Bennett 1998) to one that is more neutral (Haider-Markel, Allen, and Johansen 2006) or multifaceted (Goldman and Brewer 2007). A major determinant of this shift was the emergence of a consensus in the medical and scientific establishments that homosexuality is not a disease or disorder (Zaller 1992). But by no means are trends in the tone of coverage consistent across social issue domains, making generalizations difficult. Coverage of debates over euthanasia shifted in a conservative direction in the mid-1990s (from the use of the phrase "right to die" to "assisted suicide") as the media focused on the Jack Kevorkian controversy (J. A. Green and Jarvis 2008). In contrast, in the past decade, the tone of news coverage on the death penalty has moved in a liberal direction, focusing more than ever on the exoneration of defendants and flaws in the criminal justice system (Baumgartner, De Boef, and Boydstun 2008). One commonality found regarding media coverage of social issues arises from rulings by the Supreme Court, which typically raise the salience of these issues (Flemming, Bohte, and Wood 1997; Ura 2009). Given that Americans are selecting into media such as cable news, talk radio, and Internet websites that they believe to be harmonious with their own political predispositions (for example, Iyengar and Hahn 2009; Jamieson and Cappella 2008; Stroud 2008), we might surmise that—as on other issues—voters are increasingly less likely to hear views on social issues that are opposed to their own beliefs.

# Explaining Opinion on Social Issues

What sorts of forces cause opinion on social issues to covary in such a consistent fashion—and in a way that is distinct from attitudes on economic issues? Three prominent answers to these questions have emerged in public opinion research. A tradition of scholarship with a particularly long lineage locates the source of opinion on social issues in the extent to which individuals' personalities fall on the spectrum between tolerance and *authoritarianism*. More recent work examines how attitudes on social issues are the consequence of deeply held *core values*—values that may be in conflict with one another and thus produce ambivalence. Finally, many scholars have shown that social issues are no different from others in the way that *elite leadership of opinion* can affect individual attitudes. Of course, these three explanations are not necessarily mutually exclusive. In the following discussion, I outline each of the arguments in turn.

## Authoritarianism

A crude—but nevertheless accurate—way to sum up people's stances on most social issues is the extent to which they dislike certain *groups* and disapprove of certain *behaviors*. The strong relationship between these two bundles of attitudes suggests the concept of *authoritarianism* as a natural point of departure for explaining opinion on social issues. The study of authoritarianism has improved tremendously since the concept was introduced in Adorno et al.'s *The Authoritarian Personality* (Adorno, Frenkel-Brunswik, Levinson, and Sanford 1950), but the basic claim has remained the same: some people have a fundamental orientation toward in-group favoritism, conformity, and thus the maintenance of established social order, leading them both to reject efforts to flatten social hierarchies and to favor the policing of private behavior (Altemeyer 1996; Duckitt 1989; Stenner 2005). Authoritarian predispositions appear to be activated by actual or perceived threats to the established order. High authoritarians react to such threats by becoming less tolerant of out-groups and more punitive of morally aberrant behavior. This may provide micro-foundations for the finding that controlling for a society's level of economic development, its level of economic inequality—and, presumably, an accompanying perceived breakdown of the social order—is associated with intolerance toward homosexuality (Andersen and Fetner 2008). Hetherington and Weiler (2009) present evidence that among white Americans, low and high authoritarians are increasingly sorted (respectively) into the Democratic and Republican parties. A group that is a notable exception is African Americans, who tend to be high authoritarians. Their attitudes on some social issues, such as same-sex marriage, can be unusually conservative for being such strong Democrats (Lewis 2003).

The value of scholarship on authoritarianism for those interested in opinion on social issues is quite substantial: this theory alone tells us why social issues might inhabit a separate dimension of public opinion. By differentiating authoritarianism from conservative attitudes about the welfare state, it provides a compelling explanation for why coalitions between liberals and conservatives on economic and social issues are never set in stone.

## Values in Conflict

Social issues are distinctive from other issue domains in that the underlying core value of *moral traditionalism* (Conover and Feldman 1986) plays a strong role in shaping attitudes on these issues (for example, P. R. Brewer 2003; Carmines and Layman 1997; Layman and Green 2006). Of course, moral traditionalism is not the only core value Americans invoke when constructing their opinions on social issues. In particular, we might expect values regarding egalitarianism and limited government (Feldman 1983) to respectively affect attitudes on issues involving women and minorities on the one hand and the regulation of private behavior on the other. Scholars have documented the ambivalence in opinion that results when core values are in conflict on social issues such as abortion (Alvarez and Brehm 2002; Craig, Kane, and Martinez 2002) and gay rights (Craig, Martinez, Kane, and Gainous 2005).

One reaction to these findings is to wonder how exactly we can distinguish a case of true ambivalence from one in which an opinion just happens to be not so strongly held (J. Miller and Peterson 2004). Furthermore, without studies that look for evidence of ambivalence in a consistent way across different issue domains, we cannot say for sure the extent to which the level and nature of ambivalence in the realm of social issues is distinctive—or whether it is similar to the ambivalence Americans appear to exhibit in other issue domains due to conflicts in core values (for example, Feldman and Zaller 1992; Keele and Wolak 2006).

## Elite Opinion Leadership

John Zaller's celebrated theory of opinion change holds that opposing messages transmitted by political elites interact with individual ideological predispositions and interest in politics to produce a polarized public (1992). Given the fact that social issues are "easy" and that attitudes on these issues are relatively consistent over time, we might expect it to be difficult and unusual for opinion to be shaped by the messages of partisan and ideological elites in this way. Nevertheless, scholars have identified numerous instances of mass attitude change following elite shifts in opinion and others where political information plays an important role. Much of this change has its roots in the Democratic Party's embrace of civil rights in the 1960s and the party's capture by "New Left" activists in the 1970s, which yielded opportunities for Republicans to woo evangelical Christians and others who held conservative views on social issues (Brady 2001; Layman 2001). Partisan trends in mass opinion followed elite divides. Some of this change is undoubtedly due to shifts in party affiliation and cohort replacement, but panel survey data demonstrate that aggregate change is also due to partisans changing their attitudes to conform with their party's position on the issue (Layman and Carsey 2002b). Other studies report evidence of this sort of conversion of attitudes among party activists, as well (Layman and Carsey 1998; Carsey and Layman 1999; see also Carmines and Woods 2002; Wolbrecht 2002).

But the direction of causality in the relationship between partisan attitudes on social issues need not necessarily run from the former to the latter—and the process is often reciprocal. For example, Bill Clinton successfully shifted opinion on gays in the military among his followers but he also lost popularity among those originally opposed to his policy change (Bailey, Sigelman, and Wilcox 2003). More generally, Carsey and Layman (2006) find that those who feel strongly about an issue tend to change their partisanship if they correctly perceive that they disagree with their party's position on the issue, while those who do not attach importance to an issue are likely to change their issue attitudes to align with their partisan identification—a pattern that is consistent across economic, social, and racial issues. The argument corresponds to research showing that masses can follow elites on any issue that divides the elites of the two parties—but only after the issue becomes part of the underlying basis for party identification (Hill and Hurley 1999; Hurley and Hill 2003; Levendusky 2009; Lindaman and Haider-Markel 2002).

# How Distinctive is Opinion on Social Issues?

The three groups of explanations discussed here—authoritarianism, core values, and elite opinion leadership—provide respectively a lot, some, and little evidence that public opinion on social issues is distinctive from that on other issues. The authoritarianism literature holds that because social issues invoke a basic personality trait (namely, one's orientation toward in-group hierarchy and conformity), we should expect attitudes on these issues to covary, and quite possibly to follow a trajectory that is orthogonal to liberal and conservative conceptions of the proper size of the welfare state. By contrast, research on core values holds that social issues are no different from other issues in that attitudes are affected by deeply held values. What makes social issues distinctive, however, is that moral traditionalism shapes attitudes on just about all of them. Less clear is whether conflicts in core values produce an unusually high degree of ambivalence on social issues compared to other issue domains. Finally, studies of opinion leadership tell us that there is nothing particularly unusual about attitudes on social issues: political elites and political information play the same strong roles that they do in other issue domains. The opinion leadership literature tells us that to the extent that contemporary social issues are distinctive from other issues, it is because they are relatively new arrivals to partisan politics. This makes it more likely that we will witness the generic processes of opinion leadership, partisan sorting, and cohort replacement in contemporary politics on social issues than on issues where the platforms of the two parties have been in place for a longer period of time.

## CONCLUSION

Scholarship is scant that compares the authoritarianism, core values, and opinion leadership explanations head to head. Research indicates that party affiliation and affect for political leaders can change people's core values (Goren 2005; McCann 1997), and analysts have shown that the power of authoritarianism in shaping attitudes persists even after controlling for a core value like moral traditionalism (Feldman and Stenner 1997; Stenner 2005). But scholarship is lacking that explores questions such as: can opinion leaders raise the specter of a threat to activate authoritarianism and turn citizens sour on "deviants" and other minorities? How stable is authoritarianism across the life span, and how does its stability compare to that of party identification and core values? Do the ways we think about values change depending on which issues happen to be salient? And what happens when—as in campaigns on referenda over abortion, gay rights, and drugs—political leaders bombard voters with opposing messages that invoke conflicting core values? Should we expect ambivalence (as the core values literature predicts) or polarization (as indicated by research on opinion leadership)?

In answering these questions, scholars will need to continue to take care in how they define the domain of social issues with criteria that are theoretically grounded and empirically documented, rather than designated a priori based upon convention or popular conception. In determining the causes of attitudes on social issues and their salience in the public sphere, consideration should be given to the varying incentives faced by candidates, activists, and parties either to fold these debates into the primary left–right axis that defines American political conflict or, by contrast, to forge new coalitions. From these starting points, we can better determine whether the processes that shape public opinion on social issues are similar to those associated with other attitudes regarding public affairs—or, rather, if there is something special about this set of controversies, which mobilizes, excites, and inspires so many Americans in contemporary politics.

## References

ABRAMOWITZ, A. I. 1995. It's Abortion, Stupid: Policy Voting in the 1992 Presidential Election. *Journal of Politics*, 57/1: 176–86.

ADAMS, G. D. 1997. Abortion: Evidence of an Issue Evolution. *American Journal of Political Science*, 41/3: 718–37.

ADORNO, T. W., FRENKEL-BRUNSWIK, E., LEVINSON, D. J., and SANFORD, R. N. 1950. *The Authoritarian Personality*. New York: Harper & Row.

ALTEMEYER, B. 1996. *The Authoritarian Specter*. Cambridge, MA: Harvard University Press.

ALVAREZ, R. M., and BREHM, J. 2002. *Hard Choices, Easy Answers: Values, Information and American Public Opinion*. Princeton: Princeton University Press.

—— and NAGLER, J. 1995. Economics, Issues and the Perot Candidacy: Voter Choice in the 1992 Presidential Election. *American Journal of Political Science*, 39/3: 714–44.

—— —— 1998. Economics, Entitlements, and Social Issues: Voter Choice in the 1996 Presidential Election. *American Journal of Political Science*, 42/4: 1349–63.

ANDERSEN, R., and FETNER, T. 2008. Economic Inequality and Intolerance: Attitudes toward Homosexuality in 35 Democracies. *American Journal of Political Science*, 52: 942–58.

ANSOLABEHERE, S., RODDEN, J., and SNYDER, J. M., JR. 2006. Purple America. *Journal of Economic Perspectives*, 20/2: 97–118.

—— —— —— 2008. The Strength of Issues: Using Multiple Measures to Gauge Preference Stability, Ideological Constraint, and Issue Voting. *American Political Science Review*, 102/2: 215–32.

BAILEY, M., SIGELMAN, L., and WILCOX, C. 2003. Presidential Persuasion on Social Issues: A Two-Way Street? *Political Research Quarterly*, 56/1: 49–58.

BARTELS, L. M. 2006. What's the Matter with *What's the Matter with Kansas*? *Quarterly Journal of Political Science*, 1/2: 201–26.

BAUMGARTNER, F. R., DE BOEF, S. L., and BOYDSTUN, A. E. 2008. *The Decline of the Death Penalty and the Discovery of Innocence*. New York: Cambridge University Press.

BENNETT, L. 1998. The Perpetuation of Prejudice in Reporting on Gays and Lesbians: *Time* and *Newsweek*, the First Fifty Years. Research Paper R-21. Cambridge, MA: Joan Shorenstein Center on the Press, Politics and Public Policy, Harvard University.

BENOIT, K., and LAVER, M. 2006. *Party Policy in Modern Democracies*. London: Routledge.

BRADY, H. E. 2001. Trust the People: Political Party Coalitions in the 2000 Election. In *The Unfinished Election of 2000*, ed. J. Rakove. New York: Basic Books.

BREWER, M. D., and STONECASH, J. M. 2007. *Split: Class and Cultural Divides in American Politics*. Washington, DC: CQ Press.

BREWER, P. R. 2003. The Shifting Foundations of Public Opinion about Gay Rights. *Journal of Politics*, 65/4: 1208–20.

BRICKMAN, D., and PETERSON, D. A. M. 2006. Public Reaction to Repeated Events: Citizen Response to Multiple Supreme Court Abortion Decisions. *Political Behavior*, 28: 87–112.

CARMINES, E. G., and LAYMAN, G. C. 1997. Value Priorities, Partisanship, and Electoral Choice: The Neglected Case of the United States. *Political Behavior*, 19/4: 283–316.

—— and STIMSON, J. A. 1980. The Two Faces of Issue Voting. *American Political Science Review*, 74/1: 78–91.

—— —— 1989. *Issue Evolution: Race and the Transformation of American Politics*. Princeton: Princeton University Press.

—— and WOODS, J. 2002. The Role of Party Activists in the Evolution of the Abortion Issue. *Political Behavior*, 24/4: 361–77.

CARSEY, T. M., and LAYMAN, G. C. 1999. A Dynamic Model of Political Change among Party Activists. *Political Behavior*, 21/1: 17–41.

—— —— 2006. Changing Sides or Changing Minds? Party Identification and Policy Preferences in the American Electorate. *American Journal of Political Science*, 50/2: 464–77.

CONOVER, P. J., and FELDMAN, S. 1986. Morality Items on the 1985 Pilot Study. ANES Pilot Study Report 2251. At <ftp://ftp.electionstudies.org/ftp/nes/bibliography/documents/nes002251.pdf>. Accessed Sept. 29, 2009.

CONVERSE, P. E., and MARKUS, G. B. 1979. Plus ça change . . . The New CPS Election Study Panel. *American Political Science Review*, 73: 32–49.

CRAIG, S. C., KANE, J. G., and MARTINEZ, M. D. 2002. Sometimes You Feel Like a Nut, Sometimes You Don't: Citizens' Ambivalence about Abortion. *Political Psychology*, 23/2: 285–301.

—— MARTINEZ, M. D., KANE, J. G., and GAINOUS, J. 2005. Core Values, Value Conflict, and Citizens' Ambivalence about Gay Rights. *Political Research Quarterly*, 58/1: 5–17.

D'EMILIO, J. 1998. *Sexual Politics, Sexual Communities*, 2nd edn. Chicago: University of Chicago Press.

DOMKE, D., SHAH, D. V., and WACKMAN, D. B. 2000. Rights and Morals, Issues, and Candidate Integrity: Insights into the Role of the News Media. *Political Psychology*, 21/4: 641–65.

DUCKITT, J. 1989. Authoritarianism and Group Identification: A New View of an Old Construct. *Political Psychology*, 10/1: 63–84.

EGAN, P. J., PERSILY, N., and WALLSTEN, K. 2008. Gay Rights. In *Public Opinion and Constitutional Controversy*, ed. N. Persily, J. Citrin, and P. J. Egan. New York: Oxford University Press.

ERIKSON, R. S., and TEDIN, K. J. 2007. *American Public Opinion: Its Origins, Content, and Impact*, updated 7th edn. New York: Longman.

FELDMAN, S. 1983. Report on Values in the 1983 Pilot Study. ANES Pilot Study Report 2242. At <ftp://ftp.electionstudies.org/ftp/nes/bibliography/documents/nes002242.pdf>. Accessed Sept. 29, 2009.

FELDMAN, S., and STENNER, K. 1997. Perceived Threat and Authoritarianism. *Political Psychology*, 18/4: 741–70.

—— and ZALLER, J. 1992. The Political Culture of Ambivalence: Ideological Responses to the Welfare State. *American Journal of Political Science*, 36/1: 268–307.

FLECK, R. K., and KILBY, C. 2002. Reassessing the Role of Constituency in Congressional Voting. *Public Choice*, 112/1–2: 31–53.

FLEISHMAN, J. A. 1988. Attitude Organization in the General Public: Evidence for a Bidimensional Structure. *Social Forces*, 67/1: 159–84.

FLEMMING, R. B., BOHTE, J., and WOOD, B. D. 1997. One Voice among Many: The Supreme Court's Influence on Attentiveness to Issues in the United States, 1947–92. *American Journal of Political Science*, 41/4: 1224–50.

FRANK, T. 2004. *What's the Matter with Kansas? How Conservatives Won the Heart of America*. New York: Henry Holt.

FRANKLIN, C. H., and KOSAKI, L. C. 1989. Republican Schoolmaster: The U.S. Supreme Court, Public Opinion and Abortion. *American Political Science Review*, 83: 751–71.

GELMAN, A. 2008. *Red State, Blue State, Rich State, Poor State: Why Americans Vote the Way They Do*. Princeton: Princeton University Press.

GOLDMAN, S., and BREWER, P. R. 2007. From Gay Bashing to Gay Baiting: Public Opinion and News Media Frames for Gay Marriage. In *Defending Same-Sex Marriage, iii: The Freedom-to-Marry Movement: Education, Advocacy, Culture, and the Media*, ed. M. Strasser, M. Dupuis, and W. Thompson. Westport, CT: Praeger.

GOREN, P. 2005. Party Identification and Core Political Values. *American Journal of Political Science*, 49/4: 881–96.

GREEN, J. A., and JARVIS, M. G. 2008. The Right to Die. In *Public Opinion and Constitutional Controversy*, ed. N. Persily, J. Citrin, and P. J. Egan. New York: Oxford University Press.

GREEN, J. C. 1995. The Christian Right and the 1994 Elections: A View from the States. *PS: Political Science and Politics*, 28/1: 5–8.

GREENBERG, S. B. 2004. *The Two Americas: Our Current Political Deadlock and How to Break It*. New York: Thomas Dunne Books.

GUSFIELD, J. R. 1963. *Symbolic Crusade: Status Politics and the American Temperance Movement*. Champaign: University of Illinois Press.

HAIDER-MARKEL, D. P., and JOSLYN, M. R. 2008. Beliefs about the Origins of Homosexuality and Support for Gay Rights: An Empirical Test of Attribution Theory. *Public Opinion Quarterly*, 72/2: 291–310.

—— and MEIER, K. J. 1996. The Politics of Gay and Lesbian Rights: Expanding the Scope of the Conflict. *Journal of Politics*, 58/2: 332–49.

—— ALLEN, M. D., and JOHANSEN, M. 2006. Understanding Variations in Media Coverage of U.S. Supreme Court Decisions: Comparing Media Outlets in their Coverage of *Lawrence v. Texas*. *Harvard International Journal of Press/Politics*, 11/2: 64–85.

HANLEY, J. 2008. The Death Penalty. In *Public Opinion and Constitutional Controversy*, ed. N. Persily, J. Citrin, and P. J. Egan. New York: Oxford University Press.

HETHERINGTON, M. J., and WEILER, J. D. 2009. *Authoritarianism and Polarization in American Politics*. New York: Cambridge University Press.

HIGHTON, B. 2004. Policy Voting in Senate Elections: The Case of Abortion. *Political Behavior*, 26/2: 181–200.

HILL, K. Q., and HURLEY, P. A. 1999. Dyadic Representation Reappraised. *American Journal of Political Science*, 43/1: 109–37.

HINICH, M. J., and MUNGER, M. C. 1994. *Ideology and the Theory of Political Choice.* Ann Arbor: University of Michigan Press.

HURLEY, P. A., and HILL, K. Q. 2003. Beyond the Demand-Input Model: A Theory of Representational Linkages. *Journal of Politics,* 65/2: 304–26.

INGLEHART, R. F. 1977. *The Silent Revolution: Changing Values and Political Styles among Western Publics.* Princeton: Princeton University Press.

—— 1990. *Culture Shift in Advanced Industrial Society.* Princeton: Princeton University Press.

—— 1997. *Modernization and Postmodernization: Cultural, Economic, and Political Change in 43 Societies.* Princeton: Princeton University Press.

—— and WELZEL, C. 2005. *Modernization, Cultural Change, and Democracy: The Human Development Sequence.* New York: Cambridge University Press.

IYENGAR, S., and HAHN, K. S. 2009. Red Media, Blue Media: Evidence of Ideological Selectivity in Media Use. *Journal of Communication,* 59/1: 19–39.

JAMIESON, K. H., and CAPPELLA, J. N. 2008. *Echo Chamber: Rush Limbaugh and the Conservative Media Establishment.* New York: Oxford University Press.

JOHNSON, T. R., and MARTIN, A. D. 1998. The Public's Conditional Response to Supreme Court Decisions. *American Political Science Review,* 92: 299–310.

KAUFMANN, K. M. 2002. Culture Wars, Secular Realignment, and the Gender Gap in Party Identification. *Political Behavior,* 24/3, Special Issue: *Parties and Partisanship, Part Two,* 283–307.

KEELE, L., and WOLAK, J. 2006. Value Conflict and Volatility in Party Identification. *British Journal of Political Science,* 36/4: 671–90.

KNUCKEY, J. 2006. Explaining Recent Changes in the Partisan Identifications of Southern Whites. *Political Research Quarterly,* 59/1: 57–70.

LAYMAN, G. 2001. *The Great Divide: Religious and Cultural Conflict in American Party Politics.* New York: Columbia University Press.

—— and CARSEY, T. M. 1998. Why Do Party Activists Convert? An Analysis of Individual-Level Change on the Abortion Issue. *Political Research Quarterly,* 51/3: 723–49.

—— —— 2002a. Party Polarization and Party Structuring of Policy Attitudes: A Comparison of Three NES Panel Studies. *Political Behavior,* 24/3: 199–236.

—— —— 2002b. Party Polarization and "Conflict Extension" in the American Electorate. *American Journal of Political Science,* 46/4: 786–802.

—— and GREEN, J. C. 2006. Wars and Rumours of Wars: The Contexts of Cultural Conflict in American Political Behaviour. *British Journal of Political Science,* 36/1: 61–89.

LEEGE, D. C., WALD, K. D., KRUEGER, B. S., and MUELLER, P. D. 2002. *The Politics of Cultural Differences: Social Change and Voter Mobilization Strategies in the Post-New Deal Period.* Princeton: Princeton University Press.

LEVENDUSKY, M. 2009. *The Partisan Sort: How Liberals Became Democrats and Conservatives Became Republicans.* Chicago: University of Chicago Press.

LEWIS, G. B. 2003. Black–White Differences in Attitudes toward Homosexuality and Gay Rights. *Public Opinion Quarterly,* 67: 59–78.

LINDAMAN, K., and HAIDER-MARKEL, D. P. 2002. Issue Evolution, Political Parties, and the Culture Wars. *Political Research Quarterly,* 55/1: 91–110.

LUKS, S., and SALAMONE, M. 2008. Abortion. In *Public Opinion and Constitutional Controversy,* ed. N. Persily, J. Citrin, and P. J. Egan. New York: Oxford University Press.

McCANN, J. A. 1997. Electoral Choices and Core Value Change: The 1992 Presidential Campaign. *American Journal of Political Science,* 41/2: 564–83.

McCARTY, N., POOLE, K. T., and ROSENTHAL, H. 2006. *Polarized America: The Dance of Ideology and Unequal Riches*. Cambridge, MA: MIT Press.

MANZA, J., and BROOKS, C. 1999. *Social Cleavages and Political Change: Voter Alignment and U.S. Party Coalitions*. New York: Oxford University Press.

MILLER, G., and SCHOFIELD, N. 2003. Activists and Partisan Realignment in the United States. *American Political Science Review*, 97/2: 245–60.

MILLER, J., and PETERSON, D. A. M., 2004. Theoretical and Empirical Implications of Attitude Strength. *Journal of Politics*, 66/3: 847–67.

MURAKAMI, M. 2008. Desegregation. In *Public Opinion and Constitutional Controversy*, ed. N. Persily, J. Citrin, and P. J. Egan. New York: Oxford University Press.

PERSILY, N., CITRIN, J., and EGAN, P. J. (eds.) 2008. *Public Opinion and Constitutional Controversy*. New York: Oxford University Press.

Pew Research Center 2002. Among Wealthy Nations . . . U.S. Stands Alone in its Embrace of Religion. Pew Global Attitudes Project, Dec. 19. At <http://pewglobal.org/reports/pdf/167. pdf>. Accessed Sept. 29, 2009.

—— 2003. Views of a Changing World. Pew Global Attitudes Project, June. At <http://people-press.org/reports/pdf/185.pdf>. Accessed Sept. 29, 2009.

POOLE, K. T., and ROSENTHAL, H. 1997. *Congress: A Political-Economic History of Roll Call Voting*. New York: Oxford University Press.

—— —— 1998. The Dynamics of Interest Group Evaluations of Congress. *Public Choice*, 97/3: 323–61.

STENNER, K. 2005. *The Authoritarian Dynamic*. New York: Cambridge University Press.

STIMSON, J. A. 1975. Belief Systems: Constraint, Complexity, and the 1972 Election. *American Journal of Political Science*, 19/3: 393–417.

STOKER, L., and JENNINGS, M. K. 2008. Of Time and the Development of Partisan Polarization. *American Journal of Political Science*, 52/3: 619–35.

STOKES, D. E. 1963. Spatial Models of Party Competition. *American Political Science Review*, 57/2: 368–77.

STONECASH, J. M. 2000. *Class and Party in American Politics*. Boulder, CO: Westview Press.

STROUD, N. J. 2008. Media Use and Political Predispositions: Revisiting the Concept of Selective Exposure. *Political Behavior*, 30/3: 341–66.

TREIER, S., and HILLYGUS, D. S. 2009. The Nature of Political Ideology in the Contemporary Electorate. *Public Opinion Quarterly*, 73/4: 673–703.

URA, J. D. 2009. The Supreme Court and Issue Attention: The Case of Homosexuality. *Political Communication*, 26/4: 430–46.

WOLBRECHT, C. 2002. Explaining Women's Rights Realignment: Convention Delegates, 1972–1992. *Political Behavior*, 24/3, Special Issue: *Parties and Partisanship, Part Two*, 237–82.

ZALLER, J. R. 1992. *The Nature and Origins of Mass Opinion*. New York: Cambridge University Press.

# CHAPTER 39

........................................................................

# BIG GOVERNMENT AND PUBLIC OPINION

........................................................................

## COSTAS PANAGOPOULOS
## ROBERT Y. SHAPIRO

## INTRODUCTION

........................................................................

AFTER President Barack Obama's administration entered office facing a deep recession and pursued a massive (perhaps not massive enough) economic stimulus program, the nation was enveloped in the recurring debate about the role of *big government* in the United States. The country struggled to get out of its economic trench and, as Europe pulled back and adopted austerity and balanced budget strategies, the debate in the US shifted away from large-scale federal spending to loosening the reins of government.

Big government issues go beyond the size of the American "welfare state" to include regulation of business and industry, the environment, and policies toward energy, labor unions, immigration, national defense, and other areas. (Issues of civil rights, civil liberties, race relations, and religious or moral values also bear on the scope of government action but go beyond the confines of this chapter.) We consider the following major questions and themes concerning these issues in research on public opinion toward big government: How can we best describe the public's support for expansive government to tackle economic and regulatory issues? Has there been an overarching trend in a liberal or conservative direction, or some other systematic pattern? What are some of the issue-specific dynamics that require further attention going forward? How has the salience of these issues played out in the mass media? And

* We thank Alissa Stollwerk, Anthony Daniel, Narayani Lasala Blanco, Sara Arrow, and Stephen Thompson for their assistance. Shapiro benefited much from his collaborations and communication with Greg Shaw. Unless otherwise cited, data were obtained from the iPOLL database of the Roper Center for Public Opinion Research and from the Vanderbilt University Television News Archive. We are responsible for all analysis and interpretation.

last, to what extent has the public been affected in this issue area by increasing partisan conflict in politics?

The big government continuum was the defining battleground for the New Deal partisan realignment; its demarcation became clearer as leaders in both parties became increasingly distinctive along this political axis, and *intra-party* differences on it diminished as civil rights and racial equality became part of the debate over government activism dividing the parties (see Carmines and Stimson 1989; McCarty, Poole, and Rosenthal 2006). Did the increase in partisan conflict lead to substantial divergence in the policy preferences of Democrats and Republicans in the mass public?

# The Welfare State

Entering the twentieth century, Americans generally viewed themselves as individualists of the same timber as those who settled and developed the nation. Adopted initially in response to the Great Depression of the 1930s, President Franklin Roosevelt's New Deal policies established the foundation for an American welfare state, with the enactments of Social Security retirement pensions, assistance to dependent children, and unemployment insurance. This beginning of a social safety net was substantially enlarged by President Lyndon Johnson's War on Poverty and Great Society programs: the expansion of health care through Medicare and Medicaid, "welfare" (though not its official name) assistance to poor families, along with "urban renewal" and housing programs. This expansion occurred in fits and starts, with occasional debates about retrenchment. Past observations about the public's complex opinions toward the welfare state still hold:

This configuration of preferences reflects a fundamental individualism that esteems individual responsibility and individual initiative, and relies primarily upon free enterprise capitalism for economic production and distribution. Yet it also reflects a sense of societal obligation, a strong commitment to government action in order to smooth capitalism's rough edges, to regulate its excesses, to protect the helpless, and to provide a substantial degree of equal opportunity for all.   (Page and Shapiro 1992, 118)

The emphasis on both economic protection for those in need and also individual responsibility and initiative has led to the public's *ambivalence* regarding government activism in this area. At the same time, Americans have been pragmatic and attentive to evolving circumstances, which led to support for Social Security and Medicare and Medicaid. The public's ambivalence as described by Katherine Newman and Elisabeth Jacobs in *Who Cares?* (2010) can be found in the early Gallup polls conducted in the 1930s (see also Zaller 1992). In fact, we can compare responses to the first question in the very first Gallup poll in September 1935, "Do you think expenditures by the Government for relief and recovery are too little, too great, or just about right?" (Gallup 1972), to responses fully sixty years later to the 1994 and 1996 NORC–General Social Survey (NORC–GSS) question that asked about spending "too much" or "too little" on "welfare (see Shapiro 2009). The term "relief" had a connotation similar to "welfare" payments to the "lazy" poor who were "undeserving" and took advantage of the system to avoid work; and "relief and recovery" implied an expansive government, so that we can make very rough historical comparisons (leaving aside sampling; see Berinsky 2006). It is striking that during the Great Depression year of 1935, a stunning 60 percent of the public responded that expenditures on relief and recovery were too great, the same as the 1994 and 1996 average of 60 percent who said we were spending too much on welfare. In contrast, in a July 1938 Gallup poll, 67 percent of respondents said it "is the government's responsibility to pay the living expenses of needy people who are out of work" (Erskine 1975, 260); and, again, sixty years later in a 1998 NORC–GSS survey, 60 percent said that "too little" was being spent on "assistance to the poor" (Shapiro 2009).

All of this suggests something about American values—and liberalism—when comparing "relief" and "welfare" to more consensual areas of support in the American welfare state for helping the "deserving" poor and those who genuinely could not find work. There have been similarly higher levels of support for spending on Social Security and health care as well (Shaw 2009–10; Shapiro 2009; these parallel trends in economic welfare liberalism–conservatism have been emphasized especially by Stimson 2004 and Erikson, MacKuen, and Stimson 2002).

## Social Security

On the eve of the seventy-fifth anniversary of the passage of the 1935 Social Security Act, attitudes about it have remained remarkably stable over the last three quarters of a century. Based on differently worded questions, Roper and Gallup polls in the late 1930s (see Schiltz 1970) found that very large majorities, often more than 80 percent, supported old age pensions and the "Social Security laws which provided such pensions and unemployment insurance" (Page and Shapiro 1992). Given this overwhelming consensus, pollsters stopped asking such simple support questions, focusing instead on spending levels and possible reforms, as the nation's changing demographics and economic fortunes affected Social Security's long-term funding. It was last a major focus in the media (based on the number of national network—ABC, CBS, and NBC—news stories found in the Vanderbilt University *Television News Index*) when President George W. Bush's administration proposed to reform Social Security by creating private retirement accounts.

While Americans in early 2004 had grown somewhat more optimistic (though not fully confident; Shaw 2009–10) about Social Security and Medicare's future than they had been in the 1990s (even amid some evidence to the contrary), they were divided on proposals to allow some payroll tax contributions to go to personal investment accounts ("partially privatizing" Social Security), and they opposed the government's investing Social Security funds in the then rocky stock market. The public resisted raising the age eligibility for collecting retirement benefits, as well as various other proposed reforms (Shaw and Mysiewicz 2004). In the emerging debate on Social Security reforms and the rising federal budget deficit in 2010, large majorities of essentially all segments of the public supported spending on Social Security, opposed benefit cuts (even when confronted with the need to reduce deficits), and preferred to strengthen the financing of Social Security by raising the payroll tax "cap" or other progressive taxation (Page and Jacobs 2010). These attitudes may reflect confidence in the long-term viability of Social Security, which is a much more tractable problem than more complex entitlements like Medicare and Medicaid, for which there are serious cost control issues.

The overarching trends in opinion that the nation was spending "too little" on Social Security, a proxy for support for big government on this issue, showed a fall-off into 1994 after Bill Clinton took office, which we interpret as the public applying the brakes on what it perceived as liberal government. This is a recurring pattern, in which the public is sensitive to what it sees as government overreaching, whether real or anticipated (this "thermostat" pattern was originally recognized by Christopher Wlezien; see Soroka and Wlezien 2010, ch. 2; Erikson, MacKuen, and Stimson 2002). Public support then moved upward, to an all-time high level. This is one issue area in which partisan differences have been stable and have perhaps narrowed, unlike other issues where the gaps have widened (in NORC–GSS data through 2008; see Bafumi and Shapiro 2009).

The future of Social Security is a divisive matter but more muted than others. The degree of consensus on it may reflect less abstract ideology than pragmatic liberalism in responding successfully to the once enormous problem of poverty among the elderly. American public opinion to some extent is ideologically conservative in the abstract, but operationally liberal (Page and Jacobs 2009; Shaw 2009–10 credits this observation to Samuel Lubell), although the reverse has held regarding support for limitations on the scope of some ostensibly protected constitutional rights and liberties (see Page and Shapiro 1992, chs. 3–4) and in some instances of government activism noted below.

## Assistance to the Poor

This, again, is the classic case in which the public's conservative emphasis on individual responsibility leads it to be philosophically opposed to aiding the poor, who should be able to help themselves. On the other hand, the reality may be that, through no fault of their own, individuals are in need and *deserving* of assistance. The public expresses more liberal opinions when they perceive the latter situation. Indeed, the level of public support for spending to assist the poor (not referring to "welfare") is greater than that for social security (NORC–GSS data; Shaw 2009–10; Shapiro 2009). In addition, opinions in favor of both "assistance for the poor" and "welfare" fit the "thermostat" model noted above, in which support decreases after a liberal Democratic government takes office and increases with the ascendancy of a conservative Republican administration (Soroka and Wlezien 2010; Erikson, MacKuen, and Stimson 2002).

President Ronald Reagan rode into office on a wave of a conservative opinion trend toward welfare spending, and President Bill Clinton on a liberal one. An anti-welfare opinion backlash occurred after Clinton took office which contributed to the enactment of "welfare reform" in 1996, ending payments to poor families with children as the kind of open entitlement that it had been—perceived to be fraud-ridden and stereotyping African Americans as largely undeserving recipients (see Gilens 1999). The "end of welfare as we knew it" led to a decline in opposition to such spending (for all NORC–GSS question wordings) and to George W. Bush taking office as opinion continued to move in a liberal direction during the good economic times under Clinton and, more predictably, during the economic downturn of the Bush years (Shaw 2009–10; Shapiro 2009).

This major reform raised the question of whether racism and the past stigma of welfare would diminish, and whether the economy's effect on public attitudes toward welfare policy would become less predictable (see Shapiro 2009; Soss and Schram 2007). While no sweeping changes have occurred, the potential for them warrants continued attention. What did happen unequivocally after the 1996 reforms was that "welfare" dropped off the media radar screen, with the average number of network news reports roughly in the single digits from 2007 to 2009. Also beginning in 1997, while the number of "welfare" recipients of Temporary Assistance to Need Families (which replaced Aid to Families with Dependent Children) and federal spending on this cash assistance declined precipitously as intended, other, less stigmatized forms of assistance to the poor expanded substantially to include food stamps (renamed the Supplemental Nutrition Assistance Program, SNAP) and the Earned Income Tax Credits, especially SNAP during the deep recession (Shapiro 2009). Moreover, after Obama took office, and as tracked in-depth by the Pew Research Center (2009), public support for assisting the needy and those who could not take care of themselves declined, as did the public's liberalism toward the full gamut of big government issues. Furthermore, the NORC–GSS data showed that partisan differences in these opinions (between self-identified Democrats and Republicans) widened from the 1970s to 2008 (see also Bafumi and Shapiro 2009), and the Pew surveys showed more of the same for welfare-related and many other issues into 2009.

## Medical Care

With the enactment and subsequent high level of public support for Medicare and Medicaid in the 1960s, one could argue that the public was becoming philosophically liberal in the area of health care. It strongly supported the idea that everyone should have access to affordable health care—arguably as a right (see Blendon, Brodie, Benson, and Altman 2011; Jacobs and Shapiro 2000). Moreover, a similarly growing but also larger percentage of the public has favored government spending on medical care than on Social Security and assistance to the poor (and there have been somewhat smaller partisan differences for assisting the poor; Shaw 2009–10; Shapiro 2009). Opinions, as measured by the NORC–GSS, had moved somewhat conservatively during the late 1970s but then climbed upward overall from the 1980s to 2000.

If the public had become increasingly liberal toward government's role in health care, the devil was clearly in the detail as Presidents Obama and Clinton tried to capitalize on this support to enact major reform. The public opinion story for both presidents was the same, although action on health care reform came quicker in 2009 than in 1993, and there were more stories on television network news on health care reform in 2009 than in either 1993 or 1994. For both reform initiatives support declined as the public learned (or tried to) about the specifics of the proposed legislation. Republican leaders' opposition to reform readily evoked the public's reluctance to increase taxes that might be needed. Opponents also triggered Americans' risk aversion to changing the kind of health-care coverage that most of them had and which they were reminded that they liked (because they had insurance and did not have extensive medical problems). As health-care reform was vigorously attacked, Americans increasingly perceived that the proposed changes would adversely affect the nation and their *own* health care, and support for reform declined in both cases from a clear majority to a minority.

The one difference, however, was that Obama and the Democrats were able to pass landmark reform legislation with their larger congressional majorities than Clinton had in 1993–4 and with a different political strategy and some legislative maneuvering. This reform, then, was at odd with shifts in public opinion and did not have clear majority support, though major components of it that assured insurance coverage had substantial support. The Democrats, however, were left with the political burden of showing that this was the right decision—to gain public support in the way the Medicare prescription drug expansion enacted by George W. Bush's administration caught on after initial confusion about its implementation and full benefits (see Shaw and Mysiewicz 2004; Blendon, Brodie, Benson, and Altman 2011).

## Education

Education has not usually been included with health care and income benefits as welfare state issues, but it is the one area in which the United States has been a world leader. The Obama administration's educational reform efforts made the issue salient again in national television news after the Bush administration's No Child Left Behind legislative initiative came up for renewal. There has been less political conflict on expanding such government efforts, judging from support for educational spending reaching a high ceiling in NORC–GSS surveys twenty years ago and holding steady though 2008, with significant but somewhat smaller partisan differences compared to other issues.

From 1995 to 2009, the issue of education had been covered each year on average in 100–50 network news stories, compared to more noticeable highs and lows for other issues. Some issues, as noted above, have fallen off the national agenda at times or over long stretches, but education has not been one of them. Despite the recession and rising deficits, the public has supported government spending on education versus budgetary restraint: a Gallup poll in February 2009 found that 88 percent thought it was important (or "most important") to include funding for education in the economic stimulus plan. In June 2009, consistently with NORC–GSS data through 2008, the Pew Research Center reported that nearly 67 percent would increase federal spending on education; in the same month an NBC/*Wall Street Journal* poll reported fully 80 percent favoring spending on education even when the question reminded respondents of the recession, war, and the budget deficit.

While the public has strongly supported funding education and the liberal view of promoting educational opportunity, it is less liberal, though still positive, toward active government intervention in schools. A March 2009 CNN/Opinion Research Corporation poll reported that only 56 percent favored increased spending on education if it also increased the federal government's "influence over education policies." However, when it came specifically to testing, 74 percent favored a national certification standard for public school teachers, according to the 2009 Attitudes toward the Public Schools Survey (Bushaw and McNee 2009); and 66 percent wanted tests for students in grades 3–8 to be uniform across the nation rather than letting each state choose its own tests. Support for "mandatory testing" has long been at this level or higher, but it now represents support for national standards; this suggests that problems in education are perceived as so severe that the public is looking to big government for leadership and support.

## Urban Problems and Race

The problems of American cities and how African Americans fared economically in them were once a major focus of national policymaking, leading to Lyndon Johnson's Great Society programs. Trends in public opinion toward spending on cities and improving the conditions of blacks have deviated noticeably from support for the above policies. While NORC–GSS data show that Americans have increasingly reported that the "right amount" is being spent to deal with the problems of cities and to improve the conditions of or assist blacks, the percentage of those who think "too little" is spent on urban problems has fallen off significantly (since the 1980s or 1990s, depending on the question wording). This is consistent with the apparent decrease in the kinds of stories that appeared on network news highlighting urban problems— other than crime—since the 1960s and 1970s; they largely disappeared with recent exceptions including the plight of Detroit in tandem with the auto industry and mortgage foreclosures in major urban areas as well as nationwide. While this decline in salience may be related to lower crime rates across the country and in cities since the late 1980s (with reports on crime often connected to economic problems in cities), the invisibility of "the urban issue" very much fits the conclusion that Washington has "abandoned the cities" (Caraley 1992; see also Page and Shapiro 1992, ch. 3).

The one area where there has perhaps been the strongest general support is the special case of urban education: between 1989 and 1998, Gallup surveys revealed growing numbers who felt improving inner city schools was "very important" (from 74 to 86 percent). While there have been noticeable and possibly increasing partisan differences in public support for spending to assist urban areas, the gulf between Democrats and Republicans in the percentage of those who think "too little" is spent to improve the conditions of blacks has widened dramatically since the mid-1970s (see Bafumi and Shapiro 2009). The same has occurred since the 1980s in regard to support for preferential treatment to improve the conditions of minorities. To be sure, Barack Obama's election led to more optimistic conclusions about the experiences of African Americans and the success of anti-discrimination policies; but these civil rights issues remain contentious (Pew Research Center 2009).

# Labor Unions

Americans hold liberal attitudes toward the idea of labor unions, but they are more conservative when specific issues and conflicts arise (see Page and Shapiro 1992, ch. 4). Since the late 1960s there has not been much national network news coverage of labor union issues, largely reserved for major strikes or changes of leadership in the largest unions, and 2004–9 was a low point, averaging barely one or two news stories per year. Even as the news devoted little attention to labor unions, Americans since the 1980s have maintained generally positive impressions of unions, with majorities expressing consistent support. In the early 1980s, upon hearing of a strike by a union against a large company, most Americans' "first reaction" was to side with the company over the union. By the early 1990s and later into the decade, the reverse was true, with most Americans indicating initially that they were inclined to side with unions (Panagopoulos and Francia 2008). When asked to compare big business, big labor, or big government, the proportion of the public responding that big labor represented the biggest future threat to the country dropped from about 1 in 5 in the early 1980s to less than 1 in 10 in 2005. Strong majorities between 1999 and 2005 believed that unions "mostly help" members, even as most also believed unions "mostly hurt" workers who were not members. In the 1990s the public overall believed that unions "mostly help" the US economy, that American workers still need labor unions, and that, between 1988 and 2009, unions were "necessary to protect the working person." Large majorities between 1981 and 2006 generally reported at least some confidence in organized labor as an institution and also consistently expressed at least some confidence in union leaders. In contrast, regarding the adverse political clout of unions, polls from 1994 to 2005 indicated that the public was consistently divided over whether unions had too much or too little influence in Washington (Panagopoulos and Francia 2008; Pew Research Center 2009).

The most recent trend data suggest that partisan conflict since 2003 has had some effect on the public's general favorability toward unions. While just over 60 percent of the public in 2009 agreed that labor unions were necessary to protect working people, this represented a drop of more than ten percentage points since 1997–2003—seven points from 2007 to 2009 after Obama took office. This change was driven primarily by changes in the opinions of Republicans and Independents, who have historically been less favorably disposed toward unions than Democrats (who held steady at 80 percent; Pew Research Center 2009), possibly influenced also by perceptions of strongly pro-labor Democrats controlling the presidency and Congress.

# IMMIGRATION

Immigration to the United States spiked following the liberalization of immigration policy in 1965. Over the past four decades, the number of first-generation immigrants living in the United States has quadrupled, from 9.6 million in 1970 to about 38 million in 2007 (Segal, Elliott, and Mayadas 2010). A record 1,046,539 people were naturalized as US citizens in 2008 (Lee and Rytina 2009). By 2050 the US population is projected to climb to 438 million (from 296 million in 2005), with 82 percent of the increase coming from immigrants (Garcia 2008). In 2008 an estimated 11 million immigrants—mostly from Mexico and other Central American countries—were in the US illegally (Passel 2006). Concerns about the social, political, and economic dimensions of both legal and illegal immigration, especially acute in states with significant immigrant populations (California, Texas, Florida), have catapulted immigration to the forefront of the national policy agenda. Immigration has fully captured the attention of the national media, with a notable rise in network news coverage in 2000 and then a large spike in 2006–7.

The sharp increase in immigration levels in the early part of the 1990s was accompanied by growing negativity toward them (Lapinksi, Peltola, Shaw, and Yang 1997). Public opinion over the past three decades has been somewhat split on legal immigration. Gallup surveys between 1995 and 2009 found that most Americans consistently believed that immigration should be decreased or kept at its present level. That said, Segovia and Defever (2010) note that the percentage believing that immigration should be decreased declined nearly 20 percentage points between 1995 and 2007, despite increases in the immigrant population. Large majorities have continued to express concern about illegal immigration, and growing numbers since the mid-1980s have believed most immigrants enter the US illegally (Lapinski, Peltola, Shaw, and Yang 1997). According to a question that has repeatedly been asked by CBS/*New York Times* since 1986, 49 percent of the public in June 1986 believed that most immigrants in the last few years entered the country illegally (compared to 32 percent who thought they entered legally); by June 1993, 68 percent of Americans believed most were entering illegally. By December 2001 (notably, in the aftermath of the September 11 terrorist attacks), the figure dropped to 53 percent, but it jumped to a record level by May 2007 when fully 3 in 4 Americans thought that most were entering the country illegally. Public concern about illegal immigration has remained consistently high since the 1990s, escalating between 2001 and 2007 (Segovia and DeFever 2010).

The economic dimensions of immigration have also become quite palpable, especially when the economy contracts and jobs become scarce. Overall, between 1983 and 2006 most Americans consistently believed that immigrants mostly took unwanted American jobs. Subsequently, however, there was an apparent increase in the number who perceived immigrants to be taking jobs away from American citizens. Gallup polls in September 2000 and January 2004 indicated that 13 and 14 percent of Americans, respectively, believed that immigrants were largely taking away American citizens' jobs; more than 3 in 10 consistently agreed with this view according to CBS News surveys based on responses to similar questions in 2005 and 2006. From the mid-1980s to the mid-1990s, stable majorities or pluralities thought that immigrants ended up on welfare and used a disproportionately high share of government services (Lapinksi, Peltola, Shaw, and Yang 1997). At the same time, growing numbers of Americans since 1993 believed that immigrants "pay their fair share of taxes" and "mostly help" the economy. Further complicating the picture are other perceptions that immigrants contribute meaningfully: pluralities of the public between 1993 and 2007 said that immigrants work harder than people born in the US; there was a sharp decline, after 1986, in the proportion of Americans who believed recent immigrants "cause problems" (Segovia and DeFever 2010); and on the whole, according to Gallup poll data, majorities from 2001 to 2008 believed immigration was "a good thing" for the country.

Regarding public policy, until the 2010 controversy that peaked with Arizona's enactment of tougher surveillance of possible illegal immigrants, public attitudes were less extreme compared to the 1990s. This may reflect increasingly pragmatic approaches toward immigration that acknowledge the useful functions performed by immigrants and the practical impediments to stricter and harsher policies. Majorities of Americans, however, continued to support status-checking policies and required everyone to carry identification cards, but there had been a decline in the public's support for security measures that entailed building fences and walls (Segovia and DeFever 2010). While majorities have favored some proposals to permit illegal immigrants to remain in the country, the public has held increasingly negative views about whether or not lawmakers can effectively implement immigration reforms (Segovia and DeFever 2010). Perhaps most striking is the stability of the public's overwhelming general view that "we should restrict and control people coming to live in our country more than we do." This has been drowned out by increasing partisan disagreement and hostility regarding immigration policy, which has joined the ranks of partisan issues. Whereas in the past Democrats and Republicans (e.g., George W. Bush and pre-2009 John McCain, in contrast to other Republicans) could be found on both sides of the issue, during the Obama administration immigration became, in effect, another "civil rights" issue for the parties, with opinions splitting increasingly predictably along party lines (Pew Research Center 2009; Carmines and Stimson 1989).

# ENERGY

Media attention to the issue of energy dissipated following the crises of the late 1970s, but news interest began to climb in the aftermath of the September 11, 2001, terrorist attacks, and it has remained relatively high since. In the two decades since 1990, public opinion reflected growing concern about energy, corresponding with the intensifying attention in the national press. In an August 1990 Gallup poll, about 3 in 4 Americans (73 percent) said that the energy situation was "very" or "fairly" serious; by March 2009, fully 93 percent felt that way; those saying the situation was "very" serious increased from 28 to 42 percent. Concern about energy became as high as it was during the national energy crises of the 1970s (Bolsen and Cook 2008). Between 2003 and 2007, Gallup polls found that the proportion of Americans who personally worried "a great deal" about the availability and affordability of energy rose from 27 to 43 percent, and the public became increasingly receptive to alternative sources of energy, including even nuclear power, which had fallen out of favor (Bolsen and Cook 2008; cf. Page and Shapiro 1992, ch. 4). Gallup surveys between 2001 and 2006 reported that most Americans believed that the United States was likely to face a critical energy shortage during the next five years. Bearing on this, the public has been split on opening Alaska's Arctic National Wildlife Rescue for oil and natural gas exploration. Majorities in the 1980s expressing support for increased use of nuclear power had eroded somewhat, and by 2005–6 most Americans opposed promoting greater use of nuclear power. Consistently with patterns observed in the 1990s, solid majorities have opposed constructing more nuclear power plants, but similar proportions of Americans believed that nuclear power remained an important source of energy for the nation (Rosa and Dunlap 1994). These have been partisan issues, with Republicans more supportive of nuclear energy, of drilling everywhere for new oil deposits, and of relying on business rather than government investment to develop new energy technology (Pew Research Center 2009).

Americans' perceptions of the oil industry in general have deteriorated markedly since the 1980s (without taking into account the 2010 offshore oil rig explosion and oil spill that devastated the Louisiana Gulf Coast): in 1984 a majority of Americans (54 percent) expressed "very" or "somewhat" favorable attitudes toward the oil industry, dropping to 21 percent in 2009. When asked to choose priorities for US energy policy, since the late 1980s the public has often been split among expanding energy exploration, mining, drilling, and construction of new power plants; and more energy conservation or regulation of energy. It has generally shown greater support for focusing on energy conservation: between 2001 and 2008, when asked to choose between more production of oil, gas, and coal supplies and more conservation, majorities consistently favored greater conservation. The public was supportive of government policies that encourage conservation through energy-efficient appliances, vehicles, homes, and offices (Bolsen and Cook 2008). NORC–GSS data show that there has been a gradual increase since the mid-1980s in the percentage of the public responding that we are spending "too little" on mass transportation. This is one area in which Democrats and the Republicans have differed, though not enormously (not more than 15 percentage points), and have moved in the same direction. In contrast, while support for increasing gas taxes has not been great, Democrats have been much more supportive than Republicans (Pew Research Center 2009).

# REGULATION

Regulation in a sense epitomizes Americans' outlook—and ambivalence—toward big government: Americans prefer "small government" to allow the free market to play out, but they then expect big government to deal with problems and dangers caused by free enterprise and its excesses. The problems range from health and safety in the workplace, to the quality and safety of all manner of consumer goods and products, to the protection of the natural environment. These concerns raise questions about the regulation of business, industry, and the market, broadly defined. This played out in the 2010 Louisiana Gulf crisis when the federal government and the Obama administration were blamed both for the failure in government regulation that led to the explosion and oil spill, and for the inability of the oil industry and the government to deal quickly and efficiently with the spill and the damage it caused.

There have been past cycles of regulation–deregulation–reregulation in American government policy and public opinion (see Page and Shapiro 1992; Shapiro and Gillroy 1984a, 1984b), but the latest cycle occurred with the Obama administration entering office on the crest of the most severe financial and banking industry crisis since the Great Depression. Whether the public responded to the ascendancy of what it perceived to be a liberal Democratic government that had run against conservative Republicans in a bitterly fought and highly partisan election, or to the failure of the Obama administration to take the country quickly out of a deep recession, public opinion moved in an anti-big government direction. Interestingly, however, regarding general attitudes toward business regulation, the Pew Research Center (2009, 34) concluded that "In the wake of the economic crisis and the federal government's increased involvement in the banking and automotive sectors, there is no overall shift in the balance of opinion about the effectiveness of government regulation." The most important trend was the increasing partisan divide: the gaps between Republicans and Democrats reached their highest levels for opinions that the government is inefficient and wasteful; that it "controls too much of our daily lives"; and that "government regulation of business usually does more harm than good" (Pew Research Center 2009).

# ENVIRONMENTAL PROTECTION

The environment stands out as a major area for government protection. Propelled partly by a backlash against the Reagan administration's environmental policies and the emergence of new environmental threats, the 1980s witnessed substantial increases in support for environmental protection (Dunlap and Scarce 1991; also Page and Shapiro 1992, ch. 4), despite the fact that national network news did not devote enormous attention to the environment throughout much of this period. By the late 1980s, however, the salience of environmental issues peaked and remained high through the early 1990s. Media attention to the environment fell off somewhat in the mid-1990s but the topic received additional attention from 2000 to 2002. Support for environmentalism and related measures accelerated with the emergence of new problems and controversies (global warming, pollution, contamination, and incidents like the Exxon Valdez oil spill) and remained high. Majorities of Americans since the 1980s have typically viewed environmental problems as serious, worsening, and increasingly threatening to human well-being (Dunlap and Scarce 1991). A wide range of environmental problems have consistently been perceived by majorities as at least somewhat threatening, even as the public appeared to be less concerned about air pollution and acid rain compared to the late 1980s. Still, majorities in NORC–GSS surveys have consistently responded that we have been spending "too little" on "improving and protecting the environment," peaking during the (presumably conservative) George H. W. Bush administration, falling off during the (liberal) Clinton administration, and increasing during the subsequent (conservative) Bush years.

Public attitudes toward environmental protection during the deep recession continued two compelling patterns or trends. Gallup/USA Today surveys between 1984 and 2010 and Pew Research Center surveys through 2009 revealed that many Americans favored environmental protection even if it came at the cost of economic growth. However, support falls off during periods of economic decline, with the public less willing to pay higher prices to protect the environment and to give priority to protecting the environment if it causes slower economic growth and job losses (Pew Research Center 2009). In the Gallup/USA Today polls, the distributions of opinion about this matter have become more evenly divided over time. In surveys conducted during the bad economic times of March 2009 and 2010, most Americans indicated that economic growth should be the priority. By May 2010, however, 50 percent of Americans selected the environment as the greater policy priority—very likely in response to the April 20, 2010, British Petroleum oil spill disaster in the Gulf of Mexico—compared to 43 percent who preferred to attend to economic growth. The second trend is that since the 1990s, especially by the middle of the Clinton years, the high degree of political conflict on environmental issues became strikingly apparent in the increasing partisan differences in public support for spending on environmental protection that continued at least through 2008. Moreover, from 2007 to 2009, after Obama took office, the Pew Research Center survey questions cited above showed wider partisan differences as well, reflecting the increasing divide between the two parties on the issue of environmental regulation.

Most Americans since the 1980s have generally believed that government regulation has not gone far enough concerning the environment. The public has increasingly believed businesses and industry are the major contributors to environmental problems and that the private sector cannot be relied upon to help resolve environmental issues. Overall, Americans have appeared increasingly willing to help absorb the costs of environmental protection by paying higher prices on goods and services. After the 1980s, majorities of Americans often identified themselves as environmentalists and growing majorities reported developing "ecologically responsible" lifestyles that incorporate changes in personal behavior (such as recycling and avoiding products like aerosols; Dunlap and Scarce 1991).

Last, one main area of environmental concern has been the emergence of global warming as a potential environmental threat. Analysis of opinion data gathered over the past three decades has indicated great awareness about global warming (or "the greenhouse effect"), approaching at times near-universal levels (topping 90 percent), compared to the mid-1980s, when fewer than 4 in 10 Americans reported knowing of the issue. Decades after scientists and journalists first alerted the public to global warming, few Americans have revealed confidence that they grasp its complexities (Nisbet and Myers 2007, 447). One positive indicator of awareness, however, is that the segment of the public that has reported understanding the issue "very well" doubled—from 11 to 22 percent—between 1992 and 2007 (Nisbet and Myers 2007).

Studies have found that majorities of Americans believe global warming is real, that temperatures have been rising, and that the release of carbon dioxide has been a cause; but only about 1 in 3 Americans have believed that global warming will pose a threat in their lifetime (Nisbet and Myers 2007). That said, the proportion of Americans who felt that global warming was "extremely important" to them personally more than doubled—from 7 to 18 percent—in the decade from 1997 to 2007. Majorities since the late 1980s have reported being personally worried about global warming as an environmental problem. Strong majorities also, however, oppose levying taxes on electricity to reduce the problem. Most Americans have thought that the US should participate in and abide by the provisions of the Kyoto Protocol on global warming. And again, here, partisan differences abound and have widened, not only concerning support for government action but also regarding perceptions of the severity of the problem or of whether the problem of global warming even exists (Shapiro and Bloch-Elkon 2008a). That partisan conflict has affected how different segments of the public, and even its leaders, perceive ostensibly real-world conditions speaks to a potentially deeper problem in contemporary American politics (Shapiro and Bloch-Elkon 2008b).

# Defense

Defense and national security constitute a major set of "public goods" which are the sole obligation of governments. They compete with domestic policies and spending along the lines of a "guns versus butter" tradeoff. In the early 1980s, in the wake of the Iran hostage crisis and the Soviet invasion of Afghanistan, there was a huge spike in the percentage of the public responding to the NORC–GSS and other surveys that the country was spending "too little" on national defense and the military. Public opinion reversed quickly into the first Reagan administration as defense spending rose and the initial reactions to the events in Iran and Afghanistan receded. Into the late 1980s and 1990s, Americans increasingly thought the US was spending "too much" on defense, but about one third consistently thought we were spending amounts that were "about right." Beginning in the late 1990s, the proportion of the public saying we were spending "too little" appeared to increase slowly and then more substantially after the September 11 attacks and then with the wars in Afghanistan and then Iraq. This was driven by the opinions of Republicans. From the beginning of the Clinton administration through the latest available data in 2009, the existing partisan differences on defense, national security, and related foreign policy issues increased markedly. The idea that partisan politics ended at the water's edge had fallen by the wayside and the ideological conflict among party leaders that had penetrated to the mass public applied to a full spectrum of domestic issues and defense and foreign policy issues as well (for example, see the evidence and references cited in Bafumi and Shapiro 2009; Shapiro and Bloch-Elkon 2005, 2008a, 2008b; Pew Research Center 2009).

One issue regarding national defense that was less vulnerable to partisan conflict concerned the military as an institution. Between 1981 and 2009, Americans' confidence in the military climbed significantly, with a major increase coming with the military's impressive victory in the first Gulf War in 1991. According to Gallup polls conducted in these years, the share of Americans who expressed "a great deal" of confidence in the military more than doubled overall—from 22 to 45 percent—during this period (see also Torres-Reyna and Shapiro 2002). The one aspect of defense for which there was less support was a victim of the success of the nation's all-volunteer military: 62 percent of Americans opposed (and 35 percent favored) mandatory military service according to a June 2005 Gallup poll, in sharp contrast to the 69 percent who favored mandatory service in peacetime 1955. Between 1999 and 2005, despite the military's growing popularity, a shrinking number of Americans indicated they would support a son or daughter planning to enter the military—a decline from 66 to 51 percent—almost certainly related to the dangerous ongoing wars in Iraq and Afghanistan. The proportion of the public opposing a return to the military draft also rose steadily from the early 1980s: fully 85 percent opposed returning to the draft in October 2004, compared to 59 percent in February 1980.

# Conclusion

By way of summary and synthesis, we conclude where we began: how do we best describe the public opinion toward big government in the United States? Even with evidence of high levels of public support for the American welfare state and some continuing liberal shifts, the tensions between the values of individualism and egalitarianism have continued. They have led to continuing ambivalence and sensitivity to changes in government policies that may be perceived as going too far in a liberal or conservative direction. This was apparent most recently in the conservative backlash during the first two years of the Obama administration. The divergence in the opinions of Republicans and Democrats, catching up to the sharp partisan conflicts at the elite level, has continued with no (at least short-term) end in sight. Against the backdrop of intense partisan conflict, the general notion that Americans are conservative in the abstract but operationally or pragmatically liberal has become more complicated. In some issue areas such as labor, energy, the environment, and health-care reform, Americans have appeared at times liberal in the abstract, but they have reacted conservatively to specific liberal policy proposals, the details and contingencies of which evoke real or imagined threats.

Will the overarching patterns and trends we describe in this chapter continue? We think so, but changing circumstances and conditions could alter them (see Page and Shapiro 1992). The key ones to watch are partisan conflict, changes in partisan control of government, the economy, the emergence of new domestic and foreign policy issues, and demographic changes—including generational replacement and immigration, which itself has become one of the major issues for big government and the American welfare state.

# REFERENCES

BAFUMI, J., and SHAPIRO, R. Y. 2009. A New Partisan Voter. *Journal of Politics*, 71: 1–24.

BALDASSARRI, D., and GELMAN, A. 2008. Partisans without Constraint: Political Polarization and Trends in American Public Opinion. *American Journal of Sociology*, 114: 408–46.

BERINSKY, A. J. 2006. Public Opinion in the 1930s and 1940s: The Analysis of Quota Controlled Sample Survey Data. *Public Opinion Quarterly*, 70/4: 530–64.

BLENDON, R. J., BRODIE, M., BENSON, J. M., and ALTMAN, D. E. 2011. *American Public Opinion and Health Care*. Washington, DC: CQ Press.

BOLSEN, T., and COOK, F. L. 2008. The Polls—Trends: Public Opinion on Energy Policy. *Public Opinion Quarterly*, 72/2: 364–88.

BUSHAW, W. J., and MCNEE, J. A. 2009. The 41st Annual Phi Delta Kappa/Gallup Poll of the Public's Attitudes toward the Public Schools: Americans Speak Out: Are Educators and Policy Makers Listening?, *Phi Delta Kappan*, 91/1: 8–23.

CARALEY, D. 1992. Washington Abandons the Cities. *Political Science Quarterly*, 107: 1–30.

CARMINES, E. G., and STIMSON, J. A. 1989. *Issue Evolution: Race and the Transformation of American Politics*. Princeton: Princeton University Press.

DUNLAP, R., and SCARCE, R. 1991. The Polls—Trends: Environmental Problems and Protection. *Public Opinion Quarterly*, 55/4: 651–8.

ERIKSON, R. S., MACKUEN, M. B., and STIMSON, J. A. 2002. *The Macro Polity*. New York: Cambridge University Press.

ERSKINE, H. 1975. The Polls: Government Role in Welfare. *Public Opinion Quarterly*, 39: 257–74.

GALLUP, G. H. 1972. *The Gallup Poll: Public Opinion 1935–1971*. New York: Random House.

GARCIA, A. 2008. Whites to Become Minority in U.S. by 2050. *Reuters*, Feb. 12.

GILENS, M. 1999. *Why Americans Hate Welfare: Race, Media, and the Politics of Antipoverty Policy*. Chicago: University of Chicago Press.

JACOBS, L. R., and SHAPIRO, R. Y. 2000. *Politicians Don't Pander: Political Manipulation and the Loss of Democratic Responsiveness*. Chicago: University of Chicago Press.

LAPINKSI, J., PELTOLA, P., SHAW, G., and YANG, A. 1997. The Polls—Trends: Immigrants and Immigration. *Public Opinion Quarterly*, 61/2: 356–83.

LEE, J., and RYTINA, N. 2009. *Naturalizations in the United States: 2008*. Washington, DC: Office of Immigration Statistics, Mar.

McCARTY, N., POOLE, K. T., and ROSENTHAL, H. 2006. *Polarized America: The Dance of Ideology and Unequal Riches*. Cambridge, MA: MIT Press.

NEWMAN, K. S., and JACOBS, E. S. 2010. *Who Cares? Public Ambivalence and Government Activism from the New Deal to the Second Gilded Age*. Princeton: Princeton University Press.

NISBET, M., and MYERS, T. 2007. The Polls—Trends: Twenty Years of Public Opinion about Global Warming. *Public Opinion Quarterly*, 71/3: 444–70.

PAGE, B. I., and JACOBS, L. R. 2009. *Class War: What Americans Really Think about Economic Inequality*. Chicago: University of Chicago Press.

—— —— 2010. *Understanding Public Opinion on Deficits and Social Security*. Working Paper No. 2. New York: Roosevelt Institute, June 27.

—— and SHAPIRO, R. Y. 1992. *The Rational Public: Fifty Years of Trends in Americans' Policy Preferences*. Chicago: University of Chicago Press.

PANAGOPOULOS, C., and FRANCIA, P. 2008. The Polls—Trends: Labor Unions in the United States. *Public Opinion Quarterly*, 72/1: 134–60.

PASSEL, J. 2006. *The Size and Characteristics of the Unauthorized Migrant Population in the United States*. Washington, DC: Pew Hispanic Center, Mar. 7.

Pew Research Center for the People & the Press. 2009. *Trends in Political Values and Core Attitudes: 1987–2009*. Washington, DC: Pew Research Center for the People & the Press.

ROSA, E., and DUNLAP, R. 1994. The Polls—Trends: Nuclear Power: Three Decades of Public Opinion. *Public Opinion Quarterly*, 58/2: 295–324.

SCHILTZ, M. 1970. *Public Attitudes toward Social Security, 1935–1965*. Social Security Administration Research Report No. 33. Washington, DC: US Department of Health, Education, and Welfare.

SEGAL, U. A., ELLIOTT, D., and MAYADAS, N. S. 2010. *Immigration Worldwide: Policies, Practices, and Trends*. New York: Oxford University Press.

SEGOVIA, F., and DeFEVER, R. 2010. The Polls—Trends: American Public Opinion on Immigrants and Immigration Policy. *Public Opinion Quarterly*, 74/2: 375–94.

SHAPIRO, R. Y. 2009. From Depression to Depression? Seventy-Five Years of Public Opinion toward Welfare. Paper presented at the Annual Fall Research Conference of the Association of Public Policy Analysis and Management, Washington, DC, Nov. 5–7.

—— and BLOCH-ELKON, Y. 2005. Partisan Conflict, Public Opinion, and U.S. Foreign Policy. Paper presented at the Inequality & Social Policy Seminar, John F. Kennedy School of Government, Harvard University, Dec. 12.

—— —— 2008a. Foreign Policy, Meet the People. *National Interest*, 97 (Sept.–Oct.), 37–42.

—— —— 2008b. Do the Facts Speak for Themselves? Partisan Disagreement as a Challenge to Democratic Competence. *Critical Review*, 20/1–2: 115–39.

SHAPIRO, R. Y., and GILLROY, J. M. 1984a. The Polls Regulation—Part I. *Public Opinion Quarterly*, 48: 531–42.

—— —— 1984b. The Polls Regulation—Part II. *Public Opinion Quarterly*, 48: 666–77.

SHAW, G. M. 2009–10. Public Opinion and the American Welfare State. *Political Science Quarterly*, 124: 627–53.

—— and MYSIEWICZ, S. 2004. Social Security and Medicare. *Public Opinion Quarterly*, 68: 394–423.

SMITH, M. A. 2007. *The Right Talk: How Conservatives Transformed the Great Society into the Economic Society*. Princeton: Princeton University Press.

SOROKA, S. N., and WLEZIEN, C. 2010. *Degrees of Democracy: Politics, Public Opinion, and Policy*. New York: Cambridge University Press.

SOSS, J., and SCHRAM, S., 2007. A Public Transformed? Welfare Reform as Policy Feedback. *American Political Science Review*, 101: 111–27.

STIMSON, J. A. 2004. *Tides of Consent: How Public Opinion Shapes American Politics*. New York: Cambridge University Press.

TORRES-REYNA, O., and SHAPIRO, R. Y. 2002. The Polls—Trends: Defense and the Military. *Public Opinion Quarterly*, 66: 279–303.

ZALLER, J. R. 1992. *The Nature and Origins of Mass Opinion*. New York: Cambridge University Press.

# Section Nine: Foreign Policy and Security

CHAPTER 40

....................................................................................................

# PUBLIC OPINION, FOREIGN POLICY, AND THE MEDIA

## *Toward an Integrative Theory*

....................................................................................................

DOUGLAS C. FOYLE

ALTHOUGH public opinion provides a foundation for modern perspectives on democratic governance, its influence on foreign policy remains understudied in American politics and international relations. For scholars studying American politics, while public opinion remains a core area of interest, the area of foreign policy tends not to be well integrated into the broader field although recent work suggests this effort would be productive (Berinsky 2009). Scholars of international politics have directed even less attention to public opinion, although this pattern might be changing as evidenced by the literature considering democracy and war (Chan 2010) and the diversionary use of force (Moore and Tarar 2010). Still, to the extent that international relations scholars have an interest in public opinion's role in policy formulation, they have tended to see it as a complementary factor rather than a primary focus (Foyle and Van Belle 2010). Furthermore, what continues to elude public opinion and foreign policy scholars is an integrative understanding of public opinion, the media, and foreign policy as part of the American political system on the one hand and as a determinant of international political outcomes on the other.

This review considers several areas of research relating to public opinion, the media, and foreign policy. First, my review of the existing knowledge suggests that although public attitudes on foreign policy appear reasonable and structured, significant controversies remain over its influence. I then consider the research on public opinion rallies, elections, audience costs, the use of force, and the media. The review ends with a discussion of useful future directions for research. I conclude that opportunities exist for progress in three related areas. First, public opinion and foreign policy research needs to devote more attention to how demographic variables affect public attitudes toward foreign policy. Second, I argue that the international relations and American politics literatures would benefit from greater intellectual cross-fertilization. Finally, I contend that the public opinion and foreign policy literature needs to work toward building broadly integrative models situating public opinion on foreign policy within its broader political context.

# Traditional Skepticism: The Almond–Lippmann Consensus

Research has focused on the three components of the Almond–Lippmann consensus (so named after political scientist Gabriel Almond and commentator Walter Lippmann): public opinion's rationality, structure, and policy influence (see Holsti 2004 for a summary). Portraying the public negatively, the Almond–Lippmann consensus reigned from the 1920s through the early 1970s and suggested that a largely ignorant public opinion on foreign policy reacted in an emotional rather than reasonable or rational manner, which in turn led to high attitude volatility. Furthermore, these attitudes had little relationship with each other (e.g., an individual opposed to strengthening the United Nations in general but favoring specific policies to empower it). Many proponents of this view worried little about public opinion's weaknesses since they believed the public did not influence foreign policy.

# Modern Trends: Structure and Influence

A reevaluation of public opinion in the 1970s and 1980s turned the Almond–Lippmann consensus on its head. Although few scholars would argue that public opinion is infused with knowledge of foreign policy events, the prevailing view now portrays it as possessing relatively stable attitudes and responding reasonably to foreign affairs information (Page and Shapiro 1992; Jentleson and Britton 1998).

The clearest view of these trends derives from the Chicago Council on Global Affairs periodic surveys conducted since 1974.[1] Since the end of the Second World War, Americans have consistently favored engagement in international affairs (Question: "Do you think it will be best for the future of the country if we take an active part in world affairs or if we stay out of world affairs?"). In 1947, 68 percent supported active involvement while only 25 percent suggested staying out of international affairs. The 2010 poll reflects a similar result where 67 percent favored active involvement and 31

---

[1] All polls cited here derive from the 2010 report available at ⟨http://www.thechicagocouncil.org/curr_pos.php⟩.

percent supported staying out (favorability peaked at 72 percent in 1955 and bottomed out at 55 percent in 1982).

The most favored foreign policy goals were all closely linked to national security and the domestic economy (Question: "Below is a list of possible foreign policy goals that the United States might have. For each one please select whether you think that it should be a very important foreign policy goal of the United States, a somewhat important foreign policy goal, or not an important goal at all?" Percentages are those indicating "very important"):

- protecting the jobs of American workers (79 percent),
- preventing the spread of nuclear weapons (73 percent),
- combating international terrorism (69 percent),
- securing adequate supplies of energy (68 percent),
- controlling illegal immigration (59 percent)
- maintaining superior military power worldwide (56 percent), and
- improving America's standing in the world (53 percent).

Ranking lower in importance were issues with transformational ends such as:

- combating world hunger (42 percent),
- limiting climate change (37 percent),
- strengthening the United Nations (37 percent),
- promoting international trade (33 percent),
- promoting and defending human rights in other countries (30 percent),
- protecting weaker nations against foreign aggression (24 percent), and
- helping bring a democratic form of government to other nations (19 percent).

Simply put, Americans favor foreign policy goals most closely associated with a narrow (self-interested) reading of the national interest.

American attitudes also consistently display an inclination toward multilateral action. Large majorities favored American participation in a nuclear testing ban worldwide (82 percent), the International Criminal Court (70 percent), and a climate treaty to address greenhouse gases (67 percent). The public favored complying with a hypothetical World Trade Organization ruling against the United States 72 percent to 26 percent. While the public did not prioritize "strengthening the U.N.," the public still favored a series of actions that would enhance its powers and capacities such as:

- establishing an international marshal service to arrest leaders who committed genocide (73 percent),
- empowering it to enter countries to investigate human rights violations (72 percent),
- constructing a UN agency to control nuclear fuel to limit its availability for weapons (64 percent).
- creating a standing peacekeeping force (64 percent), and
- allowing it to regulate the international arms trade (55 percent),

Although space limitations preclude a more detailed discussion of public attitudes, additional extensive surveys are available through the German Marshall Fund's "Trans-Atlantic Trends" poll of American and European attitudes,[2] the Program on International Policy Attitudes at the University of Maryland,[3] and the Pew Research Center's Global Attitudes Project[4] (also see Holsti 2004).

An extensive literature also developed regarding the question of whether a meaningful structure organized public attitudes. Although scholars disagree over how (e.g., a continuum from unilateralism to multilateralism, opposing to favoring forceful action, etc.) and the number of organizing dimensions that characterize public attitudes, most now agree that public attitudes meet the criteria set by Philip Converse (1964) of both stability (attitudes tend to stay the same) and "some form of constraint or functional interdependence" (e.g., individuals favoring multilateralism also support working through the United Nations). The most prominent analysis, by Eugene Wittkopf (1990), describes two dimensions for American public opinion: (1) cooperative internationalism refers to whether an individual favors or opposes working with other nations to solve global and national challenges; and (2) militant internationalism indicates whether the person favors forceful action, possibly unilateral in nature, to pursue American interests. Others point to a third dimension, representing a unilateralism and multilateralism continuum (Chittick, Billingsley, and Travis 1995) or a hierarchical model driven by core values (Hurwitz and Peffley 1987).

Unlike research on the stability and structure of public opinion, no consensus exists on whether and under what conditions public opinion influences policy. Although it appeared at first that research into this area would reverse the Almond–Lippmann consensus position, it has not. First, some research continues to suggest that public opinion plays a limited role in foreign policy formulation. Most notably, in a statistically sophisticated examination evaluating public opinion's effect on policy relative to interest groups and policy experts, Lawrence Jacobs and Benjamin Page (2005) found that public opinion's influence paled in comparison to other policy actors and had little or no statistical influence.

Interestingly, this finding aligns with a growing trend in US presidential studies that suggests that presidents do not respond to public preferences (Wood 2009) and use the sophisticated polling techniques available to them to limit public influence. Presidents might use polls to build support for their chosen policies (Heith 2004), to construct policies that appear to reflect popular will (while being substantively incongruent with public attitudes), or enable leaders to ensure general popular support despite pursuing unpopular policies (Jacobs and Shapiro 2000).

The influence of leaders on public opinion has also generated controversy and a great deal of research in American politics (see reviews in Goethals 2005; Rockman and Waterman 2008). Some have suggested that public opinion tracks elite opinion (Gabel

[2]  <http://www.gmfus.org/trends>.
[3]  <http://www.pipa.org>.
[4]  <http://www.pewglobal.org>.

and Scheve 2007). Since presidents will likely possess much more detailed knowledge about foreign affairs than the public, scholars have suggested that presidents can shape public opinion on foreign policy more than on domestic affairs (Entman 2004; Canes-Wrone 2006; Canes-Wrone, Howell, Lewis 2007). On the other hand, the president's ability to lead public opinion at all might be more limited than commonly thought, with George Edwards (2009) suggesting these efforts largely fail (and that any "leadership" appears because some presidents skillfully capitalize on existing public attitudes to pursue their chosen policies). In general, international relations scholars have paid much less attention to the question of the president's influence on public opinion. In large part, many international relations scholars have assumed a leader's ability to shape opinion to favor a chosen foreign policy rendering this subject intellectually uninteresting.

Second, a common finding in the literature suggests that public opinion has an important and strong influence by limiting the range of policy choices available to government leaders (Powlick and Katz 1998; Sobel 2001; Foyle 2004). Third, some research suggests public opinion spurs the adoption of particular foreign policies across a range of issues (Page and Shapiro 1992).

Finally, some scholars have emphasized a range of conditional variables that influence public opinion's influence on foreign policy, including level of public support for the policy (Graham 1994), domestic structure (Risse-Kappen 1991), elections (Gaubatz 1999), presidential attitudes toward public opinion (Foyle 1999), stage of decision-making (Knecht 2010), and presidential popularity (Canes-Wrone 2006).

# ELECTIONS AND FOREIGN POLICY

The role of elections runs throughout much of the public opinion and foreign policy literature and addresses two questions: (1) whether foreign policy affects vote choices; and (2) the influence of elections on foreign policy choices. Early analyses based on data from the 1950s and 1960s suggested that foreign policy remained at best a secondary factor in determining vote choice (Holsti 2004). As the bipartisan consensus over foreign policy broke up over Vietnam, foreign policy rose in prominence as a voting issue as partisan differences among opinion leaders emerged (Aldrich et al. 2006; Berinsky 2009; Gelpi, Feaver, and Reifler 2009). In a transformative article, Aldrich, Sullivan, and Borgida (1989) found that attitudes about foreign policy conditionally affected vote choice with the strongest influence occurring when large policy differences existed between the candidates and the campaign emphasized foreign policy. Foreign policy's influence on voting tailed off as candidate differences blurred and/or attention focused elsewhere.

Unlike the scholarly consensus that emerged over the effect of foreign policy on voting, controversy continues over the influence of elections on foreign policy. First, some scholars have found that approaching elections push leaders to make more peaceful choices (Gaubatz 1999). Second, others have argued that elections cause increased uses of force as leaders see foreign policy as a chance to either distract the public from unpopular domestic circumstances or artificially enhance public support (see the diversionary use of force section below). Third, presidents might wish to avoid foreign policy choices of any kind during election years given the inherent risks and uncertainty (Quandt 1986; Huth and Allee 2002). Fourth, principal–agent models suggest leaders who are facing difficult elections will seek "successful" conflicts to mimic "good" leaders (Downs and Rocke 1994). Fifth, some scholars argue that leaders pursue whatever policy the public prefers during election years (Geer 1996; Canes-Wrone and Shotts 2004). Finally, disputing these claims are those who portray elections as having no influence on foreign policy decisions (Ostrom and Job 1986; Meernik 1994; Gowa 1999; Derouen 2001; Fordham 2002). Given the range of findings, a consensus position seems a distant possibility.

# PUBLIC OPINION AND THE USE OF FORCE

Scholars have devoted considerable effort toward investigating the factors that influence the public's approval of the use of force (Klarevas 2002; Eichenberg 2005). First, some researchers suggest that vital national interests provide a precondition for support (Kohut and Toth 1995). Second, other scholars conclude that multilateral military operations receive more support than unilateral ones (Kull 2002). Third, some (Jentleson and Britton 1998) contend that the military mission drives public support with humanitarian interventions and instances of "foreign policy restraint" (military action against an actor who acted aggressively against American interests) receiving greater public support than interventions in the internal affairs of other countries.

Fourth, still others have emphasized the existence (or lack) of consensus among opinion leaders as cuing public support (or opposition). When consensus reigns, the public supports intervention. When disagreement emerges, the public divides behind the positions taken by leaders of the political party with which they identify (Brody 1992; Powlick and Katz 1998; Berinsky 2007).

Fifth, an extensive literature considers the effect that causalities have on public support with the bulk of the literature suggesting that as causalities go up, support for wars decrease (Mueller 1973; Larson 1995; Gartner 2008). Finally, still others have suggested that perceptions of whether the use of force is likely to succeed or not has the strongest effect on public support for war (Feaver and Gelpi 2005; Gelpi, Geaver, and Reifler 2009). Although scholars in this debate acknowledge that multiple factors determine public support, the debate between these last two views remains the most active controversy.

The related concept of audience costs (Fearon 1994) from the international politics literature observes that crises force leaders to take highly visible foreign policy stances. Unlike many foreign policy issues that receive little attention, the public would both notice and disapprove if the leader later backed down. This circumstance makes democratic leaders unlikely to retreat once they have taken a public position. Since foreign leaders will recognize this scenario and believe that democratic leaders will not change their positions in these circumstances, democratic leaders should be able to make more credible commitments and achieve more favorable crisis outcomes. The initial insight created a large literature which supported the theory's central insights (Eyerman and Hart 1996; Partell and Glenn 1999; Schultz 2001; Baum 2004; Slantchev 2006; Roselle 2010).

# WAGGING THE DOG? THE DIVERSIONARY USE OF FORCE

The rally effect concept suggests that during times of international crisis or tension an upsurge in popular approval of a nation's leadership occurs (Mueller 1973; Brody and Shapiro 1989; Parker 1995; Baum 2002; Colaresi 2007). Although no consensus exists on the cause of rallies or even that they are real, the subject continues to draw attention especially since it relates to the controversial diversionary use of force concept. The massive diversionary use of force literature evaluates whether leaders use military force to solve domestic political problems (or "wag the dog" in popular parlance). This theory suggests that leaders use international force in order to distract the public from domestic problems by "changing the subject" (and indirectly building public support) or to cause the public to "rally" around the leader (creating an artificial upsurge in the president's approval rating). Scholars have suggested that a bad economy, tightly contested elections, or elections in the midst of an ongoing war enhance these incentives (Moore and Tarar 2010 provide an extensive review). On the other hand, some scholars suggest leaders do not conceive of international threats or respond to them in the manner suggested by the theory (Foyle 1999; Hendrickson 2002). Other research strands have suggested that domestically vulnerable democracies have *fewer* opportunities to divert because potential challengers anticipate the leader's politically inspired temptation to use force and will avoid challenging these weakened leaders (Clark 2003).

# THE MEDIA, PUBLIC OPINION, AND FOREIGN POLICY

The American politics literature provides extensive and finely nuanced theoretical approaches regarding the influence of the media on attitude formation and change (see Chapters 4–16 in this volume). More so than other aspects, this work has seeped into the international politics research (Roselle 2010), with the dominant perspectives reflecting efforts by international relations scholars to integrate insights from American politics in two areas: (1) where media content comes from and how it is structured; and (2) how the media influences foreign policy attitudes.

Several prominent models portray the media's content and influence on attitudes. First, indexing models suggest that the media reflects the content, tone, and distribution of attitudes held in Washington by government officials and opinion leaders. This view portrays the media as the information transmission belt from opinion leaders to the public without providing an independent voice. This perspective is most associated with the work of W. Lance Bennett (Bennett, Lawrence, and Livingston 2007). Although not explicitly a theory of the media effects on public opinion, the implication is that elites largely shape the knowledge that the public has about foreign policy.

Second, framing (see Chapter 12) suggests an independent role for the media in foreign policy formulation. In framing, which is "selecting and highlighting some facets of events or issues, and making connections among them so as to promote a particular interpretation, evaluation, and/or solution" (Entman 2004, 5), political actors (e.g., the president, Congress, foreign policy experts) and the media interact to shape and control how an issue, problem, or situation is understood. The strongest media influence is thought to be in ambiguous situations where political leaders can compete to shape the frame. Proponents suggest that frames are potentially powerful tools in strengthening or weakening public support for foreign policies (Entman 2004). Rather than changing fundamental public attitudes about foreign policy, frames serve to "inform" the public about what a particular instance is a "case of." Since this view portrays the media as independent of government elites, it suggests the media can affect public support of foreign policies.

Third, the related concepts of agenda-setting and priming also portray the media influence on public attitudes (see Chapter 11). Cohen (1963, 13) captured the idea of agenda-setting best, saying the press "may not be successful much of the time in telling people what to think, but it is stunningly successful in telling its readers what to think *about*." Priming suggests that the media's coverage affects the standards the public uses to evaluate officials and issues. For example, media coverage of a foreign policy issue might cause the public to use that issue (rather than others) to form their overall assessments of the president. Several studies point to a strong influence of agenda-setting and priming on public attitudes and policymaker perceptions of the public's priorities in the foreign policy sphere (Iyengar and Simon 1994; Soroka 2003).

Fourth, the hegemony view contends that a virtual government monopoly on foreign policy information allows it to control media messages (and thereby public opinion) and generate public support for whatever policy it wishes to pursue (Herman and Chomsky 1988; Bennett and Palatz 1994; Rutherford 2004).

Three additional concepts merit brief attention here. First, the "CNN effect" refers to the demands that twenty-four-hour news coverage places on policymakers. The crush of breaking news is claimed to affect the foreign policy agenda and/or substantive policy decisions (causing decision-makers to choose policies that they consider to be imprudent) (Gilboa 2005). Second, scholars agree that media content does not reach

each individual equally. Bernard Cohen summarized this situation famously by saying "if little foreign affairs news was published, even less was read, on the average" (Cohen 1963, 251). This situation led Gabriel Almond to suggest that an "attentive public" consisting of roughly 10 percent of the general public ingested foreign affairs information while the vast majority paid little attention (Almond 1950). Finally, the soft news concept (foreign policy messages in ostensibly entertainment-oriented productions discussed in more detail in Chapter 8) builds on the notion of an inattentive public and posits that even these people can receive information about foreign policy despite their efforts to avoid it altogether. Soft news then allows even low-information voters to integrate foreign policy information into their vote calculations and vote consistently with their preferences (Baum 2003).

Although much has been accomplished, more remains to be done in three areas: demographic variation, cross-fertilization between American politics and international politics, and the need for greater integration and synthesis.

# The Need for More Basic Research: Demographic Variation

Research on the influence of demographic characteristics (such as race, ethnicity, occupation, economic background, religious beliefs, gender, partisanship, and ideology) on foreign policy attitudes has emphasized ideological and partisan predispositions as determinants of foreign policy attitudes (Holsti 2004). Post-cold war opinion patterns seem to be reinforcing this dynamic (Snyder, Shapiro, Bloch-Elkon 2009). Unlike American politics scholars, who have given much attention to how a range of demographic characteristics influence attitude formation and content (see Chapters 28–35 in this volume), the influence of demographic factors on opinion formation and political attitudes on foreign policy remains understudied (Berinsky 2007).

Recent research suggests that this pattern might be changing. Several works have provided general demographic analysis regarding foreign policy attitudes (Holsti 2004; Herron and Jenkins-Smith 2006; Page and Bouton 2006; Berinsky 2009). Scholars have published work on the influence on attitudes of gender (Eichenberg 2003), race (Gartner and Segura 2000), religion (Baumgartner, Francia, and Morris 2008), and occupation (Feaver and Gelpi 2005). Given the positive findings in this recent work, additional efforts regarding these variables should prove valuable. If attitudes toward foreign policy are driven primarily by partisanship and ideology most of the time, these efforts should focus on discerning when, and under what conditions, demographic factors such as race and gender rise in relative importance.

# THE NEED FOR MORE CROSS-FERTILIZATION: AMERICAN POLITICS AND INTERNATIONAL POLITICS SUBFIELDS

A stronger connection between international relations and American politics scholars would provide a mutual benefit. Much of the literature cited in this review is written by scholars who would self-identify themselves as primarily within the international relations subfield. In addition, much of the literature cited by these articles also refers predominantly to work written by international politics scholars with much less engagement with the work of American politics scholars. Although scholars in both international politics and American politics largely address the same questions, they engage the topics through a different lens. International relations scholars view public opinion as a subset of how domestic factors (e.g., elections, interest groups, the media, governmental processes, and individual decision-making factors) influence a state's international choices and behavior. American politics scholars view foreign policy as a particular substantive policy area within the much broader literature on public opinion and/or presidency studies. With rare exceptions, the opportunity for cross-fertilization between international politics scholars focusing on domestic politics and American politics scholars considering public opinion and the presidency has been missed.

Although the international relations literature tends to imply a uniform reaction to domestic concerns across leaders, a nuanced literature has developed in studying presidential responsiveness and suggests wide variation both individually and circumstantially. For example, Brandice Canes-Wrone (2006, 6–11, 123–8) usefully summarizes the range of perspectives on presidential responsiveness and decision-making from American politics, each with potentially useful contributions to existing international relations debates. She points to several views: (1) government leaders as responsive to public opinion (dynamic representation); (2) unpopular presidents seeking to align their policies with public opinion (need-based popularity); (3) a lack of policy responsiveness wedded to public relations efforts; (4) policymakers' reactions to a primarily results-oriented public (as opposed to a public that cares about the policies pursued as well as the results); and (5) the influence of election cycles. Rather than portraying leaders as uniformly responsive to the same conditions, this research suggests a level of variance which the existing international relations literature would do well to integrate.

Scholars working from the American politics subfield acknowledge the need for greater integration across these subfields with the recognition that foreign policy, rather than characterizing an exception to the "normal" policy process, progresses much as on domestic issues (Shapiro and Jacobs 2002; Druckman and Jacobs 2006; Berinsky 2009). Ironically, although much of international politics literature that has considered public opinion has dealt with United States foreign policy, this same research has largely failed to integrate findings from American politics scholars. Since international relations scholars are primarily interested in foreign policy choices and policy outcomes, this work can contribute to American politics by addressing the core question of "who governs" when and under what conditions especially as it relates to the critical issue of war and the use of force. For international relations scholars, conceptions regarding the relationships among elections, agenda-setting, legislative–executive relations, and public opinion could inform topics discussed in this review (see Edwards and King 2007, especially the chapters by Jacobson, Jacobs, and Blinder). On public opinion in particular, Manza, Cook, and Page (2002) and Burstein (2003) provide a broad range of insightful contributions engaging issues central to this field of study.

# The Need for Integration and Synthesis: Within the Study of Public Opinion and Foreign Policy

As evidenced by the extensive amount of research in this area, the field has made enormous gains in understanding the interrelationships among public opinion, the media, and foreign policy. Still, although notable attempts have been made to synthesize a comprehensive public opinion model or model of governance that integrates public opinion into foreign policymaking (Rosenau 1961; Powlick and Katz 1998; Western 2005; Baum and Potter 2008), no one approach has emerged to dominate the field. Instead, the field is best characterized as one with a diverse group of scholars focused mainly around a range of discrete issues that do not add up appreciably to a comprehensive intellectual model. The next major challenge for the field is to begin to integrate the various research strands into progressively broader and more integrative models. Needless to say, doing so in an effective and convincing manner provides an enormous intellectual undertaking. It is one that several scholars have begun to pursue.

First, in their literature review of public opinion and foreign policy literature, Philip Powlick and Andrew Katz (1998) posit a conditional model of public opinion's influence depending upon the behavior of elites and media coverage. They present a linear map of the interactions among the public, the media, and decision-makers. Although leaders anticipate public opinion in making decisions, their model largely assumes that public opinion will become engaged largely after a policy decision. Depending upon the intellectual accessibility of media coverage and whether elites disagree regarding the policy, the public will become engaged (or not). If elite disagreement emerges and the media covers it in a manner that the public can understand, public opinion will become activated, public support can become problematic, and a policy change might occur. If either the media frame is inaccessible to the public or elites largely agree, public opinion's reaction will be to acquiesce (if the debate is inaccessible given media coverage) or support the policy (when the frame is accessible and elites are supportive).

Second, Jon Western (2005), in reference to use of force decisions, presents a similar linear model of public opinion influence. Western's model emphasizes the role of competing elites in affecting political outcomes. When a potential use of force arises, competing groups of elites advocate for their respective positions. The ability of these groups to win is determined by their actions as they relate to existing "information advantages" (the presidency and executive branch cohesion, media reaction, and the organizational capacities of the groups) and existing public attitudes. The effectiveness of these advocacy groups in the context of these informational advantages and existing public opinion then determines the policy outcome. In Western's model, the advocacy groups are the primary drivers of policy as well as the media, while executive branch officials and public opinion provide the context in which these groups compete. More than Powlick and Katz, Western posits a public opinion that has preexisting attitudes on policy questions independent of (but clearly influenced by) the media and elites.

Finally, Baum and Potter (2008, 56) have suggested moving to a "foreign policy marketplace" approach that captures the interrelationships "characterized by expectations, anticipated reactions, and constant updating" among leaders, the public, and the media. This marketplace concept would suggest "the convergence of actors and information on points of equilibrium, rather than linear causal chains." Importantly, it also would place the information asymmetries that exist at various points in the policy process at the center our studies.

Developing a fully integrated model of public opinion, the media, and foreign policy remains a challenging, important, and unrealized task. As this brief review of integrative models suggests, these efforts are engaging the current scholarly thinking regarding how the various foreign policy actors interact with each other. Given the numerous contingent and variable parts involved, successful realization of this vision will remain a long-term aspiration.

# CONCLUSION

The question of whether public opinion should guide policymaking has engaged philosophers since the days of Plato's *Republic*. Scholars have made enormous progress in this field in the last several decades in their understanding of how leaders, public opinion, and the media react and interact regarding foreign policy. Most importantly perhaps is the conceptual shift from the Almond–Lippmann consensus, which portrayed only foreign policy leaders as truly independent actors in the foreign policy process. By developing the notion that both public opinion and the media can react independently of leaders in response to foreign policy, scholars have become open to conceptual breakthroughs necessary to move toward more synthesized concepts. At the same time, we are only beginning to move toward developing integrated models that can account for the dynamic nature of how these independent actors interact. Much like the parable of the blind men and the elephant, if scholars are to make progress toward more integrated models of how public opinion, the media, and leaders interact regarding foreign policy, we will need to work together across disciplinary boundaries to develop a more complete understanding.

# REFERENCES

ALDRICH, J. H., GELPI, C., FEAVER, P., REIFLER, J., and SHARP, K. T. 2006. Foreign Policy and the Electoral Connection. *Annual Review of Political Science*, 9: 477–502.

—— SULLIVAN, J. L., and BORGIDA, E. 1989. Foreign Affairs and Issue Voting: Do Presidential Candidates "Waltz before a Blind Audience?" *American Political Science Review*, 83 (Mar.), 123–41.

ALMOND, G. 1950. *The American People and Foreign Policy*. New York: Praeger.

BAUM, M. A. 2002. The Constituent Foundations of the Rally-Round-the-Flag Phenomenon. *International Studies Quarterly*, 46: 263–98.

—— 2003. *Soft News Goes to War: Public Opinion and American Foreign Policy in the New Media Age*. Princeton: Princeton University Press.

—— 2004. Going Private: Public Opinion, Presidential Rhetoric, and the Domestic Politics of Audience Costs in U.S. Foreign Policy Crises. *Journal of Conflict Resolution*, 48: 603–31.

—— and POTTER, P. B. K. 2008. The Relationships between Mass Media, Public Opinion, and Foreign Policy: Toward a Theoretical Synthesis. *Annual Review of Political Science*, 11: 39–65.

BAUMGARTER, J. C., FRANCIA, P. L., and MORRIS, J. S. 2008. A Clash of Civilizations? The Influence of Religion on Public Opinion of U.S. Foreign Policy in the Middle East. *Political Research Quarterly*, 61: 171–9.

BENNETT, W. L., and PALATZ, D. 1994. *Taken by Storm*. Chicago: University of Chicago Press.

—— LAWRENCE, R. G., and LIVINGSTON, S. 2007. *When the Press Fails: Political Power and the News Media from Iraq to Katrina*. Chicago: University of Chicago Press.

BERINSKY, A. J. 2007. Assuming the Costs of War: Events, Elites, and American Public Support for Military Conflict. *Journal of Politics*, 69: 975–97.

—— 2009. *In Time of War: Understanding American Public Opinion from World War II to Iraq*. Chicago: University of Chicago Press.

BRODY, R. 1992. *Assessing the President: The Media, Elite Opinion, and Public Support*. Stanford, CA: Stanford University Press.

—— and SHAPIRO, C. R. 1989. A Reconsideration of the Rally Phenomenon in Public Opinion. In *Political Behavior Annual*, ed. S. Long. Boulder, CO: Westview Press.

BURSTEIN, P. 2003. The Impact of Public Opinion on Public Policy: A Review and an Agenda. *Political Research Quarterly*, 56: 29–40.

CANES-WRONE, B. 2006. *Who Leads Whom? Presidents, Policy and the Public*. Chicago: University of Chicago Press.

—— and SHOTTS, K. W. 2004. The Conditional Nature of Presidential Responsiveness to Public Opinion. *American Journal of Political Science*, 48: 690–706.

——Howell, W. G., and Lewis, D. E. 2007. Toward a Broader Understanding of Presidential Power: A Reevaluation of the Two Presidencies Thesis. *Journal of Politics*, 69: 1–16.

Chan, S. 2010. Progress in the Democratic Peace Research Agenda. In *The International Studies Encyclopedia*, ed. R. A. Denemark, ix. Oxford: Wiley-Blackwell.

Chittick, W. O., Billingsley, K. R., and Travis, R. 1995. A Three-Dimensional Model of American Foreign Policy Beliefs. *International Studies Quarterly*, 39: 313–32.

Clark, D. H. 2003. Can Strategic Interaction Divert Diversionary Behavior? A Model of U.S. Conflict Propensity. *Journal of Politics*, 65: 1013–39.

Cohen, B. C. 1963. *The Press and Foreign Policy*. Princeton: Princeton University Press.

Colaresi, M. 2007. The Benefit of the Doubt: Testing an Informational Theory of the Rally Effect. *International Organization*, 61: 99–143.

Converse, P. E. 1964. The Nature of Belief Systems in Mass Publics. In *Ideology and Discontent*, ed. D. E. Apter. New York: Free Press.

DeRouen, K., Jr. 2001. *Politics, Economics, and Presidential Use of Force Decision Making*. Lewiston, NY: Edwin Mellen Press.

Downs, G. W., and Rocke, D. M. 1994. Conflict, Agency, and Gambling for Resurrection: The Principal–Agent Problem Goes to War. *American Journal of Political Science*, 38: 362–80.

Druckman, J. N., and Jacobs, L. R. 2006. Lumpers and Splitters: The Public Opinion Information that Politicians Collect and Use. *Public Opinion Quarterly*, 70: 453–76.

Edwards, G. C., III. 2009. *The Strategic President: Persuasion and Opportunity in Presidential Leadership*. Princeton: Princeton University Press.

——and King, D. S. (eds.) 2007. *The Polarized Presidency of George W. Bush*. New York: Oxford University Press.

Eichenberg, R. C. 2003. Gender Differences in Public Attitudes toward the Use of Force by the United States, 1990–2003. *International Security*, 28 (Summer), 110–41.

——2005. Victory Has Many Friends: U.S. Public Opinion and the Use of Military Force, 1981–2005. *International Security*, 30 (Summer), 140–77.

Entman, R. M. 2004. *Projections of Power: Framing News, Public Opinion, and U.S. Foreign Policy*. Chicago: University of Chicago Press.

Eyerman, J., and Hart, R. A., Jr. 1996. An Empirical Test of the Audience Cost Proposition: Democracy Speaks Louder than Words. *Journal of Conflict Resolution*, 40: 597–616.

Fearon, J. D. 1994. Domestic Political Audiences and the Escalation of International Disputes. *American Political Science Review*, 88: 577–92.

Feaver, P. D., and Gelpi, C. 2005. *Choosing Your Battles: American Civil–Military Relations and the Use of Force*. Princeton: Princeton University Press.

Fordham, B. O. 2002. Another Look at Parties, Voters, and the Use of Force Abroad. *Journal of Conflict Resolution*, 46: 572–96.

Foyle, D. C. 1999. *Counting the Public In: Presidents, Public Opinion, and Foreign Policy*. New York: Columbia University Press.

——2004. Leading the Public to War? The Influence of American Public Opinion on the Bush Administration's Decision to Go to War in Iraq. *International Journal of Public Opinion Research*, 16: 269–94.

——and Van Belle, D. A. 2010. Domestic Politics and Foreign Policy Analysis. In *The International Studies Compendium Project*, ed. R. A. Denemark, ii. Oxford: Wiley-Blackwell.

Gabel, M., and Scheve, K. 2007. Estimating the Effect of Elite Communications on Public Opinion Using Instrumental Variables. *American Journal of Political Science*, 51: 1013–28.

GARTNER, S. S. 2008. The Multiple Effects of Casualties on Public Support for War: An Experimental Approach. *American Political Science Review*, 102: 95–106.

——and SEGURA, G. 2000. Race, Casualties, and Opinion in the Vietnam War. *Journal of Politics*, 62: 115–46.

GAUBATZ, K. T. 1999. *Elections and War: The Electoral Incentive in the Democratic Politics of War and Peace*. Stanford, CA: Stanford University Press.

GEER, J. G. 1996. *From Tea Leaves to Opinion Polls: A Theory of Democratic Leadership*. New York: Columbia University Press.

GELPI, C., FEAVER, P. D., and REIFLER, J. 2009. *Paying the Human Costs of War: American Public Opinion and Casualties in Military Conflicts*. Princeton: Princeton University Press.

GILBOA, E. 2005. The CNN Effect: The Search for a Communication Theory of International Relations. *Political Communication*, 22: 27–44.

GOETHALS, G. R. 2005. Presidential Leadership. *Annual Review of Psychology*, 56: 545–70.

GOWA, J. 1999. *Ballots and Bullets: The Elusive Democratic Peace*. Princeton: Princeton University Press.

GRAHAM, T. W. 1994. Public Opinion and U.S. Foreign Policy Decision Making. In *The New Politics of American Foreign Policy*, ed. D. A. Deese. New York: St Martin's Press.

HEITH, D. J. 2004. *Polling to Govern: Public Opinion and Presidential Leadership*. Stanford, CA: Stanford University Press.

HENDRICKSON, R. C. 2002. Clinton's Military Strikes in 1998: Diversionary Use of Force? *Armed Forces & Society*, 28: 309–32.

HERMAN, E. S., and CHOMSKY, N. 1988. *Manufacturing Consent: The Political Economy of the Mass Media*. New York: Pantheon.

HERRON, K. G., and JENKINS-SMITH, H. C. 2006. *Critical Masses and Critical Choices: Evolving Public Opinion on Nuclear Weapons, Terrorism, and Security*. Pittsburgh: University of Pittsburgh Press.

HOLSTI, O. R. 2004. *Public Opinion and American Foreign Policy*, rev. edn. Ann Arbor: University of Michigan Press.

HURWITZ, J., and PEFFLEY, M. 1987. How Are Foreign Policy Attitudes Structured? *American Political Science Review*, 81: 1099–120.

HUTH, P. K., and ALLEE, T. L. 2002. Domestic Political Accountability and the Escalation and Settlement of International Disputes. *Journal of Conflict Resolution*, 46: 754–90.

IYENGAR, S., and SIMON, A. 1994. News Coverage of the Gulf Crisis and Public Opinion. In *Taken by Storm*, ed. W. L. Bennett and D. L. Paletz. Chicago: University of Chicago Press.

JACOBS, L. R., and PAGE, B. I. 2005. Who Influences U.S. Foreign Policy? *American Political Science Review*, 99: 107–23.

——and SHAPIRO, R. Y. 2000. *Politicians Don't Pander: Political Manipulation and the Loss of Democratic Responsiveness*. Chicago: University of Chicago Press.

JENTLESON, B. W., and BRITTON, R. L. 1998. Still Pretty Prudent: Post-Cold War American Public Opinion on the Use of Military Force. *Journal of Conflict Resolution*, 42: 395–417.

KLAREVAS, L. 2002. The "Essential Domino" of Military Operations: American Public Opinion and the Use of Force. *International Studies Perspectives*, 3: 417–37.

KNECHT, T. 2010. *Pulling the Reins of Power: Public Attention, Mass Opinion, and American Foreign Policy*. University Park: Pennsylvania University Press.

KOHUT, A., and TOTH, R. 1995. Intervention in the Post-Cold War World. In *Managing Conflict in the Post-Cold War World: The Role of Intervention*. Aspen, CO: Aspen Institute.

KULL, S. 2002. Public Attitudes toward Multilateralism. In *Multilateralism and U.S. Foreign Policy*, ed. S. Patrick and S. Forman. Boulder, CO: Lynne Rienner.

LARSON, E. V. 1995. *Casualties and Consensus: The Historical Role of Casualties in Domestic Support for U.S. Military Operations*. Santa Monica, CA: Rand.

MANZA, J., COOK, F. L., and PAGE, B. I. 2002. *Navigating Public Opinion: Polls, Policy, and the Future of American Democracy*. New York: Oxford University Press.

MEERNIK, J. 1994. Presidential Decision Making and the Political Use of Military Force. *International Studies Quarterly*, 38: 121–38.

——and WATERMAN, P. 1996. The Myth of the Diversionary Use of Force by American Presidents. *Political Research Quarterly*, 49: 573–90.

MONROE, A. D. 1979. Consistency between Public Preferences and National Policy Decision. *American Politics Quarterly*, 7: 3–19.

MOORE, W. H., and TARAR, A. 2010. Domestic–International Conflict Linkages. In *The International Studies Encyclopedia*, ed. R. A. Denemark, ii. Oxford: Wiley-Blackwell.

MUELLER, J. E. 1973. *War, Presidents, and Public Opinion*. New York: Wiley.

OSTROM, C. W., and JOB, B. L. 1986. The President and the Political Use of Force. *American Political Science Review*, 80: 541–66.

PAGE, B. I., and BOUTON, M. M. 2006. *The Foreign Policy Dis\*Connect: What Americans Want from Our Leaders but Don't Get*. Chicago: University of Chicago Press.

——and SHAPIRO, R. Y. 1992. *The Rational Public: Fifty Years of Trends in American Policy Preferences*. Chicago: University of Chicago Press.

PARKER, S. 1995. Toward an Understanding of "Rally" Effects: Public Opinion in the Persian Gulf War. *Public Opinion Quarterly*, 59: 526–46.

PARTELL, P. J., and GLENN, P. 1999. Audience Costs and Interstate Crises: An Empirical Assessment of Fearon's Model of Dispute Outcomes. *International Studies Quarterly*, 43: 389–405.

POWLICK, P. J., and KATZ, A. Z. 1998. Defining the American Public Opinion/Foreign Policy Nexus. *Mershon International Studies Review*, 42: 29–61.

QUANDT, W. B. 1986. The Electoral Cycle and the Conduct of Foreign Policy. *Political Science Quarterly*, 101: 825–37.

RISSE-KAPPEN, T. 1991. Public Opinion, Domestic Structure, and Foreign Policy in Liberal Democracies. *World Politics*, 43: 479–512.

ROCKMAN, B. A., and WATERMAN, R. W. (eds.) 2008. *Presidential Leadership: The Vortex of Power*. New York: Oxford University Press.

ROSELLE, L. 2010. Foreign Policy and Communication. In *The International Studies Encyclopedia*, ed. R. A. Denemark, iv. Oxford: Wiley-Blackwell.

ROSENAU, J. N. 1961. *Public Opinion and Foreign Policy: An Operational Formulation*. New York: Random House.

RUTHERFORD, P. 2004. *Weapons of Mass Persuasion: Marketing the War against Iraq*. Toronto: University of Toronto Press.

SCHULTZ, K. 2001. *Democracy and Coercive Diplomacy*. New York: Cambridge University Press.

SHAPIRO, R. Y., and JACOBS, L. R. 2002. Public Opinion, Foreign Policy, and Democracy: How Presidents Use Public Opinion. In *Navigating Public Opinion: Polls, Policy, and the Future of Democracy*, ed. J. Manza, F. L. Cook, and B. I. Page. New York: Oxford University Press.

SLANTCHEV, B. L. 2006. Politicians, the Media, and Domestic Audience Costs. *International Studies Quarterly*, 50: 445–77.

SNYDER, J., SHAPIRO, R. Y., and BLOCH-ELKON, Y. 2009. Free Hand Abroad, Divide and Rule at Home. *World Politics*, 61: 155–87.

SOBEL, R. 2001. *The Impact of Public Opinion on U.S. Foreign Policy Since Vietnam: Constraining the Colossus*. New York: Oxford University Press.

SOROKA, S. N. 2003. Media, Public Opinion, and Foreign Policy. *Harvard International Journal of Press/Politics*, 8: 27–48.

WESTERN, J. 2005. *Selling Intervention and War: The Presidency, the Media, and the American Public*. Baltimore: Johns Hopkins University Press.

WITTKOPF, E. R. 1990. *Faces of Internationalism*. Durham, NC: Duke University Press.

WOOD, B. D. 2009. *The Myth of Presidential Representation*. Cambridge: Cambridge University Press.

...............................................................................................

# CHAPTER 41

# PUBLIC OPINION, THE
# MEDIA, AND WAR

...............................................................................................

## JOHN MUELLER

AT least at the broadest level of analysis, the media do not seem to have much independent impact on public attitudes toward war. For the most part, the media are exactly that: the thing in the middle. As such they convey information, for better or worse, about what is going on and who is doing what in the war. But it is the information conveyed that chiefly matters, not the method or style of delivery.

Although the role of the media in influencing thought is often considered to be enormous, much research on the issue concludes that in the main, media reports simply reinforce or strengthen beliefs already held by its readers and viewers (Kinder and Sears 1985, 705–14; see also Zaller 1996, 17–18). This is likely to be especially true in the case of war.

War is humanity's least subtle phenomenon. Unlike many foreign policy events, it captures people's attention, and they generally have a pretty good idea about what goes on in it. They also seem to have a fairly good feeling for how to evaluate the stakes at risk in the armed conflict, and they generally seem capable of determining for themselves whether the value of the war is, or is not, worth the costs. They do need information about the war's purported stakes and about what is going on in the war. But it is the message that matters, not the media.

Indeed, people may not even need the formal media to make up their mind if they are able to collect the relevant information by other means. We have no poll data to confirm the conclusion, but it seems likely that the support of the Soviet people for their government's war in Afghanistan in the 1980s declined as Soviet casualties mounted, even though information about what was actually going on there came to them primarily through word of mouth, not through the controlled media.

The media, then, lie (or lurk) between the events they report and the customers they serve. In a free, market driven society, they must, of necessity, be sensitive to both, transmitting, rather than shaping, events and the actions of those who make the news and satisfying the demands of those who consume it. Thus, in the end, the events, event makers, and media consumers substantially call the shots. As Gladys and Kurt Lang observe in their study of press coverage of Watergate, "The main contribution of the media to moving opinion along was their extensive and full coverage of critical events" (Lang and Lang 1983, 304; see also Nacos 1990, 189; and the discussion about "audience effects" in Erbring, Goldenberg, and Miller 1980). The same, it appears, holds true for war. Thus, in an important text on public opinion and American foreign policy (not only on war), Ole Holsti scarcely ever finds cause even to mention the media (2004; see also Strobel 1997).

In this chapter I seek to determine who or what ultimately sets the policy agenda in the case of war and which sorts of facts are the ones that matter most in the process.

## FRAMING, PRIMING, AND AGENDA-SETTING

Some researchers have concluded that the media—television in particular—are important not so much because of the way they influence opinion one way or the other, but because of the important independent role they play in gate-keeping, in framing issues, and in setting or priming the agenda for public discussion. "Americans' views of their society and nation are powerfully shaped by the stories that appear on the evening news," they argue, and they find that "people who were shown network broadcasts edited to draw attention to a particular problem . . . cared more about it, believed that government should do more about it, reported stronger feelings about it, and were much more likely to identify it as one of the country's most important problems" (Iyengar and Kinder 1987, 112; see also Brody 1991, 111; Russett 1990, ch. 4; Page and Shapiro 1992, 339–48; Zaller 1992, ch. 12).

At least in the case of war, however, the notion that the media has a notable—and, in particular, lasting—independent impact in agenda-setting is called into question. To illustrate the process, the experience before, during, and after the Gulf War can be useful (Mueller 1994, 130–3), particularly because that war seems to have been special in the degree to which postmortems have been preoccupied with the role played by the media (see, for example, Smith 1992; MacArthur 1992; Taylor 1992; Lamay, Fitzsimon, and Sahadi 1991; Bennett and Paletz 1994).

Immediately after Saddam Hussein's Iraq invaded Kuwait on August 2, 1990, there appears to have been a certain wariness and confusion on the part of the public as to how to interpret the event. This evaporated a few days later when President George H. W. Bush announced troops would be sent to Saudi Arabia. At that point, the contest in the Gulf soared to the top of the political agenda, but this happened far more by the actions and statements of Bush and Saddam Hussein than by anything the media did. The media dutifully reported what was being said and done of course, and they commented extensively on it in columns and editorials, but it was the message that dominated the media, not the other way around. Moreover, when the attention of the public and the media was diverted in October 1990 to a bitter budget fight between the president and Congress, the Gulf crisis was brought back onto the agenda not by the media, but by the actions of the president when he escalated the troop commitment threateningly in November, and it was the ongoing debate between the president and his political opponents (and Saddam) that kept it there.

Once war began in January 1991, the media found that their consumers had a nearly insatiable appetite for news—especially for supportive news—and they serviced that demand assiduously, supplying their ravenous customers with huge amounts of information about the war. It proved to be the event that elevated CNN, perhaps the war's only unambiguous winner, to prominence. Serving the public mood, the coverage was characterized by boosterism, even sycophancy. One accounting finds that 95 percent of all television news sources who discussed the performance of the American military praised its effectiveness (Lichter 1992, 227). The editors at the *Los Angeles Times* war desk explicitly took their cue from the polls. Noting that the public seemed to support the war 80–20, they decided that it made sense for their coverage to be similarly weighted. That proportion would have been generous. According to one study, during the war only one out of 878 on-air sources who appeared on newscasts over the major television networks represented a national peace organization (Solomon 1991). And another found that newspapers during the first three weeks of the war devoted 2.7 percent of their space to peace activities while the comparable figure for television network news was 0.7 percent (LaMay, FitzSimon, and Sahadi 1991, 50; Lichter 1992, 224, 228).

This is hardly anything new. One of the innumerable myths about Vietnam is that the press was critical from the start. In fact, for the first years it largely conveyed the official Washington line and was rarely critical even by implication (see Hallin 1986, especially ch. 4; Page and Shapiro 1992, 226–34; Western 2005, 19).

Had the Gulf War gone badly, it is reasonable to suspect that the press would have become critical—though, as in the case of Vietnam, it would probably have followed, rather than led, political and public discontent. Without failure in the war, the media remained frozen in advocacy.

Then, immediately after the war ended in early March, the media sensed correctly that their customers' interest had shifted—without being led or primed or manipulated by much of anyone. Accordingly, the media followed them onto other issues—particularly the troubling state of the economy. A few months after the war, television network anchormen found themselves observing in a panel discussion on C-SPAN that, although they personally considered foreign affairs to be of major and increasing importance to the country, they were cutting their coverage of foreign events because their customers wanted them to concentrate on domestic issues.

While the Gulf events demonstrate in some important ways the ability of the president (if not of the media) to lead and to set the public agenda, the post-war experience suggests that even he is far from all-powerful in this respect. It was clearly to Bush's political advantage to keep the war and foreign policy as lively political issues during his reelection campaign of 1991–2, and he certainly tried to do that. But despite the advantage of his enormous post-war popularity (see Page and Shapiro 1992,

348–50), he found himself unable to divert attention to topics more congenial to him. The public had shifted its agenda and wanted now to focus on the sagging economy— something very much to the benefit of his challenger, Bill Clinton. Only occasionally did Clinton bring up foreign affairs issues—and when he did, his remarks often received little play in the media anyway.

A contrast can be made here with an observation by Shanto Iyengar and Adam Simon. Noting that, whereas 70 percent of the American public picked illegal drugs as the country's most important problem in 1989 but only 5 percent did so in February 1991 during the Gulf War, they suggest that the "most plausible explanation" for this change was that news coverage had shifted, not that the public was capable of shifting its attention on its own (Iyengar and Simon 1994, 168).

# THE FACTS THAT MATTER

The public not only substantially sets its own agenda, particularly in the case of war, but it can be quite selective, and often rather unpredictably so, about which facts about the war, as transmitted by the media, it is willing to embrace. For example, about the only time the public chose to pay much attention to the war in Bosnia, a venture much publicized and much agonized over by elites and by the media in the 1990s, was when an American airman was shot down behind enemy lines and when American troops where dispatched to the area to police the situation (Sobel 1998, 258–9; see also Western 2005, 264–5).

A somewhat similar phenomenon is found in the run-ups to the Gulf War of 1991 and to the Iraq War of 2003. In neither case was the president able, despite great effort, notably to increase public support for going to war (Mueller 1994, 29–34; Larson and Savych 2005, 136; Mueller 2008, 126–9). However, his ability to order troops into action, and thereby to commit the country's honor and destiny, was. With such moves he can make an issue important and convey a compelling sense of obligation as well as of entrapment and inevitability. As with public support for the military ventures in Korea in 1950, in Vietnam in 1965, in the Gulf in 1991, and in Afghanistan in 2001, the war in Iraq was quite notably supported by the public (and elites) as the troops were sent in as a "rally round the flag" effect took place (Mueller 1973, 208–13).

More generally, this phenomenon suggests that the president does not necessarily need the advance support of the public (or of the media or elites) to pull off a military venture. The public generally seems to be willing go along as troops are put in harm's way, but it reserves the right to object if, in its view, the cost of the war comes to outweigh its perceived value. Sometimes the public has apparently been quite support-ive of military action, as in the Second World War (after Pearl Harbor), in Korea (1950), in Vietnam (1965), in Panama (1989), in Somalia (1992–3), and in Afghanistan (2001). At other times, the public has been at best divided, as in Lebanon (1958, 1983), Grenada (1983), the Gulf War (1991), Haiti (1994), Bosnia (1995), Kosovo (1999), and the Iraq War (2003). In some cases, the ventures have been accomplished at acceptable cost, as in the Second World War, Panama, Lebanon (1958), Grenada, the Gulf War, Haiti, Bosnia, and Kosovo. In others, support dropped as costs grew, as in Korea, Vietnam, and Iraq (and, eventually, Afghanistan). And in others, the public's dismay at rising costs was met by abrupt early withdrawal, as in Lebanon in 1983 and in Somalia (Mueller 2008, 129; see also Larson and Savych 2005).

In the three cases since 1945 in which significant American casualties were suffered—Korea, Vietnam, and Iraq—support decreased as casualties—whether, variously, of draftees, volunteers, or reservists—were suffered. This suggests that Americans have a sense of, and react to, the war's increasing cost. However, they are not particularly good at estimating the actual number of casualties at any point in time, nor do the often fanciful numerical estimates correlate with war support (Mueller 1973, 62–3; Berinsky 2009, 73–84). The decline was steeper in the early stages of the war as reluctant approvers were rather quickly alienated, and the erosion slowed as support progressively became reduced to the harder-core (Mueller 2008, 132–7).

However, this does not mean the wars were equally supported as the costs accrued. Specifically, it is clear the public places a far lower value on the stakes in Iraq than it did in the earlier anti-Communist wars: for example, in 2005 the percentage finding Iraq to have been a mistake, when around 1,500 Americans had been killed, was about the same as in Vietnam at the time of the 1968 Tet Offensive, when about 20,000 had perished (Mueller 2005, 45). Casualty for casualty, support dropped off far more quickly in the Iraq War than in either of the earlier two wars. It is difficult to see why, or how, media effects could account for this key phenomenon. Nor is it likely explained by changes in cost tolerance: Americans expressed great willingness to expend lives to go after al-Qaeda in Afghanistan in the wake of the 9/11 attack.

In all this, what chiefly matters for public opinion is American losses, not those of the people defended. For example, official estimates at the end of the 1991 Gulf War that 100,000 Iraqis had been killed scarcely dampened enthusiasm at the victory and "welcome home" parades for returning troops. And support for the wars in Korea and Vietnam derived from the fact that people held those conflicts to be vital to confront the Communist threat, not to defend the South Koreans or the South Vietnamese (Mueller 1973, 44, 48–9, 58, 100–1). This public preference shows up in news coverage which routinely reports and tallies American losses far more fully and systematically than those suffered by foreigners.

The issue about which facts matter can be further assessed by an examination of Figure 41.1, which displays the trend established by a key poll question that can be used to measure support for the Iraq War after its outset in 2003. As it demonstrates, certain events seem to have boosted or depressed support within the general factual fabric of the rally rise and the subsequent erosion of support as casualties mounted. In all cases, however, event-driven change proved to be temporary: soon after each boost or drop, support levels returned roughly to their previous level and then resumed their erosion if further American casualties were registered.

Thus, support for the war dropped at the time of Hurricane Katrina in 2005 as Americans were led to wonder about the nation's priorities, but this decline was more

In fact, the most significant public opinion development in this war seems to owe virtually nothing *either* to the media *or* to opinion leadership by party leaders: the creation of a massive partisan division on the war. The public, or much of it, has viewed war through partisan lenses (Mueller 1973, 116–22; Zaller 1992; Berinsky 2009, ch. 5). However, as Gary Jacobson has documented, the partisan split for the Iraq War of 2003 was considerably greater than for any military action over the last half century (2007, 131–8). An interesting comparison can be made with the 1991 Gulf War. In the run-up to each, Democrats were predictably less likely to support the prospective wars than were Republicans, but what is surprising is that the partisan gap was *far* wider in the 2003 case than in the 1991 one even though Democratic leaders in Congress stood in strong opposition to going to the earlier war, while in the later one they mostly remained silent or were even generally supportive of the effort (Jacobson 2007, 133, 136). That is, partisan elites disagreed far more in the run-up to the earlier war, but partisan public opinion differences were far greater in the later one. The effect continued during the Iraq War itself as the Democratic base jerked a reluctant party leadership toward an anti-war stance.

# THE SPECIAL IMPACT, IF ANY, OF VISUAL INFORMATION

Insofar as the erosion of support in wars is related to casualties, the phenomenon is caused by the fact of cumulating combat deaths. Pictures in the media of dead bodies, body bags, or flag-draped coffins are not necessary. Somehow, the notion that support declines with casualties became expressed as "support drops when they start seeing the body bags," and this vivid expression apparently led, in turn, to the naive notion that for people to become disaffected they actually need to *see* the body bags. In consequence, perhaps, the military in the Iraq War of 2003 enterprisingly tried to keep pictures of body bags and flag-draped coffins out of the media presumably in the hope that this would somehow arrest the decline of support.

To insist on the importance of pictures is to suggest that people are so unimaginative that they only react when they see something visualized. Yet, Americans were outraged at the Pearl Harbor attack weeks—or even months—before they saw pictures of the event (Mueller 1995, 98–9). They hardly needed visual stimuli. Moreover, the Vietnam War was not noticeably more unpopular than the Korean War for the period in which the wars were comparable in American casualties, despite the fact that the later war is often seen to be a "television war" while the earlier was fought during the medium's infancy (Mueller 1973, 167; see also Mandelbaum 1981; Lichty 1984; Hallin 1986; Strobel 1997).

During the Gulf War of 1991, one reporter observed that "You can be certain that if saturation bombing of the Iraqi capital becomes an American tactic, stomach-churning footage of bombed-out schools and hospitals will find their way on to American screens" (quoted in Taylor 1992, 11). But the immunity the American public showed to the images of a bombed air-raid shelter in Baghdad and of the war's much publicized "highway of death" suggests there was little effect. The "highway of death" pictures do seem to have influenced American policy by inspiring concerns in the administration about how the visuals might affect public opinion. But these concerns were not justified: it appears that the public was scarcely moved by these pictures (Mueller 1994, 122).

Relatedly, during the Second World War an experiment was made to determine whether "realistic" war pictures would hurt morale. It found that those who were exposed to such pictures were not any more or less likely to support the war than an unexposed control group. Those exposed, however, did become more favorable to showing people realistic war pictures (National Opinion Research Center 1944). Moreover, efforts of the military to use vivid propaganda films during that war to indoctrinate new draftees were ineffective (Kinder and Sears 1985, 706).

## THE ROLE OF THE MEDIA: PLACING ITEMS ON THE SHELF

One view in all this would be to see the media as purveyors or entrepreneurs of tantalizing information. They report on a wide variety of topics and they are constantly seeking to turn people on—and, accordingly, to boost sales. For example, the editors of *Time* or *Newsweek* would be quite happy if every one of their cover stories became a hot button item. Not all, however, do so.

An interesting example of the phenomenon arises in the case of the Ethiopian famine that received such big play and was so affecting in the mid-1980s. This is often taken to have been a media-generated issue because it was only after it received prominent coverage in the media that the issue entered the public's agenda. But a study by Christopher Bosso (1989) suggests a different interpretation. At first the media were reluctant to cover the issue at all because they reckoned this African famine (like other ones) to be a dog-bites-man story. Moreover, the story had received some play, and it had stirred little response, thus suggesting that the customers were not interested. However, going against the consensus, NBC television decided to do a three day sequence on the story in October 1984. This inspired a huge public response, whereupon NBC gave it extensive follow-up coverage and its television and print competitors scrambled to get on the bandwagon, deluging their customers with information that, to their surprise, was actually in demand.

There is a sense, of course, in which it could be said that NBC led opinion and put the issue on the public's agenda and that the media "magnified" the event. But the network is *constantly* doing three-day stories, and this one just happened to catch on. It seems more accurate to say NBC put the issue on the *shelf*—alongside a great many others—and that it was the public that put it on the agenda and demanded the magnification. Ironically, Bosso's study is published in a book titled *Manipulating Public Opinion: Essays on Public Opinion as a Dependent Variable*. It seems clear, however, that in the case he documents, it was the media that was the dependent variable. In a very important sense, the public was manipulating the media, not the other way around.

In the case of the Gulf War of 1991, as noted earlier, the agenda does seem to have been set far more by the public (and by the dramatic events themselves) than by the media. Journalists and editors reported what was going on, and they correctly doped out that their public wanted more news about events in the Gulf. So instructed, they supplied that need, but they did not invent it, nor did they invent the issues that, for a while, so engrossed the public. Then, when the customers tired of the issue in the wake of the successful war, the media dutifully shifted their attention, despite the strenuous efforts of the previously influential President to keep the war euphoria and glow alive. The message and the customer dominated, even intimidated, the medium.

The caprice of the customer also explains a phenomenon often taken to be a great failing of the media: the lack of follow-up. Thus, in a classic book analyzing coverage of the 1968 Tet Offensive in Vietnam, Peter Braestrup takes the press to task not so much for misreporting the offensive itself as for failing to follow up, for neglecting to reassess the event in its aftermath when more and fuller information became available. Instead, the press simply let its often erroneous first impressions become the established story. There were some notable exceptions, but these were rare and they lacked resonance with the public—which, of course, explains their rarity (Braestrup 1983, ch. 13).

Something similar can be said for the Gulf War of 1991. It generated huge interest within the public during its approach and execution: indeed, a few days before the war began, 22 percent of the public said they thought about the crisis in the Gulf every few minutes and another 27 percent said they did so at least once an hour, while only 10 percent were so blasé as to claim they thought about it at most once a day (Mueller 1994, 214). However, that interest abruptly evaporated at its end, as discussed above, and, stimulated by the demands of its consumers, the once war-obsessed media quickly moved on to the next issue. The author of a book published a full year after the war observes that, "the complete story of why and how [the war] happened has gone largely untold" (US News and World Report 1992, p. vii), even as John Simpson of the BBC mused, "not many people seem interested in finding out what really happened" (1991, p. xiv). If their readers and viewers lose interest, the media will, perforce, follow suit.

## DELIBERATION, REASON, AND CAPRICE

Ultimately, democracy is based on the notion that "the people shall judge." Various "opinion leaders," including those in the media, bring out ideas and perspectives and try to sell them to the public (sometimes even by "pandering"). The public then "judges"—chooses which of the many issues before it are worthy of its attention and which of these it is willing to embrace.

The process is perhaps less one of "deliberation" than one in which reason is blended with a considerable amount of caprice, and it is distinctly inexact in part because, far from being the attentive, if unpolished, policy wonks dreamed of in so many theories about democracy, real people in real democracies often display a lack of political interest and knowledge that approaches the monumental (Mueller 1999, 183–5; Gans 1979, 226). However, as much of this discussion has suggested, people often seem quite capable of making up their minds without much reliance either on the media or on "opinion leaders" (Page and Shapiro 1992; Mueller 2002, 149–57).

As anyone who has spent time in a newsroom knows well, they are inhabited by a class of people, editors, who spend their lives assessing stories and potential stories and guessing whether their customers will ignore the story, whether the story has a lasting power of a day or so, or whether it is likely to enjoy a longer run. Every reporter has gone in with a seemingly interesting story or angle only to be greeted with the ultimate put-down: "Nah. Nobody's interested in that." Whether editors really know what they are doing in gaging their customers' likely response to a story would be an area worth investigating. One would probably want to remove from consideration those stories that are so obviously big that no predictive skills are necessary: the sudden death of Princess Diana or of pop star Michael Jackson, for example. But even with that, editors perhaps do, on balance, get it right. And, of course, if they do guess wrong, they can quickly abandon a story that doesn't stir interest while jumping on those that do.

This does not mean stories are necessarily composed solely with the market in mind—something, actually, that would be unwise because of the difficulty of predicting what consumers of the news will actually be interested in. In fact, in a study about how journalists decide what is news, Herbert Gans finds that they do not "directly take the audience into account when selecting and producing stories," but rather that they assume "what interested them would interest the audience" (Gans 1979, 229–30). Journalist Daniel Gardner substantially agrees. Reporters, editors, and producers do not calculate their stories in order "to boost revenues and please their corporate masters," he concludes. Rather, "they do it because information that grabs and holds readers grabs and holds reporters. They do it because they are human." A story is likely to be "newsworthy" if it includes "novelty, conflict, impact, and that beguiling and amorphous stuff known as human interest" (Gardner 2008, 167–8). But "human interest" means that, for the story to succeed, it must interest humans.

Then, once a story that is deemed (or calculated) to be likely to interest humans (that is, consumers) is put on the shelf, the media, as in the Ethiopia case, follow up on those items that stimulate their customers' interest. If they give an issue big play, it may arrest attention for a while. This momentary arresting of attention can be simulated in experiments, but, as suggested at the outset, the key issue is not momentary diversion, but whether the issue has legs: whether it actually *takes* (see also Zaller 1994, 201). Research in this area should examine not momentary rises in attention and interest, but ones that last.

And even more important, it is vital to avoid selection bias in which one focuses on the issues that do catch on after the media gives them play while neglecting the huge number of issues initially given equal play that never generate much of a stir at all. In his *Selling Intervention and War* John Western has looked at a variety of instances in which the people attempting to do the selling failed as well as ones in which they were successful. He repeatedly finds that the public has often "resisted persuasion," and that sales pitches work when the arguments made were ones "the public was willing to accept," when they "strike a chord" or "resonate" with the public (2005, 5, 20–1, 179, 229).

No one would seriously argue that the public paid so much attention to the deaths of Jackson and Diana because of extensive media coverage—the causal direction was clearly the opposite. Do the murders at Fort Hood by a deranged Muslim psychiatrist in 2009 capture infinitely less attention than the O. J. Simpson murders because the media is gate keeping or servicing its customers? Was there so little coverage of the Cambodian genocide of 1975–9 because the public at the time did not want to be reminded of the recently ended war in Vietnam, or because the media decided not to prime or frame (Mueller 2002, 170)? Why, despite considerable media coverage and impassioned advocacy by reporters, was so little interest roused in the public about the war in Bosnia in the early 1990s? Why did the public react to the famine in Ethiopia, but not to the far greater humanitarian disaster that has transpired in the eastern Congo since 1997? Why is the sex life of Madonna or Britney Spears or Tiger Woods of more interest than that of figures of more historic importance, or even of other celebrities? Why do the often quite colorful terrorist plots rolled up in the United States over the years since 9/11 generate only a few days of coverage? Also of research interest would be a systematic examination of the process by which the 2003 Iraq War generated partisan division far in excess of what would be expected from media and partisan elite effects (Jacobson 2010).

Like the media, public relations people are focused on predicting what people will be interested in, and they too are at the mercy of the whims and caprices of those they are seeking to "manipulate." For example, Richard Reeves's book *President Kennedy* came out in 1993. Seeking to imagine a hook for promoting the book, the publisher decided to try to link the Kennedy experience to that of Bill Clinton, an attractive, newsworthy Kennedy admirer who was then in his first year as president. As it happened, the book did come out at a commercially propitious time, but that had nothing to do with Clinton. The year 1993 just happened to be the thirtieth anniversary of Kennedy's assassination and, for some (or no?) reason, this stirred a flurry of interest that helped Reeves's book sales considerably. By contrast, there was no comparable flurry on the fortieth anniversary. Who knew? Who knows?

Promoters and "opinion leaders" have their hands full, and characteristically they fail much more often than they succeed. Indeed, if extensive purposeful promotion could guarantee acceptance, we'd all be driving Edsels. Or, put another way, anyone who could accurately and persistently predict public tastes and whims would not be writing about it, but would move to Wall Street to become in very short order the richest person on the planet.

# REFERENCES

BENNETT, W. L., and PALETZ, D. L. (eds.) 1994. *Taken by Storm: The Media, Public Opinion, and U.S. Foreign Policy in the Gulf War*. Chicago: University of Chicago Press.

BERINSKY, A. J. 2009. *In Time of War: Understanding American Public Opinion from World War II to Iraq*. Chicago: University of Chicago Press.

BOSSO, C. 1989. Setting the Agenda: Mass Media and the Discovery of Famine in Ethiopia. In *Manipulating Public Opinion: Essays on Public Opinion as a Dependent Variable*, ed. M. Margolis and G. A. Mauser. Pacific Grove, CA: Brooks, Cole.

BRAESTRUP, P. 1983. *Big Story: How the American Press and Television Reported and Interpreted the Crisis of Tet 1968 in Vietnam and Washington*. New Haven: Yale University Press.

BRODY, R. A. 1991. *Assessing the President: The Media, Elite Opinion, and Public Support*. Stanford, CA: Stanford University Press.

EDWARDS, G. C., III. 2003. *On Deaf Ears: The Limits of the Bully Pulpit*. New Haven: Yale University Press.

ERBRING, L., GOLDENBERG, E. N., and MILLER, A. H. 1980. Front-Page News and Real-World Cues: A New Look at Agenda-Setting by the Media. *American Journal of Political Science*, 24/1: 16–49.

GANS, H. J. 1979. *Deciding What's News*. New York: Pantheon.

GARDNER, D. 2008. *The Science of Fear*. New York: Dutton.

GARTNER, S. S. 2008. The Multiple Effects of Casualties on Public Support for War: An Experimental Approach. *American Political Science Review*, 102/1 (Feb.), 95–106.

GELPI, C., FEAVER, P. D., and REIFLER, J. 2009. *Paying the Human Costs of War: American Public Opinion and Casualties in Military Conflicts*. Princeton: Princeton University Press.

HALLIN, D. C. 1986. *The Uncensored War: The Media and Vietnam*. New York: Oxford University Press.

HOLSTI, O. R. 2004. *Public Opinion and American Foreign Policy*. Ann Arbor: University of Michigan Press.

IYENGAR, S., and KINDER, D. R. 1987. *News that Matters: Television and American Opinion*. Chicago: University of Chicago Press.

—— and SIMON, A. 1994. News Coverage of the Gulf Crisis and Public Opinion. In *Taken by Storm: The Media, Public Opinion, and U.S. Foreign Policy in the Gulf War*, ed. W. L. Bennett and D. L. Paletz. Chicago: University of Chicago Press.

JACOBSON, G. C. 2007. *A Divider, Not a Uniter: George W. Bush and the American People*. New York: Pearson.

—— 2010. Perception, Memory, and the Partisan Polarization of Opinion on the Iraq War. *Political Science Quarterly*, 125/1: 31–56.

KINDER, D. R., and SEARS, D. O. 1985. Public Opinion and Political Action. In *Handbook of Social Psychology*, iii, ed. G. Lindzey and E. Aronson. New York: Random House.

# CHAPTER 42

......................................................................................................

# THE MEDIA, PUBLIC
# OPINION, AND TERRORISM

......................................................................................................

BRIGITTE L. NACOS
YAELI BLOCH-ELKON

THE terrorists who attacked ten different sites in Mumbai, India, in late November 2008 killing 173 people and injuring more than 300 communicated with their operation center somewhere in Pakistan via email and satellite telephone. At one point, hostage holders in the Oberoi Hotel received a phone call from two of their handlers. "Brother, Abdul. The media is comparing your action to 9/11," one of the callers said. "Everything is being recorded by the media," added the other caller.[1] Indeed, the masterminds of the operation had reason to rejoice: the sixty-hour nightmare and its aftermath dominated the local, regional, and international news and sent shock waves around the globe. If publicity is the oxygen or lifeblood of terrorism, as has been argued by former British prime minister Margaret Thatcher and others (Graham 1986, 76; O'Sullivan 1986, 69; Nacos 1994, 10), the local, regional, and global media's attention to the Mumbai operation was akin to providing concentrated oxygen or massive blood transfusions to strengthen the perpetrators of this kind of political violence.[2]

The same would apply to a host of earlier terrorist spectaculars—although the proliferation of global TV networks, the emergence of the Internet, and other advances in communication technology increased the availability of far-reaching carriers of terrorist publicity and propaganda. When the Palestinian Black September terrorists attacked members of Israel's national team at the 1972 Olympic Games in Munich, they aimed at news coverage by the international media. As one Palestinian explained the

---

[1] The transcript of several phone conversations was made available online by the *New York Times* and is available at <http://graphics8.nytimes.com/packages/pdf/nyregion/city_room/20090109_mumbaitranscripts.pdf>, accessed Jan. 14, 2009.

[2] Terrorism is defined here as violence deliberately carried out by non-state actors against civilians or non-combatants for political ends.

necessity of staging shocking acts of political violence, "We would throw roses if it would work" (Schlagheck 1988, 69). Before the Oklahoma City bomber Timothy McVeigh selected the Alfred P. Murrah Federal Building as the target for his 1995 truck bombing, he made sure that there was "plenty of open space around it, to allow for the best possible news photos and television footage" (Michel and Herbeck 2001, 169). As he awaited his execution on death row, he was convinced that "the Oklahoma City blast was heard around the world" (Michel and Herbeck 2001, 382). And following the attacks of September 11, 2001 (9/11), Osama bin Laden gloated that "these young men [the hijackers] said in deeds, in New York and Washington, speeches that over-shadowed other speeches made everywhere else in the world. The speeches are understood by both Arabs and non-Arabs—even Chinese" (Nacos 2007, 49).

Thus the al-Qaeda leader expressed what Black September terrorists, the Oklahoma City bomber, members of the Mumbai terror operation, and terrorists at all times believe and act upon, namely, that terrorism is "propaganda by the deed" or "propaganda of the deed" as nineteenth-century anarchists claimed. More pointedly, after comparing the publicity success of Black September's attack on Israeli athletes during the 1972 Olympic Games in Munich and the 9/11 strikes, Abu Ubeid al-Qurashi, a leading al-Qaeda operative, boasted that "September 11 was an even greater propaganda coup. It may be said that it broke a record in propaganda dissemination" (Rubin and Rubin 2002, 274).

Students of terrorist violence and communication concluded that for those who carry out terrorist attacks, "the immediate victim is merely instrumental, the skin of a drum beaten to achieve a calculated impact on a wider audience" (Schmid and De Graaf 1982, 14). Recent studies detailed the sophisticated communication strategies of two very different organizations, the Red Army Faction (Elter 2008) and al-Qaeda (Corman and Schiefelbein 2006), strengthening the argument that regardless of their grievances, goals, size, and secular or religious convictions, literally all terrorist groups strive to maximize their propaganda efforts (O'Sullivan 1986; Nacos 1994, 2007; Richardson 2006). As Osama bin Laden wrote in a letter to Taliban leader Mullah Muhammad Omar, "It is obvious that the media war in this century is one of the strongest methods; in fact, its ratio may reach 90% of the total preparation for the battles."[3]

The question, then, is whether and to what extent terrorists succeed in exploiting the mass media for their media-centered publicity goals and how their various target audiences react. This chapter focuses on the links between terrorism, media, and public opinion; it will also deal—albeit to a lesser extent—with counterterrorism, as responses to terrorism figure into terrorists' and governments' propaganda and demagoguery schemes and how the media accommodate them. We review and evaluate relevant literature of various research strains in the following four categories: weapon of choice in a changing media landscape; media as agents of copy-cat terrorism; terrorism as theater: different publics and reactions; and media events, demagoguery, and ritual communications.

---

[3] Combating Terrorism Center, Document No. AFGP-2002-6000321.

# WEAPON OF CHOICE IN A CHANGING
# MEDIA LANDSCAPE

Each major act of terrorism and, in fact, even relatively minor and failed terrorist deeds result in news coverage. Louise Richardson concluded that "Publicity has always been a central objective of terrorism" and that "terrorists have been extremely successful in gaining publicity" (2006, 94). While this does not mean that the press is sympathetic to terrorists, their methods, and objectives, it is nevertheless true that terrorist strikes provide what the contemporary news media crave most: sensation, drama, shock, and tragedy suited to be packaged as gripping human-interest narratives. As a result, terrorists get precisely what they want: massive publicity and the opportunity to showcase their ability to strike against even the strongest of nation states. Media organizations are rewarded as well in that they energize their competition for audience size and circulation—and thus for the all-important advertising dollar. As one scholar put it, contemporary television "is embedded within commercial logics and structures of dominance that often implicates it in times of conflict" and struggles with the "professional raison d'être of journalism itself" (Cottle 2006, 22). In the coverage of terrorism, commercial imperatives seem to triumph over journalism ethics. Thus, while terrorists and news organizations are not loving bedfellows, "they are more like partners in a marriage of convenience" (Nacos 2007, 107).

Many scholars agree that terrorists and media organizations feed off each other. According to Walter Laqueur, "the media are the terrorist's best friend. The terrorist act is nothing; publicity is all" (Laqueur 1976). And, as Margaret Thatcher's earlier-mentioned oxygen metaphor reveals, the terrorist–media symbiosis argument is popular among decision-makers who must respond to terrorism. In the extreme, there is the notion that terrorism would cease if the media would not cover such events. Others see a variety of more complex "relational modes" that reveal "weaknesses and failings" in the way journalists report terrorism but deem it "entirely improper to make a scapegoat of them, or to lay the blame for terrorism at their feet" (Wieviorka 1993, 43–6, 51).

While the links between and the implications of terrorism, media, and communication were studied well before the more recent catastrophic terrorist attacks, most of the earlier works fall into the anecdotal genre focusing on some limited aspects of media reporting, publicity-savvy terrorists, emergency responders' handling of public information, and legal issues, such as censorship (Martin 1990; Bassiouni 1981; Miller 1982; Kupperman and Kamen 1989). Several excellent studies examined the various features of terrorism coverage comprehensively but focused mostly on domestic terrorism and to a lesser extent on the transnational variety (Schmid and De Graaf 1982; Schlesinger, Murdock, and Elliott 1984; Paletz and Schmid 1992; Alali and Eke 1991). There were also systematic content analyses of terrorism news that produced convincing evidence of the media's tendency to over-cover terrorist incidents at the expense of other equally important, or more important, news (Altheide 1982, 1987; Nimmo and Combs 1985;

Nacos 1994; Weimann and Winn 1994). One study found that from 1981 through 1986 ABC News, CBS News, and NBC News together aired more than 2,000 television stories about terrorism, an average of eleven a month per network. During this period "more stories were broadcast on terrorism than on poverty, unemployment, racial inequality, and crime combined" (Iyengar 1991, 27).

In the early 1990s, two experts in the field predicted that is was "only a matter of time before journalists will temper their enthusiasm at the theatrical prospects of terrorism coverage with an enhanced sensitivity to the impact of their reporting" (Weimann and Winn 1994, 279). Such a turnaround did not happen. On the contrary, the sheer volume of news about 9/11 and subsequent terrorism spectaculars in the West and around the world was unprecedented, as many studies documented. Summarizing this trend based on their research, Andrew Hoskins and Ben O'Loughlin characterized the mass media as "terrorists' weapon of choice" (2007, p. x).

When terrorists struck in the 1970s and 1980s, they often claimed responsibility for their deeds and communicated their motives to news organizations. More recently, the perpetrators of major terrorist attacks have more often failed to make such public claims. Some experts in the field concluded, therefore, that a new "terrorism of expression" or "expressive terrorism" had emerged which did not require publicity. According to Avishai Margalit, these terrorists "lack clearly defined political ends" but give vent to "rage against state power and to feelings of revenge. They want to inflict the greatest amount of pain on their targets" (1995, 19). Since by definition all terrorists have political goals, this explanation does not hold water. Another explanation is that governments have become tougher and increased international cooperation in reaction to terrorism so that terrorists would take greater risks if they made public claims (Hoffman 1997, 1–6).

Lost in this debate is that claims are not always made or reported immediately after terrorist strikes and therefore may be missed by organizations and individuals who search open sources for their data about terrorist incidents. Thus, after the first World Trade Center bombing in 1993 the *New York Times* received a typewritten letter that claimed responsibility and explained the motives for the strike. But the *Times* handed the letter over to the FBI and published its content a month later, after agents had found the typewriter on which it had been written by one of the plotters. Also, instead of claiming responsibility for their attacks, terrorists leave clues that reveal their motives. Timothy McVeigh, for example, did not contact news organizations to claim responsibility for the Oklahoma City bombing. But by detonating the destructive truck bomb on the second anniversary of the FBI's and other federal agents' ill-fated actions against a heavily armed group of religious extremists, the Branch Davidians, in Waco, Texas, he ensured that the media would figure out his motive—revenge for Waco. Following the simultaneous bombings of the US embassies in Kenya and Tanzania in August 1998, Osama bin Laden was covered as the likely architect of these terrorist strikes although there was no immediate claim of responsibility. However, two months earlier the Saudi exile had told journalists that Americans were easy targets and that this would be obvious in a very short time.

*New York Times* columnist Thomas Friedman suggested that bin Laden transcends the scope of a terrorist because of his geopolitical aspirations and because he and al-Qaeda employ "violence not to grab headlines but to kill as many Americans as possible" (Friedman 2002). An al-Qaeda training manual revealed otherwise in that it instructed recruits to target sentimental landmarks, such as the Statue of Liberty, Big Ben, and the Eiffel Tower because their destruction would generate intense publicity. Other documents captured in Afghanistan, Iraq, and elsewhere, as well as the steady flow of communications from al-Qaeda and like-minded groups, revealed that "Jihadis pursue these [communication] strategies using sophisticated, modern methods of communication and public relations. They segment audiences and apply some of the same PR techniques used by large corporations... They do so using a variety of sophisticated means, including traditional mass media and new media channels" (Corman and Schiefelbein 2006, 2). So much for the irrelevance of contemporary terrorists' need for publicity.

Following the Oklahoma City bombing and the nerve gas attack in the Tokyo subway system, both in 1995, policymakers, terrorism scholars, and the media began to proclaim the emergence of a "new terrorism" carried out by new types of terrorist groups and networks (Lesser 1999, 2; Hoffman 1999, 9; S. Simon and Benjamin 2001, 5–6; Laqueur 2003, 9). But others questioned and rejected the idea of a fundamentally different kind of terrorism (Rose 1999; Ferguson 2001; Spencer 2006). Martha Crenshaw concluded that "Differences among groups and differences in patterns of terrorism over time do exist, but many of these shifts are due to a changing environment, largely associated with what is termed globalization" (2006, 6).

We suggest that the environment in which terrorists in the twenty-first century operate has changed far more dramatically than terrorism itself. The advances in, and growth of, global media and communication technology in particular offer transnational and domestic terrorists significantly more, and more effective, opportunities to magnify their "propaganda of the deed." Consider that during the 1990s Western television and radio networks, wire services, and leading print outlets still dominated the global media market. At that time, bin Laden had no choice but to give interviews to Western reporters to get his messages across to friends and foes. Thus, his fatwas, or religious edicts, of 1996 and 1998 that declared war against the United States, Western crusaders, Israel, and Zionists were first published by the London-based newspaper Al-Quds al-Arabi. Since the first Arab global TV network, al-Jazeera, emerged as the first non-Western global television network at the beginning of the war in Afghanistan in late 2001, al-Qaeda has no longer depended on direct contact with the Western press; instead, the group's leaders have made videotapes and other communications available to the Arab network. From there, these propaganda statements have been picked up by news media around the world. Most of all, the Internet allows contemporary terrorists to circumvent media outside their control to post their propaganda tracts on their own websites or those of friendly organizations and individuals. As Bruce Klopfenstein noted, when they relied on the old broadcast and print media in the past, terrorists could not control "mediated communication," but now, "for the first time in history, terrorists can take whatever message and images they decide straight to the online world, and that world is of global reach" (2006, 108).

Today's terrorists can perpetrate violence and report their deeds themselves. This was practiced in Pakistan, Iraq, and Saudi Arabia, when terrorists beheaded their hostages, filmed the scenes, and posted videotapes of the brutal killings on Internet sites. Thus, terrorists were the source and the reporters of terrifying news; the traditional media were left to report on terrorists' own news productions and spread the terrorist propaganda masquerading as news.

In essence, then, there is nothing new when it comes to terrorists' emphasis on publicity and propaganda except for the enhanced opportunities brought about by the proliferation of global media and communication networks.

## MEDIA AS AGENTS OF COPY-CAT TERRORISM

In the late 1960s and early 1970s Palestinian terrorists staged a number of spectacular hijackings of commercial airliners, exploited the often prolonged hostage situations to win massive news coverage of their political grievances, and seemed to inspire other groups to carry out hijackings and take hostages. Ever since, contagion theories have been forwarded and rejected with respect to terrorism–media links. While some scholars deny such relationships (Picard 1986; Schlesinger, Murdock, and Elliott 1984), the notion of mass-mediated contagion seems commonsensical and is supported by both anecdotal accounts and systematic research (Schmid and De Graaf 1982; Weimann and Winn 1994).

More than twenty years ago Robert G. Picard attacked the news-as-contagion theory as "backed by dubious science" and argued, "The literature implicating the media as responsible for the contagion of terrorist violence has grown rapidly, but, under scrutiny, it appears to contain no credible supporting evidence and fails to establish a cause–effect relationship" (Picard 1986, 1). He cited the minimal press effect findings of social scientists in the 1940s and 1950s in support of his rejection of the media contagion theory (Picard 1991, 55–6). What he failed to mention was that ample and far from "dubious" research, starting in the 1960s, found far stronger media effects on audiences (most notably with respect to agenda-setting, framing, and priming) than the minimal effect school. Writing with Northern Ireland and domestic terrorism in mind, Schlesinger, Murdock, and Elliott (1984), too, rejected the idea that the media are spreading the virus of political violence as ignoring the intelligence and good judgment of news consumers and especially television audiences.

However, based on their quantitative analysis of media reporting (or non-reporting) of terrorist incidents and subsequent terrorist strikes of the same type (e.g., hijackings, kidnappings) Gabriel Weimann and Conrad Winn concluded that their data "yielded considerable evidence of a contagion effect wrought by coverage." More specifically, these scholars found that "television coverage was associated with a shortened lag time to emulation in the case of kidnapping, attacks on installations, hijackings, bombings, and assassinations" (1994, 277).

contagion is possible at two levels, and can happen in two ways. On one level a group might copy a particular terrorist technique, and on another level a group might copy a general terrorist strategy. Either of these might happen directly or indirectly. All these forms of contagion take place. The primary form, however, is the adoption of a general terrorist strategy without direct contact. All other forms of contagion are secondary to this.    (2007, 102)

The most recent, most lethal, and geographically most diffused inspirational virus originated with Afghan mujahidin fighting Soviet occupiers in the 1980s and, most importantly, with the establishment of al-Qaeda and its rapidly expanding terrorism network. It is hardly surprising that the contagion effect tends to be far stronger among those individuals and groups that share the cultural and religious background of organizations and leaders with inspirational ideologies. Whereas kinship and friend-ship brought the members of the al-Qaeda central organization together (Sageman 2004), the mighty "Afghan wave" that reached literally all continents in the post-9/11 years is now mostly driven by (mass-mediated) inspirational contagion (Sedgwick 2007, 106–7). As Marc Sageman noted, "The present threat has evolved from a structured group of al Qaeda masterminds, controlling vast resources and issuing commands, to a multitude of informal local groups trying to emulate their predecessors by conceiving and executing operations from the bottom up" (2008, p. vii). Without the global media and communication environment, the inspirational diffusion of terrorist ideology would not be as strong as it is in the twenty-first century.

# TERRORISM AS THEATER: DIFFERENT PUBLICS AND REACTIONS

As Brian Jenkins noted, "Terrorism is aimed at the people watching, not at the actual victim. Terrorism is theater" (1990, 34). While the theater metaphor remains instruc-tive, it has been displaced by that of a global reality hit show that is seen by record audiences on television and computer screens. In short, contemporary terrorists can reach huge audiences that their predecessors could only dream of. Moreover, today's terrorists have the communication means to direct the same messages to people around the world or "segment audiences and adapt their message to the [particular] audience" they want to reach (Corman and Schiefelbein 2006). The question is how various publics react to the "propaganda of the deed," threats of further terror attacks, and other communications by terrorists. Moreover, one wants to know whether public reactions further terrorists' media-centered objectives, namely, to get the attention of foes and friends and to intimidate the targets of their violence; to publicize their motives and the reasons for their determination to fight for what they proclaim to be just causes; and to win or increase sympathy and support among those in whose interest they claim to act.

## Attention and Intimidation

Three decades ago, a student of terrorism suggested that over time the news value of terrorism diminishes as a result of frequent and repetitious incidents and reporting (Jenkins 1981, 7). That seems no longer the case in the age of catastrophic terrorism. Literally all Americans followed the news of the 9/11 attacks and terrorism in general to one degree or another, hour after hour, day after day. This universal interest did not diminish quickly. Oral and written reports, combined with mass-mediated images of the burning and collapsing twin towers in New York and the partially destroyed Pentagon outside of Washington, triggered American's concerns of future terror attacks and fears that they or their families could become victims of terrorism (Huddy, Feldman, Taber, and Lahav 2005; Nacos, Bloch-Elkon, and Shapiro 2007). As time went by, these worries declined but there were frequent escalations in reaction to reports about new threats from al-Qaeda, major terrorist strikes abroad, foiled plots, and terror alerts by the Bush administration. The heightened public attention to and awareness and salience of terrorism precedes the era of catastrophic violence of this sort, applies to domestic and transnational terrorism, and is not specific to the United States (Downes-Le Guin and Hoffman 1993; Josiger 2006).

Since the news media tend to be the most likely source of information about terrorism and often the most trusted one as well (Lemyre, Rutner, Lee, and Krewski 2006), one wonders whether and to what extent the public agenda reflects the media agenda. Systematic research has demonstrated that the volume of news about events, issues, or developments and the placement of stories affect how the public assesses the importance of news items (Iyengar and Kinder 1987). More specifically, researchers found that when the media cover terrorism heavily and prominently, the public ranks this kind of political violence high on its list of most important national problems; when terrorism coverage declines and/or is less prominently displayed, the public is less inclined to rank terrorism high on its agenda (Iyengar and Kinder 1987; Nacos 1994). In the post-9/11 years, "levels of public concern [about terrorism] roughly reflected the volume of terrorism coverage in the major TV-networks' evening news" (Kern, Just, and Norris 2003, 290).

Heavy consumers of television news tend to perceive the threat of terrorism to be significantly higher than light watchers (Kushner 2005). About three years after 9/11, 43 percent of survey respondents who said they paid high levels of attention to TV news about national politics and the war on terror believed that another terrorist attack would take place in the United States within the next twelve months, whereas only 31 percent with low-level and 37 percent with moderate news consumption reported such fears (Nisbet and Shanahan 2004). How individuals perceive the threat of terrorism and to what degree they feel anxieties or anger matters because these assessments and feelings affect their support for (or opposition to) counterterrorist policies (Lerner, Gonzales, Small, and Fischhoff 2003; Nisbet and Shanahan 2004; Huddy, Feldman, Taber, and Lahav 2005; Kushner 2005). Whereas increased threat perceptions were found to coincide with heightened support for tough government actions at home and abroad, high levels of anxiety related to support for American isolationism (Huddy, Feldman, Taber, and Lahav 2005, 604). There are also indications that fear and anger result in different policy preferences. Thus, "experimentally primed anger activated more punitive preferences, and fear enhanced preferences for conciliatory policies and investment in broadly applicable precautionary measures" (Lerner, Gonzales, Small, and Fischhoff 2003, 150).

In sum, then, terrorists are quite successful in getting the attention of the publics they target and, in the process, intimidating them. No wonder that Osama bin Laden followed and seemed to be pleased about the American public's preoccupation with 9/11 and fears of further terrorist strikes. In one of his videotapes, he exclaimed and probably exaggerated that "America has been filled with terror from north to south and from east to west, praise and blessings to God" (Lawrence 2005, 104).

## Publicity for Terrorist Grievances

Terrorists commit violent acts in order to make target societies aware of their motives and affect public opinion in ways that put pressure on governments, especially in democracies, to adopt particular policies. To further this goal, they need news coverage of their grievances. Some thirty years ago, a leading terrorism scholar concluded that terrorists "obtain much publicity through the news media, but not the propaganda they usually want. The news media focus on the incident, not the grievances nor the objectives of the terrorists' cause" (Jenkins 1981, 3). While this was based on mere observations, Michael Kelly and Thomas Mitchell studied the news coverage of a random sample of 158 terrorist incidents between 1968 and 1974 in the *New York Times* and *The Times* (London). They found that fewer than 10 percent dealt with the causes and grievances of the perpetrators and concluded that terrorism "is not a very effective way to propagandize if one wants issues and goals to be known or understood" (Kelly and Mitchell 1984, 284). Case studies of the Iran hostage crisis (1979–81) and the TWA hijacking of 1985 also found that about 10 percent of the coverage in leading American newspapers addressed the grievances and motivations of terrorists (Nacos 1994, 64–5). It seems to us that terrorists are quite successful in inducing news about their motives when some 10 percent of total terrorism coverage is devoted to the "why" behind their violence.

However, media attention to terrorist grievances does not mean that target audiences sympathize with terrorists' motives and policy goals. Distinguishing between revolutionary and nationalist terrorism in domestic settings, a study of "fragmentary" survey data from five countries (Uruguay, Spain, Italy, Germany, and Northern Ireland) concluded that public attitudes toward political violence are not affected by terrorist actions and campaigns or government responses but rather by the historical features of particular cases (Hewitt 1990). Even if applied only to domestic terrorism in the five selected countries, this finding is not convincing with respect to public attitudes toward counterterrorist measures. In Germany, for example, the public became more supportive of tough government positions against the Red Army Faction in 1975, after the group kidnapped a mayoral candidate in Berlin and freed him only after the authorities released five jailed terrorists (Katzenstein 1990) and paid ransom money. The kidnapping and killing of former prime minister Aldo Moro in 1978 had similar effects on the Italian public and support for tough government action (J. D. Simon 1994).

At times, opinion changes seem responsive to terrorists' grievances as expressed in their communications. Thus, several weeks after the Iran hostage crisis began in 1979, one in four Americans agreed with the statement that "[the Ayatollah] Khomeini and his followers [presumably including the hostage holders] have a lot of right on their side when it comes to their accusations against the United States government and its support of the Shah regime" (Nacos 1994, 71). Hinckley (1992), too, found evidence for changing public attitudes and policy preferences with respect to terrorism and counter-terrorism during the Reagan years.

# Winning Support in Communities that Terrorists Claim to Represent

Terrorists are aware of their different audiences and try to communicate with them. Literally all terrorists claim that they act for a larger community that has been oppressed or otherwise wronged. Richardson has noted, "Terrorists strive in complicit societies. Without recruits they cannot grow" (2006, 215). Therefore, they need to be in touch with "the communities from which they derive their support." Sustaining community support ranks high on the agenda of terrorist groups (Bloom 2005; Reuter 2004). It has been reported that after suicide attacks, Hamas and Islamic Jihad deliver martyrs' videotapes to community groups to inspire new recruits, sermons in mosques, and public demonstrations in honor of these martyrs (Hassan 2001, 39). Al-Qaeda and related groups, too, make great efforts to get their messages across for the sake of social and religious legitimization in communities in which they operate and/or claim to act for (Corman and Schiefelbein 2006). However, Osama bin Laden and al-Qaeda have taken the communication of powerful messages to unprecedented levels in terms of quantity and global reach (Nacos 2007; Lawrence 2005).

While a significant part of these communications were transmitted outside the traditional news media, the latter continued to be important carriers of relevant news that in the post-9/11 era tried to answer a question asked by President Bush in a speech before a joint session of Congress: "Why do they hate us?" There was a wave of stories about the roots of deep-seated opposition to US foreign policy in the Arab and Muslim world that repeated the charges made by bin Laden's written and spoken statements. As Peter Ford wrote, "the buttons that Mr. bin Laden pushes in statements and interviews—injustice done to the Palestinians, the cruelty of continued sanctions against Iran, the presence of US troops in Saudi Arabia, the repressive and corrupt nature of the US-backed Gulf governments—win a good deal of popular sympathy [among Arabs and Muslims]" (2001, 1). This was a summary of the most important grievances expressed in bin Laden's communications. Whereas the US media paid little or no attention to the growing anti-American sentiments among Muslims and Arabs before 9/11, this changed dramatically thereafter (Nacos 2007, 53–5).

Even the best-laid communication strategies do not insure that terrorist groups win sympathies and support among those they claim to represent. Germany's Red Army Faction was especially media-savvy and developed sophisticated communication campaigns but was unable to muster meaningful support in their own community. Perhaps the early arrests of the RAF's founders deprived the organization of its most effective communicators. When the last members of the third RAF generation announced in 1998 that the group had disbanded, their communiqué recognized the inability to build a movement as one of the reasons for the RAF's failure.[4] In stark contrast, al-Qaeda's "propaganda by the deed" and communication strategy resulted in sympathy and support for bin Laden and his group among a significant number of people in Muslim and Arab countries. The much-publicized events of 9/11 in particular made bin Laden and al-Qaeda "into household words all over the world" (Richardson 2006, 95) and earned them admiration in those communities for which they claim to wage jihad. While survey and news organizations reported declining support for bin Laden beginning in 2005 compared to his high approvals in 2003, poll data revealed continued quite solid approval of the al-Qaeda leader and his organization in the following years. In Muslim countries vast majorities were well aware of the grievances articulated by bin Laden and other al-Qaeda leaders and, most importantly, agreed consistently "with nearly all of al Qaeda's goals to change US behavior in the Muslim world, to promote Islamist governance, and to preserve and affirm Islamic identity" (Kull et al. 2009, 20).

In sum, then, while some terrorist organizations are successful in winning sympathy and approval among those they claim to represent, others are not. Groups that succeed on this count have a good chance of enlisting significant support for their policy goals in the same communities, as the example of al-Qaeda attests to.

# MEDIA EVENTS, DEMAGOGUERY, AND RITUAL COMMUNICATIONS

The original definition of "media events" (e.g., John F. Kennedy's funeral, Olympic Games, royal weddings) was reserved for major ceremonial occasions that are televised live, pre-planned, pre-announced, and jointly produced by broadcasters and organizers, governments, or other public organizations (Dayan and Katz 1992; Katz and Liebes 2007). Following a series of terrorist spectaculars in the 1980s, Gabriel Weimann suggested that "there are attributes shared by certain terrorist events and the

---

[4] The text of the communiqué "RAF-Auflösungserklärung" is available in German at <http://www.rafinfo.de/archiv/raf/raf-20-4-98.php>, accessed Oct. 31, 2010.

conceptualization of media events" (1987, 21). Finally, with 9/11 and subsequent catastrophic terror attacks in mind, Elihu Katz and Tamar Liebes concluded that disruptive, threatening events, such as disasters, terrorism, and wars, have actually upstaged
ceremonial "media events," and that terrorism events "are obvious co-productions of
perpetrators and broadcasters" (Katz and Liebes 2007, 164).

While the era of terrorist media events preceded 9/11 by some three decades, the attacks
of that day added up to a "megaevent in a global media world, a society of the spectacle,
where the whole world is watching" (Kellner 2006, 167). Communication scholars distinguish between communication as transmission and communication as ritual. Transmission here means disseminating information "farther and faster, eclipsing time and
transcending space" (Carey 1992, 17). It is this instant transmission of communication
from any place to the rest of the world that casts terrorist media events into perfect stages
for ritual communication in the sense of "sacred ceremony that draws persons together in
fellowship and communality" (Carey 1992, 18). However, there are also "rituals of excommunication" that divide and separate communities rather than draw them together (Carey
1998). Both the purveyors of terrorist violence and the purveyors of counterterrorism
utilize ritual communication to draw communities together on the one hand and divide
and demonize on the other. When it comes to terrorism and counterterrorism, demago-
gues tend to be masters of ritual communication.

Patricia Roberts-Miller defines demagoguery as "polarizing propaganda that motivates members of an in-group to hate and scapegoat some outgroup(s)" (2005, 462).
While all terrorists embrace the "us" versus "them" divide (Sprinzak 1990; Bandura
1990) and target governments cast terrorists as communal outcasts as well, the mass-
mediated communications of Osama bin Laden and George W. Bush in the post-9/11
era were a particularly instructive example. Whereas bin Laden's declarations attempted to unite the global Muslim and Arab community of anti-American extremists
and moderates, President Bush tried to unite a shell-shocked nation behind him with
patriotic appeals. But besides such ritual communications of fellowship and shared
sentiments, both sides also conveyed ample messages of division and excommunication within and among communities. For bin Laden and his circle, apostates within the
Muslim community were just as dangerous enemies as the Crusaders and Zionists. For
President Bush and his supporters, critics of his counterterrorism policies within his
own country were abettors of terrorists or no different from them.

It was not only President Bush who "articulated the escalating patriotism, vilification
of the terrorists, and demand for stern military retaliation," as Kellner (2006, 165) put it.
The news media, too, followed a melodramatic story-line that pitted the victimized
nation against the ultimate villain. Based on her qualitative content analysis of Fox
News on the afternoon of September 11, 2001, Elisabeth Anker concluded, "Melodrama
defined America as a heroic redeemer with a mandate to act because of an injury
committed by a hostile villain" (2005, 35). While the virtuous nation and its heroes
received a great deal of prominent news coverage, so did the villain-in-chief bin Laden
and his followers who killed themselves as they killed thousands of innocent Americans. Indeed, in the months immediately following the 9/11 attacks, bin Laden was

mentioned more often in US TV network news than President Bush (Nacos 2007). This degree of attention to bin Laden's messages of hate and threat fit the story-line about "the evil-doer," as President Bush called the al-Qaeda chief; it provided a perfect contrast to the commander-in-chief who dispatched forces to Afghanistan to hunt down bin Laden and, later on, ordered the invasion of Iraq to remove from power another threatening source of "evil," Iraq's president Saddam Hussein. The result of both sides' propaganda of polarization and a media narrative that amplified the in-group versus out-group rhetoric was unprecedentedly high approval ratings for President Bush at home (Hetherington and Nelson 2003). While public support for heads of governments is quite common during and after massive terrorist strikes (Nacos 1994, 2007), it is not automatic but depends on support or opposition by political elites as reflected in the mass media (Brody and Shapiro 1989). Moreover, public attitudes are not static but are affected by events and relevant information, especially with respect to foreign policy (Page and Shapiro 1992, ch. 8). This may explain why the hero-versus-villain narrative no longer resonated as strongly with the news media and the public after Saddam Hussein was captured and authoritative sources began to express criticism about the conduct of the post-invasion phase of the Iraq War.

It was a different story abroad, and particularly in the Arab and Muslim world, where Bush was portrayed as the villain. Using survey data from nine Muslim countries, researchers found that attention to television news contributed "significantly to anti-American perceptions" and that in this respect the differences between those who watched al-Jazeera or Western networks were not as significant as some critics of the Arab network claimed (Nisbet, Nisbet, Scheufele, and Shanahan 2004). As described above, there was significant support for bin Laden and al-Qaeda and even more so for their policy goals among Arabs and Muslims. This seemed an affirmation of Samuel Huntington's argument that there is little or no evidence "to support the assumption that the emergence of pervasive global communications is producing significant convergence in attitudes and beliefs" and that "people interpret communications in terms of their own preexisting values and perspectives" (1996, 59).

## CONCLUSION: THE STATE OF MEDIA AND TERRORISM RESEARCH

Thanks to several excellent studies, the centrality of communication, media, and propaganda in the terrorist calculus was quite well understood before the attacks of September 11, 2001. Subsequent research added to and deepened that knowledge, although much of the relevant literature remains anecdotal. Systematic research was and remains segmented in that it focuses on media and communication, or public opinion, or political actors (governments and terrorists) and not on the important and complex relationships between two or more of the parts. Edited volumes that address in separate chapters terrorism in the context of media, public opinion, and government responses cannot fill the gap.

Also, while the utilization of the Internet by terrorists is well studied, little is known about the effects of different messages of hate and terror on various audiences. While the testimony of some reformed or captured terrorists has revealed how new media have served increasingly as instruments for the recruitment of terrorists, one would want to get more first-hand explanations, especially concerning the Internet. As for the overall communication strategy of terrorist organizations, interviewing terrorists themselves, say those caught and imprisoned, seems the best prospect for adding to our understanding of this crucial part of political violence by non-state actors.

# REFERENCES

ALALI, A. O., and EKE, K. K. (eds.) 1991. *Media Coverage of Terrorism: Methods of Diffusion.* Newbury Park, CA: Sage.

ALTHEIDE, D. L. 1982. Three-in-One News: Network Coverage of Iran. *Journalism Quarterly,* 59: 482–6.

—— 1987. Format and Symbols in TV Coverage of Terrorism in the United States and Great Britain. *International Studies Quarterly,* 31: 161–76.

ANKER, E. 2005. Villains, Victims, and Heroes: Melodrama, Media, and September 11. *Journal of Communication,* 55: 22–37.

BANDURA, A. 1990. Mechanism of Moral Disengagement. In *Origins of Terrorism: Psychologies, Ideologies, Theologies, States of Mind,* ed. W. Reich. New York: Cambridge University Press.

BASSIOUNI, M. C. 1981. Terrorism, Law Enforcement, and the Mass Media: Perspectives, Problems, Proposals. *Journal of Law and Criminology,* 72: 1–51.

BERKOWITZ, L., and MACAULAY, J. 1971. The Contagion of Criminal Violence. *Sociometry,* 34: 238–60.

BLOCH-ELKON, Y. 2007. Trends: Preventing Terrorism after the 9/11 Attacks. *Public Opinion Quarterly,* 71: 142–63.

BLOOM, M. 2005. *Dying to Kill: The Allure of Suicide Terror.* New York: Columbia University Press.

BOSCARINO, J. A., FIGLEY, C. R., and ADAMS, R. E. 2003. Fear of Terrorism in New York after the September 11 Terrorist Attacks. *International Journal of Emergency Mental Health,* 5: 199–209.

BRODY, R. A., and SHAPIRO, C. R. 1989. A Reconsideration of the Rally Phenomenon in Public Opinion. In *Political Behavior Annual,* ii, ed. S. Long. Boulder, CO: Westview Press.

CAREY, J. W. 1992. *Communication as Culture.* New York: Routledge.

—— 1998. Political Ritual on Television: Episodes in the History of Shame, Degradation and Excommunication. In *Media, Ritual and Identity,* ed. T. Liebes and J. Curran. London: Routledge.

COLEMAN, L. 2007. The Copycat Effect. blogspot.com, Apr. 19, 1. At <http://www.lorencoleman.com/copycateffect>. Accessed Nov. 6, 2010.

CORMAN, S. R., and SCHIEFELBEIN, J. S. 2006. *Communication and Media Strategy in the Jihadi War of Ideas*. Report No. 0601. Tempe: Consortium for Strategic Communication, Arizona State University.

COTTLE, S. 2006. Mediatizing the Global War on Terror: Television's Public Eye. In *Media, Terrorism, and Theory*, ed. A. P. Kavoori and T. Farley. Lanham, MD: Rowman & Littlefield.

CRENSHAW, M. 2006. The American Debate over "New" vs. "Old" Terrorism. Unpublished paper.

DAYAN, D., and KATZ, E. 1992. *Media Events: The Live Broadcasting of History*. Cambridge, MA: Harvard University Press.

DOWNES-LE GUIN, T., and HOFFMAN, B. 1993. *The Impact of Terrorism on Public Opinion*. Report. Santa Monica, CA: Rand.

ELTER, A. 2008. *Propaganda der Tat: Die RAF und die Medien*. Frankfurt: Suhrkamp.

FERGUSON, N. 2001. Clashing Civilizations or Mad Mullahs: The United States between Formal and Informal Empire. In *The Age of Terror: America and the World after September 11*, ed. S. Talbot and N. Chanda. New York: Basic Books.

FORD, P. 2001. Why Do They Hate Us? *Christian Science Monitor*, Sept. 27.

FRIEDMAN, T. L. 2002. No Mere Terrorist. *New York Times*, Mar. 24, sect. 4, 15.

GRAHAM, K. 1986. The Media Must Report Terrorism. In *Terrorism: Opposing Viewpoints*, ed. B. Szumski. St Paul, MN: Greenhaven.

HASSAN, N. 2001. An Arsenal of Believers. *New Yorker*, Nov. 19.

HETHERINGTON, M. J., and NELSON, M. 2003. Anatomy of a Rally Effect: George W. Bush and the War on Terrorism. *PS: Political Science and Politics*, 36: 37–42.

HEWITT, C. 1990. Terrorism and Public Opinion: A Five Country Comparison. *Terrorism and Political Violence*, 2: 145–70.

HINCKLEY, R. H. 1992. *People, Polls, and Policy Makers: American Public Opinion and National Security*. New York: Lexington.

HOFFMAN, B. 1997. Why Terrorists Don't Claim Credit. *Terrorism and Political Violence*, 9: 1–6.

—— 1999. Terrorism Trends and Prospects. In *Countering the New Terrorism*, ed. I. O. Lesser, B. Hoffman, J. Arquilla, D. Ronfeldt, M. Zanini, and B. M. Jenkins. Santa Monica, CA: Rand.

HOSKINS, A., and O'LOUGHLIN, B. 2007. *Television and Terror: Conflicting Times and the Crisis of News Discourse*. Houndmills: Palgrave Macmillan.

HUDDY, L., FELDMAN, S., TABER, C., and LAHAV, G. 2005. Threat, Anxiety, and Support of Antiterrorism Policies. *American Journal of Political Science*, 49: 593–608.

HUNTINGTON, S. P. 1996. *The Clash of Civilizations and Remaking of World Order*. New York: Simon & Schuster.

IYENGAR, S. 1991. *Is Anyone Responsible? How Television Frames Political Issues*. Chicago: University of Chicago Press.

—— and KINDER, D. R. 1987. *News that Matters: Television and American Opinion*. Chicago: University of Chicago Press.

JENKINS, B. 1981. *The Psychological Implications of Media-Covered Terrorism*. Paper. Santa Monica, CA: Rand.

—— 1990. International Terrorism: The Other World War. In *International Terrorism: Characteristics, Causes, Controls*, ed. C. Kegley, Jr. New York: St Martin's Press.

JOSIGER, W. J. 2006. Fear Factor: The Impact of Terrorism on Public Opinion in the United States and Great Britain. Paper delivered at the Annual Meeting of the International Studies Association, San Diego, Mar. 22.

KATZ, E., and LIEBES, T. 2007. "No More Peace!" How Disaster, Terror and War Have Upstaged Media Events. *International Journal of Communication*, 1: 157–66.

KATZENSTEIN, P. 1990. *West Germany's Internal Security Policy: State and Violence in the 1970s and 1980s*. Occasional Paper No. 28. Ithaca, NY: Center for International Studies, Cornell University.

KELLNER, D. 2006. September 11, Social Theory, and Democratic Politics. In *Media, Terrorism, and Theory*, ed. A. P. Kavoori and T. Fraley. Lanham, MD: Rowman & Littlefield.

KELLY, M., and MITCHELL, T. 1984. Transnational Terrorism and the Western Elite Press. In *Media Power and Politics*, ed. D. A. Graber. Washington, DC: CQ Press.

KERN, M., JUST, M., and NORRIS, P. 2003. The Lessons of Framing Terrorism. In *Framing Terrorism*, ed. P. Norris, M. Kern, and M. Just. New York: Routledge.

KLOPFENSTEIN, B. 2006. Terrorism and the Exploitation of New Media. In *Media, Terrorism, and Theory*, ed. A. P. Kavoori and T. Fraley. Lanham, MD: Rowman & Littlefield.

KULL, S., RAMSAY, C., WEBER, S., LEWIS, E., and MOHSENI, E. 2009. Public Opinion in the Islamic World on Terrorism, Al Qaeda, and US Policies. World Public Opinion.org., Feb. 25. At <http://www.worldpublicopinion.org/pipa/pdf/feb09/STARTII_Feb09_rpt.pdf>. Accessed Oct. 31, 2010.

KUPPERMAN, R., and KAMEN, J. 1989. *Final Warning: Averting Disaster in the New Age of Terrorism*. New York: Doubleday.

KUSHNER, S. A. 2005. Threat, Media, and Foreign Policy Opinion. Paper prepared for the Annual Meeting of the Midwest Political Science Association, Chicago, Apr. 7–10.

LAQUEUR, W. 1976. The Futility of Terrorism. *Harpers*, 252/1510, Mar.

—— 2003. *No End to War: Terrorism in the Twenty-First Century*. New York: Continuum.

—— and ALEXANDER, Y. 1987. *The Terrorism Reader: The Essential Source Book on Political Violence both Past and Present*. New York: NAL Penguin.

LAWRENCE, B. 2005. *Messages to the World: The Statements of Osama bin Laden*. London: Verso.

LEMYRE, L., TURNER, M. C., LEE, J. E. C., and KREWSKI, D. 2006. Public Perception of Terrorism Threats and Related Information Sources in Canada: Implications for the Management of Terrorism Risk. *Journal of Risk Research*, 9: 755–74.

LERNER, J. S., GONZALES, R. M., SMALL, D. A., and FISCHHOFF, B. 2003. Effects of Fear and Anger on Perceived Risks of Terrorism: A National Field Experiment. *Psychological Science*, 14: 144–50.

LESSER, I. O. 1999. Changing Terrorism in a Changing World. In *Countering the New Terrorism*, ed. I. O. Lesser, B. Hoffman, J. Arquilla, D. Ronfeldt, M. Zanini, and B. M. Jenkins. Santa Monica, CA: Rand.

LUZMA, L. M. 2000. Trends: Terrorism in the United States. *Public Opinion Quarterly*, 64: 90–105.

MARGALIT, A. 1995. The Terror Master. *New York Review of Books*, Oct. 15.

MARSDEN, P., and ATTIA, S. 2005. A Deadly Contagion? *The Psychologist*, 18: 152–5.

MARTIN, J. L. 1990. The Media's Role in Terrorism. In *International Terrorism: Characteristics, Causes, Controls*, ed. C. W. Kegley, Jr. New York: St Martin's Press.

MICHEL, L., and HERBECK, D. 2001. *American Terrorist: Timothy McVeigh & the Oklahoma City Bombing*. New York: Regan Books.

MIDLARSKY, M. I., CRENSHAW, M., and YOSHIDA, F. 1980. Why Violence Spreads: The Contagion of International Terrorism. *International Studies Quarterly*, 24: 262–98.

MILLER, A. H. 1982. *Terrorism, the Media and the Law*. Ardsley, NY: Transnational.

NACOS, B. L. 1994. *Terrorism and the Media*. New York: Columbia University Press.

NACOS, B. L. 2007. *Mass-Mediated Terrorism*. Lanham, MD: Rowman & Littlefield.

—— 2010. *Terrorism and Counterterrorism: Understanding Threats and Responses in the Post-9/11 World*, 3rd edn. New York: Longman Pearson.

—— BLOCH-ELKON, Y., and SHAPIRO, R. Y. 2007. Post-9/11 Terrorism Threats, News Coverage, and Public Perception in the United States. *International Journal of Conflict and Violence*, 1: 105–26.

NIMMO, D., and COMBS, J. E. 1985. *Nightly Horrors: Crisis Coverage in Television Network News*. Knoxville: University of Tennessee Press.

NISBET, E. C., and SHANAHAN, J. 2004. *Restrictions on Civil Liberties*. Media and Society Group Special Report. Ithaca, NY: Cornell University, Dec.

—— NISBET, M. C., SCHEUFELE, D. A., and SHANAHAN, J. E. 2004. Public Diplomacy, Television News, and Muslim Opinion. *Press/Politics*, 9: 11–37.

NORRIS, P., KERN, M., and JUST, M. 2003. *Framing Terrorism: The News Media, the Government, and the Public*. New York: Routledge.

O'SULLIVAN, J. 1986. Media Publicity Causes Terrorism. In *Terrorism: Opposing Viewpoints*, ed. B. Szumski. St Paul, MN: Greenhaven.

PAGE, B. I., and SHAPIRO, R. Y. 1992. *The Rational Public: Fifty Years of Trends in Americans' Policy Preferences*. Chicago: University of Chicago Press.

PALETZ, D. L., and SCHMID, A. P. 1992. *Terrorism and the Media*. Newbury Park, CA: Sage.

PICARD, R. G. 1986. News Coverage as the Contagion of Terrorism: Dangerous Charges Backed by Dubious Science. Paper presented at the Annual Meeting of the Association for Education in Journalism and Mass Communication, Norman, Oklahoma, Aug. 3–6.

—— 1991. News Coverage as the Contagion of Terrorism: Dangerous Charges Backed by Dubious Science. In *Media Coverage of Terrorism: Methods of Diffusion*, ed. O. A. Alali and K. K. Eke. Newbury Park, CA: Sage.

REUTER, C. 2004. *My Life Is a Weapon: A Modern History of Suicide Bombing*. Princeton: Princeton University Press.

RICHARDSON, L. 2006. *What Terrorists Want*. New York: Random House.

ROBERTS-MILLER, P. 2005. Democracy, Demagoguery, and Critical Rhetoric. *Rhetoric & Public Affairs*, 8/3: 459–76.

ROSE, G. 1999. It Could Happen Here: Facing the New Terrorism. *Foreign Affairs* (Mar.–Apr.). At <http://www.foreignaffairs.org/19990301fareviewessay1030/gideon-rose/it-could-happen-here-facing-the-new-terrorism.html>. Accessed June 2, 2007.

RUBIN, B., and RUBIN, J. C. 2002. *Anti-American Terrorism and the Middle East*. New York: Oxford.

SAGEMAN, M. 2004. *Understanding Terror Networks*. Philadelphia: University of Pennsylvania Press.

—— 2008. *Leaderless Jihad*. Philadelphia: University of Pennsylvania Press.

SCHLAGHECK, D. M. 1988. *International Terrorism*. New York: Lexington.

SCHLESINGER, P., MURDOCK, G., and ELLIOTT, P. 1984. *Televising Terrorism: Political Violence in Popular Culture*. New York: Charles Scribner's Sons.

SCHMID, A. P., and DE GRAAF, J. 1980. *Insurgent Terrorism and the Western News Media: An Exploratory Analysis with a Dutch Case Study*. Leiden: Center for the Study of Social Conflicts, Dutch State University.

—— 1982. *Violence and Communication: Insurgent Terrorism and the Western News Media*. London: Sage.

Sedgwick, M. 2007. Inspiration and the Origins of Global Waves of Terrorism. *Studies in Conflict & Terrorism*, 30: 97–112.

Simon, J. D. 1994. *The Terrorist Trap: America's Experience with Terrorism*. Bloomington: Indiana University Press.

Simon, S., and Benjamin, D. 2001. The Terror. *Survival*, 43: 5–18.

Spencer, A. 2006. Questioning the Concept of "New Terrorism." *Peace Conflict & Development*, Issue 8 (Jan.) Available at <http://www.peacestudiesjournal.org.uk/dl/Feb%2006%20SPENCER%20version%202.pdf>. Accessed Nov. 5, 2010.

Sprinzak, E. 1990. The Psychopolitical Formation of Extreme Left Terrorism in a Democracy: The Case of the Weatherman. In *Origins of Terrorism: Psychologies, Ideologies, Theologies, States of Mind*, ed. W. Reich. New York: Cambridge University Press.

Weimann, G. 1987. Media Events: The Case of International Terrorism. *Journal of Broadcasting & Electronic Media*, 31/1: 21–39.

—— 2006. *Terror on the Internet: The New Arena, the New Challenges*. Washington, DC: United States Institute of Peace.

—— and Winn, C. 1994. *The Theater of Terror: Mass Media and International Terrorism*. New York: Longman.

Wieviorka, M. 1993. *The Making of Terrorism*. Chicago: University of Chicago Press.

PART V

# DEMOCRACY UNDER STRESS

CHAPTER 43

........

# THE DEMOCRATIC
# PARADOX

## *The Waning of Popular Sovereignty and the Pathologies of American Politics*

........

ROBERT Y. SHAPIRO
LAWRENCE R. JACOBS

## INTRODUCTION

........

IN 1960 E. E. Schattschneider published *The Semi-Sovereign People*, one of the enduring studies of how the opportunities in the United States for citizen direction of government were often diminished by the dominance of interest groups. Schattschneider's conclusion that American politics typically limits the form and degree of democratic influence may appear too pessimistic. Indeed, this volume has demonstrated the substantial and growing attention to public opinion, as reflected in the astronomical expansion of polling since the publication of *The Semi-Sovereign People*. It has also described the vast and growing diversity of information available today. Although these developments have created the potential for expanding American democracy, their actual effects have exacerbated the pathologies of American politics that have contributed to further constricting popular sovereignty.

* We thank Yaeli Bloch-Elkon, Martha Crum, Robert Erikson, Susan Herbst, Hélène Landemore, Joanne Miller, Brigitte Nacos, Russ Neuman, Benjamin Page, Paul Sniderman, and Charles Taber for useful discussions and communications.

# THE STRAINS ON AMERICAN DEMOCRACY

## Celebrating Democratic Responsiveness

A substantial body of quantitative and qualitative research has challenged Schattsch-neider's dour portrayal of American democracy by reporting evidence to support a more optimistic account of American democracy—the responsiveness of government policy to public opinion (see the reviews by Burstein 2003; Glynn et al. 2004, ch. 9; Wlezien and Soroka 2007). Concluding a review of this research, James Stimson noted that "quasiexperimental studies find clear evidence of responsiveness as do time series analysis of either policy domains or global attitudes and policy" (2007, 861). Methodo-logically diverse research over the past several decades has reported that the electoral process holds officeholders accountable by removing those who are unresponsive or motivating elected representatives to anticipate future electoral removal by responding to the "median voter" and therefore moving toward the midpoint of public opinion (for example, Downs 1957; Pitkin 1969; Erikson, MacKuen, and Stimson 2002).

A more recent and commonly cited explanation for government responsiveness is the proliferation of public opinion polling and its availability to political leaders and everyday Americans (Geer 1996; Frankovic, Panagopoulos, and Shapiro 2009). The number of polls has sharply increased during the last third of the twentieth century and is now readily accessible in the media and through online sites such as Polling Report, Pollster, and Real Clear Politics. While presidents were initially able to monopolize polling data for their own use and capitalize on them as a strategic tool, public opinion data are now widely available in accessible formats to everyday citizens and to political leaders in Congress (Jacobs 1993; Jacobs and Shapiro 2000; Eisinger 2003).

The proliferation of highly visible and easily accessible polling results may help to explain the "congruence" or "consistency" between majority opinion and policy, or between changes in opinion and changes in policies (for example, Monroe 1998; B. I. Page and Shapiro 1983). Although some rational choice models of political decision-making stress that limited information about voters induces risk aversion, the reality is that candidates and government officials have access to and confidence in extensive research on public opinion in order to respond to the median voter in reaching policy decisions and designing their election campaigns, if they choose (Druckman and Jacobs 2006).

As polling and reports of poll results have become increasingly visible to the public at large, the positions of elected officials and candidates have faced scrutiny when they departed from public opinion. In the case of salient decisions by government officials—such as the passage of health reform in 2010 or the House impeachment of Bill Clinton in 1998—their divergence from public preferences has become a focal point of debate, with the media and citizens raising questions about democratic accountability and politicians, on occasion, offering justifications for their positions. Although cases of public debates about departures from democratic accountability are uncommon, critical "publicity" may illustrate expanded public monitoring of government and greater government responsiveness to public opinion.

In short, American politics—as Paul Quirk and Joseph Hinchliffe (1998) forcefully claim—may now be enveloped by the "hegemony of public opinion." The institutional mechanism of elections and the availability of ample, trusted, and readily accessible polling data through the media and online sources may enable politicians to respond to public opinion and equip Americans to punish those who do not.

## The Paradox of American Democracy

Many of the chapters in this volume and related research point us to a sober and quite different conclusion: Schattschneider's pessimism has stronger—rather than weaker— justification today than it did in 1960. Although the institutional mechanisms of elections and an increasingly pluralistic information environment do create opportunities for democratic policymaking, government responsiveness to public opinion is conditional, selective, and no more frequent and quite possibly less frequent than before the 1980s. Indeed, what would seem to be new opportunities for democracy (the proliferation of information and polling) have, paradoxically, introduced new or newly intensified obstacles to popular sovereignty. Below we discuss three major *pathologies* related to political leaders and other elites, the media, and public opinion that weaken or at times short-circuit democratic accountability.

## PATHOLOGIES OF AMERICAN DEMOCRACY

......................................................................................

### Political Elites

*Strategic Communications, Unintended Consequences, and Manipulation*

A long-standing theme in age-old discussions of orderly government is the role of "benevolent" leaders in educating the public to sacrifice its narrow, selfish instincts in favor of policies that advance the public good and the national interest. "The king" was presented as a symbol of the nation that acted in its overall interests (Pitkin 1969). The framers of the US Constitution, of course, revolted against monarchy and harbored a suspicion of human nature, but they nonetheless assumed that the proper balancing of personal motivation and institutional checking would induce elected representatives to serve the nation's interests. In Federalist Paper No. 10, James Madison argued that the "public voice, pronounced by the representatives of the people... will be more consonant to the public good than if pronounced by the people themselves." One of the clearest statements of elected representatives as benevolent leaders comes from

Edmund Burke, a British Member of Parliament, who insisted that "Your representative owes you, not his industry only, but his judgment; and he betrays, instead of serving you, if he sacrifices it to your opinion."

Decades of research demonstrate, though, that the "public good" is rarely self-evident but is rather the product of multiple and competing interpretations, which often arise from divergent policy goals and philosophies, clashing interests and values, and differing personalities (Dahl 1989). Presidents and their advisers as well as other elected officials are influenced by core personality traits such as their self-esteem and need for positive reinforcement and their level of energy and engagement. James David Barber's (1972) analysis of presidential character, for instance, contrasts the strong self-esteem and energetic engagement of Franklin Delano Roosevelt, who forcefully reached and communicated the dramatic decision to lead America through the Great Depression and Second World War, as opposed to the low-esteem and compulsively driven personality of Richard Nixon, who engaged in lawbreaking, manipulation, and deception in directing the cover-up of the Watergate Hotel and expansion of the Vietnam War into neighboring countries.

In addition to personality, policy goals and partisan philosophies have increasingly motivated American politicians. Since political parties formed competing camps in the early nineteenth century, the split between parties has varied over time and, since the 1970s, has sharply widened along ideological lines with Democrats becoming more consistently liberal and Republicans more conservative with regard to the scope of government across the full range of economic issues—including taxation, spending, and regulation (Chapters 36 and 39 in this volume examine these issues; see McCarty, Poole, and Rosenthal 2006; Fiorina with Abrams 2009; Fiorina with Abrams and Pope 2011). This polarization was evident during the presidency of Barack Obama when nearly all Democrats voted to enact national health reform and all Republicans voted in opposition. Civil rights and social issues (including those related to women's rights, abortion, and religious practice) instigated or reinforced the polarization (see Chapters 37, 38, and 39 in this volume; Carmines and Stimson 1989). During the Bush administration (through this writing, 2001–10), the partisan division extended further than in the past to foreign policy and national security issues—most notably the war in Iraq (Shapiro and Bloch-Elkon 2006, 2007; Snyder, Bloch-Elkon, and Shapiro 2009; Jacobson 2010). Southern Democrats in Congress, who had staunchly opposed civil rights and liberal labor policies, were gradually replaced by Republicans or more liberal Democrats, or they switched parties. Moderate to liberal Republicans on social issues went through a similar conversion, as past leaders like Senators Jacob Javits, Edward Brooke, Charles Percy, and Clifford Case have become nearly extinct within the GOP.

Partisan loyalty is a primary driver of the agendas and policy formulations of authoritative political figures. Research shows that the intense views of partisans influence the positions of presidents more than majority opinion (Wood 2009). This pattern of partisan-driven policymaking defies both the expectations of "benevolent" leaders devoted to the overall public good and the norms of popular sovereignty—that is, responsiveness to the policy preferences of the mass public.

The movement of the major political parties into divergent and ideologically consistent programmatic organizations pushed the United States toward the "responsible two-party system" model that many political scientists in the 1950s recommended to enhance accountability (American Political Science Association 1950). Despite the hopefulness of earlier political scientists, contemporary partisan polarization in the US has contributed to a partisan deadlock that requires super-majorities to move most legislation of significance (McCarty 2007) and erodes the ability of elites to accurately assess and design policies to respond to the world around them. Although government officials are more experienced in designing policy and the public may defer to them (Hibbing and Theiss-Morse 2002), they may also suffer—especially in the ideologically polarized and emotionally charged environment that has emerged—from misperceptions (Jervis 1976) and closed-mindedness or "epistemic closure," that distorts their analysis and prevents them from critically evaluating assumptions, tracking real-world conditions, or understanding alternative perspectives (e.g., as some conservatives themselves have debated; Douthat 2010). They are as vulnerable as the public, as we shall see below, to biases resulting from "motivated reasoning" and related processes. Recent research by Philip Tetlock (2005) has shown that elite-level "expert" judgments and predictions can vary widely, producing results that may, on average, be no more accurate than those of non-experts.

Obsessive-compulsive and withdrawn personalities and divergent policy goals among government officials, as well as heightened perceptions of risk, can spur the most serious threat to democracy—outright manipulation and deception. Effective control over the content and flow of relevant information has most often occurred on foreign policy and national security issues and, especially, during the initial formulation of policy because the executive branch can often control access to intelligence and prevent the opposition from challenging the president's accounts (Schuessler 2010; Page and Shapiro 1992, chs. 9–10; on manipulation more broadly, see Le cheminant and Parrish 2010). Confidential documents released as part of the Pentagon Papers revealed that President Lyndon Johnson deliberately misled Americans about the Vietnam War; he simultaneously instructed the Defense Department to increase US troop levels (a decision that would ultimately deploy 500,000) and to "minimize any appearance of sudden changes in policy."

Political elites understand that increasing the perception of national threat can increase the public's *fear* and susceptibility to being manipulated (Koh 1990; Nacos, Bloch-Elkon, and Shapiro 2011; see Chapter 25 in this volume on risk aversion). Government officials may be especially prone to deviate from accepted norms of democratic governance when they harbor strong convictions about the threat to the national interest and face intense pressure from supportive partisans, organized interests, and campaign contributors (Winter and Page 2009).

## Growing Challenges to Effective Democratic Governance

Political elites are a source of distortion and, at times, outright deception. Hopeful accounts of benevolent elites who selflessly serve the national interest have given way to accumulating evidence of manipulation and the routinized processes of polarization that corrode the notion of a consensual "public good" and "expert answers" of which technocrats and elite theorists once dreamed (Dahl 1989). The determined efforts of presidents and other political leaders to move (rather than follow) public opinion to rally support for partisan agendas raise sobering questions about the nature and scope of democratic accountability. The threat of elite devotion to narrow, particularistic policy goals and to using manipulation and deception to forestall public backlash is an age-old one.

Today's intensified interdependence of information development and distribution, which this volume has charted (see Chapter 1), increases two contemporary threats of political elites to democratic accountability. The first is that political leaders enjoy increased capacities to deliberately short-circuit citizen oversight directly or indirectly by misleading the media and ordinary citizens. While changes in traditional and online media have made possible a new level of social networking and empowered everyday citizens as co-producers of socially shared information, they have also increased the opportunities for elites to reach citizens and enhanced their ability to unify their base of political support. The second threat is inadvertent and relates to the interaction of a large, diverse, and often uncoordinated set of operations and organizational routines that generate the information that reaches most Americans. The information about policy and politics that reaches individuals is often merely the accidental by-product of a complicated chain of events: the crafted statements and actions by presidents and other government authorities trigger disparate reactions by the traditional and online media that often defy the plans of political elites. Although the information that reaches Americans is often unplanned by political leaders, it nonetheless affects the mass public in ways that foster misunderstandings, distractions from real-world developments, and inflated fears, which in turn diminish the capacity of citizens, fan political conflict, and complicate efforts to govern. We focus next on how the organizational designs of the media and the dynamics of public opinion interact with the mobilization and communications strategies of political elites, often in unintended ways.

## Media Reflexes

Political leaders and the public alike have been quick to blame the media for their dissatisfaction with politics—for reporting on news in ways that stoke the flames of conflict and for infusing public debate with triviality (from haircuts to sporting preferences). Appearing on CBS News's *Face the Nation* on September 29, 2009, President Obama complained that the new media era in which cable news and Internet blogs operate around the clock "focus on the most extreme elements on both sides. They can't get enough of the conflict—it's catnip to the media right now." The consequence, he charged, is that "it is more difficult to solve the problems." Obama's complaints were echoed by his predecessor, George W. Bush, who fingered the media "filter" for fuelling political conflict and public confusion. The complaint of political elites—and a genuine strain on democracy—is that citizens are not accurately monitoring societal problems and the actions of government and its leaders. Despite the efforts of political elites to shift responsibility, the sources of this breakdown rest with them: false and misleading information launched by one of the warring factions in American politics is reported and distributed by traditional and especially online media, which in turn spurs misperceptions and reinforces growing partisan perceptual biases and reinforces elite divisions.

There are two reasons that today's 24/7 information environment fosters and amplifies political conflict and public confusion perhaps more so than in the past. The first are the "silos of bias" that have emerged among traditional and online media. Traditional media have long been scrutinized to detect a liberal or conservative bias, especially when the increasing concentration of ownership and control of news outlets potentially limited the range and diversity of news available to the public to receive. This past accusation that "the media have a liberal bias" or "a conservative bias" has become moot. The reality today is that cable news and online options have proliferated options to serve a wide range of political perspectives from liberalism (ably served by MSNBC and other traditional and online media) to conservatism, which is supplied by Fox News and other media (Baum and Groeling 2008, 2010; Groeling 2008; Groseclose and Milyo 2005; Gentzkow and Shapiro 2006). These media outlets have used their political orientation to attract ideological niches that generate revenues and economic success, reversing the earlier business model that embraced "objectivity" and "neutrality" as a recipe for building the largest market share possible (Hamilton 2004; Gentzkow and Shapiro 2008, 2010). This ideological segmentation of the media market parallels the emergence of the partisan press in the nineteenth century and serves a similar function: it enables political elites to reach their core supporters, which in turn perpetuates or further exacerbates the polarization that many observers and some government officials lament.

The proliferation of partisan information sources has redefined the organization and control of information. The long-standing fear that large businesses would buy up media organizations to concentrate control over information and entertainment and reduce diversity and competition has resurfaced as media magnates have attempted to buy up multiple news outlets in the same market (see Baker 2006). Although concentration has increased, the expansion of traditional and online media sources may have outstripped the capacity of any one organization to literally control what individuals learn. The structure of today's information prevents the monopolization of information as was previously feared. Indeed, arguably the greater risk today is the dispersion (rather than concentration) of divergent streams of information, with segmented concentrations on the left and right as illustrated by MSNBC and Fox News.

The second and related threat to today's information environment and the needs of a democratic citizenry is the decline of independent investigative journalism. The decline of newspapers and "hard" news television reporting in reaction to shrinking audiences and revenue from advertising has come at a cost: although the quality of news reporting over the past three decades should not be overstated, its news gathering did monitor most major societal problems and many government policies (as Michael Schudson suggests in Chapter 4 in this volume; see also Downie and Schudson 2009). The decline of traditional news media and their labor-intensive (and therefore expensive) "shoe-leather" journalism has diminished quality reporting as a primary source for most Americans, a development that is compounded by the fact that many online information sites rely on (selectively) reposting the reporting by the traditional press—a supply that is shrinking and losing its depth.

## Public Opinion: Public Competence and Elite Dissonance and Deceit

Today's informational interdependence widens and strengthens the impact of political elites and the media on public opinion, with significant costs to American democracy. One of the most striking contrasts has occurred between the degree of public agreement on many social and economic issues and problems (Fiorina with Abrams and Pope 2011; Page and Jacobs 2009; see Chapter 39 in this volume) and the wide polarization among political elites that precludes compromises in enacting changes in public policy (Fiorina with Abrams 2009; Brownstein 2007; Jacobs and Shapiro 2000). The answer to this puzzle lies in the effects of elite mobilization strategies and communications and the inadvertent consequences of today's information system, which have diminished and distorted the provision of quality information that allows citizens and community groups to assess the real-world challenges facing them and to consider appropriate remedies. In today's world of informational interdependence, citizens often do not receive and process the best available information and, as a result, the quality of public opinion is compromised, leaving Americans ill-informed or unaware of critical national challenges.

Detecting the culpability for today's new information system rests on a fundamental question: are citizens up to the task of serving as informed and enlightened influences on government policy? Put another way, should we blame citizens for the ills of American politics today?

Although elite and media commentary tend to blame citizens for their lack of knowledge and engagement, decades of research have found that the opinions of the public are rational based on the information that is available. The culprits for what ails American politics today are political elites and the system that organizes and distributes information. We begin by reviewing research on the competence of everyday Americans and then turn to the ill-effects of political elites and today's information system.

### The Rational Public

Research on the nature of public opinion has focused on three dimensions: knowledge, coherence, and stability. From the framing of the US Constitution through the 1960s, the prevailing elite view of the mass public was that it was irrational and not to be trusted as a guide to government policymaking. The Constitution's framers repeatedly warned that ordinary individuals were prone to flights of intolerant "passion" and lacked the knowledge and experience to reach sensible policy judgments; this was the primary motivation for adopting a "scheme of representation" to stand in as the "voice" of the people. Leading political observers—most notably Walter Lippman (1925)— derided the competence of everyday citizens, pointing to their inattention and igno- rance about specific issues and politics more broadly and fickle tendencies to change their preferences. Some of the earliest and most influential research on public opinion and voting was also quite critical of the public's competence to play a constructive role in democracy, reporting that it was ignorant and lacked knowledge of key issues and political figures, tended to be volatile in its views, and held opinions that seemed idiosyncratic and lacked coherence across issues (Campbell, Converse, Miller, and Stokes 1960; Berelson, Lazarsfeld, and McPhee 1954; and other critics cited in Page and Shapiro 1992, chs. 1–2). This "public as ignorant" account was crystallized by Converse (1964), who portrayed the views of individuals as "nonattitudes" that lacked ideological coherence and suffered from extensive instability, making them ill-suited to guide the policy deliberations of government officials.

The early dim view of public opinion has been largely replaced by a growing body of research that reports that public opinion and the behavior of voters make sense, and are largely stable *given the information that is available* and therefore worthy of serious attention in the political process (Page and Shapiro 1992; Popkin 1991; Erikson, MacK- uen, and Stimson 2002; Sniderman, Brody, and Tetlock 1991). This view of public opinion as rational finds that the mass public responds reasonably to new information rather than remaining fixed to outdated views; that changes in public opinion are infrequent, are tied to new information, and do not involve wild fluctuations; and that the public draws meaningful distinctions among issues and alternative policies based on a consistent set of underlying values and beliefs, and information "heuristics" or shortcuts (see Popkin 1991; Sniderman, Brody, and Tetlock 1991; Lupia and McCubbins 1998). The most persuasive evidence is based on *aggregate* public opinion data— namely, the overall percentages in polls—that document the rationality of *collective* opinion. For instance, the decline in support for Barack Obama during 2010 can reasonably be traced—as news reports often do—to the slow and uneven economic recovery and other disappointments. The rationality of aggregate opinion partly reflects the "miracle of aggregation"; that is, the views of individuals responding to real-world developments cancel out those who are distracted and errors in measure- ment are also canceled out (for example, Page and Shapiro 1992). Another explanation is that collective deliberation about events and changing conditions equip the diverse public to learn through the media and interactions with others (Jacobs, Cook, and Delli Carpini 2009; Landemore forthcoming; S. E. Page 2007).

Although there is now wide agreement about this interpretation of aggregate public opinion (especially in the media's own narratives; but cf. Chapter 16 in this volume), the stability and competence of individual-level opinion has been the subject of serious questions. Some research has found fluctuations and mistaken evaluations by individuals as they react to policy issues and politicians (compared to more "enlightened" opinions; Chapter 35 in this volume; Althaus 2003; Bartels 1996; Caplan 2007; Luskin 2003). These, however, may reflect elite deception or inadvertent priming or framing (see below), or understate the extent to which individuals consistently use their values and *constructive* information shortcuts or heuristics (including partisanship until recently, which we return to below; Shapiro and Bloch-Elkon 2008). In addition, some research at the individual level has questioned whether members of the general public harbor dogmatic, authoritarian, or ethnocentric personalities (Hetherington and Weiler 2009; Kinder and Kam 2009). On the other hand, there are variations in the impact of emotion and personality, which can contribute to rational rather than irrational psychological processes (see Chapter 24 in this volume; Sniderman, Brody, and Tetlock 1991; Marcus, Neumann, and MacKuen 2000). Moreover, there is evidence that segments of the population with higher levels of knowledge hold different opinions than lower-knowledge subgroups (including greater support for rights and liberties) and may reach different evaluations of candidates (Chapter 35 in this volume; Althaus 2003; Gilens 2001; Bartels 1996). These differences, however, have not been very large: the degree of *changes* over time in informed versus ill-informed opinions has rarely differed by much (though even small differences can determine close elections; Erikson 2007).

In short, the public exhibits substantial competence based on the information available to it. This capability, however, does not preclude the possibility that the measures of their views may be flawed. The veracity and value of polling has long been questioned (see Chapter 16 in this volume; Rogers 1949; Bishop 2005). In addition, reliance on single questions, as a referendum, to assess the public's attitudes will often miss the complexity of public opinion (see Chapter 22 in this volume; Schuman 1986).

## The Ill-Effects of Political Elites

Because public opinion relies on the content and tenor of the information that is available, political elites and the media exert enormous influence on the public. We discuss two interrelated processes that affect public opinion: elite strategies to drive the public and the inadvertent interactions of the information system and the public's political attitudes.

*Elite mobilization strategies.*   Under certain conditions the efforts by political elites—especially authoritative government officials—to influence public opinion can succeed. As in the cases of Johnson's concealment of his decision to send more troops to Vietnam, the dependence of the media and ordinary individuals on the White House for information on national security policy makes them particularly vulnerable to manipulation and deception. The public's reaction to Johnson's escalation of the war remained relatively compliant for several years after his decision due to the administration's control over information.

The routine operations of the White House and other senior government officials to develop strategies to "control the flow of information" (according to a Clinton administration advisor) can affect the government agenda—the issues and topics that receive sustained attention. The White House's use of nationally televised speeches by presidents—including their State of the Union addresses at the beginning of the year— are often quite effective tools for agenda-setting through their effects on the subjects covered by the press and the concerns of Americans (Cohen 1997). For instance, the Obama White House successfully used a national presidential address in September 2009 to refocus the debate over health reform on unmet needs and excessive costs after the "Tea Party" protests dominated press coverage in August (Jacobs and Skocpol 2010).

*Information system effects and public attitudes.* Today's interdependent information system spans not only the large, diverse, and spread-out traditional media but also a sea of innumerable individual and organized online operations. While the ownership patterns, shared organizational models, and pyramidal networks of the information system that operated through the 1990s produced similar reporting patterns, the information produced and distributed by the new mass media system is largely uncoordinated and often discordant. It generates effects on public opinion that are often not the intention of political elites. We point to two.

First, the interaction of political elites and the media leads to processes of *priming*, which boosts the public's attention to specific issues, and *framing*, which orchestrates how an issue is presented to the American public (see Chapters 11 and 12 in this volume). During 2010 Barack Obama preferred to focus public attention on the scheduled troop withdrawal from Iraq rather than on a languid economy, and the White House developed a variety of tactics to prime the press and thereby the public to achieve its objectives. But political opponents who were intent on attacking the President to boost their opportunities in the mid-term elections, as well as the media, which "indexed" the genuine conflict in Washington (Bennett 1990), focused attention on the level of unemployment and other worrisome economic indicators; Obama's follow-through on his commitment to withdraw 100,000 troops in Iraq received little sustained attention.

In addition, the White House works hard to frame particular issues to drive how they are presented. For instance, Richard Nixon portrayed protesters against the war in Vietnam as disruptive and dishonoring US troops while the protesters attempted to present themselves as honorable dissenters lawfully exercising their constitutional rights. How the press organized their stories about the protesters determined if they attracted broader support (as in the latter frame) or opposition (former frame). The media also use frames on political and policy developments. Although both Bush's drive to reform Social Security and Clinton's attempt to enact health reform sought to focus on the merits of policy change, the press often framed its presentation of these reform episodes in terms of political conflict, which tended to evoke the public's cynicism as they worried that reliable retirement benefits and their existing access to health care were under threat (see Chapter 39 in this volume; Jacobs and Shapiro 2000; Cappella and Jamieson 1997; Iyengar and Kinder 1987).

The second and perhaps most striking effect of today's information environment relates to its impact on ideological partisanship ("partisan sorting") and misperceptions.

Among everyday Americans, those who identify as Democrats or as Republicans have long differed in their baseline political opinions and policy preferences, and partisanship is the single most influential determinant of vote choice (Campbell, Converse, Miller, and Stokes 1960). Recent research demonstrates that the information system's reaction to the polarization among officeholders has had significant effects that have accentuated the political divide among ordinary Americans, contributing to deadlock in the governing process and muted government responsiveness to majority opinion.

The efforts of partisan leaders combined with the press coverage of them and the associated conflict has increased the intensity of political conflict between Republicans and Democrats as well as liberals and conservatives. The top-down national strategies of political elites to mobilize sympathetic partisans has prompted Democrats to self-identify more consistently as "liberal" and Republicans as "conservative," and to adopt corresponding positions on economic, social, and foreign policy issues (for example, Levendusky 2009; Fiorina with Abrams and Pope 2011; Layman, Carsey, and Horowitz 2006; Bafumi and Shapiro 2009; Abramowitz 2010; Shapiro and Bloch-Elkon 2006, 2007). The partisan strategies in major recent political episodes—from the impeachment of President Bill Clinton, the fight over who won the 2000 presidential election, and the divisive 2004, 2006, and 2008 elections—widened the partisan and ideological gap among Americans (Jacobson 2010). Echoing and accentuating the messages and strategies of dueling political elites, the traditional media—and increasingly the Internet—have magnified the political divide and deepened the emotional reactions of partisans and ideologues (see Mutz 2006; Sunstein 2007, 2009; Prior 2007; Lawrence, Sides, and Farrell 2010; Stroud 2010).

The traditional and online media have not only accelerated the sorting of Americans into opposing political camps but have also fueled selective or faulty perceptions of *objective reality and facts*. Ideally, one might expect individuals to collect facts from all easily available sources, assess them, and then develop a reasoned set of preferences about specific policy prescriptions and general approaches to policy remedies. By contrast, the new systems of informational interdependence have reversed this chain of reasoning: partisanship and ideology operate increasingly as misleading heuristics, leading to selective exposure to information and producing a degree of perceptual bias that had not previously existed (cf. Bartels 2002; Gerber and Green 1998, 1999). Although cognition has long been considered a means for "thinking through" issues and candidate choices based on information instead of reflexively making flip decisions based on emotions and pre-set attitudes, a growing body of research shows that motivation shapes reasoning and information gathering. The increasingly emotional and high-decibel divisions among partisan elites that are conveyed and amplified by the media have produced "motivated reasoning" and "motivated skepticism," which affects the exposure, acquisition, acceptance, and use of new factual information (see Chapters 9, 15, 23, 27 in this volume; and the reviews in Taber and Lodge 2006; Mutz 2007; Shapiro and Bloch-Elkon 2008; Manjoo 2008; Slothuus and De Vreese 2010).

Instead of individuals with higher levels of education and cognitive engagement exercising the greatest resistance to the winds of passion (as the Constitution's framers assumed), they are most vulnerable to perceptual biases—their prior theories and political attitudes determine how they seek out and evaluate new information rather than the other way round (see Chapter 1 in this volume; Bennett and Iyengar 2008, 2010). It turns out that having the cognitive ability to construct ostensibly reasonable justifications makes the better-educated and -informed more prone to reject new information that clashes with their strongly held partisan and ideological positions. Research has shown that the better-educated and -informed who support a host of distinct issues (from gun control and affirmative action to cracking down on crime and welfare) seek out information that confirms their preexisting opinions and dismiss reports that contradict them (Taber and Lodge 2006; Taber, Cann, and Kucsova 2009; Shapiro and Bloch-Elkon 2008). The best-educated Republicans, for example, were especially resistant to acknowledging evidence that repudiated the primary rationales for invading Iraq—weapons of mass destruction and connections with the al-Qaeda terrorists who attacked the US on September 11, 2001 (Shapiro and Bloch-Elkon 2006; Jacobson 2010; Gaines et al. 2007). Although economic conditions are ostensibly objective information that can be used to evaluate politicians' performance, individuals with strongly held partisan attitudes have tended to take note of economic conditions to reward only their preferred party's officeholders in power when times are good and to punish only those of the *opposition* party in power when they are not good; this helps explain the continued strong support of Republicans for Bush and of Democrats for Obama during periods of economic decline (Lebo and Cassino 2007; Achen and Bartels 2006). Conservatives with greater education and more engagement with politics have been much *less* likely than other conservatives to acknowledge the evidence of increasing income differences (Bartels 2008). What is also striking is that these and other significant misperceptions can persist (Nyhan and Reifler 2010; Redlawsk, Civettini, and Emmerson 2010).

For Americans who are not hard-core partisans, the partisan press and the media's more general preoccupation with political conflict prompts many to turn to *non-political* media and information options (see Prior 2007). This helps to explain the odd juxtaposition of inflamed partisans and disinterested spectators.

In short, motivated reasoning triggered by elite mobilization strategies and media reporting has produced a worrisome pattern in which accurate factual information may neither be perceived nor accepted by Americans with strongly held political attitudes, including the most educated and inclined to follow public affairs. Partisans have polarized because they literally see different worlds: they follow and absorb dramatically different portrayals of policy debates and real-world developments, which reinforce preexisting perceptions and assumptions about threats and opportunities. These dynamics have sobering effects on American democracy. The flames of partisan conflict among the public, lit by political elites and fueled by the media, feed back on politics; they contribute to partisan deadlock in government and to greater responsiveness to comparatively extreme partisan and ideological activists and favored interests than to the public writ large (McCarty 2007; Bartels 2008; Wood 2009; Jacobs and Shapiro 2000; Jacobs and Page 2005).

# CONCLUSION: THE PHANTOM ELITE

Many of the problems with American democracy today originate with its political leaders and other elites. The role and impact of government officials and their allies that have emerged from decades of research depart dramatically from the benevolent leader accounts which had portrayed them as beacons of the public good and the foundation for a working democracy. Instead, we have found that partisanship, ideology, special interest bidding, and other factors drive the policy goals of political elites. In response, the traditional press and new online media have focused their attention on the strategic manipulations of political elites and often the mobilization of counterfactions. And the ostensible guardians of American democracy—the best-educated and most engaged and political leaders themselves—turn out to be particularly susceptible to emotional reasoning and to reaching views that are not consistently wise or "correct."

The hope for American democracy lies with reform at the top. The first challenge might be to change the behavior of traditional media outlets and to tap the new online outlets in the service of democracy. One recommendation is for government or non-profit foundations to subsidize reporting that is devoted to public service (Downie and Schudson 2009); these could in theory moderate the news media and counterbalance current reporting and commentary that cater to the ideological extremes. Although an intriguing proposal, there is strong opposition to government funding of the media and several foundations have already invested heavily in public media outlets with only modest overall effects in improving democratic processes. Another possibility is to capitalize on technological breakthroughs in online media as they begin what will likely be a series of innovations in business models and news platforms.

The starting point, though, for more substantive press reporting and reality-based citizens lies with political elites and the need to change the current behavior of highly partisan leaders and in turn their effects on public opinion. It is possible that expanded partisan conflict may open the door to centrist third party candidates, which may put pressure on party leaders to temper their more extreme elements. Another possibility is to change the party primaries to *open* them to all voters in order to encourage and aid candidates in each party who appeal to median voters.

Although remedies are elusive, what is clear is that the burden of democracy has shifted from skepticism about the competence of citizens to doubts and concerns about the wisdom and responsibility of their political leaders.

## REFERENCES

ABRAMOWITZ, A. I. 2010. *The Disappearing Center: Engaged Citizens, Polarization, & American Democracy.* New Haven: Yale University Press.

ACHEN, C. H., and BARTELS, L. M. 2006. It Feels Like We're Thinking: The Rationalizing Voter and Electoral Democracy. Paper presented at the Annual Meeting of the American Political Science Association, Philadelphia, Aug. 31–Sept. 3.

ALTHAUS, S. L. 2003. *Collective Preferences in Democratic Politics: Opinion Surveys and the Will of the People.* New York: Cambridge University Press.

American Political Science Association. 1950. *Toward a More Responsible Government: A Report of the Committee on Political Parties. American Political Science Review,* suppl. 44 (Sept.), pt 2.

BAFUMI, J., and SHAPIRO, R. Y. 2009. A New Partisan Voter. *Journal of Politics,* 71: 1–24.

BAKER, C. E. 2006. *Media Concentration and Democracy: Why Ownership Matters.* New York: Cambridge University Press.

BARBER, J. D. 1972. *The Presidential Character: Predicting Performance in the White House.* Englewood Cliffs, NJ: Prentice-Hall.

BARTELS, L. M. 1996. Uninformed Votes: Information Effects in Presidential Elections. *American Journal of Political Science,* 40: 194–230.

—— 2002. Beyond the Running Tally: Partisan Bias in Political Perceptions. *Political Behavior,* 24: 117–50.

—— 2008. *Unequal Democracy: The Political Economy of the New Gilded Age.* New York: Russell Sage; Princeton: Princeton University Press.

BAUM, M. A., and GROELING, T. 2008. New Media and the Polarization of American Political Discourse. *Political Communication,* 254: 345–65.

—— —— 2010. *War Stories: The Causes and Consequences of Public Views of War.* Princeton: Princeton University Press.

BENNETT, W. L. 1990. Toward a Theory of Press–State Relations in the United States.

—— and IYENGAR, S. 2008. A New Era of Minimal Effects? The Changing Foundations of Political Communication. *Journal of Communication,* 58: 707–31.

—— —— 2010. The Shifting Foundations of Political Communication: Responding to a Defense of the Media Effects Paradigm. *Journal of Communications,* 60: 35–9.

BERELSON, B. R., LAZARSFELD, P. F., and MCPHEE, W. A. 1954. *Voting: A Study of Opinion Formation in a Presidential Campaign.* Chicago: University of Chicago Press.

BISHOP, G. P. 2005. *The Illusion of Public Opinion: Fact and Artifact in American Public Opinion Polls.* New York: Rowman & Littlefield.

BROWNSTEIN, R. 2007. *The Second Civil War: How Extreme Partisanship Has Paralyzed Washington and Polarized America.* New York: Penguin.

BURSTEIN, P. 2003. The Impact of Public Opinion on Public Policy: A Review and an Agenda. *Political Research Quarterly,* 56: 29–40.

CAMPBELL, A., CONVERSE, P. E., MILLER, W. E., and STOKES, D. E. 1960. *The American Voter.* New York: Wiley. Repr. Chicago: University of Chicago Press, 1976.

CAPLAN, B. 2007. *The Myth of the Rational Voter: Why Democracies Choose Bad Policies.* Princeton: Princeton University Press.

CAPPELLA, J. N., and JAMIESON, J. H. 1997. *Spiral of Cynicism: The Press and the Public Good.* New York: Oxford University Press.

CARMINES, E. G., and STIMSON, J. A. 1989. *Issue Evolution: Race and the Transformation of American Politics.* Princeton: Princeton University Press.

COHEN, J. 1997. *Presidential Responsiveness and Public Policy-Making: The Public and the Policies that Presidents Choose.* Ann Arbor: University of Michigan Press.

LUSKIN, R. C. 2003. The Heavenly Public: What Would a Fully Informed Citizenry Be Like? In *Electoral Democracy*, ed. M. B. MacKuen and G. Rabinowitz. Ann Arbor: University of Michigan Press.

MCCARTY, N. 2007. The Policy Effects of Political Polarization. In *The Transformation of American Politics: Activist Government and the Rise of Conservatism*, ed. P. Pierson and T. Skocpol. Princeton: Princeton University Press.

—— POOLE, K. T., and ROSENTHAL, H. 2006. *Polarized America: The Dance of Ideology and Unequal Riches*. Cambridge, MA: MIT Press.

MANJOO, F. 2008. *True Enough: Learning to Live in a Post-Fact Society*. Hoboken, NJ: Wiley.

MARCUS, G. E., NEUMANN, W. R., and MACKUEN, M. B. 2000. *Affective Intelligence and Political Judgment*. Chicago: University of Chicago Press.

MONROE, A. D. 1998. Public Opinion and Public Policy, 1980–1993. *Public Opinion Quarterly*, 62: 6–28.

MUTZ, D. C. 2006. How the Mass Media Divide Us. In *Red and Blue Nation?* i: *Characteristics and Causes of America's Polarized Politics*, ed. P. S. Nivola and D. W. Brady. Washington, DC: Brookings Institution; Stanford, CA: Hoover Institution.

—— 2007. Political Psychology and Choice. In *The Oxford Handbook of Political Behavior*, ed. R. J. Dalton and H.-D. Klingemann. New York: Cambridge University Press.

NACOS, B. L., BLOCH-ELKON, Y., and SHAPIRO, R. Y. 2011. *Selling Fear: Counterterrorism, the Media, and Public Opinion*. Chicago: University of Chicago Press.

NYHAN, B., and REIFLER, J. 2010. When Corrections Fail: The Persistence of Political Misperceptions. *Political Behavior*, 32: 303–30.

PAGE, B. I., and JACOBS, L. R. 2009. *Class War? What Americans Really Think about Economic Inequality*. Chicago: University of Chicago Press.

—— and SHAPIRO, R. Y. 1983. Effects of Public Opinion on Policy. *American Political Science Review*, 77: 175–90.

—— —— 1992. *The Rational Public: Fifty Years of Trends in Americans' Policy Preferences*. Chicago: University of Chicago Press.

PAGE, S. E. 2007. *The Difference: How the Power of Diversity Creates Better Groups, Firms, Schools, and Societies*. Princeton: Princeton University Press.

PITKIN, H. 1969. *Representation*. New York: Atherton Press.

POPKIN, S. L. 1991. *The Reasoning Voter: Communication and Persuasion in Presidential Campaigns*. Chicago: University of Chicago Press.

PRIOR, M. 2007. *Post-Broadcast Democracy: How Media Choice Increase Inequality in Political Involvement and Polarize Elections*. New York: Cambridge University Press.

QUIRK, P. J., and HINCHLIFFE, J. 1998. The Rising Hegemony of Mass Opinion. *Journal of Policy History*, 10/1: 6–28.

REDLAWSK, D. P., CIVETTINI, A. J. W., and EMMERSON, K. M. 2010. The Affective Tipping Point: Do Motivated Reasoners Ever "Get It"? *Political Psychology*, 31: 563–93.

ROGERS, L. 1949. *The Pollsters*. New York: Knopf.

SCHATTSCHNEIDER, E. E. 1960. *The Semi-Sovereign People: A Realist's View of Democracy in America*. New York: Holt.

SCHUESSLER, J. M. 2010. The Deception Dividend: FDR's Undeclared War. *International Security*, 34 (Spring), 133–65.

SCHUMAN, H. 1986. Ordinary Questions, Survey Questions, and Policy Questions. *Public Opinion Quarterly*, 50: 432–42.

SHAPIRO, R. Y., and BLOCH-ELKON, Y. 2006. Political Polarization and the Rational Public. Paper presented at the Annual Conference of the American Association for Public Opinion Research, Montreal, May 18–21.

—— —— 2007. Ideological Partisanship and American Public Opinion toward Foreign Policy. In *Power and Superpower: Global Leadership and Exceptionalism in the 21st Century*, ed. M. H. Halperin, J. Laurenti, P. Rundlet, and S. P. Boyer. New York: Century Foundation Press.

—— —— 2008. Do the Facts Speak for Themselves? Partisan Disagreement as a Challenge to Democratic Competence. *Critical Review*, 20/1–2: 115–39.

SLOTHUUS, R., and DE VREESE, C. H. 2010. Political Parties, Motivated Reasoning, and Issue Framing Effects. *Journal of Politics*, 72: 630–45.

SNIDERMAN, P. M., BRODY, R. A., and TETLOCK, P. E. 1991. *Reasoning and Choice: Explorations in Political Psychology*. New York: Cambridge University Press.

SNYDER, J., BLOCH-ELKON, Y., and SHAPIRO, R. Y. 2009. Free Hand Abroad, Divide and Rule at Home. *World Politics*, 61: 155–87.

STIMSON, J. A. 2004. *Tides of Consent: How Public Opinion Shapes American Politics*. New York: Cambridge University Press.

—— 2007. Perspectives on Representation: Asking the Right Questions and Getting the Right Answers. In *The Oxford Handbook of Political Behavior*, ed. R. J. Dalton and H.-D. Klingemann. Oxford: Oxford University Press.

STROUD, N. J. 2010. Polarization and Partisan Selective Exposure. *Journal of Communication*, 60: 556–76.

SUNSTEIN, C. R. 2007. *Republic.com 2.0*. Princeton: Princeton University Press.

—— 2009. *Going to Extremes: How Like Minds Unite and Divide*. New York: Oxford University Press.

TABER, C. S., and LODGE, M. 2006. Motivated Skepticism in the Evaluation of Political Beliefs. *American Journal of Political Science*, 50: 755–69.

—— CANN, D., and KUCSOVA, S. 2009. The Motivated Processing of Political Arguments. *Political Behavior*, 31: 137–55.

TETLOCK, P. E. 2005. *Expert Political Judgment: How Good Is It? How Can We Know?* Princeton: Princeton University Press.

WINTER, J. A., and PAGE, B. I. 2009. Oligarchy in the United States? *Perspectives on Politics*, 7: 731–51.

WLEZIEN, C., and SOROKA, S. N. 2007. The Relationship between Public Opinion and Policy. In *The Oxford Handbook of Political Behavior*, ed. R. J. Dalton and H.-D. Klingemann. Oxford: Oxford University Press.

WOOD, B. D. 2009. *The Myth of Presidential Representation*. New York: Cambridge University Press.

ZALLER, J. R. 1992. *The Nature and Origins of Mass Opinion*. New York: Cambridge University Press.

# Name Index

Includes all referenced authors.

# SUBJECT INDEX